THE LIFE OF RICHARD WAGNER
1813-1848

WAGNER IN THE PARIS PERIOD

FROM A DRAWING BY ERNST KIETZ

ERNEST NEWMAN

The Life of

RICHARD

WAGNER

VOLUME ONE : 1813–1848

NEW YORK · ALFRED · A · KNOPF · MCMLXVI

PUBLISHED JANUARY 25, 1937
REPRINTED FIVE TIMES
SEVENTH PRINTING, MAY 1966

THIS IS A BORZOI BOOK,
PUBLISHED BY ALFRED A. KNOPF, INC.

Manufactured in the United States of America and distributed by Random House, Inc. Published in Canada by Random House of Canada, Limited

TO
VERA

FOREWORD

ANOTHER LIFE of Wagner may seem to many people a super-fluity at this time of day. My justification for the present attempt is that as yet no satisfactory Life of him exists, for one reason, among others, that during the last twenty years or so, and still more during the last ten or even the last five years, so much new and vital first-hand matter has come to light that one's old conception of the story has had to be modified at a hundred points. The life of no artist — indeed, of very few men in any walk of life — is so copiously documented as that of Wagner. He himself has left us, in addition to the *Autobiographical Sketch* of 1843 and the *Communication to my Friends* of 1851, an autobiography running to nearly 900 pages, though it covers only the first fifty-one of the seventy years of his life. He was one of the most indefatigable of letter-writers, and every few years sees an addition to the published number of these. When Wilhelm Altmann, in 1905, brought out what was intended to be the definitive edition (in the form of abstracts) of Wagner's letters, he had at his disposal 3,143 of these. When, nine years later, Julius Kapp and Emerich Kastner embarked upon yet another " complete " edition, the number of available documents had increased to 5,000. Since that time there have appeared the volumes of letters to Frau Julie Ritter (1920), to Hans Richter (1924), to Albert Niemann (1924), and to Mathilde Maier (1930), as well as a number of isolated letters in various periodicals. In addition we have had, during the last few years, the second volume of Sebastian Röckl's *Ludwig II und Richard Wagner*, with its new documents relating to the Munich epoch; Du Moulin Eckart's *Cosima Wagner*, again with a mass of first-hand material relating to this and the later period; Woldemar Lippert's *Richard Wagners Verbannung und Rückkehr, 1849–*

1862, with a large number of new letters and of other documents relating to those years; the *Richard Wagner und seine erste " Elisabeth "* of Julius Kapp and Hans Jachmann, containing much material that had hitherto been unpublished; several new letters in Frau Elisabeth Förster-Nietzsche's *Wagner und Nietzsche zur Zeit ihrer Freundschaft;* and the many still unpublished letters the contents of which are summarised in the Catalogue of the Burrell Collection. In further addition to all this there has been published, in one book or another on other subjects, a mass of new material bearing directly or indirectly on Wagner; while the intensive research of the Munich and other archives is constantly adding to our first-hand knowledge of the personalities and the events of this or that period of the story. Furthermore, while most of the older editions of the Wagner letters were subjected to plentiful deletions, the gaps thus made in our knowledge of the full facts of the case are gradually being filled in: Mr. Elbert Lenrow, for instance, has not only given us, for the first time, the authentic text of the letters to Pusinelli that appeared, under the aegis of Wahnfried, in 1909 in the *Briefe an Freunde und Zeitgenossen,* but has published in full a number of letters from Wagner to Pusinelli that were omitted from that book, as well as several from Pusinelli to Wagner.

When Nietzsche said that most of what passed for Wagner biography was " *fable convenue,* or worse," he spoke more wisely than he knew. It is not so much that the existing records were tampered with by partisans — though there has been a fair amount of that — as that events were narrated and conclusions come to on the basis of records that were lamentably imperfect. Everybody who has attempted original research in the field of biography will agree sadly with Walpole's refusal to let his son read some history to him: " Not history! " said the shrewd old man; " that is sure to be false! " His experience at the centre of politics for so many years had shown him how little the facts, as the world at large knew them, or thought it knew them, corresponded with the facts as known to those who had taken an active part in the events. In the vast majority of cases we know far too little of the personalities, the outer and inner lives, and the environment of musicians to be within a measurable distance of compiling authentic biographies of them. As a rule we have records, such as they are, of only one side of the case. Even a man's letters, though they may have survived by the thousand, are at the best only the equivalent of our listening to one end of a telephone conversation.

The rule that no man is to be accepted as judge in his own cause, and, indeed, not always as the advocate in it, is blandly forgotten by musical biographers. Flaubert's Bouvard and Pécuchet, in the course of their pathetically vain itinerary through all the arts and sciences, came to the same rational conclusion as Walpole — that what passes for history and biography is largely legend, fiction, or guesswork. They had innocently planned a life of the Duc d'Angoulême; but their comic inability to find out, within the narrow circle of their own household, " who had drunk the Calvados, how the chest got broken, what Madame Castillon wanted when she was calling Gorju, and whether he had dishonoured Mélie," led them to the sage if sad reflection, " We are not able to tell what is happening in our own household, yet we lay claim to discover all about the hair and the love affairs of the Duc d'Angoulême! "

They had the sense to see, what no musical biographer, with an honourable exception or two, has ever had the sense to see, that one side of a story is, after all, only one side of a story, and that our verdict might be quite different did we know the other side. Biographers of Mozart have become almost speechless with indignation over Archbishop Colleredo's treatment of that refractory young man. They have not paused to reflect that, as in the case of all disputes between master and servant, the statements of the latter, made in whatever good faith, cannot be accepted *en bloc* without our hearing the other side. That rule ought to hold good for all history and all biography: as Pécuchet put it, " We should have a different idea of Caesar had we the Commentaries of Vercinge-torix." It is conceivable that we might take quite another view of the conduct of Leopold Mozart and his son if we possessed the Memoirs of Colleredo. The older biographers accepted far too unquestioningly Wagner's account of his dealings with other people and his estimates of their characters and motives: even had he been ideally free from bias in these matters it would still have been prudent to suspend judgment till the depositions of the other parties to the case had been taken.

Two modern historians, MM. Charles Seignobos and C. V. Langlois, in their invaluable *Introduction aux études historiques*, have shown how infinitely difficult it is to arrive at the truth in any matter of history whatever, even when the documents seem copious enough, and even when the documents are contemporary; and from the case of Wagner alone a scientific text-book could be compiled to illustrate the difficulty of writing an authentic biography of any artist, even when the documents are as plentiful as they are here. Again and again one finds that there is no truth in this story or that, that has been accepted as gospel partly because it seemed on the face of it credible, partly because, for romantic or partisan reasons, we were all too willing to accept it without question. One of the best known stories in the Wagner record is that of the Munich treasury officials paying Wagner the loan of 40,000 gulden, granted to Wagner by King Ludwig, in silver coins, and compelling Cosima to cart the money through the streets of the town in sacks, their object being to stir up public feeling against the pair. I myself, in my *Wagner as Man and Artist*, took the truth of all this for granted. I now discover, however, that as long ago as 1904 Karl Dürck, in his book *Richard Wagner und die Münchener, 1865*, proved, from the Munich archives, that the story is false — a fact which did not prevent the later German Wagner biographers, who, being more or less on the spot, can hardly be forgiven for their ignorance of Dürck, from repeating it in their books, as Wolfgang Golther, Du Moulin Eckart, Glasenapp, the editor of Wagner's letters to Mathilde Maier, and several others have done. A single experience of this kind is enough to shake our faith in almost everything that has come down to us in the way of musical biography: we have the uncomfortable feeling that most of the stories we read, could we put them to the test of contemporary documentary evidence, would turn out to be *fable convenue*, or worse.

There can never be too many documents in these matters: the trouble is that we rarely possess documents enough, or that, even when they exist, the biographer is too rarely acquainted with them all. Every conclusion we come to is liable to be upset by the later discovery of some fresh document or other. Here is a simple instance. Minna, in one of her letters (from Paris, to Emma Herwegh, on the 24th March, 1860), after expressing her resentment of Wagner's fondness for Blandine Ollivier (the sister of Cosima), continues thus: " Hans von Bülow has been here nearly two months and during that time has given four concerts. . . . You will have met his wife in Berlin. She is another rather dissolute [*lüderliche*] creature. It is her fault that [Karl] Ritter left his wife; the poor young thing is pining away. Bülow looks perfectly wretched." This has generally been regarded as only another evidence of how Minna's mind was so unhinged by jealousy, suspicion and illness as to lead her to see a non-existent wickedness in all the young women who fluttered round her husband. But quite recently there has come to light a document that fully establishes her veracity in this matter. As everyone now knows, Wagner's published letters to Mathilde Wesendonk are merely a selection, made by that lady in her old age in order to present her association with Wagner in a purely ideal light. Julius Kapp recently had access to the still unpublished letters; and in one of these (which appeared in the *Berliner Illustrierte Nachtausgabe* of the 25th November, 1930), Wagner tells Frau Wesendonk of a confidence he had just received (in September 1858) from Karl Ritter: after a visit to Blandine in Geneva, Cosima, in an outburst of passion for Karl, implored him to kill her; he refused to do this, but offered to die with her. She was about to throw herself from a boat into the lake, and only desisted from her purpose when she saw he was resolved to follow her. Minna's story of Cosima having been the cause of Ritter's estrangement from his wife is therefore confirmed.

The example in itself is trivial, but it is typical: a seemingly incredible story is liable to be confirmed at any moment by some unexpected piece of evidence, a story perfectly credible on the face of it is liable to be shown to be untrue. This difficulty confronts us all through the Wagner record. The biographer can at no stage hope to have reached the final truth. All he can do is to make sure that whatever statement he may make, whatever conclusion he may come to, shall be based on the whole of the evidence available at the time of writing. This I have endeavoured to do in the present Life. It makes no pretensions to finality: it is merely an attempt to bring, for the first time, all the available Wagner documents into the one focus, and so to make the way a little easier for some better qualified student a few years hence. The present Wagner biographies are mostly hindrances rather than helps towards the ideal end. They are practically all second-hand Glasenapp. No student in this field can feel anything but gratitude to Glasenapp for his tireless industry. But virtually every document that was available for him is accessible to us, while we now possess a vast amount of material of which he knew nothing. Even the valuable first-hand research of later students like Röckl and Koch has been supplemented at many points since they wrote. And there is all the more need to-day to traverse the ground afresh on one's own account because Glasenapp was so blind a partisan that his interpretation of a document, the amount of selection he may make from it, or the general use to which he may put it, can never be relied upon.

It is in connection with the period to be dealt with in the second and third volumes of the present Life that so many fresh documents have come to light during recent years as to necessitate a re-writing of the whole story. In the nature of the case, there can be little hope of any vital new material relating to Wagner's earlier years being discovered now. The familiar material, however, can still be looked at from another point of view and correlated in new ways. After the middle of the nineteenth century we are dealing with a world not notably different in essentials from that of to-day. But the world in which the lot of the youthful Wagner was cast was one so different from ours that we constantly go astray if we apply our modern conceptions to it. I have accordingly devoted a fair amount of space to an attempt to reconstruct for the reader the musical, economic, and social conditions in Europe during the first part of Wagner's life, and the more significant of the personalities with which he was brought into contact. I have also given detailed consideration to the question of Wagner's debts. In this, I am sure, I would have had the approval of Balzac, who knew the infinite importance in a man's life of his finance. We have been told, in great detail, the story of " The Women in Wagner's life." But much more important than this is the story of the thalers in Wagner's life: that record may not be so piquant as the other, but it is decidedly more vital.

If it be found that the tone and the conclusions of the present volume are not always those of my *Wagner as Man and Artist* of some twenty years ago, I may perhaps be allowed to plead that the deeper one goes into the Wagner story, the more one tries to understand the man, the less one is inclined to err on the side of harshness of judgment. The most unfortunate event in the whole story, for him, was the publication of *Mein Leben* in 1911. The often unpleasant tone of that book, and its many obvious departures from the truth, could not fail to stir up, even among the admirers of the artist, a certain prejudice against the man. A truthful biographer can in no case ignore the more unpleasant features of his subject's character; but the offences against good taste and good feeling were so plentiful and so gross in *Mein Leben* that people who had to deal with Wagner just about that time can perhaps be excused for over-stressing his weaknesses here and there, for saying to him what the centurion in *Androcles and the Lion* says to the snivelling Spintho as he manhandles him — " You're the sort that makes duty a pleasure, you are! " But in the course of time one comes to the conclusion that it is unfair to let so exceptional a book as *Mein Leben* weigh too heavily against its author — a great artist maddened beyond endurance at the time of writing the book by sufferings that were not always his own fault, and embittered by recent enmities on a scale and of a vileness to which there is no parallel in the life of any other composer. Moreover, in estimating Wagner as a man we do well to bear charitably in mind that few men's private lives have been laid so cruelly bare to the world as his. Apart from the copious records that other people have left of him, we have letters of his own to the number of nearly 6,000. That means about 120, on the average, for each year of his life from the twentieth to the seventieth — one every three days; and many of the letters are the length of an ordinary newspaper article. The character of no human being, not even were he a saint, as saints go, could come unflecked through so microscopic an examination as is possible, and indeed necessary, in the case of Wagner; episodes that remain unrecorded in the case of other men, explosions, revelations of weaknesses that would be for ever veiled from the prying world, are in his case exposed to full view, open to every degree of hatred, malice, and uncharitableness in interpretation. The task of the modern biographer is, while abating nothing of the desire to get at the truth, to try to see the man as if, instead of being a divine artist from whom the world rather unreasonably expects a super-saintliness in his private life, he were just one of ourselves — perhaps, if the full truth about each of us were known, just oneself.

The present volume carries the record down to the crisis in Wagner's artistic and more especially his financial affairs in the summer of 1848. It has been the practice of his biographers to draw a dividing line at his flight from Dresden in May 1849. I have preferred to reserve the complete story of his revolutionary activities for another volume. The flight was an external rather than an internal crisis in his life: and the crisis was a cumulative one from the middle of 1848 onwards. The second volume will carry the record down to about 1864, and the third down to 1883.

I may be reproached for a certain inconsistency in my manner of reference to musical works. The plan I have adopted is to retain the foreign title in most cases, but to use the equivalent English one whenever English people would adopt that practice in conversation. No one would refer to *Das Liebesverbot, Der Freischütz, La Favorita, Il Trovatore, La Forza del Destino, La Bohème,* or *Tod und Verklärung* by any but their original titles. On the other hand, we talk not of *Robert le Diable* but of *Robert the Devil,* not of *Der Streit zwischen Phoebus und Pan,* but of *Phoebus and Pan,* not of *I Giojelli della Madonna* but of *The Jewels of the Madonna,* and so on.

I make no apology for the rather copious documentation of the work. There is nothing more exasperating, for the serious student, than a work every statement in which depends, or is supposed to depend, upon some document or other, but in which no clues are given as to sources. It is the duty of the historian or the biographer to remember that some other student may wish to traverse the ground after him on his own account, and to make it as easy as possible for him to do so. The " Sources " given in the following list do not, of course, exhaust the authorities upon which a modern Life of Wagner must be based: they represent only those to which specific reference has been made in the ensuing pages.

My warm thanks are due to my friends Professor H. G. Fiedler and Mr. H. W. Acomb for their kind help in connection with one or two points, and to Mr. William R. Steinway for his generous assistance in the search for recent Wagner documents in the German Press.

E. N.

Tadworth, 17th August, 1932.

CONTENTS

[xv]

ILLUSTRATIONS

SOURCES FOR VOLUME I

English translations exist of the works marked with an asterisk.

A

ABB   = A. W. AMBROS: *Bunte Blätter; Skizzen und Studien für Freunde der Musik und der bildenden Kunst.* 2 vols. Leipzig, 1872, 1874.

AM   = COMTESSE D'AGOULT (DANIEL STERN): *Mémoires (1833–1854)*; *avec une introduction de M. Daniel Ollivier.* 7th ed. Paris, 1927.

AMZ   = *Allgemeine Musikzeitung.* (Cited by year of issue and number.)

B

BAMC   = HECTOR BERLIOZ: *Au milieu de chemin, 1852–1855. Correspondance publiée par Julien Tiersot.* Paris, 1930.

BAS   = HANS VON BÜLOW: *Ausgewählte Schriften, 1850–1892. Zweite, vermehrte Auflage.* Leipzig, 1911.

BB   = HANS VON BÜLOW: *Briefe.* 7 vols. Leipzig, 1899–1908.

BBL   = MARIE VON BÜLOW: *Hans von Bülows Leben, dargestellt aus seinen Briefen. Zweite Auflage.* Leipzig, 1921.

BBLW   = MARIE VON BÜLOW: *Hans von Bülow in Leben und Wort.* Stuttgart, 1925.

BBW   = Bayreuther Blätter: *Deutsche Zeitschrift im Geiste Richard Wagners. Herausgegeben von Hans von Wolzogen.* Various years.

BCI   = HECTOR BERLIOZ: *Correspondance inédite, 1819–1868, avec une notice biographique par Daniel Bernard.* Paris, n.d.

BDM   = DIETRICH BELLMER (Ed.): *Deutsche Meisterbriefe aus fünf Jahrhunderten.* Halle, 1925.

BHB   = ADOLPHE BOSCHOT: *Hector Berlioz.* 3 vols. Paris, 1906, 1908, 1912.

BKMK   = HANS VON BRESCIUS: *Die Königl. Sächs. Musikalische Kapelle von Reissiger bis Schuch, 1826–98.* Dresden, 1899.

BLG   = OTTO BOURNOT: *Ludwig Heinr. Chr. Geyer, der Stiefvater Richard Wagners.* Leipzig, 1913.

BM*   = *Mémoires de Hector Berlioz.* 2 vols. Paris, n.d.

BMC   = HENRI BLAZE DE BURY: *Musiciens contemporains.* Paris, 1856.

BNB*   = HANS VON BÜLOW: *Neue Briefe, herausgegeben und eingeleitet von Richard Graf Du Moulin Eckart.* Munich, 1927.

BPMO   = CHARLES DE BOIGNE: *Petits Mémoires de l'Opéra.* Paris, 1857.

BRR   = ROBERT BORY: *Une Rétraite Romantique en suisse; Liszt et la Comtesse d'Agoult.* Paris, 1930.

BRW   = MARY BURRELL: *Richard Wagner, his Life and Works from 1813–1834.* London, 1898.

BRWB   = HANS BÉLART: *Richard Wagners Beziehungen zu François und Eliza Wille.* Dresden, 1914.

C

CBC   = *Catalogue of the Burrell Collection of Wagner Documents, Letters, and Bibliographical Material.* London, 1929.

CGN   = DR. CABANÈS: *Grands Névropathes; Malades immortels — Baudelaire, Byron, Chateaubriand, Molière, Pascal, Shelley, Wagner.* Paris, 1930.

CL   = *Chopin's Letters, Collected by Henryk Opieński;* translated from the original Polish and French by E. L. Voynich. London, 1932.

CMGM   = HENRY F. CHORLEY: *Modern German Music.* London, n.d. (1854).

CPC   = CARL MARIA CORNELIUS: *Peter Cornelius, der Wort- und Tondichter.* 2 vols. Regensburg, 1925.

CRW*   = HOUSTON STEWART CHAMBERLAIN: *Richard Wagner.* Munich, 1896.

CTYR   = HENRY F. CHORLEY: *Thirty Years' Musical Recollections,* edited by Ernest Newman. New York, 1926.

D

DA   = KARL VON DITTERSDORF: *Autobiography;* translated by A. D. Coleridge. London, 1896.

DBET   = *Briefwechsel zwischen Eduard und Therese Devrient, herausgegeben von Hans Devrient.* Stuttgart, n.d. (1909).

DEE   = HEINRICH DORN: *Ergebnisse aus Erlebnissen. Fünfte Folge der Erinnerungen.* Berlin, 1877.

DGG   = ALFRED DÖRFFEL: *Geschichte der Gewandhauskonzerte.* Leipzig, 1884.

DJE   = THERESE DEVRIENT: *Jugenderinnerungen. Dritte Auflage.* Stuttgart, n.d.

DM   = *Die Musik.* (Cited by volume number.)

DML   = HEINRICH DORN: *Aus meinem Leben.* 3 vols. 1870–1872.

DRFM = EDUARD DEVRIENT: *My Recollections of Felix Mendelssohn-Bartholdy;* translated from the German by Natalia Macfarren. London, 1869.

E

ELW = WM. ASHTON ELLIS: *Life of Richard Wagner.* 6 vols. London, 1900–1908. (The first three volumes are mainly a translation of Glasenapp.)

EMHL = F. G. EDWARDS: *Musical Haunts in London.* [London, 1895.]

ERWL = ERICH W. ENGEL: *Richard Wagners Leben und Werke im Bilde.* 2nd ed. Leipzig, 1922.

EU = *Europa, Chronik der gebildeten Welt . . . herausgegeben von August Lewald.* Stuttgart, 1837, etc.

F

FE = HERMANN VON FRIESEN: *Erinnerungen aus meinem Leben.* 2 vols. Dresden, 1880.

FH = NEWMAN FLOWER: *George Frideric Handel, his personality and his times.* London, 1923.

FLT = HERMANN VON FRIESEN: *Ludwig Tieck. Erinnerungen eines alten Freundes aus den Jahren 1825–1842.* 2 vols. Vienna, 1871.

FNWN* = ELISABETH FÖRSTER-NIETZSCHE: *Wagner und Nietzsche zur Zeit ihrer Freundschaft.* Munich, 1931.

FWW = HENRY T. FINCK: *Wagner and his Works.* 2 vols. London, 1893.

G

GBC = GEORGE M. GOULD: *Biographic Clinics.* 6 vols. London and Philadelphia, 1900–1907.

GOHM = HANS GAARTZ: *Die Opern Heinrich Marschners.* Leipzig, 1912.

GRML = KARL GUTZKOW: *Rückblicke auf mein Leben.* Berlin, 1875.

GRW* = CARL FR. GLASENAPP: *Das Leben Richard Wagners.* 6 vols. Leipzig, v.d.

GWH = JUDITH GAUTIER: *Wagner at Home; fully translated by Effie Dunreith Massie from the French.* London, 1910.

GWKZ = EDUARD GENAST: *Aus Weimars klassischer Zeit; Erinnerungen eines alten Schauspielers. Neu herausgegeben von Robert Kohlrausch.* Stuttgart, 1905.

H

HAPD = MARCEL HERWEGH: *Au Printemps des Dieux; Corréspondance inédite de la Comtesse Marie d'Agoult et du poète Georges Herwegh.* Paris, 1929.

HED   = HEINRICH HUBERT HOUBEN: *Emil Devrient, sein Leben, sein Wirken, sein Nachlass.* Frankfurt a/M, 1903.

HGCW   = EDUARD HANSLICK: *Geschichte des Concertwesens in Wien.* Vienna, 1869.

HKL   = FERDINAND HILLER: *Künstlerleben.* Cologne, 1880.

HLLC   = MORITZ HAUPTMANN: *The Letters of a Leipzig Cantor,* ed. by A. Schöne and F. Hiller. Translated by A. D. Coleridge. London, 1892.

HMNA   = E. T. A. HOFFMANN: *Musikalische Novellen und Aufsätze, herausgegeben und erläutert von Edgar Istel.* 2 vols. Regensburg, n.d.

HNNZ   = EDUARD HANSLICK: *Aus neuer und neuester Zeit.* Berlin, 1900.

HMP   = FERDINAND HILLER: *Musikalisches und Persönliches.* Leipzig, 1876.

HMS   = EDUARD HANSLICK: *Musikalische Stationen.* Berlin, 1880.

HRMG   = [EDWARD HOLMES]: *A Ramble among the Musicians of Germany.* London, 1828.

HSW   = HEINRICH HEINE: *Sämmtliche Werke.* 11 vols. Hamburg, 1862.

J

JKJ   = JULIUS KAPP UND HANS JACHMANN: *Richard Wagner und seine erste "Elisabeth," Johanna Jachmann-Wagner.* Berlin, 1927.

JKJW   = JULIUS KAPP: *Der Junge Wagner; Dichtungen, Aufsätze, Entwürfe, 1832–1849.* Berlin, 1910.

JKRW   = JULIUS KAPP: *Richard Wagner, eine Biographie. Völlige Neuausgabe* (22nd). Berlin, 1929.

JKWF*   = JULIUS KAPP: *Richard Wagner und die Frauen. Völlige Neuausgabe, 15. Auflage.* Berlin, 1929.

K

KGT   = EMIL KNESCHKE: *Zur Geschichte des Theaters und der Musik in Leipzig.* Leipzig, 1864.

KM   = GEORG RICHARD KRUSE: *Giacomo Meyerbeer.* Leipzig, n.d.

KN   = GEORG RICHARD KRUSE: *Otto Nicolai, ein Künstlerleben.* Berlin, 1911.

KRLS   = KARL THEODOR VON KÜSTNER: *Rückblick auf das Leipziger Stadttheater.* Leipzig, 1830.

KRW   = ADOLPH KOHUT: *Richard Wagner: Neues und Intimes aus seinem Leben und Schaffen.* Berlin, 1905.

KVJ   = KARL THEODOR VON KÜSTNER: *Vierunddreissig Jahre meiner Theaterleitung in Leipzig, Darmstadt, München und Berlin.* Leipzig, 1853.

KW   = GUSTAV ADOLPH KIETZ: *Richard Wagner in den Jahren 1842–1849 und 1873–1875; Erinnerungen, aufgezeichnet von Marie Kietz.* Dresden, 1905.

L

LCS   = BERTHOLD LITZMANN: *Clara Schumann: an artist's life, based on material found in diaries and letters.* Translated and abridged from the fourth [German] edition by Grace E. Hadow. 2 vols. London, 1913.

LGB   = ALBERT LORTZING: *Gesammelte Briefe, herausgegeben von Georg Richard Kruse.* Regensburg, n.d.

LRRG   = J. G. LEGGE: *Rhyme and Revolution in Germany; a Study in German History, Life, Literature and Character, 1813–1850.* London, 1918.

LRS   = *The Letters of Robert Schumann, selected and edited by Karl Storck.* Translated by Hannah Bryant. London, 1907.

LSAS   = ERNEST LEGOUVÉ: *Soixante Ans de Souvenirs.* 2 vols. Paris, 1887.

LWV*   = WOLDEMAR LIPPERT: *Richard Wagners Verbannung und Rückkehr, 1849–1862.* Dresden, 1927.

LZB   = *Franz Liszts Briefe, gesammelt und herausgegeben von La Mara.* 8 vols. Leipzig, 1893–1905.

LZBHZ   = *Briefe hervorragender Zeitgenossen an Franz Liszt, herausgegeben von La Mara.* 2 vols. Leipzig, 1895.

LZCA   = *Briefwechsel zwischen Franz Liszt und Carl Alexander Grossherzog von Sachsen, herausgegeben von La Mara.* Leipzig, 1909.

LZPR   = FRANZ LISZT: *Pages romantiques; avec une Introduction et des notes par Jean Chantavoine.* Paris, 1912.

M

ME   = A. B. MARX: *Erinnerungen: Aus meinem Leben.* 2 vols. Berlin, 1865.

MECW   = RICHARD GRAF DU MOULIN ECKART:
     * I. *Cosima Wagner, ein Lebens- und Charakterbild.*
     II. *Die Herrin von Bayreuth.*
     2 vols. Munich, 1929, 1931.

MGML   = ALFRED MEISSNER: *Geschichte meines Lebens.* 3rd ed. 2 vols. Vienna, 1884–1885.

MH   = CAMILLE MAUCLAIR: *La Vie Humiliée de Henri Heine.* Paris, 1930.

MKRW   = MAX KOCH: *Richard Wagner.* 3 vols. Berlin, 1907–1919.

MMNJ   = A. B. MARX: *Die Musik des neunzehnten Jahrhunderts und ihre Pflege.* Leipzig, 1855.

MRB   = *Reisebriefe von Felix Mendelssohn-Bartholdy aus den Jahren 1830 bis 1832, herausgegeben von Paul Mendelssohn-Bartholdy.* Leipzig, 1862.

MRMM = Ignatz Moscheles: *Recent Music and Musicians, as described in the diaries and correspondence of I. M.* Edited by his wife, and adapted from the original German by A. D. Coleridge. New York, 1879.

MVA   = Ignaz Franz Mosel: *Versuch einer Aesthetik des dramatischen Tonzatzes* (1813). Reprint, edited by Eugen Schmitz. Munich, 1910.

N

NBV   = Otto Nicolai: *Briefe an seinen Vater, herausgegeben von Wilhelm Altmann.* Regensburg, 1924.

NFF   = Ernest Newman: *Fact and Fiction about Wagner.* London, 1931.

NH   = Max Nietzki: *Heine als Dichter und Mensch.* Berlin, 1895.

NMA   = Otto Nicolai: *Musikalische Aufsätze, zum erstenmale herausgegeben von Georg Richard Kruse.* Regensburg, n.d.

NRS   = Frederick Niecks: *Robert Schumann.* London, 1925.

NT   = *Otto Nicolais Tagebücher, nebst biographischen Ergänzungen von B. Schröder.* Leipzig, 1892.

NW   = Ernest Newman: *Wagner as Man and Artist.* 2nd ed. New York, 1925.

O

OB   = Alexandre Oulibicheff: *Beethoven, ses critiques et ses glossateurs.* Leipzig and Paris, 1857.

P

PAMZ = Friedrich Pecht: *Aus meiner Zeit: Lebenserinnerungen.* 2 vols. Munich, 1894.

PFL*   = Guy de Pourtalés: *La Vie de Franz Liszt.* Paris, 1925.

PGHD = Robert Prölss: *Geschichte des Hoftheaters zu Dresden, von seinen Anfängen bis zum Jahre 1862.* Dresden, 1878.

PJB   = J. G. Prod'homme: *La Jeunesse de Beethoven (1770–1800).* Paris, 1927.

PW   = Ferdinand Praeger: *Wagner as I knew him.* London, 1892.

R

RFT   = Friedrich Rochlitz: *Für Freunde der Tonkunst.* 4 vols. Leipzig, 1824–1832.

RGB   = Romain Rolland: *Goethe and Beethoven.* Translated from the French by G. A. Pfister and E. S. Kemp. London, 1931.

RLL = Peter Raabe: *Liszts Leben.* Stuttgart and Berlin, 1931.

RMWF = *Wagner et la France:* Numéro Spécial de *La Revue Musicale,* 1 Oct., 1923.

RWAP = *The Letters of Richard Wagner to Anton Pusinelli,* translated and edited with critical notes by Elbert Lenrow. New York, 1932.

RWBV = Richard Wagner: *Briefwechsel mit seinen Verlegern.*
    1. Mit Breitkopf und Härtel.
    2. Mit B. Schotts Söhnen.
    2 vols. Leipzig, 1912.

RWFB* = *Familienbriefe von Richard Wagner, 1832–1874.* Berlin, 1907.

RWFP = *Richard Wagner an Ferdinand Praeger. Zweite, neu durchgesehene Auflage, herausgegeben mit kritischem Anhang von Houston Stewart Chamberlain.* Leipzig, 1911.

RWFZ = *Richard Wagner an Freunde und Zeitgenossen, herausgegeben von Erich Kloss.* Berlin, 1909.

RWGS* = Richard Wagner: *Gesammelte Schriften und Dichtungen. Vierte Auflage.* 12 vols. Leipzig, 1907.

RWHB = Richard Wagner: *Briefe an Hans von Bülow.* Jena, 1916.

RWJF = *Richard Wagner-Jahrbuch, herausgegeben von Ludwig Frankenstein.* Leipzig, 1906.

RWJK = *Richard Wagner-Jahrbuch, herausgegeben von Joseph Kürschner.* Erster Band. [No further issues.] Stuttgart, 1886.

RWKK = *Richard Wagners Gesammelte Briefe, herausgegeben von Julius Kapp und Emerich Kastner.* 2 vols. Leipzig, 1914. (The two volumes so far published bring the letters down to July 1850.)

RWLB = *Richard Wagners Lebens-Bericht.* (The German version of the article, "The Work and Mission of My Life," originally published in the *North American Review,* 1879.) Leipzig, 1884.

RWLZ* = *Briefwechsel zwischen Wagner und Liszt. Dritte erweiterte Auflage, herausgegeben von Erich Kloss.* Leipzig, 1910.

RWML* = Richard Wagner: *Mein Leben, kritisch durchgesehen, eingeleitet, und erläutert von Wilhelm Altmann.* 2 vols. Leipzig, n.d.

RWMW* = *Richard Wagner an Minna Wagner.* 2 vols. Berlin, 1908.

RWMW* = *Richard Wagner an Mathilde Wesendonk; Tagebuchblätter und Briefe, 1853–1871. Zweite Auflage.* Berlin, 1904.

RWTA* = *Richard Wagner an Theodor Apel.* Leipzig, 1910.

RWUF* = *Richard Wagners Briefe an Uhlig, Fischer, Heine.* Leipzig, n.d.

S

SA   = *Louis Spohr's Autobiography;* translated from the German. London, 1865.

SDH   = AL. SINCERUS: *Das Dresdner Hoftheater und seine gegenwärtigen Mitglieder.* Zerbst, 1852.

SHJ   = FRIEDRICH SCHULZE: *Hundert Jahre Leipziger Stadttheater: Ein geschichtlicher Rückblick.* Leipzig, 1917.

SIM   = *Sammelbände der Internationalen Musikgesellschaft.* (Cited by year and page.)

SKHD   = GOTTFRIED SEMPER: *Das Königliche Hoftheater zu Dresden.* Braunschweig, 1849.

SMMW   = ALBERT SOUBIES ET CHARLES MALHERBE: *Mélanges sur Wagner.* Paris, 1892.

SR   = STENDHAL: *Vie de Rossini,* ed. by Henry Prunières. 2 vols. Paris, 1922.

SRW   = GEORGES SERVIÈRES: *Richard Wagner jugé en France.* Paris, n.d. (1887).

SS   = CH. SÉCHAN: *Souvenirs d'un homme de théâtre, 1831–1855; receuillis par Adolphe Badin.* Paris, 1883.

SSC   = O. G. SONNECK: *Suum cuique; Essays in music.* New York, 1916.

STS   = ALBÉRIC SÉCOND: *Le Tiroir aux Souvenirs.* Paris, 1886.

SWL   = EUGEN SEGNITZ: *Richard Wagner und Leipzig, 1813–1833.* Leipzig, 1901.

SWM   = EDUARD STEMPLINGER: *Richard Wagner in München, 1864–1870: Legende und Wirklichkeit.* Munich, 1933.

SWS   = EDWARD SPEYER: *Wilhelm Speyer der Liederkomponist, 1790–1878.* Munich, 1925.

T

TGV   = FRANCIS TOYE: *Giuseppe Verdi, his life and works.* London, 1931.

TRW   = WILHELM TAPPERT: *Richard Wagner, sein Leben und seine Werke.* Elberfeld, 1883.

TWSK   = WILHELM TAPPERT: *Richard Wagner im Spiegel der Kritik. Dritte Auflage des Wagnerlexikons.* Leipzig, 1915.

U

UMS   = THEODOR UHLIG: *Musikalische Schriften, herausgegeben von Ludwig Frankenstein.* Regensburg, n.d.

V

VMBP   = LOUIS VÉRON: *Mémoires d'un Bourgeois de Paris.* 6 vols. Paris, 1853–1855.

VTP   = Louis Véron: *Paris en 1860: Les Théâtres de Paris depuis 1806 jusqu'en 1860*. Paris, 1860.

W

WBB   = Carl Maria von Weber: *Briefe an den Grafen Karl von Brühl; herausgegeben von Georg Kaiser*. Leipzig, 1911.

WCMW* = Max Maria von Weber: *Carl Maria von Weber, ein Lebensbild*. 3 vols. Leipzig, 1864–1866.

WEFR   = Alfred Weise: *Die Entwicklung des Fühlens und Denkens der Romantik, auf Grund der romantischen Zeitschriften*. Leipzig, 1912.

WEW   = Hans von Wolzogen: *Erinnerungen an Richard Wagner*. Leipzig, n.d.

WHW   = Hans von Wolzogen: *E. T. A. Hoffmann und Richard Wagner: Harmonien und Parallelen*. Berlin, n.d.

WL   = Felix Weingartner: *Lebenserinnerungen*. 2 vols. Zürich, 1928–1929.

WM   = M. E. Wittmann: *Marschner*. Leipzig, n.d.

WRB   = *Reise-Briefe von Carl Maria von Weber an seine Gattin Caroline, herausgegeben von seinem Enkel*. Leipzig, 1886.

WRW   = William Wallace: *Richard Wagner as he lived*. London, 1925.

WSD   = Alfred von Wolzogen: *Wilhelmine Schröder-Devrient: ein Beitrag zur Geschichte des musikalischen Dramas*. Leipzig, 1863.

WSS   = *Sämtliche Schriften von Carl Maria von Weber; kritische Ausgabe von Georg Kaiser*. Leipzig, 1921.

Z

ZIMG   = *Zeitschrift der Internationalen Musikgesellschaft*. Leipzig. (Cited by year.)

Note. — The same initials (RWMW) have inadvertently been given to both the Wagner-Minna and the Wagner-Wesendonk letters. The context, however, will, it is hoped, make each reference clear.

THE LIFE OF RICHARD WAGNER
1813-1848

CHAPTER I

PATERNITY AND ANCESTRY

1

ON HIS father's side, the parentage of Richard Wagner is still a matter of dubiety; to the end of time, in all probability, it will never be definitely known whether he was the son of the Leipzig Police Actuary Carl Friedrich Wagner or of the actor Ludwig Geyer. The evidence for the former paternity would at first sight appear to be conclusive; there is a strong facial resemblance between Richard Wagner and his fourteen-years-older brother Albert, who was born before Geyer had even made the acquaintance of Carl Friedrich and his wife: there is a certain, though remoter, resemblance also between Richard Wagner and Adolf Wagner, the younger brother of Carl Friedrich. (The alleged similarity between Adolf's handwriting and Richard's may mean anything or nothing; for the child might consciously have modelled his own penmanship on that of the literary uncle of whom the family had such good cause to be proud.) [1] Anna Zocher (see p. 19) told Mrs. Burrell that Carl Friedrich Wagner " was small and slightly crooked, but had a fine head." " I have often thought," says Mrs. Burrell, " in looking at Richard Wagner, that he had a narrow escape of deformity: he was not in the least deformed, yet the immense head was poised on the shoulders at the angle peculiar to hunchbacks." This is particularly noticeable in a photograph taken in Paris in 1860.[2] There is a suggestion of it again in a photograph of 1865.[3] In other photographs it is not so observable, perhaps because in the camera; while of course the portraits by painters more or less conventionalise the set of the head.

---

[1] Mrs. Burrell gives facsimiles of Adolf's writing and Richard's. For my part I can see no great resemblance between the two hands, but this is perhaps a matter strictly for graphologists.

[2] See ERWL, p. 277.

[3] See ERWL, p. 335.

[3]

The twist is most pronounced in the Paris photograph of 1860; and in a letter of Wagner's to Frau Wesendonk of the 23rd May of that year there is a curious reference to this photograph, with which, it is evident, he was not greatly pleased. He compares it with one taken a little later in Brussels, that is more to his liking; " I had been photographed," he says, " before that in Paris [i.e. the photograph now under discussion], and, without my being aware of it, the brute of an artist had seen fit to pose me in a most affected attitude, with my eyes twisted sideways. The resulting portrait is abhorrent to me; I said it made me look like a sentimental Marat. This wretched counterfeit was reproduced in *L'Illustration,* and — still more distorted — has since gone the round of the illustrated journals (even in England). Well, my abhorrence of it instinctively led me, at the Brussels operation, to adopt another and more comely expression, so that, without any affectation, I there have a tranquil, reasonable look."

The Brussels portrait is in profile, and Wagner is obviously composing his features for the occasion. The Paris photograph is *en face,* with the head turned slightly to the left. It is one of the two or three most veracious portraits of Wagner, one of the two or three in which we feel that not merely the features but the mentality and character of the man have been caught to the life. Evidently the photographer was an artist of genius, quick to read his sitter and to sense the pose that would bring out all that was most personal and vital in the head, face and eyes. Wagner's comical dislike for the photograph probably came from the recognition that it not only showed him strained and made pugnacious by his hard experiences in Paris — which is precisely the incomparable virtue of it for us to-day — but that it gave him a slight suggestion of that almost-deformity of which Mrs. Burrell speaks.[1]

The family likenesses mentioned above have led many writers to declare categorically that, as Julius Kapp puts it, " Richard Wagner was undoubtedly the body-child of Carl Friedrich Wag-

---

[1] Gould (see p. 37) would have seen in the Paris photograph a confirmation of his theory of an optical defect in Wagner. "Torticollis, or Tilted Head," he says: "a twisted or tilted position of the head may be caused by a displacement of the axis of astigmatism of the dominant eye." GBC, III, 488. Following Gould, Cabanès gives a murderous reproduction of the Paris portrait, and invites us to "observe the deviation of the eye." CGN, p. 362.

ner." [1] The matter, however, is not quite so simple as all that. We have to take count of the awkward fact that the composer himself, in the soberest years of his maturity, believed in at any rate the possibility of Geyer having been his father.

Some people have fancied they can detect a hint of this belief in the opening pages of *Mein Leben,* where Wagner describes how Carl Friedrich, who was passionately devoted to the theatre, used to be scolded by his wife for keeping lunch waiting while he paid court to a celebrated actress of the day, Wilhelmine Hartwig — his excuse being the usual male one that he had been detained at the office — how Carl Friedrich was " not free from a gallant warmth of feeling " for other local actresses, and how, " while the Police Actuary was spending his evenings in the theatre, the worthy actor Geyer generally filled his place in the family circle, and, it seems, had often to appease my mother, who complained, rightly or wrongly, of her husband's inconstancy." [2] Assuming, as we are bound to do, this sentence to have been written when *Mein Leben* was first embarked upon, and further supposing that, as some contend, it hints at a certain suspicion even then on Wagner's part, this suspicion must have taken shape in his mind at least as early as 1865, when the autobiography was begun. Four or five years later there is practically no doubt as to his entertaining such a suspicion. At Christmas, 1869, his half-sister Cäcilie — herself the legitimate child of Geyer — sent him copies of some old letters from her father to various members of the family, including their mother; and on the following 14th January Wagner wrote to Cäcilie that from these letters " it was possible for me to gain a deep insight into the relations of the two [i.e. Geyer and the widow Wagner] in difficult times. I believe I see now with absolute clearness, though I must consider it extremely difficult to express myself on those his self-sacrifice for the whole family [i.e. the struggling actor's

---

[1] JKRW, p. 22.

[2] *Flatterhaftigkeit* may carry also the stronger meaning of " infidelity." I may perhaps be permitted to quote here from a former article of mine on this subject: "It does not seem to have occurred to anyone to ask — though obviously the question is of some importance — how Wagner knew this. Precocious child as he was, it could hardly have been from personal observation, as he was only six months old when Friedrich Wagner died. It is hardly likely that Geyer took him into his confidence, if for no other reason than that Wagner was only eight years old when Geyer died. Who then was his informant, and when did this information reach him?"

[5]

taking on himself the burden of the widow and her seven children],
believed to atone for a guilt (*eine Schuld zu verbüssen*)." It has
been argued that *Schuld* here signifies not " a guilt " but simply a
money debt; and there happens to be evidence that in his younger
and more giddy days Geyer, like most of the impecunious German
artists of his epoch, was rather given to borrowing. On the 22nd
December, 1813, i.e. a month after Carl Friedrich's death, we find
Geyer writing to the widow and offering her, by way of partial discharge of a debt, the money coming to him for a newly finished
portrait, and promising her the remaining 30 gulden [1] when she
comes to see him in Dresden. We gather also, from his letters to her
of the 18th and 28th January, 1814, that Johanna had been accustomed to reproach him for his habit of incurring debts, and that
he had at last reformed in this respect. It is hardly likely, however,
that the fifty-six-years-old Wagner, in his letter to Cäcilie, would be
discussing merely a debt of *this* kind with such gravity, such emotion, and such a sense of difficulty in the choosing of words of befit-
ting delicacy to describe the relations between his mother and
Geyer. It is at least a fair presumption that he was using the term
Schuld in the sense of moral guilt. When we further consider that
Geyer must have been cohabiting with the widow Wagner within
six months after Carl Friedrich's death,[2] and that their marriage,
which took place on 28th August, 1814,[3] was undoubtedly hastened
in order to legitimise the coming child,[3] who was the result of an
intimacy that must have commenced in the preceding May at the
latest, we have probably some collateral justification, however
slight, for taking *Schuld* in a graver sense than the merely financial
one.[4]

---

[1] The approximate values of the currencies with which we shall have to deal in the
following pages may be taken as follows:
  1 gulden = 2/-.
  1 thaler = 3/-.
  1 Louisdor = 16/-.
  1 Friedrichsdor = 16/9.
  1 ducat = 9/4.
[2] Carl Friedrich had died on November 22nd, 1813.
[3] Cäcilie was born on February 26th, 1815.
[4] So far as my own reading goes, no German writer on the subject takes *Schuld* in
the sense of "money debt." Altmann, in his edition of *Mein Leben*, quotes the vital
passage from the letter of the 14th January 1870 to Cäcilie as throwing light on the
references to Geyer in the autobiography (RWML, p. 3), and adds the comment:
"Whoever reads these remarks about Geyer without prejudice must come to the con-

That Wagner, until fairly late in his life, was not quite comfortable about the obvious implication of these dates is suggested by the fact that they were handled, in the earlier Wagner biographies, if not with a deliberate attempt to deceive, at any rate with a decided lack of frankness. In *Mein Leben* he tells us that Geyer married the widow " a year after his friend's death " — a statement which there is difficulty in believing he did not know to be untrue. The first biographers of Wagner were plainly either in the dark as to the true date of the second marriage or were cloaking the real facts: Wagner's faithful henchman Tappert, for instance, in a Life published in 1883, merely says that " Frau Wagner married Geyer after a certain time," — the peculiar wording suggests knowledge of something like the true facts on his part — and then proceeds to give the correct date of birth of their child Cäcilie.[1] Glasenapp, in the first edition of his official Life of Wagner (1876, i.e. seven years before the composer's death), actually says that the second marriage took place *two years* after the death of Carl Friedrich; while he abstains from even mentioning the year of Cäcilie's birth. Now Glasenapp had been a visitor at Wahnfried for at least two years before 1876. Wagner and Cosima had placed a good deal of material at his disposal for what was intended to be the definitive Wagner biography; and we must assume either that Glasenapp was deliberately misleading the world as to the dates of the second marriage and the birth of Cäcilie or that they had not been confided to him at that time. Houston Stewart Chamberlain, another member of the inner Wagnerian circle, in his voluminous biographical study published in 1896,[2] tells us no more than that " Ludwig Geyer married the widowed mother in 1814," and does not even mention the birth of Cäcilie.

As late as the third edition of Glasenapp (1894) the facts, it is tolerably clear, are uneasily concealed or deliberately confused: the earlier erroneous statement, to the effect that the marriage took place " two years " after Carl Friedrich's death, does indeed disappear now, but in its stead we merely get the evasive remark that " in

---

clusion that Richard Wagner regarded him as his actual father" (RWML, p. 1008). It will be noted that in the passage quoted above from the letter to Cäcilie—the unquestioned child of Geyer—Wagner speaks of "our father Geyer."

[1] TRW, p. 2.
[2] CRW, p. 33.

Geyer's soul a resolve that was worthy of him had ripened to clearness in the months since the death of his unforgettable friend — the widow quietly became his wife." [1] Still no date is mentioned, but this time Glasenapp gives the date of Cäcilie's birth. As he had been by now accurately informed of that, we may presume that he knew also the date of the marriage; but the Wagner family was presumably still reluctant to let the world draw the conclusion it would be certain to draw had this date also been in its possession. And then, as in the winter of 1869–70, the Geyer letters that had been sent to Wagner by Cäcilie once more played a vital part in the story. Glasenapp's fourth edition appeared, as has been said, in 1905; and in this edition we read what amounts to an open admission of Wagner's belief — or at any rate half-belief — in the Geyer paternity.[2] "The idea," says Glasenapp, "that the deceased [Geyer] might even have been his real father he [Wagner] repeatedly expressed as a possibility in conversation with intimate friends, of whom we could name several." " And yet," he continues, " *if* there was a secret here to be preserved, then his mother took it with her into her grave and never confided it either to him or to any of the other grown children." Glasenapp is obviously fencing; he wants to repel in advance the assumption that such light as Wagner had on the matter had come to him direct from his mother, yet he also wants to make it fully clear that the composer himself, in his later years, believed in at any rate the possibility of Geyer having been his father. Manifestly Glasenapp, who, as his words intimate, had known long before of those " conversations with friends " — he himself was probably one of the friends — had at last been unmuzzled, and we may conjecture the reason for the unmuzzling to have been twofold: in the first place Cosima, as the years went on, was disposed to release more and more of the truth about Wagner, and in the second place the publication of the *Family Letters* [3] had been decided upon about that very time. These appeared, under Glasenapp's editorship, in 1907.[4] Included in them

---

[1] The sentence remains unchanged in the fourth edition (1905).

[2] The added matter appears at the end of what was Chapter III of the third edition (4th edition, pp. 77, 78).

[3] I.e. Wagner's letters to his mother, his brother Albert, his sisters, the latters' husbands, etc.

[4] Glasenapp was living in Bayreuth in 1906, working at the final stages of the Life, and no doubt preparing the *Family Letters* for publication. (See MECW II, 796.)

was that letter of Wagner's of the 14th January, 1870, to Cäcilie from which I have already quoted, and the deduction from which is fairly obvious. The expansive frankness of Glasenapp in 1905 is explained, then, by the fact that the forthcoming publication of this letter would be bound to stimulate certain enquiries which, it was now felt, had better be answered, more or less frankly, in advance.

The upshot of it all is not that it is now certain that Wagner was the son of Geyer — certainty on that point could come only from the mother, and the sentence quoted above from Glasenapp suggests that Wahnfried wanted to place it on record once for all that she had carried the secret, if there was a secret, with her to the grave — but that *Wagner himself believed in the possibility* of Geyer having been his father. With this fact definitely established, both the evidence for that theory and the arguments against it take on a new aspect. The argument from the resemblance between the composer and his elder brother and uncle, on which the opponents of the Geyer theory lay such stress, is bound to lose something of its former weight. For it goes without saying that no one could have been better informed as to these resemblances than Richard Wagner himself; and if, in spite of all this, he still believed that he *might* be Geyer's son, and had no hesitation in confessing this belief to a number of his intimates, the inference is irresistible that he must have had stronger reasons for that belief than have been so far communicated to the world. He may still have been mistaken, of course. We can be certain neither one way nor the other; all we can do is to insist on the fact that Wagner himself, in his later years, inclined to the belief that Geyer was his father, though he must have been as fully acquainted as any of us to-day with all that can be urged in support of the theory that he was the son of Carl Friedrich.[1]

Opponents of the Geyer theory lay stress on the formality of address in his letters to Johanna,[2] and especially on the fact that

---

[1] The reader will find a fuller discussion of this subject in NW, pp. 321–350.

[2] The four letters from Geyer to the widow that are the basis of such knowledge as we have of the relations of the pair during the months immediately following the death of Carl Friedrich are given in BRW. They are dated 22nd December, 1813, 14th January, 28th January and 11th February, 1814, all from Dresden. One of the 29th December, 1813, is reproduced in BLG, p. 31.

It should be noted that when the Avenarius family (i.e. the descendants of

Geyer uses *Sie* instead of the more intimate *Du;* is it likely, it is asked, that this formal manner would be adopted by a man to a woman whose lover he had been? Here again we have to remind ourselves that Wagner himself was perfectly well aware of this formality, and that it does not appear to have weighed with him in the least. He comments, indeed, in his letter to Cäcilie, on " the delicate, fine, and highly cultured tone of these letters, particularly of those to our mother." He cannot understand, he continues, how this tone of " genuine culture " can have become so lowered in the later intercourse of the members of the family with each other. It is immediately after saying this that he remarks " *At the same time,* however, it was possible for me, from these letters to Mother, to gain a deep insight into the relations of the two in difficult times." That is to say, the formality of the letters does not, for him, negate what he believes to be the inner significance of their contents.

It would be interesting if some student of German manners in the early nineteenth century could inform us whether there is anything to be surprised at in the formal style of these letters. Weingartner tells us that he has in his possession some letters written by his father to his mother during their courtship — i.e. about 1860, a full half century later than these letters of Geyer. He describes them as " delicate, amiable, heartfelt outpourings in the flowery, somewhat ceremonious style of that time, when engaged couples of good society still addressed each other as *Sie.*" [1]

Wagner was as sensible as any modern writer on the subject can be of the " tone " of the Geyer letters: as we have seen, he expressly remarks on it in his letter to Cäcilie. Once more, then, if, in spite of this and of his undoubted knowledge of the facial resemblance between himself and his brother Albert, he persisted in his belief that he may have been the son of Geyer, for us to regard these two simple considerations as utterly ruling out such a possibility is surely being more royalist than the king. [2]

Cäcilie) placed these four letters at Mrs. Burrell's service in the eighteen-nineties, only a portion of that of 22nd December, 1813, was sent to her; the last page actually breaks off in the middle of a word. It would be interesting to know what was in the latter portion of the letter.

[1] WL, I, 4, 5.

[2] Bélart (BRWB) who insists that Wagner was Geyer's son, makes a great parade of pseudo-science—tracing all kinds of resemblances between Wagner's face

2

Both the Wagner and the Geyer families have been traced back for several generations.

Of the male Wagners known to us, four were schoolmasters or school assistants, and in some cases, no doubt, church organists also. These were —

1. Samuel Wagner (1643–1705), of Thammenhain.
2. Emmanuel Wagner (1664–1726), son of the foregoing; of Colmen, then schoolmaster in Kühren for twenty-two and three-quarter years.
3. Samuel Wagner (1703–1750), second son of the foregoing; schoolmaster at Müglenz.

The father of the first-named — himself a Samuel — is also conjectured to have been a village schoolmaster.

The Müglenz Samuel's son, Gottlob Friedrich (February 1736–1795), is supposed to have become a student of theology in Leipzig University in 1759, though this is not certain. In 1767 he became an assistant excise officer. He married, two years later, Johanna Sophia Eichel, the daughter of a Leipzig schoolmaster; he had already had by her, in 1765, a son who died in infancy. The first-fruit of the marriage was Carl Friedrich Wilhelm Wagner (17th or 18th June, 1770 — 22nd November, 1813), the legal father of the composer. The second son, Gottlob Heinrich Adolf (14th November, 1774 — 1st August, 1835), was the " Uncle Adolf "

---

and Geyer's, for example—but his chatter is finally quite worthless as a serious contribution to the subject.

In BDM will be found several instances of old-fashioned formal politeness in the form of address of intimates, or even lovers, to each other. Goethe uses the "Sie" in his letters to Frau von Stein, and Johann Heinrich Voss to his fiancée Ernestine Boie (16th June, 1773): "How delightful," he says, "is the passage in which you [Sie] give me permission, if I am good, to call you Ernestine always." Charlotte von Lengefeld, at the end of 1788, uses the "Sie" in a letter to her "lieber Freund" Schiller, whom she married fifteen months later. Friedrich Wilhelm of Prussia is still addressed as "Sie" by his bride Luise a few days before their marriage in 1793; while calling him her "Heissgeliebter" ("ardently beloved one"), she speaks of her letter as being proof of her "tender and sincere friendship." Grillparzer, in 1830, uses the "Sie" to Kathi Fröhlich, with whom he was passionately in love. Gottfried Keller addresses Luise Rieter as "Sie" in the letter in which he makes a proposal of marriage—in 1847. As late as 1877 Detlev Fritz von Liliencron uses the "Sie" to the "gnädiges Fräulein" for whose hand he is asking.

It looks, then, on the whole, as if the "Sie" in Geyer's letters to Johanna is not inconsistent with something more than mere ordinary friendship.

who figures so largely in the story of the early years of Richard's life. There was also a daughter, Friederike (born in 1778), who resembled her famous nephew in " the abnormal size of her chin." Carl Friedrich became a scholar at St. Thomas's School, Leipzig, on the 22nd December, 1780, and nine years afterwards he entered some university or other, — not, however, according to Mrs. Burrell, that of Leipzig, as the older biographers have supposed: they had been misled by the name in the school lists of another Carl Friedrich Wagner (born 7th May, 1770, son of the grazier Michael Wagner).

It was probably on the 2nd June, 1798, that Carl Friedrich married the twenty-four-years-old [1] Johanna Rosine Paetz [2] (19th September, 1774 — 9th January, 1848), the daughter of a Weissenfels master baker. Nine children were born to them:

1. Albert (2nd March, 1799 — 31st October, 1874). He became a singer, then a stage manager. He had three children:
    a. Johanna (13th October, 1826 — 16th October, 1894), the famous singer. She married (2nd May, 1859) Alfred Jachmann.
    b. Franziska (28th August, 1829 — 20th June, 1895). She married, on 12th September, 1854, the composer Alexander Ritter, a brother of the Karl Ritter with whom Wagner was so closely associated about the middle of the century.
    c. Marie (25th January, 1831 — 19th May, 1876). She married, on 27th January, 1851, the merchant Carl Jacoby.
2. Carl Gustav (21st July, 1801 — 12th November, 1802).
3. Rosalie (4th March, 1803 — 12th October, 1837), who became an actress. She married, on the 24th October, 1836, the Leipzig University Professor Gotthard Oswald Marbach, and died a few days after having given birth to a daughter.
4. Carl Julius (7th August, 1804 — 29th March, 1862). He became a goldsmith.

---

[1] Mrs. Burrell, who was extremely scrupulous about dates, insists that she was born on the 19th September, 1774, and that she was consequently between thirty-eight and thirty-nine when Richard was born. Her birthday was always kept in the Wagner family on September 20th.

[2] The spellings in the older biographies—Pertz, Bertz, Berthis, Peitz, etc.—are incorrect.

5. Luise (14th December, 1805 — 2nd January, 1872), who became an actress, leaving the stage, however, in 1828, when she married the well-known Leipzig publisher Friedrich Brockhaus.

6. Klara (29th November, 1807 — 17th March, 1875). She became an operatic singer, but had to abandon her profession at an early age, owing to the loss of her voice. She married, in 1829, Heinrich Wolfram, who was then a singer, but who later settled in Chemnitz as a merchant.

7. Maria Theresia (1st April, 1809 — January, 1814).

8. Ottilie (14th March, 1811 — 17th March, 1883). She married, in 1836, the philologist Hermann Brockhaus, a younger brother of the above-mentioned Friedrich Brockhaus.

9. Wilhelm Richard, the composer (22nd May, 1813 — 13th February, 1883); baptised at St. Thomas' Church, Leipzig, 16th August, 1813.[1]

We possess no portrait of Carl Friedrich Wagner, and little is known of him except that he was a man of education and good literary taste, with a particular passion for the theatre: he named his daughters after Goethe's and Schiller's heroines. He had studied jurisprudence as a young man, and at the age of twenty-three had been admitted as a notary. In 1794 he became Vice-Actuary, or Deputy Registrar, at the Town Court of Leipzig, and in 1805 Actuary. In 1806 Saxony had concluded an alliance with Napoleon, and there was a legend in the Wagner family that in December of that year Carl Friedrich, who had a sound knowledge of French, was entrusted by Marshal Davoust with the reorganisation of the Leipzig legal system, and made provisional chief of the newly formed Police for Public Safety. Mrs. Burrell doubts this story; according to her, Carl Friedrich's knowledge of languages did indeed secure for him a post in the police service, but not until 1810. His salary, from then to the time of his death, was 1,045 thalers a year. The French campaign in Saxony in 1813 threw a great deal of extra and exhausting work upon him. In August of that year the short truce arranged between Napoleon and his enemies expired;

---

[1] Not, as Wagner says in *Mein Leben*, "two days after" his birthday. He was born in Leipzig, in the house known as the "Red and White Lion," in the Brühl. The building was later numbered 88. In 1886 it was replaced by a new building.

Saxony had thrown in her lot with the French, and Leipzig, with the King in it, was invested by the Allies on the 16th October. The three-days' battle of Leipzig, that ended in a decisive check to Napoleon, ended on the 18th; during the battle the Saxon army deserted to the Allies, and King Friedrich August was made a prisoner. The devastation in the city threw still more work on Carl Friedrich Wagner; in his enfeebled condition he fell a victim to the hospital fever (typhus) that broke out — mainly as the result of so many corpses being left unburied — and died on the 22nd November, six months after the birth of Richard.

Carl Friedrich was not only a patron of the Leipzig theatre, which was situated only a few paces from his home: he was an amateur actor, taking part in the performances given by the local company of theatrical amateurs whenever a member of the royal family visited the town. He was an ardent supporter of the local " privileged " theatre,[1] which held a high place among the German theatres of the day, for the central position of Leipzig, its famous University, and its annual book fairs enabled the town to play a leading part in German culture. It was at Leipzig, on the 17th September, 1801, that Schiller's *Jungfrau von Orleans* had received its first performance, at which Carl Friedrich Wagner and his wife were present. It was through their association with the theatre that they made the acquaintance of Ludwig Geyer.

3

The Geyer family has been traced back to one Benjamin Geyer, who, at the commencement of the eighteenth century, was Town Musician at Eisleben. One of his sons, also a Benjamin (1682–1742), was organist at St. Andrew's Church, Eisleben, from 1703 until his death. The latter's son Gottlieb Benjamin (1710–1762), studied music and philosophy in Leipzig some time between 1732 and 1738, and it is conjectured that he may not only have heard Sebastian Bach play but have had lessons from him on the organ.

---

[1] I.e. not a State or municipal theatre, but one run by a speculative impresario under license from the town or the government. It would sometimes be occupied by a local company, sometimes by a visiting troupe. Dresden (the Saxon capital) and Leipzig were at this time catered for chiefly by the Seconda companies, of which we shall hear more shortly.

He married the daughter of the cantor of St. Anne's, Eisleben, about 1737, and in the following year succeeded to his father-in-law's post. In 1750 he became organist and cantor of the neighbouring church of St. Nicholas.

With this Gottlieb's son — Christian Gottlieb Benjamin (1744–1799) — a break was made with the Church as a profession. Christian Gottlieb studied law at Leipzig, where, in 1764, he figures in the books of the University as " Dr. iur. utr. decretal. prof. ordinar. fac. iur. ordin." On his return to Eisleben in 1772 he practised as an advocate and actuary, and was appointed Clerk " beim Kurfürstlich Sächsischen Ober-Aufseheramte." In 1776 he married a lady who would apparently be regarded as of some standing in the provincial German world of that day, the daughter of no less a person than a former cook to a Dresden Commandant. Their second child was a son, Ludwig Heinrich Christian (21st January, 1779 — 30th September, 1821), who was destined to take a place in history as the " Father Geyer " of the Wagner story. Of another son, Karl Friedrich Wilhelm (born 27th March, 1791) we shall hear later, when he comes for a moment into the story of Richard Wagner's childhood.

Shortly after Ludwig's birth his father removed to Artern, a small town in Thuringia; and here, it is believed, a visiting painter from Leipzig first detected the boy's aptitude for the arts of design. We hear of his being educated in Eisleben from 1793 to the spring of 1797, and then we lose sight of him until May, 1798, when he entered the Leipzig University as a student of law, at the same time taking lessons in art at the Painting Academy. He would almost certainly have made painting the prime object of his life but for a series of family misfortunes. His father sustained heavy business losses towards the end of 1798, and with a view to retrieving his fortunes removed to Dresden to take up an appointment as " Ober-Steuer-Calculator." This affair having, apparently, been satisfactorily concluded, he was returning to Artern, when, outside the gates of Leipzig, he was involved in a carriage accident, from the effects of which he died, in the presence of his son, some time in the first half of 1799.[1] He left behind him nothing but debts.

---

[1] In all details concerning the Geyer family I have followed BLG. Bournot has corrected the errors of Glasenapp and other earlier investigators.

The support of the family now devolved upon Ludwig, who, at the age of twenty, and while still a mere student, was forced to practise his barely acquired art as a painter professionally. He was consequently never able to develop his genuine talent to the full; all his life, seemingly, he remained, as a painter, something of a brilliant amateur. After a brief visit to Artern to wind up his father's affairs he returned to Leipzig in the latter half of 1800. It is probable that he had already, as a student, made the acquaintance of the Wagner family, for in the *Leipziger Anzeiger* of 3rd September, 1800, there appears an announcement in which " Vice-Actuarius C. F. Wagner recommends to his friends a young portrait-painter who, by the blows of fate, has been suddenly forced to abandon his juristic studies, and whose pictures attain the highest degree of likeness." [1] It is true that Geyer is not mentioned by name, but the announcement can hardly refer to anyone else: in all the contemporary notices we have of Geyer as an artist, particular stress is laid on the fact that his portraits are " speaking likenesses."

He now gave up law and its prospects entirely, toured the country for a time as a portrait painter, and then settled in Leipzig, where he became a house-intimate of the Wagners: the eager young artist must have been stimulated by the culture and the enthusiasm of the eight-years-older Carl Friedrich. We soon find Geyer making an appearance among the company of amateur actors to which Carl Friedrich belonged, and revealing such talent for the stage that he was easily persuaded to take up acting professionally. He joined the Magdeburg troupe at the beginning of 1805, being content to study his new art in minor parts for some time, till ultimately he took a fairly high place in his profession. At the end of 1805 he left Magdeburg for Stettin: the company broke up in the autumn of 1806, as a result of the economic disasters that came in the train of Jena and Austerlitz, and Geyer settled in Breslau till August, 1809. Then he removed once more to Leipzig, where he was hospitably housed under Carl Friedrich's roof. As the result of a couple of successful guest-appearances in October, 1809, he was engaged as a permanent member of the Seconda troupe.

At the end of the eighteenth century and the beginning of the nineteenth, many of the German theatres and opera houses were

---

[1] BLG, p. 22.

still not only under Italian influence as regards taste but actually in Italian hands. The theatrical fare in Leipzig had been for some time provided by an impresario named Bondini. He was succeeded by his secretary, Franz Seconda, whose brother Joseph ran a complementary company in Dresden. Franz's company devoted itself almost entirely to the drama; it had the use of the Royal Theatre when in Dresden. Here, too, was housed the Italian Opera. Joseph's troupe was partly concerned with German opera; and as this, in the eyes of the Italianised Saxon Court, was an inferior branch of the art, it was barred from the Royal Theatre, its performances being given in the small theatre in the Linke'sches Bad.[1] No musician from the Royal Theatre was allowed to take part in these performances. Towards the end of 1814 the Russian authorities who were then administering the affairs of the town annulled the contract of Franz Seconda and declared the theatre a State institution. It was placed under the supreme control of Court Marshal von Racknitz, with Privy Secretary Winkler[2] as Intendant. King Friedrich August the Just, on his return to his capital in 1815, continued this arrangement, Count Heinrich Vitzthum, however, being substituted for Racknitz: Franz Seconda was given the minor rank of Economic Councillor. Out of Joseph Seconda's company there was constructed, later, the Court German Opera, of which Weber was appointed the first head in 1817.

In virtue of his membership of the Franz Seconda company, Geyer thus became, in the autumn of 1817, a " Royal Saxon Court Player." The public of Leipzig and that of Dresden were served alternately by the Seconda brothers, Franz's theatrical troupe playing in Leipzig in the summer and in Dresden in the winter, Joseph's operatic troupe in Dresden in the summer and in Leipzig in the winter.

During the visits of the company with which he was connected to Leipzig, Geyer seems always to have had his quarters in the Wagner house. Mr. O. G. Sonneck, anxious to load the dice against

---

[1] This "Bad" was a favourite country resort of the Dresdeners in the summer. Towards the end of the eighteenth century the gardens belonged to the Excise Councillor Linke, who built a theatre there in 1776.

[2] A man of many activities, who dabbled in literature under the pseudonym of Theodor Hell. He plays a not inconsiderable part in the life of Richard Wagner up to 1849.

any possibility of the truth of the theory that Geyer may have been Richard Wagner's father, demands irrefragable proof that Geyer was " in Leipzig from six months, at the very latest, to nine months before Wagner's birth on May 22nd, 1813." " I know very well," he continues, " that the Seconda theatrical company usually played at Leipzig from the Oster-Messe until the Michaelis-Messe (that is, from spring to fall), but it must be proved . . . that this was also true of the year 1812." [1] But this seems to be carrying scepticism to an extreme. We know that Geyer was a member of the theatrical company from 1809 till his death in 1821, and that this engagement was the main source of his livelihood. Although the events of his career have been traced in fair detail by Bournot, there is not the slightest suggestion by his biographer, or by anyone else, that in this one summer, 1812, he failed to appear with the company in Leipzig as usual, though we do know that the summer of 1813 was spent by him in Teplitz, Seconda having decided to play there instead of at Leipzig, about which town the war-clouds were now gathering. All in all, the burden of proof that Geyer, by solitary exception, was absent from Leipzig during the summer theatrical season of 1812 would appear to lie upon those who would fain establish that convenient proposition.[2]

Geyer had hoped that, as he could not visit Leipzig as usual in the summer of 1813, the Wagners, with the recently-born Richard, would join him for a holiday in Teplitz; but this proved impossible. When war was resumed, on the 15th August, all strangers were ordered to leave Teplitz. Geyer, and presumably the rest of the company, returned to Dresden for the winter. And there, in due course, the news reached him of the death of his friend Carl Friedrich Wagner in Leipzig on the 22nd November.

---

[1] SSC, p. 197.

[2] It remains to be added that, even supposing Wagner to have been Geyer's child, the amount of Jewish blood in him must have been infinitesimal. The Geyers had been Protestants by faith for generations, and had always married into pure German families. Geyer himself bore the very un-Semitic name of Ludwig Heinrich *Christian:* he was baptised at Eisleben (Luther's town) on the 23rd January, 1779.

CHAPTER II

GEYER

1

APPARENTLY ALL that the widowed Johanna had at the moment on which to support herself and her eight [1] children was some £40, being the current quarter's salary of her deceased husband,[2] which would become payable on the 16th December. The " pension " of which some biographers speak is described by Mrs. Burrell as " a myth." But friends, Geyer among them, came quickly and energetically to the rescue. Mrs. Burrell tells us, on the authority of Anna Zocher,[3] that Geyer at once made the journey to Leipzig, in spite of the difficulty and perhaps danger of it at that troubled time, to bring consolation and help. " It is certain," says Mrs. Burrell, " that she had no money, and what she owed for rent and war tax was wiped out, which proves her inability to pay it." Geyer's own position just then must have been an exceedingly anxious one. " You cannot have the smallest conception of the wretched state of Dresden," he writes to Johanna on the 22nd December. " People here have no spirit left to go on living, and yet are afraid of death, though they could not do anything more suitable than die. I myself would like to be a dormouse this winter; but I have resolved to fight resolutely against this world-irony, the fools of which we are." ("Irony" was a favourite catchword of the Romantics when speaking of the disparity between the tragic world of reality and the ideal world of their dreams.) He placed Johanna in a new apartment, where she could make a trifle by sub-letting. Her son Albert, who was now fourteen, was left at school in Meissen. Rosalie

---

[1] Their number was soon reduced to seven, the little Theresia dying in the following January.

[2] See her receipt for the amount of 261 thalers, 6 groschen, in BRW, p. 16.

[3] Anna Zocher (later Frau Doktor Rose) and Emmy Zocher (later Frau Baumgarten) were the daughters of Albert Wagner's friend Gustav Zocher. Mrs. Burrell made the acquaintance of these two ladies in the eighteen-nineties, and took down their reminiscences of the young Richard and his relations.

and Luise were sent to Dresden, where Luise was taken charge of by Carl Friedrich's actress friend, Frau Hartwig. According to Bournot, Geyer, on his return to Dresden, kept urging Johanna to come to him there, " as he had something important and personal to say to her." From a letter of his of the 11th February, 1814, it would appear that she was then about to make the journey: " I have a great deal to say to you," he writes, " and I impatiently await the time when I can have a heart-to-heart talk with you on the cosy sofa "; and Bournot is right in saying that " the tone and the contents of these letters will convince anyone who had studied them that besides the most upright friendship there was also a particular attraction, which led to the marriage of the pair on the 14th [1] August, 1814, in the parish church of Bödewitz [Poetewitz], near Weissenfels," — not, as might have been expected, in Leipzig. As we have already seen, intimacy between them must have begun not later than the preceding May, for Cäcilie was born on the following 26th February (1815).[2] According to Saxon law, a widow could not re-marry in less than ten months after her husband's death. Ten months from the 22nd November, 1813, however, would be the 22nd September, 1814.

The few letters of Geyer to Johanna that have been published contain veiled allusions to matters upon the nature and significance of which, at this distant epoch, we can only speculate. A letter of the 29th December, 1813 — only five weeks after the death of Carl Friedrich — seems to hint at a previous slight estrangement. " Dear Friend," it runs, " I once more hold out my hand to you in trust,[3] with a warm hand-press let every recollection that overcasts our life be blotted out, especially the remembrance of our recent correspondence, let us look for the purer metal in us, not the dross, I am now susceptible to everything good, how otherwise could I bind myself so firmly to you and your dear ones? Over the sarcophagus

---

[1] The correct date, however, is the 28th August.

[2] According to Glasenapp, shortly after the widow had "quietly become" Geyer's wife, she "returned to Leipzig, whither he followed her about Easter." As we have seen, Glasenapp's dates for this period are—perhaps designedly so—ambiguous. This visit of Johanna to Dresden, her return to Leipzig, and the journey of Geyer thither, must all have been *before*, not after, the marriage in August, 1814. Glasenapp's German, however, is not quite clear; it may mean either that Geyer became engaged to Johanna or that he married her, as Ellis translates it.

[3] I retain the punctuation of the original.

of the year 1813 let us bind our friendship's bond even closer, the summons to do so is great and noble. And so I exterminate all jealousy that could still cling to me. Do you do the same, and let us face each other in strength and truth." Bournot will not have it that by " recollection that overcasts our life " Geyer can possibly have meant " anything deep-reaching "; " only unimportant incidents," he says, " small disagreements, could be the ground for explanations of this kind. The concluding portion of the letter, the ' abandonment of all jealousy,' and the whole tone of the letter, clearly indicate what the matter is that is in question — some jealousy on Geyer's part, that had led to a retort in kind from the wounded Johanna." We are still, however, left searching for an explanation why mutual " jealousy " so serious in its temporary consequences as this should be troubling Carl Friedrich's friend and Carl Friedrich's widow within a month or so of Carl Friedrich's death.

We may conjecture that Uncle Adolf looked with no friendly eye on his sister-in-law's second marriage. He had seen a good deal of Geyer during the last thirteen years, and we gather that he did not, at that time, share the good opinion of him held by the world in general — though it is possible that the tendency to frivolity he deplored in him was really nothing more than the ordinary *sans gêne* of theatrical life. Adolf was a scholar who loved the drama but disliked the stage. He was a man of high literary reputation, commanding great respect in his own day — the pure type of German scholar of the old school, scorning delights and living laborious days, taking the whole field of literature, history, philosophy and philology for his province, and asking little more of life than that it should provide him with material substance enough to sustain him in his intellectual work. He had known Schiller and Fichte, and was intimate with Tieck and other celebrities; he did good service to German culture by his translations from and into various languages and by his studies of the poets and philosophers of antiquity. There was, indeed, the same breadth of mental span in him as in his greater nephew, but without anything of Wagner's genius; as Mrs. Burrell says, " the description of Adolf's varied gifts looks as if the family had already tried to produce a Richard and failed." An ascetic and a strict moralist, he mistrusted the atmosphere of the theatre, while the breadth and depth of his sober intellect made him despise the facile arts by which the actor substitutes illusion for reality. He seems, indeed, to have held the rather extreme opinion that the actor's constant feigning upon the stage must necessarily lead to a corresponding insincerity in the serious things of life; and he was particularly set against the theatre as a career for women. " When I look closely into his calling," he wrote, " I cannot but regard a life devoted to it as thrown away. No one who knows the actor's life needs to be told how it burns a man out, pumps him dry, makes him shallow; how it brings with it so-called fortunes and adventures that are too paltry to be of any use in the forming of a man, but serious enough in any case to pervert the mind and manners of a woman. The wild whirl of the outer life and the lying jugglery of the inner involve too sharp an antithesis, too violent a strain, not to dislocate and subvert the nature of a woman."

Holding opinions such as these, Adolf would see in the new marriage only a greater, and perhaps irresistible, temptation to Carl Friedrich's children to adopt the stage as their profession; and as four of the seven children were girls, he had an extra reason to feel perturbed. Rosalie, the eldest of the girls, had indeed been marked out by her father for an actress, though he had laid it down that she was not to commence until she was at least fifteen or sixteen; while Luise had been given that name in a spasm of enthusiasm for Frau Hartwig's playing of the part of Luise in Schiller's *Kabale und Liebe*, and already the child was so closely connected with the popular actress in the family sentiment that, as we have seen, it was to Frau Hartwig that she was sent after the death of the father. Geyer, however, had himself no more real liking for the stage than any intelligent man has for the profession by which fate has compelled him to earn a living, but of which he has seen too much from the inside to have any of the romantic illusions about it that outsiders have. In the end, the tug of the theatre proved too strong to be resisted by most of the children, brought up, as they had been first of all, by a father whose passion was the stage and whose intimates were mostly connected with the stage, and then turned over to a stepfather who, earning his living mostly as an actor, was bound hand and foot to the theatrical machine. But Geyer knew too much of the difficulties and dangers of that life to be at all anxious to thrust any of the little ones dependent upon him into it. Albert, the eldest, after a short period of study of medicine, decided to become an actor, no doubt because it suggested to his notoriously practical mind better prospects of an early income, however small; whereupon Geyer warned him in the most serious tones against the perilous " comedianism " of the new world he was about to enter.

2

For the moment, however, no such questions as these arose to trouble the new household in Dresden, where Johanna settled at Michaelmas, 1814. Johanna had a temperament that does not seem to have been given to fretting overmuch or overlong about anything. We may take it that she was born on the 10th September, 1774; [1] her father, Johann Gottlieb Pätz, had married Dorothea Erdmuth Iglisch, a tanner's daughter, on the 11th January, 1763. Johanna was the fourth child of the marriage: she was little more than fourteen years old when her mother died (on the 5th January, 1789). We may perhaps detect a little hint of mystery in Wagner's story of so much as he had been able to glean from her about her early days. " She never," he says, " gave any of her children any definite information about her extraction. She came from Weissenfels, where, she admitted, her parents had been bakers.[2] Even in regard to her maiden name she spoke with a strange embarrassment, giving it as ' Perthes,' whereas, as we discovered, it was really ' Bertz.' [3] The curious thing was [4] that she had been placed in a

---

[1] This seems to be the correct date, not 1778 or 1779, as given in various biographies. See the article in RWJF, II, 19 ff., by Stephan Kekule von Stradonitz, who examined the Weissenfels records.

[2] Wagner adds in a footnote, "According to more recent information, mill-owners."

[3] As a matter of fact it was neither, but Paetz, or Beetz. Mrs. Burrell explains this and similar confusions as being due to the Saxon habit of pronouncing B as P, and P as B. She found that Johanna's name was entered at various times in the church books of St. Thomas, Leipzig, as "geborene Betz, Pez, Beez, Beetz, Betz, and Beetz"; while her father was married "in the same church in the same village, firstly as Pätz, secondly as Bätz, and thirdly as Pätz, and finally died as Bätz, all according to the accent of the book-keeper." The comedy, according to Stephan Kekule von Stradonitz, was continued to the very end. Johanna died in Leipzig in 1848. In the register of burials she is described as *geborene Pätz*. Over this is written the correction *Bertz*. This in turn is crossed out, and in the margin is written, "The deceased Frau Geyer was not *geborene Bertz* but *geborene Pätz*."

[4] Was the "curious thing" the fact that a daughter of a Weissenfels small tradesman should have been sent to be educated at a select Leipzig school? Was the mysterious "fatherly friend," perchance, her real father? Note that Wagner puts

select educational institution in Leipzig, where she enjoyed the advantage of the care of one whom she called ' an exalted fatherly friend,' [1] to whom she afterwards referred as being a Weimar prince who had been of service to her family in Weissenfels. Her education in this establishment seems to have been interrupted by the sudden death of this fatherly friend." Presumably she was not long enough at the Leipzig school to obtain much education before she married Carl Friedrich Wagner in 1798, for even her son Richard has to admit that " her education was very faulty." Carl Friedrich took her to Lauchstädt in June, 1803, to see the first performance of Schiller's *Die Braut von Messina;* on which occasion her husband, as she informed Richard later, " rebuked her warmly " for her ignorance of Goethe and Schiller, whom he pointed out to her on the promenade.

Mrs. Burrell, on the strength of information supplied to her by Albert Wagner's daughter Johanna (the first Elisabeth in *Tannhäuser*), tells us that " Richard seems to have resembled his mother in nothing but his small size and electric disposition." She was " a tiny, eccentric woman, so diminutive . . . that when she visited her daughter-in-law [Minna] in 1845 at Dresden the maid took her on her arm like a baby and ran up the stairs with her." She suffered from " head-gout," and " wore nine caps one over the other to keep her head warm." We are reminded of Richard's abnormal sensitiveness to cold, necessitating a certain amount of luxury, for which he has been rather unfairly criticised, in the matter of silk underclothing and padded dressing-gowns.

Whatever Johanna lacked in culture she made up for in mother-wit. Wagner describes her chief characteristics as being " a droll humour and a good temper "; she was a " peculiar mixture of domestic bourgeois efficiency and extreme intellectual sensibility." The new establishment does not seem to have been badly off for its station in life, for Geyer was always able to supplement his salary

---

this part of the phrase—*die Sorge eines von ihr sogenannten "hohen väterlichen Freundes"*—in inverted commas, and rather pointedly repeats the *"väterlichen Freundes"* a few lines later. Mrs. Burrell heard a tradition, coming from more than one source, that Johanna "was chosen by [Duke] Karl August and Goethe for the Weimar stage, and it was through Goethe that Friedrich Wagner made her acquaintance and married her."

[1] In the English version of *Mein Leben* this is mis-translated as "one of her father's influential friends."

as an actor (1040 thalers) by his portrait painting, for which com-
missions were fairly plentiful. The family in his immediate charge
was a relatively small one. The eldest child, Albert, who had been
at school at Meissen, now went to Leipzig University to study medicine. Luise, though living in the same town as her mother, was still
under the care of Frau Hartwig. Theresia had died, at less than the
age of five, in January, 1814. Rosalie, however, was under the maternal roof once more.

Until 1816 Geyer's duties with the Royal Court Players took him
to Leipzig each Easter; afterwards the company confined its operations to Dresden, though Geyer made frequent guest appearances
in various other towns. As an actor he was undoubtedly competent.
The " idealistic " school of acting that Goethe had imposed upon
Weimar, and that had spread thence to other German stages, was at
this time being energetically challenged by a more naturalistic
method, the leading representative of which was Friedrich Ludwig
Schröder of Hamburg. A third group, of which the chief figures
were Ludwig Devrient, Ferdinand Esslair, and Sophie Schröder
(the mother of the famous Wilhelmine Schröder-Devrient who
played so large a part in the early stages of Wagner's operatic career), aimed at combining the virtues of both schools, reproducing
the accents and the gestures of nature, but still giving them a certain
plastic composition instead of letting them sink to the level of crude
realism.[1] This was Geyer's ideal of acting also. His general intelligence, his wide culture, and the liveliness of his temperament made
him particularly admirable in ordinary character parts. In the more
heroic figures he was hampered by the smallness of his person and
the relative weakness of his voice; but he had brains enough to
achieve a certain success even in parts of this kind. His exceptional
culture, indeed, seems to have brought on him the dislike of some
of his colleagues whose own intellectual equipment was no more
remarkable than has been usual from time immemorial in the
theatrical profession. In addition, Geyer, with his painter's instinct
and technical experience, was peculiarly skilled in designing his
own costumes.

---

[1] For an account of these various schools see GWKZ. Genast was the son of the
regisseur (stage manager) of the Weimar theatre under Goethe: his own life was
mostly spent in Weimar, first as an actor, then as regisseur.

He even took a minor singing part occasionally. He had already displayed his agreeable, if not specifically trained, tenor voice once or twice in the Seconda company; and Weber thought enough of it to make use of it, at a pinch, for purely operatic ends. In 1817, as we have seen, Weber had been entrusted with the task of founding a German opera in Dresden. The Court favour, however, was still bestowed mostly on the Italian opera; and Morlacchi, the Italian Kapellmeister, kept so jealous a hold on the singers that Weber, in sheer desperation, had sometimes to resort to whatever material he could lay his hands on for his purpose in the theatrical portion of the German Court company. Geyer, if he had had no formal musical training, must certainly have had some natural aptitude for music; and Weber was glad to use him for small parts in some of the lighter German Singspiele and French comic operas.

Geyer further dabbled with some success in dramatic composition. For important events in the domestic circle he was accustomed to write little pieces [1] in which the children played parts appropriate to their ages and abilities. One of these, *Die Überraschung*, written for Johanna's birthday in 1816,[2] has come down to us, and from its innocent lines we can form some idea of the characteristics of the children at the time. The fifteen-year-old Rosalie had evidently assumed an authority over her juniors that was not to their liking. This is how she appeared in their eyes:

> Die will überhaupt hier schalten und walten,
> Das Beste ist ihr immer genug,
> Ja, sie hält sich allein für klug,

---

[1] The earliest that has survived (in the possession of the Avenarius family) was written for the celebration of Johanna's forty-first birthday, 20th September, 1815. It is entitled *Frauenlob* (*Praise of Woman*). According to the analysis of it given by Bournot, Geyer, after exercising his satirical wit on the failings of womankind, declares that his Johanna shares only two of them with the rest of her sex—grumbling and sulking. But it is only with her lips, not in her heart, that she sulks and grumbles; and her husband concludes with the affectionate assurance that if Heaven will only grant him length of days with her she can grumble to her heart's content. "Johanna," says Bournot, "is depicted as a woman of character and *savoir faire*, though of rather quick temper." "We see in these verses a virtuous, faithful wife, a provident and circumspect housewife, a kindly, charming woman, of whom we can well believe that in her lively way she had made a happy home for the poet. And the teasing enumeration of all the failings of woman abundantly shows that, as Geyer himself was a man of blithe wit and humour, the family relations in general were carried on in the same tone." BLG, p. 53.

[2] Not in 1818, as given in Koch's and other biographies. The manuscript, according to Bournot and Mrs. Burrell, is clearly dated 1816.

Und tut sich gewältig Anseh'n geben,
Und Richard hat immer den härtesten Stand,
Den schuppt sie manchmal an die Wand.
Aber wenn sie auch den Arm abschleckt,
Es hat vor ihr doch alles Respekt.

(" She is always ordering and bossing: the best is good enough for
her. She thinks she is the only one with any sense, and puts on a
mighty lot of airs. Richard always has the hardest time with her:
she often pushes him into a corner. But when she raises her hand,
she awes them all.")

What parts were played by the tiny Richard and the still smaller
Cäcilie in this domestic entertainment we do not know at first hand,
as their powers were apparently not looked upon as being equal to
the learning of a spoken rôle. But Richard is drawn for us in some
lines delivered by Albert:

Wir werden die Eltern so glücklich erblicken,
Dass sie am Ende vor Wohlstand ersticken.
Mit Richarden, glaub' ich, hat's auch keine Not,
Der wird ein zweiter Paul Butterbrot.
Der geht seinen Weg so ganz im stillen,
Und sucht sich nur immer den Magen zu füllen.
Ein guter Fresskünstler ist auch nicht so dumm,
Er findet nicht minder sein Publikum.

(" We will see our parents so happy that in the end they will burst
with comfort. As for Richard, there's no need to worry about him.
He will be a second Paul Bread-and-Butter. He goes his own way so
quietly, and thinks of nothing but filling his stomach. A good glutton-
artist, anyhow, is no fool: he will find his public.") [1]

On a more ambitious scale were certain pieces written for the
theatre, one of which, *Der bethlehemitische Kindermord* (*The Mas-
sacre of the Innocents*), had quite a little success during Geyer's
lifetime: it was produced for the first time at Dresden on 20th February, 1821, whence it made its way during the next few years to
Breslau, Hamburg, Berlin, Brunswick, Leipzig and other towns.
The charming serio-comedy is plainly a picture of the struggling
artist's life as Geyer himself had come to see it — the artist Klaus,
wholly absorbed in his visions of great pictures to be painted, being

---

[1] For a full analysis of the action of *Die Überraschung* see BLG, pp. 57–59.

perpetually brought down to earth by the material necessities of his family and the practical admonitions of his more realistically-minded wife Sophie.[1] Cosima delighted Wagner at Christmas, 1869, by making him a present of a copy of the play, which had recently been republished in a theatre almanac: and on his sixtieth birthday (22nd May, 1873) it was produced by her for his delectation at the old theatre of the Margravine Wilhelmine in Bayreuth.

Many a line and situation in it must have reminded him ruefully of his own life with Minna during the Zürich period. Minna could never understand why Richard should be wasting his time writing prose works which it was doubtful that anyone would read — the ponderous *Opera and Drama* and so on — and planning impracticable revolutionary theatrical works like the *Ring*, when he might have been producing good, sound pot-boilers for Paris. As Sophie puts it in Geyer's comedy, musing in her husband's studio during his absence:

> Ob er ein Bild entwirft? Ob lies't er oder schreibt?
> Ach, wollt' er endlich doch auf Nützliches sich legen!
> — Am Ende macht er Gold? — Da geb' ich meinen Segen,
> Gott weiss! das brauchen wir.

("Is he sketching a picture? Or reading? Or writing? Oh, if he would only devote himself to something profitable! What if he is making gold? I would give my blessing to that: God knows we need it!")

> Du hast stets dummes Zeug, nie Broterwerb vor Augen,

she reproaches him.

("You are always occupied with some stuff and nonsense or other, instead of thinking of our living.")

She dubs him "Hans ohne Sorgen" (Johnny Don't-Care), an epithet that would have summed up admirably poor Minna's opinion of Richard after 1849.

Wagner, for his part, must often have answered Minna as Klaus answers Sophie.

> Vom Himmel ziehst du mich beständig doch herunter,
> Erschlaffst die Phantasie mit lauter Alltagsplunder.

---

[1] The play is still well worth reading to-day. There is a convenient cheap reprint of it in the Reclam Series.

Der liebe Ehestand — ach, ja! es ist wohl wahr,
Ist stets ein Feind der Kunst — das zeigt sich offenbar.
Du schlägst mit Prosa tot, was ich begeistert fühle,
Sprech' ich von meiner Kunst, drehst du die Kaffeemühle.
Liegt mir ein grosser Plan zu einem Bild im Kopf,
So klagest du und zeigst den leeren Buttertopf.
Will ich durch Mittheilung an Raphael mich pflegen —
Was ist dir wichtiger, als Gurken einzulegen?
Nie kann ich ungestört der hohen Kunst mich weihn,
Denn immerfort steckt Eins die Nas' zur Thür herein;
Geld ist das Losungswort — das summt vor meinen Ohren;
In der Alltäglichkeit geht meine Kunst verloren.
Und nun beruh'ge dich, die Not hört jetzo auf,
Mein Bild — es *wird* berühmt, ich biet es aus zum Kauf.
Das Publikum wird sich darum entsetzlich reissen.
Ich werd' ein reicher Mann — du kannst von Silber speisen.

("You are continually dragging me down from the skies, enervating my imagination with the mere trash of everyday things. Alas, marriage is the enemy of art! You kill all my inspirations with your prose. If I talk about my art, you turn the coffee-mill. When I conceive a big plan for a picture, you set up a wail and show me the empty butter-pot. When I try to teach Raphael [one of Klaus's little sons], all you can do is to pickle a cucumber. I never get a chance to devote myself undisturbed to high art, for someone is sure to stick his nose in at the door. 'Money' is the word that is always being dinned into my ears. My art is ruined by all this triviality. But don't worry: our troubles will soon be at an end. My picture *will* be famous: I will put it up for sale: the public will fight like mad over it: I will be a rich man, and you will eat off silver.")

One of Sophie's complaints is that Klaus, instead of sticking to his job, mixes himself up with politics — quite like Richard. His reply — again in the true Wagner vein — is to tell the poor wretch gaily to go and get a bottle of good Burgundy for the dinner to which he has invited a guest — and a bottle of champagne for the dessert. She even surprises him in the act of embracing a fair sitter — for reasons, of course, rooted solely in his artistic enthusiasm — ("It isn't the first time," says Klaus in a mournful aside: "Goodbye, model!"); "So this," she says, "is why you asked a guest — to keep me busy in the kitchen!"

Had Geyer been gifted with prophetic vision he could not have painted a truer picture of poor Richard and Minna in the troubled years following the flight from Dresden.[1]

3

Der bethlehemitische Kindermord was Geyer's last literary work. The strain of his double artistic life was now decidedly telling on a constitution that had never been particularly strong. Not that he was overworked at the theatre. At that epoch plays were given in the Dresden theatre only four evenings a week, the Italian opera occupying the stage each Wednesday and Saturday, and no performance taking place on Friday: in addition the theatre was closed during Lent and Advent and other church seasons, as well as when the Court was in mourning. The actors consequently had a good deal of leisure for study and relaxation.[2] Geyer's flawed constitution probably suffered more from his confinement to his studio than from his exertions in the theatre. We have a hint of failing health as early as the *Überraschung* of 1816, in which reference is made to the father's need of more fresh air and his desire for horse exercise. A contemporary letter of his to Frau Hartwig speaks of the hypochondria to which he has become a prey, and that makes it more difficult than usual for him to provide for the needs of his large family.[3] In 1817 he tried a cure at Carlsbad that was only partially successful. A letter of September 1820 shows the clouds gathering fast about his brave spirit: " I am at present very hypochondriacal, and need some distraction, but dear livelihood calls out to me from every corner, and so I cannot just remain in my hypochondria, whether I want to or not." In the winter of that year he stayed for some time in Leipzig with Adolph Wagner, who, after the death of his mother in 1814, had taken apartments with his sister Friederike and Fräulein Jeannette Thomä in the famous old Thomä house.[4] Geyer vexed

---

[1] Mrs. Burrell obtained from Frau Baumgarten the manuscript of a portion of another work by Geyer, *Der Parnass*. (It had been written — 9th February, 1821 — for the birthday of Frau Baumgarten's father — Gustav Zocher — and of "Theodor Hell"; the latter was Cäcilie's godfather.) Mrs. Burrell prints Apollo's part from this in her biography of Wagner. Of the remainder of the work we are ignorant. Otto Bournot seems to have tried to consult the manuscript, and to have been informed that it was lost.

[2] See Friesen's account of the Dresden theatre at this period, in FLT, Vol. I.

[3] BLG, p. 70.

[4] Familiar to readers of Goethe as "Apel's House." The vast building had

Adolf somewhat by what the latter took to be moodiness, but which was really a morbid depression resulting from his overwrought condition and the swift inroads of the malady of the chest that was already undermining him. He was able to take up his theatrical work in the Dresden theatre again in the following February, and to play the part of Klaus in his own comedy;[1] but it was ominous that after the production of it on 20th February the work was not given again for some weeks, Geyer being too unwell to appear in it.

He was gladdened by reports of the success of his play in Breslau, and betook himself thither for four happy weeks, renewing old theatrical associations. But an attempt to take up his stage work in Dresden again on his return led to another partial breakdown: a newspaper criticism of 5th September records that during the performance " Herr Geyer was visibly fighting against physical disabilities." He fled to the near-by Pillnitz with Rosalie, and for the first time since their marriage he was absent from the domestic rejoicings on Johanna's birthday. His letters to Albert had been increasingly serious in tone for some time; and at last, from Pillnitz, there came one in which he seems to be conscious that the end was near: " Honour these well-meant and perhaps last words as a holy testament of your father, who would have you consider that you will be called upon to perform the duties that are now mine." The explanation of this is that Albert, who had taken up opera-singing as a career, had been misusing his voice; and Geyer, with the bitter consciousness of how his own vocal weakness had stood in the way of his advancement, and of the added strain it had been on his health in recent years to make the failing lungs and throat do what he required of them, warned Albert anxiously against the imprudent use of his own organ.[2]

---

become the property of the wealthy Commissary of the Exchequer Andreas Friedrich Thomä, who left it to his unmarried daughter Jeannette. It was "the regular abode" of the Saxon royal family when they visited Leipzig.

[1] The part of one of the children was taken by Klara, now thirteen years old.

[2] There has also come down to us a poetic epistle of Geyer's to Albert the exact date of which is uncertain. Max Koch attributes it to 1821, but probably in that year Geyer would not have blended so much humour with his advice and warnings as he does here; so that the epistle may perhaps be more justly dated 1820. Albert's light way of living and his reckless use of his voice were a constant trouble to Geyer. He warns Albert against the wiles of women, exhorting him to study music seriously — "stick your nose in thorough-bass" — so that he may not have to "gnaw at hunger-threads instead of beef" when he is no longer good for singing. The future,

On 20th September he sent a despairing letter from Pillnitz to Johanna:

" Dear Wife,
The weather is dreadful, and I am getting worse rather than better; so to-morrow morning or afternoon, immediately after dinner, take a carriage and bring a basket in which we can pack the things most necessary, and fetch me away. Even if everything is not in order in our house I prefer to be there, where I shall have more comfort and a warm room. . . . Fulfil this wish of your faithful husband."

He had only ten days more to live. Back in his Dresden home, he still busied himself hopefully with business affairs of the moment, planning, for instance, to have a lithograph made of his portrait of the King of Saxony. But he was becoming weaker daily, and suffering grievously from attacks of asthma. The little eight-year-old Richard had been for a year or more at the village school in Possendorf, a few miles out of Dresden. He has himself told, in *Mein Leben*, the story of those last days:

" One day . . . a messenger came from the town to ask the pastor to take me back to my parents' house in Dresden, as my father was dying. We did the three hours' journey on foot: I was exhausted when I arrived, so that I scarcely understood why my mother was in tears. The next day I was taken to my father's bedside: the extreme weakness of his voice, together with all the precautions taken in the last desperate treatment of his trouble — an acute hydrothorax — gave me the feeling that it was all only a dream; I believe I was too frightened and amazed to cry. In the next room my mother asked me to show what I could play on the piano, hoping the sound would divert my father somewhat. I played *Üb' immer Treu' und Redlichkeit*, and my father said to her, ' What if he has a talent for music? ' In the grey dawn the next morning my mother came into the big night nursery, and coming to the bedside of each of us in turn told us, with sobs, that our father was dead, and gave each of us a message with his blessing; to me she said, ' Of you he hoped to make something.' In the afternoon Pastor Wetzel [the schoolmaster at Possendorf] came and took me

---

he continues, is dark, the present dull; the public is weary of the theatre. As for the family, the mother is still struggling with her moods and spasms; Rosalie still has a bad throat, and restores herself with plum jam; Luise is getting bigger and fatter and hardly ever gets out of bed; Klara is as rude as ever, and Ottilie as given to gossiping; Richard is growing up and becoming very learned, while Cäcilie cheerfully dispenses with wisdom. See the whole poem in BLG, pp. 61–63. This was one of the Geyer documents that moved Wagner so deeply when Cäcilie sent him copies of them at Christmas, 1869.

back to the country. We walked all the way, and did not arrive until nightfall. On the way I asked him many questions about the stars, about which he gave me my first intelligent notions."

In the *Autobiographical Sketch* contributed by Wagner to the Dresden *Zeitung für die elegante Welt* in 1842 he adds one or two minor details. In addition to *Üb' immer Treu' und Redlichkeit* he played for Geyer the lately published *Jungfernkranz* (from *Der Freischütz*). He adds, " I remember that for a long time after I used to imagine that something would become of me."

It was the 30th September, 1821. For the second time in his brief eight years of life the boy was fatherless.

CHAPTER III

THE CHILD

1

JOHANNA, THOUGH poor enough, was not left in such dire need after her second widowhood as she had been after her first. She is alleged by some biographers to have been granted a small pension by the Court; but there appears to be no evidence for this. There were many of Geyer's pictures to sell. Albert, now twenty-two, had taken to the stage a year or so earlier, and was now maintaining himself in Breslau. Carl Friedrich Wagner's wish that Rosalie should not tread the boards until she was fifteen or sixteen had been respected; it was on the 2nd March, 1818, two days before her sixteenth birthday, that she made her first appearance in Dresden in her step-father's play *Das Erntefest* — the one serious drama of his that has come down to us [1] — in which she took the part of a fourteen-year-old child bearing the same name as herself. She showed so much talent as an actress that on 1st May, 1820, she was admitted to the company of Royal Court Players at a salary of 824 thalers; she made her début with the troupe twenty days later. A hint of the strength of her character has already been given us in the little play that Geyer wrote for the family circle in 1816. In the dark days immediately following the death of her step-father, we learn from a contemporary letter of a friend of the family, she was the only one able to master her grief:

"The most sober-minded of them all," we read, "was Rosalie. She bore herself with the utmost gravity. She exhorted her mother and her sisters to be calm and yield to God's will. 'He was too good for us,' she said, 'and that is why God has taken him from us and raised him above us; but we will try to be worthy of him. I swear to you, mother,'

---

[1] A summary of the plot is given in GRW, I, 64. BLG (p. 69) calls the play a failure, Geyer, in his opinion, having no gift for the tragic. Glasenapp discovered a copy of the play in 1878, and sent it to Wagner, who did not care greatly for the "Dresden Kotzebue" genre it represented. See MECW, I, 844.

LUDWIG GEYER
(*Courtesy, J. B. Lippincott Co.*)

ADOLF WAGNER
(*Courtesy, J. B. Lippincott Co.*)

she continued, 'that I will truly fulfil my duty as a daughter; God will give me strength and bless my endeavours. Yet must all of you,' she said (Richard was there with the others), 'stand by me, and God will bless you as he will me.' And so she maintains an appearance of firmness and tranquillity, so as to impress her mother and the other children, but when she is away from them she weeps, and at times gives free expression to her grief for the father she loved so much."

Plainly there was little need for the mother to distress herself about Rosalie; she was well able to take care not only of herself but of the others.

Luise, as we have seen, had been taken charge of by the actress Frau Hartwig, who was manifestly determined that she should adopt her own profession. The child made her first appearance at the age of about nine (in 1814); three years later she played the part of a ten-year-old child in a comedy, *Das Mädchen aus der Fremde*, specially written for her by Geyer under the pseudonym of E. Willig; Geyer himself acted in the piece. Soon after the death of her father she received an engagement at the Breslau theatre. Rosalie had studied for a time with the actress Frau Schirmer, between whom and Frau Hartwig there was no love lost. Emmy Zocher told Mrs. Burrell that the mutual jealousy of the two older actresses communicated itself for a while to their pupils, and the two Wagner sisters would not remain in the same room with each other at a party.

The boy Julius, who was now turned seventeen, had been apprenticed some time before to Geyer's younger brother, Karl Friedrich Wilhelm, a goldsmith at Eisleben. Julius was never of more than minor importance in Richard Wagner's life.

The Dresden household, therefore, now comprised, in addition to the mother, Rosalie, Klara, Ottilie, Richard and Cäcilie. Klara had already, at the age of thirteen, taken a child's part in the production of *Der bethlehemitische Kindermord* in 1821. She was now being trained as a singer; she made a successful début at the Italian Opera in Dresden on 1st May, 1824, as Angiolina in Rossini's *La Cenerentola*. In spite of her decided natural gifts and her early successes, however, her stage career was short, her voice soon showing the ill effects of the strain put upon it before it was fully developed. In 1828 she married the Magdeburg operatic singer and producer, Wolfram, and a few years later retired from the stage. Wolfram's own small vocal talent also deserting him in time, he gave up the stage and became manager of a machine factory at Fürth, near Nuremberg.

The problem of the family, at the moment, was little Richard. If Geyer had wanted to " make something " of him, that was because there had been signs already that he was different from the others. Physically and mentally he was made of more sensitive, perhaps more precarious, stuff than they. He was a tiny fellow with a large head, and blue eyes that were one of the secrets of his fascination in later life: Judith Gautier speaks of them as being " as blue as the lake of Lucerne," and again as " beaming eyes, where blended the most beautiful shades of sapphire." [1] As for his stature, there may be something in Balzac's theory that the great men of history have generally been small: " the head has to be near the heart if the two powers that govern the human organisation are to function well." As has been the case with many another man of genius, it seemed unlikely that Richard would survive early childhood; and all his life he was one of those men who are rarely well, but whose endurance and capacity for work are endless, and whose fundamental vitality of constitution actually comes to seem, in late middle age, to be proof against the assaults of time and the most exhausting labour. Cosima, in the happy days of the late eighteen-sixties at Triebschen, used to assure Richard that he would be doing his best work at ninety. So, in all probability, he would have been, equalling or surpassing the record of Verdi, but for the fact that his heart, which had already been damaged by the strain and the vexations of the Vienna and Munich periods, was unable to bear the terrific burden imposed upon it first of all by the creation of Bayreuth, secondly by the organisation of the two festivals there in 1876 and 1882. If, like Verdi, he could have made money easily in his young days, and, like Verdi, nursing an inveterate dislike of the mean theatrical world into which the fates had thrown him, had retired to the country, emerging only when it was necessary to force the latest of his works through in spite of the inertia and lack of understanding of the human instruments through which alone the dramatist can work, there can be little doubt that he would have

---

[1] GWH, pp. 33, 63.

achieved more than one masterpiece after *Parsifal,* if not in the field of music drama, at any rate in that of the symphony, towards which his thoughts were tending more and more in his last years.

He tells us in *Mein Leben* that after an illness in his early boyhood he was so weak that his mother almost wished him dead, so impossible did it seem that he would ever be strong again, but that Geyer's courage and patience pulled him through, and his later good health astonished his parents. He was afflicted at intervals during his life with a kind of erysipelas that, during the periods of the attacks, made existence a misery to him. An American doctor, George M. Gould, has tried to trace most of his troubles to an error in the refraction of his eyes; according to this theory, much of his ill health, his pessimism at periods, even his cutaneous malady, could have been set right by a proper pair of spectacles. Whether the matter was quite so simple as that we may take leave to doubt. Gould, as his six volumes [1] show, belonged to the familiar type of medical specialist that sees all human maladies in terms of its own special pursuit, and explains them — to its own satisfaction — in terms of its own pet theory. Wagner never passed through his hands: and in dealing at second hand with his case in the second volume of his *Biographic Clinics* Gould merely followed the easy course of picking out from the composer's biography everything that suited his theory and then regarding his application of his theory to the case as being self-evident. [2] Laymen who have suffered under mistaken diagnoses originating in monomania on the part of medical specialists are inclined to be a trifle sceptical of explanations like this of Gould, who would have us believe that eye-strain is answerable for most of the troubles of famous and unknown men. It is certain, however, that Wagner worked far too many years without consulting an oculist. In London, in 1877, at the age of sixty-four, he saw the famous ophthalmologist, Sir Anderson Critchett, who found him to be suffering from " a dioptric of myopic astigmatism " in each eye. Critchett prescribed the appropriate glasses: and on his return to Germany Wagner wrote him that the symptoms that had troubled him in London — " severe

---

[1] GBC. See especially, for Wagner, Vols. II, III and VI.
[2] It is to be hoped that the layman is duly impressed when he learns from Gould that Schopenhauer's habit of taking two hours' brisk walking exercise each afternoon, no matter what the weather, was "an astigmatic sign"!

frontal headaches, insomnia and inability to work for more than short periods without distress " — were " much relieved," which is not quite the same thing as totally cured.[1] Gould and Cabanès are probably right in attributing Wagner's better health and greater happiness at Triebschen (between 1866 and 1872), in large part to the simple fact that Cosima took upon herself the immense burden of his correspondence and literary work, to the great relief of *his* eyes, and to the damage, in the years to come, of hers.[2]

In *Mein Leben* he tells us that, like many another sensitive and imaginative child, he suffered from night terrors.

> " Even in my latest boyhood years," he says, " not a night passed without my waking out of some ghostly dream and uttering the most frightful shrieks, that could be put an end to only by the sound of some human voice; and then the most severe scolding or even beating seemed a blessed relief. None of my brothers or sisters would sleep anywhere near me. I was put to sleep as far as possible away from the others; they did not reflect that in consequence my cries for help against the ghosts would only be the louder and longer. In the end, however, they got accustomed to this nightly nuisance."

As befitted a true son of the Hoffmann epoch, one sense in him flowed over into another; in later life this was to lead to an astonishing enrichment of his art, in which poetry, music, gesture and scene all co-operate towards the one aesthetic effect. In his childhood's years this tendency showed itself in an imaginative projection of his own life into the inanimate objects around him. One of the curious and most pathetic features of his later psychology was his dislike of being alone: it was not mere egoism that made him exact from his friends so much devotion, so much sacrifice of their own time and work and interests, but a fundamental inability to endure solitude except during the hours when he was composing — perhaps because even at ordinary times solitude brought up out of the subconscious depths of him all kinds of old lurking fears. It is significant that in describing one of his childhood's regular agonies he should tell us that it always descended upon him when he was

---

[1] ELW, VI, 41–55; GBC, VI, 228.

[2] CGN, p. 361; GBC, II, 124. "One eye at last went out of function," says Gould, "and this helped also to establish relief." Gould, by the way, does not seem to be aware that, after being free of his erysipelas for some years, Wagner had a return of his old malady.

alone: "If I was left alone in a room for long, and my attention became fixed on inanimate objects, such as the furniture, they would suddenly seem to be alive, and I would shriek out with fright." The complex must have played a large part in him all his days for him thus to dwell upon these childish manifestations of it when dictating his biography in middle life.

Wagner was no infant prodigy: indeed, it would probably have been possible to associate daily with him from his fifth to his twentieth year without receiving the impression that he had a special gift that would carry him to decided distinction in any sphere of life or of art. But we can see now that his absence of early definition of bent was due to both the richness and the depth of the soil from which the later Wagner was to spring. In the main, the characteristics of the man are all observable in the boy. As is the case with so many men of superabundant intellectual energy, he had a strongly erotic side to him; and this side was fostered by the lax theatrical life into which he was flung from childhood. The romantic make-believe of the theatre had the attraction for him that it has for most children; but in his case the attraction was deepened by the peculiar intensity of his imagination on the one hand and by the free-and-easy undress of stage life on the other.

"What particularly attracted me to the theatre," he tells us in *Mein Leben* — " by which I mean also the stage itself, the rooms behind the scenes, and the dressing-rooms — was not so much the desire for entertainment and distraction, as it is with the theatrical public of the present day, but the provocative delight of being in an element that opposed to the impressions of everyday life an absolutely different world, one that was purely fantastic, and with a touch of horror in its spell. Thus to me a stage setting, even a wing representing merely a bush, or a costume, or even a characteristic part of one, seemed to me to come from another world, to have a sort of ghostly interest, and I felt that the contact with it must be a lever to lift me from the commonplace reality of the routine of daily life to that enchanting demon-world. Everything connected with a theatrical performance had for me a mysterious, intoxicating attraction; and when, with the help of my playmates, I tried to imitate the performances of *Der Freischütz*, and zealously sought to reproduce the costumes and masks by grotesque paintings of my own, the nicer portions of my sisters' theatrical wardrobes, with the fitting-up of which I had often seen my family occupied, exercised a subtle charm and excitement over my imagination: the mere handling of them would make my heart beat wildly and fearfully."

He was a bundle of energy — Geyer's name for the wild little imp had been "the Cossack" — and as a child he was no doubt full of winning ways, especially for women. The harder and rougher elements latent in his complex nature had not yet had any occasion to show themselves; the development of the less likeable side of him, under the buffetings and deceptions of life, it will be our task to trace in the following pages. That the egoistic tenacity of the doughty warrior of the after years was already there, however, is shown by an anecdote of his boyhood. With wrath in his little heart he once followed a dog through the streets of the town; even a kick in the chest from a passing horse was not sufficient to turn him from the chase. This seems a strange proceeding for the Wagner whose exquisite sensibility where animals were concerned was one of the most loveable features of his character. But this particular dog had committed an unpardonable offence: it had made off with a bone that the boy regarded as his own. Many a man in the later years was to learn, to his cost, that it was not permissible to rob Richard Wagner of a bone, or even to cling to a bone legitimately his if Richard Wagner coveted it.

His chief companion in his young days was Cäcilie. Between them, indeed, there was a special affection that endured to the end of their days; Cäcilie generally meant more to him than any of his other sisters or his brothers. When the two met in maturer life they loved nothing so much as to recall adventures of their childhood; and it is to the reminiscences of Cäcilie that we are indebted for much of our knowledge of Wagner as a boy. Ottilie was only two years older than he, but there does not seem to have been any special comradeship between them. The next senior member of the family was the six-years-older Klara, the next the eight-years-older Luise; and Rosalie was already a sober-minded young woman while Richard was still a child. He and little Cäcilie were thus predestined playmates; and the pair were associated in many pranks in the town and in the neighbouring country. The love of animals and of nature was common to them; and the madcap Richard was always getting Cäcilie and himself into messes, and invariably redeeming the situation and escaping punishment by his plausibility, his ready inventiveness, and those powers as an actor that astonished all who knew him in later life.

2

Geyer had been powerless to keep some of the elder children from the theatre as a profession; but for Richard he had had special plans which the widow, who also had good reason to look with foreboding upon the adoption of the stage as a career, was willing enough to carry out to the best of her ability. For a time Geyer had hoped to make a painter of Richard. But the boy showed no special aptitude in that line, and Geyer wisely gave up the attempt to force him against his inclination. Wagner's experience with the brushes was brief and conclusive. Like most budding geniuses, he could learn only in his own way, which in his case was the way of exciting his imagination with a plan far beyond his powers at the moment, and then, by a combination of intuition and sheer hard work on original lines dictated to him by his genius, acquiring a technique of his own with which to realise it. The young adventurer who was planning dramas on a Shakespearean scale almost as soon as he had learned to read, and dreaming of continuing the work of Beethoven before he had anything more than the most rudimentary knowledge of musical technique, of course wanted to begin his career as an artist by painting pictures on the scale of those he saw around him in his father's studio. Geyer damped his ardour by setting him at elementary outlining; instead of portraits, the boy had to limit himself to drawing eyes; and the mediocre result of his efforts in this line quickly convinced Geyer that whatever the Cossack might become, it would certainly not be a Raphael.

There was never any question of making an actor of him. He appeared in that capacity only once in his life — on the 19th September, 1820, at the age of seven, when he deputised for a little girl who was to have played the part of William Tell's youngest son Wilhelm in Schiller's drama. Geyer was playing Gessler; Klara was the elder son, Walther. Little Richard's part ran to only five words. In the first scene of the third act, in which Tell bids farewell to his wife, taking Walther with him, Wilhelm clings to his mother, saying, " Mother, I stay with you! " But when Richard saw Klara leave the stage with Tell he cried, " Klara, if you are going, I'm going too," and ran after her, leaving the play to take care of itself. Fortunately the curtain descends at that point. Geyer's dry comment was that Richard evidently had a gift for improvisation.

Geyer had always grieved over the interruption of his own studies in his twentieth year, that had resulted, as he sorrowfully recognised, in his never being much more than a gifted amateur artist to the end of his life. He was anxious that Richard should have a sound education before being thrown into the world to earn his living: perhaps the boy's general eagerness, his abnormal quickness of apprehension, and the torrential fluency of speech that always distinguished him held out hopes of success in one of the learned professions. But at the time of Geyer's death Richard was too young for any definite decision to have been come to with regard to him. And for the moment, no doubt, the only consideration was how to lighten as far as possible the heavy burden that had so suddenly been thrown on the widow. Geyer's brother Karl Friedrich Wilhelm, who had set up in business in Eisleben as a goldsmith, had come to Dresden for the funeral, and had promised to take the boy and be responsible for his education. Richard was accordingly brought back from Possendorf once more, this time by his goldsmith uncle in a carriage: and the sensitive child noted, with some wonder, an unaccustomed note of tenderness that had suddenly come into the speech and the manners of the rather quarrelsome family. The generally untrustworthy Praeger may probably be believed for once when he tells us that on arrival at some intermediate station where the horses were to be changed, the boy caressed the poor lean animals that had brought him thus far: [1] the story is too characteristic of the Wagner we know to be an invention of Praeger's.

At Eisleben he found his brother Julius, who was apprenticed to their uncle; Karl Friedrich Geyer's bachelor household also included his mother. The old lady was in so poor a condition of health that it was judged unwise to let her know of her son Ludwig's

---

[1] PW, p. 10. Praeger professes to have had the story from Wagner's own lips at Zürich in 1856.

death; so the tell-tale crape was removed from Richard's coat by
the servant and economically stored for a little while, till at last it
could be worn for father and grandmother at once. Small towns
always pleased Wagner more than large ones, no doubt because
humanity there gave him the illusion that it was nearer the primitive virtues and simplicities; and he seems to have been happy in
Eisleben, where, as a member of a Protestant family that had always been out of tune with the catholicism that filtered down to
Dresden from the Court, he was duly impressed by the associations
of Luther with the town. Kolter, the most famous tight-rope walker
of his day, was a resident in Eisleben; and little Richard practised
that difficult art in emulation of one who was probably regarded
as the town's most distinguished citizen. Imaginative biographers
have conjectured that it was to the storing up of impressions of his
goldsmith uncle and the workshop that we owe the portrait of
Pogner in the *Meistersinger;* but the theory seems a trifle far-
fetched. According to *Mein Leben,* Richard was sent to the private
school of a man named Weiss; and in the late fifties he was touched
to read in a musical paper an account of a concert in Eisleben, consisting of selections from *Tannhäuser,* at which his old master was
present. (Glasenapp, however, makes no mention of this Weiss (or
Weise), but tells us that Richard, after a little teaching from his
uncle, attended the school of Pastor Alt. The explanation of the apparent contradiction seems to be that while the school was Alt's,
Weiss was the head master from 1820 to 1822.)

Wagner remained in Eisleben only about a year: his uncle having taken it into his head to marry, fairly late in life, a new home
had to be found for the boy in September 1822. Apparently there
was a suggestion that Uncle Adolf in Leipzig should take him; but
Adolf felt that his bachelor habits, the demands of his literary
work, and his inexperience of children unfitted him for the charge.
Mein Leben does not wholly agree with Glasenapp at this point; and
we may no doubt follow the account in the former, according to
which the boy went to Leipzig for a few days, staying with Uncle
Adolf and Aunt Friederike in the big Thomä house overlooking the
market-place, enjoying the crowds by day, but scared to death at
night by the vastness of the room in which he was put to sleep and
by the ancient portraits in it. A bed had been fitted up for him in

one of the state rooms, the furniture and decorations of which dated from the days of Augustus the Strong.

" There was only one part of the decorations of the rooms of the house," he says, " that I could not bear at all, — the various portraits, especially those of high-born ladies in hooped petticoats, with youthful faces and white powdered hair. These appeared to me absolutely like ghosts, who, when I was alone in the room, seemed to come to life again, and filled me with the utmost fear. To sleep alone in this big room, that was so far away from the others, in an ancient bed of state, close to these uncomfortable pictures, was a terror to me; I did indeed try to hide my fears from my aunt when she lighted me to bed in the evenings with her candle, but never a night passed in which I did not lie sweating with fright, a prey to the most awful ghostly visions."

All in all, the boy must have been glad when he could leave the strange old house and the three elderly oddities who occupied it, and return to Dresden. There he found the family as comfortable as could be expected, in the house in the Waisenhausgasse (No. 412 II, later Neubar No. 24), in which Geyer had died.[1]

---

[1] Mrs. Burrell contradicts the generally accepted story that the family ever lived in the Jüdenhof (the present Galarieplatz), either before or after Geyer's death.

CHAPTER IV

THE KREUZSCHÜLER

1

ON 2ND DECEMBER, 1822, — in the middle of the term, therefore, — he entered the old Dresden Kreuzschule under the
name of "Wilhelm Richard Geyer, son of the Dresden Court
player." There was nothing unusual at that time in this assumption
of his step-father's name; the children of a woman by her second
marriage were generally entered under the living husband's name,
for conformity's sake in case there happened to be other children
of his at the school. Richard was placed in the second division of the
fifth (the lowest) class; his formal education, therefore, we may
assume not to have been very advanced at the age of nine-and-a-
half. He was a day scholar, living at home.

At school he applied himself very casually to the subjects that
did not interest him, while he appears to have made no exceptional
progress in those that did, because of his congenital inability to
learn except in his own way, which, as has been said, was to begin
with a rush to the centre of a subject, find out, to his annoyance, that
his desires were beyond his powers, and then go back and master
the rudiments, but all the more quickly now because he saw clearly
what it was he wanted and the shortest route to the acquisition of it.
He was attracted to Greek because his imagination had been stirred
by stories from the Greek mythology and he wanted to re-create
these ancient figures dramatically according to his own excited
vision of them; but as he confesses that he found the grammar of
the language only " a bothersome obstacle," of no interest in itself,
it seems probable that he made little progress with it. In his open
letter to Nietzsche of 12th June, 1872, on the subject of German
educational institutions, he claims that no boy could have been
keener about classic antiquity than he was, that he was so attracted
to Greek that he neglected his Latin, and that his master, Professor

[45]

Sillig, was so pleased with his work, which (according to *Mein Leben*) consisted of "metrical translations and some original poems," that he urged the boy to adopt philology as his profession. But as he also confesses in *Mein Leben* that his study of languages was never thorough, that this accounted for his so soon abandoning this field in later years, and that when at length he became really interested in languages through his reading of Jakob Grimm it was too late for him to apply himself systematically to them, it is difficult to decide how far he actually advanced with his Greek. But of his interest in Greek mythology there can be no doubt; and he was able to enter into the world of the Greek drama by a side door, as it were, by way of the pseudo-classical tragedies of Uncle Adolf's friend August Apel.

It took him until Easter, 1825, to move up to the fourth class at the Kreuzschule, but we are assured that from that time not only was his promotion regular but his industry was unceasing. In a roundabout kind of way he was becoming more directly interested in music also. *Der Freischütz*, which, after being produced in Berlin on 18th June, 1821, had reached Dresden by the following 26th January, had set young Germany on fire, and Richard was infected by the general enthusiasm. But he appears to have received no regular instruction in music even as late as this. Two of his sisters were learning the piano, and perhaps he did a little furtive strumming on his own account. At last, he tells us, a tutor, — one Humann, — who was taking him through Cornelius Nepos, gave him something in the nature of formal piano lessons. Characteristically enough he had hardly mastered the first five-finger exercises before he began practising, mainly by ear, the *Freischütz* overture; his teacher, happening to overhear one of his appalling performances, declared that nothing would come of him. "He was right," says Wagner; "in my whole life I have never learned to play the piano." The fact has been generally overlooked that this often-quoted reference to his "whole life" was written in 1842, when he was twenty-nine; and a good deal of perhaps quite mistaken obloquy has been cast on Wagner's piano-playing. That he was never a virtuoso is beyond question; but in the course of the years he must have achieved some sort of correct fingering. He probably learned, in the end, to play as well as most musicians who have no occasion to set up as public pianists need to play for their own delectation and for purposes of musical illustration among friends. In his own inner circle he used to play a good deal in this expository way in his later years, and we even read of his performing one day " a difficult composition by Liszt."

2

In September 1826, Rosalie having left the Dresden theatre for a more profitable engagement in Prague, the mother and the remaining children removed there also, Richard being lodged out in Dresden with a family named Böhme, whose sons were among his schoolfellows. The Böhme house was in the Oberseegasse, which became later the Ferdinand Strasse. He himself notes that " with my residence in this rather noisy, poor, and not particularly well-behaved family began the *Flegeljahre* of my life. More and more I lost the quiet necessary for work, and the gentle imaginative influence of my sisters' companionship. These were exchanged for a turbulent life, full of horseplay and quarrels." Knowing the later Wagner as we do, and his constant flight to women to console him for the rough handling of men, we can readily imagine this sudden change for the worse in his environment intensifying his need for feminine sympathy. And as a matter of fact he himself tells us of a curious awakening of the erotic in him under these very circumstances.

" Nevertheless," he continues in *Mein Leben*, " it was there [in the Böhme house] that I experienced the influence of the gentler sex in a way hitherto unknown to me, as the small and poorly-furnished rooms of the house were often filled with the grown-up daughters and their female friends. My first recollections of boyish love date from this time. I remember a very beautiful, well-behaved young girl, whose name, if I am not mistaken, was Amalie Hoffmann, who, on the rare occasions when she visited us in her neat Sunday clothes, used so to astonish me that for a long time I would remain speechless. On other occasions I remember pretending to be quite unconscious with sleepiness, so as to be carried up to bed by the girls, with all the efforts apparently necessitated by my condition, because I had once found, to my excited surprise, that similar circumstances brought me into immediate and gratifying contact with the female nature (*mit dem weiblichen Wesen*)."

In the middle of the winter his mother returned to Dresden to take him back with her to Prague for a holiday: owing to her refusal to use the mail coach — she was given to being rather eccentric in these matters — it took them three days, in bitterly cold weather, to cover the ninety miles or so in an uncomfortable hackney carriage. But the nature-loving boy found compensation in the romantic scenery of the Bohemian mountains; and Prague itself, with its ancient enchantment and the novel types of humanity and the strange costumes he saw in the streets, was an intoxication to him. Here he found himself promoted to rather better society, apparently, than the family had been accustomed to keep in Dresden. Ottilie had been taken into the good graces of the aristocratic Pachta family: and the two natural daughters of Count Pachta, Jenny and Auguste Raymann, the leading beauties of the neighbourhood, made a great impression on the susceptible heart of young Richard. In addition he met several of the intelligentsia of Prague, through whom he made his first acquaintance with the tales of E. T. A. Hoffmann, which were then beginning to make a stir in the German literary world. Richard at once fell a victim to them: they coloured his thinking for many years; he made their fantastic conception of the world his own.

3

It was probably, in the main, the lure of Jenny and Auguste that drew him to Prague again in the following spring (1827). This time he set out on foot, accompanied by his friend Rudolf Böhme. The footsore youths were compelled to ride from Teplitz to Lobositz; then, their funds being exhausted, they plodded along again all day in the scorching heat, hungry and weary, till at length an elegant travelling coach drew near them. Richard, representing himself to be a travelling workman, boldly begged an alms from the occupants, the embarrassed Böhme hiding himself in the ditch the while. It is the first instance recorded, and that by himself, of Wagner's lifelong practice of borrowing. He seems to have had as little scruple on this first occasion — in itself, of course, harmless enough — as on all the others. Apologies have often been made for his habit of laying his friends under contribution, on the ground that he thought himself, with some justice, entitled to financial support, private or

public, in order that he might have the leisure and the comfort necessary for him to produce masterpieces for the world. Whatever
validity there may be in that plea as regards the later Wagner, it
will hardly hold good for the earlier. We have to recognise frankly
that as a borrower he was born, not made, without the least scruple
in asking even strangers for whatever he might want, and with an
optimism that never deserted him as to the certainty of his soon
being able to repay the loan without any disagreeable sacrifices on
his part. Of reluctance to ask for money there is nowhere in his
record the faintest trace; he seems to have been singularly lacking
in the normal man's delicacy and sense of discomfort in these
matters.

It was decided that the windfall from the occupants of the carriage should be spent not on a bed but on a supper. While the boys
were engaged on this, a strange-looking being entered the inn. He
was returning from Hanover to his home in Prague; " he wore a
black velvet cap with a metal lyre stuck in it by way of cockade; on
his back was a harp." The strolling player had the invincible high
spirits of his profession; over supper he joked with the boys, whom
he amused with his constant repetition of his favourite motto, " non
plus ultra." The three agreed to continue their journey together
next day; but the harpist had drunk so much Czernosek wine in between his jokes, his solos, and his " non plus ultra " that in the
morning he could not be roused. The boys left him sleeping on the
straw that had served them for their bed, and set out alone for
Prague, confident that he would soon overtake them. Meanwhile
Richard had had the foresight to borrow of him a trifle of forty
kreutzers (ninepence), conscientiously making sure that the Prague
address of his mother was duly noted in his creditor's pocket-book.
" It was not until several weeks later that the extraordinary fellow
turned up at my mother's [Richard had left Prague by that time],
less with the purpose of asking repayment of his loan than of getting
news of his young friends; he appeared really grieved at having
missed us."

When at length they drew near the suburbs of Prague, the boys
were hailed with astonishment by the occupants of a fine carriage:
they were the two dazzlingly beautiful Pachta sisters. Wagner still
remembered in later life his boyish mortification at being thus seen

by them before he had had the opportunity to garb himself less like a tramp and rid himself of his disfiguring sunburn. Two days' seclusion, spent in applying parsley poultices to his face, achieved the latter end, and then he gave himself up once more to the delights of Prague society. He does not tell us so expressly, but we surmise that it was grief at parting from the entrancing girls that caused him, on the way back, to burst into tears, throw himself on the earth, and for a long time resist his astonished companion's attempts to induce him to continue their journey. " I was serious," he adds, " for the rest of the way." He was too young as yet to realise that an un-licked cub of his low social status had been admitted into the aristo-crat's house only as a kindness, and that the brilliant daughters were never likely to take his calf-love seriously. This, to his vast mortification, he was made to realise later.

In the following summer he tramped with a number of his school-fellows the forty-five miles from Dresden to Grimma, doing the remaining fifteen miles to Leipzig with becoming dignity in open carriages. Except for one brief visit, Richard had not seen his native town since he was eight. The more thoughtful side of the boy's character came uppermost for a while when he renewed acquaint-ance with his studious uncle; [1] and he learned, to his joy, that a whole caseful of books left by his father was his by right. He ar-ranged for several of them, principally works by Latin authors, poetry, and essays in belles lettres, to be sent to Dresden. This visit to Leipzig seems to have played a decisive part in making him dis-contented with his life in Dresden.

4

For the moment, however, he made a show of settling down there again in the old groove. At Easter, 1827, he rose to the second class in the Kreuzschule, and on 8th April he was confirmed in the Kreuz-kirche, on which occasion, apparently, he bore the name of Geyer for the last time in any official document. His connection with Dres-den, in fact, was almost over: he was soon to return to his native town, where, among people who had known Carl Friedrich Wagner,

---

[1] Adolf had married, on the 18th October, 1824, Sophie Wendt, the sister of an old friend, Amadeus Wendt, and had left the Thomä house for an apartment of his own.

he could hardly continue to go by the name of his stepfather. Luise, who had been acting in Breslau for some years, and latterly in Berlin for a brief period, was just then offered an engagement at the Leipzig theatre. This she accepted (June 1827); and the mother shortly afterwards seized the opportunity to settle in Leipzig once more with such of the children as were now under her roof, except, for the moment, Richard. Her new house was in the " Pichhof," outside the Halle Gate.

He was probably by this time beginning to be a bit of an anxiety to her. His recent visit to the lively Leipzig had given him an appetite for a " student " life very different from that of decorous Dresden and its Kreuzschule. The ardent imagination of the adolescent was quivering under the impact of Hoffmann and other romantic writers, and he was already commencing to turn against what he now regarded as " drier " studies. " The impressions of the theatre and those of Prague," he says, " were now reinforced by a new fantastic element — the so-called swagger of the undergraduate world." The picturesque costume of the Leipzig students had attracted him long ago as a tiny child. But the German students had changed with the changing times. They had become more defiantly self-conscious under the régime of repression that followed the collapse of Napoleon and the re-establishment of Court despotism. Everywhere they were beginning to taste of the heady wine of revolt. As early as 1815 they had formed the *Burschenschaft* — a Students' Union extending to all the universities, its object being " to substitute a pan-German organisation for the clubs which had hitherto split up the students into their various German ' nations.' . . . The colours of the Union, sufficiently indicating its political complexion, were, in distinction from the Prussian black and white, the old German colours, black, red and gold, which Jahn [the leader of the movement] interpreted, with the true German instinct for swelling phrases, as signifying ' out of the black night of slavery through bloody strife to the golden dawn of freedom.' " [1] In October, 1817, the students had held a three days' " sacred festival " in the Hall of the Knights of the Wartburg; there were seven or eight hundred of them, gathered from all parts of Germany. There were dinners,

[1] LRRG, p. 21.

suppers, processions with banners, burnings of books and objects — such as " a bag-wig, a guardsman's stays, a corporal's cane," typical of despotism — and much speech-making.

> " When general silence was obtained a student delivered a speech on very much the following lines: he spoke of the aim of this assembly of educated young men from all circles and all races of the German Fatherland; of the thwarted life of the past, of the rebound, and the ideal that now possessed the German people; of hopes that had failed and been deceived; of the vocation of the student and the legitimate expectations which the Fatherland founded upon it; of the destitution and even persecution to which a youth devoting himself to science had to submit; finally, how they must take thought to introduce among them order, rule, and custom, in a word, student-form, must earnestly and together take thought for the ways and means of facing worthily the duties of their calling, to divert in their direction the regard, at once comforted and encouraging, of grown-up people who unfortunately could attain to nothing more themselves, and to be to them in days to come what they would that young men should be. The audience, and we men among them, were moved to tears, tears of shame that we had not so acted, of pain that we were the cause of such distress, of joy over this intellectual message, so beautiful, so clear, joy too for that we had so brought up our sons that they should one day win the victory where we in our folly had failed." [1]

These were noble ideals. The more conservative elements in Germany, represented by Goethe, who wrote to Zelter expressing his repugnance towards " the horrible smell of the Wartburg fire," looked askance at them; and the more cynical, represented by the Mephistophelean Heine, soon came to see only the more grotesquely sentimental side of them. In 1819 Heine, then aged twenty, and, like the other students, on fire for the ideals of the *Burschenschaft,* attended a similar meeting on the Drachenfels. His enthusiasm did not long endure: he has left us his final disillusioned word on the proceedings in a satirical sonnet in which, after describing the scene on the Drachenfels at midnight, the patriotic songs, the drinking of Germany's health in Rhine wine, the romantic ruins, with the north wind blustering through them, the screeching of the owls, the shiver

---

[1] LRRG, p. 22. The quotation is taken from a rare contemporary account of the proceedings — it was confiscated by the authorities and destroyed — by a professor who was present, Lorenz Oken of Jena. It was printed by that publishing house of Brockhaus into which Wagner's sister Luise married in 1828.

given them all by the sense of ghosts and dead knights of old and phantom women all around them, he finished up with the characteristically deflating remark that he went home with a cold in the head:

Um Mitternacht war schon die Burg erstiegen,
Der Holzstoss flammte auf am Fuss der Mauern,
Und wie die Burschen lustig niederkauern,
Erscholl das Lied von Deutschlands heil'gen Siegen.

Wir tranken Deutschlands Wohl aus Rheinweinkrügen,
Wir sahn den Burggeist auf dem Turme lauern,
Viel dunkle Ritterschatten uns umschauern,
Viel Nebelfrau'n bei uns vorüberfliegen.

Und aus den Trümmern steigt ein tiefes Ächzen,
Es klirrt und rasselt, und die Eulen krächzen;
Dazwischen heult des Nordsturms Wutgebrause. —

Sieh nun, mein Freund! so eine Nacht durchwacht' ich
Auf hohem Drachenfels, doch leider bracht' ich
Den Schnupfen und den Husten mit nach Hause.

Ludwig Börne was still more unfortunate: his watch was stolen by some fellow-enthusiast for German emancipation. Börne's philosophical comment was that he would very much like to find the patriot who relieved him of his watch; when their party came into power he would make him head of the police and diplomacy. The watch, he says, is well worth the reward of 100 louisdor he is going to offer for the return of it — " if only as a curiosity; you see, it is the first watch stolen by German Freedom. Yes, we too, Germania's sons, we too will wake up from our drowsy honesty. . . . Tremble, tyrants, we can steal as well! "

Thirteen years later there was another festival, this time at Hambach, that gave Heine the opportunity to remark that it " denoted a great step in advance, especially when one compares it with that other festival which once took place upon the Wartburg, equally in glorification of the interests of the people. . . . The spirit which manifested itself at Hambach is fundamentally distinct from the spirit, or rather the spectre, which haunted the Wartburg. There, at Hambach, modern time shouted its sunrise songs and drank brotherhood with all mankind; but here upon the Wartburg the past croaked its raven ditty, and follies were spoken and enacted which were worthy of the silliest days of the middle ages." [1] It was not till 1849 that the more idealistic Wagner lost *his* faith in the regenerability of mankind in general, and German mankind in particular, through the medium of politics. In the early thirties of the century he took his little part with the other students in the struggle against reaction; but even this aspect of student life was probably beyond him in 1827. What attracted him to it then was the picturesque costume of the Leipzig students, their evident satisfaction with themselves and with their union, and their contempt for the bourgeoisie. They were regarded, for their part, by the bourgeoisie with good-tempered tolerance as " a proud, honourable-minded, and obliging set of harum-scarum fellows, made up of that warmth of disposition and independence of character the overflowing of which is in youth always pleasant " — even if their swagger sometimes took the ob-jectionable form of poisoning respectable citizens with the fumes of their pipes.[2] Wagner was at a dangerous age for a fatherless boy of his superabundant energy and complexity of nature, with his mind inflamed by the make-believe of the theatre, by Hoffmann-esque and other Romantic literature, and by the first prompt-ings of sex, and seething with vague plans which as yet he had not the capacity to realise. Student life, he tells us, represented for him at this time " emancipation from the restraints of school and family." He was driven to " headstrong attempts to make a change in my condition." He had left the Böhmes three months before and gone to live by himself in a small garret, where he was waited on by a " Court dish-washer's widow," who gave him little else in the way of nourishment but " the well-known thin Saxon coffee all day long." Here, to the presumable neglect of his studies, he wrote verses and a " colossal tragedy," to which we shall come presently.

" I soon," he says, " made use of an opportunity that had come my way to bring about a breach with the Kreuzschule,[3] so as to force my family to let me go to Leipzig. To ward off what

[1] LRRG, p. 109.

[2] See HRMG, pp. 83, 250, 251.

[3] Mrs. Burrell denies that there was any breach with the Kreuzschule; according to the school reports, which she examined, his conduct there was good. It seems safer, however, to follow Wagner's own account of the matter.

I considered an unjust punishment that threatened me from the assistant master, Baumgarten-Crusius, for whom otherwise I had a real respect, I pretended to have received a sudden summons to join my family in Leipzig, hoping thus to be discharged from the school." His ruse was successful; and he left Dresden at Christmas 1827. No doubt his mother, whose abandonment of him in Dresden to live such a life at such an age seems oddly callous, was beginning to be alarmed for him. As a matter of fact, the family's troubles with him were about to begin; and they were to last for many years. As was always the case with him, he had to go through a series of convulsions in his ordinary life in order to reach a fresh stage of temporary poise as an artist. This was a law of his being: we see it in operation in these early years of wildness, terminating in his first discovery of himself as an artist; again in 1839, when disgust with the smallness and superficiality of provincial German theatrical life drove him to Paris; again in 1849 and 1850, when his adventures in politics and his fever over Jessie Laussot were the necessary preliminary to the new mental phase out of which came the *Ring;* again at Zürich, when the passing infatuation with Mathilde Wesendonk was necessary to assist him to be delivered of the stupendous *Tristan;* and finally in Vienna in the early sixties, when a new orientation of his perpetually developing mind was heralded by a complete loss of anything like balance in the conduct of his everyday life.

CHAPTER V

THE LEIPZIG STUDENT

1

RICHARD ARRIVED in Leipzig at the end of December, 1827. Shortly before he left Dresden he had been visited by Luise, of whom he had not seen much in recent years; and we get a side-light on the hardness of the life he had been living of late in his remark that " for the first time a sister treated me with tenderness." One gathers from scattered hints in his autobiography and his letters that the normal manners of the Wagner family with each other were a trifle rough in those early days. Luise seems to have been rather more finely-bred than one or two of the others. She soon made an advantageous marriage and retired from the stage: at the age of twenty-three she became the wife of Friedrich Brockhaus, a well-known and prosperous Leipzig publisher. The affable bride-groom was apparently willing to mix freely with his " penniless bride's " poor relations; but Luise seems to have developed rapidly the instincts of a social climber. " Her desire to establish herself solidly in the higher bourgeois circles," says Wagner, " brought about a marked change in her manner, which had formerly been so gay and genial; and in the course of time I became so bitter about this that at one period I fell out with her completely." The probability appears to be that Luise resented the discredit that was brought upon her middle-class husband's respectable family by the wild behaviour of her rapscallion young brother during the next few years and by his later immersion in the ragged theatrical life of the smaller provincial towns; while still later she and her husband discovered to their cost that it was dangerous for any acquaintance of Richard Wagner to have money while he had none.

When Luise had left the maternal house, in June, 1828, the Geyer household consisted only of the mother, Ottilie, Richard and Cäcilie. The old St. Thomas School being in process of reconstruction at this time, Richard was sent on the 21st January, 1828, to the St. Nicholas School. Three times at least in his later life he blamed his Leipzig teachers for setting him against classical studies. In the *Autobiographical Sketch* of 1843 he told his readers that he was so " embittered " at being placed in the third form at St. Nicholas's, after having attained to the second at Dresden, that " from that time I lost all love for philological studies." In *Mein Leben* he tells us that his " discontent at having to lay aside Homer — of whom I had already made written translations of twelve books — and go back to the easier prose authors, was indescribable: [1] it cut me deeply, and had as result that I never made a

---

[1] Mr. William Wallace pours derision on Wagner's account of his Greek studies as a boy; and indeed the story that at the age of thirteen years or so he translated twelve books of the *Odyssey* in some seven months is frankly incredible. (See WRW, 13–20, 283–297.) It is practically certain that for his studies of Greek literature and antiquities Wagner relied all his life on translations. Mr. Wallace, however, overshoots the mark when he derides Wagner for the following passage, supposedly taken from *Mein Leben* ". . . I could see the *Oresteia* with my mind's eye, as though it were actually being performed, and its effect upon me was indescribable. Nothing, however, could equal the sublime emotion with which the *Agamemnon* trilogy inspired me, and to the last word of the *Eumenides* I lived in an atmosphere so far removed from the present day that I have never since been able to reconcile myself with modern literature."

On this Mr. Wallace comments: "Wagner said that while he was stirred by the *Oresteia* it was the *Agamemnon* TRILOGY that 'inspired him with sublime emotion.' The *Oresteia* and the *Agamemnon* TRILOGY which Wagner alluded to as two different groups of plays are ONE AND THE SAME THING. As well say that *Twelfth Night* is one play and *What You Will* another. All this bombastic talk about the Greek drama vanishes into thin air when Wagner shows us that he did not know that the *Agamemnon* is the first part, and the *Eumenides* the third part, of the *Oresteia*."

But Wagner knew this perfectly well. Mr. Wallace has blundered through relying too trustfully on the English version of *Mein Leben*. The main trouble comes from the word "however" in the sentence "Nothing, however, could equal . . ." It is *this* that makes Wagner appear to be distinguishing between the *Oresteia* and the *Agamemnon* Trilogy as two distinct works; but there is nothing whatever corresponding to the fatal "however" in the German original. (RWML, I, 468.) Moreover, it is the English translator, not Wagner, who speaks of the "*Agamemnon* Trilogy*." Wagner speaks only of the "*Agamemnon*," i.e. the first of the three plays constituting the *Oresteia* trilogy. So far from Wagner betraying his ignorance of the fact that, as Mr. Wallace says, "the *Agamemnon* is the first part, and the *Eumenides* the third part, of the *Oresteia*," that is precisely what the German implies: "In my mind's eye I could see the *Oresteia* as vividly as if it were being performed. . . . Nothing could equal the shatteringly-sublime effect of the *Agamemnon* on me: to the end of the *Eumenides* I remained in an atmosphere, etc., etc."

I may add that an enterprising German has called attention to the fact that the melody of Tannhäuser's cry to Venus, "Ach, schöne Göttin! Wolle mir nicht zürnen!" can be fitted to some words in the fifth book of the *Odyssey*, addressed by Odysseus to Calypso in a similar situation. The discoverer of the analogy points

friend of any teacher in the school." And a few years after writing this he told Nietzsche that his teachers at the Nicholas and Thomas Schools " entirely rooted out " of him his former taste for Greek. There can be no question that two of the main reasons for his neglecting his studies in Leipzig were his sudden passion for the ordinary dissipations of youth and the fact that his head was becoming filled with all kinds of fantastic plans for poetical and musical creation. But to suppose that in later life he was merely seeking to place the responsibility for his slackness on his teachers instead of on himself is to fail to understand him. A grievance of this kind does not rankle in a man for something like half a century without its having a strong foundation in fact. All his life Wagner was quick to take offence at anything that hurt his self-esteem. In 1873, when King Ludwig of Bavaria conferred the Maximilian Order on him, he was sufficiently irritated at " the official way in which the President summoned him to his bureau [in Munich] to receive the decoration "; but when he learned that Brahms also was to receive the order he would have returned his own in his rage had not Cosima dissuaded him.[1] And when a German town invited him to attend the fiftieth performance of *Tannhäuser* in the place, he declined, in a bitter letter, because a similar honour had recently been paid there to Gounod on the strength of his *Faust,* which Wagner regarded as a Gallic outrage on the German spirit, and the success of which in Germany was a constant irritation to him. All in all, there can be no doubt that, whatever other causes may have been operative in 1827, his child's pride was deeply wounded by his being relegated to a lower form in Leipzig, and that this would be quite sufficient to make him turn obstinately against his classical studies.

On the intellectual side the needs of his nature were fully met by his walks and talks with his uncle, whose conversation had more sprightliness and grace than, unfortunately for him, he could ever

out the "quite un-German, Latin imperative construction" of the "wolle . . . nicht" — it occurs again, by the way, in the line "O Göttin, woll' es fassen" — and opines that, consciously or unconsciously, Wagner has reverted to a line in his boyhood's *metrical* version of Homer. See Eugen Mehler in RWJF, V, 332.

That Wagner retained some faint memories of his Greek in later life is shown by his appending three words in that language to his letter of the 7th January, 1862, to Bülow. (RWHB, p. 173.) He adds, however, "Geht nicht mehr — griechisch!"

[1] MECW, I, 677.

achieve in his writings. Wagner always remembered affectionately the stimulus given him by the fine intellect and the high character of his uncle. " God, when I think of Uncle Adolf! " he said to Cosima in 1874. " I should have been proud to introduce you to him and say to you, ' This is the race from which I sprang.' The delicacy and softness of his speech, the noble, liberal cast of his mind! He was so truly a product of the school of Goethe." [1] The boy probably learned nothing very definite from these talks, for most of the subjects and his uncle's treatment of them must alike have been above his head at that time; but Adolf's well-stocked mind and his large library were rich in vague stimulation for the boy. Richard was already subconsciously aware that a breach with his family over the matter of his future career was inevitable some day; and he was actor enough to deceive them for some time as to his outer life while he worked in secret at his illicit musical and literary schemes. In Dresden he had begun a tragedy on a vast scale, a mixture, as he himself tells us, of *Hamlet, Richard III, King Lear, Macbeth,* Goethe's *Götz von Berlichingen,* Kleist, and heaven knows whom and what besides. His only confidante was Ottilie, whom he used to impress to the point of terror by his dramatic readings from the marvellous manuscript. Upon this *Leubald* of his he always looked back with amusement; and few passages in his prose works are better known than the one in the *Autobiographical Sketch* in which he says that forty-two characters died in the course of the gigantic work, so that he was compelled to bring the majority of them back as ghosts, as otherwise he would have been short of characters for the later acts.

We know now that this is a slight exaggeration. Wagner always thought the manuscript of the play had been lost. Mrs. Burrell, however, acquired it along with a large number of other early Wagner documents that she bought from Minna's daughter Natalie, and in her biography of the composer she prints some selections from the play, together with a list of the dramatis personae. From the latter we discover that Wagner's memory was slightly at fault when he said that forty-two persons died in the course of the drama: there are only twenty-two principal characters in the cast. Still, the mortality is abundant. The story is one of wholesale revenge on

---

[1] MECW, I, 694, 695.

the part of Leubald for the murder of his father by Roderick. The comprehensive and painstaking young man disposes of Roderick, his sons, and apparently all his male relations, and then sets out to find the one person still lacking to make the job of extinction a thoroughly good one. This person is Roderick's daughter Adelaide, who had been saved from the family carnage by a suitor whom, however, she hated. The energetic Leubald, having blotted out this unfortunate gentleman and his relations, proceeds to the castle of a robber-knight who has complicated matters by abducting Adelaide. Leubald is taken prisoner; but in a subterranean dungeon of the castle he meets with the young lady, who is working out a scheme for her own escape. Flying into the wilderness together, they suddenly realise, after falling in love with each other, that they ought to be deadly enemies. The shock of this discovery is too much for so highly-strung a young man as Leubald. An insanity that was already incipient begins to make alarming strides in him, its course being accelerated by his father's ghost, who persists in coming between what might otherwise have been a reasonably happy pair. The other deceased members of Adelaide's family also appear as ghosts; and for the laying of them the distracted Leubald is forced to call in the services of a sorcerer named Flamming. This professional practitioner summons one of the *Macbeth* witches to lay the spirits. Her work in this line failing to give satisfaction, Leubald kills her also. With her dying breath she launches a whole crew of fellow-spirits upon him; and under the combined attentions of these and the ghosts for whom he had been directly answerable, Leubald's reason at last gives way. He stabs Adelaide, finds peace in the approved later Wagner manner, lays his head in her lap, and passes away in a gratified *Verklärung* under her blood-stained caresses. Adelaide's faithful maid, Gündelchen, dies at her feet like another Brangaene; and when all are dead, Astolf, like another King Marke, comes to deliver an oration upon Leubald, who, it seems, was " one who loved and hated, and furious in murder; yet regret deranged his mind, and anguish brought him madness." [1]

---

[1] "Ein Mann, der geliebt und gehasst,
　　Im Morde gerast.
　　Doch machte ihn Reue verrückt,
　　Qual hat ihm Wahnsinn geschickt."

The great work being at last completed, Richard sent it to Uncle Adolf, accompanied by a letter in which he grandiloquently announced his resolve not to let " any school pedantry hamper his free development." Adolf was to communicate the good news to the family. The results, however, were different from what the boy had anticipated. Mother and sisters bewailed his folly and his neglect of his studies; even Adolf, who, as a man of letters himself, might have been expected to give a sympathetic welcome to this first effort of a junior colleague, greeted the masterpiece with a marked lack of enthusiasm. He even blamed himself as being in part responsible, in that he had indulged the boy in conversations that were beyond his years.

2

The stock theatrical company that had served Leipzig as a Town theatre under the directorship of Küstner since 1817 [1] was disbanded in May, 1828, the house being re-opened in August of the following year as a Royal Court theatre under the general control of the Dresden Intendant, one Remie becoming the local Director. [2] Luise Wagner retired when Küstner did, marrying Friedrich Brockhaus on 16th June, 1828. To the Wagner household, however, Rosalie was soon added: after a successful career in Prague and other towns she joined the new Leipzig theatre at its opening in 1829; it fell to her to speak the prologue on the first night, when Shakespeare's *Julius Caesar* was given. Richard was no doubt present then, as also a few weeks later, when, as part of the nationwide celebrations of the poet's eightieth birthday, Goethe's *Faust* was staged, Rosalie playing Gretchen. To what extent Richard was at this time acquainted with Goethe, or what degree of influence the poet had on him, it is difficult to say. A schoolfellow, Franz Ludwig Siegel, declared at a much later time, when his memory may have betrayed him, that Richard kept *Faust* under his school desk so that he might dip into it whenever the teacher was not looking, and that he talked of writing an opera libretto on the

---

[1] See Küstner's own story of his directorship, in KVJ, Chapter I.

[2] The theatre was not a success in its new form. It was closed, with a deficit of 60,000 thalers, in May 1832. See SWL, 17, 29 ff. For interesting details concerning the Leipzig theatre see KRLS and SHJ.

THE LIFE OF RICHARD WAGNER

subject of the Witches' Kitchen, but on a grander scale and in a more voluptuous style than Goethe's.[1] According to *Mein Leben*, Richard had wanted to read *Faust*, but, to his annoyance, had been told by his uncle that he was too young to understand it. In a conversation with Cosima at Bayreuth in 1873 he said that at the time of the old poet's death (1832) he still knew very little about him, but regarded him just as " one of those people who are always pouring out books." At that time he thought far more of Schiller; Goethe's *Die Wahlverwandtschaften* he found " tedious," while the scenes in *Egmont* in which the folk appear were only " an imitation of Shakespeare." " Such is youth," the old man added philosophically.[2]

Had the family only known it, the boy was already slipping further down the steep incline that was to land him in the theatrical swamp his mother had always dreaded for him. It was his ambition to be not only a poet but a composer. In Dresden he had been thrilled by the music of Weber, particularly that of *Der Freischütz*; and the first piece of music he ever copied out was Weber's *Lützows wilde Jagd*. Mozart, at that time, made small appeal to him, partly owing to a curious boyish prejudice against the Italian text in the scores. In Dresden he had heard, and been impressed by, the *Fidelio* overture in E major; but apparently it was not until he settled in Leipzig that he really flung himself into Beethoven's music. In Leipzig he profited by the Gewandhaus concerts, such as they were at that epoch, to hear a great deal of music that had not been accessible to him in Dresden. The foundations of his Mozart worship were now laid by a hearing of the *Requiem*. He found a score of *Egmont* that belonged to Luise; this fired him with the desire to know the Beethoven piano sonatas. One gathers from all this that in spite of his having had practically no teaching, the boy was already an excellent reader of music. The climax to this phase came on 17th January, 1828, when, at the Gewandhaus, he heard Beethoven's seventh symphony for the first time; the effect on him, he says, was " indescribable." He was fascinated by the tragic features of the composer, of whom lithographs existed every-

---

[1] RWJK, p. 72. Siegel added that Wagner "was not precisely loved" by his schoolfellows, on account of "his sharp tongue, his irritability, and his vehemence (*Heftigkeit*)." "The others were careful not to 'come up against him,' for he knew how to back up his opinions." All this sounds authentic enough.

[2] MECW, I, 657.

where. " I soon formed an image of him in my mind as a being of elevated, supernatural originality. This conception coalesced with that I had of Shakespeare; I used to meet them both in ecstatic dreams, saw them and spoke to them; on awakening I was bathed in tears."

Egmont made it clear to him that he must have music to his *Leubald*. He set about the study of the mysteries of composition in secret, for he knew that after the reception his grand tragedy had had from his family he could not expect from them much sympathy with his musical ambitions. From the lending library of Friedrich Wieck, the father of the future Clara Schumann, he borrowed Logier's *Method of General-bass*. He humorously dated his lifelong financial embarrassments from that time. He had hoped to pay for the few weeks he anticipated needing the book by means of savings from his pocket-money. But the weeks ran into months, till finally, after Wieck had sent him many little reminders, and the cost of the loan of the book amounted almost to the price of it, he had to appeal to his mother for help. The shock of having to discharge the debt would of itself have been enough for the poor woman, but in addition she now realised that her difficult son was neglecting his school studies for music. Plans were formed for a closer supervision of him: none of the family as yet realised that, however long he might remain at school, his days of formal " education " were already over.

In the summer of 1829 he was left alone in the house for some time; he seized the opportunity to bury himself in music. It is not clear whether it was at this time that he took some lessons in harmony from Christian Gottlieb Müller, a violinist in the theatre orchestra, and director of the concerts of the Euterpe Society, or whether these lessons had come earlier. Müller, although Wagner spoke fairly respectfully of him later, merely succeeded in filling his impatient pupil with disgust for the dry bones of music. Perhaps the teacher's interest in the pupil waned a little when he found that payment of his modest fees was always being postponed: Wagner confesses that the ultimate settlement of this secretly incurred debt by his relatives was a further cause of ill-feeling between him and them. The boy was finding, as so many others of his age and type have done, great difficulty in bringing into the one focus the vivid impressions he was daily receiving from music as an art and the seemingly useless, and here and there incomprehensible, routine of the text-book and the class-room. His brain was seething with the fantastic musical creatures of Hoffmann's stories — Kreisler, Krespel, and the rest of the immortal crew. He found, in one Flachs, a figure who might have stepped out of Hoffmann's pages: Richard thought him a reincarnation of Kreisler. But the man was little more than a mountebank, and the boy, to his shame, soon discovered that, like Titania, he had been enamoured of an ass.

In his amateurish way he was now composing busily. He seems to have begun with a piano sonata in D minor, an aria for soprano, and the music to a pastoral play on the model of Goethe's *Laune des Verliebten,* in which he accomplished the curious feat of writing the words and music simultaneously. Though he knew nothing of instrumentation, he somehow managed to score the work for orchestra; he seems to have studied orchestration after a fashion of his own from a full score of *Don Giovanni* which had come his way. The attempt to grapple with a quartet by Haydn had shown him the necessity of learning to read the viola clef; having mastered this, he gaily proceeded to the composition of a string quartet of his own, in D major. None of these works has survived. During a visit, in the summer of 1829, to his sister Klara Wolfram in Magdeburg he obtained from his brother-in-law a manuscript copy of Beethoven's last-period quartet in E flat, the parts of which had been published in 1826. On his return to Leipzig he fell once more from his musical dreams into cold reality; the family discovered, to its horror, that he had not attended school for the last six months.

Evidently something would have to be done with the obstinate and wilful boy. A family council of war was held, and there seemed nothing for it but to let him indulge his bent towards music in return for a promise on his part to go back to school. For any bourgeois family, of that or any other epoch, " music," of course, has meant playing some instrument or other. Friedrich Brockhaus proposed to send Richard to Weimar to study the piano with Hummel. But this the lad energetically refused to do, though he consented to take some lessons on the violin from a member of the Leipzig orchestra, Robert Sipp,[1] and for a time tortured his mother and sisters with

---

[1] He was only seven years older than Wagner. He was invited as a guest of

the sounds he drew from his anguished instrument; they soon had good reason not to insist on his keeping up his practising. The compromise agreed upon did not work; Richard was now too full of music to be capable of taking any interest in school routine. In his explanation of the circumstances in *Mein Leben* he once more recurs to that curious Greek obsession of his: an adequate elucidation of it would indeed be interesting. He tells us that as a school task he wrote a choral song in Greek on the subject of the recent war of liberation; it was " mockingly rejected " by his teacher " as a piece of impudence." As we have already had occasion to remark, the grown man would hardly have kept harping on his grievance over Greek unless there had really been something in his school life in this connection that had left a rankling wound in him. There was no doubt a genuine desire in him to master Greek in order to enter more fully into the enchanting world of antiquity; but he seems at no time to have had any great gift for languages, ancient or modern, and he was probably unable to learn anything whatever by being " taught " in the usual way. Knowing the later Wagner as we do, we can readily conceive that these repeated blows to his sensitive self-esteem would result in a blind hatred of the men and the system that had dealt him them, a rancour that endured subconsciously for the remainder of his life and was ready to spring into full being again whenever anything touched the sore spot. The immediate effect of this last irritation was that in inner fact, if not yet in outer form, his connection with school " education " was now at an end. " After this," he says, " I have no further recollection of my school. My continued attendance was a pure sacrifice on my part out of consideration for the family: I did not take the slightest notice of what was taught in the lessons, but secretly occupied myself during them with reading, which had a particular attraction for me." And all the while he kept hammering away at his musical education in a muddled fashion of his own.

---

honour to the first Bayreuth festival in 1876. He survived Wagner by sixteen years, dying, at the age of ninety-three, on 21st December, 1899. The indefatigable Mrs. Burrell hunted him out; the old man told her that Wagner was his very worst pupil: he "understood very quickly, but was lazy, and would not practise."

There has been a vast amount of thoughtless talk in academic circles about Wagner's training as a musician — indeed, even about his aptitude for music. Writers with an imperfect sense of the infinite complexity of aesthetics, who would restrict the " legitimate " operations of the musical faculty to " the weaving of tonal shapes," whatever that glib phrase may mean, would have us believe that a composer who tries to realise " poetic " concepts in his music is at best only half a composer. Academic enemies of Wagner have fastened gleefully upon his declaration that as a child he " determined to become a musician " after hearing Beethoven; according to these complacent schoolmen, this is a sure proof that he became a sort of a musician by an act of the will rather than by the grace of God. It must be admitted that in the middle period of his career he played into the hands of superficial theorists of this kind by his perpetual insistence, in his prose works, on the importance of the dramatic and poetic sides, as against the musical side, of the total art-work as he then conceived it. The assumption was at once made that Wagner was merely a semi-musician who began with a " literary " idea and then consciously searched about for a musical illustration of it. Nothing could be further from the truth, which is that it was always the musician in Wagner that dominated and directed the poet. This is not the place for a demonstration of that simple truth, which can easily be established in two ways — (a) by an examination of Wagner's own pronouncements upon music and of his all too rare hints as to his method of constructing his music dramas from the music upwards, and (b) by an analysis of the purely musical " form " of his works.[1] In his earlier theoretical writings he was driven to over-insist on the dramatic side of his composite art-work for the simple reason that this was the side to which it was most important to direct the thinking of the misguided operatic public of that day. All his life he seems to have talked relatively little about the musical part of his work, taking this more or less as a matter of course. He could not fail to be aware

---

[1] This has been done lately by Alfred Lorenz in three remarkable books on *Das Geheimnis der Form bei Richard Wagner*. As regards (a), see Wagner's letters to Gaillard, in RWFZ.

WAGNER'S BIRTHPLACE (REBUILT)

ROSALIE WAGNER

of the originality of his musical vocabulary and craftsmanship. But he seems never to have thought all this worth much talking about, the truth being that he was far too much of a natural musician to be impressed by his own originality to the point of insisting on it. In these matters he had nothing of the excessive self-consciousness of the greatest of his contemporaries — Berlioz — who was for ever drawing his correspondents' and the public's attention to the novelty and ingeniousness of this or that musical effect in his works. Wagner knew quite well that in the *Ring* and in *Tristan*, and more particularly in the latter, he was changing not merely the face of the musical drama but the face of music itself, by purely musical processes. But though an expression now and then escapes him in his letters that shows he was aware that *Tristan* especially was something the like of which the world had not yet seen, he nowhere and at no time launches into a full formal discussion of the novel elements in the melody, the harmony, the orchestral colour of his music. He took all this as a matter of course; his musical vocabulary and his technical devices were for him not calculated, ponderable things to be detached from the general body of the art-work and dissected and commented upon admiringly for their own sake, but merely the natural, inevitable flowering of his unconscious musico-poetic being.

And while the academic commentators who have never really understood either Wagner or aesthetics have thus failed to perceive the true nature of his musical constitution, they have never grasped the process by which he made so consummate a technician of himself. It is natural that the people who teach in conservatoires, with no more than the standardised musical equipment normally provided by those no doubt admirable institutions, should be unable to understand how any composer can compose at all, still less become a great composer, without having had the benefit of instruction of the type they themselves are accustomed to impart or to receive. A distinguished English writer on musical subjects has even gone so far as to regret that Wagner never really learned how to compose.[1] One would have thought that events have

---

[1] It is sometimes said that he "composed at the piano." The origin of this legend seems to be the fact that he had constructed for him in the 'sixties a piano that was also a writing desk: Judith Gautier (GWH, p. 36) describes it as "a piano of a special design (almost an altar), furnished with drawers and a plane like a table.'

demonstrated that he somehow managed to learn an astonishing lot about composition; and if he succeeded in doing so without the assistance of the professors, and if the results were of a type and on a scale to which the professors themselves have never attained, the inference would seem to be that the professors do not know all there is to be known about the art of composition. In a discussion of English educational methods, Mr. G. K. Chesterton once said that in these days the authorities would insist on Sam Weller being " educated "; whereupon, said Mr. Chesterton, the question at once arises, " Who among the ' teachers ' could teach Sam anything? " And when we find the academics deploring that Wagner was never properly " taught," we are constrained to enquire who, in the conservatoires of that day or this, could have taught him anything vital about music that he could not discover for himself.

We know little about the first formal studies of Wagner and Berlioz, but it is manifest that each of them must have put in an immense amount of quiet work in his young days. A young man does not come up from the country, as Berlioz did, ignorant of everything but the veriest rudiments of music, and in three or four years make for himself an instrument of self-expression which, while markedly different from that in common use, was so admirably adapted to the needs and the purposes of his special musical constitution, without having addressed himself long and seriously to technical problems. Both Berlioz and history are silent as to what really went on in those years of his association with Lesueur and of his ranging through the scores in the Conservatoire library; but there can be no question that Berlioz was doing a huge amount of quiet experimentation in his own way. Wagner, too, must have worked at technique not less assiduously than the average student at the conservatoire but immensely more. But he worked in a way of his own. The basic school-principles of musical procedure can be mastered by any intelligent student in a few months: after that,

Only people with the most rudimentary notion of the processes of composition can imagine that a work like *Tristan* can be " composed at the piano ": if they persist in saying that it can, one can only suggest that they be shut up for a few months with a piano and allowed to try. Wagner, like every other composer, liked to test out on the piano what he had done; and his specially constructed apparatus, one third piano, one third desk, and one third drawers, was merely another illustration of his practical common sense: he had everything under his hand with the minimum expenditure of energy and of time.

how far he will carry those principles, and what he will achieve in the personal application of them to composition, depends entirely on himself, on the amount and the quality of the music that Nature has implanted in him; and *that* phase of his education as a composer is not only one that lasts, if he happens to be a man of genius, for the remainder of his life, but one in which no professor, no text-book, can be of the slightest use to him, for a craftsmanship that really matters is not something that can be reduced to a recipe and bottled in a conservatoire and carried away by a student for external application to the problems of artistic creation, but a personal thing that comes from the special nature of the individual's thinking.

For the most part, Wagner was able to supply out of his own resources all that he needed in order to become a composer. His experience was plainly that of many another gifted student who has managed to evade the conservatoire routine. His first teachers were utterly unable to teach him anything, because they could not explain and justify things to him in terms of his own intellect. Every intelligent autodidact has gone through much the same experience: able to read music from childhood as a natural language, without knowing when or how the initiation began, and familiar, from his score-reading, with music as it reveals itself in the works of the great composers, the boy is merely perplexed by an educational routine that seems to him to have been designed only to " teach " music to people who are unmusical by nature. Mentally he is already far beyond the stage at which the text-books would have him begin. He is able to follow, in his own way, the operations of the musical mind as revealed in the music of this or that great composer in whom he has revelled, without as yet understanding fully the technical processes by which the music has been made, though he has an intuitive inkling of them. And this particular understanding, which is all he now requires, he finds his teacher and his text-book cannot give him. He is given " rules " of which he does not merely fail to see the reason, but which his experience tells him have not been observed by the composers he admires. Having already learned to follow with ease the most advanced language of music as the great composers speak it, he is confronted with " exercises " written in a jargon that seems to him to have no connexion whatever with music as he has come to understand and feel it. He cannot reconcile music as he knows it with music as it is taught him: he feels that there must surely be a bond between them somewhere, but what it is, or how to find it, he can neither discover for himself nor can his teacher or his text-book show him. He is dogmatically told a number of things, some of which appear to him to be untrue, for they are contradicted by the music he knows, while the others are so elementary that he wonders why anybody should need to be " taught " them. His teacher can neither justify his own method of teaching nor enter into the student's mind so far as to be able to see precisely what his difficulties are, or to show him the con-nexion between these, his studies of the moment, and the infinite world of music that lies beyond, and into which the student has already won unaided the glorious right of entry.

This was manifestly Wagner's case. Like every other really musical boy, he could read complicated music, as a kind of natural language, without the slightest difficulty before he had grasped more than the rudiments of school craftsmanship. Within a year or two after the death of Beethoven, while as yet the average profes-sional mind could make little of this new music, he was steeped in the master's quartets and symphonies.[1] A sound instinct led him to one of the surest ways of penetrating to the secrets of composi-tion — the copying of scores. He was no more than seventeen when, after copying out the full score of the Ninth Symphony, he made an arrangement of it for piano solo — nothing of the kind existed in 1830 — and sent it to Schotts: the publishers did not think the time was commercially ripe for such a venture, but, after a second approach on his part in the following year, retained his work and sent him in exchange, to his great delight, a full score of the Mass in D.[2] There would be something comical in the spectacle of so

---

[1] On this point we have the testimony of Heinrich Dorn, the friend of his youth and afterwards his bitter enemy. " I doubt," says Dorn in his reminiscences, " whether there has ever been a young composer more familiar with Beethoven's works than the eighteen-year-old student Wagner. He had copies, made by himself, of the full scores of most of the master's overtures: he went to bed with the sonatas and rose with the quartets: the songs he sang, the quartets he whistled, for he made no progress with his playing: in short, it was a veritable *furor teutonicus*."

[2] The manuscript remained in Schotts' possession until 1872, when Wagner reclaimed it. They wished now to trade on his reputation and publish the arrange-ment; but this he would not allow. See RWBV, II, 6.

advanced a student of music as he plainly was already being unable to make head or tail of what the worthy Müller was trying to " teach " him, did not more than one of us know from his own childhood's experience that that tragic phenomenon is quite a common one.

4

After the compromise agreed upon between Wagner and his family in the matter of general study, consent was given to his receiving lessons in harmony from that very Müller to whom he had already been resorting in private, by whose teaching he had been utterly unable to profit, and whose bill was still unpaid. The new lessons, we may conjecture, were no more successful than the old ones had been. The boy was now in a mental state that was not to be satisfied by anything that a plodding teacher of harmony could give him. He was receiving a fresh set of vivid impressions from the dramatic and operatic performances given at the Leipzig Court Theatre under the new management. He could always obtain admission through Rosalie; and he heard not only a good deal of Shakespeare and Schiller but several of the latest romantic operas, such as Marschner's *Der Vampyr* and *Der Templer und die Jüdin* and Auber's *Masaniello*, which last affected him as powerfully as it did that generation as a whole.[1] The most shattering experience of all, however, was the Fidelio of Wilhelmine Schröder-Devrient, who had come from Dresden to Leipzig for some guest performances. This great artist, who was destined to occupy a position of some prominence in Wagner's later story, was the daughter of a baritone, Friedrich Schröder, who was the first to sing the part of Don Giovanni in German, and Antoinette Sophie Bürger, who was considered the greatest actress of her day. Wilhelmine, who was born in 1804, had married the actor Karl Devrient in 1823; the unhappy marriage was dissolved five years later. She was not quite eighteen when, at the revival of *Fidelio* in Vienna on the 3rd of November, 1822, she astonished every one by the combination of

---

[1] In an article (*Erinnerungen an Auber*) written after the French composer's death in 1871, he analysed searchingly the reasons for the contemporary effect of *Masaniello*, and for Auber's subsequent decline. See RWGS, Vol. IX. Rosalie took the part of the dumb girl Fenella in the Leipzig performances of September, 1829.

vocal beauty and dramatic fire in her Leonora. She had joined the Court Theatre at Dresden in 1823, and remained connected with the company more or less continuously to the end of her operatic career.

She had done much to spread the vogue of *Fidelio* in Germany. She appears to have had a passion for interspersing her arias with spoken interjections. Berlioz found this objectionable, indeed " execrable." But that was in 1842, when, no doubt, her vocal powers already being on the decline, (Berlioz, indeed, speaks of her voice as being " not very flexible," and " worn in the upper register,") she may have resorted too often to speech to help her out of a technical difficulty.[1] It was precisely by an effect of this kind that she had thrilled her hearers at the commencement of her career. In the prison scene in *Fidelio*, at the point where Leonora presents the pistol at Pizarro's head with the words, " One more word, and you are *dead*," Schröder-Devrient used to send a shudder through her audience by pronouncing the final word in her speaking voice. Writing many years after (in 1871), Wagner gave a rational explanation of the effect. He did not deny, any more than Berlioz would have done, that this kind of thing in music is a " transgression." But he saw that there are exceptional cases in which ordinary aesthetic reasoning is overridden by emotional forces stronger than itself, which forces, purely emotional and perhaps irrational as they may at first sight appear, nevertheless have a temporary super-reason of their own. The sublimity of the effect, and its " indescribable effect on the hearer," came from " the headlong plunge from one sphere into another," with the result that the spectators were given, " as by a lightning-flash, a glimpse of the ideal and the real together. Plainly the ideal was for a moment unable to bear a certain load, and discharged it upon the other." [2] In *Mein Leben* he gave it as his opinion that Schröder-Devrient, especially in the days when he saw her first, was an artist " whose like I have never seen on the stage since." In an essay on *Actors and Singers* pub-

---

[1] This device of hers was evidently a stone of stumbling for many musical listeners of the period, and no doubt it became a more and more pronounced mannerism with the years. Lortzing, in 1838, writes from Leipzig to a friend that "Schröder-Devrient is with us again at the moment, and, apart from the *Huguenots*, is playing off all her old dodges on us." See LGB, p. 73.

[2] *Über die Bestimmung der Oper*, in RWGS, IX, 152.

lished in 1872 he pays her his finest tribute. He sweeps away impatiently the doubting question that was often put to him as to whether her voice " was really so remarkable." He resented the question because it seemed to put Schröder-Devrient " in the same category as the female castrati of our opera." His answer is, " No, she had no voice, but when we heard her we thought of neither voice nor singing, so moving was her dramatic appeal."

In after years he declared that his first experience of her, in the Leipzig *Fidelio* performance of 1829, was the most powerful impression of his whole life. After the performance he rushed home, and, like the very young man he was, wrote the actress an enthusiastic letter assuring her that his life had assumed for him its true significance from that day, and that if ever the world should hear of him it was she who had made him what, he now swore, it was in his destiny to become.

She retired from the stage in 1847, but, in spite of her voice being sadly impaired, still managed to create an effect by her art in the concert room. Like so many of the best German artists of that period, she had been rushed into an operatic career before her voice had been thoroughly trained,[1] and she had to pay the penalty later. Her power over her listeners seems to have come in part from a peculiarly moving quality in the voice, in part from her passionate dramatic temperament.

Chorley, who was an excellent judge of these matters, says that

" within the conditions of her own school she was a remarkable artist. She was a pale woman. Her face — a thoroughly German one — though plain, was pleasing, from the intensity of expression which its large features and deep tender eyes conveyed. She had profuse fair hair, the value of which she thoroughly understood, delighting, in moments of great emotion, to fling it loose with the wild vehemence of a Maenad. Her figure was superb, though full, and she rejoiced in its display. Her voice was a strong soprano — not comparable in quality to other German voices of its class (those, for instance, of Madame Stöckl-Heinefetter, Madame Bürde-Ney, Mademoiselle Tietjens) — but with an inherent expressiveness of tone which made it more attractive on the stage than many a more faultless organ. Such training as had been given to her belonged to that false school which

---

[1] See WSD, pp. 97 ff. Wolzogen, like others of his epoch, blamed Wagner's music for contributing to the decline of Schröder-Devrient's vocal powers. But even he is constrained to admit that few Germans of that epoch could really sing.

admits of such a barbarism as the defence and admiration of ' nature-singing.' Why not as well speak of natural playing on the violin or other instrument which is to be brought under control? . . . But on the rock of this difficulty the German singers and composers for voices have split. . . . Sontag and Jenny Lind . . . had learned to sing: Madame Schröder-Devrient not. Her tones were delivered without any care, save to give them due force. Her execution was bad and heavy."

But he goes on to pay a high tribute to her acting, especially in *Fidelio:* and on another occasion he says that Malibran's Leonora could not be compared, for emotional effect, with that of " a singer incomparably inferior to her, Madame Schröder-Devrient." [1]

She had little success, even as Fidelio, in Paris, where the critics and the public were accustomed to a higher standard of singing than generally obtained in Germany.[2] She must have damaged her voice, midway in her career, by attempting coloratura parts.[3] By 1849 her voice seems to have failed her completely, and in the concert room (she had left the stage by this time) she resorted to tricks that were an annoyance to sensitive listeners. Thus Bülow, in a letter of the 28th January, 1849, to Raff, says that in Schubert's *Am Meer* she delivered the words " Die Möve flog hin und wieder " with a pseudo-dramatic

while " vergiftet " became " verrrrgiftet "; and so on.[4] All in all, it seems probable that Wagner was so impressed by her dramatic ability in her best days that he was blind to her defects as a singer.

5

He had obstinately set his mind on going to the Leipzig University, less for purposes of study than in order to realise his dominant ambition at this time — to bear the glorious title of " student," and to enjoy all the privileges attaching to it in the Germany of

---

[1] See CTYR, pp. 9, 38, etc.
[2] See BMC, p. 84.
[3] GWKZ, Part II, Chapter 5.
[4] BB, I, 147.

the epoch following the wars of liberation. But as he was in too ill
odour with the masters at St. Nicholas to have any hopes of recommendation from that quarter,[1] it was decided that he was to leave
the school at Easter, 1830, study privately for six months, then
enter at St. Thomas's, and make this a leaping-off ground for the
University. Still so curiously, pathetically ardent for Greek, he
once more, he tells us, read Sophocles with a tutor. But again the
cruel Fates intervened between him and the object of his desire:
this time it was the intolerable odour of a tanyard, upon which
the tutor's windows looked, that put him out of humour with the
Greek language!

He entered St. Thomas's in the June of 1830 — not, as he says
in *Mein Leben,* in the autumn. There his masters had as little reason to be satisfied with him as those at St. Nicholas's had had; and
at the end of the first half-year he was as far as ever from having
earned the right to promotion to the University. There was another
council of war at home: Richard settled the matter by propounding
a plan for entering the University, with the passive connivance of
his teachers, by the simple device of enrolling himself as *studiosus
musicae,* which he did on the 23rd February, 1831. " Having
passed no leaving examination at St. Thomas's," says Mrs. Burrell,
he " must have entered the University of Leipzig as what is now
termed a ' second class student,' who could attend the lectures but
was not eligible for a State examination, and consequently could
never hold any appointment under Government." He was not likely
to fret himself over that; he had achieved his double object: he had
qualified for the delightful corps-life of a " student," and he had
forced the family to accept music as the central aim of his existence. Meanwhile, in spite of a good deal of youthful dissipation,
he had somehow or other found time for composition and for pushing his claims to public performance. In after life he recalled, as
belonging to this period, an overture in C major, in 6/8 time, and
a piano sonata in B flat major, for four hands, which latter, as it
had taken the fancy of Ottilie, he scored for orchestra. Both manuscripts are lost, as are those of a *Political Overture,* inspired by

---

[1] Mrs. Burrell gives facsimiles of the school reports on him, which confirm his
own account of his neglect of his studies. He had bad marks for Conduct, Industry,
and Progress. He did not do his written task at the end of the 1829 term: "non
scripsit absens," says the report.

the repercussions in Saxony of the Paris Revolution of July, 1830, and an overture to Schiller's *Braut von Messina*.

Another work, however, an overture in B flat major, has survived. This was apparently the result of his study of the Ninth Symphony. His own music had all kinds of mystic Hoffmannish meanings for him, and these he wanted to make clear to the eye, as a preliminary to their realisation by the ear, by using a different-coloured ink for each of its constituent " elements." Black was to be used for the brass, red for the strings, and green for the wood wind: no green ink, however, happened to be obtainable. He showed the score to his friend — afterwards his enemy — Heinrich Dorn,[1] who was Kapellmeister at the Leipzig theatre from 1829 to 1832. In later years Wagner was inclined to suspect that the more experienced Dorn only accepted the work for performance in order to play a bad joke on him in public. But there seems no reason to attribute any particular malice to Dorn in the matter; at that time he was genuinely interested in the boy, whose acquaintance he had made through Rosalie. Dorn appears to be in error when he says that Wagner had shown him his piano sonata in B flat major, " in the style of Haydn, afterwards published by Breitkopf, and dedicated to his teacher," for the teacher in question, under whose eyes the work was written, was Weinlig, with whom Wagner did not begin to study till a later date than the one at which we have now arrived. (Perhaps Dorn, writing in 1877, was confusing this sonata with

---

[1] 1804–1892. He was one of several companions of Wagner's youth who could not forgive the raw cub of the thirties, whom they had been used to patronise, for becoming the genius of the sixties, who had so outgrown them all both as conductor and composer. Their honest puzzlement is sometimes quite comical. Dorn tells us how, whenever he and "the older German Kapellmeisters" foregathered, they used to discuss Wagner's extraordinary popularity, and could find no explanation of the mystery. Were they all of them, he asks pathetically — Abt, Esser, Krebs, Franz and Ignaz Lachner, Rietz, G. Schmidt, Taubert, etc., etc. — "all blind and deaf" when they could not believe that the one and only dramatic verity was incarnated in Wagner, and that "everything in opera before him had been only a preparation for him"? (See DML, p. 12.) They would have been astonished had they been told that their names would mostly be remembered now merely because they happen to come into the Wagner story.

Dorn had been specially nettled by a remark made about him by Wagner during his visit to Berlin in 1871. Asked what he thought of the three Kapellmeisters at the Berlin Opera at that time, Wagner replied: "One of them is not unmusical, but he is phlegmatic; the second is not phlegmatical, but too unmusical; the third [i.e. Dorn] ought to have learned how to conduct, for he saw me conduct in Riga thirty years ago, but he *hasn't* learned." See DEE, p. 161.

that for four hands, in the same key, the manuscript of which Wagner may have shown him.) In the sonata, says Dorn, there was not a trace of individuality. Since writing it, however, Wagner had absorbed himself in Beethoven, and the result was this extraordinary overture, which, according to Dorn, was written on small octavo pages, with the three sections of the orchestra characterised by black, red and blue ink. (Elsewhere Dorn says that the score was written in *two* inks.) The music was " equally abnormal," but as there was something in it that merited attention, Dorn decided, he says, to give it at the theatre " as an interlude between two comedies."

In the main, his account of the performance agrees with that of Wagner in *Mein Leben* and elsewhere. In the *Autobiographical Sketch* of 1843 the composer humorously assures us that by the side of this mighty overture the Ninth Symphony was a mere Pleyel sonata. Dorn says that he had great difficulty with the orchestra at the rehearsals, the players imploring him not to inflict the insane composition on them and on the public; but he stuck to his guns. The performance, according to Wagner, took place on Christmas Eve, 1830,[1] not as part of an ordinary theatrical evening but as the first number (anonymous, under the title of " a new Overture,") of a concert for the benefit of the poor. He tells us that at each fourth bar of the allegro the kettle-drummer had to come in with a volley on the second beat. After a little while, the delighted audience had no ears for anything but this; and the poor composer, knowing only too well how many more of these bangs there were to come, waited for each of them in an agony of apprehension. He awoke, he says, from his nightmare to find that the overture, to which he had disdained to give the usual formal ending, had suddenly come to an unexpected close. This agrees with Dorn's account: " The effect of this maiden speech was fabulous; the puzzled audience did not know what to make of it all when the players, after a long and confused passage, suddenly put their instruments down, their task being over; the public was still waiting hopefully for something more agreeable to come." Wagner slunk

---

[1] Really, as the theatre bill (reproduced in facsimile by Mrs. Burrell) shows, Christmas Day. The occasion was a "Declamatorium," i.e. a medley of musical numbers, recitations, extemporised anecdotes, etc.

out of the pit, not daring to look the dazed audience in the face. He had with difficulty obtained permission to enter by assuring the man at the door that he was the composer of the new work to be played that evening: the pained reproachful look in the man's eyes as Wagner passed him on his way out haunted him for years afterwards, and it was a long time before he ventured into the pit of the theatre again. Dorn tells us that he prevailed upon his friend Herlossohn to say a few kind words about the work in the *Comet*, but that, apart from this, the papers were silent about it.[1] In this, however, he was in error: a notice appeared in the *Leipziger Tage-blatt* of the 28th December, which ran thus — " The first part of the concert opened with a ' new Overture,' which, I was assured — for unfortunately I arrived too late to hear it myself — made a good deal of sensation and created considerable astonishment, especially by reason of the kettledrum effect and the startling conclusion."

6

Wagner's boyish imagination had been captured by the bragga-docio of the Leipzig students, who, after coming into conflict with the authorities in the excited days that followed the July (1830) Revolution in Paris and similar risings in Brussels, Warsaw, and other towns, had made themselves immensely popular in the town by doing more or less useful police work during some proletarian disturbances. He forced himself into the company of some of the most notorious bloods, and as a result of his usual quick temper and uncontrollable impetuosity of speech soon found himself booked for half a dozen duels. As some of his opponents-to-be were skilled swordsmen, there is a fair probability that had any of these contests materialised, the world would have had to do without *Tristan* and a few other masterpieces. But the Fates intervened, as they always did in some mystic way or other, when it was a question of saving Richard Wagner for posterity. Of the first three formidable duellists with whom he had engagements, the first was disabled by the sever-ing of an artery in his arm in a previous encounter; the second went off to Jena to fight a duel, and was killed therein; the third, for

---

[1] DE, pp. 157–159. According to Dorn (DML, p. 2), Wagner, "who at that time was of a diffident nature, and not at all arrogant," laughed at the fiasco himself.

whom Wagner actually waited on the duelling ground, quite prepared never to see mother and sisters again, or at all events to be
carried back with a dangerous wound, was unable to keep the appointment — full of virtue and of beer, he had made an attack on
a house of ill fame the night before, and had been so maltreated by
the scandalised occupants that he was now in hospital. The remaining potential antagonists were removed from Wagner's path by
events the details of which he could not remember in after life.

One gathers that he was drinking rather heavily at this time, absenting himself from his home for days and nights at a stretch, and
gambling at the clubs that used to meet in some of the less reputable
taverns. His primary object in gambling, no doubt, was to make
money enough to repay the debts he had already contracted. At last
he decided on a desperate throw: he would gamble with his mother's
pension, of which he was " trustee of a fairly large sum." That night
he lost all of it but a single thaler; in despair he staked this on a
card, won, ventured his winnings, won again, and, luck being with
him, continued the process till he had made a considerable amount
— enough not only to restore his mother's money but to pay off his
debts as well. It all ended in one of those cathartic emotional and
moral crises that were to be so frequent in his life. He crept into the
house in the small hours of the morning, slept soundly, woke physically refreshed and mentally purified, and made a clean breast of
the whole matter to his mother. We can imagine the scene: no one
ever enjoyed the luxury of repentance more than Richard Wagner;
the ecstatic glow of it always made delightful sin more than ever
worth while. He tells us in *Mein Leben* that he was now free of the
fascination of gambling for ever. This, however, is not strictly true,
for in a letter to his friend Apel, dated from Rudolstadt, 13th September, 1834, he laments that he has been gambling and has lost
persistently.

There were other drunken and hooligan follies during this year
or so of adolescent madness; he records that he was one of a mob
that attacked certain houses of ill fame one night. Whatever the
motive of the rest of the crowd may have been, in his case, as he
admits, the moving force was simply the infection of mob passion
and of the blind mob impulse to destruction. When he woke up the
next morning from this debauch it all seemed a nightmare to him;

he would probably not have believed in the reality of it had he not found in his room a torn red curtain that he had evidently brought home as a trophy. His escapades, which were in the main those of youth in all ages, need not be taken more seriously by posterity than they were by his own indulgent elders. They are of interest to us, however, as evidence that he was at this period very susceptible to mass influences in his environment. This susceptibility endured in him till 1849; it was this that made him an ardent admirer of Italian music for a few years after 1833, when he was dragged into the theatrical life of the smaller German towns, and that caused him, in his later Dresden days, to throw in his lot with the political revolutionaries. After 1849 he was a different being; from that time to the end of his life he swam not with but against the stream; friends, the public, Intendants, statesmen and monarchs had either to go his way or be flung angrily aside by him. It was his Dresden experiences of all kinds between 1842 and 1849, in the theatre and outside it, that brought about this gradual hardening of his nature. As a boy he was apt to take on the colour of any company in which he happened to find himself, to be now a sober student with Uncle Adolf, now a gambler and a swashbuckler with the young bloods of the Clubs. The one persistent strain in him at this time is the musical: nothing could turn him from his resolution to become a musician, and even in the intervals of his boyish debauches he still found time for composition.

Mrs. Burrell held that Wagner's account of his excesses is " transparently unreal, the exaggeration of a physically diminutive youth with his head inflated by some *Studentenroman* whose hero's exploits he wished to be supposed to rival." A good woman, however, often does not know all that a bad boy, even if physically diminutive, is capable of in the way of naughtiness. Mrs. Burrell thought these escapades inconsistent with the amount of musical composition done by Wagner during this period. Obsessed with the utterly untenable idea that Wagner was " not responsible " for *Mein Leben* (that book, according to her, being the detested Cosima's work), she was reluctant to believe anything she read there that seemed to reflect on the moral character of her idol. There is not the slightest reason, however, to doubt the veracity of Wagner's account of his youthful follies.

His surrender to the mob aspects of student life was probably due, as he himself notes, to the fact that as yet he had no real friend of his own age and type: the first friend he ever had, in his own sense of the term, was Theodor Apel, who did not come on the scene till later. Wagner's conception of friendship always involved the complete surrender of the friend to himself, as we shall have occasion to observe many times in the later story of his life; the ideal friend, from his point of view, would have been one who refused food when he was away; in the Triebschen years he even tortured Cosima with his jealousy of her own father! Not, of course, that he would have agreed with that summary of the case. On the contrary, his naive view was that it was always he who gave himself unselfishly and superabundantly, while the others for the most part drew back from a corresponding generosity. He needed a receptacle for the volcanic outpouring of his ideas, and encouragement in the realisation of them; and the true friend, from his point of view, was one who gave himself up most completely to the rôle of listener and helper. In a sense he was, like all men who tower above their fellows, too big for ordinary friendship: there can be no genuine friendship between the central mountain and the surrounding hills — only a looking up to in the one case and a looking down upon in the other. " A deplorable law governing genius," says Romain Rolland very truly, " seems to decree that, with the superior mind, a strong dose of mediocrity in the other is required to satisfy the needs of friendship. A genius will form only a passing friendship with his peers." [1]

The grown Wagner, indeed, dictating his autobiography, paints a youthful portrait of himself in these very terms. He cannot remember, he says, that " any particular inclination or attraction " determined him in the choice of the friends of his youth; and then he proceeds to the innocent admission that he " cared only for some one to accompany me in my excursions to whom I could pour out my inmost feelings to my heart's content, without caring what the effect was on him. The result was that when, after a long outpouring on my part to which the only response was my own excitement, I at

[1] RGB, p. 23.

last came to the point when I looked at my friend, I usually found, to my astonishment, that there was no question of response at all, and as soon as I set myself to the task of drawing a corresponding something from him, of stimulating him to the communication of something that was not really in him, there was generally an end of all relation between us, no trace at all being left on my life." Understanding him as we now do, it is a tolerably safe surmise that what he unconsciously demanded of each companion, under the guise of a corresponding confidence on the part of the latter, was in reality merely the launching of the appropriate second-subject to Wagner's first, so that a working-out on purely Wagnerian lines would be made possible. We are reminded of the story of an eminent living violinist who, meeting a friend in the street, talked about nothing but himself for a good hour, and then said, " Well, that's enough about me. Now let's talk about you. What did you think of my playing last night? " It was easy enough for the later Wagner, the hypnotic genius, to draw within his orbit listeners who were more than willing, who were positively compelled, to sink their personalities in his, to admit none but his premises and agree that his conclusion was the only possible one. But it was a little too much to expect this adoration from one schoolboy towards another. The consequence was that, as Wagner says, he was driven into the general whirl of student dissipations because from the mass he did not expect any intimate individual response, and so felt no disappointment in not receiving it.

In a certain sense, he goes on to say in *Mein Leben,* his strange relationship with Flachs was typical of the great majority of his ties in after-life. When he says that " in consequence no enduring personal bond of friendship ever found its way into my life," it is not quite clear whether he means his life at that early time or his life as a whole. But his remark is certainly applicable, in the main, to the latter: in spite of all that had been done for him by Apel, Liszt, Bülow, Frau Ritter, the Wesendonks, Cornelius and many others, his friendship for none of them survived the stage at which they had nothing more to give him in the intellectual or emotional sense. It is a phase of his being that has been rather misunderstood, because it has been regarded from the point of view of character instead of that of constitution. The charge of ingratitude that has been so freely levelled against him is not merely a posthumous one, based on the copious records posterity possesses of his life. It was one that was freely and publicly made during his life-time. Dorn, for instance, in that book of his of 1877 to which reference has already been made, did not hesitate to say publicly that while the " eccentricities " of Wagner's art and his theories were one thing, to be accounted for and perhaps excused in normal ways, his personal character was quite another. " One gross and ugly failing," says Dorn, " of which Wagner has always been guilty, no one can pardon in him; and this failing is so much the worse because it cannot be grounded in a man's character, but because the actions resulting from it were done deliberately, just as by deliberation they might have been avoided. I refer to the cold, heartless ingratitude that Wagner has always exhibited. I will here mention only the names of [King] Friedrich August in Dresden, Meyerbeer in Paris, Wesendonk in Zürich, Bülow in Munich. . . ." [1] All this in a public imprint in Wagner's life-time!

Even some of his admirers as an artist were under no delusion as to his ability to forget his benefactors when the flow of benefits from them had ceased. " Wagner remembers people only for as long as he needs them," Cornelius wrote to his fiancée. Brother Albert once indulged in unusually plain speaking to him. Richard, in 1853, was indiscreet enough to ask his niece Johanna, who was then a successful singer, for a loan of 1,000 thalers; whereupon her father Albert seized his pen and said what he had no doubt been itching to say for years: " I will not dwell on that [i.e. certain misunderstandings about *Tannhäuser* in Berlin], for I am used to seeing you respect people only *if* and *as long as* they can be useful to you; when the usefulness is over, the person also no longer exists for you. Gratitude for the past is unknown to you: all that is merely an infernal obligation! It has always been so — towards Brockhaus, the King, Lüttichau, Pusinelli, Tichatschek, and everyone else who has helped you in one way or another. Greatly as I value and love your talent, it is just the opposite as regards your character. Since your last letter the first sign of life you give Johanna is — give me 1,000 thalers! A mere trifle! " [2]

It was plainly the view taken of him by the whole contemporary

---

[1] DEE, p. 169.   [2] JKJ, p. 69.

German world outside a small circle of admirers whose fidelity to
him was unshakable. Nevertheless it may be suggested that perhaps
the world was, and still is, a little wrong on this point — wrong not
as to the facts but as to its interpretation of them. The explanation
probably is that Wagner was so possessed by his daemon that he
never saw, and could not possibly see, the matter of friendship and
gratitude as ordinary men see it. He was driven onward by a colossal will-to-create that was insatiable in the demands it made upon
life and men for material that would nourish its own blood-stream.
Nothing angered and perplexed him so much as this charge of ingratitude: as the matter presented itself to him, it was the others
who had fallen short of the highest ideal of friendship, by failing,
from poorness of spiritual material or from lack of will, to yield
the answering fire he would fain have struck from them. His constant error lay in forgetting that other men had their own lives to
live, humbler destinies to fulfil than his, no doubt, but at any rate
their own, and therefore dear to them. And in these passages from
Mein Leben dealing with his student years we have evidence that
even then he was consumed with hunger for a sympathy that no one
could give him of the quality and in the measure he longed for. It
was the refusal of the world to give him this sympathy, to which he
felt he was entitled, that in the later years was to make what was
originally an idiosyncrasy of nature come to seem a defect of character. Nature dealt with him with her usual far-seeing vision; with
each wound he grew a thicker skin, in the face of each new obstacle
he developed a new hardness not only of physical but of moral
tissue. Since only by the most ruthless assertion of himself could he
reach his destiny-appointed goal, his daemon saw to it that he gradually became compact of the only right stuff for the long and bitter
conflict.

8

His floundering attempts at composition had shown him that there
was something he had to learn before he could really express his
emotions and give shape and consistency to his ideas. After the
fiasco of his overture he hoped to reinstate himself in the graces of
the public with what he held to be a better work — the already-
mentioned overture to *Die Braut von Messina;* but the directors of

the Leipzig theatre were not inclined, at the moment, to run any more risks with him. He wrote seven pieces inspired by Goethe's *Faust* — 1. " Lied der Soldaten " (" Burgen mit hohen Mauern ") ; 2. " Der Schäfer putzte sich zum Tanz "; 3. " Es war eine Ratt' im Kellernest "; 4. " Es war einmal ein König "; 5. " Was machst Du mir vor Liebchens Tür "; 6. " Meine Ruh ist hin "; 7. Melodrama, " Ach neige, Du Schmerzensreiche." These are now accessible in volume 15 of the Complete Edition of his musical works, published by Breitkopf & Härtel. He made an honest attempt to interest himself in the lectures on philosophy and aesthetics he was supposed to be attending at the University, but soon gave it up; neither the subjects nor the treatment of them could he work up into his own mental tissue. The whole of his intellectual energy was manifestly directed now upon music; and his family had the good sense to let him make one more effort to find a teacher who would be of some use to him.

This time he had the good fortune to find the man he needed in Theodor Weinlig; perhaps also the teacher was fortunate in that the pupil came to him just at the moment when he at last realised subconsciously what it was he needed to learn, and how to learn it. Weinlig (1780–1842) had been, since 1823, Cantor at St. Thomas's Church, a post formerly occupied by Johann Sebastian Bach. According to a contemporary letter of Wagner, he was regarded, at any rate in Leipzig circles, as the greatest of living contrapuntists.[1] His first experience with the boy was no happier than those of Müller had been. Richard no doubt thought that a ready-made key to the art of composition would be instantaneously provided him: when he found that he was once more set at dry exercises in four-part harmony, the proud composer of overtures and sonatas revolted. As he was visibly neglecting his work, Weinlig refused to have anything more to do with him; but apparently it was just at this time that Richard came to a sense of the folly of the life he had been living in taverns and gambling dens, and in a mood of general repentance he besought Weinlig to forgive him and begin again. The teacher no doubt recognised the essentially musical nature of the boy's mind, and confined himself to familiarising him with the fundamental relationships of harmony and principles of counter-

---

[1] Letter of 3rd March, 1832, to Ottilie, in RWFB.

point, letting him work out the tasks set him in his own way, and then going over them with him and showing how *he* would have worked them out — the only real way by which composition can be "taught," as Wagner himself said in later years. His interest in technique was now thoroughly aroused; at last he saw the reasons for certain procedures. He worked hard at fugue for eight weeks, astonished to find how quickly the time flew; then Weinlig allowed him to pass on to a different kind of thematic weaving in works of the sonata type. All in all he was with Weinlig some six months, from about October 1831 onwards; at the end of that time his teacher dismissed him with the remark that though he would probably never have to write canons or fugues he had mastered Independence — and showed his satisfaction with his pupil by refusing to take a fee from the mother for the six months' teaching.[1]

During this time Richard wrote a piano sonata in B flat major which Weinlig, by way of encouragement to the boy, prevailed upon Breitkopf & Härtel to publish at Easter, 1832;[2] Richard received a welcome 20 thalers for it. It was of course dedicated to his teacher. A Polonaise in D major for piano (four hands) was issued, as opus 2, by Breitkopf in the same year. A second piano sonata, in A major, the manuscript of which is now at Wahnfried, has never been published. To this period belongs also a Fantasia for the piano in F sharp minor, in which a good deal that is characteristic of the later Wagner can be detected in embryo; it was first published, by C. F. Kahnt, Leipzig, in 1905.

His passion for more or less academic study was no doubt increased by the perplexity into which he was thrown about this time by some of his experiences of Beethoven's music at the Gewandhaus

---

[1] Some fifty years later, when a conversation had turned on to the subject of the "dissonances" that were even then disturbing the minds of conservatives like himself, Wagner told Cosima that Weinlig had warned him against dissonances. They were "dubious" things to have to do with, said his teacher, for either they sounded bad or they simply were not heard at all. The young Wagner had accordingly resolved not to indulge in them: he might have risked their sounding bad, he said; but if they were not to be heard, they might as well be avoided. MECW, I, 861.

[2] In *Mein Leben* he expresses a certain annoyance that this work had "lately been re-issued through the indiscretion of Messrs. Breitkopf & Härtel." They professed to have "had several enquiries for it lately": the truth probably was that the firm wished to profit by his present vogue. Wagner, of course, could have no voice in the matter, the copyright being Breitkopf & Härtel's. See their letter of the 8th November, 1862, in RWBV, I, 211.

concerts. As will be shown in a later chapter, the vast majority of public performances of music at that epoch must have been hopelessly inadequate according to more modern notions. Naturally the greatest and most advanced music suffered most, for here the technical incompetence of players and conductors was reinforced by the lack of anything in the nature of a tradition of interpretation. We have no difficulty in comprehending the slow spread of Beethoven's later works when we realise that most contemporary performances of them must have been of the type described by Wagner in his account of this period of his life. At the Gewandhaus, which already prided itself on being one of the best German institutions of the kind, symphonies and other instrumental works were given without a conductor, such guidance as there was being supplied by the leader of the violins; the conductor only made his appearance at the desk when the vocal part of the concert began. In 1830 the Ninth Symphony was given at Leipzig.[1] The orchestra scrambled through the first three movements as best they could without any direction; for the vocal finale the worthy but incompetent Pohlenz appeared at the conductor's desk. At the rehearsal, Wagner had been horrified at the muddled noises emitted by the orchestra in the three-four section that introduces the finale, especially in the trumpet fanfares, and at the preposterously slow tempo adopted by Pohlenz, for sheer safety's sake, in the recitative of the double-basses. Some measure of sense was only brought into the delivery of this when the veteran leader of the basses, " in bluff and energetic language," prevailed upon the conductor to put the baton down and let the passage take its own course. The result of the chaotic performance as a whole was to make the young Wagner doubt whether he had been mistaken in finding the marvellous meanings he had done in the work. For the time being the puzzled boy gave up the problem as insoluble, and, under the influence of Mozart and of Weinlig's contrapuntal teaching, turned to simpler musical matters. An overture of his in D minor, conceived under the influence of the *Coriolan* overture, was performed at a Declamatorium on the 25th December, 1831; it was probably the same work that was given again, and favourably

---

[1] Wagner speaks of "the annual production of the Ninth Symphony." These performances, however, were not strictly annual affairs. The one to which Wagner is referring must have taken place on 14th April, 1830.

received, at a Gewandhaus concert on the 23rd February, 1832. (It had been finished, in its first form, on the 26th September, 1831, and then recast, the revised version being completed on the 4th November.)[1] An overture in C major with a concluding fugato (written between the 3rd and 17th March, 1832) was given at a concert of the Dresden Italian opera singer Matilde Palazzesi on the 30th April, 1832, after having first of all been tried out at a concert of the less ambitious Euterpe Society, under the composer's own direction.[2] (The Euterpe Society had been founded in 1824. It began as an occasional private meeting of professional and amateur players — mostly the latter — who " ran through " this work or that for their own amusement; later it gave public concerts, under that Müller who had vainly tried to teach Wagner the art of composition. The Society never ranked higher than a kind of stepping-stone to the more important Gewandhaus concerts; and its performances, by modern standards, must have been appalling.)[3] Through Rosalie's influence an overture of his to Raupach's *König Enzio* was performed at the theatre on several occasions as an introduction to the play. In *Mein Leben* Wagner tells us that " out of prudence it was not announced on the programme the first time," the composer's name being revealed only after the success of the work with the public had been assured. According to the theatre programme of 16th March, 1832 (the second performance of the play), " the overture and the music at the end of the fifth act have been newly composed for the occasion by Richard Wagner." This was the first occasion on which his name appeared in a theatre bill.

A month or so later, on the 22nd April, a " Scena and Aria " of his (now lost) was sung by Henriette Wüst, a pupil of Dorn, at a Declamatorium in the Court Theatre.

The crowning work of this period was a symphony in C major, the further history of which will be narrated later. According to a letter of 16th December, 1832, to Apel, this had been written in six weeks.

---

[1] This overture, that in C major, and that to *König Enzio* have all been published in recent years.

[2] This work was played at Bayreuth as a birthday compliment to Wagner on 22nd May, 1873, and under Bilse, in Berlin, on 30th November, 1877. It will be found in Vol. XX of the Complete Musical Works.

[3] See KGT, pp. 290–297.

His growing disgust with student excesses and the Philistine student mentality was deepened by the failure of his boon companions to share his enthusiasm for the Poles, whose struggle against Russia was arousing general sympathy at this time. (Warsaw had fallen on the 7th September, 1831.) Friedrich Brockhaus was president of a committee that had undertaken the care of the Polish refugees who had flocked to Leipzig after the disastrous battle of Ostrolenka, and at Brockhaus's house Wagner met the most distinguished of these exiles, Count Vincenz Tyszkiéwitcz, whose aristocratic bearing and fine breeding made the boy more than ever critical of the brainless swagger of the hobbledehoy students. The excitable boy was now taking his first draught of the heady wine of politics; he particularly remembered in after life a dinner given to the Polish refugees on the anniversary of the third of May, at which the enthusiasm for the Poles reached its climax. The ultimate musical outcome of this enthusiasm was the overture *Polonia,* the actual composition of which, however, belongs to a later date (1836).

Tyszkiéwitcz must have taken a liking to the eager youth, and, learning that he wished to see something of the great world, and of Vienna in particular, he offered him a place in his own luxurious travelling carriage as far as Brünn, whence Richard made his way alone to Vienna by coach. One of the paradoxical advantages of the relatively undeveloped musical state of Germany at that time, and of the low standard of performance with which the public was content, was that there was less hesitation about performing new works than there is in more critical and cynical times and places. The ambitious young man therefore took with him hopefully the scores of the three overtures that had been given in Leipzig and the as yet unperformed symphony. At Brünn he had a recurrence of the night terrors that had assailed him as a child. The cholera was raging in the town when he arrived. Far away from friends, shut up by himself in a bedroom in a lonely wing of the hotel, his congenital horror of isolation and his sudden dread of cholera combined to keep him in a state of numb hysteria all night. It was probably as a result of his reading of Hoffmann and other Romantics that in the darkness of his room he *saw* the cholera as an actual living

[89]

thing; it even crept into his bed and embraced him. " My limbs,"
he says, " turned to ice; death crept up to my very heart." But
sleep must have stolen upon him unawares, and when he woke up
next morning he was astonished to find himself feeling so remarkably well. The episode was characteristic of him; many a time in
his later life he was to astound his associates and himself by the
strange calm and sense of well-being that suddenly came over him
just when his nerve appeared to be broken and all seemed lost. One
of the things that puzzled and angered poor Minna most was the
extraordinary serenity that used suddenly to descend upon him at
the point in their quarrels when his blind rage and his wounding
bitterness of speech had reached a climax that was beyond her
bearing. There was a kind of compensatory mechanism in him that
always came automatically into operation just in time to save his
sanity in moments of trial; and his strange blitheness after
" scenes " with Minna and others did a good deal to create the
impression, among people who were not sympathetic towards him,
that he had no heart. But the root of the phenomenon was the same
" watchspring " temperament that always made Napoleon seem
preternaturally serene immediately after Fate had dealt him one
of its hardest blows; the very excess of electricity in the storm of
Wagner's nerves led to a quick dissipation of it and the coming
of a new feeling of inner harmony and strength.

He arrived in Vienna in the midsummer of 1832. According to
Mein Leben he stayed there six weeks, but his memory probably
played him false as to the time, for in a letter of 16th December of
the same year to his friend Apel he gives the period as four weeks.
He had been well provided with introductions, and he enjoyed
himself thoroughly in the lively Austrian capital, listening to the
waltzes of Strauss Vater and revelling in the fantastic fairy plays
that had been the delight of the Viennese public ever since the days
of Schikaneder and the *Magic Flute*. He found the unmusical public mad over the then novel *Zampa*. He heard Gluck's *Iphigenia in
Tauris* with a first-rate cast; but the work bored him on the whole,
though he hardly dared to confess as much to his friends. As yet he
did not know Gluck's masterpiece, and he had perhaps formed an
excited but not very accurate notion of it from reading Hoffmann's
story *Ritter Gluck* (in the *Fantasiestücke in Callots Manier*).

And, as he says, he missed in the performance the special kind of thrill that Schröder-Devrient's acting had given him in *Fidelio*. He nonchalantly informs us that in Vienna he "contracted some debts," which he paid off when he was Kapellmeister in Dresden. As he did not enter upon that appointment until the beginning of 1843, by which time he was further in debt in Magdeburg, Königsberg, Leipzig, Riga, Paris, and several other places, one does not know which to admire most — the time-proof patience of his Vienna creditors or his own happy forgetfulness where monetary obligations were concerned.

Having been introduced to one of the professors at the Conservatoire, he persuaded him to get the students to rehearse the D minor overture. But apparently it was too much for them, and, as he philosophically records, they soon gave up the attempt. All in all, his sojourn in Vienna, agreeable as it must have been to the young pleasure-seeker in various ways, brought him nothing that was of any value to him either as artist or as man.

10

From Vienna he went by coach to the estate of Count Pachta at Pravonin, a few miles from Prague. There the erotic adolescent once more came under the spell of the two pretty daughters of the house, Jenny and Auguste. In *Mein Leben* he tells us that he left them "undecided whether he was in love or angry with them." The girls had little in their charming heads but the idea of making advantageous marriages; and Richard was constantly irritated by the kind of company they kept — mostly sporting young landowners of the neighbourhood, whose conversation ran chiefly to horses. He tried to induce the girls to give up reading bad novels and singing trashy Italian arias, and generally to improve their minds; but the damsels were not at all anxious to be improved. Wagner was no doubt made to feel, by the well-to-do cavaliers who infested the house, that he was not of their class; and this sense of social inferiority combined with frustrated passion to rouse even at that age the critic and the revolutionary in him. With characteristic Wagnerian assurance the raw youth took it upon himself to advise the girls to mend their ways, to take a more serious view of life, and to marry educated men of the solid middle class; and when they showed signs of resenting the fatherly interference of this young bourgeois from Leipzig in their private affairs he became, as he admits, " harsh and offensive," rather tactlessly reminding them of what had happened to the aristocrats in the French Revolution. When, on a later page of *Mein Leben,* he refers once more to this stay of his at Pravonin, he admits that the family had been " irritated " by his " love of wrangling." At Pravonin, at the age of nineteen, he was plainly the zealot, Bible in one hand, sword in the other, we are so familiar with in later years, with the same impatience of contradiction, the same forgetfulness of good manners and polite speech when his will was crossed or his theories not accepted instantly.

His contemporary letters to Apel, however, show that matters were much more serious than he paints them thirty-odd years later in *Mein Leben.* He was very much in love with the black-eyed Jenny. In a letter of the 12th October he tells Apel how one evening he was sitting by her side at the piano.[1]

" Suddenly my emotion flowed over. To conceal my tears from her I ran out into the open air, to the castle. The evening star shone on me: I fastened my gaze on it: it drank up my tears. I became calmer, yet still could not give a name to my feelings. Then the evening bells pealed out. They revealed me to myself; it was the same feeling that possessed you when you wrote your *Abendglocken.* I hurried to my room, took the poem out of my pocket-book, and improvised on it at the piano; afterwards I wrote it out, and I think it is good."

From Leipzig, in the following December, he gave Apel further particulars of his experiences during his five weeks' stay at Pravonin.

" Oh, what heavenly days! For not only Nature but Love surrounded me. Imagine Jenny — an ideal of beauty — and my glowing imagination, and you know everything. In her beauty my passion believed it saw everything else that could make her a glorious apparition. My idealising eye saw in her all it wanted to see, and that was the misfortune! I thought I was sure of a return, and in fact there

---

[1] For some reason or other the letter was not dispatched from Pravonin at the time it was written. Wagner came across it among his papers in Würzburg five months later, and sent it to Apel then. In the margin opposite the description of the episode at the piano with Jenny he scribbled, "This is stolen from *The Sorrows Werther!*" RWTA, p. 1.

needed on my side only a bold advance to be sure of her response. But what a response! An anxious presentment held me back; and yet what a struggle I had to go through with my tempestuous passions! My dreams at night were disturbed; I often awoke dreaming I had avowed my love, and I found nothing but the night, that crushed me with painful foreboding. At last — for it could not, *could not,* endure any longer — at last it became clear to me! We went to Prague, and ah, you can imagine all the wounds an ardent love can feel; but how it can kill is more frightful than anything! Understand it, then, and send me your sympathy. She was not worthy of my love! "

This was to be the refrain to most of his burnt-out passions in later life: Jessie Laussot, Mathilde Wesendonk and several others, the moment of erotic madness past, were " not worthy of his love."

" A deathly cold," he continues, in the flowery romantic style of the German novels of that epoch, " descended upon my spirit. Oh, if I could only have renounced at once all my beautiful hopes, if only I could have become numbed with cold, I should have thought myself happy! But to feel every spark of the once so bright flame die out one by one, to see each atom of a blossoming hope slowly die, to see, hour by hour, the glory of spiritual beauty melt away, oh, this wrings tears from one, the bitterness of which can only be felt but never expressed! When I tried to warm myself with the last remains of my glow, and felt it dying out the more under the breath of death, how paralysed was my glance back into the fiery stream of the past, into the icy vault of the future! Enough, enough, and already far too much! For in spite of the infinite emptiness in my heart, I still feel a longing for love in me; and what I rebel against most is that I appear to be so extremely sound and well! "

He sought relief for his bruised heart in the sketching of the poem for his opera *Die Hochzeit,* and left Pravonin. When next he met the two young ladies, in Prague, in the summer of 1834, their father was dead. Jenny and Auguste, though illegitimate, had been left fairly well provided for. He saw them for the last time, apparently, in the autumn of 1843, on the occasion of a brief visit to Prague. In the interval they had made aristocratic and happy marriages, after having prudently placed themselves for a time under the protection of two gentlemen of the neighbourhood.[1] A kindly fate had saved them from being hitched to Richard Wagner's star.

---

[1] See Wagner's letter to Apel of 21st August, 1835: "I was in Prague again, and met the mistresses of Count Baar and Baron Bethman — the girls whom we knew formerly as Jenny and Auguste."

[93]

From Pravonin, in November, he went to Prague, where he met several of the local musicians, including the Bohemian composer Tomaschek and the sturdy old conservative Dionys Weber, the director of the local Conservatoire of Music, who had never been able to tolerate any work of Beethoven's later than the second symphony.[1] Richard brought into operation the diplomacy he could command occasionally; he tactfully agreed with all Weber's views on music, and pointed to his own symphony as evidence of his devoted study of Mozart. The bait took: the symphony was rehearsed by the students of the Conservatoire, and performed before a few friends of the gratified composer, among them being old Count Pachta, who was President of the institution. It is probable that it was after hearing the work in Prague that Wagner made a cut of forty bars in the finale; at some time later a further fifty bars or so were excised.

He left Prague hurt and angry; the Countess, who had seemingly noted his jealousy of the suitors, had artfully kept the plebeian youth with her in an ante-room one evening while the daughters, beautifully dressed for the occasion, flirted in the salon with the aristocratic cavaliers whom he hated. Certain tales of Hoffmann, dealing with the subject of " satanic love-intrigues," which till then he had imperfectly understood, now found a horrible personal application in him; and he set out for Leipzig with his mind poisoned against the society in which such things as had happened to him were possible.

11

As we have seen, it was under the spell of Jenny's beautiful eyes that he had set to music the *Abendglocken* (*Glockentöne*) of Apel,

---

[1] According to Wagner, Dionys Weber had not the slightest feeling for the characteristic difference between Mozart and Beethoven, and took the opening movement of the Eroica in the strict time of a Mozart symphony. Ambros narrates that at a performance he heard of the Eroica under Weber in 1842 — it seems to have been the first in Prague! — while the celebrated dissonance between the horn and the violins was "corrected" in the way then usual, by making the second violins play G instead of A flat, at a later stage of the movement the first hornist added an unexpected horror to the proceedings by forgetting to change from the E flat crook to the F. See ABB, II, 107. From Dionys Weber, however, Wagner learned the right tempi for some of Mozart's works, which the old man had heard under Mozart himself. See Wagner's *On Conducting* (RWGS, Vol. VIII), and *Artist and Critic* (RWGS, Vol. XII).

being apparently influenced in mood and manner by Beethoven's song-cycle *An die ferne Geliebte*. This work of his is lost. He had used the last of his spare time in Prague to complete the sketch of the poem for his first opera, *Die Hochzeit* — a gruesome romantic tale of a lady who, being assailed on her wedding night by an unwanted lover, had summoned up enough strength to hurl him through the window into the courtyard below; at the funeral of the knight the mystery of his death was explained by her suddenly falling lifeless on his corpse. Apparently the subject had been derived by Wagner from J. G. Büsching's *Ritterzeit und Ritterwesen,* published in Leipzig in 1823: Büsching's story was based on the medieval poem *Frauentreue.*[1] Still under the influence of Hoffmann, Wagner had at first meant to turn the subject, or one resembling it in essentials, into a novel; but this plan came to nothing. On his return to Leipzig he sought Rosalie's approval of his libretto; but the subject failing to appeal to her, he showed his affection for her and his confidence in her judgment by destroying the manuscript. He had already written the music for the opening scene — including an orchestral introduction, a chorus, and a solo septet. The music for this he showed to Weinlig, who was pleased with the clarity of it.[2]

In Leipzig he had the gratification of hearing two performances of his symphony in C major, the first — a kind of trial trip — at a concert of the Euterpe Society in the humble Schneider-Herberge, the second at a Gewandhaus concert on the 10th January, 1833, under Pohlenz.[3] At the latter concert a little girl who was destined

---

[1] Wagner's treatment of the subject, however, differs at several points from the original. Max Koch finds evidence of the influence of Shakespeare's *Romeo and Juliet* and Herold's *Zampa.* See his article *Die Quellen der Hochzeit* in RWJF, 1912, p. 105 ff. (It will be remembered that Wagner had seen *Zampa* in Vienna just before he drafted *Die Hochzeit.*) See also Arthur Seidl's article, *Analogien, Parallelen, Harmonien,* in RWJF, 1912, pp. 98, 99.

[2] So much of *Die Hochzeit* as was written has been published in Volume XII of the Collected Edition of Wagner's musical works. He finished the composition on the 5th December, 1832, the scoring on the 1st March, 1833. The text will be found in JKJW, and RWGS, Vol. XI.

[3] The oft-told story of how Wagner *lent* the score of his symphony to Mendelssohn, who lost or concealed or destroyed it, requires some modification now. Mendelssohn became conductor of the Gewandhaus concerts in 1835. Wagner's letter to him of the 11th April, 1836, from Magdeburg, shows that he sent the score to Mendelssohn *as a present,* asking him to read it at his leisure, as a specimen of his industry and aspirations at eighteen. (RWKK, I, 89.) Mendelssohn never performed the work, the score of which seems to be lost for ever. But the parts used at

to become one of his most irreconcilable enemies — Clara Wieck, afterwards the wife of Robert Schumann — played a piano concerto by Pixis; she was thirteen years old at the time. A letter from Clara to Schumann, of the 17th December, 1832, gives us an interesting account of how the symphony struck her father. " Listen," she says, " Herr Wagner has got ahead of you; a symphony of his was performed, which is said to be as like as two peas to Beethoven's symphony in A major. Father said that F. Schneider's symphony, which was given in the Gewandhaus, was like the freight-wagon which takes two days to get to Wurzen, always keeping to the same track, and a stupid old waggoner with a great peaked cap keeps on growling to the horses: ' Ho, ho, ho, hotte, hotte.' But Wagner drives in a gig over stock and stone, and every minute falls into a ditch by the road, but in spite of this gets to Wurzen in a day, though he looks black and blue." [1]

The symphony was favourably received by both the public and the critics; and Wagner particularly remembered in after life a notice of it by Heinrich Laube in the *Zeitung für die elegante Welt*, of which Laube was the editor. This notice, however, did not appear after the first performance, as Wagner says, but more than three months later, in the issue of 27th April. Laube, who already had a considerable reputation in Germany as a publicist, was at that time a person of some importance in the intellectual life of Leipzig. He was another of the influential acquaintances Richard had made through Rosalie. Frau Wagner used to consult Laube anxiously as

Prague (with the exception of those of the trombones) were found in Dresden in November, 1877, in a trunk left behind him by Wagner when he fled from the town in 1849. From these parts a score was put together by Anton Seidl, and the symphony was performed privately in the Fenice Theatre, Venice, on Christmas Day, 1882 (Cosima's birthday), Wagner himself conducting the first two movements, Humperdinck the remainder. The work was posthumously performed in many places in the winter of 1887–8, the Wagner family having sold to the Hermann Wolff Concert Direction the performing rights for one year, for 50,000 marks. This money was allotted to the Bayreuth Stipendiary Fund — a fund, started in 1882, for providing poor students and enthusiasts with seats at the Festival performances, and, in some cases, with travelling expenses also.

The score of the symphony was published in 1911.

While it is certain that the score was not lent but given to Mendelssohn, it is difficult to account for its not being found among his papers after his death, except on the supposition that he destroyed it. In 1874 Wagner told Cosima that he thought Mendelssohn must have done so, "perhaps because he detected in it a talent that was disagreeable to him." MECW, I, 692.

[1] LCS, I, 50.

to the probable gifts and possible future of her headstrong son: she was nervously set against his adopting a musical career. Laube describes Richard, in these Leipzig days, as " wild " (*ausgelassen*) and " fantastic " when it came to the subject of music as a profession. " He had received the sound musical training that was customary in Leipzig since Bach's day, and was bursting with confidence." Laube himself, positive, pushful, plausible, experienced in the ways of the world, had a good deal to do with infecting the youthful Richard with the superficial notions of the " young Germany " of the epoch, with its catchwords of " freedom " and " the emancipation of the flesh." Laube seems, however, to have sensed the unusual quality of the boy, and offered to provide him with a libretto, originally intended for Meyerbeer, on the subject of Kosziusko. But the book was too much in the conventional style of the day for Richard, who was already feeling that he alone was capable of supplying the precise kind of opera text he needed to kindle his musical imagination. Accordingly Laube's offer was politely declined; but for prudence' sake the refusal was not made in person but by letter. As Wagner says, his journey to Würzburg came in very usefully for this purpose. He had been invited to pay a visit to his brother Albert, who was singing tenor parts at the theatre there, and who had persuaded the local Musical Society to ask Richard to conduct one of his overtures at a concert. He had another reason for wanting to leave Saxony for Bavaria: he was anxious to escape military service. In the third place, it was time for him to begin to think of earning a little money. In August 1831 he had asked Breitkopf & Härtel and the Leipzig Bureau de Musique (afterwards the publishing house of Peters) for work, offering to read proofs, make piano arrangements, and so on, for less than the current rate of pay. To Breitkopfs he submitted at the same time a piano arrangement of a Haydn symphony, which he proposed to follow up with arrangements of all the other Haydn symphonies published by the firm. But nothing came of all these approaches, and at the age of twenty he was still dependent on his mother and Rosalie for even his bread and butter. At Würzburg there was the possibility of his combining a holiday with a little business. Thither, accordingly, he went a few days after the production of his symphony at the Gewandhaus.

[97]

CHAPTER VI

WÜRZBURG

1

ALBERT WAS a person of some importance in tiny Würzburg, where he had made his début, as George Brown in Boieldieu's *La dame blanche,* on 1st October, 1830. Though his voice could have been no better trained than that of the average German tenor of the time, it was apparently a serviceable organ enough in his early days before the defects of a bad method began to tell on it; and he seems to have had something of the histrionic ability of his younger brother, who would probably have become an eminent actor had he chosen the stage as a profession. In addition to singing high tenor parts in the local opera, Albert made himself useful as stage manager; and he occupied himself entirely in the latter capacity in later years, when — after about 1841 — his voice had failed him. He was blessed with a wife, a former Elise Gollmann, whose qualities as woman and spouse were apparent to no one but himself. She had been an actress in Mannheim, and is described as being " immensely tall." " Everyone agrees," says Mrs. Burrell, who had pumped survivors of the Wagner circle for their reminiscences of her, " that she was a hideous woman," — a diagnosis amply confirmed by a photograph we possess of her — " with a sinister expression, very untruthful, and a perfect fury. Why Albert married such a Gorgon is a mystery. She was deeply pockmarked, highly rouged, and Richard's horror." Of the three girls she had borne to Albert, the eldest, Johanna, was only six years old at the time of Richard's arrival in Würzburg. He would have been surprised had he been told that in another ten years he would be writing a leading part for her in an opera that was destined to be world-famous.

It had become necessary for the now nearly twenty-years-old Richard to make a start at keeping himself; and as it was obvious by this time that he was unfitted for anything but music, the sooner he began to learn the practical business of the theatre the better. Albert found him his first engagement: even if, as Mrs. Burrell says, Richard was not appointed officially to the then vacant post of Solo- and Chorrepetitor (solo and chorus rehearser) at the Würzburg theatre, he acted in that capacity at a salary of ten gulden a month for three months, the season finishing at the end of April. After staying with his brother in the Untere Wöllergasse for the first few weeks, he took humble lodgings for himself at the corner of the Hübnergasse and the Kapuzinergasse, opposite the Hofgarten. The salary could have barely sufficed to keep him on the most modest scale; and knowing him as we do, it is a fairly safe surmise that once more he ran into debt.

The provincial German operatic public of that day, though perhaps it did not realise it, was not very particular as to the quality of the performances it listened to, for it had had little opportunity of developing a standard in these matters. Travelling was rather difficult; good German singers were scarce. A small town as a rule either maintained a stock company of its own, or relied upon the seasonal visits of travelling companies; and in either case economic conditions made even a reasonably high standard of performance impossible. Occasionally a star singer from one of the bigger centres would delight the natives by making a guest appearance in some favourite part. But precisely because the standard of performance was low and the taste of the public unexacting, the repertory was extensive; as the economic and artistic resources of these small-town theatres were barely adequate for tolerable singing, orchestral playing, staging or dressing in any opera, it really did not matter much how many operas were ventured upon. The Würzburg company, during Richard's first three and a half months' sojourn there, intrepidly produced such works as Weber's *Freischütz* and *Oberon*, Auber's *Masaniello* and *Fra Diavolo*, Rossini's *Tancredi*, Cherubini's *Water-Carrier*, Beethoven's *Fidelio*, Paer's *Camilla*, Herold's *Zampa*, and several others; while the season finished up in a blaze of glory with the production, at the end of April, of Meyerbeer's massive *Robert the Devil*, which had first seen the light in Paris only two years earlier. Marschner's *Der Vampyr*, which was then a comparative novelty (it had been first produced at Leipzig in March, 1828) was also, according to *Mein Leben*, given during the season.

The inexperienced boy must have found his task in the theatre anything but an easy one at first. He had to begin his chorus-training — the chorus numbered fifteen all told! — with *Camilla*, of which he did not know a note. After a passing doubt as to whether he was really fitted for his job he settled down to it in earnest; and from all that we know of him as a practical worker in the theatre it is certain that he performed his duties conscientiously. He was always able to do this because each task was not merely the routine job it was for the others, but a fascinating field in which he could work out the new ideas that were always springing up in him. The technics of the theatre interested him enormously from the first; and there can be little doubt that his rationalising and organising brain got to work at once even in the humble surroundings of Würzburg. We are probably safe in the surmise that it was Würzburg he had in mind when, forty years later, in an essay on *The German Musical Stage of To-day*, he described a characteristic attempt on his part to convince a provincial Kapellmeister of the error of his ways. It used to be the custom for a fermata to be introduced just before the end of an operatic aria, in order to allow the singer to indulge in showy flourishes of his own to make sure of an applause-catching exit. The practice must have jarred on the dramatist Wagner from the beginning. In the essay referred to he tells us that he once remonstrated with a Kapellmeister for allowing the singer of Roger, in Auber's *Le Maçon* (in its German title, *Maurer und Schlosser*), to indulge in this kind of clap-trap in the aria in the third act. The Kapellmeister pleaded, in excuse, the taste of the public and the impossibility of inducing the singers as a whole to abandon the practice — for of course no single one among them would be likely to give it up so long as his rivals were winning easy applause by it. Wagner took it upon himself, he says, to prove to the Kapellmeister that this " obliging and very talented singer " could easily have held the public's attention to the full, without the fermata, had the Kapellmeister taught him — and assisted him, by the adoption of the right tempo — to sing the aria in such a way that itself, as a totality, not merely the final bars of it, would rouse the audience to enthusiasm. " I proved this to him by myself singing the aria to him in the right tempo and with the appropriate expression, and then, for purposes of comparison, singing it in the wrong tempo the singer had adopted, and in his scampering manner. My demonstration had so drastic an effect on the Kapellmeister that for once I was admitted to be right."

We know that the part of Roger was one in which Albert particularly shone, so that it is quite credible that the incident took place at Würzburg. If so, we can guess that thus early in his career the young reformer must have begun to make enemies for himself in the opera house by trying to break down the hoary routine, and by imprudently letting Kapellmeister, singers and players see that he ranked their capabilities none too highly in comparison with his own. His zeal and his uncompromising frankness in this respect were destined to make the path of his own works a thorny one in later years.

2

At the conclusion of the season, early in May, the company disbanded till the autumn; Albert, with his wife, left for Strasburg, where he had a starring engagement that lasted two months. During the summer Richard seems to have had an offer of a post as conductor at the Zürich theatre. His family was anxious that he should accept it; his reason for declining it may have been either that he did not as yet feel himself competent for such a task, or, which is still more probable, that he was reluctant to suspend work on the new opera of his own on which he was then engaged. He accordingly remained at Würzburg all through the summer. At the end of September the theatre opened again with *Der Vampyr*, which was followed shortly by *Hans Heiling*. It was the pleasant custom in those days for a theatre to regard a composer's work as its own property once he had sold it the right of performance, and to alter, curtail or add to it in any way that the conductor or the singers thought would improve it. Albert, who sang Aubry in *Der Vampyr*, did not think the ending of the aria in the third act (*Wie ein schöner Frühlingsmorgen*) effective enough. Thereupon Richard wrote for him a new ending of 142 bars to take the place of the 58 bars of the original; the words, as well as the music, were of course his own.[1]

---

[1] The fragment will be found in Volume XV of the Complete Works.

The interpolation had a great popular success at the performance of 29th September, and this went far to console Richard for the slighting criticism Albert had passed on a previous little effort of his. Albert had wanted to use, in Bellini's *La Straniera*, an aria from the same composer's *Il Pirata*. As there was only a piano score of the aria available, Richard was asked to make a version for orchestra. In his inexperience of the technique of this genre, however, he scored the aria so thinly that it proved ineffective in performance, and the notoriously frugal Albert reproached him bitterly for the useless expense he had been put to in the copying of the parts.

The opera at which Richard was working during the summer was *Die Feen*, which he had sketched out before leaving Leipzig. The story was taken, in its essentials, from one of Gozzi's *fiabe* — *La donna serpente*. Fantastic subjects of this nature were popular in Germany just then, in large part, no doubt, as a result of Hoffmann's enthusiastic recommendation of Gozzi's works for operatic purposes. Wagner had undoubtedly been influenced by Hoffmann's story *The Poet and the Composer*, in which the author protests against the feeble kind of romantic opera in which fairies, spirits, and wonders of all sorts make their appearance simply to amaze the ignorant among the audience: the true romantic opera would blend this fantastic world with that of real life, showing the reactions and interactions of the two — which is exactly what the youthful Wagner aims at in *Die Feen*. " Only in the genuine romantic is the comic so intimately blended with the tragic that the total effect is one and indivisible, and the soul of the spectator is moved in a special and wonderful way." [1] Wagner certainly had this ideal in view when he planned the comic characters and episodes of *Die Feen*. He completed the work in full score on the 1st January, 1834.[2] Albert, while, singer-like, not altogether approv-

---

[1] *Der Dichter und der Componist*, in HMNA, I, 311, 318, etc.

[2] In the Burrell Collection are two musical manuscripts, (a) the scene between Ada, Farzana and Jemina, followed by Ada's aria, from the second act of *Die Feen* (commencing with *O Grausame*, p. 191 of the vocal score published by Heckel, and ending with *mich befrei'n*, p. 206); (b) the same passage in short score, together with the orchestral parts, the music being substantially the same as that of (a), but the words slightly different. In her biography of Wagner Mrs. Burrell says that she possessed a manuscript of the latter part of this aria (*Begeistern wird auch ihn die Liebe*) arranged for voice and violin, preceded by a different recitative, and headed

ing of the composer's writing for the voice — a point on which great stress was laid in those days — thought well of the work in general and of the tenor rôle in particular; and Richard, who at this stage of his career never missed an opportunity to be heard, persuaded the local Musical Society to let a couple of selections from the opera be given at its concert of the 12th December, 1833. Mademoiselle Friedel, an amateur, sang Ada's aria from the second act, and joined Albert and a young bass in the terzet from the same act. The Society had already performed Wagner's symphony on the 27th August, and his C major overture on the 22nd April. It has been surmised that the *Hochzeit* music, of which there exists a copy, in Wagner's handwriting, dated 1st March, 1833, with a dedication to the Würzburg Music Society, was also performed; but there is no record of anything of the kind. A curious by-product of the Würzburg days is an Adagio for clarinet, with accompaniment for strings, which is to be found in Volume XX of the Complete Edition of his works. It was written for the clarinettist Rummel in Kissingen, no doubt during one of those excursions referred to in the next paragraph.

3

During the absence of Albert and his wife in the summer, Richard seems to have occupied their house as the nominal guardian of the three children. He admits having neglected his duties with regard to them, preferring, on the days when he was not working at *Die Feen*, to enjoy himself with boon companions in the local taverns and in excursions into the country. He found also the facile conquests of the minor theatrical life very much to his taste as an amorist. As he admits, he could not remain insensible to the charms of some of the ladies of the company. Forgetting Jenny Pachta for the moment, he describes as his " first love affair " an episode with one Therese Riegelmann, the daughter of a grave-digger. She had a good voice, and, though only a chorus girl, was ambitious

Scene und Arie aus der Oper Die Feen von Richard Wagner. The handwriting, she held, was that of 1832 rather than 1834, for which reason she thought it probable that part of the opera may have been written in the former year, i.e. before Wagner went to Würzburg. She conjectures that this may have been the scena and aria sung by Fräulein Wüst at the Declamatorium in the Leipzig theatre on the 22nd April, 1832.

to become a great singer; and Wagner gave her lessons on a method of his own which, he says, remained a mystery to him ever after. He was not quite sure how much he was in love with her, her defective education being a source of trouble to him; while she further gave him cause to be jealous. Her family seem to have tried to bring matters to a formal engagement; but this he had the wisdom to avoid.

An affair with Friederike Galvani was more serious. She was the daughter of a mechanic of Italian origin, had made a successful début at the theatre, and was engaged to a simple fellow who played first oboe in the theatre orchestra. Richard tells us, with a somewhat self-satisfied smirk, that about this time he was beginning to realise his attractiveness to women, and his power over them in virtue of the vivacity of his temperament. At a country wedding in the neighbourhood, where the wine had been flowing freely, he snatched the susceptible Friederike from the very arms of her fiancé. " I at length behaved quite openly as her lover. Late in the night, in fact when dawn was breaking, we all drove home to Würzburg together. This was the snug triumph of my delightful adventure: while the rest of them, including, in the end, the anxious oboist, slept off their debauch in the oncoming dawn, I, with my cheek against Friederike's, with the larks singing around us, watched the rising of the sun. During the days that followed we had scarcely any consciousness of what had happened. A certain not unbecoming shame kept us away from each other; yet I easily won access to her family, and was from that time forward daily welcome there, when for some hours I would linger in unconcealed intimate intercourse with her in the very domestic circle from which the unfortunate bridegroom was barred." (For some reason or other, while the family sanctioned the engagement to the oboist, he was not admitted to the house.) The curious situation was accepted by Friederike and the family without embarrassment, and there was no attempt to substitute Richard formally for the other lover. There was a tearful leave-taking when he finally left Würzburg; but he did not correspond with Friederike. " Two years later, when I was making a short tour of the neighbourhood, I called on her again. The poor child approached me utterly shamefaced. Her oboist had remained faithful to her; but although marriage between them was

still impossible, she had become a mother. I have never heard anything of her since."

This is the tale as told in *Mein Leben*. The later visit to Würzburg to which Wagner refers was made in 1835; in a letter to Apel
dated the 21st August of that year we read: " I was also in Würzburg. My maiden has had a child: a clown of a peasant was my
fortunate rival."

He left Würzburg for Leipzig on the 15th January, 1834, taking
with him the score of *Die Feen:* the composition of the first act had
been finished on the 6th August, that of the second on the 1st December, and that of the third by the end of the year, the overture
being scored by the 6th January, 1834.

CHAPTER VII

THE LAST SIX MONTHS
IN LEIPZIG

1

FROM A letter of Richard's to Rosalie, of the 11th December, 1833, we gather that as usual the family had been worrying about him: he had been almost a year in Würzburg, he had earned very little money, he had refused to go to Zürich, and at the age of twenty and a half he was still without the least prospect of a career. The good Rosalie had kept him in pocket money during the months when he was unemployed at the theatre, where his engagement had apparently not been renewed on the re-opening in the autumn; [1] and her brave belief in the possibilities of his opera was a great support to him. He was optimistic enough to believe that he could get this work produced at Leipzig; and for that purpose he returned home in the middle of January, 1834, after having paid a visit to sister Klara and her husband in Nuremberg. On his arrival in Leipzig he found that his brother Julius, after a fairly long period in Paris, had settled in business as a goldsmith in his native town.

Richard was in excellent spirits when he returned. He expounded and played and sang his opera, in his own fashion, to Rosalie and various friends, and was gratified by the impression it made on them. Rosalie at once began to use her influence in the theatre to get the work accepted for performance. The Leipzig theatre had by this time been given up by the Dresden Court, and was now once more a town undertaking, run by the impresario Ringelhardt, who, by dint of giving the public the simple French and Italian fare it wanted, was making the embarrassed institution pay its way again. He seems to have placated Rosalie with one of those facile promises that, in the theatre, mean everything to him who receives it and

---

[1] After his brother's return for the winter season, Richard again took lodgings for himself, this time at Lochgasse, 34.

nothing to him who gives it. That the word had gone round that *Die Feen* was to be produced is shown by an announcement to that effect in March in Laube's *Zeitung für die elegante Welt*. But the usual postponements and excuses followed, other new or unfamiliar works from abroad took up all the time and money of the theatre, and in the end it became clear enough that *Die Feen* stood a very thin chance of performance in Leipzig.

Ringelhardt staved the young composer off at first by referring him to the regisseur, Franz Hauser. Glasenapp treats this official with characteristic unfairness in his account of the episode. He calls him an old fogy — though Hauser was only fifteen years older than Wagner — glances with a sniff at his career as a singer and actor, quotes from a contemporary article on him (1834) a reference to his " intelligence, artistic education, musical understanding, penetrative study of rôles, and rightly characteristic reading of vocal parts," and adds the peevish comment, " Can't one see the sheer nonentity in the very vagueness of the praise dealt out to him? " Hauser, however, could hardly have been a sheer nonentity. He is mostly remembered now, perhaps, as the addressee of the majority of the published letters of the celebrated theorist Moritz Hauptmann. The latter did indeed fail to keep pace with some of the new developments of music in the later part of his life. But in his own way and his own sphere he was a man of remarkable intellectual power and unusually profound musical understanding; the discussions of musical, aesthetic, and cultural problems in his letters reveal a fine character and a penetrating mind. The man to whom these thoughtful letters were addressed for preference must certainly have himself been of an intellectual quality above the ordinary. If people like Hauptmann and Hauser were " reactionaries," that was only because, in a rapidly changing musical world, in which, as yet, no new standard of values had definitely established itself, they chose to delve deeper and deeper into the great music of the past with which they had an elective affinity, trying daily to understand better the workings of the minds of the old masters they loved, and to work out for themselves a rationale of musical technique and a philosophy of musical history. The ordinary music current in their day was too shallow for them. The later Beethoven they could not understand, partly

[107]

because, like everyone else, they had too few opportunities of hearing adequate performances of his works, partly because the passionate struggle for freedom in the expression, and still more in the forms, of his last works, seemed to their minds, absorbed as they were in the older and stricter order of the fugue, a mere lapse into anarchy. For each of them the ideal of music was summed up in Bach and one or two others of the classical polyphonists. It was a misfortune for each of them, and no doubt for those with whom they were brought into professional contact, that hard economic conditions drove them, for mere livelihood's sake, into careers in which there was no correspondence whatever between their outer and their inner lives. Hauptmann, until, in 1842, at the age of fifty, he became Cantor of the St. Thomas School in Leipzig, had to scrape away on his fiddle in the orchestra of the Cassel Opera, playing in works the mental emptiness and the technical flimsiness of which became more apparent to him each night. Hauser, who had a good bass voice, had also been driven into the world of the theatre for a living; in Leipzig his general capacity had won him the post of regisseur in addition. A scholar and a thinker of a conservative cast of mind, he was perhaps the last man to whom a new work of the type of *Die Feen* ought to have been submitted. It was one thing to produce resignedly, because the uninstructed public wanted it, this or that established French or Italian success, contemptible as, in his heart of hearts, he knew it to be. But the judgment of a new German work was a different matter. In these things there were as yet no standards to guide him. German opera, for many of the most thoughtful minds of that day, fell between two stools: it had neither the practised ease of handling and the facile melodic appeal of foreign opera, nor the solidity of tissue and profundity of thought of the instrumental music that was recognised to be the real glory of the German spirit.[1]

Wagner, after some conversations with Hauser on the subject of *Die Feen*, wrote him a long letter of which we possess the draft.[2] Apparently Hauser, while unable to take the work to his heart, and frank in his criticism of it, had been quite polite and friendly and

---

[1] A sympathetic account of Hauser, by Hanslick, will be found in HNNZ, pp. 262–293. As Hauser did not die until 1870, he witnessed Wagner's steady rise to universal fame.

[2] RWFZ, pp. 1–8.

even sympathetic towards the ambitious young composer. The letter shows Wagner in the best possible light, in his turn perfectly courteous to the older man, yet quietly sure of himself. It gives us a hint of what he might have become, as a man, had his way been made easier for him in his early years; it is one evidence among many that the worsening of his character in later years was largely the result of the instinctive necessity he was under of hardening himself to the point of the most uncompromising roughness if he were not to go under in the struggle. He speaks of his studies with Müller and Weinlig, of his unwearying efforts to master the technique of his job as a composer — this, no doubt, by way of letting the classically-schooled older man see that Richard was no mere amateur with ambitions beyond his powers — of the approval by Weinlig, who was held in universal esteem in Leipzig, of the works written under his tutelage, of the performances of his overtures and the favourable public reception of them. He tells Hauser frankly, but politely, that the latter's disapproval of the opera is due to his approaching it from the standpoint of an ideal of art that is inapplicable to it: Hauser's judgment was a foregone conclusion, for it came from the clash between one view of the nature and function of music and another that is irreconcilable with it. Hauser found in it all the faults of the time because he was fundamentally out of tune with the spirit of the time. He objected to the scoring because it was not like Haydn's; nay, even Mozart did not wholly find favour in his eyes. He had reproached the young composer with lack of technical knowledge, and with aiming at effect at all costs: he had not perceived the complete sincerity of the expression. Wagner recognises the impossibility of making a convincing reply to all this: the capacity for conviction is simply not there, he says. He cannot agree that his opera would be especially difficult to produce. A practised singer (his brother Albert) while at first critical as to the " singableness " of a few passages, had shown the liveliest interest in the work; and he cannot see that there are any more difficulties in his opera than, say, in one of Marschner's, who has had successes everywhere. Two extracts from the work had been performed without difficulty in Würzburg; while the success of the music he had written by way of addition to the *Vampyr* aria once more proved that his own opera, which was wholly in the style of that experiment, was well within the scope of the singers. He asks Hauser to reconsider his verdict, as the production of the opera is a vital matter for him and those who believe in him. He would like to have the score back so that he may submit it officially to the Kapellmeister (Stegmayer).

What Stegmayer's verdict was we do not know, but at any rate the production, if not refused out and out, was postponed. August was mentioned as the first practicable date: but in July Wagner had already left Leipzig to take up new duties at Magdeburg. With the consequent withdrawal of his personal pressure upon the management, reaction and theatrical apathy had their way. *Die Feen* was never performed; [1] and soon the composer had a new work in hand in which he was even more interested.

2

Meanwhile he had been going through some significant inner changes as a musician.

In the spring of 1834, Schröder-Devrient, appearing as a guest-artist from Dresden, drove Leipzig wild with enthusiasm as Romeo in Bellini's *I Montecchi ed i Capuletti*. The experience set Wagner thinking. On the one hand he realised once more the extent to which dramatic genius in the actor could atone for musical feebleness in an opera: on the other, the mere fact that such music as Bellini's could constitute the basis of an undeniably successful work of art seemed to indicate that in opera the Italians had a secret that was as yet hidden from the Germans. In the *Autobiographical Sketch* of 1843 he told his readers that he now " became doubtful as to the choice of the means that lead to great successes; for though I could see no great merit in Bellini, yet the stuff out of which his music was made seemed to me to be better suited to the spreading of the warm glow of life than the painfully calculated pedantry with which we Germans, as a rule, achieved only a laboured make-believe. The flabby lack of character of our modern Italians, equally with the frivolous levity of the latest Frenchmen, appeared to me to challenge the serious, conscientious German to master the more happily

---

[1] That is to say, in Wagner's lifetime. It was first given on the 29th June, 1888, in Munich. Pohlenz produced the overture at a Gewandhaus concert on the 10th August, 1834.

chosen and cultivated means of his rivals, in order then to surpass them in the achievement of genuine works of art."

The change going on in him was a threefold one. He was twenty-one, and full of zest for life. He had been fired by the new spirit in the German literature of the time, and had had his young blood excited by the reading of Heinse's *Ardinghello* and other works of that order, in which the warm south was painted in glowing colours. He was reacting against the burdensome pressure of thought in German music such as Beethoven's, and beginning to feel the intoxication of the Italian and French music that went so much more lightly on its feet and took the world as something to be sensuously enjoyed for the moment and be done with, not philosophised about and brooded upon in the heavy German manner. The young composer who only a few months earlier had been convinced of his mission as a German now came out as a confessed recusant in an article on *German Opera*, which he contributed anonymously to Laube's journal, the *Zeitung für die elegante Welt*, in June, 1834. The Germans, he said, occupied a sphere that was peculiarly their own — that of instrumental music. But they had no German opera, for the same reason that they had no German drama.

> " We are too intellectual, too learned, to create warm human figures. Mozart could do so, but he animated his characters with the beauty of Italian song. Since we have come to despise this, we have wandered further and further from the path that Mozart beat out for the salvation of our dramatic music. Weber never knew how to handle song, nor does Spohr understand it much better. But song is the organ through which a human being can communicate himself musically; and so long as this is not fully developed he lacks genuine speech. This is where the Italians have an enormous advantage over us; with them, beauty of song is second nature, and their figures are as sensuously warm as they are poor, for the rest, in individual significance. . . . I shall never forget the impression lately made on me by a Bellini opera, after I had become heartily tired of the eternally allegorising orchestral bustle and at last a simple, noble song came forth again."

Not that he wishes French and Italian music to drive out German; but the good in all schools must be recognised, the Germans must rid themselves of their " self-satisfied hypocrisy," give up brooding over fifths and ninths, and seize upon the warmth of life. " We must throw ourselves on our epoch and try hard to cultivate its new forms; and he will be the master who writes neither Italian nor French — but also not German."

In a similar vein was an article of his entitled *Pasticcio*, and signed " Canto Spianato," that appeared in Schumann's journal, the *Neue Zeitschrift für Musik*, of the 6th and 10th November of the same year. It may best be dealt with here as further evidence of its author's mood at this period. Wagner laments the poor singing that is prevalent in Germany:

> " To-day," he says, " one hardly ever hears a really beautiful and technically correct trill; very rarely a perfect mordent; very rarely a rounded coloratura, a genuine, unaffected, soul-moving portamento, a complete equalisation of the registers, a steady intonation through all the varying nuances of crescendo and diminuendo. Most of our singers, as soon as they attempt the noble art of portamento, go out of tune; and the public, accustomed to faulty execution, overlooks the defects of the singer, if only he is a skilled actor and knows the routine of the stage."

The Italian refuses to sing a part if it is not " vocally grateful," whereas the German will make an attempt at anything, whether it is vocal or not, whether it suits his kind of voice and his technique or not. An instrumental composer has to study the special nature of each instrument before he writes for it; but German opera-composers recklessly write for the voice without any study of *its* individuality as a musical instrument. " The instruments ought to form a guard of honour to the voice; but with us they have become the singer's constables, putting him in irons the moment he tries to give free expression to his feelings." German music, in fact, has become too exclusively instrumental since the time of Bach, who, indeed, was largely answerable for the submerging of the singer by the instruments. Only pedants would insist on a plain, straight-forward metrical rendering of a melody; the artist in song must be given full liberty to indulge in ornaments.

> " The public is at sea as regards art, and the artists as regards the public. Why is it that no German opera composer has made his way to the front of late? Because none of them has known how to win for himself the voice of the people; that is to say, *none has seized upon true, warm life as it is.* . . . Our modern romantic noodles are nothing but stupid lay-figures. Away with them all — let us have *passion.*

. . . Grasp the time, ye composers, and try honestly to cultivate new forms; he will be the master who writes neither Italian, French, nor even German."

A third article, belonging to a much later date, may also be taken into consideration here. It is the one entitled *Bellini*, contributed to the Riga *Zuschauer* of 7 (19) December, 1837. The thesis is roughly the same — that flimsy as the melody of Italian opera may be, still it is *melody*, grateful at once to the singer and to the listener, and in its own way more capable of stirring the soul than "the fumes of prejudice and pedantry" and the learned contortions of the average German composer.

3

These youthful essays of Wagner have been rather misunderstood by the biographers. While there are hints in them of the later reformer, they are generally regarded as regrettable personal aberrations on the part of a fundamentally good young man who, in music as in life, had temporarily forsaken the path of virtue. But neither in their excellencies nor their absurdities are the essays anything more or less than the re-statement of ideas that were everywhere in the air in the Germany of that epoch. The later Wagner's glory does not consist in having formulated a new theory of the musical drama, but in having realised one. All through the early years of the century there had been an immense amount of speculation, in the books and the periodicals of the time, on the problem of the ideal combination of the arts in opera. In the very year of Wagner's birth, and in his native city of Leipzig, one Ignaz Franz Mosel had published an exhaustive examination of the problem from every angle;[1] and the speculations of E. T. A. Hoffmann and others are known to most students of the epoch. Long before Wagner came to full consciousness of himself, the union of all the arts in one comprehensive art-work had been an aspiration of thousands of thoughtful Germans.

---

[1] See the modern reprint of Mosel, MVA. A summary of his argument will be found in NW, pp. 229, 230. For a convenient summary of the parallels between Wagner and Hoffmann see WHW. For evidence of the great interest taken in the theory of opera in the Germany of the early part of the nineteenth century see Rochlitz's dialogue *Der Frühlingstag*, in RFT, II, 230–280.

" In spite of the successes won by poetry and music, each in its own sphere, since their severance," says a writer in the journal *Orpheus* (1825), " neither of the two arts can give us of itself that lofty satisfaction which their combination can afford to susceptible spirits. Poetry, even at its best, lacks melodic movement; on the other hand music, without poetry, lacks harmonic definiteness and significance. It has been reserved to the new epoch to apply this beneficial union of poetry and music to the drama also, and so aim at the greatest possible artistic effect through the co-operation of almost all the arts. . . . The opera should be regarded and treated not merely as a succession of *musical numbers,* not as a mere *musical* drama, but as having the value of *poetry,* a poetry of so noble a kind that it rises, as the art of arts, freely and high-mindedly above them all, and, in the form of *dramatic poetry,* as the exhibition of an action in its highest potency, of so elevated a kind that ordinary speech, ordinary ways of thinking and behaving, no longer seem adequate, but speech is raised to the power of music, events are raised to that of the marvellous, men to the height of gods; and this highest order of opera, the romantic, must be a poetry in which all that is holiest and most mysterious is incarnated in shapes of the utmost sensuous richness, a poetry in which everything that is beautiful in the arts is blended in one harmonious action, in which the rhythm of speech is exalted by the magic of music, in which these glorious creations of the mind pass before the eye of the delighted spectator in all the charm of a setting in which pictorial and architectural beauties combine with miming and the dance." [1]

Here we have summarised in advance practically the whole theory of the Wagner of the eighteen-fifties. The trouble at an earlier stage of German history was merely that no composer of that time was capable of converting all these admirable theories into practice; that achievement had to wait for the unique combination, in Wagner, of poet, dramatist, opera composer, and continuer of the instrumental music of Beethoven.

In the German literature of the time, again, we find, in one form or another, all that Wagner has to say in his three youthful essays. The country was in a critical stage of its evolution, not only politically and culturally but musically. The national feeling liberated by the struggle against Napoleon was heading towards a new culture in art and letters, but as yet it lacked unity and even clear and complete consciousness of itself; while there was a lurking sense in

---

[1] Quoted in WEFR, pp. 179, 180.

many of the best German minds of the time of a certain national inferiority as compared with other nations. As early as 1807/8, in the thick of the national struggle, Fichte, in his *Addresses to the German Nation,* contending against this inferiority complex, had insisted passionately on the alleged racial homogeneity and purity of the German breed, the innate superiority of the race, the individual and unique virtues of the German language as a medium for philosophy and poetry, the exceptional closeness of the race to nature, the high destiny of the nation, and the necessity of working out that destiny along its own pre-appointed lines. He regretted the national tendency to regard the Latin civilisation as superior to the Teutonic, to see something " vulgar " in what was German.

" Naturalness on the German side, arbitrariness and artificiality on the foreign side, are the fundamental differences. . . . This unnaturalness comes of itself into the life of foreign countries, because their life has deviated from nature at the beginning and in a matter of the first importance. But we Germans must first seek it out and accustom ourselves to the belief that something is beautiful, proper and convenient which does not appear so to us by the light of nature. The main reason for all this in the case of the German is his belief in the greater distinction (almost stylishness) of non-German and Romanised countries, together with the craving to be just as distinguished. . . ." [1]

Hegel preached that the world had known four Ages — the Oriental, the Greek, the Roman, and the German; and that " the German Spirit is the Spirit of the New World." " Not Herrmann and Wodan," says a writer in the journal *Athenaeum* (about the end of the eighteenth century), " are the national gods of the Germans, but art and science: think of Kepler, Dürer, Luther, Böhme, and then again of Lessing, Winckelmann, Goethe, Fichte." " The spirit of our old heroes of German art and science," says another writer in the same journal, " must be ours also, as long as we remain Germans. . . . Honest, sincere, profound, punctilious, and thoughtful is this character, and at the same time innocent and somewhat awkward. Only among the Germans is it a national peculiarity to worship art and science for art's and science' sake alone." The rôle of Germany, another writer of that epoch holds, is to " regenerate " Europe, to be to the rest of modern mankind what the East once was

---

[1] I avail myself of the translation in LRRG, p. 82.

to mankind of old. " Germany is the real Orient of Europe, in which the iron strength of the North and the light and heat of the East will attain their desired harmony." [1]

But these and similar outbursts of the swelling national consciousness were generally recognised to be aspirations towards an ideal future rather than an accurate description of the present. The more thoughtful among the Germans were rather painfully conscious of a touch of gaucherie, of provinciality, in themselves when they came into contact with the outer European world. " I have lately travelled," Moritz Hauptmann writes to Hauser from Rome in December, 1829, " in company with English, French, Italians and Germans, and I find that in assurance and *aplomb* our dear compatriots are far behind them all. We are at our worst when, in the society of Frenchmen, we try to affect the French *tournure*. I never saw a Frenchman affecting a German or an English *tournure*, or an Englishman trying any other than his own." [2] There was a dim sub-consciousness in them that music *ought* to be a specifically German art, combined with a frank but uneasy recognition of the practical superiority of the French and Italians in opera. The mass of the people, geographically penned in and immobile as they were, had no standards in performance, because they had no opportunities for comparison; but travelled Germans, and those in the larger towns that supported an Italian opera, knew well enough that the foreigners were generally the superiors of the Germans in technique and style. In Italy, Hauptmann discovered, " the opera houses are much finer and better built than ours. Now and then one hears a German fiddler who is up to the mark, but it cannot be denied that the Italians have a better tone, both in singing and in playing. Grating bass voices like Föppel's, untuneful tenors like Albert, [two members of the Cassel company] are not to be found here, and they never aim at making effects unless they are sure of them." [3] The Italians, as Nicolai, who lived among them, noted in 1837, were content to remain ignorant of any music but their own:

> " The whole nation believes that it alone can write operatic music, and that the Ultramontanes are barbarians. The Italians will not even make an attempt to perform German vocal music, or to listen to it:

[1] Quoted in WEFR, pp. 24, 57.   [3] HLLC, I, 56.
[2] HLLC, I, 54.

there are no Italian translations of German operas, and the names of Beethoven, Weber, Spohr, Marschner, etc., are completely unknown to them. What they do know of German opera music they reject as being incomprehensible, unmelodious, unsingable, and mere school-exercises; and is there not some truth in this? "

But, says Nicolai, the Italians are at any rate unified in their musical impulses and taste, whereas Germany is distracted by the conflict between this school and that, this theory and that:

" Our public, as regards its judgment and its taste, is split up into a multitude of parties. The learned Herr Dr. W[interfeld] and Dr. B[ellermann], who speak with authority and have influence, will listen to no music that has not been covered with classical dust for a few centuries. Major R[adowitz] loves war, therefore he must have fugues; he will listen to nobody but Sebastian Bach. A large academic party will listen to nobody but Handel. Gluck has his own public, Mozart his, Beethoven his — and a big one — but Rossini also has a big one, and the Schneidermamsells all sing the songs of Rudolf Gernchen. . . . But when a nation's taste is so dispersed as this, the artist does not know in which direction to turn."

To win a success in his own country in that epoch, a German opera composer must first have been accepted in Italy. And, in those pre-Wagnerian days, the Italian opera occupied a position of almost unquestioned superiority. Criticise it in detail as much as they liked, the Germans had to recognise that it had a form of its own that was both consistent and theatrically efficient, and that it had a unique power of human appeal in its melody. Nicolai said what the young Wagner was saying and what thousands of other Germans thought — that the ideal opera would be a blend of the Italian and the German. The German composers might be more thoughtful than the Italians, but the simple expressiveness of the latter went direct to the public heart. Italian operatic melody sounded just as well on an instrument, because it was purely and simply melodic, while German melody lost something of its force when divorced from the words that had called it into being. German opera, compared with Italian, had more philosophy, but less music. And German composers, continued Nicolai, with their bias towards the instrumental, were not so good as the Italians in casting their opera music into simple, self-sufficing, and instantaneously seizable forms. The upshot of it all was, once more, that the new opera should take as its

[117]

ideal a fusion of all that was best in the theory and the practice of both schools.[1]

Even German musicians of the splendid solidity of Hauptmann were constrained to admit that, unsatisfactory as Italian opera might be in many respects, it at all events had a unity of purpose, a definiteness of aim, and a routine of form that made it, for what it was, superior to the distracted experimentation of the Germans. From his desk in the Cassel orchestra under Spohr, where he had nightly opportunities to study the operas of all schools, Hauptmann formed the opinion that the French and Italians at any rate understood their business in a way that the Germans did not.

> "I prefer," he wrote to Hauser in 1829, "even the *Stumme* [i.e. Auber's *Masaniello*] to the middle German, or middling German ware, which is about as indigestible as a stale Monday bun. Strip the *Stumme* of all the foreign frippery, spangles, tinsel and rouge, and there is still a vital element, a fruitful germ, which I value more highly than the pure harmony and good part-writing they make such a fuss about; for 'pure' and 'good' are epithets misapplied often enough by quacks and ignoramuses. Bad, clumsy patchwork by bungling tailors and apprentices, thorough-bass and no thoroughness — i.e. by gentlemen absolutely ungrounded. For downright blunders, commend me to German composers; Spohr may say what he likes, I declare the Italians are far more correct. The Germans understand (or rather misunderstand) so much that they take music to be the outcome of a bare intellectual process."

Opera, he said in 1821, is in "a piteous state": "If it's a question of a good German opera, text and music must go together — you cannot divorce them." The difficulty, however, was how to find a really good subject for opera and a really good handling of it by the librettist, and then to write music for it that should express it drastically without becoming too ponderously philosophical in the German way.

> "Even supposing the Italian opera were inferior to ours, I should prefer it as not being German, for I had rather not parade our poverty. We are in the midst of a period like that which followed on the days of Bach and Handel: the period of the Rolles, Schweizers, Harrer, Homilius, and that galaxy of nobodies, amongst whom Graun was a star of the first magnitude."

---

[1] See the essay *Einige Betrachtungen über die italienische Oper, im Vergleich zur deutschen*, in NMA, pp. 78–92, etc. The date of the essay is apparently 1837.

For this reason Hauptmann

" will not join in this wholesale depreciation of Rossini. I admire his
facility in the formal arrangement of his numbers, as such, though
I admit his poverty of thought, and cannot but see how unsuitable
the whole thing is from a dramatic point of view. Still, by his long-
winded periods, and the way in which he keeps the parts distinct from
each other, he not only gives the singer room to move and to do something on his own hook, but he enables the listener to enjoy it."

Hauptmann, like Wagner, saw that the Italians obtained greater
freedom for their own expressive type of melody by simplifying
harmony to the point of downright poverty. But at any rate they
achieved the one thing they set out to do, whereas the Germans
were so intent on extending the resources of harmony that they did
not know how to manage a melodic cantilena. The Germans, said
Hauptmann, had no feeling for recitative, partly because their
language was not propitious to it, partly because, from Bach onward, they had been inclined to insist too much on instrumental
expression.

" Our *répertoires* prove in a general way the non-existence of German opera; for one German, we have twenty French or Italian operas.
Is it only because the German operas are too good? I doubt that fact;
the fault lies elsewhere. There is too much somehow — too much
music, too little speech. Italians and Frenchmen, with their classic
origin, are born speakers; the most commonplace among them could
make a better extempore speech than the majority of our learned
pundits. As a makeweight, we have our symphony, quartet, and sonata,
which they have not got; we are radically and intrinsically more
musical." [1]

There was nothing in the least remarkable or personal, then, in
Wagner's suddenly declared preference for " Italian song " in
opera, in his discontent with the excess of " learning," the " eternally allegorising orchestral bustle," that marred German opera.
He was merely expressing ideas that were everywhere current in
the Germany of that period.[2] German music was as yet not fully

---

[1] See HLLC, pp. 16, 25, 36, 37, 66, 84, 85, etc.

[2] Friesen, the friend and biographer of Tieck, tells us how the world was divided,
in his youth, between the partisans of Italian and those of German music; while
the Italians "relied on the grace of melody," "some of the German composers tried
to restore their rights to profound harmony and feelings." See FLT, I, 232. One is
apt to wonder, in these days, who the "profound harmonists" of that epoch were.

conscious of its destiny. There was a vague sense that its pre-appointed career lay along a path that diverged from that of other nations, and in particular that for its greater " inwardness " and superior weight of thinking the best medium was either instrumental music or some form in which the music would derive its life from poetic or dramatic suggestion. But the new impulse that Beethoven had given to music had not yet had time to fill the veins of German art, nor were his extended and complex forms within the scope of the comprehension, to say nothing of the practice, of any composer of that day. The result of it all was a general feeling of unsatisfactoriness, of living in an age of transition that felt an aspiration towards something new and something better than Italian opera, without the ability to realise it. Meanwhile Italian opera was there, in solid possession, a self-contained, self-satisfied, and on the whole not unsatisfactory unity — a routine of form and of expression that had proved its vitality by the mere fact of its long survival, and that had, to support it, an art of singing that was superior to anything of the kind outside its own genre. So powerful was the contemporary Italian current that even the young Wagner, with his ardent Beethoven study on the one hand and his enthusiasm for the specifically German art of a Weber on the other, was carried away by it for a time. And his sudden surrender to it in Leipzig in 1834 was made more or less enduring by the circumstances of his life in the next few years, during which his lot was cast exclusively in the small theatrical circles in which the shallow Italian ideals reigned supreme, while he was removed not only from the steadying influence of his former study of the great composers of his own race but from the society and the conversation of people of culture. The " brooding seriousness," as he calls it, of his earlier years was rapidly becoming an alien thing to him; " just as, in my student days, I had sown wild oats as a man, so now I boldly rushed into the same course as regards the evolution of my artistic taste." [1]

But our wonder diminishes somewhat when we learn that the Italians, who, ignorant as they were, were no more ignorant than thousands of Germans whose taste had been Italianised, thought Mozart "violent," and his harmony too "scientific." Rossini's vogue was regarded as a victory over the "pedants," who persisted in using nasty dissonances instead of agreeable consonances: Stendhal thought that the model blend of "antique melody" and "modern harmony" was to be found in *Tancredi*. See SR, Introduction, Section 4; Chapter VII; etc.

[1] In his *Lebens-Bericht* (1879), which is profoundly interesting and valuable as a

4

Theodor Apel, a fellow student at the St. Nicholas School, now becomes a definite factor in his life. This young man, who was some two years Wagner's junior, had been left very well off by the death of his father, the famous metrist, who had been a close friend of Adolf Wagner. His mother had married again: her second husband was a Leipzig lawyer, and apparently they were both anxious to turn Theodor from the poetry in which he dabbled and induce him to take up law as a profession. In this scheme she hoped to gain Richard's support, knowing his influence upon her son; this probably accounts for Wagner's entry at this time into these higher circles of Leipzig society. But her calculations went sadly wrong; the two young enthusiasts merely encouraged each other in the determination to devote their lives to art. Moreover Theodor Apel possessed the unique virtue, from Wagner's point of view, of being not only well provided with money but altruistic with regard to it.

In May the two friends set out on a trip to Bohemia, travelling comfortably in a carriage of their own, for which, of course, Apel must have paid. They made first for Teplitz, where they ate well of the local trout, drank well of Czernosek wine, indulged in long drives, and gave free vent to their youthful energies in every way. From Teplitz Richard took his companion to Prague; there they found the Pachta girls, who had had to leave Pravonin on the death of their father. Their position was still one of some slight anxiety. A rich and obviously enamoured young man like Apel must have looked like a way out of their temporary difficulties for at any rate one of them; and their mother seems not only to have tried to draw Theodor into her net but to have hoped that Richard would abet her in her plans. But Richard's own Pravonin fever was by now a thing of the past. Conscious of his emancipation and of his recently acquired knowledge of the world, but feeling something of the old annoyance rankling in him still, he took a line with the girls and their mother of mad gaiety and man-of-the-world cynicism. The exuberance of the two young men occasionally got them

perspective view, in his old age, of his long inner development as man and artist, he tells us of his half-unconscious struggle, in the 1830's, to square his life with his art. The former was then out-running the latter: *Das Liebesverbot* was a desperate attempt to find a musical form for the reconciliation of the two. See RWLB, pp. 18 ff.

into difficulties, as when they received one morning, at their hotel, a visit from the police to ask them for an explanation of their bellowing the forbidden *Marseillaise* at the top of their voices the night before, and no doubt of other conduct calculated to scandalise the sober burghers of Teplitz. But the danger passed, and the merry pair set out in search of fresh adventures on their roundabout route to Leipzig. There was a kind of anticipatory poetic justice in Richard's wildness during these weeks. They were, as he was soon to discover, the end of the first chapter in his life, and the opening of another — a very different and less delightful one. As he himself says, " With my return home there definitely closed the really cheerful epoch of my youth. If, till then, I had not been wholly free from wildnesses and passionate agitations, now care came for the first time into my life."

In the midst of his gaieties at Teplitz he had worked out the plot of *Das Liebesverbot,* taking the subject from *Measure for Measure,* but dealing with it in a way of his own that was more consistent both with the ideas of young Germany and with his own hectic outlook on life. He intended the work to scourge " puritanical hypocrisy " and " exalt unrestrained sensuality." Under the influence of Laube, he was passing through a phase of " freedom from convention " and " emancipation from the past," being about equally contemptuous, with his mentor, of the " old-fashioned " Mozart, of the " too-romantic " Weber, and of " pig-tails " like Goethe — the sempiternal tomnoddyism of youth, that always believes the real history of the world to have begun only with itself. As Pecht said, the movement was more truly " Young France " than " Young Germany," for, as is the eternal way again with youth, it was to an alien culture that these bright spirits looked for national salvation. The new literary and artistic spirit lent itself accommodatingly to youth's natural desire for erotic experience; and Wagner, like so many of his boyhood's friends, inflamed his imagination with the reading of Heinse's *Ardinghello* (1785), though how he could have derived any voluptuous stimulus from that rather sober work it is difficult for a later and more sophisticated generation to conceive. Obeying the dim instinct of so many of the literary Germans of that and an earlier period towards the light and heat of the south, he changed the scene of his drama to Sicily; and the

young censor of morals vented his wrath at the hypocrisy of his
fellow-countrymen by turning the hypocritical Angelo into the
German Friedrich. On the musical side his imagination seems to
have been fired by *Masaniello* and other operas that dealt with the
passionate south. But for the moment he got no further than the
first rough draft of his subject, which he sketched out one morning
when he happened to be alone among the Schlackenburg ruins.

5

On his return to Leipzig he found that during his absence he had
been offered the post of musical director of the Magdeburg theatrical troupe. The Director of the company, being dissatisfied with his
present conductor, had applied to Leipzig for help in finding a
successor; and, as Wagner afterwards suspected, Stegmayer
thought he saw an easy way out of his difficulties in connection
with *Die Feen* by recommending Richard for the post: he would
both place the young man and his family under an obligation to
him, and get rid of the composer who was pestering him to do the
impossible and perform his opera. Before deciding, Richard
thought he would first like to see something of Lauchstädt, the little
watering place in which the Magdeburg company was performing
during the summer months. The Director was a curious old character of the name of Heinrich Edward Bethmann (1744–1857),
who continued, after the death (in 1815) of his first wife, the
famous actress Friederike Unzelmann, to enjoy the financial favour
the King of Prussia had been accustomed, for reasons of his own,
to bestow on that lady. In *Mein Leben* Wagner gives us a shrewdly
observed and admirably painted picture of Bethmann and his company — a picture that is probably representative of most of the
small theatrical companies of the time. Old Bethmann, whose
special talents seem to have been for drink, bankruptcy,[1] and
matrimonial infelicity, received him in dressing-gown and cap.
Complaining of the sad state of his interior, he sent his son
to a neighbouring shop for a comforting dram, handing him

---

[1] At an earlier stage of his chequered career he had been Director in Aachen,
which town he left heavily in debt. When Director in Leipzig (1828–9), he lived
in the theatre, protected by two town guards, in order to escape his creditors, until
the day of his benefit arrived. See SHJ, p. 68 ff.

ostentatiously a real silver groschen, the sight of which was in-tended to impress his visitor favourably as to the financial stability of the company. His second wife, who was lame in one foot, reclined on an extraordinary couch; by her side, smoking a pipe, was an elderly bass, about whose attentions to the lady Bethmann com-plained quite openly to Wagner. After a little conversation, the Director took him to his regisseur, Schmale, who lived in the same house. Schmale, a " toothless old skeleton," kept reaching through the open window to pick cherries from a tree outside, mumbling the fruit, and ejecting the stones noisily, the while he calmly told the newcomer of one or two of the most recent of those little diffi-culties that are always cropping up in theatrical circles. *Don Gio-vanni*, it seemed, had been put in the bill for the next Sunday; but unfortunately the Merseburg town band, who constituted the or-chestra, refused to come to Lauchstädt on the Saturday to rehearse. Bethmann, he said, was up to his usual trick of dodging a difficulty by turning it over to him, Schmale. Wagner, who by this time had taken the tiny measure of Bethmann and his troupe, told him that if they were counting on *him* to produce *Don Giovanni* on Sunday under these circumstances they were mistaken in their man. He loftily gave Schmale to understand that he had come to Lauch-städt for reasons quite unconnected with the Bethmann company, and was returning to Leipzig at once " to put his affairs in order." He thought it quite safe to take this lofty line, as he had no inten-tion of ever seeing Lauchstädt again. But the Fates, in their dubious wisdom, had decided that this hour in Lauchstädt was to determine one of the main currents of his life for the next thirty years.

He needed a lodging for the night; and a young actor in the com-pany, whom he had known at Würzburg, took him to a house in which, he assured him, he would have for housemate the prettiest and nicest girl in the place: apparently he knew, from of old, Rich-ard's taste in these matters. She was a Fräulein Minna Planer, who played juvenile lead in the non-operatic section of Bethmann's company.

" As luck would have it," says Wagner in *Mein Leben*, " the prom-ised damsel met us at the door of the house in question. Her appear-ance and bearing formed the most striking contrast possible to all the unpleasant impressions of the theatre that I had received on this fatal morning. She looked fresh and charming: and her composure and the grave assurance of her manner gave an agreeable and attractive dignity to the friendliness expressed in her face. Her scrupulously clean and tidy dress completed the startling effect of the utterly unexpected encounter. After I had been introduced to her in the vestibule as the new musical director, and she had taken stock, with an astonished air, of the stranger who seemed so young for such a post, she recommended me kindly to the landlady of the house, asking her to look after me well. Then, calmly and proudly, she walked across the street to the rehearsal."

The die, as he says, was cast. " I engaged the room on the spot, promised to conduct *Don Giovanni* on the Sunday,[1] regretted greatly that I had not brought my luggage with me from Leipzig, and hurried back there, in order to return to Lauchstädt as quickly as possible." A whim of sex, that in other circumstances would have come and gone as others had already done, and as many others were destined to do later, had made him musical director of a wretched little operatic company, and changed the whole tissue and direction of his life.

---

[1] This would be 3rd August, 1834.

CHAPTER VIII

THE STATE OF MUSIC
IN GERMANY

1

WHAT WAS the theatrical and operatic world into which this ardent but innocent young adventurer had now plunged? An understanding of the true nature of Wagner's later reforms, of the forces against which he had to struggle, nay, even of the man himself, and particularly of his financial difficulties, is impossible without some preliminary insight into the musical, social, and economic conditions of the Germany of the first half of the nineteenth century. The economic conditions are especially important for our study of Wagner, not only as artist but as man. For he was destined not only to change the face of German music but to be the living symbol of a revolution in the status of the German musician. We begin to look a little less harshly on his juvenile thoughtlessness in the matter of money obligations when we have realised the economic condition of the average German opera composer of the period; we discover that Richard Wagner was no more constructed to fit into the existing economic than into the existing musical condition of things. In every sense he is a colossus bestriding a century. The musical companions or rivals of his nonage — the Spohrs, the Webers, the Marschners, the Nicolais, the Lortzings and all the rest of them — seem almost, in the light of his later development, to be not so much his contemporaries as inhabitants of another epoch and another world. The economic distance between him and them is equally remarkable; not one of them ever dreamt that a German opera composer would ever have the theatre authorities grovelling at his feet as Wagner had long before the end of his career. It is true that towards the end of the eighteen-sixties composers in general found themselves placed in a new and stronger legal position relatively to publishers and impresarios; but apart from that, the standing of Wagner in the economic and social as well as in the musical world in the last two decades of his life was evidence that the status of the German opera composer had changed enormously since the eighteen-thirties. And to this change Wagner contributed not only by the excellence of his musical dramas but, paradoxical as it may seem, by what the commercial world would regard as his faults as a man. It could be quite plausibly argued that had he been as scrupulous in the matter of money as Nicolai and Lortzing and a hundred other struggling German composers had been he would never have realised his artistic ideals. It almost seems as if Nature, with a definite artistic goal in view, had made him, in a sense, so magnificently complete that there was no fear of his artistic ideal ever coming to shipwreck through an undue sensitiveness on his part to certain conventions of ordinary life. The plain fact is that if he had been less willing to live at other people's expense he would never have accomplished a quarter of the work he was sent into the world to do. And that he should have been constitutionally incapable, from the commencement, of conforming to the economic standard so humbly accepted by other German composers was just another sign, as we now see, that in Richard Wagner Nature had thrown up a being as different from the generality of German musicians in ordinary human substance as he surpassed them in genius.

The modern world is apt to look at Wagner's borrowings from rather the wrong angle. With few exceptions, the German composers and men of letters of the early years of the nineteenth century lived in a state of chronic impecuniosity. Borrowing from friends, especially in the difficult first part of a career, was not an exception but the rule; and there were few of these people who had not at some time or other made the acquaintance of the local pawnbroker. Hauptmann borrowed from his friend Hauser: E. T. A. Hoffmann borrowed from his friend Hippel; the list might be lengthened considerably. The difference between Wagner and all these others was in the first place that he was never in the least reluctant to incur debts not merely for necessities but for luxuries, and in the second place that he would have been quite content to go on owing money to the end of his days had his creditors not reminded him occasionally of his obligations to them.

2

Let us first of all take a glance at the German musical world of the first part of the nineteenth century.

The ordinary music lover of to-day, lacking a historical perspective, naturally assumes that musical conditions in the not very remote past were very much as they are now. This mistaken notion lies at the root of the fallacious theory that the great musician has always had to contend with the " conservatism " of his purblind contemporaries, and has suffered martyrdom in the process. No partisan of this romantic theory, so dear to the heart of the sentimental modern biographer, seems to have set himself to discover what opportunities the great man's contemporaries had of becoming acquainted with his music. The chances of hearing it at all may have been rare; and when people did hear it the performance may have been of a kind that made it a hindrance rather than a help to the understanding of the work. The reader, and too often the writer, of to-day is apt to assume that as the musical world is now, so, more or less, it has always been, with opera and concert institutions flourishing everywhere, with a fairly high level of performance everywhere, with the present facilities for publication, and with the composer occupying much the same economic position towards the publishers and purchasers and performers of his music as he does now. But to suppose all this is to have a completely wrong conception of the musical world as it was even so recently as a hundred years ago, or less.

In the eighteenth century the German composer was almost entirely dependent for his living upon aristocratic patronage, or upon the possession of a practising post of some kind, either as church organist or director of the town's music — which latter meant nothing so grand as presenting the public with the finer contemporary productions of the art, but simply the provision, for trifling fees, of music of a sort for weddings, funerals, dances, and other occasions of the kind — or as part of the domestic establishment of a king or of one of the many princelings scattered over the country. Comparatively little high-class music was published, except by subscription. The composer's direct contact with the general world of music was relatively limited, except in the case of opera or oratorio. The result of all this, and especially of the composer's frequent reliance for his livelihood on the favour of an aristocratic patron, was a certain standardisation of taste, a certain limitation of personal intellectual adventure in music, and, as corollary to these two, a certain practical restriction on difficulty of performance, for obviously there would have been no sense in a composer's writing much beyond the technical capacity of the average executant.[1] This condition of virtually stable equilibrium received its first severe shock from the dynamic personality of Beethoven, who not only made music say a hundred things it had never said before, but made it say them in a way that placed the performance of many of his works beyond the powers of the average executant of that period. In the course of time the composers of the first half of the nineteenth century, aided in large part by new developments in instrument-construction, succeeded in imposing a new technique not only directly upon virtuosi but indirectly upon the ordinary practising musician — the violin technique of Paganini, Spohr, Rode, Vieuxtemps and others, the piano technique of Liszt, Chopin and Schumann, the orchestral technique of Weber, Berlioz, Wagner and Meyerbeer. But the first result of the new energy pumped into the veins of the old music by Beethoven was that both the amateur and the professional performer found themselves suddenly confronted with problems of technique that were beyond their previous experience and their capacity; and until the new technical problems were solved there could be little hope of any general understanding of the new music.

When we read of the blank amazement created here and there by the chamber music of Beethoven, especially the posthumous quartets, we have to remember that the people who were amazed and confused by this music never really heard it as it was, for the simple reason that hardly anyone could play it. It is doubtful whether, in the whole of Europe, there was in Beethoven's own day a string quartet capable of dealing faithfully, according to our modern notions, with one of his works in that genre, with the exception of the Schuppanzigh combination in Vienna, composed of personal friends of the composer; and there are hints in contemporary records that even these enthusiasts occasionally failed to do justice to

[1] Works written expressly for outstanding virtuosi — certain arias and concertos of Mozart, for example — were in a different category.

this audacious music. Incredible as it may seem to us now, it took a long time for the simple conception to become firmly established that a quartet is a work for four instruments of equal standing, of equal importance in the presentation of the musical thought. The general view in the early nineteenth century was that a quartet was a work for a soloist with an " accompaniment " by the three other instruments. We get a measure of the unique musical intelligence of the technically almost untrained young Wagner when we read of his studying the posthumous E flat quartet of Beethoven *in the score;* for the general notion was that the gist of a work of this type lay in the first violin part. Writing in 1834 (at the age of thirty-one), Berlioz, who devoured the Beethoven quartets in the library of the Paris Conservatoire, said of the last quartets that " the first violin part bristles, as a rule, with strange figures, with unexpected modulations, with broken phrases, that give it, at first sight, the aspect of a page of Sanskrit." As M. Boschot pertinently says, " This is a notable avowal. Berlioz did not play the violin: why then did he read *this* part and this part *alone?* Why does he speak of the aspect of a page of this part, not of the *aspect of a page of the score?* " [1] Strange as the conclusion may seem, it is irresistible: Berlioz, like most musicians of his day, was at that stage of his career attempting to grasp a posthumous string quartet of Beethoven from the first violin part! No complete score, indeed, lay before him; the Conservatoire library contained only the separate instrumental parts; and Berlioz, instead of making a full score of his own from these, thought the reading of the first violin part a sufficient approach to the quartets. Our surprise at this may perhaps be abated somewhat when we discover how Habeneck dealt with the symphonies of Beethoven. One of the best known passages in Wagner's prose works is that in which he tells us how the Beethoven symphonies, that had sounded merely chaotic to him in Germany, became for the first time clear in performance when he heard them, during his sojourn in Paris between 1839 and 1842, given by the orchestra of the Conservatoire under Habeneck.[2] But we are driven to the conclusion

---

[1] See BHB, II, 223, 224.

[2] This was Hiller's experience also. In Weimar, where he spent his boyhood, "Hummel sat comfortably at the head of his orchestra: everything went along smoothly and cheerily, and it all seemed so natural to me that I did not indulge in the slightest critical examination. It was the Conservatoire concerts in Paris that

that such clarity as there was in these performances came simply from the fact that the players were competent technicians and the works had been assiduously rehearsed; for we have the assurance of Berlioz that not only Habeneck but his successors conducted the symphonies *from the first violin part*.[1] In Italy, again, it was the custom, says Hauptmann, to conduct an opera from " a part with two lines — which represents something, of course, but not much." [2]

We meet with abundant evidence as to this conception of the quartet as a violin solo with three accompanying parts in the auto-biography of Spohr. Nowhere does Spohr betray any notion of a Beethoven quartet as a whole, as a complete organism with its life subtly distributed through all its parts; again and again he tells us that *he* played a quartet — that is to say, he exhibited himself as the violin virtuoso, the others " accompanying " him more or less efficiently. He was requested, in 1804, to " perform something " at a large evening party in Leipzig. " I selected for the occasion," he tells us, " one of the finest of Beethoven's six new quartets,[3] with my [*sic*] performance of which I had so frequently charmed my audience in Brunswick. But already after a few bars I remarked that those who accompanied me were as yet unacquainted with this music, and therefore unable to enter into the spirit of it." He saw nothing strange in a star violinist choosing three other players at random to " accompany " him in a quartet; both he and his listeners were perfectly content with the procedure so long as the " accompaniment " constituted a reasonably efficient support for the star. In this particular case the results were evidently beyond either his or the company's bearing; so he broke off, but conciliated his auditors by giving them something more within their capacity and that of his colleagues; " I therefore willingly resumed my violin and played

---

first showed me what could be done with a magnificent and conscientiously exercised orchestra." HKL, p. 9.

[1] See BM, II, 248. Berlioz is discussing the qualifications of the orchestral con-ductor, among which, he insists, must be the ability to read a score — evidently a gift by no means universal among the conductors of his day. "The conductor," he says, "who uses a *reduced score*, or merely *the violin part*, as is done in many places to-day, especially in France, is incapable of discovering the majority of mistakes in performance; and when he points out a fault, he lays himself open to the musician whom he is censuring replying 'What do you know about it? My part is not in front of you.'"

[2] HLLC, I, 57. Hauptmann is writing in 1829.

[3] I.e. op. 18, published in 1801.

Rode's quartet in E flat, which the musicians knew and therefore well accompanied. On the conclusion of the quartet so many things were said to me of my playing that I was now induced to parade my hobby-horse, the G major variations of Rode." He flatters himself, later, on having " obtained a hearing " for the Beethoven quartets in Leipzig: " I succeeded in obtaining a full appreciation of their excellence by my style of execution " — the three other parts evidently being a minor consideration in his eyes, those of the other players, and those of the audience.[1]

In Berlin it was the same story: *he* played the Beethoven quartets, but as the Berlin musicians who " accompanied " him knew as little of them as their brethren in Leipzig, the works naturally made no effect; the 'cellist Romberg, indeed, bluntly asked him " how he could play such stuff." Romberg, of course, took the same view of a quartet as Spohr did, the only exception being that as he was a 'cellist he made the 'cello part the centre of gravity; at Prince Radziwill's he " played," says Spohr, " one of his quartets with 'cello obligato." In Hamburg, Spohr made a sensation with " his " quartet playing; " I . . . excited much sensation by my truthful rendering of the distinctive characters of each " (i.e. certain quartets of Mozart and Beethoven). A rich Jew banker " who had heard my quartet-playing much praised," asked Spohr to exhibit his powers at his house. Spohr consented on condition that " the best artists of Hamburg should be invited to accompany me." This was agreed to, and on this occasion all might have gone well but for a trifling error on the part of the host: in his ignorance of music he had gathered together three other *violinists* for the other parts of the quartet. In Frankfort, in 1816, Spohr had to give up the attempt to play quartets because " the accompaniment was so bad ": at Strasburg things were a little better. Hummel " was pleased to hear that a lady (Mrs. Anderson) had repeatedly played in public his septet for the pianoforte," [2] the other parts evidently being a matter of relatively minor importance even in the composer's eyes. So also with Clara Schumann, who " played Hummel's septet " in 1833.[3] Chopin went to a party in Warsaw to hear Prince Galitzin " play Rode's quartet "; [4] while Chopin himself " played Spohr's quintet for piano, clar.,

---

[1] See SA, *passim.*
[2] See HRMG, p. 263.
[3] LCS, I, 50.
[4] CL, p. 80.

fag., *valtorn* [*sic*] and flute." [1] The supreme height of virtuoso absurdity in these matters was reserved for Paganini, who used to
play the theme of the rondo in the violin part of a Beethoven piano-
and-violin sonata in flageolet octaves (double-stopping), besides
strewing the violin part in general with ornaments. [2] We get a last
echo — in the main, perhaps, only a verbal one — of this strange
conception of a quartet in a letter from Joachim to Liszt as late as
1852, in which he says that at his first appearance at the Ella concerts in London he " played the Schubert quartet," the other performers being apparently collected at random to " accompany " the
star of the evening. [3] In Leipzig, in the early years of the nineteenth
century, Mathäi, the leader of the local orchestra, used to give regular quartet performances with three other members of the band, [4]
and no doubt this happened also in other towns; but the results were
probably of a kind that would hardly commend themselves to modern ears. It was no doubt performances of this type that led even so
good a musician as Hauptmann to say that he never wanted to hear
the late Beethoven quartets again, though he thought he had heard
them " well played." [5]

3

The general level of German musical culture was evidently a low
one, not at all from any lack of interest in the art but simply because
economic and other factors stood as yet in the way of a wide diffusion of difficult and thoughtful music and the adequate performance
of it. There was a good deal of music-making in private houses, and
virtuosi like Spohr were touring the country and demonstrating the
higher powers of this or that instrument or of the voice. Most towns
had a local concert organisation of some kind or other; but the general standard of performance was so low that only the strongest
national enthusiasm for music and the soundest natural aptitude for
it could have enabled the audience to perceive at any rate something
of the quality of a great work through the general badness of the

---

[1] Ibid., p. 105. "Beautiful, but dreadfully unpianistic" is his comment on the
work.
[2] See Speyer's letter of the 17th September, 1829, to Spohr: SWS, p. 103.
[3] See LZBHZ, I, 223.
[4] KGT, p. 229.
[5] HLLC, I, 81, 85.

performance.[1] The same holds good of the opera, which flourished more or less in every German town of any consequence. The opera organisations fell into four main categories. There were the smaller Court opera houses, supported entirely by the ruling prince, a part of his establishment on which he prided himself as an evidence of his culture. Of this class of theatre, that of Weimar in the earlier years of the nineteenth century may be taken as typical. There the public was admitted to the dramatic and operatic performances, but merely as an act of condescension; the performances were entirely under the direction of the Court and for the satisfaction of the Court, and no public criticism was permitted in the Press.[2] There were some larger Court operas, such as that of Vienna, which were leased to impresarios — at that time generally Italian. There were the stock companies working under the control of this or that town council, or perhaps, as in the case of Leipzig in the late twenties, under the ultimate aegis of the Court. Finally there were the touring dramatic and operatic troupes, mostly serving in rotation the smaller towns that had neither the population nor the means to support a theatrical entertainment for more than a few weeks in each year. Of this type was the Bethmann troupe that Wagner joined in Magdeburg.

In all but two or three of the largest German cities the orchestral and vocal material and technique must have been quite inadequate for the performance of anything but the simplest works. It is true that operas and oratorios on a would-be grand scale were frequently given; but the results must often have been of a kind of which the modern musician can hardly think without a shudder. As late as 1853, Liszt, after having produced at Weimar the earlier works of

---

[1] In 1811 Weber began to compile a sort of guide to musical conditions in the various German towns, mainly for the benefit of touring performers — *Ideen zu einer musikalischen Topographie Deutschlands, als Versuch eines Beitrages zur Zeitgeschichte der Kunst, und zunächst als ein Hilfsbuch für reisende Tonkünstler*. He gives some curious particulars of the state of music in this town or that, the halls available, the prices that can be charged, the local musical forces that can be drawn upon, and so on. The Basel contributor to the guide says that good singers will be listened to there with pleasure, for their visits are rare. It is a long time since Basel had the opportunity to hear any good piano playing; and pianists who may think of going there to give a concert are warned that not only is the hall "unfavourable" to their instrument, but there is not a single good piano to be obtained in the town. See WSS, pp. 15 ff.

[2] See Hiller on Weimar in his young days, HKL, p. 21.

Wagner, had to complain to the Grand Duke Carl Alexander — who was perhaps the most enlightened of the rulers of the smaller German principalities, and sincerely anxious to preserve for his capital the position in the intellectual world it had won for itself under a previous Grand Duke and Goethe — that the forces at his disposal did not permit him to give the representative operas of the day the kind of performances they needed if their true quality was to be made evident to the public. He particularly lamented the smallness of the chorus in the *Flying Dutchman*, and said that it would be impossible, with such a body, to perform properly the works of Meyerbeer and Spontini. Though kind things had been said about the Weimar orchestra, he continued, it could not, without radical changes and additions, hope to bear comparison with those of Leipzig and other towns.[1] An earlier letter of his to the Grand Duchess (14th January, 1852) gives us some idea of the justice of Wagner's perpetual complaints at that period about the imperfect nature of the performances his works received in most German towns, and shows that he had good reasons for refusing his permission to give the works unless he had some guarantee, by the presence of either himself or Liszt at rehearsals, that the production would come somewhere near adequacy. Let us remember that Weimar was exceptionally fortunate, in comparison with other German towns of the same size,[2] in that it had a genuinely art-loving prince

---

[1] See LZCA, p. 41 (letter of the 16th February, 1853, to the Grand Duke).

[2] It is not generally realised to-day, however, how tiny and sleepy were some of the German towns that make so gallant a show in the musical records of that period. In 1843, when Liszt began to think seriously of settling there, Weimar had only some 11,823 inhabitants and 1,011 houses. In 1859 there were 13,154 inhabitants and 1,055 houses: that is to say, in sixteen years new houses had been built at the average rate of only about three a year! This little capital maintained at least seven other Court establishments besides that of the Grand Duke; and it had resident ambassadors from Prussia, Bavaria, Russia, Austria, Belgium, France, and the Netherlands. A decided line was drawn between the nobility and the people of the town; in the theatre they sat on different sides.

Guy de Pourtalès, in the chapter on "Weimar, the city of the Muses," in his Life of Liszt, falls into a common modern error when he tells us that the Weimar Kapelle numbered 75. (PFL, p. 119.) The official record for 1843 shows it to have consisted of 8 Kammermusiker, 26 Hofmusiker, and an Accessist — in all 35. The chorus numbered 23, i.e. 10 men and 13 women; occasionally extra voices would be drafted in from the theatrical company. The ballet consisted of 2 men and 2 women. In 1851, when the young Joachim was the leader of the violins, the orchestra still numbered only 35, but the chorus was now 29, and the ballet 7. The figures for 1855 were respectively 37, 35, and 6; and for 1859, 39, 27, and 4. (See RLL, p. 100 ff.)

Thus during the whole period of his Kapellmeistership at Weimar, Liszt never

who was willing to do all that lay in his power for the theatre, and that the director of the opera was Liszt, whose competence as a musician and whose enthusiasm for Wagner were beyond question, and we shall realise how near the impossible must have been any attempt in most other places to obtain a performance adequate to the composer's intentions. Not only, says Liszt in his memorial to the Grand Duke, had the Weimar orchestra been unequal to its task, containing as it did " more than one invalid and infant who exhaust the time and the patience of the others and still spoil the effect," but the chorus and the *mise en scène* had been equally imperfect. For the large choruses on which *Lohengrin* depends for so much of its effect he should have had at least a dozen more choristers — a very modest demand! For lack of " supers " he had had to perpetrate, in the second act, the absurdity of playing a processional march without any procession. The imposing personal *cortège* of Lohengrin had consisted of four peasants. The scenery of the third act was the dilapidated remains of some settings from the epoch of Herold and Boïeldieu. The costumes, he said bitterly, need not necessarily have been expensive, but they could easily have been made of better stuff than what one is accustomed to find on the sofas of the hotels that let furnished rooms; while the furniture might have been " less patriarchal than Elsa's chair in the third act, that stood on four bare legs," and the swan and the boat might have been " better adapted to harmonise with the gorgeous illusion created by the music in the minds of the audience." [1]

had even an orchestra of 40 under him. We must constantly bear facts and figures of this kind in mind if we are not to get an utterly false notion of the musical conditions in the German world in which nearly the first forty years of Wagner's life were spent. It was at Weimar, under these conditions, that *Lohengrin*, an enormously difficult work for that epoch, was first performed: and because new and revolutionary works of this sort, making exceptional demands on the technique and intelligence of the performers and on the slender resources of the German opera houses, were not instantly understood and hailed as masterpieces under conditions such as these, our modern writers jump to the conclusion that "no great composer is ever appreciated at his true merit by his contemporaries"! The wonder is how Liszt managed to give *Lohengrin* at all. He had for it an orchestra of 5 first violins, 6 seconds, 3 violas, 4 'cellos, 3 basses, 2 flutes, 2 oboes, 2 clarinets, 2 bassoons, 4 horns, 2 trumpets, 1 trombone, 1 tuba, and 1 kettledrummer — a grand total of 38 men!

[1] LZCA, pp. 36, 37.

4

If this was the unsatisfactory state of affairs in the cultured Weimar of the fifties, the general condition of music in Germany in the first three or four decades of the century can be imagined. Nowhere, outside Berlin and Vienna and two or three of the other largest towns, was it possible to get a performance of any big work that would not be regarded in these days as a libel on it. Germany in general had neither the orchestral players, the singers (other than Italians, who were, of course, useless for any music but their own), nor the conductors necessary for a thoroughly competent performance.[1] We need not be surprised to learn that audiences found Beethoven's symphonies incomprehensible when they were played, as they were at the Gewandhaus concerts in Leipzig in Wagner's youth, by an orchestra of about thirty, without a conductor, such leading as there was being given by the first violin. Many of the German orchestras were composed partly of professional players, whose technique, apart from the leaders, could rarely have been remarkable, partly of local amateurs with probably no technique at all. It was with orchestras of this calibre that the great musical festivals in Germany and the neighbouring German-speaking countries were given, the players being recruited from all the surrounding districts. It was an orchestra of this kind, numbering no less than a hundred and six, that figured at the Frankenhausen festival of

---

[1] A wealth of interesting detail as to the resources and repertory of the Leipzig theatre during the Küstner régime (1817–1828) will be found in KRLS. The orchestra and chorus at their largest were only 33 and 30 respectively; at first they numbered only 27 and 20; and Küstner, writing in 1830, proudly describes orchestra and chorus as being "both as complete as one finds them in the best Court theatres" (KRLS, p. 235). With these forces the Leipzig theatre indulged in a repertory that included Gluck, Dittersdorf, Winter, Mozart, Weigl, Beethoven, Spohr, Weber, Marschner, Paisiello, Cimarosa, Cherubini, Spontini, Rossini, Grétry, Boïeldieu, Herold, and Auber. In the sixteen months from August, 1817, to December, 1818, Küstner gave 374 performances of 114 works (plays, operas, and ballets). In 1819 there were 220 performances of 117 works, and in 1826, 283 performances of 137 works. (Ibid., pp. 44–154.)

Küstner, who was a man of great experience in these matters, thought that the German theatres in general attempted too much for their limited resources. The smaller towns, he held, should be content with the spoken play, not attempting opera at all.

Leipzig, at this period, had a population of only 35,000, but many strangers came to the Fairs. For further details of the opera there in the first four decades of the 19th century see SHJ.

1810, when Spohr produced the *Creation,* Beethoven's C major symphony, and a number of other works after one rehearsal.[1] At Carlsruhe, in 1815, he found that the orchestra was " still mediocre," in spite of the fact that " several distinguished artists " had latterly been engaged for it: " a few good members cannot cloak the weak points of the rest." [2] At Strasburg the orchestra for Spohr's concert was composed, he says, " half of dilettanti and half of skilled musicians, the string instruments tolerably good, the wind instruments for the most part bad. As the latter had a good deal to do in my compositions, they [the compositions] therefore got sadly mishandled." [3] At Colmar the orchestra, " which was almost wholly composed of dilettanti, was very bad; I was compelled to renounce my playing any of my own compositions and chose some of easier accompaniment by Rode and Kreutzer." [4] At Basel the orchestra of the Musikverein was composed entirely of amateurs with the exception of three or four, and " the accompaniment of my solo pieces, particularly by the wind instruments, was fearful. How poor Tollman [the local Director of music] is to be pitied, to be obliged to hear such music all the year round! " And yet, he was told, the orchestras in the other towns of Switzerland were still worse. " If that is the case, then indeed music is in a more pitiable condition in Switzerland than in Alsace. The good folks here are enraptured still with compositions such as in Germany even in Pleyel's time were considered intolerable. Mozart, Haydn and Beethoven are scarcely known by name to the majority." [5] At Zürich the local Musikverein was again hopelessly at sea, but " by dint of innumerable repetitions of the most difficult parts [at rehearsal] I at length succeeded in making them sound like music; but in the evening the orchestra got so frightened that it upset everything again. Fortunately the audience did not appear to notice anything of it, for they evinced the greatest satisfaction with everything they heard." [6] At Berne the orchestra was " if possible still worse than in Basel and Zürich, and the public, with the exception of very few, yet more uncultivated." At the festival in Freiburg, at which the *Creation* was given, the orchestra was " fre-

---

[1] SA, I, pp. 142–150.
[2] I, 224.
[3] I, 228.
[4] I, 232.
[5] SA, I, 234, 235. This was in 1816.
[6] I, 235, 236.

quently not heard at all," and when it was, the sound was " awful."
" The intonation of the violins was unbearably false, and the wind
instruments, particularly the horns and trumpets, produced tones
that sometimes excited general laughter." [1]

In Cologne, in 1825, Speyer heard a performance of Spohr's
opera *Jessonda*. The orchestra, he says, was composed of " 10
violins, 1 viola, 1 'cello, 1 bass, *no* trombones, 2 horns, 1 bassoon,
etc. Almost all the tempi were murdered. The war-dance of the
Portuguese was downright comical: ten soldiers marched on with
muskets and side arms and went through their exercises. . . . It
was enough to make you burst your sides. . . ." The marvellous
orchestra " consisted almost entirely of graybeards, all of them
sixty to seventy years old. The house was full, and the applause
throughout terrific." [2]

Even in London, where the orchestras were large and the players
well paid, Spohr found it impossible to get an ensemble as good as
the best in the German theatres, mediocre as that must have frequently been. At the Philharmonic concerts the conductor sat at the
piano; though he had the full score before him he had no influence
on the performance, the beat and the tempi being given by the first
violin; but as this gentleman had only his own part in front of him
all he could do was to work conscientiously through that and let
the remainder of the orchestra follow as best it could. It was under
conditions such as these that the path-breaking symphonies of Beethoven were first given to the world: and posterity naively wonders
that they were not understood *in toto* from the beginning! Spohr
only managed to secure decent performances of his own works by
conducting from the score at the rehearsals, and at the concert,
where etiquette demanded that he should sit at the piano, exercising
from there some reminiscent influence on the players.

At the Italian Opera in London, where the same system ruled,
Spohr kept dreading every instant that the orchestra would break
down. At a benefit concert of the singer Mara, a pianist was to play
the C major piano concerto of Mozart with trumpets and drums.
Only at the actual concert was it discovered that the piano was tuned
so high that the wind instruments could not be used; but a trifle of

---

[1] I, 248.
[2] See Speyer's letter of the 12th May, 1845, to Spohr, in SWS, p. 87.

that kind could not daunt English players or an English audience. The wind parts were simply omitted, only a violin and a 'cello occasionally touching-in the first oboe and first bassoon parts.[1]

Chorley has a similar tale to tell à propos of the Brunswick festival of 1839 and other gatherings. " At these German musical festivals," he says, " as was formerly the case at our English ones, the orchestra is compounded of unequal materials, being assisted by many persons unused to practising together. Here, too, [in Brunswick] it was largely amateur." [2] Even in the early forties some of the most accredited opera orchestras in Germany were plainly unequal to their task, either in numbers or in technique. Berlioz tells us that in all the German towns of the second order — by which he means towns of the size and ambitions of Frankfort, Carlsruhe, Mainz, and so on — the orchestra consisted of some forty-seven musicians in all, made up of 8 first and 8 second violins, 4 violas, 5 'cellos, 4 basses, 2 flutes, 2 oboes, 2 clarinets, 2 bassoons, 4 horns, 2 trumpets, 3 trombones, and 1 kettledrummer. At his concert in Stuttgart, at which he gave the Symphonie fantastique and the Francs-Juges overture, he had only 4 first violins and 4 seconds. The Hanover orchestra had only 7 first violins, 7 seconds, 3 violas, 4 'cellos and 3 basses; and some of the violinists were " infirmes." He very rarely found an orchestra with a harp or a cor anglais; even the Leipzig orchestra did not possess the latter instrument. For Berlioz's concert one was unearthed somewhere in the town, but it was found to be so dilapidated and out of tune that he had to dispense with it, its important solo being given to the first clarinet. In few towns did he find bassoonists who could play in tune; the technique of the other wind players varied from place to place, a really good complete orchestra being discoverable nowhere.[3] In many places the reed instruments were of so faulty a make that correct intonation on them was impossible. At Weimar, in 1843, the chorus in Marschner's Vampyr, according to Berlioz, was composed of " a lot of wretches squalling out of tune and out of time; I had never heard anything like it ": while he refused even to speak of the female soloists, " out of gallantry — poor

---

[1] See Spohr's letter to Speyer of the 17th April, 1820, in SWS, p. 49 ff.
[2] CMGM, I, 10.
[3] See BM, II, 13, 22, 26, 44, 55, 143, 225, etc.

women! " At Prague, he says, both orchestra and chorus were small in numbers and poor in quality, so that large-scale works suffered grievously in performance. At Dresden, in 1843, during Wagner's Kapellmeistership there, Berlioz found that the leader of the 'cellos had to lead the double-basses also, " for the bassist who reads with him is too old to be able to play some of the notes of his part, and indeed can barely support the weight of his instrument. I have met," he continues, " with many instances in Germany of this mistaken regard for old men, which leads Kapellmeisters to entrust them with musical duties that have long been beyond their physical strength, and this, unfortunately, until they die. More than once I have had to put on the armour of complete insensibility and insist cruelly on the replacement of these poor invalids by other players." And if we bear in mind that Berlioz's published comments on the German orchestras he met with during his tour of 1842 and 1843 were tactfully toned down so as not to give offence, in view of the fact that he hoped to return to Germany later, we realise that the average German opera or concert performance must have been a very imperfect affair.

In Vienna, as late as 1837, while concerts were frequent enough, there was no concert orchestra of more than third-rate quality. Concerts, indeed, had to suffer for the benefit of the Opera: no public concerts could be given in the evening, while private concerts were not allowed to be publicly advertised. Concerts were regularly given by the *Gesellschaft der Musikfreunde* (founded in 1812), but the orchestra consisted mostly of amateurs, professionals being employed only for the wind and double-basses, and the conductors were also dilettanti.[1] To ease the intellectual strain on the audience, arias from Italian operas were sung between the movements of symphonies. In 1833 Franz Lachner had given four concerts with the orchestra and singers of the Vienna Opera; but the venture was poorly supported and led to nothing permanent. The establishment of first-rate concerts in Vienna was largely due to Otto Nicolai, who, when Kapellmeister at the Opera in 1842, began a series of concerts with the Opera orchestra, and by his gifts as a conductor and his insistence on adequate rehearsal laid the foundations of a new concert style. But other towns were slow

---

[1] See HGCW, Book I, Chap. I.

to follow the example of Vienna. A few years later Nicolai found Berlin, in spite of its excellent Opera, quite unready for first-rate concert music: " the Berliners," he wrote in 1848, " have not as yet the slightest notion of symphony performances such as those I gave with the Philharmonic in Vienna; yet they believe that they do this sort of thing better than the rest of the world! " [1]

When Spohr was in Munich in 1819 he noted with approval that the Royal orchestra (a large one) gave a *whole* symphony at each of its concerts — " which is the more praiseworthy from its becoming unfortunately daily more rare, and the public for that reason are losing more and more the taste for that noble kind of instrumental music." [2]

5

Apart from a few really skilled players, the standard of individual orchestral technique must everywhere have been a rather low one. Edward Holmes, while assuring us that Spohr's band at Cassel was " excellent," containing as it did " one of the best clarinet players I have heard," tells us also that the orchestra was " half filled with officers, who fiddled in their regimental uniform without considering it derogatory to the dignity of their profession " [3] — gratifying evidence, no doubt, of the love of music on the part of the military, but hardly a guarantee of a first-rate performance. In the original score of Marschner's *Heinrich IV* there is a note by the composer to the effect that if the wood wind cannot play a certain passage consisting of sextolets, they are to hold the main note and leave the sextolets to the violins — and this in a slow tempo, and with the Dresden orchestra of 1820! [4] In Carlsruhe, in 1843, Berlioz had to cut out the finale (the Orgy) of *Harold in Italy* because not only were the violins of the Opera orchestra too few but the trombones were simply incapable of playing their notes. And the extent to which the current Italianism had corrupted some of the players is indicated in Berlioz's story of the flautist in the Stuttgart orchestra, who annoyed him by decorating his part with trills and gruppetti according to his own fancy. [5] At Dresden —

[1] KN, p. 208.
[2] SA, I, 213.
[3] HRMG, pp. 276, 277.
[4] GOHM, p. 14.
[5] BM, II, 23.

Wagner's own opera house! — the first oboe indulged at the rehearsal for Berlioz's concert in trills and mordents in his solo at the commencement of the *Scène aux champs* in the *Symphonie fantastique*. Berlioz pointed out to him the error of his ways; but at the concert the oboist, knowing that the composer could not interfere with him then, indulged to his heart's content in his favourite pastime of embroidering the melody in the Italian fashion, regarding the maddened Berlioz all the time with a cunning air. It was under such conditions as these that new works of the difficulty of those of Berlioz and Wagner were introduced to the public; and it is on the not always favourable reaction of the public and the critics to these non-representative performances that certain modern writers base their pet theory of the inability of a great man's contemporaries to recognise his greatness!

In several towns there had sprung up, in the years following the conclusion of the Napoleonic wars, choral societies that did a great deal to raise the level of public knowledge and understanding, especially by their performances of the older masterpieces. But one suspects that their musicianship was not always equal to their zeal. At Brunswick, in 1843, the women of the choir could not master the simple enharmonic modulations in the choral interludes in the Sanctus of Berlioz's *Requiem:* after three days of agonised struggle with them the ladies implored him not to expose them to public disaster, and the excerpt had to be deleted from the programme of the concert.[1]

The solo singers in general must in all probability have been even worse than the orchestras. One suspects that a singer like Schröder-Devrient owed at any rate part of her success to the fact that in her great days she was one of the best of a not very distinguished lot. Germany had indeed produced a few native singers of the first class; but in the main it was to the Italians, or to Germans who had studied in Italy and who specialised in Italian opera, that German audiences had to look for tolerable singing; and Weber tells us (in 1812) that a great part of the Dresden public stolidly refused to believe that a German could either sing or teach singing.[2] Even a fairly good German opera singer could command a salary twice as large as that of her Kapellmeister. When Weber was

---

[1] Ibid., II, 83.   [2] WSS, p. 30.

commencing his task of founding a German opera in Dresden, in 1817, he drew up, for the guidance of the Court authorities, a list of the singers who would be indispensable — three first sopranos at a salary of 3,400, 2,000 and 1,500 thalers respectively, a first tenor at 2,000 thalers, and a first bass at 1,600 thalers; his own salary as Kapellmeister and Director of the opera was only 1,500 thalers. " Really good singers," he remarked in his report, " are so scarce, and so much sought after, that only a quick decision can secure them." [1]

It was no wonder that the public as a rule preferred the Italian opera that the Courts had foisted on them, for in an epoch when few of the rough German throats had as yet learned to discipline themselves it was mostly only from the Italians that reasonably good singing could be expected. This lack of competent German singers was one of the greatest obstacles with which the nascent German opera had to contend in the first half of the nineteenth century; even as late as 1843 Berlioz, on his tour through Germany, could praise Sabine Heinefetter as being " almost unrivalled among German singers, for she knows how to sing "; and even *her* high notes he found it " often difficult to endure." The solo singers at the Hanover Opera he thought " more than mediocre." We realise how scanty was the supply and how low the standard when we find even a composer of music as unexacting as Lortzing's complaining that it was difficult for this town or that to provide an adequate cast for his works. In 1847 he laments that none of his operas except *Czar und Zimmermann* had made much headway in Vienna: " performers for my works are everywhere hard to find, and in Austria they simply do not exist." [2] In a letter of 1839 to the editor of the Berlin *Freimüthige* he says that he wrote *Czar und Zimmermann* without a prima donna part because he had " had to cut his coat according to his cloth "; the work had been planned to suit the modest capacities of the Leipzig opera, of which he was at that time Kapellmeister. [3] In 1843, writing from Leipzig, he says that *Figaro* is possible in few German opera houses because " the performers do not exist: where will you find a Count, a Figaro, a Susanne, equal to the demands made on them by the drama and

[1] WSS, pp. 39–43.
[2] LGB, p. 198.
[3] Ibid., pp. 75, 76.

the music? " [1] In 1844 Nicolai was asked by the Intendant of the Berlin Opera to let him have the score of his opera *Die Heimkehr des Verbannten* for possible production there; but the composer declined on the grounds that even a theatre of the standing of that of Berlin did not possess the necessary vocal material: " Fräulein Marx," he notes in his diary, " could sing the part of Leonora well; but the bass, Böttiger, is hardly good enough for his: the tenors are Bader, who is too old, and Mantius, who is more of a *Spieltenor* — almost a contra-alto." [2] He attributed the failure of this opera of his in Vienna to the poor quality of the German singers there, as the work had been a European success in its Italian form, with Italian singers.[3] It was impossible, says Nicolai, to get an adequate German performance of *Figaro* or *Don Giovanni* even in the leading theatres, because these works required several principal singers, " and even in the largest theatre so many singers of the first rank cannot be found "; while a theatre in which they do exist has not the artistic sense to employ them all simultaneously in a work of this kind, but ekes out all but the leading parts with singers of the second class.[4]

Prague, towards the end of the eighteenth century, had had a vigorous musical life of its own, and had been especially famous for its passion for Mozart. In the early years of the nineteenth century its musical culture had declined sadly, largely owing to the economic difficulties created by the Napoleonic wars.[5] Three years of vigorous work by Weber, who had been Kapellmeister there from 1813 until his appointment to Dresden in 1816, had restored the town to something approaching its old standing; but after his departure the theatre sank again to the low level of the rest of Germany. Passing through Prague again in 1823, on his way to Vienna to produce *Euryanthe*, Weber heard a German performance of *Don Giovanni* that filled him with dismay — " voices like threads," he wrote to his wife, " and acting that was pitiable." The house was almost empty, and he left at the end of the first act.[6] After a few days at Vienna he had to confess, after seven years of frenzied struggle to set German opera on its feet in Dresden, that the singers

---

[1] Ibid., p. 100.   [4] Ibid., p. 155.
[2] NT, p. 140.   [5] WSS, p. 149 ff.
[3] Ibid., p. 153.   [6] WRB, p. 8.

in the Italian opera were so vastly superior to the Germans every-where that the public could be forgiven for preferring the alien art. He heard Lablache and Mde. Fodor in *Il Matrimonio Segreto,* and was enchanted with their " pure perfection " both of voice and style, their combination of technique and expressiveness. " You would have dissolved in tears," he wrote to his wife.[1] The public is right, he continues a day of two later, in holding that no one wants to hear a German sing. The Viennese, this most ardent of German musical patriots is compelled to confess, are not really one-sided; if the Italian opera calls forth so much more enthusiasm than the German, it is because the public knows what is best.[2] And his patriotism received a further shock when, on his way to London in the early part of 1826, he saw an Auber opera at the Théâtre Feydeau in Paris, with an excellent orchestra, singers " far better than he had expected," and an art of acting of which he had had little experience in Germany.[3] At the Paris Opéra he was again made to realise the provinciality of even the best stages of his own country — a splendid building, he tells his wife, enormous stage forces, a magnificent orchestra, " with a power and a fire the like of which I have never met with before." [4]

The rank and file of the average German theatre were expected to make themselves useful in the opera as well as in the drama. The public was accustomed to both forms of entertainment: and as the finances of the theatre did not permit of two entirely separate establishments, a good part of the personnel had to be capable of service in them both. Genast tells us that " German singers were rather scarce, but operas had to be given: therefore hardly any actor was engaged unless he had a passable voice that would fit him for small operatic parts or for the chorus ";[5] and though he is speaking specifically of the Weimar stage about the turn of the century, his words are broadly applicable to the smaller German theatres as a whole in the eighteen-twenties and thirties. Genast himself, though principally an actor, had had his voice trained to an extent that permitted of his singing, after a fashion, a variety of operatic parts. When he joined the Leipzig theatre, about 1823,

---

[1] WRB, p. 13.
[2] Ibid., p. 29.
[3] Ibid., p. 89.
[4] Ibid., p. 91.
[5] GWKZ, p. 58.

he was engaged both as actor and as first baritone: later he sang in Weber's German Opera in Dresden, taking such parts as Don Giovanni and Kaspar (in *Der Freischütz*).[1] In the Weimar theatre, to which he was permanently attached later, he sang not only baritone but deep bass parts (such as Sarastro), and, when the first tenor, Moltke, died, such tenor parts as Masaniello! His operatic repertory further included Fra Diavolo, Zampa, Figaro (in Rossini's *Barbiere*), Orestes (in Gluck's *Iphigenia in Tauris*), Tell in *William Tell,* and Bertram in *Robert the Devil.* Naturally the deep bass and the tenor parts had to be " adapted " to his baritone range.[2] We can well believe that, as he says, the average German actor of that epoch had to sink his own individuality and aim at universality; but the artistic results in opera must sometimes have been decidedly queer.

The famous actor Emil Devrient was only one of many who tried to combine opera with the spoken drama, only to find, after a few years, that lyrical rôles were impossible for him, owing to the lack of proper training of the voice. During his engagement in Bremen, in 1822, he played one hundred and forty-seven times in eleven months and learned ninety-eight parts, twenty of which were operatic: they included such exacting rôles as Kaspar and Don Giovanni.[3] The zeal of people of this kind is beyond praise; but one shudders at the thought of what the opera performances in which they took part must have been like.

The country was genuinely musical at heart. However mediocre the average performance may have been, the concert and opera habit was already ingrained in the German public. An operatic performance usually began at six o'clock and ended about nine, after which, on summer evenings, the audience would resort to the public gardens, where they would be regaled with still more music. At Leipzig a short instrumental concert was given from the balcony of the Town Hall on three mornings in each week, after which the merchants and shopkeepers would go back to their business. There was excellent music in many of the German churches, a full orchestra being employed, for instance, in the Lutheran service at Leipzig and at Dessau. The average German composer

---

[1] Ibid., pp. 158, 206, 212.   [3] HED, p. 9.
[2] Ibid., pp. 224, 225.

may have been a dull dog, but he was at least well schooled, according to the standard of the day; and there was considerable musical culture even among the dilettanti in the large towns, where, if the popular taste was superficial, as it was in Vienna and Munich, they would form private societies for the practice of music of the better kind. The musical mentality in many places was quite primitive: at Darmstadt, for example, the Grand Duke, seated in his box exactly opposite the stage, would give signs to the conductor and the singers that had to be rigorously obeyed.[1] The public was everywhere keen enough about music, but the art was kept down by paternal regulations from above. Weber tried in vain to assert the rights of the specialist as against the Kings and Dukes and Intendants. Wagner was to make a winning fight of it, but only after a struggle in which, for a time, he seemed to be routed.

---

[1] HRMG is a mine of information with regard to music in Germany about 1830.

CHAPTER IX

THE ECONOMIC AND
SOCIAL STATUS OF THE MUSICIAN

1

THE CHANGE in the status of the German composer during the nineteenth century is summed up in the proud words of Wagner after the first Bayreuth festival of 1876, that had been attended by such a crowd of notabilities as had never visited a theatre simultaneously before: In former times, he said, the artist used to dance attendance on emperors and princes: now, for the first time, the emperors and princes had come to the artist. This improvement in not only the composer's artistic but his social and economic standing was in the main the work of Wagner himself, who, in this field as in all others, destroyed an old world and created a new one. Given a character of less power, and, be it added, one more scrupulous in matters of money, even his genius would not have saved him from the fate of all the other German opera composers and many of the literary men of the régime under which he was brought up — either slow starvation, or a humble suppression of his own personality and a resigned acceptance of whatever favours a Court or an impresario might fling at him, or both.

In the eighteenth century the composer, with one or two exceptions such as Gluck and Handel — who were exceptionally strong in themselves and sure of the public support — was more or less simply a servant producing music for a master; it made little difference whether the master was a town council, a private patron, a monarch, or the Intendant of a Court theatre. Everyone knows how Mozart, on the days when his Salzburg archbishop dined in state, sat at the house servants' table. For the greater part of his life, Haydn was a lackey of genius, though he had much more independence of character than his older biographers credited him with. Dittersdorf, when his prince removed to another palace in Vienna, was immensely gratified not only by an increase of his salary to thirty-seven gulden a month, but by dispensation from " the menial duties " hitherto imposed upon him, he being now absolved from wearing a uniform like the other servants.[1] He thought himself lucky when, after playing a mild musical joke at a party on an ambassador who had pretended to a knowledge of music, instead of receiving the box on the ear he had expected from his master he was magnanimously handed the prince's own plate " with a glass of Tokay and five or six biscuits on it "; under the plate were ten ducats, the prince's tribute to a risky *jeu d'esprit* that had happened to commend itself to him.[2] Having run away to evade his debts, Dittersdorf was brought back by a policeman, on a warrant signed by the Statthalter of Prague, to answer for the crime of having " run away from the Prince's service." He remained under arrest for three days, was then tried, and sentenced to a fortnight's arrest in the porter's house, with bread and water every fourth day. " My tears choked me," he says in his account of the affair; " I could scarcely find words to express my gratitude to so generous a Prince "; and he dissolved in tears when, on the evening of the third day, his noble employer condescended to forgive him for " the shame he had brought on both of them." [3]

Beethoven was able to assert himself against this degrading view of the musician partly in virtue of his own sturdy combativeness, partly because, in a world that was surely, if slowly, changing, the success of some of his music brought him into more immediate contact with the general public than the majority of his predecessors had been able to achieve. But the old tradition of the essential intellectual and social inferiority of the composer died hard; and in a country in which public concerts were few as yet and comparatively little music was published, while the impresarios and the publishers bled the unfortunate composer unmercifully, even a composer of genius was in a net from which there was no escaping. Unless he were also, like Spohr, a virtuoso upon some instrument or other, he could generally look forward to nothing but a life of hard and ill-paid toil. The eagerly desired goal of most of them was

---

[1] DA, p. 75.   [2] Ibid., p. 85.   [3] Ibid., pp. 92–100.

a Court Kapellmeister's post, with a life-appointment and a pension at the end: the salary might be small, but at any rate it was certain.

Even when allowance is made for the relative cheapness of living in the Germany of that epoch,[1] the German musician must have had to live very frugally. His fees for teaching were derisory; and even as Kapellmeister his salary was unbelievably small, by present-day standards. Spohr commenced life as Kammermusicus at the Court of Brunswick, at the age of fifteen, at a yearly salary of 100 thalers, for which he had to play regularly in the theatre orchestra and at the Court concerts. Later, being promoted to the post of first violin, he was granted an additional 200 thalers, and the nineteen-year-old young man notes with pride that he can now live " respectably and free from care." Two years later (1805) he went to Gotha as concert director at the ducal Court, with a salary of nearly 500 thalers, to which a further 200 thalers were added in 1809. When, in 1822, by which time he was world-famous as a violinist, he became Kapellmeister and director of the Court Opera at Cassel, he congratulated himself on an engagement that assured him 2,000 thalers for life [2] — a salary to be had in few German theatres at that time.

---

[1] It is amusing to observe the provincial awe with which Weber, in 1826, contemplated the high prices of London and the general wealth and what seemed to him an extravagance of the great city. He lived in London for the most part cost-free, thanks to the hospitality of Sir George Smart and the usual passion of high London society not only to see the latest artistic lion but to pay him handsomely for exhibiting himself. But once or twice during his three months' stay in this country he was compelled to dine at his own expense at a restaurant; and when he did, the frugal Teuton was horrified at the size of the bill. He tells his wife that a little dinner for himself and Fürstenau (the Dresden colleague who had accompanied him to London), consisting of two portions of soup, one portion of fish, and two portions of mutton cutlets, with beans and beer, cost them the huge sum of two thalers, 21 neugroschen, 4 pfennigs in good Dresden money — rather more than six shillings in ours — without, he groans, the tip to the waiter. "I tell you, it's awful!" There were, however, places in London where one could dine both fairly cheaply and well; Fürstenau, it appears, used to get a good dinner for 17 neugroschen, 4 pfennigs (two shillings). On another occasion Weber, dining alone at a restaurant, and consuming soup, beef, vegetables, macaroni and wine, blenched when he was called upon to pay nearly three thalers. "It is enormous: thank heaven it doesn't happen very often!" About the only thing that he found cheaper in London than at home was a hair-cut, he writes to his wife. This operation cost him 8 groschen (a shilling), which was apparently below the Dresden price — an illuminating economic detail that perhaps accounts for the traditional long hair of the German musician of that and a later period. See WRB, pp. 136, 174, 196.

[2] SWS, pp. 63, 64.

Spohr was one of the lucky ones; his concert tours, especially abroad, brought him in a good deal of money. For Kapellmeisters who had nothing, or next to nothing, but their salaries to rely upon, life must have been one long self-denial in the attempt to balance the family budget. When Nicolai became Kapellmeister at Vienna, in 1837, his assured engagement was for no longer than thirteen months, at a salary of 100 gulden a month. The cost of living was relatively high in Vienna; for the three rooms of his lodging he had to pay 20 gulden a month. At Vienna, one of the two or three leading cities in the German musical world of that epoch, a Kapellmeister received the equivalent of about £120 a year! Nicolai soon found that he was unable to live on his salary, and he was compelled to take up teaching in addition to his other work. He was already 100 gulden in debt when he went to Vienna, and had to ask for an advance on his salary from the theatre. In 1842, when he had become a person of some importance in the German musical world, he was appointed first Kapellmeister at the Vienna Court Opera, for something like three years, at a salary of 2,000 gulden a year, payment to be stopped, however, if he were ill and unable to discharge his duties for more than a fortnight. He congratulated himself on his bread and butter being secure for a while at least: his financial condition may be surmised from a letter of the 6th February, 1842, to his ever-borrowing father, in which he says that the 10 thalers he is sending are the half of his total possessions — the product of the pawning of a brilliant ring given him by the heir to the Russian throne. In 1844, at the age of thirty-four,[1] he had been able to lay by nothing at all for sickness or old age, a prospect that filled him with terror. In December, 1847, he could congratulate himself heartily on being appointed Kapellmeister at the Berlin Royal Opera at a salary of 2,000 thalers a year, less the payments for a small pension for his mother and sister.[2]

Even more tragic was the case of Lortzing, from which we realise that in the first half of the nineteenth century it was possible for a German composer to have his operas performed everywhere and yet die of hunger and misery. But for the full understanding of a situa-

---

[1] He died in 1849, two months after the production of *The Merry Wives of Windsor*.
[2] See NBV, pp. 201, 213, 216, 224, 225, 293, 321, 330, 377, etc.

tion of this kind we must know the economic conditions under which the opera composer of the time had to work.

2

One need not be astonished at a Mozart dying of privation when one realises the normal economic circumstances of the musician of the epoch, especially if, like Mozart, he did not happen to be a good business man. Rochlitz, who had the particulars direct from the composer and from the latter's widow, tells us that for *Figaro* the impresario Guardasoni paid Mozart 100 ducats, this to convey full property in the score as a whole as well as in the individual numbers: Mozart was barred from possessing a manuscript copy of his own. He sold *Don Giovanni, Così fan tutte, La Clemenza di Tito* and *Die Zauberflöte* on the same terms. In the case of the last-named, Mozart had the right, in case of a great success, to sell manuscript copies of the score to other theatres. But when the success was certain, other theatres gave the work from pirated copies; and by the time ten performances had been given in Vienna, Mozart was dead. Until he received, a few months before his death, the modest appointment of Kapellmeister at St. Stephen's Church, Mozart's assured income was only 800 gulden a year: and his house-rent amounted to 600 gulden.[1]

Matters were not quite so bad as this in the nineteenth century, but it still remained true that in Germany only a composer of solid reputation could hope to get even reasonable conditions out of the publishers and impresarios of the period. When the youthful Spohr offered his first work to Breitkopf & Härtel, he was fully prepared to go without payment, stipulating merely for a few free copies; but the only terms on which Breitkopf's would issue the work were that the composer should buy one hundred copies at half the published price. The system of royalties seems hardly to have been in vogue: the composer almost invariably sold his work outright, generally for a ridiculously small sum. For the vocal score of the successful *Vampyr*, Marschner received from the publisher a mere 220 thalers.[2] Lortzing, in 1839, offered his opera *Caramo* to Breitkopf & Härtel for 100 Friedrichsdor, but the offer was refused.

---

[1] RFT, II, 258–260. [2] WM, pp. 39, 40.

His *Czar und Zimmermann,* that had been produced in 1837, had proved so popular that by 1845 Breitkopf & Härtel had issued eight editions of it; but all that the composer had ever received for it was 40 Friedrichsdor.[1]

Nor could a composer look to the theatres for a return proportionate to the work he had put into an opera and the time he had taken over it. With the exception of one or two theatres, such as those of Berlin and Leipzig, which occasionally offered a composer his choice of a lump sum or continuing royalties, the practice was for the theatre to buy a manuscript copy of the full score and the libretto for a fixed sum, which entitled it to perform the work as often as it pleased. The fees normally paid for this privilege could hardly be considered handsome. For one of his early operettas Lortzing, in 1835, asked of the Weimar Court theatre the modest sum of 40 thalers. For the successful *Der Wildschütz,* which had already been given in Dresden, Brunswick, Hamburg, and Breslau, he received from the Coburg theatre 6 Friedrichsdor. The price for an opera was a matter of bargaining with the individual theatre, abatements having necessarily to be made in the case of the smaller theatres: and Lortzing's fee for *Czar und Zimmermann* varied from 10 to 20 Louisdor, the average being about 12.[2]

It might take years for an opera to establish itself in even a few of the German opera houses,[3] and as the first payment from each town was also the last, it is evident that not much income could accrue to a composer from even a popular work. The theatres might be coining money with it, but *he* became no better off in consequence; he had sold his birthright once for all.

The galled feeling of the German opera composer found relief on one occasion in a historic letter of Weber's. On June 18th, 1821, *Der Freischütz* had been produced in Berlin. Thanks in part to the charm of the music, in part to the romanticism of the subject, that chimed so perfectly with the spirit of the time, in part to the rapidly developing national consciousness of the German people, the work

---

[1] LGB, p. 165.

[2] LGB, pp. 69, 70, 76, 82, 83, 86, 88, 97, 103, 117, 126, 141, etc.

[3] Marschner's successful *Der Vampyr,* for instance, was first given in Leipzig and Berlin in 1828, in Brunswick, Weimar, Mannheim and Bremen in 1829, in Frankfort in 1832, in Würzburg in 1833. Then its progress was stopped for a time, Dresden ultimately producing it in 1838, Hamburg in 1840, Munich in 1841, Schwerin in 1844, Dessau in 1848, and Darmstadt in 1851.

at once created all over Germany an enthusiasm to which there had been nothing comparable in the history of German music until then. At the head of the Berlin Opera, though his authority was imperilled by the machinations of Spontini, who was at that time first Kapellmeister in Berlin, stood Count Karl von Brühl, one of the most enlightened of the Court officials of the period, and a warm admirer of Weber, whom he had vainly sought to attach to his own Opera. For the rights of *Der Freischütz* the composer received what was then considered the large sum of 80 Friedrichsdor. In January, 1822, Berlin sent him a further 40 Friedrichsdor as an act of grace, in consideration of the continuous success of his work. Weber accepted this, but when, a year later, a further supplementary honorarium of a beggarly 100 thalers was offered him on the occasion of the fiftieth Berlin performance of the opera, he wrote Brühl a letter that must have astonished the Opera authorities. Weber confessed that the offer had " wounded him deeply." " In view," he said, " of the publicity that attends everything nowadays, this offer is bound to become known. Imagine, therefore, an article on these lines: ' The fiftieth performance of *Der Freischütz* in the course of eighteen months was publicly celebrated by our honoured Opera management. This so rare case in theatrical history deserves signalising in a special way, especially as, according to report, these fifty full houses must have brought in 30,000 thalers.[1] Accordingly a gratuity of 100 thalers has been given to the composer.' This, then, is the reward, people would say, the distinction, to be expected by a German composer, the Kapellmeister of a neighbouring Royal opera house, living in circumstances that raise him above money cares, from the leading German royal art-institution, from whose director native talent receives such warm protection — when the aforesaid composer has achieved a hitherto unheard-of success! " [2]

The composers raged against their economic helplessness, but in vain. First of all the would-be opera composer had difficulty in finding a good libretto. Having found one that appeared to him suitable, he had to buy it outright from the poet, and take his chances of the work ever coming to anything.[3] Finally, the opera

---

[1] Weber was not far wrong: the receipts for the first fifty-one performances were 37,018 thalers.

[2] WBB, p. 38.

[3] A reasonable price for a libretto was 10 Louisdor. See HLLC, I, 90.

being written and accepted, the most he could hope for in the way of financial return was a few hundred gulden by way of first and last payment from perhaps some half dozen theatres. It was only a composer like Weber, who had managed to create not only a national but an international sensation, who could make, within reason, his own terms with the theatres. The honorarium of 80 Friedrichsdor he received from Berlin for *Der Freischütz* was of itself a testimony to his exceptional standing in the Greman operatic world of the period. The stupendous success of this work of his enabled him to demand 300 Friedrichsdor from the Vienna impresario Barbaja for the first rights in *Euryanthe*, this sum including 60 Friedrichsdor for travelling and for the expenses of several weeks' stay in Vienna. From Berlin he received a fee of 800 thalers for the new work. Kemble paid him £500 for the British rights in *Oberon,* including the right to publish the piano score; nowhere in Germany could the composer have made so much money in two years, either by his music, his conducting, or his social engagements, as Weber did during the few months of his stay in London. But by this time Weber was the most distinguished figure in German musical life, with the possible exception of Beethoven; and he was business man enough to take full advantage of his reputation. The German rights in the piano score of *Oberon* he sold to Schlesinger for 1,500 thalers.[1]

It was no wonder that the hungry German composer of the time looked longingly towards Paris, and still more so towards London, where money was abundant. Baron Max von Weber, in his biography of his father, speaks resentfully of the difference between the German and the English view of art in the early nineteenth century. In London, he says, there was no such private cultivation of music as in Berlin, Vienna, Munich, Dresden, etc., " where Princesses would sing at a social gathering, and rulers were proud to walk arm in arm with great artists." In London, art was a mere matter of luxury and fashion, not of general culture; and the musician was just hired like any other person or commodity.

" The artist invited to a house bought a position for himself by his talent, but not in real social circles; the honourable diploma of his God-given genius did not suffice there to make him worthy to

---

[1] See WRB, pp. 74, 174.

tread the same floor with the latest-created baronet. His performance was just one ware among others. . . . He performed, was paid, and then had to leave without being regarded as one of the guests of the house. The insolent lackeys served him differently from the ' guests,' and would have blushed at the idea of offering him refreshments in the drawing room. His host greeted him condescendingly and pointed out to him his place, which, in many salons, was separated by a cord from that of the guests. . . . And so, in spite of the loud and lavish applause he had received, the artist generally left the house hurt and angry, only too easily consoled by the clink of the lightly-won guineas in his pocket." [1]

It is all very sad, no doubt; but at any rate uncultured London paid the German artist then, as it still does, handsomely — perhaps too handsomely in many cases — for his services, instead of expecting him, in the German fashion, to feel amply rewarded by being allowed to pace the floor arm in arm with some petty princeling or other.

The position of composers less fortunate than Weber was a hopeless one. " The Germans," Nicolai writes in his diary, " expect from me — a German — after *Die Heimkehr des Verbannten*, something rather better than a translation of *Il Templario*,[2] and I must admit they are right. But how is one to find text-books in a country like this, where, in the first place, there are no poets with the slightest conception of how to go about a work of this kind, and where, in the second place, nothing is done for new operas and next to nothing is paid for them? Scribe demands 12,000 to 20,000 francs for a new French opera text, and Germany pays for a new opera, the book included, either nothing at all or at the most 500 florins, which was the amount stipulated for my new work. And that is considered a great deal! Germany would rather put up with the worst Italian or French opera than pay anything for a German opera.[3] Consequently it does not deserve

---

[1] WCMW, II, 658, 659.

[2] An opera he had written for Italy.

[3] The preference of the public for foreign opera was a constant grievance among German composers. Marschner, who was Musical Director at Dresden from 1824 to 1826 (under Weber), was so discouraged by the public's attitude towards the native composer that he set on foot a scheme for producing German operettas with amateur performers, in the hope of gradually making an audience for specifically German art. He issued an appeal to the German poets and composers to help him, but received very little support. See WM, pp. 33, 34.

to have an opera literature, and as a matter of fact does not possess one, and will have some difficulty in ever getting one until the Government does something for this branch of art, as is the case in France and Italy. Sad, sad fate, to be a German opera composer! " [1]

Lortzing was not a composer of the first class, but he had a vogue that ought to have brought him in a decent income from his operas. As early as 1840, two years or so after the production of *Die beiden Schützen* and *Czar und Zimmermann,* the latter of which had quickly spread through Germany, we find him complaining of the wretched pay of the German opera composer. The larger theatres tried to beat him down; from the smaller travelling companies Lortzing received only 30 thalers for an opera, a great part of which he had to expend on the copyist. In 1845 he writes bitterly to his friend Düringer: " You think things are going badly with me, because I do not write to you. Things are not really good, but at the same time they are not so bad, for I and my family are not yet starving, and so long as the German composer — especially if he has a reputation — can say that for himself, he is to be congratulated, and he ought to sing the praises of his fatherland." And a couple of months later: " I have made a small 270 thalers [by a concert in Leipzig] and am well satisfied. . . . Germany does not let its composers starve, for I have enough to live on for at any rate a few months! " In 1846 he became Kapellmeister at the Theater an der Wien, Vienna, at a salary of 1,200 gulden a year, out of which he had to pay 520 for his lodging. It is little wonder that we find him lamenting that out of what is left he can hardly buy food for his rather large family. " O my dear friend," he cries in February, 1848, " the poor composer who is dependent on the proceeds of his works is lost; he does not know what to do." The Vienna impresario, Pokorny, is in difficulties, salaries are paid irregularly, and Lortzing and his family are on the verge of starvation. No one will advance him money on a bill, so he has had to resort to the pawnshop. At the age of nearly fifty, after having filled various posts in the theatre, he is compelled, for mere bread's sake, to go back to his first profession of actor: and he has the bitter consciousness that the gaping public flocks to see not the actor but the

[1] NT, p. 153.

celebrated composer of *Czar und Zimmermann* and *Der Waffen-schmied*.

In 1850, leaving Leipzig in debt, he obtains a post as conductor at the Wilhelmstadt Theatre in Berlin at a salary of 600 thalers.

" You would not recognise me," he writes to his friend Düringer in August, " in the life I am now living. You know how fond I used to be now and then of a drink at a tavern. There is no chance of that now. . . . I confess to you, what I have not done yet to anyone else, that as the result of these last fatal years, my many changes of residence, the many times I have been out of an engagement, and, above all, the three years during which I have drawn nothing for an opera, I am so poor that Germany ought to blush for shame, if it had any shame in it. God and my family know I have always worked; but in the last three years I have had bad luck with three new operas, — that is to say, none of them has failed, but they have not done as well as people expected, and the Intendants, Directors, stage managers and other vermin, unless they smell out a success like that of *Der Freischütz* or *Czar und Zimmermann*, leave the German composer in the lurch — just because he is a German. How they angle for French operas! What fees Bote and Bock have paid for Halévy's *Val d'Andorra* — a work that has not done well anywhere. Oh, if only there could be a revolution in the theatre! Like the murderers of Latour and Lamberg I would lay a hand to the work and help to string up the gentlemen I have named. . . . My small savings have gone, my bits of silver and jewellery were long ago pawned; and on top of it all I owe some hundreds of thalers in Leipzig. My tiny salary of 600 thalers (without a benefit) of course hardly buys us food, and I have even to ask for part payment in advance, which will have to be repaid in instalments by deduction from my salary. I assure you that often I am in need of the veriest necessities, for I have nothing more to pawn, and yet I cannot expose my condition to the world, for I am ashamed — of the world! I am working simply for the publishers, am trampled on by these hounds, and must let myself be trampled on." [1]

In a later letter to the Intendant of the Weimar Court theatre, after quoting Lessing on the artist's need for bread — " I find myself compelled to agree with him," he says, " and so have many of my German colleagues " — he humbly asks if it is possible for the fee for his *Czar und Zimmermann* to be paid him in advance of the production. " There are times in one's life — but there, in the above quotation [from Lessing] everything is said that a

---

[1] LGB, pp. 269–271.

German composer, that is to say, a poor devil, *can* say on this subject." [1] Less than two months later he was dead — literally and simply sent to the grave, at the age of fifty, by privations beyond bearing.

The truth is that the German composer of the early nineteenth century was a victim of economic and social maladjustment. The times had changed; but while he continued to produce the same commodities as of old, the market, so to speak, was no longer artificially supported as it had formerly been. He had technically won his emancipation; but, like other freed slaves in the history of the human race, he found himself temporarily worse off when he no longer had the protection of a master to rely upon, but had himself to find a purchaser for his wares at whatever price whoever might want them would be prepared to offer for them. The French Revolution of 1789 and the Napoleonic wars made a great economic difference to the average European prince or aristocrat. He was no longer able to maintain certain luxury-portions of his establishment, such as his private Kapelle or opera-house, with the result that many a composer who would have existed comfortably in the old days as a kind of musical house-servant had now to go out into the open and fight for his living. Mozart died before the great change had time to make its effects felt. Haydn received his discharge when Prince Anton Esterhazy gave up his Kapelle in 1791, but was fortunate enough to be pensioned, and his great reputation enabled him to make large sums in England. Beethoven had to be supported in Vienna by a small syndicate of patrons, and was driven into a desperate fight with publishers for payment for his works. It is to the economic strain of the period that we owe the rise of the instrumental virtuoso: a violinist or a pianist, instead of composing for a patron or a town, and using his executive gifts as a side-line, found he could make more money by touring Europe as a performer. [2]

People who were living about the middle of the nineteenth century had a clearer perception of these economic and social changes, and all they implied for the musician, than we have to-day. Oulibicheff points out that " before the French Revolution of 1789 the

---

[1] LGB, p. 279.
[2] See the discussion of this subject in PJB, p. 172 ff.

musicians, in Germany especially, formed a strictly plebeian caste, hardly distinguished by its education and manners from many simple artisans. Many of them were notorious for the disorder of their behaviour. Those whose talents admitted them into aristocratic circles *amused* this society without ever becoming part of it. . . . If Gluck and Handel were treated in a manner more worthy of them [i.e. in comparison with the merely domestic status of a Haydn or a Mozart], the first in France, the second in England, that was because the nobility of these two countries, richer and more cultivated than that of Germany, far less Gothic in its aristocratic prejudices, already understood that to honour such men was to bring credit on themselves." [1] When the great change came, the German composer, in general, was held in the old patronising disesteem as a plebeian whose function it was to provide entertainment for his betters, to take orders from Court Intendants and speculative impresarios and be thankful for any bone that was flung to him, while as yet he could not outflank these enemies economically by a direct appeal to the general public. He was almost invariably of the people, and poor: he had to live from day to day, and dared not refuse a fee that at any rate would enable him to support existence from to-day until to-morrow: and the result was that Intendants and impresarios and publishers saw to it that he was paid just enough to keep him for ever hopefully at work, but not enough to make him independent of them.

As regards his rights in his own work, the law of copyright was an even more scandalous form of legalised public plunder of the artist and man of letters than it is now. The composer in general, and the German composer in particular, was not much better off as regards his copyright than he was in the eighteenth century, when a Walsh could make so much more money by pirating Handel's operas than the composer could by writing them as to extract from Handel the grim remark, " De next opera, you shall write it and I shall publish it." [2] Almost to the end of his days, Wagner was

---

[1] OB, pp. 87, 88.

[2] Walsh *père* and Walsh *fils* both made fortunes, "and when they could not fix a contract with a composer they pirated him. The Walshes would have made a capital pair of convicts in these days, but in Handel's epoch a music publisher was a prowler, with dishonourable intent most of the time, and if he did fix up a contract with a composer it was an accident of conscience usually on the right side as regards

pursued by embarrassments and disputes over questions of copy-right in this country and that. The various laws and regulations were beyond the understanding of the average German composer, and the pitfalls beyond his foresight. Beethoven more than once got into trouble through selling the same work to different publish-ers with the object of protecting his rights in more than one coun-try.[1] Weber was the victim of a robbery so gross that it became a *locus classicus* in its epoch. He had neglected to engrave the score of *Der Freischütz* in Paris, but had sold copies of the German score there. This deprived him of all French rights in his own work. Castilblaze made a monstrous re-hash of his own of the opera, that brought him in a fortune: the French *Robin des Bois* was legally *his* work, and Weber could not collect a penny of the large fees it earned.[2] Honour among music publishers was a thing almost un-known in those days. As we shall see later, as soon as Wagner made a success with *Rienzi* in Dresden, Schotts took advantage of a legal technicality to issue a pirated edition of his song *Les deux grenadiers,* which had been printed in Paris in 1841. In 1836 the firm of Hoffmeister in Leipzig (which later became the present C. F. Peters), published a monstrously mutilated piratical version of Berlioz's *Francs-Juges* Overture for piano duet — and the com-poser had no redress.[3]

The lot of the German composer in those days was the worst of all: he might consider himself lucky if a crumb or two were thrown him from the meal that the publishers and the others made of his work. As regards the theatres, while in France and England he re-tained, if he knew how to protect himself legally, a continuous right in the product of his labours, in Germany it was for a long time only in Berlin that he and his heirs could count on receiving royalties for an opera as long as it remained in the repertory: this concession was due to the efforts of Meyerbeer and his influence with Friedrich Wilhelm IV of Prussia. Elsewhere in Germany the operatic composer's lot, as we have seen, was a sorry one. Before

---

himself." Walsh *père* left £30,000, Walsh *fils* £40,000, mostly made by swindling composers. See FH, pp. 97, 183, etc.

[1] See PJB, pp. 249, 250.

[2] See the details in BM, I, 87; BCI, p. 121.

[3] See Berlioz's long and indignant letter to the pirates in BCI, p. 113 ff. For an account of Verdi's troubles with pirates see TGV, p. 95.

we censure Wagner unduly for his habits of borrowing, we would do well to remember that there need have been no occasion for a considerable portion of his debts had he been paid an equitable price for his work.[1]

3

The composers of the eighteenth and early nineteenth centuries mostly endured their miseries with comparatively little complaint; they felt them to be part of a cosmic ordinance from which there was no escape. But about the time when the young Wagner was making his first plunge into public musical life there were signs here and there of a coming revolt. The upheaval of the French Revolution, followed by democracy's assertion of itself in the Paris revolution of July, 1830, had given a few of the bolder artists a sense of their own worthiness with which society would before long have to reckon. A new type of artist was springing up — men of natural refinement and culture like Chopin and Liszt, who felt themselves to be the equals of the aristocrats who patronised them, and were galled by the slighting forms this patronage sometimes took. Their talents admitted them into the richest society;[2] but

---

[1] Conditions were no better in Italy. Otto Nicolai, who lived in Italy in his young days, received in 1838 a commission to write a serious opera for Turin. He was to receive a total fee of 2,500 francs, out of which he had to pay almost the whole of the librettist's fee, the impresario contributing only 200 francs towards this. The opera was to be the absolute property of the impresario. Nicolai angrily calls this a "derisory fee" for a year's work, considering that a good singer could get 20,000 to 25,000 francs for three months' work. "The first steps of the dramatic composer in Italy," he writes to his father, "are, as they are everywhere else, very difficult, and it is almost impossible to make a beginning unless one has money of one's own to pay out. It is well known how many thousands Meyerbeer had to expend in Italy to get a start." Nicolai's *Templario* was the absolute property of the publisher Lucca: all the composer received was a small fee, varying from 120 to 240 thalers, for the first performance in this town or that, out of which he had to pay his travelling expenses and maintenance. (See NBV, pp. 233, 257, etc.) No wonder Italian and German opera composers turned a longing eye on Paris!

[2] In virtue, however, be it remembered, of their abilities as performers only. Wagner's genius as a composer did not prevent his being regarded in Dresden, by his King and his Director, as merely a servant. But when the youthful Chopin came to this same Dresden he was received by the Saxon Princesses, who promised him letters of introduction to Italy. In Berlin, Prince Radziwill offered him quarters in his own palace; and in Paris he was received by "the highest society," sitting with "ambassadors, princes, ministers." (See CL, pp. 69, 120, 168, etc.) The explanation is, of course, that then, as now, musical patronage was mostly in the hands of women, who are much more susceptible to piano playing or fiddling or singing than to creative intellectual work.

there they were made to realise that however much they might be admired as artists, there could be no question of their being accepted as social equals. Both Liszt and Chopin fell in love with young daughters of the aristocracy, and each was promptly put in his place for so doing. The youthful Chopin was tolerantly allowed his little romance with Marie Wodzinska for a while, but when it seemed likely to result in marriage her family intervened, and Chopin had to learn that the artist was still regarded as the social inferior of the people into whose houses he had been admitted as a friend with a talent for music. Liszt also dragged a youthful heart-ache about with him for years; when Caroline de Saint-Cricq's family realised that their daughter and he were in love with each other, the pianist was handed his fee by the Count and politely informed that, highly as they all esteemed him, the lessons were at an end. But the new type of artist that was coming into being was not inclined to accept rebuffs and slights of this kind as humbly as his predecessors had done.

Liszt's proud spirit was particularly unable to resign itself to the current state of affairs, and in a series of articles on *The Situation of Artists* which he wrote for the *Gazette musicale de Paris* in 1835 he protested vigorously against what he called the *subalternité* of the artist in the social world of the period. He pointed out that modern art called for more and a greater variety of gifts than the older art; the artist had now to be a man of literary and philosophical culture, and art should at last be treated as it deserved.

"To determine to-day, with precision and breadth of view, the situation of artists in the social order, to define their individual, political and religious relations, to tell the story of their sorrows and their privations, their fatigues and their deceptions, to tear the bandages from their ever-bleeding wounds and protest energetically against the oppressive iniquity or the insolent stupidity that blights and tortures them and condescends merely to use them as playthings, to examine their past, foretell their future, set forth their titles to glory, to teach the public, and this oblivious and materialistic society, these men and women whom we amuse and who *buy our wares*, whence we came, whither we are going, what it is our mission to accomplish, in a word, what we are, what these elect among men are who seem chosen by God himself to bear witness to the grandest feelings of humanity and to be the noble depositories of them . . . these initiators, these apostles, these priests of an ineffable religion, a mysterious,

[164]

eternal religion that germinates and shoots up incessantly in all our hearts — oh, to do all this, to say, to cry aloud, all these things that are crying to be said, in such a way that those most deaf shall be compelled to listen, this assuredly would be a beautiful and noble task to accomplish."

No musician, since music began, had ever talked to the world like this; Liszt's angry and impassioned cry was that of the herald of a general revolt.

How is it, he goes on to ask, that while music itself has always had an influence upon men, and its praises have been sung by the poets from time immemorial, musicians now live under " the yoke of a deplorable inferiority "; " by what fatality is it that those who were the first have deigned to become the last? " Since " the glorious proclamation of the Charter of 1830 " a new " aristocracy of intelligence " has indeed been recognised, composed of writers and lawyers; but what rôle has been allotted to the musicians in this new order? He inveighs against the excommunication that is still pronounced in France against many of them, and the shameful system by which, " in the aristocratic houses of London, artists of the first rank, such as Moscheles, Rubini, Lafont, Pasta, Malibran, and others are forced to enter by the service stairs."

" Alas," he cries, " music and musicians still live merely a factitious and mutilated life on the surface of society. Condemned, by I know not what fatality, to vegetate without any common possession, without dignity, without consecration, the artists are at the mercy of the first comer even as regards their material existence; and as for what I have called institutions, society has scarcely more regard for them than for individuals. Bonaparte, by a stroke of the pen, cancelled one half of the professors and pupils of the Conservatoire, and reduced the funds allotted to it by 100,000 francs. Immediately after the July revolution, His Citizen Majesty, by way of economy, dismissed, as one dismisses a useless domestic staff, the artists who constituted the royal chapel. Only eighteen months ago Choron, who had devoted his whole life to the foundation of a school intended to perpetuate in France the grand traditions of the Italian schools, died in misery. The illustrious manufacturer of the *pâte Regnault*, having become Director of the Opéra, dismissed Baillot because the great violinist refused the half-salary offered him by M. Véron."

Liszt was not exaggerating when he spoke of artists of the first rank having to enter the great London houses by the service stairs.

[165]

High society everywhere looked down patronisingly on the man who received his income from trade, even if the trade were that of music. One of the reasons for Mendelssohn's enormous success in England — and no doubt elsewhere — was that he was economically independent of his earnings as a composer and performer, a kind of gentleman farmer of music. His wealth, rather than his music, made him socially " possible " in a way that no musician could become by his music alone. Aristocratic London society might pay Weber high fees to appear at its soirées; but though the lion of the hour was sought after as the lion of the hour always is in London, the fact was never lost sight of that the lion was *paid* to do his tricks for the company. But high society felt that Mendelssohn was one of themselves, a gentleman who could play the piano and compose just as well as any of the professionals, but who really had no need to do that sort of thing for a living. He made, says his friend Eduard Devrient, a sensation in London in 1829: " in the higher circles it gave him a peculiar distinction that at their large parties, embellished by the famous artists of the season at high remuneration, he lent his aid without accepting any money, and thus belonged to the company. He was quite indignant at the way in which the paid artists were isolated from the guests, nor could he forget having seen Malibran sit in a remote corner of the drawing-room, shut out and looking miserable." [1] In these great London houses the musicians, however eminent they might be, were separated, as Baron Max von Weber complained, from the guests proper by a cord stretched across the room. One night, in one of the great houses, Lablache let this cord down; no one present had the courage to replace it, and from that time the system of segregating the artists from the guests began to fall into disuse.

Liszt sums up the situation thus:

" For the artist — sufferings, debasement, bitterness, poverty, solitude, persecution. For the art — shackles, exploitation, economic reforms, institutions, the Opera, the schools, and so on, that are either imperfect or baneful, gags and handcuffs. Everywhere, among all classes of executant musicians, professors, composers, we hear complaints, recantations, expressions of discontent or rage, vows of change or reform, aspirations towards a future that shall be broader and

---

[1] DRFM, p. 77.

more satisfactory, aspirations that are sometimes vague and contradictory, but that witness all the same to the fermentation of the new leaven. More or less openly, more or less profoundly, all are suffering. Whether it be in their contact with the public or with society; whether it be through the theatre directors, the critics, the government clerks, the music sellers; whether it be, in a word, in their civil, their political, or their religious relations, or in their relations one with another, — no matter: *all suffer,* and many among them feel that they suffer unjustly, iniquitously as a rule, but often also as the result of real wrongs, by reason of their isolation, their egoism, their lack of faith. . . . Whenever the artists — instead of uniting, whether to resist oppression and wrongful demands or to march in concert to a goal that has been destined for them by Providence — become divided among themselves, reject the consciousness of their own dignity, and, one by one, day by day, submit to all the consequences of a tacitly accepted *subalternité,* the fault must be held to be in great part theirs."

Replying to a contemporary critic of one of these articles, who had reproached the writer of them with ingratitude, in view of the fact that he at any rate had nothing to complain of as regards his acceptance by high society, Liszt said: " Certainly it would have been strangely ungrateful on my part to deny the flattering benevolence exercised towards me. And yet, since my honourable colleague challenges me so directly, I will not conceal the fact that often, both in public and private concerts and in the receptions to which, *in spite of my being an artist,* I have been exceptionally invited, I have been mournfully conscious of my solitude and of my *subalternité* as a musician," for he has been saddened by the evidence of a total lack of taste and culture in his audience.[1] Sincerely as he may have regretted, however, the intellectual and artistic shortcomings of his auditors, what rankled most in him, we surmise, was the knowledge that because he was a performing artist he was admitted to aristocratic gatherings only by way of condescension, and that, apart from his music, a line, nowhere outwardly defined but none the less tacitly clear both to his patrons and to him, was drawn between them.

Probably at the very time when these articles were pouring from his pen in a white heat of indignation he was being made to feel, by the aristocratic relations and acquaintances of the Comtesse

---

[1] See the whole series of articles, *De la situation des artistes et de leur condition dans la société,* in LZPR.

d'Agoult, that, although as a brilliant pianist he might be admitted among them, he was certainly not of them. It was their hauteur, indeed, that was largely instrumental in driving Marie d'Agoult into closer association with him, out of sheer angry reaction. When the Marquise L. V., at whose house Liszt was accustomed to make music, saw how matters were shaping themselves between the pair, she herself was sufficiently liberal-minded not to frown upon the association; but a relation of hers, " a sage and discreet man, ventured upon some remarks concerning the eccentricities of artists and the inconvenience of admitting them into one's house on terms of equality. These remarks," says the Countess d'Agoult in her account of the affair, " annoyed me, and I was grateful to the Marquise for not taking any notice of them." The Marquise praised Liszt for his noble character and his charity to the poor, and thought Marie would be justified in permitting him to pay his respects to her at her own house. " Her relation made a gesture that signified ' How unbecoming! ' This gesture decided my answer: I asked the Marquise for Franz's address, and as soon as she had left I wrote inviting him to my reception." But she had noticed a certain reserve in his part towards highly-placed company.

" Three times I made an attempt to write a note of three lines. I could not satisfy myself as to its wording: either I laid too much stress on the pleasure it would be to see Franz at my house, or my tone was too ceremoniously polite. I had noticed in him, during our conversation of the evening before, a curious suspicion, a kind of haste to remind himself of differences of rank, as if he were afraid of being made to feel them.[1] The remarks of the Marquise and her relation had

---

[1] Robert Bory is no doubt right when he says that although both Liszt and the Countess believed themselves to be perfectly sincere in their romantic passion, "never for a moment did she cease to be the brilliant aristocrat of the Faubourg and become really in love. The liaison with Liszt was immensely flattering for her. It was the epoch of *grandes passions:* would anyone dare to throw a stone at a lady of quality who gave herself freely to a man whom all Paris admired? She dreamed in secret of being his muse, his inspiration." See BRR, p. 21. It is certain that at no time during their nine years' union did she let Liszt forget the difference in rank between them. For a study of the whole affair in the light of the most recent documents, see NFF, pp. 207–222.

When the pair fled to Geneva, in August, 1835, the story current in Paris, so the historians tell us, was that Liszt had carried Marie away in a grand piano. I suspect that this was merely the malicious Parisian way of stressing the despised professionalism of Liszt. What particularly scandalised Paris high society was on the one hand the audacity of a mere piano player in abducting an aristocrat, on

made me conscious of something I had not thought of before — the differences of name, of blood, and of fortune that we owed to the accident of birth and that gave us a superiority over other people. At that moment I felt myself embarrassed by this seeming superiority in my relations towards a man whose immense talent, and what I thought I already knew of his character, placed him, in my opinion, so much above me. I was afraid, when writing my letter, that the customary formulae of my world towards an artist who was not of it might make me seem haughty, whereas I only wanted to say the right thing; and yet I feared, by neglecting these formulae, to exhibit more interest than would be thought proper in these new relations with a man so young and so much a stranger to everyone connected with me." [1]

So difficult was it in those days for a *grand dame* to admit a mere musician to her company on terms of anything like social equality, even when the musician was a man of Liszt's fame, culture, and natural breeding and distinction of manner! Liszt was fully conscious of all these hesitations and condescensions; he smarted under them, and his life-long predilection for the society and the love of aristocrats was no doubt due in part to the gratified sense they gave him of a victory won, of having forced the world to accept an exceptional artist at a proper valuation. Admitted as a raw boy into the houses of the richest of the Parisian aristocracy, in an epoch when not only titles but costume and formal manners and etiquette counted for more than they do to-day, he must have suffered many a wound to his pride. When he settled in Geneva with the Countess, he renewed his acquaintance with the Boissier-Butini family, whose daughter Valérie, afterwards the Comtesse de Gasparin, had been his pupil in Paris in 1832, where the mother had seen a good deal of the twenty-one-year-old youth. M. Robert Bory was recently given the opportunity to consult a diary left by Mme. Boissier, which contains some piquant comments on the Liszt of 1835. [2] The highly-bred lady notes, with approval, his " distinguished air," and is gratified to see that he no longer dresses " with the bad taste that was noticeable in him in Paris; it is easy to see that he had had some good feminine advice." After he had dined with the family, she is delighted to be able to record that " he has acquired a greater

the other hand the atrocious "bad form" of the aristocrat in allowing herself to be abducted by one so immeasurably below her socially.

[1] AM, pp. 23, 24.
[2] See BRR, pp. 30 ff.

ease of manner and of command of the ways of society." Liszt's
rather overdone ceremoniousness in the later years, his tendency
to over-insist on the formulae of polite address, especially with
aristocrats, are no doubt to be explained by the fact that these things
were an acquired, and a painfully acquired, language with him,
not a natural one, and that in his desire to speak the language with
impeccable correctness he was apt at times to become a trifle over-
punctilious. With all Liszt's great qualities, there was an ineradi-
cable tendency in him to overdo most things, whether in the matter
of musical emotion in his own works, in his professed admiration
of others, in the grand seigneur pose of his early days, or in the St.
Francis attitude of his later. Some of his little failings came from
an incurable kindness of heart allied to a reluctance to do anything
that would make him disliked. But the explanation of his occasionally too elaborate display of fine manners is probably that in his
early years he had been galled by the knowledge that he was being
condescended to by rich and stupid people for his plebeian birth,
and his sensitiveness and pride had made him resolved to show
them that an artist could be not only their equal but their superior
even in the practice of the stilted formulae of their own caste.

It is probable that Liszt's lavish way of living in his early years,
and his superb benevolence in all good causes, was the result not
merely of his natural generosity of spirit, but came, in part, from
his desire to show the aristocratic world that he had a soul above
considerations of pelf. For in the days when trade was looked
down upon as something not quite suitable to a gentleman, the paid
performer was necessarily regarded as at bottom a trader. One of
the *mots* of Liszt that went the rounds in the eighteen-forties was
his reply to the Princess Clemens Metternich, who had hurt him
by innocently asking whether he was " doing good business " with
his recitals. " Only bankers and diplomats do good business,
Princess," was his lofty reply. And the young Hans von Bülow,
who was an impecunious Prussian Baron, was dreadfully embarrassed when he had to take his fee from his piano pupils: payment
for any kind of service rendered always seemed degrading to him.
" During a concert tour in 1855 [he was then twenty-five] he gave
lessons in Posen to a charming Polish Countess, and in spite of
the fact that he was always short of money, ' I either do not take

a fee,' he writes, ' or I buy a very expensive Album and send it to her, because I am so pleased with her.' " [1] His hope that he would be invited to play at a Court concert in Stuttgart was not realised, the King " finding it disagreeable to see an aristocrat by birth appearing as an artist." [2] This was in 1861!

Liszt and Chopin received a particular social stamp and colour from the fact that their initiation into the great world took place in Paris, at that time the centre of Continental wealth and culture: their fight, too, was made easier for them by the fact that they were composers for, and incomparable performers on, an instrument that was within the comprehension of all intelligences, a common denominator of all tastes. They would have found it much harder to make the same social headway in the stiff little semi-feudal Courts of Germany, while nothing like the same success would have come to them had they been merely composers for the theatre, for the German opera composer, as we have seen, was in an economic net from which there was no escaping. The young Wagner had none of the social advantages of Chopin and Liszt. He played no instrument that could give him the entry to fashionable circles. He inspired no romantic attachments in excitable high-born women. His speech, his clothes, his manners, and his accent were those of the Saxon bourgeoisie. He had nothing but his unique creative gift; and with that alone he not only changed the face of German music in the space of some ten years but brought into operation a new scale of values, drawing the world-shaking Liszt, for example, into his orbit, and making a willing satellite of one who had till then been an independent star of the first magnitude. In the political sphere, Wagner was destined to force the new conception of the artist upon the bureaucrats in a way that Liszt, for all his Saint-Simonism, all his passionate mysticism, had found impossible. Before he was forty, Wagner, poor and proscribed as he was, was haranguing and dictating to the Opera Intendants in a style that Weber or Marschner or Nicolai or Spohr would have shrunk from in terror. A man was needed to focus in himself all the elements of revolt, artistic, political and social, that had been slowly forming in German music during the last half century, and in Richard Wagner Nature threw up the man. She endowed him

[1] BBLW, pp. 47, 48. [2] BBLW, p. 49.

not only with superlative genius but with a tireless vigour of organisation, a pride and confidence in himself, an obstinacy of purpose, a passion for domination, that made him deal with obstacles such as Princes, Intendants, Directors, Kapellmeisters and star singers as they had never been dealt with before in Germany; and though it must often have seemed as if he would be broken in the struggle, it ended in their being broken. Nature's crowning foresight was to make him at once luxurious and self-indulgent in his tastes and completely indifferent as to the way in which he found the means to indulge them. Richard Wagner would never die of hunger, or even live in penury, so long as friends had both kind hearts and money, and optimistic tradesmen were willing to give credit. The moralist may regret the insensitiveness of Wagner the man in these matters: the historian is bound to recognise that without that insensitiveness Wagner the artist would have gone under.

Not for another ten years or so, however, was the Richard Wagner of history to come into sight of the world. From 1833, when he went to Würzburg, to 1842, when he returned from Paris to Dresden, his story is, in the main, that of any other struggling German musician of his epoch, fighting desperately for his mere bread and butter, and thankful to theatre directors for the smallest mercies. Between 1842 and May, 1849, when he fled from Dresden to Zürich with a price on his head, he became, not only musically but politically, the living symbol of a new Germany. And after the middle year of the century he was the centre of a development, entirely of his own achieving, that seemed to relegate his operatic contemporaries of only ten or fifteen years before to a strangely distant epoch in the annals of music.

CHAPTER X

MAGDEBURG

1

THE FIVE years from 1834 onwards, apart from odd intervals of unemployment, were to be spent by Wagner in small provincial theatres. So far as the prime object of this activity was concerned — the desire to earn a living — it all ended in worse than failure, in sheer disaster; for the normal meagreness of his pay, the frequent uncertainty of its receipt, and his hunger for a comfort beyond his means combined to make him pile up a load of debt that was to weigh heavily upon him for many years to come. In addition, he plunged into an imprudent marriage. His long sojourn in the theatres had only two good results for him: it made a skilled conductor of him, and, by reaction from the excess of foreign superficiality with which he was daily brought into contact, he became in time a thoughtful German musician once more.

At first sight, his assurance in taking on, at the age of twenty-one, a job in which he had had no practice seems to amount to temerity. But he was a born score-reader, and the young man who had steeped himself in the Beethoven of the Ninth Symphony and the last quartets would not be likely to find anything to baffle him in the average operatic score of that or an earlier epoch. He must have attended many a theatrical and concert rehearsal in Leipzig, while in Würzburg, besides training the chorus, he had probably assisted at the production of some of the operas in the repertory. At the conductor's desk he had the coolest of heads and an unshakeable confidence in himself. Each theatrical company with which he was connected soon found that this under-sized young man understood his job thoroughly: above all he had the combination of dash and aplomb that gives confidence to players and singers who are none too intelligent or too industrious, and hides from the dazzled audience the thinness of the ice over which the performance has been skating. For his part, he acquired a technical command and an insight into the intentions of composers in their works that were to make him, at a later stage of his career, the founder of a new art of conducting.

On his temporary return to Leipzig, in August, 1834, for the purpose of gathering together his belongings, he found Laube in trouble with the authorities: the political reaction had commenced, and this free-spoken writer had been ordered, at the behest of Prussia, off Saxon soil. Theodor Apel's estate at Ermlitz, though in Prussian territory, was within a few hours of Leipzig, with which town Laube wished to keep up, if he could, the literary connections on which he mostly depended for a livelihood. Wagner accordingly asked his friend to harbour Laube at Ermlitz. Apel consented, but the next day, under pressure from his family, withdrew a promise that might have had serious consequences for him. In after years Wagner still remembered the curious expression that flitted across Laube's face when he communicated this decision to him; Wagner himself was one day to learn what it was to be cold-shouldered by friends who, with the best will in the world, could not at the moment undertake the responsibility of harbouring him. Laube had to leave Saxony: in a little while he was arrested for his former association with the Students' League, and thrown into prison in Berlin.

Sad at heart, feeling vaguely that life in every direction was taking a new and more serious turn for him, Wagner went back to Lauchstädt [1] to conduct the performance of *Don Giovanni* to which he had committed himself. Although it was the first opera he had ever conducted, he came through the ordeal with perfect composure. When the repertory afterwards sank to its normal low level he could not quite still the voice of his conscience, which protested against this prostitution of his musical ideals; but he

---

[1] Lauchstädt, according to Genast (GWKZ, p. 21) was "a small watering place near Merseburg, Halle and Naumburg, that was very popular with the Saxon nobility and the patrician families of Leipzig." A new theatre had been erected there, at Goethe's instance, in 1802: it was opened by the Goethe company from Weimar. It must have been quite small: Genast (p. 81) describes it as consisting of a "parkett" (next to the orchestra), a parterre, and "back seats": over the latter was a semicircular balcony, holding about sixty people. The prices in 1802 were only 16, 12, 8 and 4 groschen. When full, the house would hold 300 thalers. This was the theatre in which the Bethmann troupe performed under Wagner.

was young enough to find some consolation in the company of
Minna and other pretty actresses and in that of a tenor of
the troupe, one Friedrich Schmitt, a mediocre actor but a man
of a mentality superior to that of the majority of his theatrical
associates.

After a few weeks in Lauchstädt the company moved on to Rudolstadt. Wagner was forced to surrender the pleasure he had
promised himself of making the journey in Minna's society: stern
financial necessity drove him to Leipzig, where once more he drew
upon his anxious mother's slender resources. He took in Ermlitz
on the way. Apel, who had called for him at Lauchstädt, gave a
wild carouse at the local hotel in his honour. Wagner's health
must have been drunk right royally; for in the morning a big
Dutch tile-stove was found to have been smashed to pieces by
Richard and one of the other guests, without any of the company
being able to remember precisely how it had happened.

In Rudolstadt, Wagner's duties consisted solely in rehearsing the
light musical pieces that mostly formed the staple fare of the little
town, the actual performances being under the direction of the
conductor of the Royal Kapelle. In a letter of 13th September to
Apel he professes to be utterly bored with his life and his company. He has had to knock Bellini's *Montecchi e Capuletti* into the
heads of two completely unmusical women singers in a day or two;
and he fretfully opines that the only reason God could have had
for the creation of music was to annoy *him*. He has been gambling,
and has lost persistently. Altogether, the world is nothing but dust
and ashes in the mouth. Only one thing could cheer him up — a
visit from Theodor, whose good fortune he enviously compares
with his own bad luck in the lottery of life. Still, he manages to
get a little reading done occasionally, and he has begun a symphony.[1] A couple of days later his spirits have so far revived that

---

[1] In E major, commenced in Lauchstädt on the 4th August, and finished, as
far as it was ever destined to be finished, at Rudolstadt on the 29th. He completed
the first movement, but got no further with the slow movement than the twenty-
ninth bar. He tells us in *Mein Leben* that he wrote the work under the influence of
the Beethoven Seventh and Eighth: but he soon came to the conclusion that there
was no future for music along the lines of his great model, and so he turned with
renewed keenness to opera. Wilhelm Tappert analysed the sketches for the E major
symphony in Nos. 40 and 41 of the *Musikalisches Wochenblatt*, 1886.
    Further sketches for this symphony were found (among sketches for *Lohengrin*)

he symbolises the rosier tint the world has taken for him by the playful use of red ink; the psychological change is due to the fact that the next day is pay-day. Once more he begs Apel to visit him: he has two fine rooms, he says, one of them with no less than six windows, from which one gathers that the impecunious music-director, as usual, was treating himself quite handsomely. If Apel will come for a few days, he will go back with him to Leipzig, and thence for awhile to Ermlitz, in which " paradise " he would like to spend the remainder of the summer before going off to Magde-burg and the " flat, despicable north." These dreams, however, were not to be realised. The company moved off to Bernburg for a short spell, where once more the local Kapellmeister took charge, and then to Magdeburg for the winter. (It was not his first visit to the town: he had spent an autumn holiday there with his sister Klara and her husband in 1830.) There Wagner reigned in full and undisputed glory as conductor of the operatic repertory. He soon won the complete confidence of the performers and of the public, and if only money had been a little more plentiful he would probably have been not too unhappy. But even his scanty salary was not always forthcoming on pay-day; and he soon realised the truth of the cynical axiom current in the company that the only way to be sure of one's wages was to pay attentions to Bethmann's wife. It was because of his skill and assiduity in this quarter that the bass, Kneisel, was the only one in the troupe who drew his salary regularly.

For the New Year's Day of 1835 Wagner wrote the music for a cantata, *Beim Antritt des neuen Jahres*, the text of which was by the regisseur, Schmale. Wagner's contribution consisted of an over-ture, two interludes and two choruses: in the overture he uses the theme of the andante of his C major symphony.[1] The work

in Zürich, and were published by Aloys Obrist in AMZ, 1905, No. 20.

In 1910 there came into the market some Wagner sketches that have been analysed by Edgar Istel in DM, 1913, No. 15. The pages of the score that have survived are numbered 182 to 193. The presumption therefore is that they are from the finale of a symphony; and as they are in E *minor*, they can hardly belong to the E major symphony. The conclusion of the movement is lost.

[1] The work was revived at Bayreuth as a compliment to Wagner on his sixtieth birthday (22nd May, 1873). Peter Cornelius wrote a new text — *Künstlerweihe* — for the music, basing it on reminiscences Wagner had given him of his conversations with the painter Genelli during his Dresden days. In the *Künstlerweihe*, Cornelius describes Wagner as being depressed by doubts and despairs about his art, whereupon

had such a success that it was repeated at a concert on the 3rd January, at which Wagner conducted also Mendelssohn's *Calm Sea and Prosperous Voyage* overture, and, what was then a novelty in Magdeburg, the overture to Rossini's *William Tell*. At a further concert, on the 10th, he gave the overture to *Die Feen*. One of the compositions dating from this Magdeburg period is an overture to the *Columbus* drama of his friend Apel, which, after the regulation number of theatrical delays, was produced by the company in February, 1835. Wagner waxes ecstatic over the superlative merits of the play in his letters to his friend, and in spite of the fact that he was already in Apel's debt and doubtless looked forward to further financial favours, we may perhaps take it that he admired the work as vastly as he says he does. Bethmann, of course, was not at all inclined to let so rich a prize as young Apel slip through his fingers. He had nothing to lose and everything to gain by producing the work: the proud author was easily induced to pay for special scenery and costumes, which could be put to other uses of the company afterwards. So all was for the best: Bethmann was happy for the reasons just stated, Apel was happy in having seen a play of his actually put on the stage, Wagner was happy in the consciousness that he had strengthened a valuable bond of affection between them; while his *Columbus* overture became quite popular in the town. It was performed later at a Gewandhaus concert in Leipzig, under Pohlenz (who had given the *Feen* overture a year before that), on the 2nd April, 1835.[1] This was perhaps the last of the services the kindly Pohlenz was able to render the young composer: he was dismissed from his post in April to make way for Mendelssohn, with whose advent to power a new clique was formed in the town, a new direction given to the public taste, and a less sympathetic eye turned on the efforts of Richard Wagner.

Genelli points to the musical drama as the source of salvation, conjuring up before the composer's eyes pictures that blend with the spirit of the music. See GRW, V, 84, and MECW, I, 658. The music will be found in Vol. XVI of the Complete Edition.

[1] Wagner conducted the work himself in Leipzig a few weeks later, at a concert of the singer Livia Gerhardt on the 25th May.

2

In the theatre, the young conductor made an ever-growing impression of thorough competence by his leading of such works as Rossini's *Otello* and *Barbiere*, Gläser's *Adlers Horst*, Weber's *Preziosa*, *Der Freischütz* and *Oberon*, Auber's *Fra Diavolo* and *Masaniello*, Paisiello's *La Molinara*, Cherubini's *Water-Carrier*, Marschner's *Der Templer und die Jüdin*, and Bellini's *Montecchi e Capuletti*. In April, 1835, Schröder-Devrient descended upon the town for a series of guest-performances, during which she appeared as Romeo in Bellini's opera, Leonora in *Fidelio*, Desdemona in *Otello*, and Agathe in *Der Freischütz*. Wagner's old enthusiasm for her dramatic art was revived. She, on her part, was so attracted to the young conductor, whose genius she seems to have been one of the first to recognise, that she promised to appear at the benefit concert that was now due to him under the terms of his engagement. This concert was originally fixed, and announced, for the 24th April, but apparently the singer was recalled to her duties in Leipzig; she generously undertook, however, to return on the 2nd May. Wagner counted on the attraction of the famous singer to fill the house and provide him with the wherewithal to discharge at any rate the more pressing of his debts before leaving the town at the end of the season. It seems probable that even he was none too sure of her being able or willing to keep her promise, for in the final announcement of the concert her name is not mentioned, but Beethoven's *Battle of Vittoria* is held out as the great attraction of the evening. The canny Magdeburgers steadily refused to believe that a star of Schröder-Devrient's magnitude would really come to their town again solely to assist an unknown young conductor: the bruiting of her name was regarded as merely a device to decoy them into the concert room at enhanced prices. The result was that the great singer had a distressingly small audience to greet her when she did come. This she took good-humouredly: but the *Battle of Vittoria* was another matter. Wagner had gathered together an extra contingent of brass instruments to do justice to the fight between the French and the English; and the noise they made in the small and over-resonant room — it was the salon of a hotel — was unendurable. Schröder-Devrient, to prove to the public her goodwill towards the young conductor, had taken a front seat in the house after singing her own pieces. The audience, reeling under the shock of the battle, was one by one creeping silently to rest. At last even Schröder-Devrient, unable to bear any more, fled in terror: this was the signal for a general *sauve qui peut,* and, according to Wagner's humorous account of the affair in later years, Wellington's victory was finally celebrated in a confidential outburst between himself and the orchestra alone.

In the morning, when he went to the hotel to make up the reckoning of his receipts, he discovered that not only were there no profits but he had still a small sum to pay. He found, in addition, his creditors gathered in force; he had to run the gauntlet between a double file of them. The situation was saved by a Madame Gottschalk, a Jewess, who was presumably one of the large creditors. The case being put before her, she saw at once that nothing was to be gained by violence of either action or language. Wagner's relations in Leipzig would have to come to his rescue; and by dint of argument and abuse she succeeded in getting the other creditors to disperse and leave the conductor free to try his luck in his native city.[1] Thither, accordingly, he went early in May, accompanied, of course, by the dog of the moment, a " very intelligent brown poodle." And there he was joined by Minna, whose place in his life at this period must now be set forth in some detail.

---

[1] He revisited Magdeburg in 1872 with Cosima. He took her to the theatre, which was still unchanged since 1835, and told her how proud he had been when he conducted there in a sky-blue swallow-tail coat with huge cuffs. He showed her the hotel, the "Stadt Braunschweig," in which the meeting of his creditors took place, and the street in which Minna had lived. MECW, I, 641.

CHAPTER XI

MINNA

1

C HRISTINE WILHELMINE PLANER was born on the 5th September, 1809, and was consequently three and a half years older than Wagner. Her parents were poor: her father, a mechanic, was a native of Oederan in the Erzegebirge. He had invented an improved card for the carding of wool. A manufacturer in Chemnitz had given him a large order for these cards; but the client went bankrupt, failing to pay him for the goods already delivered and used, and leaving a further large quantity on his hands. The ruined Planer betook himself to Dresden with what was left of the wire that had been intended for the cards, and the ten-year-old Minna hawked them among the milliners for use in making flowers. Her exceptional beauty soon attracted the attention of men: she was seduced by a Herr von Einsiedel, and became a mother when she was barely seventeen. The child — a daughter of the name of Natalie — always passed in the world as her sister; but the secret was confided to Wagner at an early stage of their acquaintance, and he kept it scrupulously to the last. It appears that not only Minna's father but the child herself was kept in ignorance of the facts. This ignorance on the part of the daughter, indeed, was the cause of considerable trouble in the Wagner household in later years; for when Natalie had grown up she resented what she took to be an unwarrantable claim on a mere elder sister's part to regulate her conduct for her.

For the bulk of our knowledge of Minna we have to rely on Wagner's account of her actions and his analysis of her character. Very few of her own letters have been published. Wagner's letters to her have been issued in a form the incompleteness of which has aroused unfriendly comment among biographers, but is now capable of a simple explanation. About 1883, the year of Wagner's death, the Hon. Mrs. Burrell began collecting material for a life of the composer.[1] She managed to obtain from the widow of Bonfantini, the Italian printer in Basel who, between 1870 and 1875, had set up the private edition of *Mein Leben* (limited to fifteen copies), an extra copy of that work which Bonfantini had surreptitiously struck off for his own benefit. *Mein Leben* set Mrs. Burrell on the track of a number of people mentioned therein who were still alive, or whose heirs would be likely to possess valuable Wagner documents. She acquired a large number of these documents, some of them of the highest interest.[2] From *Mein Leben* she discovered that Natalie was not Minna's sister but her daughter. She traced her to the " sort of ladies' almshouse " in which, now an old woman, she was living, gradually won her confidence — for at first Natalie thought she was a cunning agent of Wagner and Cosima, both of whom she hated — and at last bought from her the Wagner memorials still in her possession. Minna seems to have cherished carefully not only her husband's letters but all sorts of odds and ends relating to her own life and Wagner's. When, about the eighteen-seventies, Wagner began collecting all the material he could trace relating to his early life, he of course applied to Natalie for the letters he had written to her mother. Natalie reluctantly yielded to pressure, but kept back a number of letters and other documents relating to the earlier years of the association of Wagner and Minna, giving Wagner to understand that these had been destroyed. This accounts for the fact that the earliest letter from Wagner to Minna in the official edition of the letters is that of the 21st July, 1842. Mrs. Burrell acquired the letters that had been thus withheld by Natalie: as yet they are still unpublished, but their general purport is summarised in a line or two in the Catalogue of the Burrell Collection.

With this material, meagre as it is at present, and with the help of Wagner's letters to Apel, which were published in 1910, we can check fairly well the account given in *Mein Leben* of the events that led up to the marriage of Wagner and Minna. The result of a careful comparison of all the available documents is to confirm the

---

[1] She died in 1898. The first volume of her biography was then ready, and was issued by her husband and daughter in that year. It carries the story of Wagner's life down only to 1834.

[2] The entire Burrell Collection is now (since 1931) in the possession of Mrs. Edward Bok, of Philadelphia.

accuracy of Wagner's account of the outer details of the affair at practically every point. For the vital dates he could rely on memoranda made at the time; but his memory must have been exceptionally good to place in their proper psychological order, and see clearly in their relative significance, emotional crises that had taken place thirty years before. But a further question now arises. To what extent is he to be trusted in the reading of his own and Minna's motives and character? Once more we are driven to the conclusion that, in the main, that reading is correct. This judgment of the biographer has nothing to do with the moral aspect of the domestic relations of the pair during their thirty years' association: that subject will more appropriately come up for discussion later. Here we are concerned only with what happened between August, 1834, when the pair first met, and November, 1836, when they entered upon a marriage that was to mean little but disillusion and misery for both of them. And after having made all allowances for Wagner's constitutional inability to see any matter from any other standpoint but his own, we are driven to believe, in the end, in the substantial accuracy of his diagnosis of the case.

We are not doing him justice, indeed, unless we recognise that in this one instance he shows an objectivity of judgment that is not to be met with elsewhere in the whole of his record. In every other episode of his life, his view was that he was entirely in the right and the others entirely in the wrong. This is the solitary instance in which he recognises mournfully his own faults, and sees in them a justification for much of the conduct of Minna. He could not have taken this objective view of the basic forces in the tragic drama at any other period than that at which he dictated his autobiography. He could not have done so in the late 1830's, when, blinded with passion, he was too interested and tortured an actor in the drama to see it from the outside. He could not have done it in the 1850's, when, deceiving and lying to the wife of whom he was intellectually tired, though he was still fond enough of her in a prosaic domestic way, the imperious daemon that was driving before it the artist in him had deprived the man of something of his normal humanity. The detachment exhibited in *Mein Leben* was possible to him only in the late sixties, when, Minna having died, she had ceased to be a physical exasperation to him, when the prickings of his conscience no longer led him to stiffen in self-defence, but had passed into a sphere in which, as an artist in dramatic psychology, he could savour the full bitter-sweetness of them. At that later stage he undoubtedly saw, for the first time, those distant early years in the round. The more we study the documents of the case the more we are forced to the conclusion that in this instance, and this alone in the whole of his career, he sees himself, and one who had both wounded and been wounded by him, as, in the main, they really were. When we remember the facility with which his easily-bruised sensitiveness could not merely make him forgetful of the kindnesses, the self-sacrificing devotion, shown him by several of the men and women who played a leading part in his life, but could make him savagely unjust towards them, we are the more struck by the impartiality he attempts, and in the main achieves, in his portrait of Minna and his account of their earliest relations.

2

When he took up his appointment at Lauchstädt he was twenty-one — a dangerous age for a man of his romantic imagination, inexhaustible vitality, and strong bent towards the erotic. At home, in Leipzig, the wilder part of him had been kept in partial check by his studies in the more serious music, by his desire to deserve the good opinion of his uncle Adolf, and by his profound love for his mother, that led to an acute fit of remorse after each of his student follies or debauches. Away from all these sobering influences, pitched headlong into the superficial life and the easy sexual contacts of the minor theatrical world, he at once took on the colour of his new surroundings. Würzburg had given him his first taste of freedom; he himself records how pleasant the ladies of the company made life for their lively young chorus-trainer. He had no sooner accepted the Bethmann engagement than his imagination revelled in the anticipation of the delights appropriate to a spark of his age. Though, as we have seen, he was fascinated by Minna at their first meeting, there is no evidence that his intentions towards her, then or for some time afterwards, were in the smallest degree serious. On the contrary, we may surmise that at first he saw in her only the possibility of a flirtation of the usual facile kind. On the

8th August, a few days after he had settled in Lauchstädt, he writes to Apel urging him to visit him and bring some friends with him: " I will try to give you and whoever you may bring with you here the most delightful time. All my lady singers shall be at your disposition. God, what I will do in the way of offering you allurements of the senses to conjure you here! "

Unless the published letters to Apel have been manipulated wholesale — which there is no reason to believe — there is no evidence for a considerable time that Wagner took Minna any more seriously than the other ladies of the troupe; and we have to remember that Apel, the one boon companion he had of his own age, was the recipient of all his confidences in these matters. On the 15th September, 1834, Wagner tells him that " at the moment I am practically without any love affairs. I have no time for them: I am still a little attached to Toni." Who Toni was we are not informed; the indications are that it was the theatrical lady of anything but spotless reputation referred to on page 189. In the general tone of his letters at this time there are no hints of any depth of attachment to Minna, or any planning of his future life to include hers. On the contrary, in his gayer moments, when pay-day is imminent and he is not fretting about his debts, he is full of schemes for a gay bachelor existence with Apel. Thus on the 27th October he optimistically outlines a scheme that was always in his head at this period: *Die Feen* is to be given at three or four theatres, to pave the way for *Das Liebesverbot*; this latter will bring him fame and money, and in the spring of 1836 he and Apel will go to Italy; there he will write an Italian opera, or more than one if possible; and then they will go to Paris, where he will write a French opera, make a lot of money, and no longer be a " German Philistine." " This career of mine must be yours also," he concludes. In December he expresses his delight in the " merry comedian folk " among whom his lot is cast: there is still no suggestion that Minna or any other woman is regarded by him as an essential factor in that lot. Now and then, in his soberer moments, he breaks out into bitter laments over what he feels to be his wasted life and the narrowness of his circumstances, and especially over the follies that have plunged him into debt — these laments being almost invariably accompanied by requests for more money from Apel — but nowhere does he so much as hint at a consuming passion for Minna. Her name appears for the first time in a letter to Apel of the 13th December, in which the bare name of " Planer " occurs in the cast for the projected production of Apel's *Columbus.*

3

It looks as if for a comparatively long time he had made no particular impression on the tranquil Minna. She was thoroughly versed in the ways of her own little world, and knew how to take care of herself: she must have had innumerable flies of Wagner's type buzzing round her during the last eight years or so, knew exactly what their attentions meant, and was determined that nothing of this kind should stand in the way of her one object in life, which was to secure her livelihood and maintain her position in the theatre against her rivals. Wagner assures us that she had no culture — not even much education — and no talent as an actress. His verdict on the latter point may seem at first sight to be negated by the documents in the Burrell Collection, which show her to have been in considerable demand from the theatres. She had begun with amateur theatricals in Dresden. There her good looks and youthful charm had attracted the attention of the Director of the Dessau theatre, who at once offered her an engagement with his company. As is the innocent way of theatrical people, she carefully preserved all the papers that bore flatteringly on her modest career, in which she evidently took the regulation pride. Four programmes of the Eumorphia Theatre in Dresden, now in the Burrell Collection, show her to have taken part in performances there between 1831 and 1833. A programme of the Dessau theatre of the 7th November, 1832, may possibly relate to her first appearance there; while a letter of the 26th December of the same year from the Director discusses an engagement for the following spring. Other documents show her to be either playing in, or, in the great majority of cases, receiving offers from, Coburg in November 1833, Gotha in December 1833, Dresden in August 1833, Dessau in February 1833, Schwerin in January 1835, Magdeburg in December 1833, Brandenburg in January 1834, Bremen in May 1834, Bamberg in August 1835, Lübeck in September 1834, Aachen in August 1835, Brandenburg again in September 1835, Leipzig in September 1834, Berlin in October

[185]

1835, Königsberg in March 1836, and Altenburg in March 1833 and May 1836. Manifestly, while it may be true that, as Wagner says, she had no passion whatever for the stage, and saw in the theatre only a means of maintaining herself and her dependents fairly easily, she was in considerable demand; whether she had any particular talent or not, she exercised an indubitable attraction over audiences, perhaps mainly by reason of her mere face, figure and manner. Wagner's judgment of her modest talents was no doubt that of a hypercritical connoisseur.

In his account of her attitude towards life in general and the theatre in particular Wagner was either painting, in the manner of the novelist, a purely imaginary psychological portrait, or he was drawing accurately, from the life, a woman whom he understood through and through. There is not the slightest reason for assuming the former, while there is every reason for accepting his analysis of her as substantially accurate. It is an analysis that will hold equally good of thousands of young women in her position. According to Wagner, her sober commonsense had worked out for her a consistent and effective scheme of conduct, all planned to the one end. Sobered and placed on the alert by her first staggering experience of the realities of the world, she held herself aloof from the ordinary life of the stage folk around her. Her instincts were kept well in hand; she had no intention of getting herself " talked about." But she was a woman, an actress, and an excellent business woman. She knew well enough that her main assets were her beauty and her charm — a charm that must have been all the more potent because it was allied with a modesty and a reserve, both of conduct and speech, that were rare in her particular world; and she consciously and deliberately made the best commercial use of her attractiveness, not so much to win lovers for her for their own or for her sake, as simply to advance her material interests in circles that could be useful to her. It was a safe and simple and commendable philosophy of life and conduct as far as it went, and in so far as it concerned herself alone. Complications only arose when, as in Wagner's case, a fiery, jealous, egoistic and exacting lover forced himself within the stout bourgeois ramparts she had built round herself for her own security and profit. Wagner's point of view and hers were fundamentally irreconcilable; and as each was honestly incapable of placing himself at the standpoint of the other, misunderstandings, and, in time, the bitterest recriminations were inevitable. Wagner thought her way of handling men " inconsistent " and " indelicate "; she, for her part, thought her conduct perfectly natural for a woman with her particular way to make in the world and her particular problems to solve. And above all she was inclined at first to resent the assumed right on the part of this young man, who was probably only one of scores she had been amiable with, to run her life along his lines rather than her own. She was older than he, much more experienced, and, in the matters that most immediately concerned them both, much more perspicacious. Romance was all very well in its way, but it must be kept in its proper place. Food and clothing for herself, her child and her parents, present peace of mind and security for the future, were matters not of romance but of plain business; since men were obviously susceptible to her looks and her ways, she felt she was fully justified in using these, in a business-like but respectable way, for her advancement in the theatre. She was not permanently tied to the Magdeburg or any other company: at any moment she might be offered a more advantageous engagement elsewhere. Why then should she change her philosophy of living at the behest of a wild and penniless little newcomer, a beginner in his own line, who in all probability would soon pass out of her life as others had done?

4

But the Immortals who were playing so cunning a game with them made use of all that was best in her to draw her into the trap they had set for the pair. It may well be, as Wagner always maintained afterwards, that she never had any real love for him — love, that is to say, in the exalted sense in which he understood the term — that her nature, indeed, was incapable of that kind of love. But she was certainly capable of a vast devotion and pity; and it was these, rather than a consuming passion on her side, that in the end sealed her fate and Wagner's. It was her very virtues that brought about her undoing and his.

At Lauchstädt and Rudolstadt he seems to have astonished her by his sudden infatuation, while she, on her side, showed him not only courtesy but womanly kindness, at the same time prudently avoiding doing anything that would give the rest of the company an excuse to gossip about them. At Rudolstadt there seemed to be a possibility of her becoming engaged to a certain Herr von O., a young man of good family but without means; but they both realised the impossibility of a marriage. This affair, however, must have operated for the time being to make her hold the too impetuous new music-director at arm's length; and we gather from his account of this period that he was made to realise that Minna was not going to be the easy kind of conquest he had been accustomed to. He had assumed too much: she might be in the theatrical world, but she was not of it: she had no intention of carrying the romantic fantasies of the stage into real life. As Wagner puts it, " After closer consideration I recognised that *Young Europe, Ardinghello,* and *Liebesverbot* [1] did not apply here; between the Fairy Amorosa in her merry theatrical caprices and the daughter of a decent bourgeois in pursuit of a respectable living there was a decided gulf fixed "; and so he plunged, for satisfaction of his instincts at that time, into pleasures more easily accessible to him — those of the wine cup, the beer glass, the gaming table, and, one gathers, though he does not specifically say so, the society of ladies who did not draw a ring fence about them as the level-headed Minna did. He avows that between him and her there was a " rupture " in Rudolstadt, as a result of which they were for a time " to some extent lost to one another."

5

Their friendship was renewed soon after their return to Magdeburg, but they were still cool and distant with each other. Clearly she had repulsed him as not fitting into the life she had calmly planned for herself; as the documents in the Burrell Collection show, she was corresponding with other theatre managements about this time, and it was quite on the cards that her path and Wagner's might at any moment diverge, perhaps for ever. In Magdeburg he must have renewed his importunities and plagued her with his jealousies: as usual, she was the object of the attention of several

---

[1] Symbols for him, at that time, of freedom from convention in matters of the sexes.

men of the upper class of the town, and though, as Wagner testifies, her conduct was always above reproach, though in public she was the soul of discretion and reserve, and though she protested to him that the conduct of these gentlemen towards her was much more modest and decent than that of the theatre patrons of the bourgeois class, and especially, she added pointedly, of " certain young music-directors," he plagued her " bitterly and quarrelsomely," as he admits, with a jealousy he had certainly no right to feel. " So we spent three unhappy months in ever-increasing estrangement from each other, during which time, in semi-desperation, I pretended to take pleasure in the most undesirable company, and in every way behaved with such extreme frivolity that Minna, as she told me afterwards, felt the deepest and most sympathetic anxiety for me." The psychologist and actor in him had hit upon the surest way to break down the barrier of her reserve and circumspection towards him. All his life long, women who pitied him felt an impulse to mother the highly-strung, self-torturing little man who was visibly incapable of running his own life with ordinary prudence; and more than once this impulse was the insidious opening chord in the overture to a drama of love. His tactics were half instinctive, half calculated, and they varied slightly according to circumstances; but they were generally successful. Minna's was the first case in which we see them operating with signal success.

Minna's " sympathetic anxiety " for him was increased by the fact that the other ladies of the troupe, and one in particular whose reputation was not spotless, were setting their caps at the influential young music-director. From this time onward Minna made herself more approachable by him, though still, if we are to believe Wagner, keeping entirely within the terms of her own nature, showing " no passion, or even genuine love," but being kind, admiring, and solicitous for the brilliant and likeable young wastrel. The climax came with another exercise of Wagner's rare psychological technique where women were concerned. Once more he played his best card — acting in a way that would be sure to awaken pity and concern for him in the gentle Minna. He had promised to take tea one evening with her and Madame Haas, a member of the theatre company in whom Laube was especially interested. Wagner's first liking for this lady had gradually turned to strong dislike. He went first of all to a whist party elsewhere, got completely drunk, and when, on reaching Minna's, he found, to his annoyance, Madame Haas still there, he behaved with such outrageous rudeness and coarseness that she left the house in disgust. Realising, no doubt, that it would do the music-director no good to be seen in the town in such a condition, Minna, whose conduct had hitherto always been regulated with the nicest concern for her reputation — she used to have her bedroom door locked each night by her landlady — gave up her own bed to the fuddled youth.

" There I slept," he says, " until awakened by the wonderful grey of dawn. When I recognised where I was, the sunrise threw a clearer and clearer light on what I saw to be the beginning of a long and infinitely momentous period of my life. Foreboding care had entered into my life. Without any levity, any jesting, without wantonness or joking of any description, we breakfasted soberly and decorously together, and, at an hour when we could do so without attracting attention, we went out for a long walk beyond the city gate. Then we parted. From that day onward, as openly acknowledged lovers, we gave ourselves up freely and without embarrassment to our tender interest in each other." [1]

We can date this episode with fair accuracy, for on the 4th February, 1835, Wagner writes to his brother Albert announcing his betrothal to Minna, whom, with the usual convenient forgetfulness of the past on the part of young lovers, he describes as the only woman who has ever interested him. In *Mein Leben* he tells how, when he had an attack of the erysipelas that plagued him at various periods of his life, and his swollen and disfigured face made him sensitive about leaving his room, Minna visited him and nursed him, and the good soul, to convince him that even the unpleasant rash around his mouth did not repel her, kissed him in friendly fashion on the lips. Now on the 13th March he writes to Apel that he has erysipelas, and is " disfigured and neglected." We are tolerably safe, then, in assuming that it was some six months after his

---

[1] Wagner's language, here as elsewhere in these pages, is somewhat cloudy. We have to remember that he was writing his autobiography at the request of King Ludwig, and was anxious all through the recital of the earlier phases of his career not to shock the chaste young King, who had so romantic a belief in him, by unnecessary realism of either fact or speech. He discussed this difficulty with Cosima, who communicated it to the King: Cosima urged him to tell everything in connection with his young days, saying that she was sure the King would understand. See MECW, I, 320.

settling in Magdeburg that he and Minna became recognised lovers. The earliest love letter known to us is the No. 49 of the Burrell Collection, which is still unpublished. It is dated from Leipzig, May 6th, 1835. In view of the fact that Minna preserved very carefully all her papers of this and a later period,[1] we may take it that this was really the first of Richard's letters to her. There would of course be no occasion for him to write while they were both in Magdeburg.

In May of that year the opera season ended, but although Beth- mann was now bankrupt, the dramatic performances still continued for a time. Minna consequently had to remain in Magdeburg, while Wagner, now without an appointment and therefore without a salary, went back to Leipzig to live at the expense, apparently, of the good-hearted Rosalie, and to try to raise money by hook or by crook for the satisfaction of some of the more pressing of his credi- tors. As soon as she was free, Minna went to her parents in Dresden, calling at Leipzig on the way and being introduced to some mem- bers, at any rate, of the Wagner family. "Minna was here," he writes to Apel (who was then in Frankfort) on the 6th June, "and for my sake stayed three days, in the vilest weather, without know- ing another soul in the place, and with nowhere to go — purely to give me pleasure. That is moving: it is remarkable what an influ- ence I have acquired over the girl. You should read her letters: they are burning hot " — which rather contradicts Wagner's later asser- tion that she *never* felt any passion, or even genuine love, for him — " and, as we both know, that is not inborn in her."

6

To escape from his miseries in Leipzig he went to a music festival at Dessau, then to Magdeburg, presumably on business, then to Naumburg and Kösen, in which latter place he saw the liberated Laube again. In Dessau, the town in which Minna had made her début, he heard her spoken of by some " frivolous young men " in terms disparaging to her reputation; the heat with which he de- fended her against the " scandalmongers " revealed to himself the strength of his passion for her. On his return to Leipzig he at once

---

[1] With the exception, perhaps, of one letter to the significant absence of which attention will be drawn later. See p. 232.

set out for Dresden to see her. His coach met another in which she and one of her sisters were on their way to Magdeburg; and he persuaded them to return to Dresden with him. There, with his usual recklessness, he borrowed some money from a friend and took the two girls on a tour, lasting several days, of the Saxon Alps; this merry excursion stood out ever after in his memory as on the whole the happiest time in his life as a young man. The trio returned to Leipzig, whence Minna and her sister made their way at last to Magdeburg: Richard went once more to his family, but prudently told them nothing about his visit to Dresden and the excursion to the mountains. One thought alone possessed his jealous mind — to be where the maddeningly-attractive Minna was. This meant re-engaging himself to Bethmann: there was little difficulty about that, as the director knew by this time the value of his young conductor, and knew also that where Minna was, Richard would want to be, salary or half salary or no salary. So back he went to Magdeburg, where he found, as he tells Apel on the 16th July, that matters were looking up with Bethmann. The King had agreed to continue his financial support, on condition that the affairs of the theatre were put in the hands of a responsible town committee. Wagner was actually re-engaged at a higher salary, on paper, than before: and, full of enthusiasm at the prospect opening out before him, he is on the point of setting off, he tells Apel, on a tour through Germany to engage new singers for the opera. He foolishly undertook to do this at his own expense, his reward to be a benefit at the end of the season — an arrangement that suited the sagacious Bethmann admirably, but turned out disastrously for Wagner.

He had hoped to borrow the necessary funds easily from Friedrich Brockhaus, but that sober business man was not in the least dazzled by the young enthusiast's glowing account of the royally protected Magdeburg opera, and it was with great difficulty that he was induced to part with enough money to start Richard on his journey. Passing through Teplitz and Prague he hurried on to Karlsbad, where he had the ill luck to engage a bass singer who, when he appeared in Magdeburg, proved hopelessly incompetent judged even by the anything but exacting standard of Bethmann's troupe. From Karlsbad, on the 25th July, Richard wrote a letter to his mother in which he bitterly reproached Brockhaus for the " hu-

miliation " he had been forced to undergo at his hands, a humilia-
tion for which he vows he will get even with him some day. His resentment against his relatives is now obviously at its height; he does
not think they are doing their duty towards him. He " feels independent " at last, he says; he had made a great mistake in looking
to anyone but Apel for financial backing. But these hard experiences will have been useful to him — they will correct the excessive
softness of his nature. One thing alone constitutes his refuge and his
hope — the certainty of his mother's love.

By way of Eger and Bayreuth, which latter place he entered on a
summer evening when the little town was gloriously lit up by the
setting sun, he arrived at Nuremberg, where, of course, he found
Klara and her husband Wolfram, both of whom he succeeded in
inducing to accept engagements at Magdeburg. Schröder-Devrient
happened to be in the town; and once more he had an opportunity
of admiring the dramatic art with which she could give life to musical material quite insignificant in itself: this time it was the part,
familiar to her from her earliest days as a singer, of Emmeline in
Weigl's faded old opera *Die Schweizerfamilie*. At Nuremberg, too,
he had an experience that lingered in his memory till in the end it
took a glorified artistic form in the finale of the second act of the
Meistersinger. A merry party in a tavern had been amusing themselves by cruelly baiting a local simpleton who fancied himself
absurdly as a singer: they had even succeeded in passing Wagner
of on him as the great Lablache, who, it appeared, was anxious to
hear a Nuremberg celebrity of whom he had been told so much.
The poor butt was not even made suspicious by the fact that Wagner's voice was obviously a tenor, while Lablache's was a deep bass;
nor by the further fact that the giant Lablache was nearly twice the
bulk of the diminutive stranger. The evening ended in a tipsy riot
in the street, that came to a climax with one of the company laying
another out with a blow between the eyes. Thereupon the crowd
melted away as if by magic, leaving Wagner and Wolfram to stroll
home in sudden quiet through the moonlit streets of the entrancing
old town.

From there he went on to Würzburg, where, as already mentioned, he saw the unfortunate Friederike Galvani again, and
thence to Frankfort; then to Leipzig, where he picked up his brown

dog, with which he set off to Magdeburg, there to take up his duties again on the 1st September. At Frankfort he killed time by recording in a large red pocket-book exact dates and details in his career " for my future biography "; evidently he had no doubt even then that some day the world would want an authentic biography of him! He carefully continued the record through the later years; and the pocket-book lay before him when he was writing *Mein Leben*.

He returned to Magdeburg with, on the whole, quite a good bag of singers, obtained, however, at the cost of a few more personal debts, for his own meagre funds could hardly have sufficed for his travelling expenses, even after he had sold or pawned, as he tells us, a gold ring given him by Apel for composing the *Columbus* music, and a snuff-box, presented to him by another friend, which he had trustfully believed to be of platinum, but which turned out to be made of a less valuable metal. All in all, matters were so much better in Magdeburg this season that he was able both to enlarge the operatic repertory and to raise the standard of performance above anything the town had yet known; in spite of Bethmann's opposition he managed to have the tiny orchestra augmented in places.[1] But trouble was looming in connection with Minna. She had brought her mother to live with her; the old lady, who appears to have been of a rather coarse type, interfered with him as if she were already his mother-in-law, while Minna was frankly less anxious for marriage than for an improvement in his and her financial condition. He, for his part, if we are to take his account in *Mein Leben* as an accurate description of his state of mind at this time, was " filled with anxiety " at the thought of marriage at his age and in his circumstances: " a naive, instinctive feeling prevented me from thinking of the serious possibility of a step that would have had such consequences for my whole life." Once more there is no reason to doubt the general accuracy of his account of the matter: he not only wanted Minna but needed her, but at the same time he must have realised, in cooler moments when the physical urge was dormant, that to tie himself for life to a woman so fundamentally different from him in mentality and so

---

[1] On his return from his tour in search of singers he exchanged his former lodging in the corner house of the Margaretenstrasse, No. 2, for one in the Breiterweg, No. 34, fourth floor.

much below him in culture would be a mistake for which he would have to pay dearly sooner or later.

7

Outer events forced his hand. Had he continued to live for long in the same town with her, in daily association with her, the purely physical infatuation of each of them might before long have burnt itself out. But the Fates gave an extra and determining strength to his passion by the simple process of removing Minna from Magdeburg and so from him. Her position in the theatre was being threatened by a rival, Madame Grabowsky, who had a tactical advantage over her in the fact that her husband was the head regisseur. Wagner tells us that " at the beginning of the winter Minna received advantageous offers from the Director of the Königstadt Theatre in Berlin . . . and seized the opportunity to break completely with the Magdeburg theatre." Once more the documents in the Burrell Collection and the letters to Apel confirm his story. The Collection contains the very letter of Cerf, the Königstadt Director, in which the suggested engagement was discussed: it is dated the 4th October, 1835. On the 27th October Wagner had written to Apel:

" Don't get too many fancies into your head with regard to Minna. I leave everything to fate. She loves me, and her love means a great deal to me now: she is now my central point: she gives me consistency and warmth: I cannot give her up. I only know that you, dear Theodor, do not yet know the sweetness of such a relationship; it has nothing common, unworthy or enervating in it; our epicureanism is pure and strong — not a miserable illicit liaison; — we love each other, and believe in each other, and the rest we leave to fate; — this you do not know, and only with an actress can one live thus; this superiority to the bourgeois can be found only where the whole field is fantastic caprice and poetic licence." [1]

On 5th November, agitated at the prospect of losing her, he writes again to Apel:

" Minna left for Berlin early yesterday. I cannot tell you how I feel about it; this is not being in love, it *is* love. She is guesting there: perhaps she will stay there altogether, as she has been coming into

[1] RWTA, p. 62.

many collisions here with a Madame Grabowsky. What a state I am in! My God! My God! If I wanted to be modern, this would be the very moment to effect a separation, but there you are. My heart is broken, in real bourgeois fashion broken. Do me the kindness to imagine the rest for yourself; we will *talk* about it some other time."

"In passionate unrest," he says in *Mein Leben*, "I wrote to her, urging her to return, and, to move her not to separate her fate from mine, I formally proposed marriage as soon as possible." The full tale of this vital period in their relations can be told only when the letters in the Burrell Collection are published; here it is possible only to quote the summaries of them given in the Catalogue of the Collection:

4th November, 1834 (i.e. the very day she had left Magdeburg): "Love letter. This is a most interesting letter, for in discussing the conflict between his love and his ambition he sets out all his plans in life, and they were exactly what he was to carry out. . . . He reproaches her bitterly," — presumably for leaving him.

5th November. "He implores her to marry him, and signs himself 'Your bridegroom.' Letter shows clearly that Minna did not want to marry Richard Wagner."

6th November. "He begins his letter 'My sweet bride,' and urges her to marry him at Easter. He is going to write to her every day till she consents. She had left Magdeburg secretly — a pretty clear index of her feelings."

7th November. "Love letter. He upbraids her for leaving him. He informs her no woman has ever been loved like her. He swears to take her away by force. He thinks (quite rightly) that she had left him at Magdeburg without any intention of returning to him."

8th November. "Love letter. It is the tale of his misery in her absence."

9th November. "Love letter. She has written only two letters to his six — an infidelity, he says."

10th November. "Love letter. Richard Wagner tells her he has won over her mother. Implores her to return to Magdeburg."

11th November. "Love letter. 'I have brains and ability, and in possessing you I will have a serious incentive to use them.'"

12th November. "This is a love letter. 'My dear bride . . . I have just hung up my silhouette in your room. . . . If luck is good, I shall produce my opera [*Das Liebesverbot*] in Berlin in February.' "

This daily bombardment seems to have reduced a fortress that was already virtually undermined: Minna returned to Magdeburg. She must have made a good impression in Berlin, for in the Burrell Collection there is a letter, dated 26th November, from the prompter of the Royal Theatre (not the Königstadt, which was in the suburbs), sounding her as to an engagement. According to *Mein Leben*, Wagner's brother-in-law Wolfram, who had already cancelled his engagement with the impecunious Bethmann in disgust, and had likewise gone to the Königstadt, sent his wife a letter describing Minna's conduct in the theatre and in her hotel in very disparaging terms. Klara showed this letter to Richard, who thereupon wrote to Wolfram begging to be told the truth. Whether Wolfram had been in error in the first place, or whether he was diplomatically unwilling to make mischief now that he realised how serious was Richard's passion for Minna, it is impossible to say; but he now told Wagner that on investigation he had found himself to have been mistaken, and that on nearer acquaintance with Minna he had formed so high an opinion of her character that he sincerely hoped Richard would marry her. Wagner thereupon implored her to return; and as she was weary, he says, of the frivolity of Berlin theatrical life, she was not inclined to renew her engagement at the Königstadt. He now attacked Bethmann and the Magdeburg regisseur with such vehemence that the committee, before whom the matter came, agreed to the re-instatement of Minna, in spite of her breach of her agreement with them. Again the letters to Apel fill in the outline of his story. " You should have seen me," he writes on the 25th November, " during the fortnight when Minna was away from me. Great God, how the girl has captured me, without her having really meant to do so! She has come back for my sake, in spite of the fact that a brilliant engagement was offered to her in Berlin. What do you think of that? " He goes on to describe Wolfram's favourable account of her character, and continues, " She made a sensation in Berlin; she refused more than four parts that were offered her. The devil! That moves one! "

In March 1836 came the *Liebesverbot* catastrophe, which will be described later. The season was now over, and neither he nor Minna wished to remain any longer in Magdeburg. She had already been in negotiation with the Königsberg (East Prussia) theatre: the actual contract, dated 28th March, is in the Burrell Collection. Richard, worried by his creditors — who were trying to have him imprisoned, — and aching at this fresh separation from Minna, who had already gone to Königsberg to try to pave the way for Richard's engagement as conductor there, went to Berlin on 18th May, with the prime object of getting *Das Liebesverbot* accepted at the Königstadt Theatre. Buoyed up with promises that, as usual, meant nothing, he launched out into a style of living that must have involved him in further debt. From Königsberg also the news was not good. Hopes had been held out to him and Minna that he would receive the desired conductorship, which was expected to be vacant shortly. But the man in possession, Louis Schuberth, showed no signs of leaving, and the wretched Wagner, for whom separation from anyone he loved or in any way needed was always a torture beyond bearing, was at last driven to leave Berlin for Königsberg. The letters in the Burrell Collection bearing on this stage of the story are the following: they are all from Wagner in Berlin to Minna in Königsberg:

21st May, 1836. " Love letter assuring her of eternal devotion."

23rd May. This letter is not described in the Catalogue.

29th May. " A burning love letter; ' arrange everything so that I can come very soon and we can get married quickly.' " The letter is continued on 1st June.

3rd June. " Another reproachful love letter."

5th June; continued on the 12th, and again on the 20th. " A huge and splendid love letter. It affords convincing proof that Richard wanted to marry Minna, but that Minna did not want to marry Richard; she thought his material circumstances did not justify marriage."

22nd June. " This is a supreme effort to make her marry him. It mentions his Magdeburg debts and his acquaintance with Dorn."

Jealousy now added fuel to the flames that were consuming him.

In Berlin his acquaintance was cultivated by a Jewish tradesman named Schwabe, who till then had lived in Magdeburg, and whose interest in him, he found, was due to Schwabe's having been in love with Minna. Wagner could discover nothing to make him assume real infidelity on her part, but he was suspicious, hurt, and angry. He felt that he must end his tortures by making Minna definitely his own. Estranged from his family, with hardly a single friend to whom he was really attached, loaded with debts, with as yet no better prospect in life than ill-paid engagements for a portion of each year at this miserable provincial theatre or that, secretly aware that he was wasting both his material and spiritual substance on people and things that were unworthy of him, he instinctively turned for consolation and help, as he was to do throughout his life, to the Eternal Feminine, which, for the moment, assumed the somewhat dubious incarnation of Minna Planer. He was fully conscious of her intellectual limitations — even at this stage of their association he never ventured to talk about his innermost self to her, for her placid nature had no idealism in it — but the sensual attraction over-rode his reason; while her balance, her practical good sense in ordinary matters, and her housewifoly virtues promised him a haven against the particular life's storms that he was by nature unable to cope with himself. In whatever concerned the artistic or the intellectual side of him he never had need of anyone; all his life he was prepared to fight theatre directors, journalists, public and princes single-handed and never yield an inch of ground. But to replenish his forces and sustain his courage for these conflicts he needed the cosy placidities of a home, and the cosseting and comforting of a devoted woman. The Fates laid the craftiest of traps for him when they thus threw in his way, in his inexperienced youth, a woman who was exceptionally rich in just the qualities he sought in woman as a domestic animal.

On the other side, the sensual attraction must at this time have been equally strong for Minna. In spite of the insignificance of his person, or perhaps, in part, paradoxically by reason of it, he exercised all his life a remarkable spell over women. They were no doubt at once perplexed and fascinated by the blend in him of bold erotic ardour and manifest helplessness in real life. Even more dangerous for all these women than the love he kindled in them was the pity he inspired: he held them to him by a double cable. While it may be true that Minna would have preferred not to be tied to him irrevocably by marriage, for she must have been fully conscious of his weaknesses as a man — his violent temper, his recklessness in money matters, the lack of self-control that made a debauchee and a gambler of him when things were going wrong, all failings that must have frightened the prudent, bourgeoise Minna — there can be no doubt that he roused in her at this time a passion that was very different from the calculating, businesslike coquetry with which she handled the other men who crossed her path. We have already seen that Wagner, in his letter of the 6th June, 1835, to Apel, speaks of a passion in her letters which he and his correspondent know to be hardly native to her. Nowhere in these letters does Wagner discuss Minna in relation to his deeper self; for both of them, evidently, the infatuation was almost wholly a physical one.

Wherein his charm for women may have consisted we do not know precisely; but it is certain that he was highly-sexed, and that it took only a few adventures in his youth to give him a feeling of self-satisfaction and confidence where women were concerned. " I have become conscious," he writes to his confidential friend and doctor Pusinelli nearly thirty years later, when he is contemplating a divorce from Minna and re-marriage with a woman of means, " through sufficient and strangely flattering experiences up to the present time, that soulful feminine natures cling to me easily to the point of wildest adoration, and through this become capable of the most extreme surrender." [1] And that his sexual needs were strong is shewn by his remark to Pusinelli, in this same highly confidential and long-suppressed letter, that the wife he is in quest of must be of an age " to suit my own, and therefore cause me no embarrassment in the future " — as poor Minna had done by ageing too rapidly for him.

9

Maddened by jealousy, unable to bear the separation any longer, he resolved to pursue her to Königsberg. Laube, whom he had met again in Berlin, evidently saw the misery that was gnawing at him,

[1] RWAP, p. 146.

and the danger he was in: he bestirred himself on the practical side, raising money from his own friends to give to Wagner for the journey; but he also warned him against letting his young life take on too much of the colour of the wretched theatrical environment in which his lot was momentarily cast. Concealing his real purpose from his clear-sighted older friend, Wagner set off, on the 7th July, on the long and fatiguing journey to Königsberg. His heart sank when he found Minna lodged in an ugly house in a poor and depressing suburb; but his sombre mood was soon dissipated by the placid good nature that radiated from her as usual.

The practical difficulty facing him in Königsberg came from the fact that the conductor, Louis Schuberth, who had taken up the post temporarily while the Riga theatre, to which he was really attached, was re-building, had fallen in love with the Königsberg prima donna, Henriette Grosser, and showed no disposition to leave. Moreover, by his intrigues he set the public and the orchestra against his young assistant, whose competence, no doubt, he feared. The situation soon became intolerable for both Wagner and Minna. They were on the point of accepting an engagement offered them in Danzig, where Klara and her husband were now living, when the Königsberg Director Hübsch, who did not like the idea of losing Minna for his theatre, undertook to appoint Wagner formally as conductor from the April of the following year (1837), with the further promise of a benefit for their wedding. But while Minna was now seemingly reconciled to the idea of their union, Wagner, as the time for it grew nearer, became more than ever conscious of the danger involved in the fundamental diversity of their natures. But once more jealousy increased his desire for possession of her. He came across Schwabe's letters to her; they quarrelled violently over the affair, and over the practice, in which she was still indulging, of permitting, for the sake of her advancement in her profession, familiarities from other men that were distasteful to him. Their quarrels at this time were typical of many that were to darken their later life. Neither really understood the other. When the unhappy lover protested against conduct on Minna's part that he thought humiliating for him, she could always confound him with the unanswerable rejoinder that their association was not really of her seeking, and that she was making a sacrifice by letting her fate be involved in that of a young wastrel who could not even keep himself, while she had refused more than one advantageous offer for his sake. Their disputes invariably ended in his shocking her with the insulting bitterness of tongue that was habitual with him when he had lost his temper. Then, seeing how he had distressed her, even to the point of damaging her health, he would be sincerely repentant, but still with the perplexed feeling at the back of his mind that it was he who had been the worse used, he who had the greater grievance against fate. He frankly admits that under the strain of these quarrels not only did Minna's health suffer grievously but her character underwent, in the course of the years, a radical change: the gentle, placid creature became, under constant provocation, a nagging fury inflamed with a sense of intolerable wrong. With this change in her, Wagner in turn lost something of his love and regard for the woman whose main charm for him had been her sweetness of disposition and her unfailing serenity of manner. And so the vicious circle went on ever widening itself, leaving each of them, at the tragic centre of it, more and more wounded and perplexed.

Quarrels seem to have been frequent between them in the weeks preceding their marriage. One of the most fruitful causes of differences between them was the fresh set of debts that Richard blithely incurred in order to make their future home as comfortable as he desired it to be. Optimistic as ever, he was confident of soon establishing himself firmly in the world as conductor and composer; Minna, on her side, shrank from this reckless mortgaging of a problematic future. They quarrelled even in the house of the clergyman to whom they had gone to arrange for the marriage, being put out of humour by the wretchedness of the rainy November day and by their having been kept waiting for some time in the hall. They were actually on the point of separating when the reverend gentleman at last opened the door; then the grim humour of the situation seized upon them. That night Wagner took his benefit: the opera was *Masaniello*, in which Minna took the part of the dumb girl Fenella, in which she was always exceptionally successful.[1] The perform-

---

[1] The actual script from which she studied the part is now in the Burrell Collection.

ance brought him in an agreeably large sum, meditating happily upon which, no doubt, he went off alone to the house he had furnished so comfortably. Not wishing to profane the bridal bed by his solitary presence, he slept and froze on a hard sofa.[1] The next day he set off to the little Tragheim church dressed in a new suit — for which some trusting tailor had no doubt given him credit — a conspicuous feature of which was a dark blue frock-coat with gold buttons. Minna looked her best, in spite of the fact that she wore a dress selected for her by her bridegroom. There was a large and frivolous congregation; Wagner notes sadly that there was not a real friend among them all. He listened as if in a dream to the parson's nuptial address, his wandering mind — intent, perhaps, on his debts — only coming to attention when he heard the reverend gentleman say something to the effect that in the dark days that were no doubt ahead of the couple there was one friend to whom they could always turn for help. Wagner pricked up his ears at so welcome an announcement, and looked enquiringly at the clergyman: a friend who could always be guaranteed to help was precisely what he was in search of. But when he found that the " friend " was merely Jesus, he lost all further interest in the clerical discourse. He was not, he quaintly says, " insulted, as people thought, but simply disappointed." He was so absent-minded that when the pastor held out the closed prayer-book to receive their rings, the practical Minna had to nudge him hard to get him to follow her example.

"At that moment," he says, in what is perhaps the gravest and saddest passage in his autobiography, " I saw clearly, as if in a vision, my whole being divided into two cross-currents that dragged me in completely different directions: the upper one, that faced the sun, swept me on like a man in a dream, while the lower one held my nature captive in a great and incomprehensible fear. The incredible levity with which I at once chased away the perception that kept pressing in on me of the twofold enormity I was committing, found full support and excuse in the really heartfelt ardour with which I looked on the girl, in her own way and especially in her own environment so rare and individual, who was thus binding herself so unreservedly to a young man with no means of support. It was eleven

---

[1] The newly married pair took up their abode in a house at the corner of the Mankenstrasse and the Steindamm, No. 111.

o'clock in the morning of the 24th November, 1836: I was twenty-three and a half." [1]

It has been said by some biographers that this " vision " was merely the imaginative projection, thirty years later, of his mature experience and reflection upon the scene at Tragheim. But there is no real reason for assuming this. From all we know of him and his frame of mind at this epoch, it is not in the least improbable that he was fully conscious all the time, with the more rational half of his being, that marriage with Minna was an error he would have cause to regret, but that his physical passion for her and his genuine admiration of her special womanly qualities overbore his reason.

His irrepressible spirits re-asserted themselves on the way home from the church, and the " rich banquet," as he calls it, to which he had invited the friends of both contracting parties, passed off merrily. But the next morning he had to appear before the magistrate to answer the demands of his Magdeburg creditors. Acting on expert advice, he pleaded infancy under Prussian law; and though the magistrate was justifiably astonished, seeing that Wagner had obtained his marriage licence only on presenting proof that he was of age according to the law of Saxony, he seems to have gained time by the manœuvre, and time was all that Richard Wagner generally wanted on these occasions. He notes, however, that " the vexations that pursued me for a long time after from this quarter began with the first day of my marriage." His debts were in all probability so large already that there was not the least likelihood of a young man in his circumstances clearing them off for many years. We know that he had borrowed frequently from Apel, and it is extremely doubtful whether he ever repaid the loans: in any case he could not possibly have done so except by further borrowing in some other quarter. He had clearly left a pile of debts behind him at Magdeburg. He had even laid the humble members of his orchestra there under contribution: we have a letter of his to Morath, the contrabassist at the theatre (who had done some music-copying for

---

[1] The pair seem to have fibbed right royally over their ages. According to the church register, Wilhelm Richard Wagener [sic] declared himself to have been born on the 22nd May, 1812; he thus made himself out to be a year older than he actually was. Minna gave her age as twenty-three: in reality she was nearly twenty-seven and a quarter — supposing, that is, the date of birth given on her tombstone (5th September, 1809) to be correct.

him), dated the 4th January, 1843, in which he apologises for
having kept him waiting so long — a matter of some seven or eight
years! — speaks of his financial difficulties at Dresden, recognises
that of all his creditors none is so necessitous as poor Morath, and
" makes a beginning " by sending him 35 thalers. We can imagine
the torment it was to the honest Minna, year after year, to live under
a sky that seemed to rain demands and threats and writs.

CHAPTER XII

KÖNIGSBERG AND RIGA

1

WAGNER'S CAREER in Magdeburg, as in practically every
other town with which he was associated for any length of
time, ended in disaster. He had finished the music of *Das Liebesverbot* by the New Year of 1836. As we have seen, he was entitled
to a benefit by way of recouping the expenses he had foolishly taken
on himself in the preceding summer, when he had toured the country engaging singers for the Bethmann troupe. This benefit would
naturally take place at the conclusion of the season, which had been
planned for the end of April. Before that time, however, the unfortunate company was well on the way towards dissolution; the
worried Bethmann had more reason than ever before to say that he
" would rather be a cab-horse in Berlin than a theatre director in
Magdeburg." Salaries, as usual, were in arrears, and by March
such of the actors and singers as could get engagements elsewhere
were already preparing to abandon the sinking ship. It was only
out of personal liking for their young musical director that the
singers necessary for *Das Liebesverbot*, which Wagner had chosen
for his benefit, consented to remain in Magdeburg until the end of
that month. But the wily Bethmann tricked the young greenhorn into
agreeing that the second performance should constitute the benefit,
the first being intended to cover the expenses of such new scenery
as had been necessary for the work. And apparently the opera
would never have performed at all but for Minna, who sold a brace-
let to raise funds to redeem the parts, which had been placed under
legal arrest until the copyist was paid. The grimly humorous account of the ensuing catastrophe in *Mein Leben* is one of Wagner's
best pieces of descriptive writing. In spite of his assurance that the
singers took unusual pains over the study of their parts, we may

reasonably doubt whether they regarded very seriously the preparation of a work in which none of them was ever likely to have to
appear again. Wagner's technical address at the conductor's desk
carried them safely through the rehearsals; but neither he nor they
appear to have realised that on " the night " he would not be able
to sing with them and shout at them and give them the audible leads
on which they had come to rely.

The first performance, on the 29th March, must have stood out
for heartbreaking ineptitude even in the annals of the German provincial theatre of the time. In spite of the zeal with which Wagner
so kindly credits them, none of the singers knew their parts. The
tenor who played Luzio fell back, when his memory failed him, on
what he could remember of *Fra Diavolo* and *Zampa*. As the cynical
Bethmann had neglected, for financial reasons, to have the libretto
printed in time, the audience could get no more than the vaguest
idea of the action and the psychology of the work, the subject of
which was new to them. The orchestra was as incompetent as the
singers. The word must have gone round the town that the thing had
been a fiasco, for at the second performance — which was also to
be the final night of the theatre — the house was empty. According
to Wagner, a quarter of an hour before the time fixed for the commencement there was no one in the place but Madame Gottschalk
and her husband (who were no doubt interested less in *Das Liebesverbot* as a work of art than in the amount of money the young
composer might have the next day to devote to the payment of his
debts), and a strange-looking Polish Jew in full dress. But before
a note of the overture was sounded, bedlam broke loose behind the
scenes. The husband of the leading lady, the charming Frau Pollert, made for her lover (the second tenor, who played Claudio),
and smote him on the nose, concentrating a whole season's marital
rancour in the blow; and poor Claudio had to retire to his dressing
room to wash off the blood that was pouring down his face. Frau
Pollert, who was to have played Isabella, tried to appease her en-
raged husband, received a castigation that was no doubt well deserved, and went off into hysterics. The rest of the company took
sides according to their sympathies in the case, the occasion being warmly welcomed, without any superfluous enquiry into first
causes, as a heaven-sent one for working off all the professional

animosities and jealousies that had been accumulating since the commencement of the season.

Herr Pollert's untimely matrimonial ban upon love proved more efficacious than that of Friedrich in the opera: there was nothing for it but for the manager to appear before the curtain and inform the infinitesimal audience that owing to unforeseen circumstances there would be no performance that evening. Nor was Wagner to be any more successful with the opera elsewhere. The subject was rather too risky a one for the sober Germany of that epoch. The Magdeburg police had already taken objection to the title of the work, which, to these stern moralists, was particularly unsuitable for the week before Easter, a time when frivolous productions were not allowed in the theatre; Wagner had only managed to have the opera produced at all by assuring the magistrate that it was founded on a very serious drama by the immortal Shakespeare, and by changing the name of the opera to *The Novice of Palermo*, which seemed, on the face of it, to be a certificate of religious propriety. When, later, Wagner tried to induce Ringelhardt to give the work at Leipzig, and pointed out how admirably the part of Marianne would suit the latter's daughter, the scandalised director assured him that even in the unlikely event of the Leipzig magistrates passing the work for performance, he, as a respectable father, would decidedly refuse to allow any daughter of his to be seen in it.

Wagner never heard his *Liebesverbot*. After the failure of his attempt to get it produced in Paris in 1840 he lost all interest in it, for his genius had by then taken a new flight that left this immature work of his far behind. He presented the score to King Ludwig in 1866, with a dedicatory poem in which he apologised for this "sin of his youth." Finck tells us that in 1891 he called on the great Wagnerian tenor Heinrich Vogl, according to whom a plan had been set on foot for producing the work in Munich after the success of the performances of *Die Feen* given there in 1888 (five years after the composer's death). But a five-hours' rehearsal convinced everyone of the impossibility of a revival. "The arias and other numbers," said Vogl, "were such ludicrous and undisguised imitations of Donizetti and other popular composers of that time that we all burst out laughing, and kept up the merriment throughout the rehearsal. I was for giving the opera, in spite of this, as a curiosity, and because it could, of course, not injure Wagner's reputation; nor was the Intendant quite averse to giving it. Ultimately, however, we all agreed that it would be better to leave it alone, less on account of the music than because of the licentious character of the libretto. So the manuscript was shelved again." [1]

A vocal score of *Das Liebesverbot* was first published in 1922, the full score in 1923; and about that time the work was given, as a historical curiosity, in several German theatres.

In 1879 Wagner played the overtures of his first two operas to Cosima. She preferred that to *Die Feen:* he, for his part, thought there was more " genius " in that to *Das Liebesverbot*.[2]

2

The Magdeburg fiasco of *Das Liebesverbot* may or may not have been a catastrophe for German art, but it certainly sounded the knell of the hopes of Wagner's creditors. The hounds were out, the hunt was up, in no time. Every time the musical director came home he found a fresh summons nailed to his door; his creditors actually went to the length of trying to have him arrested, and even from the excusably reticent account of the matter in *Mein Leben* we gather that Wagner found it prudent to keep away from his own dwelling and take up his quarters elsewhere, probably with Minna. But he still found time and energy to push his interests in quarters outside Magdeburg. A fortnight after the catastrophe (on the 11th April), he sent the score of his symphony to Mendelssohn; and on the 19th he despatched to Schumann a bright account of Magdeburg musical life for insertion in the *Neue Zeitschrift für Musik*. Naturally, he says in his letter, he has had to say something of himself in the article, for how could he omit mention of the local music director in an account of the place? Besides, he has to give the world news of his opera, for no one else will! " It's a great pity that one has to look after oneself! " He gives a humorous account of the deplorable state of music in the town, the good Magdeburgers being fonder of food than of music. Still, there is a " big orchestra," that can do wonders when it likes, an excellent singer (Frau Pollert), and " a conductor full of fire and nuptial bliss " (himself, of course: the

---

[1] FWW, I, 47.   [2] MECW, I, 860.

article did not bear his name). Everybody admits that during the
past winter Magdeburg has had such an opera season as never before — yet everybody has refrained from patronising it. Where
else is a company to be found to compare with this one, a company
that can put on three such sopranos as the Pollert, the Limbach and
the Schindler in Auber's *Lestocq*, to say nothing of the admirable
leading tenors and bass? " When you consider, moreover, that a
young and expert artist like the musical director, Richard Wagner,
put all his brains and skill into making a fine ensemble, you will
see that we could not fail to get genuine artistic treats from our co-
operation." The season had come to an end with a new opera by
Richard Wagner, *Das Liebesverbot*. Owing to one unfortunate circumstance and another, the performance had not been a good one:
" but even had it been otherwise, I cannot understand what could
have induced the composer to allow a work like this to be produced
for the first time in Magdeburg." It grieves the writer that he cannot discuss the opera in detail — " what is a single performance,
and an unclear one at that? " " I know this, however, that if the
composer is fortunate enough to get a good performance of it in
some town of standing, the work will make its way. There is a good
deal in it, and what pleases me, it all *sounds*, it is music and melody,
which are rather lacking in our German operas of to-day. But from
the case of Herr Wagner and myself I see clearly, however, what
torture it is to feel life tingling in every nerve and vein and to have
to live in this city of trade and war." [1]

That he still kept up his spirits to some extent is shown by a letter
of the 20th April, in which he gaily asks Apel to send him " a
small cask of 1834 ": " I still owe my chorus," he explains, " the
promised glass of wine for my opera, but I can't pay for it myself." If Apel means to pay him his contemplated visit, he continues, he must do so quickly. " For it might so happen that soon
I shall be in gaol, and in that case I couldn't offer you much in
the way of company." A fortnight later we find him declaring that
" his horizon is becoming more clouded daily," and accepting
Apel's offer of an asylum at Ermlitz; but apparently this project

---

[1] *Aus Magdeburg*, in GS, Vol. XII. The article appeared in the *Neue Zeitschrift*
on the 3rd May, 1836. It is not to be found in the English translation of the Prose
Works.

of escape came to nothing, for on the 31st May, writing from Berlin, he tells his mother resentfully that Apel had informed him that they were rebuilding at Ermlitz, and consequently there would be no room for him there. He was still slow to see that no one who had had experience of his cumulative demands upon him in the past was anxious to be settled with him indefinitely.

He sent a desperate appeal for help to his brother-in-law Wolfram, but received no answer. A brief visit to Leipzig, undertaken in the hope of raising a loan among his friends and relations there, proved fruitless, unless, as is probable, the ever-faithful Rosalie came to the rescue as usual. All his anxious mother could do was to warn him against the irreparable mistake of a too early and improvident marriage. Back in Magdeburg once more, he had to live, for safety's sake, in the strictest retirement with Minna, every day bringing with it some fresh blow or the apprehension of one. His dog deserted him: this he took as a bad omen. One day he and Minna saw a poor wretch drown in the river; on another occasion, after he had bidden a sorrowful farewell to Minna, he watched with gloomy thoughts the crowd pouring out of the town to witness a criminal being broken on the wheel; and in the evening, taking what was to be his last meal in Magdeburg at the inn, the conversation ran on this ghastly affair and on the sinister elegance of the dress and the manners of the executioner from Halle.

Minna having left for Königsberg, to try to arrange for an engagement there, Richard went to Berlin, where he arrived, for the first time in his life, on the 18th May. He saw Laube once more, who advised him to call on Cerf, the Director of the Königstadt Theatre, with a view to the production of *Das Liebesverbot* — a project that must have seemed all the more feasible from the fact that some of the Magdeburg singers were now working at the Königstadt. This Cerf was a strangely ignorant creature who, taking advantage of the temporary decline in the popularity of the Royal Theatre, was filling his own house with performances of operas of the lighter type. He assured the hungry and hopeful Wagner that he was about to make many changes in his company, and offered him the post of conductor during the absence of Kapellmeister Gläser, the composer, famous at that time, of *Alders Horst*.

[211]

Das Liebesverbot was to be put into rehearsal immediately, and in due course Richard was to step into Gläser's shoes. It soon became apparent, however, that Cerf meant nothing whatever by all he had said to the gullible young man; Wagner had merely wasted in Berlin some valuable weeks of his time. The only compensation brought him by his stay in the Prussian capital was a performance of Spontini's *Ferdinand Cortez*. Though he was not greatly impressed by either the singing or the acting, the drill of the company, the precision of Spontini's conducting, and the general splendour of the production gave him a new standard in opera. As he himself admits, this performance counted for much in the subsequent planning of his own *Rienzi*. Bülow's remark that " *Rienzi* is Meyerbeer's best opera " is excellent as a *mot;* but in sober truth that work owes more to Spontini than to Meyerbeer.[1] Wagner was no doubt also influenced, in *Rienzi,* to some extent by Halévy, whose *La Juive* he saw in Dresden in June, 1837. And as one of the operas he rehearsed and conducted during this period was Auber's *Masaniello,* that work also no doubt played its part in the shaping of the exuberant *Rienzi.*

His only hope now was Königsberg, where Minna had by this time definitely settled down. Thither, accordingly, he went on the 7th July. He found Minna already popular there, and possessing sufficient interest with the theatre management to make them listen to her suggestion that her lover should be engaged as musical director. The post was nominally held at the time by Louis Schuberth, whom Wagner had known, in days gone by, as first 'cellist in the Magdeburg orchestra. In actual fact Schuberth, as we have seen, was attached to the theatre at Riga; but that institution being temporarily closed, he had accepted an interim engagement at Königsberg. He was too competent a man for the Director to be willing to dismiss him out of hand for Wagner's sake. At the same time it was a convenience to have in reserve a second string of Wagner's proved capacity; and so Richard was given a small re-

---

[1] This was clear enough to the contemporaries of Wagner and Spontini. See, for instance, the comments of A. B. Marx, in ME, I, 256. Spontini's influence is particularly evident in the noisy orchestration of *Rienzi*. It is more than likely, too, that the young Wagner picked up on this occasion many a hint as to opera management; for Spontini, unlike the other Kapellmeisters of the period, was not content with merely conducting the music, but took command of the whole production. See ME, I, 220 ff.

taining fee, with the promise that he should step into Schuberth's shoes when the time came for the latter to return to Riga. But Schuberth was in no hurry to leave, for he found the charming Henriette Grosser better company than his wife, whom he had left in Riga, and there was no immediate prospect of the latter theatre re-opening. Schuberth seems not only to have intrigued against Wagner but to have set the orchestra against him. On one occasion, hoping to discredit his dangerous young rival beyond repair, he pleaded illness during a rehearsal of *Euryanthe*, calculating that Wagner would fail abjectly with this difficult work, the score of which he hardly knew. Wagner, however, showed such command and resource at rehearsal that Schuberth found himself sufficiently restored to health to conduct the performance himself.

Wagner's Königsberg sojourn was the most miserable of all his youthful experiences so far, grievous as these had often been. He was tortured by jealousy of Minna, yet reluctant to tie himself to her for life, fretted by his debts, miserably poor, and completely out of touch with everyone at the theatre. In August the company went to Memel for a little time. Wagner crossed the Kurische Haff, in bad weather, in a small sailing boat; in his utter wretchedness of body and soul he was further depressed by the sight, across the sands, of the castle of Runsitten, the scene of one of E. T. A. Hoffmann's best-known stories, *Das Majorat;* the sight of it brought up all kinds of melancholy memories of his fantastic romantic boyhood.

It was to Memel that he asked Dorn to send a reply to a letter he had addressed to him on August 7th, a letter which, as usual when Wagner had a favour to ask, begins and ends with protestations of the writer's profound respect for his correspondent and his undying gratitude to him. He tells Dorn how he, Richard Wagner, " visionary and *ci-devant* Beethovenianer," having two years ago taken up the performance of music as a career, had acted as musical director in Magdeburg. " I can boast of having done so well in this capacity that some former members of the Leipzig opera company could recognise me as your true pupil and emulator, while at the same time I must confess that you would be vastly astonished at the musical transformation that has taken place in my extremist musical views." He tells Dorn how Schuberth stands in his way at

Königsberg, and asks whether there is likely to be a reasonably good theatre at Riga in the autumn, and whether he could possibly get the post of musical director there, in which case his fiancée, Fräulein Planer, would follow him to Riga. She has already, in fact, had an offer from there, but naturally will not accept it unless he can be there with her. He asks Dorn to reply to him at the Memel *poste restante*, and assures him that his attitude towards him will always be " that of the protected towards the protector and bene-factor." [1] Unspeakably wretched in his company and his work, and suffering acutely from the bleakness of the climate, his one consolation was Minna. It was through her that the next decisive change in his fortunes came. On the return of the company to Königsberg, about the middle of September, he and Minna were offered engagements at Danzig, where the perpetually wandering Wolfram and Klara were now settled for a time. Richard had found a good friend in Königsberg in one Abraham Möller, a citizen of the place whose passion was the theatre, and who, though he had lost his one-time large fortune, was still a person of im-portance in the theatrical life of the town. Möller now played skil-fully upon the Director's fear of losing Minna; and to retain her, a fresh contract was signed, giving Wagner the definite promise of the post of musical director from the following Easter. By this time his marriage with Minna had been decided upon, and for the wed-ding he was promised a benefit at the theatre, for which he chose *Masaniello*. The marriage, as we have seen, took place on the 24th November, 1836.

His connection with the Königsberg theatre as musical director was destined to be a short one, and his residence in that town was almost completely barren so far as his inner artistic development was concerned. He wrote his *Rule Britannia* Overture (it was fin-ished on the 15th March, 1837), and sketched another work of a similar kind on Napoleon, which, however, came to nothing — because, according to his own humorous account, he could not settle for himself the grave question whether the fate of the Em-peror at Moscow should be indicated by a stroke on the tom-tom

---

[1] DEE, pp. 158–161. Wagner sought Dorn's advice because the latter was him-self at Riga at that time, and would know all there was to be known about the theatre and the town.

or not. We possess also some sketches of his — a March and a Chorus of Priests — that apparently relate to incidental music supplied by him to some play dealing with the conflict between ancient Prussian paganism and Christianity. They are interesting by reason of the anticipation, in the incantation melody, of the " Question " motive in *Lohengrin*, and therefore of certain passages in the *Ring* that have an affinity with this.[1] Warned by the catastrophe of *Das Liebesverbot* of the danger of flying too high in the German provinces, he worked out the plan of a light opera, in two acts, that should make no demands on soloists and chorus that could not be met by a company of the modest resources of that of Königsberg. This was *Männerlist grösser als Frauenlist, oder Die glückliche Bärenfamilie (Woman Outwitted by Man, or The Happy Bear-Family)*, the subject of which he discovered in one of the stories in the *Arabian Nights*. The text will be found in Volume XI of his Collected Works; the music, which he intended to be in the light French style, was never written, though he appears to have made a few sketches for it. According to his own account, he turned against the subject when he discovered that it was leading him to the composition of still more music " *à la* Adam." [2]

To the Königsberg epoch belongs an article *On Dramatic Song*, which was published for the first time, from a manuscript that had somehow survived, in the *Allgemeine Deutsche Musik-Zeitung* in 1888 — five years after Wagner's death. In this article he finds fault with most German singing: not only is the German throat less adapted by nature for singing than the Italian, but the majority of German singers take up opera with insufficient technical training, trusting to their power of *Affekt* to see them through. The result is that the voices mostly break down in a few years: Schröder-Devrient had made this mistake at the commencement of her career, and, faced with the possibility of a total loss of voice, had

---

[1] See Tappert's article, *Perkunos-Lohengrin*, in the *Musikalisches Wochenblatt*, 1887, pp. 414, 415, and GRW, I, 274–276.

[2] In this libretto Wagner seems to have turned a humorous eye, in Geyer fashion, on the Wagner family circle. The name of the "rich jeweller," Julius Wander, is an obvious side-glance at his peripatetic goldsmith brother Julius, whose wanderings never brought him fortune. The acrobatic bear, who is named Richard in the opera, is of course Wagner himself. The name of the bear-leader, Gregor, is alliteratively suggestive of Geyer.

had to give up her work and go through a course of severe training. A technique of any kind, says Wagner, must be acquired before, not during, the practice of the art. He compares Mozart, who had mastered the technique of composition so thoroughly as a child that in his later years he could take the most difficult problems in his stride, solving them as if he were unconscious of them, with Weber, who began his serious study of technique rather too late in life ever to have an easy command of it.[1]

In the winter he seems to have given a series of orchestral concerts of his own in the town; we know for certain that he conducted one, at which he probably produced his *Rule Britannia* Overture. At the beginning of April Schuberth left Königsberg, and Richard was at last able to assume full charge of the opera. He set himself, with his usual energy and conscientiousness, to improve the quality of the performances and to overcome the enmities that his predecessor had created for him in the town; but it soon became evident to everyone that the theatre was bankrupt, and in May the Director, Hübsch, announced that he had no alternative but to close down. Wagner, however, succeeded in inducing him to make a further effort to continue. The attempt to save the sinking ship meant a more drastic discipline in the theatre, which did not improve the young Kapellmeister's popularity there; but he sought relief in his work from his growing domestic troubles, for Minna's resentment at the straits to which he had reduced her, combined with her usual too accommodating behaviour towards the well-to-do patrons of the institution, had by this time led to an estrangement between the ill-assorted pair, and Wagner mostly preferred to be anywhere but in his own home.

3

Matters between them came to a crisis in May, 1837. On the 31st of that month, when he was leaving the house in the morning, expecting to be detained at the theatre till late in the afternoon, he was surprised and disturbed at the passionate and tearful way in which Minna and her daughter Natalie, who had been living with them for some time, took leave of him. On his return, worn out with

---

[1] The article will be found in RWGS, Vol. XII. It is not in Ellis's English version of the Prose Works.

the labour and the annoyances of the theatre, he was astonished to hear that the pair had not yet returned from their walk. Absent-mindedly opening Minna's work-table, he found it empty. A glance in the wardrobe showed him that that too had been emptied: Minna had planned her flight so cunningly that even the maid was un-aware of it. Through Möller, Richard soon discovered that a rich local merchant named Dietrich, a patron of the theatre, who had already annoyed Wagner by his attentions to Minna and by the familiar, quasi-possessive way in which he spoke of her in public, had also left Königsberg that morning by special coach, taking the road to Berlin. Wagner's jealousy of Dietrich had already led to more than one quarrel with Minna, but she had always baffled him with her customary assumption of an air of injured innocence. He made an attempt to pursue the ordinary mail coach by which Minna was presumably travelling, but his funds were insufficient to carry him further than Elbing, and for the moment he had to return, in utter misery, to Königsberg.

This was the last straw. It was Minna alone who had made the town — a hundred miles from German civilisation,[1] as he put it in one of his letters — tolerable to him; now his one thought was to get away from a place that was full of bitter memories and held out no hope for the future. Already, in the spring of 1837, he had had to appeal to the Königsberg Law Court to suspend the distraint that had been ordered on his furniture (which was already under seal), as he could confidently promise to satisfy his creditor (a musician named Brenner, in Magdeburg) within three weeks.[2] If he actually succeeded in doing this, it could only have been by further borrowing; and week by week he must have been getting deeper and deeper into the mire. Small as his salary from the theatre may have been, it should have been enough, in conjunction with that of Minna, to keep them in the modest comfort that was as much as the minor theatrical artist of that day was accustomed to expect. But with a top-heavy pile of debts in every town in which he had ever lived, and with his creditors becoming more and more

---

[1] Königsberg is nearly four hundred miles, as the crow flies, from Dresden — an enormous distance in those days — and rather more than that from Magdeburg. The next step in Wagner's itinerary as a conductor was to carry him to Riga, still further from "German civilisation."

[2] RWKK, I, 102.

pressing as the months went on, he could never have had a groschen of his salary to call his own, while it is clear that Minna must have had to submit to an incessant drain on her own slender resources. By this time she was completely disillusioned with regard to him. She had always been able to maintain herself and her daughter, and to contribute to the keep of her parents, out of her own earnings. She now saw herself not only reduced to positive privation by his follies and his lack of delicacy where borrowing and repaying were concerned, but with her simple bourgeois standard of moral values in these matters incessantly outraged by conflicts with tradesmen, creditors, and the minions of the law. She fled from him because, for the moment, she could endure no more of him: the marriage had not been of her seeking, and she must have realised that any further association with him meant the sure ruin not only of herself but of those dependent on her, for she was nearing her thirties, and the outlook was consequently none too reassuring for a woman who had nothing with which to hold her own against her rivals in the theatre but her youth and her looks. It would have been better for both her and Wagner, in the long run, if she had steadfastly refused to live with him again, or he had declined to take her back. But he not only wanted Minna — and when Wagner wanted anything he managed to get it, sooner or later, by hook or by crook — but he was so pitiful an object that in the end the impulses of her heart once more over-rode her reason.

For the moment, indeed, his anger at having to play the rôle of the deceived and abandoned husband before a cynical world getting the upper hand of even his vast self-pity, he contemplated moving for a divorce. He neglects to tell us this in *Mein Leben*, but his contemporary letters place it beyond doubt. Minna had of course gone to her parents in Dresden, Dietrich, as Wagner discovered later, having accompanied her only part of the journey, "ostensibly to help her in a friendly way." Somehow or other, perhaps by selling his wedding presents, Richard managed to get to Leipzig, whence we find him, on the 7th June, writing to Schindelmeisser,[1] who at that time was Kapellmeister at the Königstadt Theatre in

---

[1] Louis Schindelmeisser was the younger step-brother of Dorn. Born in 1811, he was virtually the same age as Wagner, whom he had known since the latter's Leipzig student days. He acted as Kapellmeister in various towns in later life, and was always a good friend to Wagner and a warm admirer of his genius. He died in 1864.

Berlin, urging him to do all he can to help him to conclude a contract with Holtei, the theatre director at Riga. He wants a salary of
1000 silver roubles, the engagement to be for two or three years;
he can go there in mid-July. That he had no thought at this time
of linking his fate with that of Minna again is shown by his telling
Schindelmeisser that his wife does not come into the matter at all.
A few days later, writing now from Dresden, on the 12th June,
1837, he tells Schindelmeisser that he is that day addressing to
the Königsberg tribunal a demand for divorce. " I am breadless,"
he continues; " I *must* get Riga." He was then staying at his sister
Ottilie's house; it was no doubt on the advice of some of his relations that he contemplated separating from Minna. He sought
her out: she was living with her parents, who greeted him coldly.
At the sight of her his heart melted; he admitted the wrong he
had done her, and spoke hopefully of the prospective Riga engagement, which, if it materialised, would constitute the foundation of a new and better life for him. She, on her side, while her
manner towards him was evidence of the conflict of emotions within
her, was touched, as she always was, by his patent misery of body
and of soul, and by the obvious sincerity of his repentance.

After spending " a painful and anxious week " with her without
wholly succeeding in winning her over, he went on to Berlin, where
he signed the agreement with Holtei for Riga, at a salary, however, of only 800 roubles. On his return to Dresden he found Minna
so much better disposed towards him that he prevailed upon her to
leave her parents' house and live with him in modest lodgings a
few miles out of the town, at Blasewitz. For a few weeks all was
well: then, he tells us, he " found the situation worsening again
without any visible reason." Minna told him that she had had advantageous offers from several theatres, and one day surprised him
with the announcement that she was going on a short pleasure
excursion, to last a week, with the family of one of the girl friends
of her youth. Perturbed, yet unable to protest, he accompanied her
to Dresden, left her at her parents' house, and returned to Blasewitz. A few days later he received a visit from her eldest sister, who
asked him for the necessary written permission to enable his wife
to apply for a passport. Suspicious and alarmed, he went back to
Dresden to get what information he could from Minna's parents.

They greeted him roughly, reproached him for being the cause of all their daughter's troubles, and returned only evasive answers to his enquiries. Back in Blasewitz once more, the harassed man found a letter from Möller that seemed to explain everything: Dietrich had left Königsberg for Dresden. Hurrying to the hotel mentioned in Möller's letter, he found that Dietrich had indeed been there, but had left again; Minna, too, had vanished. " I now knew enough," he says in *Mein Leben*, " to demand of the Fates why, at so early an age, I should have to go through this terrible experience, which, as it seemed to me, would poison my whole existence." [1]

---

[1] Altmann (RWML, II, 1017) thinks that Wagner's chronology is wrong — that it was after this *second* flight of Minna that he addressed to the Königsberg Tribunal the petition for divorce referred to in his letter to Schindelmeisser of the 12th June. But that is impossible. Minna had fled from Königsberg on the 31st May. Wagner left that town in pursuit on the 3rd June. His letters show him to have been in Leipzig on the 7th, and in Dresden on the 12th. It must have been after that that he went to Berlin, where he fixed up the Riga engagement with Holtei. From there he proceeded to Dresden once more, and then, for a few weeks, as he says, to Blasewitz. He was in Riga by about the end of August. The story as told in *Mein Leben* is plainly correct in every detail. The matter has been confused by either ignorance or carelessness or disingenuousness on Glasenapp's part (GRW, 1st edition, I, 239). He puts it that "In the summer of 1837 Wagner went to Dresden for a short time, via Berlin." This conceals the fact that Wagner went first of all to Dresden, then to Berlin, and then, "for a short time," to Dresden once more. The matter is further complicated by Ashton Ellis, who, in his English version of Glasenapp, refers to the letter of the 12th June to Schindelmeisser (which had been published after the appearance of Glasenapp's volume), but says the letter shows that Wagner "stayed en garçon for a few weeks at Dresden with his sister Ottilie and her husband Hermann Brockhaus." There is nothing whatever in that letter to warrant Ellis's addition of the words "for a few weeks." The "few weeks" of Wagner's stay in Dresden were those *after* his visit to Berlin, when he once more either stayed with Ottilie, or at all events spent the bulk of his time in her and Hermann's company. See ELW, I, 225.

In his fourth edition (1905) Glasenapp repeats his first erroneous statement that Wagner went direct from Königsberg to Berlin, and from there to Dresden, and then refers to the two letters to Schindelmeisser as showing that Wagner went from Dresden to Berlin — without seeing that the two statements are in direct conflict with each other and with the dates. The publication of the letter of the 12th June, 1837, having made further concealment of the divorce plan impossible, Glasenapp now quotes the vital passage, but without comment. Though he must surely have known all the circumstances (he had been given access to the material at Wahnfried as early as 1873 for his official biography), he loads the dice against Minna in this matter, without any reference to Wagner's own admissions, in *Mein Leben*, that he had tried the poor woman beyond endurance.

This letter to Schindelmeisser was first of all published in the *New York Tribune* in 1899, then in the *Allgemeine Musikzeitung* of the same year, then, in 1903, in the *Bayreuther Blätter*, the literary organ of Wahnfried. In spite of the fact that a full text had previously been made public in the *New York Tribune* and the *Allgemeine Musikzeitung*, the passage relating to the contemplated divorce was omitted from the reprint in the *Bayreuther Blätter!* This little incident is typical of the difficulties that were needlessly placed in the way of impartial Wagner research in those days.

4

He came daily from Blasewitz to Dresden to see Ottilie and her husband, who had a delightful house in the Grosser Garten. There he found not only consolation in his boundless misery but a new intellectual stimulus. Hermann Brockhaus was at once one of the kindest and one of the best learned of men; Ottilie was full of sisterly sympathy and tact. A period of spiritual convalescence set in for Richard; unable, by his very nature, to succumb to depression for long, a new range of intellectual and artistic interests was already opening out before his resilient spirit. He was impressed by performances of Halévy's *Jewess* and Spohr's *Jessonda* at the Dresden Opera. During the last days with Minna he had been reading Bulwer Lytton's *Rienzi;* and now the subject began to take shape within him as an opera with the most fascinating possibilities. He sent the score of the *Rule Britannia* Overture to the London Philharmonic Society, with some vague idea of obtaining a footing in London. In Magdeburg he had sketched out an opera based on Heinrich König's novel *Die hohe Braut.* With his eye already on Paris, he had had the sketch turned into French for him, and sent the manuscript to Scribe, from Königsberg, in the autumn of 1836, suggesting that this most celebrated of French libretto manufacturers should cast it into verse on condition that he secured for Wagner a commission to compose the music for the Paris Opéra! Having received no reply to his letter, he wrote again in the spring of 1837, this time sending to Scribe, as a specimen of his musical powers, the score of *Das Liebesverbot,* which, he suggested, Scribe should submit to the judgment of Meyerbeer and Auber. If their opinion was favourable, then Scribe, he modestly suggested, might adapt a text to it for production at the Opéra-Comique. At the same time he wrote to August Lewald, in Stuttgart, telling him what he had done, and sending him a copy of the Carnival Song from the opera. Lewald not only published the Song in his quarterly journal *Europa* but gave the young composer a welcome piece of publicity.

To return to the original point of this footnote: so far from Wagner being wrong in his chronology of this period, it is clear that he is correct both in his account of the actual events between the 31st May and the middle of August and in his psychological analysis of Minna and of himself.

He told his readers that the Song was out of an opera which the Music Director in Königsberg had sent to the great Scribe with a view to a production in Paris — a bit of information that no doubt impressed them hugely. The composer, it seems, had turned over the author's rights in the libretto to Scribe, so as to avoid the "intrigues" normally to be expected from French authors when a foreigner invaded their literary territory. "As soon as I hear the result of the steps taken by my young friend," continued Lewald, "I will communicate them to the public. . . . If the state of things in Germany does not alter; if it is to become almost more difficult for the talented composer to force his work into the smallest local theatre in Germany than into Paris itself; if the German theatre authorities are to go on disdainfully turning down the good and deserving that still springs up here and there, and theatrical criticism is to be left, as a shameful trade, to the ignorant, the only course left to the young aspirant is to appeal to Abroad." [1]

The further history of *Die hohe Braut* and the copy of *Das Liebesverbot* sent to Scribe may as well be given here. When, seemingly in 1839, his sister Cäcilie became engaged to Eduard Avenarius, who acted as agent of the Brockhaus firm in Paris, Wagner wrote to this gentleman asking him to see Scribe about the matter. Avenarius did so. Scribe, he discovered, had not only received the score of *Das Liebesverbot* but had had part of it played over to him by a pupil of the Conservatoire; he must at any rate have glanced at the first act of *Die hohe Braut,* for he dimly remembered the episode of the harp-player (Brigitta). Little as this really meant, the encouraging fact that Scribe was actually aware of his existence played its part in determining Wagner's journey to Paris in the summer of 1839. In November, 1838, he tried to induce Lewald to use his "influence" — though it is not very clear what "influence" Lewald could have in a matter of this kind — to extract an answer from Scribe about the libretto of *Die hohe Braut.* But still no word came from Paris, and the libretto remained on Wagner's hands till his Dresden period, when he offered it to his colleague Reissiger, who had been complaining of his difficulty in getting a good subject for an opera. Richard took the trouble to

---

[1] EU, 1837, II, 240. I have the feeling that Lewald is repeating the actual words of Wagner's letter to him. The letter, however, has apparently not survived.

turn his sketch into verse form for him, but for some reason or other Reissiger fought shy of it; Wagner believed later that he had been set against it by his wife, who suspected some cunning trick on his younger rival's part. Wagner then offered the book to his friend Kittl, who, in 1842, had succeeded Dionys Weber as head of the Prague Conservatoire. Kittl set the libretto to music; and, after the Austrian Court authorities had made several alterations in the text, his work was produced at Prague, with considerable success, on the 19th February, 1848, under the title of *Bianca und Giuseppe, oder die Franzosen vor Nizza*.[1] In *Mein Leben* Wagner humorously notes that a Prague critic was so impressed by the excellence of the libretto that he thought it a mistake on Wagner's part to dabble in composition; while Laube, on the other hand, after hearing *Tannhäuser*, thought it a pity that so good a composer did not get some "experienced dramatist" to supply him with his texts.

5

To the period of the despatch of the score of *Das Liebesverbot* to Scribe belong a letter and an essay both of which, until quite recently, have been mis-dated. In No. 18 of the *Berliner Tageblatt* (*Zeitgeist*), 1886, there was first published a letter from Wagner to Meyerbeer that apparently exists only in the form of a draft. It is addressed to "Monsieur Meyerbeer, compositeur et chevalier de légion d'honneur à Paris," and begins "Most honoured Sir and Master." Wagner, "an unknown man, writing from a foreign place," apologises for writing to Meyerbeer.

"I am as yet not twenty-four years old: I was born in Leipzig: while attending the University there, I decided, some six years ago, to devote myself to music: I was driven to this by a passionate veneration for Beethoven, by reason of which my earliest productive energy took an infinitely one-sided direction: since that time, and especially since I entered upon real life and practice, my views upon the present standpoint of music, especially dramatic music, have undergone a significant change: and shall I deny that it was precisely *your* works that pointed out this new direction to me? This would be decidedly the most inappropriate of places for me to launch out into awkward praise of your genius: I will only say that in you I recognised the

---

[1] The text will be found in RWGS, XI.

complete fulfilment of the mission of the German, who took as his model the best features of the Italians and of the French school in order to make the creations of his own genius *universal.*"

He would like, he continues, to go to Paris. He has sent the score of his opera *Das Liebesverbot* to Scribe, asking him to submit it to Meyerbeer, whose opinion he eagerly awaits.[1]

At one time this draft was held to date from the Riga period: but there can be no question that the letter was sent from Königsberg in 1837. It links up, in a curious way, with the draft of a never-published article of Wagner's on *Les Huguenots,* the autograph of which was offered for sale by the Berlin book-dealer, Leo Liepmannssohn, in 1886. Max Kalbeck gave some extracts from the article in the *Neues Wiener Tageblatt* in 1892. Julius Kapp published as much as could then be collected of the article in the second April issue, 1911, of *Die Musik.* In this form it was reprinted in Volume XII of RWGS. (It is consequently not to be found in Ellis's English version of Wagner's Prose Works, the final volume of which was issued in 1899.) Later a complete copy of the article (the manuscript of which was the property of a private collector) came into the possession of the editor of the *Gesammelte Schriften,* and the portions that had been omitted from the reprint in the body of the text were added in an appendix (RWGS, XII, 420–422).

It has always been supposed that this article, unpublished at the time of the writing of it, belonged to Wagner's Paris days: even in the latest edition of his Life of Wagner [2] Julius Kapp dates it 1840, and describes it as a continuation of the article on *German Music.* (See Chapter VII.) There can be no question, however, that the editor of Volume XII of the *Gesammelte Schriften* is correct in saying that the article manifestly belongs to an earlier epoch. The opinion of Meyerbeer expressed in it was one that Wagner assuredly did not hold in 1840, while it is certainly true of the Wagner of 1837. Moreover, the view of Meyerbeer's successful eclecticism expressed in the letter quoted above is the very thesis of the article, of which the following is a summary:

The starting-point of the article is *Les Huguenots,* which had been produced in Paris in February, 1836. Like Handel, Gluck,

---

[1] RWKK, I, 101.   [2] JKRW, p. 216.

and Mozart, Meyerbeer is a German; and it is of these great Germans that he reminds us. He is not only a master of technique but a man of culture. Like so many other German composers, he had to leave Germany to perfect himself in his art. In Italy he learned beauty of form. In France he found flourishing an extraordinary development of the pure French genius, the culmination of which is Auber's unsurpassable *Masaniello*. Into this new territory Meyerbeer has made his way, without losing his native virtues as a German. The French national manner was tending to become a mannerism: Meyerbeer adopted what was best in it and raised it to the dignity of the universal: his style has its foundations in the hearts and ears of the folk. Neither in France nor in Italy did he become the slave of the foreign spirit, because he never lost touch with his German heritage: this heritage is particularly evident in his bent towards the religious and the philosophical. His style, as the result of the admixture of all these elements, has attained to a noble, ideal independence: his forms are gigantic, the finest flower of his genius in this regard being the conjuration scene in the forth act of *Les Huguenots*; yet everything is simple and clear. To go beyond Meyerbeer is impossible: that phase of dramatic music has ended with him: he closes an epoch and a genre as Handel, Gluck, Mozart and Beethoven had done: but " Time, in its unresting creative energy, must produce a new direction, along which what these heroes did in their way must be done again in another. Nevertheless, he is still living, and in the fullness of his powers: and so let us not anticipate, but await the new birth of his genius."

The draft of the article seems to exist in two forms. The passages added in the appendix to the reprint in RWGS contain some remarks about Rossini having broken up the older moulds and inaugurated a new epoch of dramatic music, and a lament over the " non-existence " of the German nation: its geniuses are driven abroad to realise themselves; there it is their function to endow foreign limitations with universality; the German's lack of nationality is compensated by the naïveté and the purity of his feeling, which keep him sane and sound through all aberrations.

The whole article throws a significant light on the Wagner of this period. His superficial theatrical experiences had given him something of a distaste for the heavier German music, and so made him peculiarly susceptible to the expert eclecticism of Meyerbeer: but at the same time there were the drawings in him of that purely German nationalism which Riga was to foster and Paris and the *Flying Dutchman* to consolidate for good. Why the article was never published we do not know.

6

At the end of August, 1837, it was time for Wagner to leave the pleasant and comforting society of Ottilie and her husband, and make arrangements for taking up his new job in Riga. At first there was some difficulty in connection with his passport; we find him asking, but in vain, a certain Dr. Schellwitz, of Leipzig, to obtain for him a passport from that place. His failure to do his year of military service no longer counted against him, it is true, now that he was married. He had left Saxony for Prussia three years before without a passport, and had returned without one. He could not obtain one from his last place of residence in Prussia — Königsberg — without returning there; and his debts in the place made that impossible unless he were prepared to run the risk of never getting to Riga at all. He avoided Leipzig, being out of tune with his relations there; and so, to his eternal regret, he missed his last opportunity to see his beloved Rosalie, who died in the following October, after little more than a year of marriage. He went from Dresden to Berlin, where he somehow managed to obtain a passport, and received his final instructions from his new Director, Karl von Holtei. In Berlin he ran across Minna's sister Amalie; he confided his matrimonial troubles to the good-hearted girl, and the pair found relief for their feelings in copious weeping at a performance of *Fidelio* which they attended together. At Schwerin he had a half-hope of hearing something of Minna, but was disappointed. From Lübeck he had to go to Riga by boat, the sea passage being cheaper than the land journey. At Travemünde he had to wait a week for a favourable wind: Wagner spent the time in a wretched sailors' tavern, finding refreshment in a reading of the story of *Till Eulenspiegel*, which turned his restless mind in the direction of a German comic opera; he tells us that the book and the tavern were often in his thoughts when, in later years, he

[226]

was drafting the text of his *Jung Siegfried*. At last, after a four days' passage, he landed, at Bolderaa, on Russian soil.

He was gratified to find himself at Riga, where he first of all took lodgings in the Schmiedestrasse, a few minutes' walk from the theatre, in a German colony, that provided the funds for the running of the theatre. Its patrons wanted only the lightest fare; for that reason they had placed the direction of the theatre in the hands of Holtei, a man of chequered career who, himself a dramatist of sorts, was notoriously not overburdened with artistic idealism. He had been appointed Director of the local theatre, which had just been reorganised financially, in January, 1837. His only reason for engaging Wagner was that Richard was young and supposed to be enamoured of the light French and Italian style of music for which the Riga theatre patrons clamoured. Unfortunately for Holtei, just at this time Wagner's taste was undergoing a secret and silent change; the recent mournful events of his life and the mysterious chemistry of genius were combining to purge him of the musical superficialities and frivolities of his reckless youth. He addressed himself, however, to his new task with the energy and scrupulousness that were normal with him where the work of the theatre was concerned.

He found the company as yet incomplete, and everything in the theatre in confusion. The season was to have opened on September 16th with *Norma*. The singer of the chief part not having arrived, however, and one difficulty or another cropping up in connection with most of the other available operas of the repertory, *La Dame Blanche* had at last to be put on as a stop-gap. He gives Schindelmeisser an account of the personnel of his company in a letter of the following day: a good tenor (Köhler), a first-rate bass-baritone (Günther), the rest passable, the chorus good enough as far as their voices are concerned, but ruined by their exertions in the spoken drama, the orchestra still in the making, the new members being better than the old; the ensemble, too, had still to be made. The stage, the theatre and the audiences were all tiny. The population of Riga at that time was only about 70,000; and the total clientèle of the German theatre was estimated at some 3,000. The orchestra was small, but not quite so small as a careless reading of *Mein Leben* has led some people to believe. Wagner says there that " the orchestral space was calculated only for two first violins, two seconds, two violas and a double-bass for the string quartet." This does not mean, as the makers of the English version of *Mein Leben* and several other writers, have supposed, that the *orchestra* consisted merely of these seven players. It stands to reason that no operatic work could have been given under such conditions. What Wagner means is that the orchestral *space* was so small that the string nucleus had to be kept down to a total of seven; but of course there was the usual wood-wind and brass, though on a correspondingly small scale. As a matter of fact, the orchestra numbered twenty-four all told. There was an assistant conductor Franz Löbmann, who had been in Riga since 1834. Wagner managed to have some additions made to the slender orchestral force, but earned Holtei's displeasure in so doing. Irrepressible as ever, he actually planned to give concerts in the winter.[1]

Apart from working at the first two acts of *Rienzi*, the first act of which was fully scored by the 2nd February, 1839, the second act being completed in the piano version by the 9th April, he composed next to nothing during his two years at Riga. For a Singspiel by Karl Blum, *Marie, Max und Michel*,[2] he wrote an additional aria — " Sanfte Wehmut will sich regen," words by Holtei — for the bass Günther, and for the other bass, Scheibler, a song for use in *Die Schweizerfamilie*. The former was published, in 1913, in Volume XV of the Complete Edition of his musical works. It is a pity that the latter aria is lost, as according to his own account its " devotional character " bore witness to the change that was taking place in his musical nature at this time. The Complete Edition (Volume XVI) also contains a National Hymn, for solo, choir and orchestra, to words by Harald von Brackel, to the music of which,

---

[1] In the Burrell Collection is a circular letter from Wagner to the Riga orchestra, dated 11th September, 1838. "This is so like Wagner," say the anonymous compilers of the Catalogue, who lose no opportunity of showing their ill-will to the composer. "No sooner conductor of an orchestra of seven [*sic*] players in an obscure Baltic town than he harangues them as if the whole world were listening." But surely his artistic zeal under such miserable circumstances does him credit. One of his objects in giving these winter concerts was to raise money to meet the pressing demands of his creditors in Magdeburg and elsewhere.

[2] This work was a comparative novelty. It had been produced in Berlin in June, 1836, for the début of Clara Stich. Eduard Devrient, who heard it on that occasion, describes it in a letter to his wife as "a pretty, sprightly operetta, with merry, crazy music." See DBET, p. 33.

he tells us, he tried to give the best possible " despotic-patriarchal colour." The Hymn had considerable success for some years after, and was sung annually in the town on the Tsar's birthday. Apparently he forgot, when writing *Mein Leben*, to mention another effusion of this period — the music for a play by J. Springer, *Die letzte Heidenverschwörung in Preussen, oder der Deutsche Ritterorden in Königsberg*, which was performed on the 17th February, 1837. This was discovered by Dr. Kurt Rattay in 1920. His other compositions of the Riga period were a setting of Scheuerlin's poem *Der Tannenbaum*, which was published as a supplement to *Europa* in 1839,[1] and a bass aria, with male voice chorus, " Norma il predesse," written for the performance of *Norma* at his first benefit in Riga. (For his second benefit he chose *Robert the Devil*.) This aria will be found in Volume XV of his Musical Works. For completeness' sake one must mention also an arrangement for small orchestra of one of Rossini's *Soirées Musicales* (the duet, *Les Mariniers*), made by him for his concert of the 19th (31st) March, 1838.[2]

The defection of the lady (Madame Ernst) who had been engaged as the prima donna of the company — she seems to have pocketed the travelling expenses and the advance made to her on her salary, and then calmly remained in Berlin — had the curious by-effect of bringing Minna once more into Wagner's life. For some reason or other he had a genuine liking for her sister Amalie; and she, on her side, " was glad to accept an engagement that would bring her near me." As the operations of the company had been hampered for six months by the lack of a leading lady, he prevailed on Holtei to engage Amalie for Riga. She was at this time staying in Dresden, and in her letter to Wagner in reply to his offer of an engagement she painted a pitiful portrait of Minna, who was now living with her parents once more. According to his own account, Wagner " naturally took very coolly " the news that she was seriously ill, " for what I had heard about her since she had finally left me had necessarily decided me to authorise my old Königsberg friend [Möller] to take the needful legal steps to procure a divorce. It was certain that Minna had stayed some time at a hotel

---

[1] EU, 1839, p. 620. The song has been reprinted by Ad. Fürstner, Berlin.
[2] See Alfred Einstein's article in ZIMG, 1912, pp. 309–311.

in Hamburg with the sinister Herr Dietrich, and had given such utterly inconsiderate publicity to the fact of her separation from me that the theatrical world was amusing itself over the story in a way that was truly calumnious of me. I simply told Amalie of this, and requested her to spare me further news of her sister."

It has been conjectured that Wagner has here made a mistake in his chronology — that what he really had in mind, when writing *Mein Leben*, was the project of divorce he had mentioned to Schindelmeisser in his letter of the 12th June. But there is no need to assume any error on Wagner's part; the truth of the affair seems to be that he contemplated a divorce immediately after Minna first left him, abandoned the idea, tried, at Blasewitz, to restore the old relations between them, and then, after her *second* flight, and with the evidence he had of her stay at Hamburg with Dietrich, made up his mind to end the matter. It is true that, apart from the letter to Schindelmeisser, we have practically no record of all this except his own account in *Mein Leben* and elsewhere. But such letters and other documents as we possess relating to this time confirm his own story of the events of his life in practically every detail. Nor need we have much hesitation in accepting his interpretation of those events. Whatever criticism we may have to make of his reminiscences of certain other people who came into his life later, his account of Minna in these early years rings true. He writes about her and analyses her during this period without venom, without even dislike; it is manifest that when he was dictating his autobiography after Minna's death he remembered gratefully all she had done for him in the early difficult years, recognised how much he himself was to blame for her occasional revolts against him, and felt a vast pity for not only himself but her. He may not have told us everything, and it would be interesting to have a contemporary account of the matter as Minna saw it.[1] But

---

[1] Mrs. Burrell obtained from Natalie not only the Wagner letters and other documents that had been left to her by Minna, but copious reminiscences of Wagner and her mother. These documents have not yet been published. While it is certain that they contain matter of the highest interest, some of them would obviously have to be scrutinised carefully before the statements in them could be accepted as quite authentic.

Wagner never liked Natalie, of whom he has painted an unflattering portrait in *Mein Leben*, p. 615; according to him, she had been "neglected and spoiled at the critical age," so that she was "undeveloped in body and mind" (*körperlich und geistig*

on the basis of the documents we possess there is no reason whatever to doubt the substantial accuracy of his whole account of the relations between Minna and himself up to the time of his flight to Switzerland in 1849.

"Hereupon," he continues in *Mein Leben*, "Minna herself approached me with a most moving letter, in which she frankly confessed her infidelity. Just as she had been driven to this by despair, so now despair over the ill fortune into which she had fallen had caused her to retrace her steps. It appeared that she had become disillusioned as to the character of her seducer, and the knowledge of her terrible position had brought her to a most painful condition, both physically and morally, in which, ill and unhappy, she turned to me again to acknowledge her guilt, to implore my forgiveness, and to assure me that, in spite of everything, she was now at last fully conscious of her love for me. Never before had I heard such sentiments from Minna, and never was I to hear them from her again, save in one moving hour at a much later time [during the Wesendonk affair, in 1858] when a similar expression affected me as profoundly and wrought the same change in me as this letter of hers had done. I wrote in reply that there should never again be any mention between us of what had occurred, for which I took on myself the chief blame; and I can pride myself on having kept this resolution to the letter."

---

schwerfällig entwickelt), "awkward and silly" (*einfältig*). The main difficulty with regard to her in the Wagner household came from the fact that she always regarded herself as Minna's sister, so that Minna had no real authority over her. "Minna's temper (*Heftigkeit*)," says Wagner, "and her increasingly rough and jeering manner towards her [Wagner is speaking now of about 1850] made the naturally very good-natured girl, in time, quite stubborn and malignant, so that the mutual behaviour of the 'sisters' often led to the most unpleasant disturbances of our domestic peace."

If, as is not unlikely, Mrs. Burrell showed Natalie these disparaging references to herself in *Mein Leben*, the latter's normal dislike of Wagner would hardly be diminished. It is not improbable that it was from Mrs. Burrell, who met her in 1890, that she learned for the first time that she was Minna's daughter. A document in the Burrell Collection shows Minna's mother (Frau Planer) signing herself "Your Mother" in a letter to Natalie as late as 1853. Minna and the Planer family kept the secret from Natalie to the end: Minna, in her will of 1865, left her property to my "sister Natalie." After her marriage to one Bilz, in 1868, Natalie bore the name of Bilz-Planer.

Her reminiscences, so far as they relate to the earlier years, would certainly have to be accepted with caution. Assuming her to have been born about 1827, she would be only some seven years old in 1834, when she first "reminiscences" of the pair began, and only thirteen when she was living with them in Paris. Even if her recollection of those days was uncoloured by prejudice, which is slightly improbable, it would be dangerous to rely implicitly on the old woman's memory, in 1891, of the events of half a century earlier. She would be a more reliable authority on the events of 1850 (the year of the Jessie Laussot affair) and later.

As it happens, Wagner's account of the matter in *Mein Leben* is confirmed, in a somewhat unexpected way, at virtually every point by a letter of his to Minna of the 18th May, 1859. Still brooding sorely over the Wesendonk catastrophe of August 1858, and with health so grievously damaged that at times she was mentally hardly normal, Minna had apparently been re-reading Wagner's *Communication to my Friends* (that had been published in 1851), and had expressed her resentment at the references there to the early relations of herself and Richard. In the course of his account of his intellectual, musical, and moral development Wagner had spoken of the price he had had to pay, as a very young man, for his " modern levity "; " I fell in love, married in a caprice of passion,[1] tortured myself and others with the unpleasantness of a poverty-stricken home, and thus fell into that misery whose nature it is to bring thousands upon thousands to the ground." Then he tells how the longing arose in him to force his way out of all this wretchedness, material and spiritual: " my domestic tribulations increased," he says, and he sought an escape from the present and its too agonising reality in the historical fiction of *Rienzi*.

This passage in the *Communication* had evidently rankled in poor Minna's mind, and Wagner's letter of 1859 is by way of a mollifying reply to her reproaches. *She* would no doubt have preferred him, as he puts it, " to give her a handsome testimonial in the eyes of the world for her loyalty and self-sacrifice." But, he explains, she has misunderstood the whole purport of the *Communication:* there he was not writing a formal autobiography of himself as a man, but merely outlining, for the information of those who were interested in him as an artist, the vital phases of his life so far as these bore upon the evolution of his art.

" So," he continues, trying his best to soothe the poor sick, distracted creature, " if anyone in future speaks to you, with a dubious look, about that passage, just laugh in his face and say: ' Well, he was so crazy that he led me a nice dance with his jealousy, and in order that no one else might come near me he insisted on marriage, and that in

---

[1] *Heirathete in heftigem Eigensinne* — which is misleadingly rendered by Ashton Ellis as "married in feverish haste." Minna might not have objected to his saying he had married in haste; what had wounded her was his telling the world that the marriage was the result of a caprice of passion on his part. She felt that this was equivalent to a public avowal that he now regretted the step.

such unfavourable and beggarly circumstances that my calm reflection told me in advance what misery we should have to go through. But what was I to do? I loved him also; and so the callow young couple that we were plunged madly into a wretchedness that soon enough became so intense, so dolorous, that I myself believed I could not bear it any longer; and so one day I ran away from my reckless, headstrong young husband, who, weighed down with debts as he was, and with the prospect before us of a summer without any earnings, plagued me in addition with the fiercest outbursts of an intolerable jealousy."

Thus, he says in 1859, she might reply. But, he goes on, developing his own case with his usual forensic skill, an explanation of this kind would only be likely to provoke from impartial listeners the rejoinder that she could not have truly loved her husband to leave him in such circumstances, seeing that his jealousy was the result of his own excess of love — the proof of the overwhelming nature of that love being the imprudence with which he had insisted on so hasty a marriage at so impossible a time. This view of her conduct, he now tells her, had actually been put to him at the time by Hermann Brockhaus.[1] But, the skilled self-advocate continues, if anyone in the future should express this view to her, she could answer him thus:

"undoubtedly my love for Richard had vanished in those critical days, but I do not believe matters would have gone so far if a man of good position and ample means had not approached me, just at that time, with so strong a seeming of heartfelt and anxious sympathy for me in my sufferings, and protested this sympathy in so seductive a manner, that under all these conflicting impressions I wavered for a while, and in Richard's love for me, that manifested itself only in such wounding excesses that I could hardly recognise it any more, I could see no adequate compensation for all the misery this unhappy, capricious and untimely marriage had brought on both of us. Yes, I must reproach myself with having for a while been made uncertain of myself by all this; and whoever takes everything into account will be able to forgive the young wife for so far yielding to temptation that at first she was alienated from her husband, treated him as an enemy, misled him as to her steps, and wavered in her choice between him and another to such a point that that other, alas, could make it appear as if she had been more favourably disposed towards him than was really the case. But it was precisely this affair that was the proving of

---

[1] This confirms the suspicion that the idea of obtaining a divorce from her in 1837 had been the result of his conversations with his relatives.

me, and in *it* I first won the full conviction of my love for Richard, which finally emerged as the fruit of that regrettable aberration. Now, when it had come to a decision, I recognized clearly how much I loved Richard, so that I prevailed on myself to confess my fault to him — who had now had to give me up entirely and had accepted an engagement in far-off Riga — and ask for forgiveness, disclosing to him that it was only my love for him, of which I had become conscious, that could have induced me to do so. Richard too had meanwhile had much to surmount, and in particular his love for me had been put to a severe test; appearances had given him the suspicion, indeed the belief, that I had completely betrayed him and given myself to another; newspapers had been sent to him from Hamburg in which he read that I had been staying with that other at *the same hotel;* what could the poor man believe than just the worst? He had even received letters in which he was positively derided for my conduct; even from the members of the theatre at which he was engaged there came to him insinuations, covert and overt, in which he was made sport of as a deceived husband. But he withstood that test, and it proved that the earlier violent and capricious passion had made place for an earnest and sincere love. He replied to me at once with devotion, forgave me everything, called me to him, and has never since breathed a word of my lapse to anyone, even under the sorest temptations that arose later. So love, loyalty and trust took up their abode with us, and the trials of our youth were surmounted, even though the hard tests of maturer life remained in store for us.[1]

It is significant that Wagner's forgiving letter of October 1837, of which he speaks in *Mein Leben,* and the existence of which is proved beyond all doubt by this letter of his of the 18th May, 1859, is *not* in the Burrell Collection. Minna preserved, apparently, every other letter that Wagner wrote to her from the beginning of their association to the end of it. Either she or Natalie must have destroyed, then, the 1837 letter, the contents of it not being of the kind that would be favourable to Minna's reputation; and the mere fact that it has been destroyed is the completest proof imaginable of the veracity of Wagner's account of the episode of her flight and infidelity. Poor Minna little foresaw that by thus covering her tracks, as she imagined, she was delivering herself up to the hunters!

---

[1] RWMW, II, 89ff.

Minna and Amalie arrived at Riga on the 19th October, Amalie making her début as Romeo in Bellini's opera on the 25th. (She appears to have had a charming voice, but to have been a mediocre actress, her short figure being a disadvantage on the stage: her star waned when, a few months later, Frau Pollert joined the company — the same Karoline Pollert whose pretty face and capacity for ultra-matrimonial affection had been the prime cause of the *Liebesverbot* fiasco.) It was agreed between Richard and Minna that the latter was to give up her professional career, a decision which, as it turned out, brought sundry unforeseen disagreeablenesses in its train, the gossip of the company and of the town maliciously ascribing it to well-founded jealousy on Wagner's part. He and Minna had now to live on one income, instead of two as formerly; and the debt-burdened Wagner found it difficult to make ends meet on his meagre salary. Finally, he incurred before long the downright hostility of Holtei. The latter, if we are to believe Wagner, had probably the minimum of interest in women, his ostentatious paying of court to them being regarded in the town as mere strategy to distract public attention from other and less reputable tastes of his. But Wagner one day learned from Minna that the Director had been pursuing her during her husband's absences at the theatre, and had been repulsed. For his own ends, Holtei wished her to become formally attached to the theatre, but she refused, though she appeared at Richard's benefit concerts on the 6th (19th) March, 1838, and the 1st (14th) March, 1839, reciting certain passages from the Schiller plays in which she had formerly taken part. She also appeared on the stage four times in April 1839: it was no doubt on one of these occasions that a local critic described her as being " extremely pleasing in appearance, graceful in bearing, and animated in her facial expression." Failing in his designs on her, Holtei had tried to force on her a certain good-looking and well-to-do young merchant of the town. It was not long before Wagner had to realise that the most deadly of all the enemies he had in Riga was his own Director.

Holtei, who lived until 1880, published his memoirs (*Vierzig Jahre*) in 1843–50, and, curiously enough, nowhere mentions

Wagner's name there, though he tells the story of his own experiences in Riga. He became, in time, an enemy of Wagner and all
that Wagner stood for; and though he nowhere refers to him by
name in any of his published books, he expressed his opinion of
him freely in private. The two were obviously unfitted by their very
nature to work together. Holtei, who regarded the theatre as being
merely a place of entertainment, the more frivolous the better, was
incapable of understanding his young Kapellmeister's passion for
perfection in performance. Wagner, he told a friend in later years,
" harassed the company with endless rehearsals, lasting for hours;
nothing was right in his eyes, nothing good enough for him, nothing
shaded finely enough. This led to complaint after complaint; singers and orchestral players came to me with their grievances against
him. I had to admit to myself that Wagner was right; but I was not
in a position to let him do just as he pleased, for he would have
killed my singers." He certainly had no reason to complain of
Wagner's zeal: fifteen operas were rehearsed and produced by the
Kapellmeister in the first year, twenty-four in the second. But
Holtei resented the young man's ill-concealed distaste for a great
part of the repertory and his obvious desire to avoid the society
of the brainless theatrical crowd; while a further offence on his
part was his refusal to write incidental music for Holtei's own
plays.

The time came when Holtei decided to leave the town in which
his reputation was daily growing more unsavoury. Before doing so
he concluded, behind Wagner's back, an arrangement for the latter's supersession by Heinrich Dorn.[1] When it was settled that
Holtei was to give up the management of the theatre, the committee
chose as his successor the tenor singer Johann Hoffmann, from
Petersburg, who was " guesting " in Riga at the time. According to
Wagner in *Mein Leben*, it was from Hoffmann that he learned that
one of the conditions imposed on the new Director by Holtei was
that an agreement already entered into by the latter for the replacement of Wagner by Dorn should stand. Dorn had been settled at

---

[1] Wagner and Dorn saw a good deal of each other in Riga, their respective
wives being very friendly. Wagner used to play his *Rienzi* music for Dorn, smashing
the strings of the piano in his ardour. Amalie on these occasions sang all the female
parts, any men who might be present doing their best with the others. According
to Dorn, Wagner at this time intended the part of Adriano for Amalie. See DML, p. 3.

Riga as cantor and director of the town's music for a few years before Wagner's arrival in the place: according to Dorn, Holtei had originally offered the theatre post to him, but he had declined it, suggesting instead the engagement of Wagner, who had already proved his competence at Magdeburg and Königsberg. Wagner himself, and following his lead, of course, partisan biographers like Glasenapp, were convinced that he was the victim of a base intrigue on the part of his " false friend " Dorn. But the latter has left us his own account of the affair, and in face of that the sensible course is to refrain from coming to a positive verdict for either side, though Dorn's narrative, which, be it remembered, was published during Wagner's lifetime, has every appearance of being the simple truth.

According to Dorn, Hoffmann approached him, early in March 1839, with an " urgent invitation " to take up the musical director-ship at the theatre, because " the pecuniary situation of the present Kapellmeister, as the result of proceedings in connection with his bills [of exchange], was now such that he could no longer remain in safety in the town." [1] This is perfectly credible: Wagner's des-perate financial condition could be no secret in Riga, and least of all in the theatre; even if he had not talked openly of his dislike for the town and his plan for trying his fortunes in Paris, which he is practically certain to have done, it must have been clear to every-one that flight from his creditors was sooner or later inevitable, and the theatre authorities would be justified in providing in advance for that contingency. No one had any criticism to make of him as a conductor, says Dorn elsewhere: " but his purely artistic tempera-ment could not accommodate itself to bourgeois affairs in so far as these were cramped by debit and credit." [2] Holtei was in a state of continual worry, never knowing the moment when his Kapell-meister would be compelled to leave Riga for legal reasons, for the committee knew that the local tradesmen had lodged many com-plaints against him. Hoffmann had been told of all this, and it was Hoffmann himself, according to Dorn, who gave Wagner notice of dismissal, as matters at the theatre were verging by now on the impossible.

[1] DEE, p. 164.   [2] DML, p. 4.

" Hoffmann," continues Dorn, " turned, with the pre-knowledge of the theatre committee, to me, as one of the people standing nearest to the threatened man, because they wanted to furnish him (totally unprovided with ready money as he was), by means of a payment of two months' salary, with both the means of flight and something to live upon; besides, they hoped that I would be more willing than anyone else to square matters with the theatre administration by serving the first two months gratuitously for the benefit of the younger colleague who could no longer remain in the post. Through a member of the committee, Herr Schwederski, who was friendly both to me and to Wagner, I became convinced of the truth of what had been told me, and I learned that a patron of art in Königsberg, Abraham Möller, had already taken steps to make Wagner's flight effective. Thereupon I accepted the proposal, and I informed Wagner, in writing, that ' not my own but his circumstances had made this change necessary.' [1] Our common friend Schwederski had great difficulty in appeasing, to some extent, the wildly agitated Wagner; a correspondence that was begun on the matter led to no further understanding." [2]

Wagner, of course, was furious at his dismissal: he could not be brought to see that, as Dorn puts it, it was not a case of one man being turned out because another wished to get him out, but of the necessity, for the theatre's sake, of choosing another because the one could not possibly remain.

On the whole we are inclined to accept Dorn's version of the affair rather than Wagner's or that of the partisan biographers. Dorn shows himself remarkably well-informed about the early stages of Wagner's career, and especially of the circumstances surrounding his flight from Riga. His reminiscences were published in 1877, while Wagner was still alive: Dorn would hardly be likely to lay himself open to public correction by giving a false version of what had occurred in 1839, for there were probably many people still alive, besides Wagner, who could have supplied that correction if need were. Wagner himself, it is unnecessary to add, remained immovably convinced that he had been the victim of an intrigue on the part of Dorn and Holtei. In a letter of the 20th September, 1840 (from Paris), to Theodor Apel he says: " I had a serious illness; a nervous fever threatened my very life. Hardly had I begun to recover when I heard that during my illness my seeming friend Dorn

---

[1] Dorn places these words in inverted commas; possibly he may have been quoting from a copy of his own letter that he had retained.
[2] DEE, p. 164.

had displaced me in the most perfidious manner." In *Mein Leben* he tells us that he " must do Hoffmann the credit of saying that he felt very deeply the treachery that had been practised on me. He told me that the contract with Dorn bound him only for a year, and that as soon as this was over he would come to a new agreement with me. Friends of art in Riga came to me with offers of teaching, arrangements for concerts, and so on, to compensate me for the loss of my year's salary as conductor." The truth of all which we can accept without subscribing in full to Wagner's charges of deliberate treachery on Dorn's part. The few friends he had in the town may well have offered to come to the rescue, and Hoffmann may have preferred him personally, both as man and as conductor, to Dorn.[1] But the final and simple truth of the matter is probably that, as Dorn says, the theatre committee saw clearly that owing to Wagner's debts his hurried departure from the place could only be a matter of time, and they sensibly laid their plans in advance.

8

Glasenapp, who was himself a native of Riga, and knew the town well, has been at pains to rebut the legend that Wagner was luxuriously housed there. He had left his first dismal lodging in the Schmeidestrasse in the spring of 1838 for a more cheerful and commodious one in the St. Petersburg suburb, at the corner of the Mühlenstrasse and the Alexanderstrasse. The house, which belonged to a Russian merchant of the name of Bodrow, had changed very little by Glasenapp's time. The proprietor occupied the ground floor, Wagner the upper one. There was an ante-chamber leading into Wagner's study, in which latter there was a hired grand piano, a divan, and the desk upon which the first two acts of *Rienzi* were written. There were in addition a salon, with two windows looking on to each street, a bedroom for Richard and Minna, and two rooms for Amalie, who was now living with them. Glasenapp stoutly denies that the situation and the quality of the house placed it beyond Wagner's means; but even with Amalie taking on herself part of the

---

[1] In the course of the years, Hoffmann became director of the Josefstadt Theatre (the Thalia Theatre) in Vienna, where he gave the first Vienna performance of *Tannhäuser* in 1857.

burden of expense he must have found it difficult, with Minna earn-ing nothing, to struggle against his mounting load of debts. Old in-habitants of the town still remembered him, and described him to Glasenapp as sitting with pipe in mouth at the open window in mild weather, characteristically robed in a dressing gown and with a kind of Turkish fez on his head. One surmises, however, that it was not often he sat at the window; he found the Riga climate extremely inclement, even when he was well, and this and his incessant la-bours at the theatre, in which he tried to find an anodyne for his bruised and embittered soul, told severely on his health. As is shown by the letter to Apel that has been quoted from above, he had had at least one very serious illness. Though he was suffering from a severe cold in the winter of 1838–9, Holtei insisted on his dragging himself with the rest of the company to Mitau, where the perform-ances were given in an ice-cold theatre. The result was a typhoid fever that threatened to be the end of him, Holtei himself coming to the conclusion that he " was on his last legs "; he was pulled through, however, by a homeopathic doctor, one Prutzer.

Minna had arrived looking ill, but in such a mood of repentance for the past and gratitude for the present that Wagner must have found it unusually easy to live with her. But the domestic storms to which he seemed to be fated soon arose again. At first the sisters were quite happy together, but for some reason or other difficulties arose between them after Amalie, whose position in the theatre had become insecure after the arrival of Frau Pollert, had had the good sense to become engaged to a young Russian officer, Captain (after-wards General) Carl von Meck, whom, a year later, she married. Whether, on the strength of this flattering match, the generally amiable Amalie began to give herself airs, or whether for some other reason not disclosed in *Mein Leben*, we do not know; but after the engagement she and Minna were always quarrelling, and for the last year or so of Wagner's stay in Riga he had to submit to the unpleasantness of living in the same house with two sisters who neither saw nor spoke to each other.

But a profound inner change in him — and in Wagner the subtle alchemy of the inner life was always of more importance in his development than the circumstances of his outer life, dramatic or picturesque as these often were — was making him comparatively

insensitive to everything that went on around him. He was almost
without friends in the town; in the theatre he was surrounded by
enemies, from Holtei downwards; he was absorbed in *Rienzi*, which
not only held out hope of a material success somewhere or other but
corresponded to the seriousness that had by now become the dominant feature of his character. He had been sobered, too, by his
matrimonial experiences and by the danger always threatening him
from his carelessness in the matter of money obligations. In the letter of the 20th September, 1840, to Apel to which reference has
already been made he outlines his own inner development at this
time as it presented itself later before his eyes in Paris. It was then
four years since he had seen Apel; and he wants to make it clear
that the present Wagner is a very different man from the Wagner
whom Apel had known in earlier and wilder days.

" Hardly had we begun to feel," he says, " that we were in the youth
of our lives than we were made to realise that this youth could be
destroyed: your flight was crippled by blindness,[1] mine by constant
penury. . . . My levity of spirit was long ago gnawed away by the
need that dogged my naturally sanguine and buoyant nature. My
fight was a hard one, full of bitter consequences, for I had to learn
to *renounce;* I had to fight down my very being. In none of my attempts to reach my higher artistic goal was I successful. I did indeed
get so far that my opera [*Das Liebesverbot*] was accepted in Berlin;
all that was needed was that I should be able to maintain myself for
six months so as to keep under my eye and my hand the weak and
vacillating director, over whom, nevertheless, I had a personal influence. But I was poor, and no one would support me. I gave it up,
as I have given up so much else since then, and went to Königsberg,
where a post had been assured to me. There I married; but penury and
distress pursued me. I could not get the place that had been promised
me; I had to shift for myself. . . . When we meet again, ask my wife
what I was like when I heard [the news of Apel's accident]. The poor
woman suffered sorely. I lost all cheerfulness, all freedom, all openness: I cannot give you a better idea of my condition than by telling
you that that was the one year in my life in which I hardly composed
a note; I sketched nothing, I conceived nothing. I was most unhappy!
After this year of suffering my position improved, at any rate outwardly; I obtained a good and honourable post as music director in

---

[1] Apel had had a fall from his horse in May 1836, as the result of which, after
two years of acute suffering from concussion of the brain, he had gone totally blind
in 1838, at the age of twenty-seven. He lived until 1867, — long enough to see his
boyhood's friend the protégé of a King and the centre of the musical life of Europe.

Riga. There I spent two fairly tranquil years; I might almost say that there I began to find myself again, but for the fact that it became ever clearer to me that I am not built to earn my bread in this way. I sought stupefaction in an almost frenzied performance of my duties; but my body was not fitted for this, the northern climate in particular being trying for me."

Then he tells Apel of the supposed treachery of Dorn, and, in a passage that will come up for quotation later, of his resolve to flee from Riga.

His financial situation in Riga must have been desperate towards the finish: in February 1839 we find him offering to take on the duties of Löbmann (who had recently been dismissed) in addition to his own — which would have meant his rehearsing and conducting not only the more serious operas of the repertory but also the lighter operas and the vaudevilles. " I will gladly work day and night for the theatre, I will undertake any duty of which I am capable, I will orchestrate whole works, and do anything else you like. . . . To sum it all up, I beg of you [i.e. Hoffmann] a complete remission of the advance made to me (except, of course, the thirty roubles I lately received from you, which is to be repaid by the deduction of five roubles from my salary each pay-day), and I offer, in return, to do anything you like to ask of me, with the exception of boot-cleaning and water-carrying, the latter of which would be too much for my chest at present: I would even copy music, were it not that I fear the effect of this melancholy occupation would be to deepen the gloom of my temperament." [1]

Yet in a paradoxical kind of way he must have been almost happy in Riga, for with the shedding of his youthful illusions and his rapidly developing artistic idealism he could bear with tolerable equanimity the loneliness of his position in the theatre and the lack of friends in the town. How little he took part in the ordinary life of Riga is indicated by a remark, in later years, of an inhabitant of the place, who, after Wagner had become the leading figure in German music, expressed his astonishment at this huge success of a man of whose importance no one had any idea during the two years he had lived in Riga. Mentally he had outgrown, by 1839, not only Riga but German provincial musical life in general. He saw

---

[1] See his letter to Hoffmann, in RWKK, I, 115–118.

that he could never realise his ideal of operatic production in theatres so small as those in which his apprenticeship had been spent. He saw, too, that there was no hope for him of the fortune that sometimes comes along with fame if he continued to pursue the ordinary path of the German opera composer. The German theatres took their cue from Italy or Paris; only by a resounding success there could he win for himself a strategic position from which he could dictate terms to the German directors. Everything conspired to turn his eyes in the direction of Paris. A success there meant not only the power to put pressure on Germany but immediate wealth, for whereas the German theatres bought an opera outright for one meagre payment, in Paris the composer drew royalties for each performance. He believed, in his provincial ignorance of the larger world, that the great Scribe was already interested in him; he thought he could count on the protection of his compatriot Meyerbeer, who, after the Paris productions of *Robert the Devil* (1831) and *Les Huguenots* (1836), was by far the most powerful figure in the operatic world of the day, even Rossini's star having paled before his. And there was a final excellent reason why it was to Paris, rather than anywhere else, that he should go in search of fame as an artist and fortune as a man. There was nowhere in Germany where he could now pitch his tent without his life being made a misery to him by the creditors he had left in his wake wherever he had sojourned. In Paris he would be legally out of their reach. To Paris, then, he was not merely led by choice; he was driven there by inexorable necessity.

CHAPTER XIII

THE VOYAGE TO LONDON

1

ALTHOUGH MINNA was considerably less sanguine than he as to the results of this bold venture, he seems to have had little difficulty in winning her adhesion to his plan. Her own career as an actress, it had been agreed between them, was at an end. Richard was now the sole breadwinner; and obviously it was as impossible for him to make a career anywhere in Germany, things being as they were with him, as it was for him to remain in Riga, tied to a post for which he had no liking, exposed to the dislike of his Director and the machinations of his enemies, and, latterly, dismissed from his job to make way for Dorn. She was as innocent as Richard of any knowledge of the hard facts of the great world outside the German provinces, and almost as ready as he to believe that a brilliant success awaited the wonderful *Rienzi* in Paris. After his dismissal in March 1839 he could not even remain in Riga till *Rienzi* was finished; with the prospect of no salary, with practically no funds in hand, and with a horde of angry creditors at his heels there was nothing for it but flight at the earliest moment possible. " I scraped together a few hundred roubles," he tells Apel eighteen months later, " and told my wife that we should have to go to Paris. She, who is never given to cherishing ardent hopes, and had a presentiment of the misery we were making for, agreed out of love for me."

Though he had received his dismissal in March, it did not come into effect until the following summer. In June the company was to go to Mitau for the usual short summer season, and though Wagner accompanied it and conducted the performances there, his plans for escape were already matured. The last opera he produced (in Mitau) was Méhul's *Joseph*. He conducted *Fidelio* there on the 24th June, 1839, and *Oberon* on the 25th: these were his last appearances at the conductor's desk until he resumed his activities in Dresden in the winter of 1842-3.

Mitau, indeed, was a more favourable leaping-off point than Riga. According to Russian law, before a passport could be granted to anyone proposing to leave the country, notice of his intention to do so had to be advertised three times in the local papers, for the information of anyone who might have financial claims on him.[1] From Mitau a less public exit was possible. As soon as flight had been decided upon, and Minna's agreement secured, Wagner began to learn French. As by that time he had only four more weeks before him in Riga, he soon realised that he could not hope to make much progress with the language; so he craftily used what were supposed to be lessons to obtain from his French master a translation of the *Rienzi* libretto, which he wrote in, in red ink, in so much of the score as was already finished. The problem now was how to raise money for the journey to Paris and for maintenance there for a time. A benefit concert and Minna's four appearances in the theatre brought in a little; his modest furniture, which may or may not have been all paid for, was sold.[2] It was perhaps all the easier for him to pocket the proceeds of all this, as, his passport having been already impounded, it could not have occurred to any of his Riga creditors that their prey could escape them. As it was out of the question that he should both satisfy the many claims on him and have funds sufficient to carry him to Paris, he required no great persuasion to fall in with Möller's business-like suggestion that he should stick to what he had, and pay his creditors after the success on which he counted so confidently in Paris. Wagner tells us that his new director, Hoffmann, knew of his plan, and facilitated it by allowing him to leave some months before the formal termination of his agreement with the company. An agreement of that or any other nature would of course not have sufficed of itself to retain Wagner in Riga. But the fact that Hoffmann was taken into his confidence — which must have meant that the theatre committee was also aware of the plan for flight, and a conniving party to it — tends to confirm Dorn's account of the episode: everyone in close

---

[1] DEE, pp. 164, 165.

[2] In CBC there is an "autograph list of furniture, 1 p. small 8vo," which, according to Mrs. Burrell's note, refers to the "furniture of Riga bedroom sold to get money to go to Paris."

touch with Wagner must have known for some time that his position was desperate, and that the only way out was by flight; and since the company might be left without a conductor at any moment, it would be mere ordinary prudence to terminate his engagement well in advance and make other arrangements for the future, at the same time placing two months' salary at his service to facilitate his exit.

2

To escape from Russia was no easy matter. Dorn tells us that " the frontier was almost hermetically sealed. At every thousand paces there was a sentry-box, in which a Cossack kept watch when he was not actually covering his ground; between these posts a picket patrolled, whose business it was to keep an eye on the sentries. It was difficult to break through this chain, though not impossible. In the late autumn of 1834 a tenor of ours, Franz Mehlig, managed to get away by being taken as contraband goods by some Polish Jews, who left him concealed for hours at night in a boggy ditch until danger was past. Franz got to Königsberg all right, but in a fortnight he was dead of a nervous fever that was the result of the strain he had undergone." Dorn's account of Wagner's flight, which he probably obtained immediately afterwards from Möller, agrees in essence with that of Wagner in *Mein Leben*. When July came Wagner and Minna and Möller were passing through the pleasant Courland country in a special coach provided by their useful Königsberg friend. Richard was in good spirits, as again, ten years later, when he fled from Dresden to Zürich; he was conscious of little else but a feeling of relief at having slipped a galling burden from his shoulders, and certain that a glorious and prosperous future was awaiting him in Paris. Actually there were four of them in the coach. In Riga Wagner had won the affection of a huge Newfoundland dog, of the name of Robber, that belonged to a local merchant. During Wagner's absence in Mitau the animal had so visibly fretted for his friend that some well-meaning neighbours sent him by coach to Richard, who was so touched by his devotion that he swore he would never part from him. There being apparently no room for him in the coach, poor Robber had to gallop alongside it, visibly suffering so much from the blazing sun that at last Wagner could endure the painful spectacle no longer: by some ingenious rearrangement of their interior he made it possible for Robber to ride with them.

On the evening of the second day the coach reached the frontier. Möller's plans had been carefully laid. The fugitives were met by a trusty friend of his from the Prussian side, to whom Möller handed over Richard and Minna for the next and most difficult stage of the adventure. This friend drove them through by-paths to a certain point, where the carriage was abandoned; they were then taken to a house that was obviously a smuggler's den, and there handed over to a " guide." After an evening spent among Polish Jews of forbidding aspect and suffocating aroma, this " guide " led them, at sundown, to within a few hundred feet of the ditch that ran along the whole length of the frontier. According to Dorn, the expert Möller had made all the necessary arrangements; the fugitives took refuge in the warm hut of one of the Cossack sentries while the normal occupant of it was out making his inspection of the ground, and there was a convenient break for a while in the regular picket patrol. In spite, however, of everything being done that money could do, there was still some danger in the situation from those of the sentries who presumably had not been favoured with the confidence of Möller and his Prussian friend. A bolt had to be made for the ditch, with the certainty that if they were observed by an unfriendly watchman they would be fired upon even after they had reached Prussian territory. Robber, about whose vocal powers they felt a little anxiety, behaved with as much intelligence as if he himself were fleeing from creditors; he loped along beside them in perfect silence. Minna, with that susceptible heart of hers pounding away as she ran, must have wondered what she had done to provoke the Fates to tie her for life to an incomprehensible lunatic like Richard. Her existence, before she had met him, had mostly been so tranquil, so happy in its own modest way; and here she was now flying like a criminal from a town in which her husband, had he remained there much longer, would probably have been thrown into prison for debt, racing towards an insane adventure in a distant country in which she had not a single friend and of the language of which she did not know a word — with the past a ghastly failure, the future a desperate gamble, and, for the immediate present, a quite promising chance of being at any minute peppered in the back by wild Cossacks.

The gamble, for the moment, succeeded; the three got through the ditch in safety, and found waiting for them, on the other side, Möller's friend with his carriage. They were driven to the inn of a Prussian frontier village, where Möller, " quite sick with anxiety, sprang out of bed to greet us, sobbing and rejoicing." He had prudently concealed from Wagner, perhaps for Minna's sake, the real difficulties of the venture, of which Richard himself was only fully conscious when all danger was at last over. The exhausted Minna was in such manifest distress of body and mind that Wagner's heart smote him; he could not, he says, find words " to convey to my utterly exhausted wife my regret for it all." It has been said, though on what authority we are not told, that the flight from Riga was really the cause of that childlessness that Wagner regretted so much in Minna in after years — that either in the dash to the coast or on the subsequent voyage to London she sustained injuries that made motherhood impossible for her.

The next day the fugitives drove to Arnau, a mile or so out of Königsberg, where they put up at the local inn; entry into Königsberg itself was out of the question, on account of Richard's creditors there. The next stage of the journey took them to the harbour of Pillau, in Prussia, about thirty miles from Königsberg. It had been decided to proceed to Paris mainly by sea, partly because economy of their scanty funds was necessary, partly because Robber would be less of a problem on a boat than crossing Europe in a coach. The resourceful Möller accompanied them to Pillau, his knowledge of the country no doubt being useful in helping them to take a route through the villages that would obviate their touching on Königsberg. In one of these villages the clumsy vehicle in which they were travelling was overturned, and Minna received so severe an internal shock that she had to spend the night in a miserable peasant's hovel to which, in utter helplessness, she had been dragged by Wagner. After a few days in hiding in Pillau, Richard, Minna and Robber set sail in the *Thetis*, a small merchant vessel bound for London, with a crew of seven men, including the captain. As Richard had no passport, the party had to be smuggled on board when the attention of the harbour watch was engaged elsewhere.

Robber had to be hauled up the steep side of the vessel — a matter of some difficulty — and there was a final anxious hour before sailing, when the fugitives had to conceal themselves below deck from the officials whose business it was to inspect the ship before it left. But at last they cleared the harbour in safety; Wagner could now forget the world that had been so full of vexations and dangers to him during the preceding six years, and hug to his soul the sweet illusion of a new life, full of honours and of fortune, in Paris.

3

But a fresh purgatory had to be gone through by them all before they finally set foot on land again. Normally the voyage to London, in the summer, was a rather pleasant affair of some eight days. For Richard and Minna it lasted at least three and a half weeks.[1] Storms more than once drove them out of their course: on the 27th July the captain was forced to seek harbour on the Norwegian coast. As the boat made its way into the sheltering fiord the cries of the crew as they furled the sails came echoing from the rocks in a rhythm that Wagner was to remember later, when he was writing the seamen's chorus in the *Flying Dutchman*. The little village at which they had landed was Sandwike, a few miles from Arendal:

" Sandwike it is; full well I know the bay,"

says Daland in the opera. On the 31st, in spite of the Norwegian pilot's warning, the captain of the *Thetis* insisted on leaving his shelter. The storm drove them towards a reef that seemed likely to split the vessel in two; but it struck it only a glancing blow, and, congratulating themselves on their escape, once more they turned her bow to the land. They set sail again on 1st August, were favoured with fine weather for four days, and then, on the 7th, ran into another storm that proved to be the worst they had yet experienced; to the terrors of the waves were added those of thunder and lightning. They all gave themselves up for lost: Minna, imploring heaven for the favour of a death by lightning rather than by drowning, begged Richard to bind him to her so that they might

---

[1] This is the figure given in the *Autobiographical Sketch* of 1843. In *Mein Leben* it is given as "more than three weeks." In the letter of the 20th September, 1840, to Apel it is "four weeks." See note, p. 251.

not be parted when they sank. Through most of the voyage, apparently, the wretched pair were sea-sick. They had nowhere to lie down but in the captain's tiny cabin, in which the solitary berth was occupied by Minna, the luxury-loving Richard having to stretch himself out on a wooden seat under which was kept the brandy cask; and as the tired and scared crew came frequently to the cask in search of strength or consolation, poor Richard, sick as he was, was kept perpetually on the move. Robber livened things up occasionally by a fight with Koske, a sailor to whom he had taken a strong dislike, and who happened to be most persistent of the tipplers; and the exhausted Wagner had often to separate the pair. Altogether one gathers that Richard was not popular on board the *Thetis*. The fact that this unwanted passenger had come furtively aboard without a passport made him an object of suspicion; the chances were that he was a particularly desperate criminal flying from justice; and when the superstitious crew found themselves in weather worse than they had ever experienced, and the voyage taking more than twice its ordinary time, they were convinced that their passenger had brought a curse on the ship.

Even the captain, whom Möller had no doubt furnished with convincing private reasons for burdening himself with the fugitives, repented of his bargain: being a simple man, with no special insight into futurity, he did not know that trouble, profound and prolonged, was the predestined lot of anyone who mixed himself up with the fortunes of Richard Wagner, and especially of anyone who tried to do him a service. He must certainly have been tempted at times to rid his ship of this Jonah. Even when the storm in the Skager Rack was over, the sun declined to appear for some days; the captain was doubtful as to his bearings, and when at last he came to the conclusion that the wisest thing he could do was to follow a ship whose movements he could just distinguish through his telescope, he narrowly escaped the fate of this vessel, which stranded on a sandbank from which it was seemingly impossible that it could ever get free. However, the long trial neared its end on the evening of the 9th August, when the English coast was sighted in the neighbourhood of Southwold. There were still sandbanks in plenty to be negotiated, but the calm of the English pilot who came on board inspired Wagner with confidence, in spite of a gale that was once more raging, and in spite of his having been charitably informed that these sandbanks accounted for about four hundred ships in the course of each year. The *Thetis* at last entered the mouth of the Thames on the evening of the 12th,[1] after Minna, frightened out of her wits by the innumerable red lights, fog bells, and other danger signals, had insisted on pointing out each of these sinister objects to the pilot and the sailors, fearing that without her watchfulness they might miss them: Richard, more sensibly, took a long and refreshing sleep. As was invariably the case with him when he had turned a difficult corner in his life, he was in the highest spirits, and intensely interested in the new sights unfolding themselves before his astonished landsman's eyes. In his eagerness to get to London with the minimum of delay, he and Minna and Robber forsook the *Thetis* for a river steamer at Gravesend. The nearer they came to the great city the more his wonder and delight increased at the spectacle of a swirl of life of the like of which he had never even dreamed. They disembarked at London Bridge, still staggering in their gait after three weeks or so on the rolling seas, and very anxious about Robber, in whom the sudden transition to land seemed to have set up a brainstorm that impelled him to whisk round every corner that presented itself,

---

[1] My friend Mr. H. W. Acomb, Librarian of the National Liberal Club, was kind enough to get me some information from Lloyds with regard to the *Thetis* and the voyage. Lloyds' records show that the vessel was a tiny one of 106 tons. It was Prussian-owned; the master's name was Wulff. The English broker in whose name the arrival of the ship in the Thames was entered was one Lee. Wagner is correct in his date of the 12th August as that on which it arrived in the Thames. It is known to have passed, or even touched at, Elsinore on the 25th July. (Wagner speaks of having "sailed past the beautiful castle of Elsinore," the sight of which revived his youthful impressions of *Hamlet*.)

Three weeks and a half from the 12th August would be about the 18th July. From *Mein Leben* we learn that "after seven days' sailing" the ship was "no further than Copenhagen," which is close to Elsinore. He mentions the 27th July as the date on which, after struggling against the storm "for twenty-four hours" after passing Elsinore, they took refuge in a harbour on the Norwegian coast. The Elsinore date obtained from Lloyds confirms the accuracy of this date of the 27th. Seven days backward from the 25th would give us the 18th day as the probable date of the departure from Pillau. Wagner's account of the duration of the voyage is thus proved to be correct. It is manifest that he kept a careful diary of his life, which fact accounts for the exceeding rarity of a mistake in a date in his account of his early years. Reference to the diary would furnish him with full particulars of his relations with Minna in Magdeburg, Königsberg and Riga; and the conclusion becomes irresistible that the facts throughout are substantially as he has given them in *Mein Leben*. It is in the period after 1849 that the autobiography becomes to a great extent unreliable.

and generally to get lost in the bewildering London traffic. The captain of the *Thetis* had recommended " the Horseshoe Tavern, near the Tower," so thither Richard and Minna, with Robber and what must have been a fair amount of baggage — for they had brought bedding and other things with them — proceeded in a London cab of the period.

What he calls the " Horseshoe Tavern " was the Hoop and Horseshoe, 10, Queen Street, Tower Hill.[1] The hostelry and the neighbourhood proving a trifle too rough for Wagner's liking, he removed almost at once, on the advice of a Hamburg Jew with whom he had struck up an acquaintance, to the King's Arms boarding house, Old Compton Street, the exact site of which cannot now be determined. The journey to what Wagner quaintly describes as " better quarters in the West End " took an hour, Minna and Richard facing each other in the narrow cab, with Robber stretched across their knees from window to window. Wagner's English was inadequate to explaining his needs to the landlady of the King's Arms, who was a sea-captain's widow: and when she tried her French on him he could only wonder which of them knew the least of that language. While they were talking, Robber, who seems to have been gifted with a curiosity equal to that of his master, took it into his head to explore London. They had to enter the house without him, and spent two miserable hours[2] lamenting the loss of the faithful hound whom they had managed to bring so far at the cost of so much trouble. At last they caught sight of him from the window, strolling unconcernedly down a side street towards home: they learned afterwards that he had been seen as far away from their lodgings as Oxford Street.

They stayed at the King's Arms a week, justifying to themselves the expense on the grounds partly that Minna needed a rest, partly that Richard ought to seize the opportunity to make some useful

---

[1] The hotel and the street have both disappeared, as Mr. F. G. Edwards feared would be the case when he went over the neighbourhood in 1895: "it is more than probable," he wrote, "that when a fresh northern approach is made to the new Tower Bridge the 'Hoop and Horseshoe' will be demolished." In 1895 the ground floor had been modernised, but the upper portion was still unchanged. An illustration of it will be found in EMHL. It was remarkable as being "the only inn in London having that particular sign, and, curiously enough, from the front of the building is suspended a large hoop encircling a horseshoe." EMHL, p. 50.

[2] Not two days, as given in *Grove's Dictionary*!

acquaintances in the London musical world. As soon as he found the earth behaving with reasonable steadiness under his feet, he tried to find Sir George Smart, the conductor of the Philharmonic Society, to whom he had sent his *Rule Britannia* Overture in 1837, and in whose house in Great Portland Street Weber had died in 1826. After some days' enquiry — in what quarter we do not know — he learned that Smart was not in town. With his usual unabashable assurance, Richard next decided to look up Edward Bulwer Lytton, to talk over with him the question of the dramatisation of his novel *Rienzi* for opera purposes. The most likely place in which to find Bulwer Lytton seemed to be the House of Commons, of which, Wagner had been told, he was a member. At the House, he and the attendants were despairing of ever understanding each other when a distinguished looking man came along, spoke to Wagner in French, discovered what he wanted, told him that Bulwer Lytton was not in London, and, at Wagner's pressing request, took him into the strangers' gallery of no less august a place than the House of Lords. The ease with which he accomplished this feat convinced Wagner that the man must be " a lord " himself. Wagner had the felicity of seeing the British parliamentary machine at work, the debate being on the negotiations with the Portuguese Government about the Anti-Slavery Bill, as he learned next day. He was astonished at the free-and-easy manner of the place and the undress conversational tone of the debates — the only speaker who indulged in the ordinary oratorical pomposities being the Bishop of London — and greatly puzzled by the fraternisation at intervals between such political enemies as Brougham and Lyndhurst. He saw not only the Prime Minister, Melbourne, in action, but the redoubtable and then almost legendary Wellington — in a grey beaver hat, with his hands well down in his trousers pockets.

Wagner's account of the affair is confirmed in full detail by Hansard. The day was Thursday, August 15th, and the debates were on " Trade on the Western Coast of Africa " and " Suppression of the Slave Trade." Melbourne, the Premier, moved the second reading of the Slave-Trade Suppression Bill — Portugal having declined to " co-operate with His Britannic Majesty " in the matter — and the speakers were Wellington, Brougham, Lord Wynford, the Bishop of London, the Lord Chancellor (Lyndhurst),

Lord Ellenborough, the Earl of Minto, the Earl of Galloway, Lord Denman, and others. Wagner, of course, could not have understood a word of what was said. He tells us that he learned the subject of the debate from the next day's papers: but as he knew no English, he probably derived his information from his friend the German captain of the *Thetis*.[1]

The presumed lord, whom he met again on his way out, kindly took him to the room in which the Commons then sat (the old Houses of Parliament having been burnt down in 1834), showed him the Woolsack and the Mace, and talked to him at such length that Wagner came away agreeably convinced that he now knew all there was to be known about the capital of the British Empire. As it was a hot August, and therefore the most inconvenient period of the whole year for listening to music, there was of course a season of Italian opera being given in London. But Wagner, even had he felt any particular curiosity regarding the repertory, had no money to spare for expensive luxuries of that kind. In the company of the captain of the *Thetis,* to whom, as a German with some knowledge of English, he would of course cling closely, he and Minna went to Gravesend Park: it was the first time either of them had been in a railway train. If Praeger is to be believed, Richard went also to Westminster Abbey, where he struck the correct attitude before the statue of Shakespeare, and to Greenwich, where, in climbing up the pilot-ladder of the old *Dreadnought,* he dropped into the river the snuff-box that Schröder-Devrient had given him, and in his vain clutch at it narrowly escaped drowning. At the Hospital afterwards, seeing a pensioner take snuff, and lamenting that he had none of his own, he was surprised at being answered in his own language, the old sailor being a Saxon by birth.[2] For the rest, he wandered about London, filled with curi-

---

[1] His curiosity with regard to the House of Lords had probably been stimulated by a couple of articles on the subject in the same volume of *Europa* (1837) as that in which his *Carnavalslied* had been published. (See EU, pp. 70 ff, 215 ff.) It is an odd coincidence, if nothing more, that in this same volume is a story of a German in Paris who takes rooms in a hotel in the Rue du Helder — where Wagner himself was to live from the spring of 1840 to April 1841. (See *Chambre garnie, eine Pariser Geschichte*, in EU, p. 529.) The raw German provincial that Wagner then was had no doubt been thrilled also by an article on *Der Lord-Major* (*sic*) *von London* in the same volume (p. 546), and by various reports of the rich musical life in Paris.

[2] A Wagner story, of course, is not necessarily untrue because it appears in the pages of Praeger. Wagner no doubt talked to him often in later years about his stay

osity, till he was exhausted, never ceasing to wonder at the vastness of the place and the contrasts of poverty and wealth in it; and he " went through the horrors of a ghastly London Sunday." On Tuesday the 20th August he and Minna and Robber took boat to Boulogne, where they landed the same evening.

in London in 1839, though Praeger was constitutionally unable to remember any conversation accurately. See PW, pp. 68–77. As bearing on the credibility of the alleged incidents at Greenwich, it is to be remembered that while Wagner himself would have no particular reason for going there, it was one of the likeliest places for him to be taken to by the captain of the *Thetis*, with whom, it is evident, he spent a certain part of his time in London.

CHAPTER XIV

THE "CONQUEST OF PARIS"

1

THE WORLD is always inclined to exaggerate the importance of outer events and the influence of mere human beings in the life of a creative artist, because it has only a vague conception of the vital inner laws of his being which the artist obeys with a kind of unconscious fatalism. And in few artists has the inner urge towards a predestined end been more pronounced or more persistent than in Wagner. An unpublished letter of his of the 4th November, 1835, from Magdeburg, to Minna in Berlin, which is now in the Burrell Collection, " discusses," we are told, " the conflict between his love and his ambition," and " sets out all his plans in life, and they were exactly what he was to carry out." [1] As Max Koch has pointed out, already in the poem of *Die Feen* there is to be found the " Redemption " motive of *Parsifal*. In Paris, in his story *A Pilgrimage to Beethoven*, he sketches the theory of the music drama that he was to bring to completion many years later in Zürich. The first faint impulses to the *Tannhäuser*, *Lohengrin* and *Meistersinger* dramas can be traced back as far as his student days. The *Meistersinger* subject grew to almost full consciousness within him while he was writing *Tannhäuser*: his preoccupation with the " hoard " of the Hohenstaufen legend during the days of his study of the Wibelungs (Ghibellines) and Nibelungs led him later not only to the central idea of the *Ring* but to the symbol of the Holy Grail. The ideas of " renunciation " that beset him in the days when he was brooding upon his *Jesus of Nazareth* and working out the relations of Siegfried-Brynhilde and Tristan-Isolde towards the world, culminated long after in the central motive of *Parsifal*. Finally, the Bayreuth idea was in him, in embryo, in the earliest days of his work at the *Ring*.[2]

---

[1] CBC, No. 53.   [2] See MKRW, I, 1–5.

The virtual certainty is that Wagner's art, and his theories of art, would have been substantially the same wherever in Germany he had lived, and whatever the people with whom he came into personal contact or the outer events in which he took part. Almost the only things that his two and a half years in Paris did for him as an artist were, firstly, to set up in him a nostalgia that gave him, for a while, certain agreeable illusions about his native land; secondly, to strengthen the process of disillusionment that had already begun in him with regard to French and Italian opera; and thirdly, to introduce him to the music of Berlioz, from which he learned a great deal of a quite new art of orchestration. His experiences in Paris, however, had a profound and lasting effect on him as a man. He not only piled up more debts, but, by the sheer pressure of necessity, developed to the nth his congenital insensitiveness in matters of this kind. He learned something of the deterioration that normal human nature undergoes in big theatrical establishments — learned that official promises mean nothing, that one has either to intrigue like the others or be lost, that it is a case of everyone for himself and the devil take the hindmost, and that an artistic ideal of the theatre, if you are going to insist on anything so quixotic, can be realised, if at all, only through very imperfect and often unwilling human instruments. He discovered, from his association with various composers and with the heads of the Paris operatic institutions, what a cynical commercial view the people who had " arrived " took of the art in which, for mysterious reasons of its own, Providence had given them so great an influence. He saw now what theatrical directorship of the ordinary kind meant to art and artists; he was to gain further illumination on this point from his experiences on his return to Dresden, and to see that he had either to resign himself to being a theatre serf, humiliated all his life and sent whimpering to a humble grave like Mozart and Lortzing and many others before him, or find some desperate way out, both as artist and as man. And finally the galling contrast between the wealth and luxury of Paris and his own poverty and subservience deepened his doubts about a state of society in which men like him, Richard Wagner, were condemned by the accident of birth and fortune to play for ever the part of the under-dog.

2

In the third and fourth decades of the nineteenth century, Paris was the centre of the operatic world. A success there meant not only fame but fortune. An opera that had succeeded in Paris was sure of being taken up in Germany; moreover, Paris paid continuous royalties to the composer on performances of his works. It was no wonder, then, that the eyes of the ambitious and impecunious Wagner were turned hungrily on this combination of Mecca and Klondyke.

The Grand Opéra, the official title of which was the Académie Royale de Musique, had taken a new lease of life in the eighteen-thirties, owing to one of those combinations of social and economic circumstances that always play a vital part in the history of the arts. A new era had thrown up new men, who put new life into the old apparatus and in part played up to the taste of the public, in part developed in it a new appetite. By about 1830 the hitherto all-conquering Rossini was beginning to lose something of his hold on the Paris public; a new society had come into being, with a vague sense of new operatic values. The composer who at once met the new demand and endowed the public with a new appetite was Meyerbeer. The old classical ideal, of which Gluck had been the older and Spontini the newer incarnation, was at its last gasp; people were tired of the mythological abstractions of the older opera, and craved for an art that should be more representative of themselves and the quick-nerved era that had followed the conclusion of the Napoleonic wars. The situation was admirably summed up by Heine in one of his letters from Paris to the German journals for which he acted as French correspondent.[1] Heine had no specialist knowledge of music, but he was a shrewd observer of men and things, and extremely sensitive to variations in the mass-movements of opinion. We may accept his account of the situation in Paris music at that epoch as being in accordance with the basic facts.

Heine draws a comparison between Rossini and Meyerbeer that explains quite satisfactorily the veering round of popular approval, about this time, from the former to the latter, and helps us, to some

---

[1] See the ninth of his letters to Lewald, *Über die französische Bühne*, written in 1837, in HSW, Vol. XI.

ALBERT WAGNER
(*Courtesy, J. B. Lippincott Co.*)

MINNA WAGNER

FROM THE ENGRAVING BY WEGER, BASED UPON A
PHOTOGRAPH

extent, to understand the admiration of the youthful Wagner for Meyerbeer. Rossini, he says, paints the joys and sorrows of the individual — love and hate, tenderness and longing, jealousy and sulkiness, all as the isolated feeling of some particular individual: in Rossini's music, therefore, melody necessarily predominates, melody being the immediate expression of sensibility in isolation. In Meyerbeer, on the contrary, it is harmony that predominates, for harmony is more communal in its nature. He expresses not man as an individual, but man as a member of society. " Meyerbeer's music is more social than individual; the grateful present, that sees reflected in his music its own inner and outer feuds, its own dissensions of spirit, its own conflicts of will, its own needs, its own hopes, celebrates in this music its own passion and enthusiasm when it applauds the master." Rossini's music, it seems, was more suited to the Restoration period, when tired and disillusioned French humanity had lost interest in communal matters and turned inwards to the contemplation of its own ego: " Rossini would never have obtained his huge popularity during the Revolution and the Empire." But after the July Revolution (1830) there had come a new society and a new spirit, an eager concentration on business and affairs of state, to the psychological expression of which the " individual " melody of Rossini was inadequate: " only when the great choruses of *Robert the Devil* or *Les Huguenots* roared harmonically, rejoiced harmonically, sobbed harmonically, did men's hearts hearken and sob and rejoice and roar in inspired accord." This is the reason, says Heine, for the unexampled, colossal success of these two operas: Meyerbeer " is the man of his epoch, and the epoch, that always knows how to choose its man, has tumultuously raised him on its shield, has proclaimed his overlordship, and celebrates in him its own joyous entry into possession."

It was in the year following the July Revolution that Meyerbeer gave Paris *Robert the Devil,* a work in which the epoch saw itself reflected, for Robert was " the hero who does not know precisely what it is he wants, who is in perpetual conflict with himself; he is a veracious portrait of the moral uncertainties of that epoch, that vacillated so restlessly and so painfully between virtue and vice, fretted itself in endeavours and galled itself against obstacles, and, like Robert, sometimes lacked the strength to withstand the assaults

[259]

of the devil." Moreover, Meyerbeer appealed to the newly awakened public by his breadth of culture, his general intellectual power. All in all, says Heine, he had brought about a huge progress in art, had endowed the opera with new forms: the *Huguenots* was a model for all future composers of opera.

The coming of Meyerbeer, with his novel psychological expression in music, his treatment in his operas of some of the vexed moral problems of the day, and his handling of large masses on the stage, coincided with a sudden improvement both in libretto construction and in theatrical decoration. We may laugh as we like now at what may seem to be the mechanics of a Scribe libretto and at the facile productiveness of that indefatigable artisan of the theatre; but the fact remains that he was not only a highly skilled theatrical workman but, in his way and for his time, an observer and a thinker. He endowed the French opera with a whole new world of sentiments, motives and types.[1] He opened up new routes not only in grand opera but in opéra-comique.[2] His powers of invention in the matter of ingenious plot and telling situation were endless; for any musical emergency suddenly confronting the composer he could turn out at a moment's notice a stanza or an episode that would both meet the dramatic case and fill out the musical tissue as desired; and he gave his delighted audiences the feeling that opera was at last getting to grips with real life. There have been few to equal and none to surpass him in technical dexterity in his own field; and none that have had anything like his astonishing range.

The Romantic movement of the thirties gave birth to a new theatrical realism and a new pomp of *décor*. " It is from Ciceri," says Charles Séchan,[3] " that we date the Romantic renovation of *décor* in 1830, which coincided with the literary and dramatic revo-

---

[1] Practically all the most successful French operas of the period, including some successes that have endured to our own day, were written to texts by Scribe: among the best known of his libretti are those of Halévy's *Guido et Ginevra* and *La Juive*, Meyerbeer's *Robert*, *Les Huguenots*, *Le Prophète*, and *L'Etoile du Nord*, Cherubini's *Ali Baba*, Gounod's *La Nonne sanglante*, Auber's *Masaniello*, *Fra Diavolo*, *Le Dieu et la Bayadère*, *Le Cheval de Bronze*, *Le Domino Noir*, *Les Diamants de la Couronne*, *La Sirène*, and *Lestocq*, Rossini's *Le Comte Ory*, Donizetti's *La Favorita*, and Verdi's *Les Vêpres Siciliennes*.

[2] See the account of him by his contemporary Legouvé, in LSAS, II, 181 ff.

[3] See SS, p. 7 ff. Séchan, who himself became one of the leading designers for the Opéra, was a pupil of Ciceri.

lution of which the leaders were Victor Hugo, Dumas, and Alfred de Vigny. Before Ciceri, the stage settings of the Opéra and of the other theatres still trailed along in the old classical rut, in which the principal rôle was played by Olympus, with its apparatus of Cupids, bows and quivers. . . . Ciceri was the first to grasp the fact that the day of the antique and classical setting was over, and to lay down the rule that clever and minutely executed details must be sacrificed to mass and broad effect." It was he who dazzled the Parisians with the novel and daring settings of the cloister in which the nuns perform their ballet in the third act of *Robert the Devil;* it was his example that led to the striking settings of *Les Huguenots, La Juive,* and other operas. Local colour, especially that of the Middle Ages, became of the first importance; for the first time, as Séchan says, the spectator was " transported to the very milieu of the epoch in which the action took place, historical personages being shown in a setting absolutely true to reality."

3

But the most important of all in this quick inauguration of a new epoch at the Opéra was the advent of a new type of impresario.

The official Opéra enjoyed several privileges at the expense of the other lyric theatres of Paris and of music in general. Not only had it a liberal subvention from the State, but no ball or concert could be given without the Opéra receiving one-fifth of the gross receipts, while the other opera houses had to pay over to it five per cent. of their takings. In spite of all this, the losses of the institution in the eighteen-twenties had been so enormous as to constitute a heavy burden on the civil list — amounting in 1827 to close on a million francs. In 1831 Louis Philippe rid himself of this incubus by turning the Opéra over to one Véron, who undertook to run it for six years, at his own risk of loss or chance of profit, in consideration of a subsidy of 800,000 francs for the first year, 760,000 francs for the second and third, and 710,000 francs for the last three. This Véron was a man of most chequered history. Born in 1798 and trained as a doctor, he had early abandoned medicine for journalism, founding the *Revue de Paris* in 1829. His medical record appears to consist mainly in having published a treatise on the maladies of children and in having made a slight mistake in his practice — summoned to bleed a patient, he had opened an artery instead of a vein — that had resulted in the death of his unfortunate client. He had also put on the market the *pâte pectorale de Regnault*, a specific of such enormous popularity in its own day that it brought its inventor a fortune. To those who know the mentality of Court officials and politicians where the fine arts are concerned, it is not in the least surprising that this amateur assassin should have been looked upon as the ideal man to conduct a national opera house, a job for which, apparently, any qualifications suffice so long as they do not include a knowledge of art in general or of music in particular. Berlioz, who had a wide and mournful experience of these strange fauna, was often astounded at the comprehensiveness of their ignorance. He tells of one of the Directors of the Paris Opéra who, when Cherubini — at that time head of the Paris Conservatoire — called on him without having himself announced, imperiously demanded of him his name and profession, enquiring if he were part of the Opéra establishment, and if so, whether he was attached to the department of the ballet or that of the machines. Of two of Véron's successors, Duponchel and Roqueplan, Berlioz said they knew about as much of music as a couple of Chinese — yet " along with the completest ignorance, the profoundest barbarism, there goes the most unbounded confidence in themselves."

Véron did not remain at the Opéra for the full term of his lease: he commenced operations in March, 1831, and was able to retire four years later with a profit of at least 900,000 francs — and this from a business from which the majority of his predecessors and successors either drew quite modest gains, or in which they were completely ruined; a Government report of some years later asserted, indeed, that of all the concessionaires in the history of the Opéra, only two (Lully and Véron) had not come to grief.[1] He owed his success first of all to his business-like habits: he delegated no functions, but kept a personal eye and hand on the details of each department. He saw what the public wanted, and gave it them; the settings, costumes and ballets at the Opéra became of a magnifi-

---

[1] Before Véron took over the Opéra, the average nightly receipts were a miserable 1,500–2,000 francs. The unprecedented success of *Robert the Devil* quickly raised them to 9,000–10,000 francs. See STS, pp. 161, 162.

cence never previously known in Paris. Music was a minor matter with him; it was just a lucky accident that the unprecedentedly successful *Robert* fell on him from the skies in the first year of his management.[1] The great thing, in his eyes, was that the public should never have the opportunity to feel bored; if the music of a work happened to be good, the *décor* was an extra spice in the cup of their pleasure, while if, as was mostly the case, the music was bad, the *décor* was an anodyne. " The name of Véron," said the satirical Heine, " will live for ever in the annals of music. He has adorned the temple of the goddess, but shown the goddess herself the door. Nothing could surpass the luxury that rules at the Opéra, which is now the paradise of the hard-of-hearing." Véron himself, in a book he published in 1860, preferred to put it differently. He owed his success, he said, in the first place to operas such as *Robert the Devil, La Juive*, etc.; in the second place to the excellent singers and dancers attached to the house at that time — Nourrit, Levasseur, Madame Damoreau, Madame Dorus-Gras, Mademoiselle Falcon, Mademoiselle Taglioni, and so on; and in the third place " to the advent of the bourgeoisie, of the national guard, a *public d'élite*, that paid for its stalls and boxes, while the old aristocratic clientèle of the Opéra had occupied theirs free." [2]

Philarète Chasles has painted for us a murderous portrait of his contemporary Véron — " a man with a high colour, a chubby face, the mere hint of a nose, scrofulous, his neck always buried in the folds of some stuff that both alleviated his malady and concealed it, his belly rotund, his eye round, bright, scintillating, greedy, the mouth laughing, the lips thick, the hair scanty, the manner that of a little lackey mincingly apeing his master and putting on drawing-room affectations; the voice high, sharp, aggressive, hissing, overbearing; supple here, impertinent there . . . ; the head thrown back, the cheeks swollen, the glance arrogant when he had nothing to gain or to fear; Scapin, Frontin and Turcaret in one, plus the glutton, the speculator and the false marquis; Mercadet and Tuffières, and even a dash of the Bourgeois Gentilhomme; such was Véron. He was not wicked, or perverse, or lacking in intelligence.

---

[1] The agreement for it had been made by Meyerbeer with Véron's predecessor. Véron had so little faith in the work that he staged it with reluctance.
[2] VTP, p. 128.

He was without principle. . . . No one in our epoch has had such a nose as Véron for the scent of profit, or such a greyhound speed for running it down. He saw that literature was becoming industrialised. He vaguely sensed a democratic stupidity that did not know what to do, that needed advertisements as a blind man needs a stick. . . . Literature was just then becoming an affair of the shop. . . . The exploiters descended on it. Véron was the first to become the commercial broker of this malady, the jobber in coarse pleasures that had a dash of the mind in them, the Mercury of an intellectual materialism. Himself neither writer, nor man of genius, nor man of talent, nor of the salon, nor even a good observer of men, of whom he made small account; unclean in his habits, playing now the vicomte, now the bourgeois; employing artifices that were on the fringe of fraud but never slipped over into it, this gross Véron, crooked as an attorney, as three attorneys, fond of women, pictures, and men of letters, played the rôle of a farmer-general. . . ." [1]

One of his strokes of genius was to throw the wings open to the rich dandies who patronised the Opéra; another was to give intimate suppers at which the great attraction was the ladies of the ballet. On one famous occasion he allowed a number of society ladies to appear in the ballet of *Gustave,* and the young *lions de la loge infernale,* dressed up in bearskins, to range at large among them. These *lions* were the aristocratic young bloods who occupied the box nearest the stage, known, in the slang of the day, as the *loge infernale.* These bright young people of the period had had specially made for them, for use during the ballets, opera glasses that magnified thirty-two times; " point de jambes si bien cuirassées," says Séchan, " qu'ils ne déchiffrassent à jupons ouverts."

Such was the Grand Opéra of Paris under the ingenious Véron, who had made it one-third temple of the Muses, two-thirds antechamber to a seraglio. It was this institution, hoary with iniquities, cynical with long experience of human cupidity and folly, towards which the green young German provincial named Richard Wagner had bent his hopeful steps from the other end of Europe.

---

[1] Albéric Sécond, who also knew Véron well, paints a more kindly portrait of him. See STS, pp. 153–167.

4

Véron had been succeeded in 1835 by Duponchel, an architect, who was still in power when Wagner arrived in Paris in 1839. Duponchel did not make such a success of the undertaking as his predecessor had done. For one thing, he lacked the business capacity of the proprietor of the *pâte Regnault;* for another, Véron had pandered so much to his rich subscribers that they had come to regard themselves as practical dictators of the establishment, and resented any change in its habits. According to Heine, " the present Director follows the basic principles of his predecessor, although his own personality forms the most divertingly sharp contrast to his. Have you ever seen M. Véron? You must often have been surprised, in the Café de Paris or on the Boulevard Coblence, by this fat caricature of a figure, with a hat stuck slantwise on the head, which is quite buried in a huge white cravat the top points of which reach over the ears (to conceal a too profuse impostume), so that the rosy life-loving face with its tiny blinking eyes is only to a small extent visible. In the consciousness of his knowledge of men and of his success he trundles along so comfortably, so insolently-comfortably, surrounded by a court of young and now and then elderly dandies of literature, whom he generally regales with champagne or young ladies of the ballet. He is the god of materialism, and his spirit-mocking glance would often cut painfully to my heart when I met him: sometimes I seemed to be watching a brood of little reptiles, viscid and shining, crawling out of his eyes.

" M. Duponchel is a lean, pale, yellow man, with a distinguished if not noble appearance, always sad, looking like an undertaker; someone described him quite accurately as *un deuil perpétuel.* From the look of him you would take him to be a curator at Père Lachaise rather than the Director of the Grand Opéra. He always reminds me of the melancholy court fools of Louis XIII. This Knight of the Rueful Countenance is now the Parisians' *maître de plaisir,* and I often feel I would like to overhear him when he is sitting at home hatching out new jests for the amusement of his sovereign, the French public, shaking his sad head like some melancholy fool, so that the bells on his black cap tinkle like a sigh, when he colours the design of a new costume for Madame Falcon, or when he seizes the red book to see if Taglioni . . ." [1]

A change had come over the Opéra under the new Director; many of its former fashionable habitués had deserted it, their place being taken by the bourgeoisie. " The Opéra," says the ironic Heine, writing in 1837, " has become reconciled with the enemies of music, and the well-to-do citizen class has made its way into the Académie de Musique as into the Tuileries, while higher society has quitted the field. The brilliant aristocracy, the élite distinguished by its rank, culture, birth, fashion and idleness, has fled to the Italian Opera, into that musical oasis where the great nightingales of art are still trilling, the streams of melody still purl magically, and the palms of beauty wave applause with their proud fans, while elsewhere, all around, stretches a pale desert, a Sahara of music." The one resounding success of the Duponchel régime was *Les Huguenots*, produced on the 29th February, 1836, its most tragic failure that of Berlioz's *Benvenuto Cellini* on the 10th September, 1838. Duponchel resigned the Directorship of the Opéra to Léon Pillet in 1841 — i.e. in the middle of the period of Wagner's residence in Paris — but remained associated with the institution as administrator. He became Director once more in 1847, in association with Roqueplan, and finally retired from the Opéra in 1849. The shortness of his terms of power suggests of itself a certain incapacity to handle the peculiar problems of the place.

According to Charles de Boigne, who knew him and the Opéra equally well, Duponchel had no literary or musical pretensions; he let librettists and composers go their own way without advice or interference from him, the responsibility for failure being their own. He had one virtue as a Director, and that a negative one: he kept no mistresses in the theatre, and so escaped many an embarrassment such as those that befell his successor Pillet, who was indiscreet enough to take the prima donna Madame Stoltz under his protection. When one of the female singers in a company becomes *la Directrice du Directeur*, as Berlioz called Madame Stoltz, neither

---

[1] For the explanation of Heine's discreet aposiopesis at this point the reader who understands German must turn to the continuation of the original text. As Heine says, the red book "ist ein curioses Buch, dessen Bedeutung sehr schwer mit anständigen Worten zu erklären sein möchte. Nur durch Analogien kann ich mich hier verständlich machen." See *Kunstberichte aus Paris*, in HSW, XI, 263.

the lot of the other singers nor of the Director himself is a happy one. " A Director in love," says de Boigne, " is bound to end by ruining both himself and his theatre. Artists, whether they are singers or dancers or actors, are all the same; — a mixture of jealousy and vanity, egoism and pettiness, that admits neither a rival nor an equal. Each artist believes himself to be a giant, treats his colleagues as pigmies, and looks upon the applause they receive as a theft from himself. But when the artist is a woman, and when this artist is adored, when she has the Director at her feet and power in her hands, then anarchy begins, the public disappears, the re-ceipts go down, and the ridiculous arrives." [1] It was owing to an indiscreet comparison, in one of his articles in the *Journal des Débats,* of the shapely figure of his own mistress, Marie Recio, with the too ample limbs of Madame Stoltz in the same rôle, that Berlioz found the Opéra closed to him as a composer during the régime of Pillet.

De Boigne's view of Duponchel was that he was better at initia-tive than at realisation. " His restless, agitated mind loved to plan for the future. He did not trouble much about the present. He loved to plan his resources and munitions a long way ahead: if, after he had foreseen everything, prepared for everything, the present escaped him, he bent his head resignedly, mounted his horse, and went for a ride in the Bois." [2] His successor Pillet, on the other hand, was a journalist of audacity and resource who by some freak of fate found himself one day at the head of the Opéra. He could manage men well enough, says de Boigne; " he forgot that at the Opéra he would be engaged in a struggle with sirens, Armidas, singers, dancers, a whole feminine army, *galant,* artful, of which he had had no experience. He had never lived that Opéra life in which it is so dangerous to launch yourself at thirty-six or forty. His serious habits, his excessively timid character, made him out of place in a world that had never been his. The Opéra is a seraglio in which, let the master throw the handkerchief where he will, it is certain never to fall to the ground. He need not pay court, he has no delays to endure, no rivals to evict, no *femmes de chambre* to bribe, no mothers to cajole: he is the Director, that is to say, the dispenser of rôles, of applause, of engagements: all hearts are open

---

[1] BPMO, p. 119.   [2] Ibid., p. 120.

to him, the whole harem opens its arms to him." He fell a victim at the start to Madame Stoltz, who ruined him and the institution. " She cost Pillet dear; he lost his own money and that of others; he neither embezzled it nor kept it; he left the Opéra with his pockets empty but his hands clean; with the reputation of a pitiable administrator, but with his character as an honest man intact. People might laugh at him, but none could point the finger at him." [1]

This, then, was the fortress the young greenhorn from Riga, without friends, without money, without even appropriate works, and almost completely ignorant of the French language, had set out to capture. Véron had given the Opéra its dubious moral colour and its low ideals: Duponchel, with a conventionally amiable letter to whom Meyerbeer had supplied Wagner, had local problems enough of his own, without being bothered by this raw little German provincial, with his halting French and his obvious ignorance of the ways of the great world: Pillet, losing money every month, would be the last man in the world to risk anything on this unknown and untried young Teuton, a not particularly impressive specimen externally of a race that was at that time held in the lowest esteem in cosmopolitan operatic circles. Wagner's venture was madness from the first; the wisest and kindest advice that the experienced Meyerbeer could have given him at Boulogne would be to scuttle back to Germany as quickly as he could and not indulge in dreams far beyond his age and his station.

5

But in the autumn of 1839 no doubts, no fears assailed the innocent young Saxon provincial. He was convinced he was marching to the conquest of Paris. He had a vast belief in his own genius. He had already written to Scribe, who was then the ruler, in a sense, of four Paris theatres; and he innocently believed that a man like Scribe would have both the time and the inclination to concern himself with a poor little unknown bourgeois from a country of next to no account in the Parisian world of music and the drama. In imagination he saw himself at once out-Meyerbeering Meyerbeer,

---

[1] BPMO, pp. 212, 213.

out-Spontini-ing Spontini at the Paris Opéra. And with a resounding Paris success to his credit he would soon be back in Germany again, with Directors and Intendants and publishers besieging his door, imploring him for the favour of his next opera on fabulous terms. He forgot that there was a business side to art, and indeed to life; and in business he was as yet no match for the men whose whole being was business, though in his later years, when he had the world at his feet and he had learned something of realities, he put the screw upon the men of business with a rigour they did not like.[1] Paris was to correct many of his idealistic notions, to teach him a good deal about the worst side of theatrical human nature, and so to harden him for the fight that was ahead of him in the later Dresden years.

For the moment, however, Hope told the most flattering of tales. What seemed to him a heaven-sent piece of luck came his way at the very outset. On the boat to Boulogne he made the acquaintance of two Jewish ladies, a Mrs. Manson and her daughter, who, being friends of Meyerbeer, and knowing that he was then in Boulogne, gave Wagner a letter of introduction to him. He hastened to call on him: there is apparently no mention of this visit in Meyerbeer's diary — no doubt it was too insignificant an occurrence in his life to be worth recording — but Wagner tells us that he was received kindly, which was only what we might have expected, for Meyerbeer was a man not only of natural but of cultivated and calculating courtesy, whose maxim was never to make even a potential enemy if he could avoid doing so by a general benevolence of speech and manner. He listened attentively while Wagner read him the first three acts of the libretto of *Rienzi;* the skilled man of the theatre perceived at once the dramatic quality of the work, and later he declared that this was the best operatic book he had ever seen. Wagner left with him the music of the two acts that had been completed, Meyerbeer graciously promising to look through it. He introduced Richard to Moscheles, who was also in Boulogne at the time, and to a then celebrated pianist, Fräulein Marie Leopoldine Blahetka. It was Wagner's first meeting with real international

---

[1] See NFF for an account of his drastic handling of the publishers and the theatre directors after the changes in copyright law (1870) had at last given the intellectual worker some protection against those harpies.

musical celebrities, and the evenings he spent in their company flattered him with the sense that at last he was making his entry into the greater world of music.

He stayed nearly a month in Boulogne, or rather, for economy's sake, some half-hour's distance in the country, in two rooms which he rented, unfurnished, in the house of a wine merchant. Somehow or other he and Minna managed to gather together enough furniture to make the place habitable, and Wagner's usual power of detachment from his surroundings enabled him to resume work on the music of *Rienzi*.

His sister Cäcilie had lately become engaged to Eduard Avenarius, an employé of the Leipzig house of Brockhaus, who had been sent to Paris to manage the branch of their book business there. Wagner had not met him as yet, but he had been kind enough, at Wagner's request, to call upon Scribe with regard to the libretto of *Die hohe Braut*, which Wagner had sent to the great man in 1836, and of which he had had no acknowledgment. Avenarius was to find, before long, that there were decided inconveniences attached to the office of fiancé of a sister of Richard Wagner. For the present, however, Wagner's demands are not on his purse but on his amiability. On the 23rd August he writes to Avenarius asking him to look out for a suitable lodging for him in Paris. It is to be mainly furnished, though he and Minna have brought with them from Riga their own bedding, linen, table ware, and so on. Minna will do her own victualling and cooking, so that only a charwoman will be required for the roughest work. The problem was no doubt anything but an easy one for Avenarius. He seems to have suggested that the Wagners should first of all take a room in a *hôtel garni*, where they would have to pay no more than 30 francs a month. Wagner found this figure so reasonable that he authorised Avenarius to go as far as 40 or even 50 francs. He was anxious to leave Boulogne as soon as possible, for living there was dear, the prices being based on the supposed income-standard of the English visitors to the town.

He and Minna and Robber set out in the diligence on the 16th September, and arrived in Paris the next day. The hotel selected for them by Avenarius was in the Rue de la Tonnellerie (No. 23), in the Halles quarter; it was a narrow side street (later demolished), running between the Rue St. Honoré and the Marché des Innocents. The house, which is now No. 31 of the Rue du Pont-Neuf, bore on its front a bust of Molière, and an inscription that the poet had been born there — a fact that did something to reconcile Wagner to the unpleasant locality. His first impressions of Paris were decidedly unfavourable, especially after London: he found it dirty, dingy, evil-smelling, and noisy, and for the first time the young German provincial must have felt a little scared, a little dubious about the wisdom of his campaign. His solitary acquaintance in the big, bustling city was Avenarius, who at once did what he could for him in the way of introductions, which was not much. Avenarius's own position was at that time a relatively humble one, and his only musical acquaintance was one Anders, a pathetic figure who would have fascinated Balzac. Anders was a German, and at that time in his fifties. Apparently he came of a noble and well-to-do Rhine family: ruined by too generous a belief in human nature, he had saved from the wreck of his fortune only a large library of books; and with these he had come to Paris, where his wide and profound culture obtained for him a subordinate post in the Bibliothèque Royale. There he dragged out a miserable existence on a salary of 1,500 francs a year, supplemented by occasional contributions to the *Gazette musicale*. Anders was an assumed name; neither Wagner nor any other of his friends ever discovered who he really was. This pathetic failure was the first man to whom Wagner unfolded his bold plan for the conquest of Paris.[1]

The German friends to whom Anders introduced Wagner were as pathetic and as impotent as himself. The chief of them was Anders' housemate Samuel Lehrs, another sober and patient German scholar who had found that a world that has never any great use for scholarship is not inclined to pay very much for the commodity. The publisher Didot had made use of Lehrs's knowledge in connection with his famous edition of the Greek classics, paying him only enough to keep body and soul together. He was not musi-

---

[1] Anders had collected a large amount of material for a Life of Beethoven. Being diffident about his own literary powers, he suggested that Wagner should collaborate with him in the work. Wagner submitted a detailed plan of the scheme, which was to run to two volumes of 480 pages each, to various German publishers, but without success. The fee asked for was the modest one of 1,000 thalers.

cal, but Wagner was attracted by the fine personality of the man and his wealth of culture. In *Mein Leben* he speaks of his friendship with Lehrs as one of the most beautiful of his whole life, which is high praise from Wagner. The young musician had even then many sides to him, and Lehrs did him great service in interesting him in matters of philosophy.

Through his sister Luise, who was in Paris with her husband Friedrich Brockhaus in November, Wagner met Ernst Kietz, a young Dresden painter of a childlike, unpractical nature, who was at that time working in the studio of Delaroche. Their friendship was to endure for many years. Wagner, with his usual dramatist's eye for salient human characteristics, has etched him to the life in a few swift strokes. Kietz seems to have been one of those men whose whole life is a preparation for something that never happens. He lived twenty years in Paris without ever mastering the grammar of the language. He spent so much time over the cleaning of his brushes and the mixing of the colours on his palette that he rarely got any actual painting done, the light having faded before he could begin. Wagner declares that, as far as he knew, Kietz never finished a single commissioned portrait. German visitors to Paris, to whom he had been recommended, would have to leave the town before the picture was half completed; while some of his more impatient sitters even died before Kietz had finished his painting of them. According to Wagner, who, of course, may be indulging in a little humorous exaggeration, the only portrait ever finished by Kietz was one of his landlord, done in discharge of arrears of rent. But Kietz had considerable facility in sketches. In July 1840 he made a drawing of Minna that is now in the Burrell Collection. He also did a pencil sketch of Wagner during the winter of 1839, working it up to relative completion some two years later. This is the first portrait of Wagner that we possess. As a record of the Wagner of that period it is no doubt authentic; in the sensitive mouth, with its humorous upturn, we see the very Wagner who bore his disappointments and privations with such courage, confidence and even gaiety, making humorous journalistic capital out of his desperate situation, and astonishing all who met him by the resilience of his temperament.

Wagner tells us it was Kietz who introduced him to a German

fellow-painter, Friedrich Pecht, who, though only a year younger than Richard, survived him some twenty years, dying in 1903 at the age of eighty-nine. Pecht, however, says that it was Laube who introduced them one day in the Louvre. He describes Wagner as being of striking appearance, the large head and expressive face compensating for the shortness of the legs. In his dress he was "particularly elegant"; while Pecht, like everyone else in those days, was enchanted with the good looks and the pleasant nature of Minna. Wagner told him the story of his voyage to London, "the words pouring out like a snow-storm." [1] It was natural that Wagner's few real intimates in Paris should have been all Germans, of whom, Pecht tells us, there were a great number in Paris at that time. He had as yet very little knowledge of the French language, for which he cherished a certain dislike all his life; [2] while Minna never seems to have mastered more than the rudiments of it. He had no money, no clothes, and no social graces [3] for the more fashionable musical and artistic world, even had he been able to secure introductions there. But for the fact that Avenarius was settled in

---

[1] PAMZ, I, 181.

[2] In spite of his claim to have made such progress with Greek as a boy, it is evident that he had no gift at all for languages. "I cannot manage English," he wrote to Praeger in 1855, after he had undertaken to conduct the Philharmonic concerts in London: "I am completely without talent for new languages." He even seems to have made relatively little conquest of French, in spite of his two and a half years in Paris; for he tells Praeger later (writing from Zürich) that he will "muster all the French he learned in London" in order to write intelligibly to Sainton. See RWFP, pp. 21, 27.

[3] His manners were never particularly polished. Even in 1859 he struck his Paris acquaintances as "having neither grace nor elegance, ignorant of [social] ways, and, like all great minds, much more preoccupied with what he had to say than with the effect he was producing." In 1839 he must have seemed to the Parisians very raw and very German, for he had had no experience at all of refined cosmopolitan circles. Schoenewerk (the successor of the music publisher Flaxland), who, being an assistant in the business of Schlesinger, saw something of Wagner in 1840 and 1841, described him to Georges Servières as being at that time "morose, unsociable, murdering the French language and abusing everybody." See SRW, p. 11, and Servières article on Les Visées de Wagner sur Paris, in RMWF, p. 93. He seems to have been introduced into none of the big houses of Paris, or even the musical circles. It will be remembered that in Boulogne he had met not only Meyerbeer but Moscheles. The latter also went on to Paris, where he at once plunged into the musical and social life of the town, seeing everything that was worth seeing, meeting everybody who was anybody. He obviously did not remember the poverty-stricken young German whom he had met at Boulogne, for he made no attempt to find him again. He was at a party at Meyerbeer's at which Halévy, Duponchel, Duprez (the tenor), Habeneck, and Küstner (then Intendant of the Munich Theatre) were present; but Meyerbeer did not think of asking Wagner. See MRMM, p. 256 ff.

Paris he would have found it difficult at first to get any company at all to his liking.

He had not been there long before he came across Laube again. A wealthy young widow, touched by Laube's misfortunes, had married him in 1836, at the commencement of the year's term of imprisonment to which he had been sentenced in Prussia; now, after a period of travel in France and North Africa, the happy pair were enjoying themselves in Paris. Wagner was glad to see him again, not for financial reasons only, though Laube was useful to him in this regard, but because at that time he had a genuine liking for the man. Neither of them anticipated that their friendship would not stand the test of the years, though it endured till as late as 1867: on the 4th October of that year Wagner writes to his old friend that he is dictating his autobiography, and recalling with pleasure his earlier relations with Laube, " you, who, after all," he says, " were the only being whom I had to thank for real friendly services: I look upon you as one of the *very* few honest men with whom I have ever come in contact. I will always think of you with heartfelt warmth." This was a polite prelude to a hint that he could do nothing to help to gratify Laube's wish to be made Intendant of the Court Theatre at Munich: Wagner neither had nor wanted any influence in these matters, and in any case, as he tells Laube in this same letter, he has the poorest possible opinion of the average German theatre of the time, from which he no longer hopes for anything in the way of furtherance of art, and with which he has no desire to be himself associated. Laube, who, like most people, misunderstood the nature of Wagner's relations with King Ludwig and Munich, took the refusal in ill part. In the following year he fell foul of the *Meistersinger* in an article in Hanslick's paper, the Vienna *Neue Freie Presse* — an article that was copied into other journals and created something of a stir in the musical world, for Laube was a man of standing. Wagner's friends were furious over it. Peter Cornelius, who had contributed an article to the *Tonhalle*, a journal edited by the famous scholar Dr. Oscar Paul, broke off relations with the editor and withdrew his article when he discovered that Laube's attack on Wagner had been reproduced there. " Laube's essay," says Bülow in a letter to Raff of the 11th September, 1868, " is merely his revenge for his not getting the Intendantship he wanted so much. We have letters that prove this." Wagner himself held his peace until the following March, when he wrote a curt and truculent note to Laube, who was at that time Director of the Leipzig theatre: " Dear Laube: You would be doing me a great favour if you would use your position at the Leipzig Town Theatre to see that my operas are never given there again. In the hope of a friendly fulfilment of this wish I remain, your obedient servant, Richard Wagner." This seems to have been the end of his dealings with Laube, who showed his resentment at what he took to be Wagner's ingratitude by handling his old friend somewhat unsympathetically in his memoirs. Like many another, he could not see that a youthful friendship with Wagner did not authorise him to expect the mature artist to abandon the ideals for which he had had to wage so endless and so bitter a fight.[1]

Laube's later attitude is humanly understandable, for he had shown Wagner considerable kindness and rendered him substantial aid in Paris and in the pre-Paris days. Minna, no doubt glad to meet again, in a strange land, a woman who spoke her own language, became very friendly with Frau Iduna Laube. It was through Laube that Wagner met Heinrich Heine and his pretty wife Mathilde; the occasion was a dinner at Brocci's restaurant, opposite the Opéra, at which Pecht also was present. We have Pecht's own account, written many years later, of the occasion. Heine was epigrammatic and sarcastic and brilliant, as usual. Wagner told them the story of his Paris ambitions, and, once more, of the dreadful voyage to London; and Heine, who knew the world in general and Paris in particular better than his guileless young compatriot did, held up his hands in pious amazement at such Teutonic simplicity. The pretty Mathilde, who had not an idea in her charming little head, quite eclipsed the two German women: Frau Laube, though " exceedingly intelligent," was " a little faded "; while in comparison with the sparkling Mathilde, the " good-hearted " Minna seemed " rather home-baked." [2] Though the poet and the musician met a few times more, Wagner was never really attracted to Heine; perhaps, for one thing, he could never

---

[1] Wagner found an outlet for his spleen in three rude sonnets on Laube, which will be found in RWGS, XII, 370, 371.

[2] PAMZ, I, 185.

quite forgive him for being a Jew. He would be chilled, too, by Heine's cynicism and his pouring of cold water on his younger compatriot's hopes: perhaps, in his worldly wisdom, Heine struck at the root of the matter when he made a double-edged remark that was no doubt repeated to Wagner — " Do you know what makes me suspicious of this talent? The fact that he is recommended by Meyerbeer " — but at that time Wagner's belief in Meyerbeer's good intentions towards him was still unshaken. He, for his part, could hardly be unaware of the clouds of suspicion that gathered round Heine's head in political and artistic circles. He was in the pay of the French secret service; and he was thought to be not above using his journalistic pen as an instrument for putting financial pressure on his friends.[1]

---

[1] See, for instance, the curious, mysterious, but faintly unpleasant episode with Liszt in 1844. Heine apparently wrote to inform Liszt that he had done an article that would appear *before* the pianist's second concert, and as there were things in it that might not please him, he thought it as well to inform Liszt of this. Precisely what happened then we do not know; but it is assumed that Heine either read to Liszt the article in its original wounding form (which has come down to us), or in a form that, milder as it may have been, was still of a character to provoke Liszt to an angry rejoinder; whereupon Heine, also losing his temper, added some extra spiteful touches to his script. According to another version of the story, Heine was irritated with Liszt because the latter had not sent him free tickets for one of his concerts. See LZBHZ, I, 68. Heine's article, dated 25th April, 1844, will be found in his *Musikalische Berichte aus Paris*, in HSW, XI, 404 ff.

According to another version of the story, it was Liszt's refusal to accept a bill for a fairly large amount drawn on him by Heine that provoked the latter to give a malicious turn to his article: he sneered publicly at Liszt's open-handed charity, attributed his success to lavish expenditure on applause and on bouquets and to the foolishness of erotic women, and so on and so on. After the appearance of this malicious and mendacious article, Liszt terminated his acquaintance with Heine. In after life he never hesitated to express his contempt for the character of the brilliant rapscallion. Wagner tells us that in Zürich, in 1856, the conversation having turned on Heine, Frau Wesendonk asked him if he did not think the poet's name would be inscribed in the temple of immortality. "Yes," said Liszt, "but in mud."

Heine's ingratitude, and his proneness to take literary revenge on people who did not do as much for him as he thought he had a right to expect, were notorious. Therese Devrient tells of a visit to Salomon Heine, the Hamburg banker, in 1930. "Who is the gentleman over there?" she asked. "Don't you know him?" said old Salomon: "that is my nephew Heinrich, the poet." Then he whispered behind his hand, "The *canaille!*" Heine began to speak of his having no money for travelling. The uncle, as everyone knew, supported him, said to him, "Eh, Heinrich, you need not complain. If you are short of money, you just call on some good friends and threaten them like this — 'I will make you so ridiculous in my next book that no respectable person will have anything to do with you.' Failing that, you abuse some nobleman or other. You have devices enough at your disposal." See DJE, p. 330, 331.

In his poem *Die Menge tut es* Heine sneered at Meyerbeer, who had not merely

Wagner met Liszt twice during his two and a half years in Paris. He was introduced to the world-conquering pianist by Schlesinger in April, 1840. Liszt was no doubt too busy then to take much notice of this insignificant caller. Wagner, for his part, secretly resented Liszt's success and wealth and his ease of manner in a world from which he himself was excluded, and so was not in a mood to open out to him. Wagner went away with a feeling of repulsion. Towards the end of March or the beginning of April, 1841, Liszt being in Paris once more, Wagner called on him at the suggestion of Laube. Liszt was as affable as he always was; but the room was full of admirers, and as the conversation was in French, Wagner could make little of it. (He had been in Paris now a year and a half: and the fact that he had still so little command of French is another proof of his lack of aptitude for languages.) From Wagner's own account of the affair one surmises that he had gone there in the hope of borrowing some money. That subject, of course, could not be broached with company present: so Wagner tried to turn the conversation on to Loewe and Schubert, but met with no particular response on Liszt's part. He left his address, and a day or two after received, from Liszt's secretary Belloni, an invitation ticket for the pianist's coming recital. He went to this: he was stunned by Liszt's virtuosity, but out of tune with the general musical mentality of the occasion; and he was irritated by the atmosphere of opulence and feminine adoration in which Liszt seemed to bathe so complacently. In his mood of deepening seriousness towards his art he felt there could never be any community of spirit between him and Liszt; and he called on him no more. He dealt cursorily and rather contemptuously with the recital in his Letter of the 6th April, 1841, to the Dresden *Abendzeitung*, dwelling peevishly on the fact that Liszt had charged 20 francs admission, had no expenses, himself being the sole performer, and had cleared 10,000 francs, and dismissing mere piano-playing as a matter that gave him more pain than pleasure: " I got such a fearful head-ache, such painful

---

lent but given him money: "the music-corrupter Meyerbeer," he calls him, the "Beerenmeyer." A quarrel came when Meyerbeer refused to pay over a further 500 francs and to set Heine's poems to music. (See KM, pp. 47, 48.) See also Heine's caddish references to Liszt in the poem *Jung-Katerverein für Poesie-Musik*.

For a searching modern study of Heine in Paris, his malice and treachery and ingratitude, see MH, Chapter VIII.

twitchings of the nerves, that I had to go home early and put myself to bed."

In a notice of Liszt's second concert which he sent to the *Abendzeitung* on the 5th May — it was a concert for the benefit of the projected Beethoven memorial at Bonn, at which Liszt played and Berlioz conducted — he made a neat little epigram about the pair (" Liszt makes money with no expenses, while Berlioz has expenses but makes no money "), but twitted Liszt for having given way to his ignorant audience so far as to play, at a Beethoven concert, his fantasia on *Robert the Devil* as an encore. Liszt himself was chagrined at the demand, and yielded to it with manifest ill-humour; but the incident no doubt confirmed Wagner in his belief that the pianist, for all his natural gifts, was too much the slave of his public for there to be any spiritual kinship between Liszt and him. And always, at the back of his mind, was the horrible thought that Liszt was making millions by his piano-strumming, while *he*, the German idealist, was starving.

Wagner was soon to discover that in the musical world of Paris an introduction, even from Meyerbeer, did not necessarily mean anything. Meyerbeer was always generous enough with his letters to influential people, but he must have known that this poor and unknown young German musician had not the ghost of a chance of having anything practical done for him at any of the Paris theatres. Still, a recommendation would do neither of them any harm: Meyerbeer, a singular mixture of kindness and calculation, could presumably count on having laid yet another colleague under an ostensible obligation to him: if Wagner made good, he would owe a debt of gratitude to his benefactor, and if he failed, well, at all events Meyerbeer could say he had done his best for him. The whole inner truth of the matter will perhaps never be known: meanwhile the safest thing is to assume that Meyerbeer really did what he could to help this innocent young enthusiast, while remaining too much a man of the world to be under the slightest illusion as to the practical result of it all. He first of all sent Wagner to Duponchel, who adjusted his monocle and read the letter of introduction with the air of a man who had seen more letters of the kind than he could remember. Wagner went away from the Presence, and never heard another word from the Director of the Opéra.

He made no attempt to reach Scribe, realising at once, from all he heard, that so important and busy a personage would have no time for anyone so insignificant as he. He called, however, on Lablache, to try to interest him in a grand aria, with chorus, which he had written in his best Bellini style. He hoped that Lablache would introduce it into the part of Orovisto in *Norma*. The great basso received the young man kindly, but declined the aria on the ground that it would be impossible to insert anything of that kind into an opera that was so well known. This aria was part of a general plan of Wagner's, during 1839 and 1840, to make a little money by turning out a few trifles in the mode of the day. In *Mein Leben* he mentions three songs written at this period — *Dors, mon enfant*, the words of which were by a friend of Anders, Ronsard's *Mignonne*, and Victor Hugo's *L'Attente* (from *Les Orientales*). These were published in 1840 in Paris by Flaxland, under the title of *Trois Mélodies: Musique de R. Wagner*, with a dedication to the Baroness de Caters. *Dors mon enfant* was issued in 1841 as a supplement to Lewald's journal *Europa*,[1] the Ronsard and Hugo songs also appearing there in the following year.[2] To this epoch belong also the songs *Les Adieux de Marie Stuart* and *Tout n'est qu'images fugitives*, a setting of a French version of Heine's *Two Grenadiers* and a chorus written for the vaudeville *La Descente de la Courtille*, which was being given at the Variétés Theatre.[3] Some of the songs seem to have had a fair success; but as Wagner saw that to achieve anything substantial in this line he would have to pay court to influential singers in order to induce them to take them up, he soon abandoned this line of attack on Paris. He never forgot or forgave the humiliations to which the singers whom he approached subjected him in those Paris days. One of them was Pauline Viardot. At Triebschen he gave Cosima a bitter account of how he called on the Viardot and was kept waiting a long time before he was admitted, only to be told, with a smile, that she would not sing his *Attente*.[4]

---

[1] EU, 1841, I, 144.

[2] EU, 1842, I, 368 and II, 304.

[3] These Paris works are mostly published in Vols. XV and XVI of the Collected Edition. For a study of them see NW, pp. 246–248. *The Two Grenadiers* was published by Schotts.

[4] MECW, I, 455.

In his desperate need of money he was prepared to do almost anything that seemed to hold out the least hope of success. He thought his frivolous *Liebesverbot*, the score of which he had with him, might appeal to French taste; so towards the end of 1839 or early in 1840 he gave the libretto, for translation, to an elderly gentleman named Dumersan, to whom he had been introduced by Anders. Three numbers from it were soon got ready for a possible audition. A little later, in response to his appeals for further introductions, Meyerbeer sent him to his man of affairs, Gouin, with a recommendation to Anténor Joly, the director of the Renaissance Theatre. A promise was actually given him that *Das Liebesverbot* would be produced there, but first of all, he was told, there would have to be an audition, by the Committee, of a few numbers from it. The hope was clearly that the tiresome business would break down at the first fence; the director had only to say — which ultimately he did — that the singers at the theatre were all too busy to learn any fresh parts, and that would be the end of the matter. This little plot was frustrated by Meyerbeer. Certain of the leading singers at the Grand Opéra were under personal obligations to him; and Gouin obtained their consent to sing at the audition. A few days later Wagner received the news that the Renaissance Theatre was bankrupt and had closed down. Cynics, of course, hinted to him later that Meyerbeer must have been well aware of the coming bankruptcy when he sent Wagner to Joly, and that he had his own subtle reasons for the double stroke of planting Wagner in a moribund theatre and detaching him from the Opéra. This is another case in which there does not seem the least likelihood of our ever knowing the whole truth.

By this time Duponchel had practically resigned the management of the Opéra, his place being temporarily filled by Edouard Monnais.[1] Wagner managed to persuade the latter to carry through the audition that had been originally arranged for the Renaissance;

---

[1] "The year 1839 witnessed an entry and an exit at the Opéra. The entry was effected by Edouard Monnais, an honest and clever fellow, a distinguished man of letters, who became co-Director with Duponchel: the affairs of the Opéra having become somewhat involved, it had been thought necessary to call to Duponchel's assistance a man of the profoundest inexperience in the matter of opera. A mathematician was needed, and it was a dancer who. ... Edouard Monnais made his entry at the Opéra, in his *flamme de punch* coat, which caused a certain sensation, and all was said: the Opéra was not saved." BPMO, p. 178.

and as the singers taking part in it belonged to the Opéra there could be no great harm done by letting this importunate little alien have his futile way for an hour or so. Wagner now called on Scribe to ask him to be present; and the manufacturer of libretti was kind enough to consent. The audition accordingly took place in the green room of the Opéra, before Monnais and Scribe. Wagner, who, as we know, was not a great pianist at the best of times, and who had probably not touched a piano for nearly a year, played the accompaniments. When all was over, nothing remained but to get rid of the tiresome young German intruder in the politest possible way. In true French fashion, the listeners declared the music to be *charmante*. Scribe generously promised to write a libretto for Wagner as soon as he was informed that the management had given the latter a commission for an opera [1] — a contingency he knew well was never likely to arrive. M. Monnais protected himself with a declaration that a definite commission of that kind was of course not possible at the moment. Wagner, in his heart of hearts, must have known that he was merely being played with; but for all that he thought it, as he says, " very nice " of these two important gentlemen to have listened to his music, and particularly kind of the great Scribe to have attended and to have said a friendly word to him.

During all these weary months he was not only working away at the music of *Rienzi* but thinking out the plan of an opera on that subject of the *Flying Dutchman* that had affected his imagination so powerfully on the voyage from Pillau. Just as in later years he was to suspend work on the *Ring* in order to produce what he thought would be not only a smaller but an easier and more immediately practical work — the said little work turning out to be none other than the formidable *Tristan* — so now he thought he was being eminently practical in abandoning for the moment the frontal attack on the Opéra with *Rienzi* and making a flank attack on it with the *Flying Dutchman*. It must have been, in large part, his artistic instinct that made him conceive the new subject in a single

---

[1] The English mis-translation of *Mein Leben* makes it appear that Scribe undertook to arrange the libretto of *Das Liebesverbot* if and when the Opéra authorities accepted that work. The meaning of the German, however, is clear enough: "Scribe announced his willingness to arrange a text for me as soon as the administration had entrusted me with a commission to write the music for it."

act,[1] but, in his innocence, he also dreamed that in this form, as a curtain-raiser before a ballet, it would stand more chance of acceptance at the Opéra. Once more he wrote to Meyerbeer, who was then in Berlin, for help. Meyerbeer arrived in Paris in the summer of 1840, and, according to Wagner, was " most sympathetic and obliging." He took Wagner to the new Director of the Opéra, Léon Pillet. As a result of the " serious confabulation " that went on in French between the other two, Wagner learned, to his surprise, that Meyerbeer thought he would be well advised to begin by co-operating with some other composer in writing a scene for a ballet. He refused to consider this suggestion, which, however, seems at least to prove Meyerbeer's good faith towards him. As he was to learn later, it was, and had been from the start, utterly out of the question that room should be found in a moment for an unknown foreigner like himself in the operatic repertory; but that he should have been asked to write anything at all appears to prove a certain amount of insistence on Meyerbeer's part with the authorities.

Before he went away from this meeting, Wagner left with Pillet the sketch of the *Flying Dutchman* subject. Some time later he learned, after many enquiries, that Pillet had taken such a fancy to the sketch that he would like to buy it from him — to be set to music by one or other of the many composers with whom he was under contract for the supply of libretti. When Wagner refused to entertain this suggestion, pointing out that the idea of the opera was his own and that no one else could work it out along the proper lines, Pillet told him frankly that there was not the ghost of a chance of Meyerbeer's recommendation of him ever coming to anything at the Opéra, as his commitments were already made for the next seven years; once more advised him, if he wanted to compose any music for that establishment, to see the ballet-master with regard to the music for a dance; and ended by urging him, in his own interest, to be sensible and sell him the *Flying Dutchman* sketch. Wagner sought the advice of M. Monnais, who recommended him to accept Pillet's offer: as he pointed out, the story itself was quite a well-known one, and anyone who chose to make an opera of it had the right to do so; as a matter of fact, Paul Fou-

---

[1] It was only in obedience to theatrical exigencies at Dresden that he allowed the work to be produced in three acts. It was given as a one-act opera at Bayreuth in 1901.

cher, a brother-in-law of Victor Hugo, was already at work on a libretto on the same subject. Since, then, the legend would be made into an opera by someone else whether Wagner approved or not, whether he surrendered his own sketch or not, the most sensible thing he could do was to take the money offered him by Pillet and be thankful. In the end Pillet paid him the not unhandsome fee of 500 francs for the sketch, so that on the whole Wagner had decidedly the best of the bargain. No one in France was likely to make a great success of the sombre theme: he, for his part, could still construct an opera of his own out of it. And above all he had 500 unexpected francs in his pocket, which were very useful to him just then.

The *Flying Dutchman* was actually set as an opera by a mediocre composer of the name of Pierre Dietsch and produced in Paris in 1842. It was a failure, so that Wagner had both his 500 francs and his revenge. He was to meet this paltry rival of his later under curious circumstances. Dietsch rose in the course of the years to the rank of conductor at the Opéra; and to him fell the task of conducting the Paris version of *Tannhäuser* in 1861. In that capacity he was thoroughly incompetent.

In the whole two and a half years of his stay in Paris Wagner heard only one of his own works, and that an inferior one, and in a mutilated form. One of the introductions Meyerbeer had given him was to Habeneck, the celebrated conductor at the Opéra and of the famous Conservatoire concerts, which had been founded in 1828. Wagner had sought him out soon after his arrival in Paris, and was greeted kindly by the older man, who acceded to his request that something of his should be run through at one of the Conservatoire rehearsals. For this purpose Wagner left with him the score and parts of his Magdeburg *Columbus* Overture. The promise was fulfilled so far as the rehearsal was concerned; but it was made quite clear to him that there was no prospect of a concert performance. A year or so later, after Wagner had become a person of some small repute in the musical world of Paris, not as a composer but as the writer of piquant articles for the *Gazette musicale*, Schlesinger, the proprietor of that journal, offered to produce an orchestral work of his at one of the concerts he occasionally gave by way of publicity for his paper and for his music publishing business. Wagner at first thought of suggesting his recently completed *Faust Overture*, but in the end decided that the quiet ending of that would be unlikely to impress a Paris audience which had had no training in music of the German poetic and philosophical kind. He learned, too, that the orchestra for the occasion would be a poor one, and that it would have only one rehearsal. So there was nothing for it but to bring out the supposedly effective *Columbus* once more. Habeneck, when Wagner went to fetch his parts from the Conservatoire library, drily but kindly warned him of the danger of trying a work of this sort on Paris. He thought it, in his own terms, " vague," by which he probably meant that it did not explain itself without a knowledeg of the poetic subject on the hearer's part.

In Germany, with its wealth of good regimental bands, it was easy enough for a composer to get together an exceptional number of brass instruments for a special occasion. Wagner found this resource not open to him in Paris. He saw he could not count on the six brave trumpets that had so dazzled his Magdeburg audience. A practical cornettist whom he consulted promised to find him four trumpeters if he would re-write the parts on that smaller scale; he added, however, that of these four only two could be relied upon to play decently. At the rehearsal Wagner found them incapable of playing the soft high notes without cracking; moreover, both the conductor and the orchestra made hardly any secret of their conviction that they thought the work crazy. Berlioz was present at the rehearsal. " He remained silent throughout," says Wagner. " He gave me no encouragement, and made no attempt to dissuade me. He merely said at the finish, with a smile and sigh, that it was difficult to do anything in Paris." Poor Berlioz knew only too well.

The performance, on the night of the 4th February, 1841, under the conductor Valentino, was, as Wagner himself admits, a complete failure, for which he blames the incompetent trumpeters, though he hints at a suspicion that the audience was bored by the work. It was the first work on the programme, which was devoted entirely to German composers. The Press was not unkind; the more intelligent listeners recognised how bad the performance had been, while the audience, which was mainly made up of subscribers to the *Gazette musicale,* many of whom were Germans, paid the composer the compliment of comparing the structure of the work with the theory of the overture that had been set out by Wagner in an article in the *Gazette* a little while before. Berlioz, in the *Journal des Débats,* preserved a prudent silence with regard to the work. If Pecht's reminiscences, written long afterwards, are to be trusted, the Overture was hissed. He had Minna in his charge, Richard being busy behind the scenes. Poor half-starved Minna, for whom the success of this first hearing for Wagner in Paris — after eighteen months' unceasing conflict — meant so much, lost her nerve, burst into tears, and almost had a fainting fit. Pecht could steady her only by abusing her roughly; he told her that he expected something more of an old theatrical hand like her than to be upset by a lot of stupid orchestral players.

Apparently Wagner had his *Polonia* Overture with him in Paris, and he may have tried to get a performance of this also. The score was found by Pasdeloup among his papers [1] in 1881, and sent to Wagner, who was at that time staying in Palermo. It was played to the company on the piano, presumably by Josef Rubinstein, on Christmas Eve of that year. [2] How the score came into Pasdeloup's possession is not stated. At the time of Wagner's sojourn in Paris, Pasdeloup was a quite unknown young man of twenty-two or so: he did not commence giving his orchestral concerts until 1851. Kapp (JKRW, p. 189) says that Wagner had presented the score to the Paris conductor Duvinage.

6

Wagner had plunged into the Paris adventure with practically no money in his purse. How then did he live during these two and a half years?

To some extent he boiled the pot by means of journalism, though his earnings from that source, considering how poorly the average writer was paid in those days, could not have been great. He seems to have become a writer for Schlesinger's *Gazette musicale* by a

---

[1] Not, as Koch puts it (MKRW, I, 288) in Pasdeloup's *Nachlass,* for Pasdeloup did not die until 1887.

[2] We are given to understand that this was the original manuscript. But a *Polonia* score had been found in 1877 in that old trunk (left at Tichatschek's when Wagner fled from Dresden in 1849) that contained the parts of the C major symphony and a score of the *Columbus* Overture. See GRW, VI, 66, 555.

kind of accident. As has been mentioned already, among the songs with which he had hoped to win an entry into the Paris concert room was a setting of a French translation of *The Two Grenadiers*. But for this, as for his other efforts, he could not find a singer: Pauline Viardot and others whom he approached were for the most part complimentary, but each had his own quite good excuse for doing nothing with regard to them. The objection to *The Two Grenadiers* was that Wagner had had, like Schumann — though some five years earlier — the idea of introducing the *Marseillaise* at the end; and that song, he was assured, could be sung in Paris only to the accompaniment of cannons and muskets. As Schlesinger would not take any of his songs, Wagner recklessly decided to publish *The Two Grenadiers* at his own expense. That, of course, was *his* euphemistic way of putting it. What really happened was that after Schlesinger had engraved the song at an agreed price of 50 francs, no copies, according to him, were ever sold, and Wagner was unable to meet his little bill in the way he had expected. Schlesinger accordingly suggested that Wagner should wipe off the debt by means of a contribution to the *Gazette musicale*. Now began for him a new period of initiation into the charming ways of the publishing world. First of all, half his fee had to go to someone who translated his articles from German into French. Then he discovered that the " sheet " for which it was understood he was to receive a fee of 60 francs became, after deduction of the space taken up by the title, the signature, and so on, only half a sheet. Authors in those days were very much at the mercy of the publishers, and the German Jew Schlesinger was a particularly good business man.

Wagner's first article for the *Gazette musicale* was entitled *German Music*. In this he gave his Paris readers an excellent account of the fundamental difference between German and other music — the former tending more towards the instrumental than the vocal, and so on — and the now homesick artist was inclined to idealise, at a distance, the very conditions in his own country from which he had fled. He dwelt lovingly and with touching exaggeration on the honest if not always brilliant musical efforts of the amateur instrumentalists in the smallest German towns, among whom music was not an affair of public show but a religion of the home. He assured his no doubt astonished French readers that even in insignificant German towns there were to be found orchestras that could perform symphonies admirably; the ordinary bandsman could generally play more than one instrument, while the amateurs were often even better than the professionals. No wonder the article drew from Anders the ironic comment that if all this were true, then Germany must be a fine place for a musician to live in.

Wagner's journalistic articles during his Paris period were as follows: the dates appended are those of their appearance in the *Gazette musicale:*

1. *German Music.* 12 and 26 July, 1840.
2. *Pergolesi's " Stabat mater."* 11 October, 1840. (A review of an arrangement of the work, for " chorus and grand orchestra," by Lwoff.)
3. *The Virtuoso and the Artist.* 18 October, 1840.
4. *A Pilgrimage to Beethoven.* 19, 22, and 29 November and 3 December, 1840.
5. *The Overture.* 10, 14 and 17 January, 1841.
6. *An End in Paris.* 31 January and 7 and 11 February, 1841.
7. *The Musician and Publicity.* 1 April, 1841.
8. *" Der Freischütz "* in Paris. 23 and 30 May, 1841.
9. *A Happy Evening.* 24 October and 7 November, 1841.
10. *Halévy's " Reine de Chypre."* 27 February, 13 March, 24 April and 1 May, 1842.

Some of these articles also appeared in German papers, as follows:

4. In the *Dresden Abendzeitung,* 30 July to 5 August, 1841.
6. In *ditto,* 6 to 11 August, 1841.
8. Wagner wrote two articles on this subject. The first appeared in the *Gazette musicale* on the dates given above; it was intended to enlighten the Paris public in advance with regard to Weber's work, the first French performance of which was given in Paris on the 7th June. The second article, written after the event, appeared in the *Dresden Abendzeitung* on 16, 17, 19, 20 and 21 July, 1841. Its object was to tell the German public what a travesty of the original the production had been.

10. In the *Dresden Abendzeitung*, 26, 27, 28 and 29 January, 1842. (Halévy's opera had received its first performance in Paris on the 22nd December, 1841.)

The following articles appeared in Germany alone:

A. *Rossini's " Stabat Mater,"* in the *Neue Zeitschrift für Musik*, 28 December, 1841. It bore the pseudonym " H. Valentino."

B. *Paris Amusements* and *Parisian Fatalities for Germans*, in Lewald's *Europa*, 2nd and 3rd quarters, 1841. Signed " W. Freudenfeuer."

C. *Letters from Paris*, in the *Dresden Abendzeitung*:

    (1) 19, 20 and 22 March, 1841.
    (2) 24 to 28 May.
    (3) 14 to 17 June.[1]
    (4) 2 to 4 August.
    (5) 23 August.
    (6) 1 and 2 October.
    (7) 4 to 8 December.
    (8) 25 December.
    (9) 10 and 11 January, 1842.

Letter from Paris, in the *Neue Zeitschrift für Musik*, 22 February, 1842.

When he was preparing the collected edition of his literary works for publication in the 1870's, Wagner included only the articles numbered 1, 3, 4, 5, 6, 7, 8, 9, and 10 in the first of the above lists, that on Rossini's *Stabat Mater*, and the second of the articles on *Der Freischütz*.

The article on Pergolesi was translated (from the *Gazette musicale*) by Ashton Ellis in the 7th volume of his English edition of Wagner's Prose Works (1898), and those on *Paris Amusements* and *Paris Fatalities*, the *Gazette musicale* article on Halévy, and the *Letters from Paris* in his 8th volume (1899) — all from the originals in the *Gazette musicale*. Julius Kapp published all these articles, that had been discarded by Wagner, in his volume entitled

---

[1] In 1913 Julius Kapp published in the *Berliner Tageblatt*, for the first time (from the original manuscript), the sketch for the well-known discussion of Berlioz's *Symphonie fantastique* that appears in this third *Letter from Paris*. Apparently the sketch "was written in the first moment of enthusiasm after hearing the work, but did not survive a later, more critical consideration, and was therefore rejected." See JKRW, p. 219.

Der junge Wagner (1910).[1] He also printed a *Letter from Paris,* dated 1 August, 1841 (No. 5 in our list), that is not in Ellis. This is also published in volume 12 of the complete German edition of Wagner's writings. It is incomplete and unsigned, but there is no doubt as to its authorship. Apparently the regular Paris correspondent of the *Abendzeitung,* Josef Mendelssohn, had left the town, and the editor, Wagner's old acquaintance Winkler, had asked the musician to send him something for the paper. Wagner was at this time not in Paris itself but in Meudon, hard at work at the music of the *Flying Dutchman;* and it looks as if he had not had the time or the patience to complete this article.

7

As will be seen, Wagner's literary activity extended over a period of nearly eighteen months, from July, 1840, to November, 1841: he suspended his journalism from time to time to get on with the composition of *Rienzi,* to do other work for Schlesinger, and to write the *Flying Dutchman* (August and September, 1841). In these eighteen months he wrote what amounts, in all, to about an ordinary volume of 300 pages or so. Many a journalist in these days writes more than that annually, year in and year out; but Wagner was not a writer by profession; it would take him some time to acquire any ease of technique, and all in all his journalism alone must have kept him very busy during this period.

But this by no means represented all the work he did in Paris. When he left Riga he had written only two acts of *Rienzi;* he had

---

[1] The reader may possibly become confused over the Halévy articles. For the most part, the articles reproduced in the German papers correspond with the French versions, allowing for a few passages altered in translation, and for others that were suppressed in the French but were restored in the German. On Halévy, however, Wagner wrote two separate articles, one for the *Gazette musicale,* the other for the *Abendzeitung;* the latter only was reprinted by him in the 1871 ff. edition of his writings. It is this article that appears in Ellis's 7th volume, while the French article, translated from the *Gazette musicale,* is given in his 8th volume. Both Ellis and Glasenapp believed that Wagner's original German version of this article was lost to the world, the manuscript having become the property of some unknown private purchaser or other. Kapp, however, had access to this manuscript, and in *Der junge Wagner* he printed the German original for the first time. (The conclusion was missing; this had to be supplied from the French.) It appears that the manuscript is now at Wahnfried, and the article is reprinted in the 12th (supplementary) volume of RWGS.

finished the scoring of the second act before he left Boulogne. The other three acts were written in Paris between the 15th February and the 19th September, 1840, the overture being completed on the 23rd October. The scoring of the opera was finished a month later. The music of the *Flying Dutchman* was written, at high pressure, in seven weeks, in August and September, 1841, the final page being dated the 13th September: the scoring and the overture were completed by the end of the year. In addition to all this he did a large amount of musical hack-work for Schlesinger; the full extent of this will probably never be known.

Schlesinger had at first engaged him to write a method for the cornet, an instrument much in favour among Parisian musical amateurs at that time. When Wagner confessed that he did not know how to set about such a task, Schlesinger suggested to him the admirable method afterwards adopted by the gentleman in *Pickwick Papers,* who turned out an essay on Chinese Metaphysics by the simple process of reading an article on China and one on Metaphysics, and then " combining the information." Schlesinger supplied Wagner with five already published methods for the cornet, the information in which, according to him, Wagner had only to combine. Fortunately for him, and perhaps for his publisher and the lovers of the cornet, before he had discovered how to begin, Schlesinger found what he wanted in another quarter. He then sent Wagner sixty operas in piano arrangements, from which he was to patch together fourteen suites of airs arranged for the cornet. But before the first group of these was engraved, Schlesinger took the precaution of submitting the arrangements to a cornet expert, who declared that Wagner knew nothing about the instrument, the keys in which he had set the airs being as a rule too high for the average amateur. The expert agreed to correct the work on condition that Wagner shared his fee with him; whereupon Schlesinger took back his sixty scores and relieved Wagner of any further responsibility in the matter.

Some time later, when Wagner's exchequer was at its lowest, Schlesinger burst into his presence with a piano score of Donizetti's *La Favorita*, which was just then enjoying a success in Paris, and, with an air of the greatest benevolence, offered him a fee for (1) a complete arrangement of the opera for voice and piano, (2) an

Heinrich Laube

WAGNER'S MOTHER AT THE AGE OF 65
(*Courtesy, J. B. Lippincott Co.*)

arrangement of the whole work for piano solo, (3) ditto for four hands, (4) a complete arrangement for a quartet, (5) ditto for two violins, (6) ditto for cornet. For all this ghastly labour the publisher offered the magnificent fee of 1,100 francs, baiting the offer with another of an immediate advance of 500 francs, which he well knew the starving young man could not refuse.[1] Wagner tells us also that he made an arrangement from Halévy's *Reine de Chypre;* and no doubt he did other work of the same degrading, exhausting, and ill-paid kind. It was probably the spectacle of his unceasing labour that kept Minna's affection for him alight through all the miseries he had brought on her. Later, in the Zürich period that followed the flight from Dresden, she became sharply critical of him when she saw him wasting his time, as she thought, on the writing of ponderous prose works which she could not imagine anyone wanting to read, instead of using the fame he had won by his three Dresden operas to advance his interests as a composer. But there can be no doubt that in these dreadful Paris days she clung to him devotedly and uncomplainingly; his obvious sufferings and the pathetic frustration of all his hopes brought out the best there was in her kind and loyal nature.

8

What he earned by his work could only have sufficed, of course, to keep them in bread and butter, and Wagner, as usual, thought himself entitled to rather more than bread and butter. It is fairly clear that Laube lent him money, besides, as Wagner himself admits in *Mein Leben,* persuading " one of his wealthy friends in Leipzig " to come to the young man's aid. Wagner does not mention the name of this benefactor; but we now know that it was one Axenfeld, a merchant in Leipzig, and a Jew. Of the latter fact Wagner could hardly fail to be aware; and we can imagine Axenfeld's feelings if he ever read later the composer's venomous attack on his race. We know that Wagner borrowed from Kietz; a letter of the 3rd June, 1840, in the Burrell Collection, is evidence of that, while a letter

---

[1] These are the figures given by Wagner in *Mein Leben.* They are practically confirmed by a document in the Burrell Collection — a statement showing that he received 1,150 francs for the *Favorita* arrangements and 230 francs for an arrangement of Halévy's *Guitarrero.*

of July, 1841, in the same collection shows him returning a loan to Kietz. Although he did not know Avenarius before he reached Paris in September, 1839, he must have begun borrowing from him very soon after his arrival; for on the 4th January, 1840, we find him asking Avenarius if the latter will allow him to *increase* his indebtedness to him by another 50 francs. He confesses that the request may seem to " border on the impudent," but pleads that in order to pay his rent he had yesterday taken to the pawnshop the last of the household things he could spare, but still without raising enough. And, as is the way with every professional borrower, he assures Avenarius that this is positively the last time he will trouble him. On the back of the letter is pencilled Avenarius's reply: " I send you, dear friend, the 50 francs you ask for, making 400 francs in all, and will see what I find your sister inclined to. But with the best will in the world I *cannot* go any further; I mention this so as to avoid any possible misunderstandings." Though Avenarius had married Cäcilie on the 5th March, 1840, and she was now settled with him in Paris, the sister referred to in this reply cannot be she. The reference must be to Luise, who was married to the well-to-do Friedrich Brockhaus. As we have seen, she had been in Paris with her husband in November, 1839, on her way to Italy, and had annoyed Wagner by buying all kinds of expensive things without showing any desire to help *him*. Whether she responded to Avenarius's appeal on his behalf we do not know, but in April, 1840, we find Wagner sending him a letter which is to be sent on to Frau Laube and Luise, giving Avenarius authority to advance Wagner 200 francs. He hopes, however, that Avenarius will take the " shorter and much less ceremonial course " of himself advancing the money then and there, recouping himself in a month out of the remittance that is to come from Leipzig. Once more this is the last time he will trouble him, but his necessity is dire. He regrets that his borrowing should have led to a certain coolness in the relations between the two households — he tells us of this, by the way, in *Mein Leben* — and he recognises fully what a plague repeated demands of this kind must be to a business man; but he has no alternative. Anyhow, as this is to be positively the last time, the family relations can now be expected to improve, a state of things which he ardently desires.

But in February of the next year he is forced to apply to Avenarius for a further 500 francs " until Easter." He tells him that he
is doing work on *La Favorita* and *Guitarrero* for Schlesinger for a
fee of 3,000 francs, of which 1,500 have been already paid to him
— which, as we now know, is a slight exaggeration. He does not
want to ask Schlesinger for any more just yet, so will his kind
brother-in-law come to the rescue until Easter? The draft of Avenarius's reply, which accompanies this letter, runs thus: " Dear
Wagner, believe me that perhaps none of your relations would be
readier than I to assist you with a loan, if I could. But I have no
money to dispose of: my salary from the business, which I draw at
regular intervals, I need for my really very modest housekeeping,
while the capital of the business is not at my personal disposal."
He advises Wagner to induce Schlesinger to accept a bill for the
Guitarrero work, which he, Avenarius, will try to get discounted
for him. Wagner tells us in *Mein Leben* that his brother-in-law was
" not well-off "; and it is easy to understand that all these borrowings distressed Cäcilie and led to a temporary coolness between her
and Richard.

9

It was a lifelong habit with Wagner to anticipate financially the
success he was sure was waiting for him round the corner. The bare
promise of Gouin with regard to a production of *Das Liebesverbot*
at the Renaissance Theatre was enough to make him leave the in-
salubrious neighbourhood in which he had first settled in Paris,
and, at Easter, 1840, take rooms " nearer the musical centre " —
on the fourth floor of No. 25 Rue du Helder, off the Boulevard des
Italiens. In *Mein Leben* he blames Lehrs for giving him " this foolhardy advice." Seemingly his funds had already been exhausted,
in spite of his and Minna's habit of dining at a cheap restaurant for
a franc, and in spite of their having first of all pawned their silver
wedding presents and what remained of Minna's theatrical wardrobe, and then sold the pawn-tickets. Only his inextinguishable
optimism, therefore, could have blinded him to the danger of taking
more expensive lodgings at a rent of 1,200 francs a year; the rooms
were unfurnished, and Wagner had to persuade a trusting carpenter
to provide him with what was necessary on credit. The consumptive

Lehrs, who was himself one of life's most grievous failures, was all for beating the world with bluff; and Wagner lent too ready an ear to his inflated talk. He was influenced also to some extent by Minna, who assured him that they could live more economically if she did her own housekeeping, instead of their living in furnished rooms and eating at restaurants. He moved into the new apartment on the 15th April. He had hardly settled in it before Anders brought him the shattering news that the Renaissance had gone bankrupt.

As we have just seen, he had had at once to borrow from Avenarius, probably to meet the first quarter's rent of his new apartment. One morning, when he was at his wits' end to find some means of raising money, a parcel arrived for him from London. Instantly assuming this to be the expected intervention of Providence on his behalf, he broke the seal, only to find that it contained the score of his *Rule Britannia* overture, which he had sent to Sir George Smart in the summer of 1837. It was now returned to him by the Philharmonic Society, with seven francs carriage to pay. As he could not raise that sum, he had to refuse to accept the parcel, in spite of the fact that he had made himself liable for the carriage by breaking the seal. The packet was returned to London. Wagner, when writing *Mein Leben*, regarded the score as lost; but it was discovered in London in 1904, under circumstances that would be described by a journalist as romantic. It had somehow, at some time or other, come into the possession of one Evan William Thomas, who in his day had been a conductor in Liverpool and Leicester. He died, at the age of seventy-nine, in a Welsh workhouse in 1892, rather inexplicably unaware that in this manuscript he had a fairly valuable piece of property. His music was bought, at second remove, by a Mr. Cyrus Gamble, of Leicester, who, on turning over the leaves of a score that bore the title of *Rule Brittania* [*sic*] *Ouvertüre*, with one of the superfluous t's crossed out and an extra n added, found in the margin of the last page the signature "Richard Wagner, den 15. März, 1837, Königsberg in Preussen."[1]

Wagner's tottering finances were helped a little by his taking as lodgers a rather trying old maid from Leipzig, rich but stingy, of the name of Leplay, and her travelling companion, who happened to be Kietz's stepmother. For all her parsimony, Fräulein Leplay

---

[1] See *The Times*, 16th May, 1904.

seems to have been touched by the misery of Minna, for in a letter from Wagner to Minna of the 28th July, 1842 — i.e. after their return to Dresden — we find the following: " When we were trembling on the verge of hunger in Paris, you had more than one opportunity to save yourself: you had only to say one word, and Frau von Zech,[1] who loved you so much, would have taken you to Gotha with her. And the Leplay, who forgot even her avarice where you were concerned, would have taken you, as her travelling companion, back to your old home."

Fräulein Leplay and her companion stayed two months with them. They were succeeded by a recommendation of Pecht's — a German commercial traveller named Brix, a decent, quiet fellow, except when he practised the flute, which must have been a trial to Wagner, who at that time was working at the score of *Rienzi*. Wagner liked him, however, and admitted him to the little home circle in which most of his evenings were spent. Ten golden napoleons dropped into Wagner's purse about this time, under circumstances that he found amusing. An elderly Russian Count was engaging in Paris a small opera company for his estate in Russia, and wanted a musical director. The ever-helpful Laube had recommended Wagner to him. At their first and only interview the pair took each other's measure quickly. The Count, who found his ideal of opera in the works of Adolphe Adam, saw at a glance that Wagner was not his man; while it probably took no great penetration on Richard's part to see that what the old gentleman was getting together was less an opera company than a small harem. The ten napoleons, however, which the Count sent him for what he was polite enough to call his services, were very welcome just then.

10

Paris had never been a bed of roses for him and Minna, but the period on which they were now entering was to prove one of the cruellest trial. The little money he had brought with him from Riga was long ago exhausted. He was in debt to Avenarius and perhaps one or two other friends, he had 300 francs a quarter to pay his

---

[1] It is not known for certain who this lady was.

landlord, and there were the instalments on his new-made furniture to be thought about, if not paid.

A diary of his has survived from this epoch: in this he explains, under the date 23rd June, 1840, how he has been driven to this usual literary refuge for the unhappy: " I hope to win, by the record of my vivid moods, and the reflections they call forth, the same solace for my being as tears afford to the oppressed heart." A poor, sick German journeyman had called on them: he had asked him to come again to breakfast, but Minna had reminded him that they had hardly enough to buy bread for themselves. He grieves over his dependency upon others, but consoles himself with the reflection that " people like Meyerbeer and Laube would not do anything for me unless they believed that I *deserved* it. But weaknesses, whims, or accidents may intervene and estrange these people from me. That is a dreadful thought; and this doubt, and still more the as yet unfulfilled accomplishment of their intentions, is painful, and makes me sick at heart! "

On the 29th June he writes in his diary: " What the next month is going to bring forth I do not know: if I have been anxious enough in the past, now I am on the verge of despair. I indeed have the prospect of making something by articles and sketches in the *Gazette musicale:* and I will send articles to Lewald in Stuttgart for *Europa,* to see if I can make a little in that way. But in the luckiest event what is now hanging over me is so strong that it is bound to bring me down. I have only 25 francs: and on the 1st July I have to meet a note of hand for 150 francs, and on the 15th to pay the quarter's rent. I have exhausted every resource. I still conceal from my poor wife how bad things are. I kept hoping that Laube would send me something: only then would I have told her that but for it we could not have carried on: I kept it secret from her so as not to add to her anxiety, for she is already quite broken with cares. But apparently nothing is going to come of it. On the first of the month I shall have to disclose everything. God help me, that will be a terrible day if help does not come! "

The next day he notes that he has told Minna everything during a walk: " I pity the poor soul from the bottom of my heart! It is a sad business! I will work! " And on the 4th August he writes a poem of three stanzas in which he laments the passing of his youth and its beautiful dreams, and sings the praises of his good wife — the best gift a man could have — but concludes, with a touch of his usual grim humour:

Ich wünsche jedem gleiches Glück,
Ich gäb' es selbst nicht weiter:
Doch denke ich zehn Jahr zurück,
So macht ich's doch gescheidter! " [1]

In the early summer of 1840 he was helped by that combination of his sister Luise and Laube to which reference has already been made. In July he began his ill-paid journalistic connection with Schlesinger. He had known from the commencement of the Rue du Helder venture that if the " foolhardy " plan advocated by Lehrs and adopted with no less foolhardiness by himself did not result in success within a year, ruin was inevitable. And so we find him, in September of this year, turning in desperation to various friends and even strangers. On the 15th September we find him writing to a rich Leipzig merchant and art patron named Heinrich Schletter,[2] begging for a loan of 1,500 francs, which, he admits, he sees no immediate way of repaying. He received the advance, which was still unliquidated in 1843.

Five days later he addresses a long letter to Apel. The two friends had not met for over four years; in the interval, as has already been said, Apel had gone blind. In the published correspondence between the two there is a blank between Wagner's letter of the 6th May, 1836 — the time of Apel's fall from his horse — and this of the 20th September, 1840. When Wagner takes up the correspondence again it is to ask for help from Apel.

" I am in the uttermost adversity, and you can help me. When I say this you will feel a sombre bitterness. But oh my God, why is it that I am in such a state that I can dare even that? What would I not dare when I have to tell you that for a year now my wife and I have had to live without my earning a groschen, without my having a pfennig to call my own? Consider all that lies in this confession and

[1] See RWJK, p. 289 ff.
[2] It would seem that he did not know Schletter personally, but the latter had been in love with Rosalie, and had wanted to marry her.

[297]

you will understand what induces me to begin in this way the first of my letters to you after so many years."

He goes on to speak sympathetically of Apel's blindness, and of his own intuition, when they parted last, that things would never be the same again for either of them. There follows the passage, relating his experiences in Königsberg and Riga, that has already been quoted on page 241; then Wagner continues thus:

"I learned that during my illness my friend Dorn had displaced me in my job in the most perfidious way. It was dreadful; in my exaltation, however, I tried to interpret God's will to be that this should be a sign to me not to remain passive, but to strive once more towards my higher life's-goal. I scraped together a few hundred roubles and told my wife that we must go to Paris; and she, who never indulges in passionate hopes, and foresaw the misery we were making for, consented out of love for me."

He then goes on to describe his voyage to London. In Boulogne he had so little money left that he did not see how they could maintain themselves for more than a few weeks in Paris. He had the good luck to meet Meyerbeer; "I introduced myself to him and showed him my compositions, and he became my friend and protector." Filled with new confidence, he went to Paris.

"Oh, what a mixture of hopes and knock-down blows my experience in Paris has been! Meyerbeer has been unweariedly true to my interests. But unfortunately his family affairs have kept him out of France for the greater part of the time; and since only *personal* influence is any use here, this could not fail to have the most crippling effect on my affairs. What kept me up was always fresh hopes; but anyone can easily imagine that my position, with a wife and not earning a heller, is the most terrible in the world. More than once I have longed for death; and at least I have become completely indifferent to it."

He had heard vaguely of Apel's sad condition, and was pained that he, situated as he was, could do nothing to console him. Then he had learned the full truth from a Leipzig lady who had been in Paris — perhaps Fräulein Leplay. He had been deeply shocked, but relieved to learn that Apel's trouble, after all, was only physical, and that consequently there was hope of a cure. He heard, too, that Apel had published a volume of poetry. He too has become a poet. The *Rienzi* about which they had talked together has become a reality. He had intended the work for Paris.

"I soon discovered, however, that I should have to wait two or three years before I could have a big work of this kind brought out, for I should first of all have to make myself known by some smaller operas; and so I decided, in order not to see my dearest work go under, to complete it in German with a view to a German theatre. I selected Dresden: in a sense it is my native town, and I have made every kind of preparation, especially with Meyerbeer's help, to ensure the opera being accepted there. Dresden has now a large and worthy opera house; Tichatschek and Schröder-Devrient are the very people for my work; so I hope to succeed there. I am going to send my score to Dresden in a month. Perhaps it can be produced there early next year, and I would go there myself." And he tells Apel of his hopes in connection with the *Flying Dutchman* — a two or three-act opera, he calls it at this stage — at the Grand Opéra.

"For the present, however, I should like to buy medicine for my poor wife. Will she survive this misery, and shall I be able to endure hers? Oh God, come thou to my aid! I do not know what to do. I have exhausted everything, everything, the very last resource of a starving man; till now, unfortunate man that I have been, I did not know humanity. Money is the accursed word that crushes everything noble· many a friend, who would like to help, cools down at this word: relations become rigid even before one mentions it. And yet, oh heaven, what is all help without this, the most effective of all? Whoever has known real need knows that only money can relieve it. In the old days, when you were making one sacrifice after another for me, I really thought I knew what need was. Oh, imbecile that I was, to take mere embarrassments for need! Now I know what need is. To have to sell one's last little trinket, one's last necessary household things, to get bread for one's wife, and still to see her helpless, sick and suffering, since even the sale of her wedding ring did not suffice to procure her food *and* medicine — what ought I to call all this, if what I went through before was need? In a word, God forgive me, I have cursed life: what more wicked could I do? My first word to my new-found friend is — Send me help with all speed! My life is in pawn; redeem it! Therefore, I ask you for *three hundred thalers*, and rest assured that if you send me them, I have already lived over eight months on that sum, for during that time I have been able to afford nothing but bread. But turn your back on me — and then I know my fate!

"See, this is my cry from the depths of my distress. Will it grow less? Shall I yet know happiness? These questions I can answer only with a bitter sigh! And yet there are times when, after a glance at the pitifulness of the state of many whom I have met, I could be proud of

[299]

my own, if it were not for the sight of my poor good wife. She has sacrificed her youth for me, and for her I can do nothing but — write this letter to you. I do so behind her back, for I know she would try to dissuade me, for she has at last lost all hope. But I write because I had to; my heart was too full; I had to wish happiness to you, who are recovering after four years full of calamity; and could I write to you without writing just in the way I have done? No; for then I should have written to you not as a friend; my letter would have been merely a visiting card. . . . If you want to give me once more a happy day, write to me by return. . . ."

11

It would seem that Apel did not reply to this pitiful appeal; perhaps the sick man, preoccupied with the spectacle of the ruin of his own life, remained relatively numb to Wagner's cry. Perhaps he did not believe that Wagner was merely telling him the plain and simple truth: he already knew him as an inveterate borrower, and as the most plausible of letter writers when it was a case of asking for money. Wagner's old debt to him was still undischarged. And perhaps during the four years of illness when the night had slowly been closing in on him he had brooded bitterly on the silence of the boyhood's friend for whom he had done so much, and the sense of grievance was not to be dispelled in a moment. The indications are that, not having received a reply, Wagner sent another passionate appeal, for we find Apel writing thus to Laube on the 22nd October: [1]

" Respected Herr Doktor,
" I enclose a letter from our unfortunate friend in Paris, in which he increases the figure of the amount he owes. As I know how interested you are in Wagner's fate, I pass this information on to you, and only regret that at present I can do no more for him than increase my recent contribution, if that can still be done in time. Be good enough to inform me whether I should place this new contribution also in your hands, and if your efforts on behalf of our poor friend have been successful. How willingly would I help him if I were able to do as much as I did a few years ago! "

---

[1] The dictated draft (Apel was then blind) has been preserved at Ermlitz. See RWTA, p. 94. Perhaps Apel had replied to Wagner not direct, but through Laube, to whom, it would seem, he sent a donation, no doubt urging him to send round the hat among Wagner's Leipzig friends.

To which Laube replied from Leipzig on the 21st of the following month, evidently after having tried to raise money among his own friends:

"I am more disconsolate than ever about Wagner, whose letter I return to you herewith. I exchanged your gift for a draft on Paris, but did not send this off at once, as I hoped to raise more money elsewhere. But in vain. If you can and will add your gift, I shall be very grateful, and so I hold the remittance back until to-morrow."

That Apel himself had no communication with Wagner seems to be indicated by the next letter in the series, which is not from Wagner but from the distracted Minna. There was an excellent reason why it should be she who was writing. Though Wagner does not mention the fact in *Mein Leben*, there seems no room for doubt that in October 1840 he was committed to prison at the instance of some creditor or another. Minna's letter runs thus:

"Paris, 28 October, 1840.

"Respected Herr Apel,

"I hope you will not be astonished at receiving a letter from me, and a letter such as this. God be my witness that I should have preferred to approach you with a word of consolation to you in your own misfortune, instead of disturbing you with a prayer for sympathy. But unfortunately I am not mistress of my fate, and I am compelled to turn to you if I am not to give way to despair. A few words will suffice to enlighten you as to the motive of my letter.

"This morning Richard had to leave me to go to the debtors' prison. I am still so dreadfully agitated that everything is in a whirl around me. The only thing that, at this very moment, enables me to collect my thoughts at all is a letter from Herr Laube that has just arrived, and which I have opened in Richard's absence. On the one hand it deprives me of all hope of succour in our trouble; on the other, it gives me courage to take my last step — a desperate one, I confess. In this letter Herr Laube says that you had been friendly and sympathetic. If you knew, good Herr Apel, how accustomed we are to the unfriendliness and lack of sympathy of those to whom we were forced to apply for help, you would understand that this news again raised my hopes to some extent. . . .

"My poor husband, who, as a foreigner, has not even the advantages that are open to a native in such circumstances, has fallen into the hands of a German who is settled here,[1] who behaves towards him

---

[1] He is supposed to have been Eduard Fechner, the uncle of Kietz, and, like his nephew, a painter. That a debt to him was still outstanding eighteen months later is shown by Wagner's furious letter to him of the 13th May, 1842.

with such severity that I cannot count on any softening on his part. What to do is at present quite beyond my thinking [*ist mir in diesem Augenblick noch ein Chaos*]. Even if I had the means to get away from Paris I would never leave Richard in this situation, for I know that he has not got into it through frivolity, but the noblest and most natural striving of an artist has brought him to this pass, to which everyone must come who cannot count on special help. It was only after much opposition that I agreed to his plan to come to Paris; but the more I know of his projects here, the more clearly I see that if he goes under without reaching his goal it is solely because of his lack of the necessary support. He has actually got so far that he is justified in counting on soon reaping the reward of his efforts, and it is only the sacrifices it has already cost him that now stand in his way. He had work, and was making almost enough to make it possible for me to run our little household frugally; but what has happened to-day brings it all to nothing.

" Latterly, for instance, he got so far that a work of his was to be given at a big concert. A fortnight hence the overture to his *Rienzi,* which he has just finished,[1] and which everyone believes will be a great success, was to be played; but without his personal presence at the rehearsal this will not be possible. Is not this enough to make one despair? What can I do? Here alone as I am, of what avail are my tears? Is this really to be the end of us? Will you, who have so long had the friendliest feeling for my Richard, allow him to be lost to us, because a greater sacrifice than usual is needed? God forgive me, but I cannot believe that this must be the end of us. Put it down to the indescribable situation in which I find myself if I perhaps overstep the limits of propriety in placing before you a request that is prompted by despair. To my horror I learned some time ago how much Richard already owes you. You used to get money for him through your credit; but what was his situation in those days compared to the one we now find ourselves in? Would not a sacrifice of this kind be much better now, when there is the prospect that a similar debt can be wiped out in a year, or two at the most? Believe me, as a rule I do not share Richard's exalted hopes; but now I know, from what his own acquaintances say, that he has only to take one more step forward to reach his goal. My God, what more can I say? I have not the peace of mind that would allow me to say clearly all I want to say; I will make up later for what I have omitted here. All I can say is Help! Help! If you can make a great sacrifice for Richard, and as quickly as possible, God will reward you for it, if Richard's grateful heart and my prayers should be too weak for that."

---

[1] It had been completed on the 23rd.

The clear inference from this would seem to be that Wagner had that day been taken to prison; and the passage relating to the impossibility of the *Rienzi* overture being rehearsed during the next fortnight without the presence of the composer points to the imprisonment being for at least that term. As it happens, there is in the Burrell Collection a draft, in *Wagner's* hand, on three scraps of paper, of this very letter. "Whole passages from this draft," say the compilers of the Catalogue, "occur in the letter" (i.e. that of Minna just quoted). But in the Catalogue the "scraps" are wrongly attributed to the year 1841. There cannot be the slightest doubt that this is a mistake, and that they should be dated 1840. The dates of Minna's two letters to Apel (the second will be quoted shortly) and of the letters that passed between Apel and Laube place this beyond question: moreover, in October 1841 Wagner was no longer in Rue du Helder (from which Minna is writing) but in Meudon. But a little difficulty now arises. Did Wagner hurriedly draft the letter for Minna on the morning he was to leave for prison, or perhaps the night before? [1] Or was the danger actually staved off for the moment, though Wagner and Minna felt that it would be legitimate to speak of it, to Apel, as a *fait accompli?* We shall see that a later letter from Wagner to Laube hints at a similar catastrophe, actual or impending, in December.

12

We come to the conclusion that, probably from motives of caution, Apel did not at first write direct to Wagner, but employed Laube as his intermediary. The Wagner household was clearly without money at this time: in the Burrell Collection is a note from Wagner to Kietz, dated the 19th October,[2] containing the words, "Bei Wagner wird's warm! 3 sous! " ("It is getting hot here! Reduced to 3 sous! " (This, it will be noted, was nine days before the letter from Minna in which she speaks of Wagner being taken

[1] Until the draft is published, we cannot say, of course, how much of Minna's published letter is her own composition, though the style enables us to make a reasonably likely guess.

[2] The year — 1840 — has been inserted by Kietz. There can be no doubt that it is correct.

to prison. On the 17th November she sends another desperate appeal to Apel. She speaks of his " silence," which she attributes to the passionate tone of her previous letter; this she excuses on the ground of her " great distress " and the " stunning blow " that had been struck her on the day she had written to him.

> " I was with Richard " [a visit to him in prison?] " and gave him your dear letter. He thanks you from the bottom of his heart for it; and I consoled him with my confidence in you, and awakened in him the hope that in view of such extraordinary circumstances you would decide on making an extraordinary sacrifice. I confess that day by day I have waited patiently for the fulfilment of my despairing prayer. Richard is ill. I would like to go to him and look after him; but as this would involve an expense that is out of the question I must leave him in God's care, and for my part try to do what I can to discharge the debt that has brought us into this situation.[1]
>
> "Richard's creditor sent to me yesterday and had the impudence to tell me that I ought to write to Richard's brother-in-law, H. Brockhaus, to get him to discharge the debt. So he knows of this relation, and now it is clear to me why he behaved so harshly to my husband. But both Richard and I would rather endure this situation for years than break our oath not to be a burden to his relations again."

So she turns once more to Apel. She can do this better than Wagner, she says, because she is pleading not for herself but for another.

> " I can put myself on a par with you, for I too have made sacrifices for him. I have given up my peaceful independent lot to bind myself to his, since it seems to be decreed that he can reach his goal only after the wildest storms and trials. . . . You say in your letter to Richard that it is impossible for you to do more for him than you have just done."

She recognises that Apel cannot do more without exceeding the limit of his own normal expenditure; but the poor woman, in her simple, honest way, now writing without Wagner to supervise her script, tells him what she, when a girl, did for her brother.

---

[1] It will be recalled (see p. 287) that nearly a month elapsed between the publication of the *Gazette musicale* article on *The Virtuoso and the Artist* on the 18th October and that of the first section of *A Pilgrimage to Beethoven* on the 19th November. It looks as if, in view of the insistence of some creditor or other on being paid, and the probability of Wagner's being arrested on or about the 28th October, he had worked in all haste at the long Beethoven article, which occupied four numbers of the paper.

" He wanted to study in Leipzig, but my parents could not support him there. I took the burden on myself, at a time when, owing to the bad state of the theatre finances, I often lacked four groschen to buy myself a dinner. I pawned my ear-rings and things of that kind, which were often indispensable to me in my theatrical work, and sent the money to my brother for his studies, keeping back only three pfennigs for a bit of bread, which I ate for my dinner during a walk through the town, having told the people with whom I lodged that I had been asked out to dinner. Is it to be only the poor and wretched who are to have the consciousness of making sacrifices of this sort? Cannot the man of means, who would find it relatively so infinitely easier, some-how out of all his wealth find the means to help in the same way? It may be answered that this was for a brother. But if it would not be too much to give up the half of what one has for a brother, surely a friend is worth the sacrifice of a hundredth part? . . . Further, . . . in Richard there is a fine talent to be rescued, that otherwise will be brought nigh to ruin, for he has already lost heart, and without that, his higher destiny is lost. Perhaps a heavy responsibility lies on those who now turn from him with a shrug of the shoulder."

And once more she implores Apel to arrange a credit *quickly* for Richard.

Either some parts of the Apel correspondence have been suppressed — which, in view of what has been printed by Apel's heirs, is improbable — or a further likely letter or two from Wagner has been lost; for Wagner's next letter to Apel comes at an interval of thirteen years, evidently in reply to a recent one from Apel that had broken the second long silence between them.

The letters just quoted are important as showing two things — the extremity of Wagner's need at this period, and the reluctance of his friends and relations, conscious as they were of that need, to go more than a certain distance towards relieving it. Two things must be remembered in excuse of them. In the first place, Wagner had already established in one quarter after another a reputation as a borrower to whose demands no limit could ever be fixed; one had either definitely to draw the line somewhere with him or be dragged step by step into loans beyond the lender's means. In the second place, the Wagner they knew was not the great artist we of to-day know. He had given no proof whatever to the world in general, or even to his friends, of genius unmistakable or even talent out of the common. Most of those from whom he asked for help were fully justified in believing that he was attempting the impossible in trying to force himself on Paris as a composer, and that the best thing he could do would be to return to his native land and earn a modest but safe living as a practising musician like other people. Even *Rienzi* was still in manuscript. Practically all that Wagner had so far produced in public was an overture or two, the symphony, the piano sonata, and *Das Liebesverbot,* which had been a palpable fiasco; and there was nothing in these to warrant the belief that he was anything more than one of the hundreds of young men who at any period can produce quite passable work in the current forms and idioms. Wagner's family had no reason whatever to believe that he was a heaven-sent genius. The practical musicians of the time were mostly either contemptuous of his youthful efforts or good-naturedly tolerant of them. Richard's mother had shown Marschner, then at the height of his fame, the score of the C major symphony, and had been told that it showed " more cerebration," as we would say nowadays, " than power of invention," and that Brockhaus was right in recommending his young brother-in-law to keep to his school and his ordinary studies.

It is this judgment of a supposed expert that no doubt accounts for the coolness of Brockhaus and other relations towards Wagner's frequent requests for money; as sensible men of the world they felt that it would be ultimately a mistake to encourage a penniless young man to devote himself to a profession in which few succeeded in making a decent living, and for which he had shown no special aptitude. His blind obstinacy could result only in his always being a burden on his friends; he should either give music up altogether or take up one of the practical sides of it, such as theatre conducting. There are good reasons enough why his friends and relations should be absolved from any charge of callousness towards him, the situation being as they saw it. But he, for his part, with his unshakable belief in his genius and in the future, at all times of his life thought it the duty of others to provide him with the means to live his life and do his work in his own way; and his rancour at what he regarded as their unkindness to him when at last they drew their purse-strings tight was sufficient to make him sadly forgetful of all that, in spite of their final refusal, they had at one time done for him. Nowhere does he mention in *Mein Leben* the number of times

Apel had rescued him from debt; these and a hundred other benefits were forgotten when he came to survey his early career in middle age. A despairing remark about him in the 'sixties, by one of the friends who had been most generous to him, to the effect that " Wagner could not be helped," rankled in him all through the years when he was dictating his autobiography. He constantly praised Cosima because she had proved that, as he said, he *could* be helped. The fact that all the others had finally had to give up the attempt as hopeless at some time or other seemed to him to relieve him of any obligation of gratitude for what they had previously done.

13

The period with which we have been dealing must be that referred to by Wagner in *Mein Leben* as the most desperate of all in Paris. Yet we have testimony enough as to the courage with which he bore his misfortunes. In the autumn of 1840 Laube had left Paris, and Pecht had taken his place in the Wagner circle. He describes Wagner as being, in spite of his " passionate " nature, never " rough or common " in his life, but always maintaining " a certain distinction of manner." The rooms of the fourth floor of the Rue du Helder were of course furnished on credit. Pecht pays a tribute to Wagner's unique faculty for borrowing — " an inborn gift for debt-making," as he puts it: Wagner had an adroitness and an inexhaustibility of technique in the raising of money such as Pecht never found in any other human being. Pecht himself, of course, modest as his means were, was laid under contribution. He lent Wagner the money that had been set aside for his travelling expenses; and he was landed in considerable embarrassment by Wagner's inability to repay the loan when Pecht had to leave Paris.

Pecht was always struck by the elasticity of temperament that enabled Wagner to recover immediately after each knock-down blow, by his strength of will, by the breadth of his culture, and by the blend of audacity and commonsense in his judgment of men and things. Then, as later, he knew his own mind on every subject, and went straight and uncompromisingly to his point. He summed up contemporary tendencies in French, Italian and German music with a positiveness and a penetration that must have surprised his listeners. Pecht remembered his saying that there was no more " immortality " in music than in anything else in this world: taste changes with each century, the technical apparatus develops, and all music must inevitably become antiquated sooner or later. Already, he said, there is much of Bach, Haydn and Mozart that cannot be enjoyed by us: only Beethoven, at present, can meet all the demands our feeling may make on him. And never, says Pecht, did he lose faith in his own future.[1]

He completed the full score of *Rienzi* on the 19th November, 1840. We possess his letter of the 1st December to King Friedrich August of Saxony, in which he begs his sovereign to order the production of the work at Dresden, and tells him that the score is being sent to the Dresden Intendant, von Lüttichau. In *Mein Leben* he tells us that he had noted the exact tempi in the score; for this he had had to borrow a metronome. He went out one day to restore it to the owner, and at the same time to try to raise some money. His story fits in at every point with the evidence afforded by the letters to Apel. He remembered that day forever afterwards as one of the strangest in his whole life. A number of bills had fallen due. These he tried to induce the holders to renew; but as the documents had passed through various hands since he had signed them he had to trudge wearily from one part of Paris to another — omnibuses were scarce in those days — shivering in his thin overcoat. " I had," he says, " to pacify a cheese-monger who occupied a fifth floor in the Cité." He called on Hermann Brockhaus, who was then in Paris, but was refused help. He called on Schlesinger and others, also without success. The normal misery of the day was intensified for him by Providence having conceived the grimly humorous idea of selecting precisely this day to let him catch a glimpse of Robber, who had either left him or, as he thought, been stolen from him a year before. He called the dog, who seemed to recognise him, but was determined not to come too close to him. Each time Wagner approached him he moved away; the pursuit went on in the fog through street after street, till in the end Wagner, with other business to attend to, was too exhausted to continue it any further. He was cut to the quick by the animal's obvious avoidance of his old

[1] PAMZ, I, 182 ff., 202 ff., 213, etc.

master, and put it down to the dog's remembering one or two thrash-
ings he had given him. The probability is that the huge beast had
found a home where at any rate he had enough to eat, and had no
intention of leaving it for the meagre fare that was all poor Wagner
had been able to supply him with.

Late at night Wagner returned home, exhausted, to the anxious
Minna, who, during his absence, had managed to borrow sufficient
from their lodger Brix to provide her husband with a meal. He
makes no reference in *Mein Leben* to the help given him at this time
by Apel, Laube, Schletter, Schlesinger and several others; his
memory of those dreadful days was perhaps too painful for him to
wish to dwell too much on the details of them. The money sent by
Apel in response to Minna's appeal of the 17th November had, it is
to be supposed, released him from prison. A little difficulty may
seem to be created for our story by the fact that in *Mein Leben*
Wagner tells us that he completed *Rienzi* by the 19th November.
That, however, is, in itself, a little misleading. The actual opera was
finished on the 19th September, and the overture written on the
23rd. *Rienzi* was thus virtually completed before his obdurate
creditor put such drastic pressure on him a day or two preceding
the dire event of the 28th; all that Wagner had to do between the
23rd October and the 19th November was to orchestrate the overture, and he may quite possibly have put the final touches to this
in the debtors' prison. Allowing a few days for Apel's money to
reach Paris and for Wagner's release, it being fairly clear from
Minna's letter of the 17th November that he was still imprisoned
then, we get within practical distance of the 1st December, the date
of his letter to King Friedrich August. Was he threatened with
further imprisonment if more money was not forthcoming? [1] This
seems probable from his letter of the 3rd December to Laube: the
authenticity of the date is established by the fact that in the opening

---

[1] It has been conjectured that on the first occasion he was removed, by reason
of illness, to the hospital of Pitié — where, by a delightful touch of irony, his maintenance would have to be provided by his creditor — and that the latter made a
second assault on him after his discharge. This might account for Minna having
been able to see him, and for his having facilities for the completion of *Rienzi*. See
Richard Sternfeld's article, *Hat Richard Wagner 1840 im Pariser Schuldgefängnis
gesessen?* in DM, XV, 127 ff. It is certainly curious that in his article *Parisian
Fatalities for the German* he should send his destitute German to the Pitié, and
describe that institution as being less clean and more scantily furnished than the
Hôtel Dieu.

lines of the letter he tells Laube that the score of *Rienzi* is " on the way " to Dresden. The opera

" has come into the world after the most atrocious birth-pangs," he continues. " No one could live through more frightful days than the first and second of this calamitous month have been for me. My poor friends here have done all that was in their power, down to their last pfennig, to postpone the threatened blow until the 15th of this month; this blow means irrecoverably an immediate distress warrant and the loss of my personal freedom. I did not believe it; but I was within a hair's breadth of it, for as an alien I have not the usual means of protest at my disposal. I must now hunt in every nook and corner till then for the necessary amount; if you can contribute anything, however little, send it immediately! God reward you for your kindness and love! "

To understand, and to make allowances for, Wagner's forgetfulness of these and other benefits, we have to remember that when he began work upon *Mein Leben,* in 1865, he was poisoned and maddened beyond endurance by the venom poured out on him by his enemies in Munich; everyone was hateful in his eyes but Cosima and King Ludwig. But it calls for all our understanding if we *are* to make allowances. A letter from Cosima to the King gives us an insight into the corroding bitterness of Wagner's spirit. " In the evenings, after tea," she writes, " he dictates his autobiography to me. We have got to the Paris time (1839–40) . . . I cannot tell you how I have been agitated by the exact knowledge of this dreadful time, and how moved I have been by the mildness with which he judges the abominable behaviour of everyone towards him. In order not to wrench him out of this beautiful, edifying mood I pretend that all these experiences are to be taken lightly, though sometimes I can hardly write for indignation and emotion." [1] But even Cosima, perhaps, had not been told the whole story as we can reconstruct it now.

14

After his tragic experiences in October and November, 1840, he had to keep his nose to the grindstone so obligingly held out to him by Schlesinger. Now and then he coquetted with an idea that was often to recur to him in later life when his situation seemed more

---

[1] MECW, I, 311.

than usually hopeless: he would go to America, where, as he assured Minna, men were free from the wretched spectres that haunted them in Europe, where opera and music were unknown, and where a reasonable livelihood could be secured by a reasonable amount of work. Minna's reply was the practical one that while all this might be true, the immediate thing was to find some means of getting bread and butter in Paris. Richard accordingly spent every possible minute slaving away at his articles and opera arrangements. By an irony of fate, Cäcilie happened to drop in on the couple just when Wagner was gleefully displaying the hundred shining five franc pieces that represented Schlesinger's advance for his labours on *La Favorita*. This welcome evidence of his earning power had so good an influence on her and Avenarius that the relations between the two families became quite cordial again, and the Wagners were often invited to dinner on Sundays. But by now Richard had neither the time nor the inclination for society. He bent his weary back to his oar. To economise fuel, they lived in a single room, where it was only a step from the bed to his work-table in the study, and he had only to turn round in his chair in the salon to be seated at the dining-room table. For his health's sake he went out for a walk every fourth day. The result of it all, he says, was the laying of the foundation of the gastric disorders that plagued him for the rest of his life.

We have a letter of his to Schlesinger that dates (14th January, 1841) from this period. He is not leaving the house, he says; he means to get on with the corrections of his work. He has to pay 300 francs on account on his " miserable bill of exchange," which falls due on the 15th, " otherwise the process will be repeated." He owes more than 200 francs to a friend: these fell due on the 8th, and as they were not paid, the bill had been protested. A further 150 francs are due to his tailor on the 15th: in addition there is his house-rent and his cost of living. Without Schlesinger, he says, he would have gone under, for he has been left in the lurch by everyone on whom he had thought he could count in his need. Schlesinger has, in a sense, saved his life: thanks to him, he now has confidence in the future. " You have already begun to raise me out of my misery. Help me further now, and you will find in me a man whose gratitude knows no limit." All this, of course, leads up to a request for a banknote for 1000 francs, in return for which he will not trouble the publisher for the next three months, except for what he needs for mere existence. And then comes a phrase that he was to repeat in more than one begging letter to more than one friend in later years: " If it is difficult for you to do this for me, look upon it as a great sacrifice that you are making for me." [1]

But through all his experiences he preserved a courage and, except in moments of exceptional strain, a gaiety that were the astonishment and the admiration of all his friends. On the night of the fiasco of the *Columbus* overture, Pecht tells us, he was so recklessly humorous that all were surprised at his quick recovery from his defeat. He covered a remarkably wide range of musical and general intellectual interests in his articles, turning a first-rate critical faculty on what he heard in concert rooms and at the Opéra, theorising and philosophising with great acumen, and, as in the story *An End in Paris* and elsewhere, dramatising his own pitiable state with a detachment and a grim humour that are equally admirable. He never wrote better than at this period of his life: his pen has a speed and a variety of rhythm that it lost in later years, when the burden of thought in him was too great for his literary faculty to carry in comfort. As a journalist he modelled himself on Hoffmann and Heine, and though he could not rival the brilliance and the dexterity of the latter, he makes a very passable second to that incomparable journalist.

As he went on working out his penance, he retired more and more from the world; he even symbolised his withdrawal from it by growing a long beard, for the first and only time in his life, much to Minna's annoyance. They were forced to dispense with the occasional services of the concierge in the rougher work of the household, Minna not only doing the cooking and the washing-up but cleaning Brix's boots as well. They celebrated the New Year's Eve of 1840–1 with a party to which the faithful Kietz, Pecht and Anders brought veal, sugar, rum, a lemon, and even two bottles of champagne that had been given to Anders by a musical instrument maker in return for a eulogistic article on his pianos. Then the pent-up spirits of Wagner found an outlet at last: under the benign influence of the punch and the champagne he stood on the table and

---

[1] RWKK, I, 155.

gave the company a madly humorous address on the absurdity of life and the virtues of the American southern States. The next day he turned soberly to his grind at *La Favorita* again.

15

A new trouble was brewing for him. He had intended to leave the Rue du Helder, but in his ignorance of local custom he was a week late in giving his quarter's notice,[1] and the proprietor held him to his agreement for another year. In his despair he sought for a new lodger, but could find none. At last the concierge found a family who were willing to take the apartment furnished for some months; and on the 29th April, 1841, Wagner moved to Meudon, in the country near Paris, where living would be cheaper.[2] Brix went with them. But Wagner's financial position grew worse throughout the summer; and he had the extra annoyance of seeing Cäcilie and her husband settle in a comfortable house quite close to his. One day he trudged all the way to Paris in the hope of borrowing a five franc piece; he was unsuccessful, and had to make the long journey back on foot. He was closely followed by Brix, who had been on a similar errand, but with no more success; in his exhaustion Brix begged Minna piteously for a piece of bread. To make matters worse, a vagrant, ne'er-do-well Leipzig acquaintance, Hermann Pfau, whom Richard had previously had to help out of his own scanty funds — for in his greatest misfortune his purse was always open to another sufferer — had chosen this day, of all days, to call on them, and Minna had already given the starving man the last bit of bread in the house. The famishing garrison was saved by a gallant sortie on the part of Minna, who somehow or other — how she did it with her rudimentary French is a mystery — managed to persuade the local butcher, baker and wine merchant to let her have all she wanted on

---

[1] His memory misgave him when he spoke of "two days" in *Mein Leben*. A contemporary letter to Laube shows the period to have been a week.

[2] Was one of his reasons for removing to Meudon the fact that he would not be subject there to arrest at the instance of a Paris creditor? Chopin tells us that Fétis used to live outside Paris, only coming into the town to give lessons, "as otherwise he would long ago have been in Sainte Pélagie for debts. . . . You must know that, according to the law, debtors can be arrested only in their domicile; so he does not stay in his domicile but goes out of town where the law cannot reach him till after a certain time." See Chopin's letter of the 14th December, 1831, to Elsner, in CL, p. 161.

credit. And then the gods indulged in another exercise of their familiar irony towards Wagner. Avenarius and Cäcilie called on them while supper was in progress, and, as Wagner drily says, were visibly relieved to find him so well provided for.

We must not, however, take *Mein Leben* too seriously on this point. It reflects the bitterness of a quarter of a century later. Wagner's contemporary letters are always a better guide to his true frame of mind at any given moment; and the letters to Cäcilie and Avenarius written in the days immediately following his return to Germany are full of affection and of regret at leaving them. A man does not write in this tone to people with whom his relations have been really strained. He knew well enough, at that time, that his sister and her husband had done all they possibly could for him, and more than he had a right to expect. It was only after his Zürich and Vienna and Munich experiences that he became obsessed with the idea that everyone from whom he might have had help had callously failed him.

He stayed in Meudon until the 30th October, 1841, taking advantage of the temporary leisure and comparative freedom from care afforded him by the 500 francs he had received for the sketch of the *Flying Dutchman* to write his own opera on that subject. (The poem had been completed between the 18th and 28th May of this year.) He now permitted himself the luxury of hiring a piano, to reassure himself, as he quaintly tells us, that he was still a composer. The opera itself, in its unorchestrated form, was completed in seven weeks in August and September: on the title-page of the score he wrote " In Nacht und Elend [In Night and Wretchedness]. Per aspera ad astra. Gott gebe es! [God grant it!]." By that time his little capital was exhausted, and he was in too much trouble of mind to embark on the overture, which was not written till after his return to Paris. It was no doubt in this period of despair that he wrote to Pecht, urging him to try to get him some work — even a post as organist! Minna's sufferings, he said, cut him to the heart: there were times when he contemplated suicide.[1]

Before he left Meudon he learned from the concierge at the Rue du Helder that the people who had taken the apartment off his hands had left, so that he was once more responsible for the rent.

[1] PAMZ, I, 213.

He ended the matter summarily by telling the landlord he would not and could not pay any more for the rooms. The landlord recouped himself by selling the furniture, most of which was still, and presumably for a long time afterwards, unpaid for. With what he somehow managed to save from the wreck, Wagner took a wretched little apartment in Paris, in the Rue Jacob, No. 14. He boldly told Kietz that *he* would have to find funds sufficient to enable him to complete the *Flying Dutchman;* and this the faithful fellow managed to do, partly by selling the contents of his portfolio, partly by borrowing from his uncle Fechner. Wagner by this time had no soles to his boots; but he remained philosophically untroubled by the melancholy sight of them, for he seldom ventured out. The campaign against Paris had failed hopelessly: his one desire now was to get back to Germany. As luck would have it, several circumstances combined just then to deepen his consciousness that he was a German. Raumer's *History of the Hohenstaufen* came into his hands; as he read it, the figures of Frederick II and Manfred came to dramatic life within him, and he sketched the plan of a five-act opera, to be entitled *Die Sarazenin (The Saracen Woman).* Before he could begin to think seriously of composing the music to this, however, a pamphlet and some other documents that fell into his hands set him on the track of the Tannhäuser subject. Appended to the pamphlet was an essay on Lohengrin, upon which theme also his imagination at once began to play, though as yet he could not quite see how to shape either this or the Tannhäuser matter dramatically. The important thing was that his thoughts were turning more and more from Paris and all things French.

An old Prague acquaintance, one Dessauer, turned up again about this time: he had been sent to Wagner by Schlesinger with the request that the former would supply him with an opera text on the lines of that of the *Flying Dutchman,* which had made so favourable an impression on all who had seen it. Wagner drafted a scenario — it is dated 5th March, 1842 — based on E. T. A. Hoffmann's story *Die Bergwerke zu Falun;* but before he could proceed further with it, news came that Pillet was repelled by the obvious difficulties of staging such a work. Dessauer now asked Wagner to prepare for him the text for an oratorio on the subject of Mary Magdalene. Wagner humoured the man, who seemed to be suffering from a kind of melancholy dementia; but the draft was never written. The *Bergwerke*, however, brought him 200 francs, which helped him through a little more of this distressful winter.[1]

16

A turn in his fortunes was now close at hand. For the leading parts in *Rienzi* he could visualise only Tichatschek, the leading German heroic tenor of that epoch, and Schröder-Devrient, both of whom were attached to the Dresden opera. To Dresden, accordingly, he had sent the score soon after its completion in November 1840, laying stress in his letter to the King of Saxony on the connection of his family with the town, in which his step-father had been a respected member of the royal company of players. He spoke of his good fortune in having Meyerbeer for a protector, and pardonably exaggerated a little when he told the King that thanks to Meyerbeer he was " in the friendliest negotiations with the Paris Opéra for a work to be composed solely for that institution." In Paris, however, he continues, he had not forgotten his fatherland; his *Rienzi* had been written with the special intention of offering it in the first place to His Majesty's Court Theatre. He had some right, indeed, to look forward hopefully to Dresden: the secretary of the theatre, Hofrat Winkler, was the editor of that *Abendzeitung* to which he had contributed so many articles, and an old acquaintance of Geyer and of the family; while Schröder-Devrient had always been well disposed towards him. The theatre committee, with the Intendant, Baron von Lüttichau at its head, was greatly taken with the work; and so, in June, 1841, *Rienzi* was accepted for performance in Dresden.

At the beginning of December, 1841, he had sent the score of the *Flying Dutchman* to Berlin, at the same time appealing by letter to the good offices of Meyerbeer, in whose diary for the 7th December is the entry: " Called on Redern [the Intendant] to recommend to him the score of *Der Fliegende Holländer* "; while under the date of the 9th we learn that Meyerbeer sent the score to

---

[1] The prose sketch for *Die Bergwerke zu Falun* ("Opera in three acts") and that for *Die Sarazenin* ("Opera in three acts") will be found in RWGS, Vol. XI.

Redern with a letter in which he said, " The day before yesterday I had the honour to speak to your Excellency about this interesting composer, whose talent and whose extremely straitened circumstances make him doubly worthy of not having the doors of the great Court Theatre that is the protector of German art closed to him." Moreover, Meyerbeer had used his good offices for him in Dresden; on the 18th March he had written to Lüttichau: " Herr R. Wagner is a young composer who has not only a sound musical training but also much imagination and a general musical culture; and his situation deserves the sympathy of his fatherland in each of these aspects. . . . Some sections [of *Rienzi*] that he played to me I found full of fantasy, and of considerable dramatic effect. May the young artist be able to rejoice in the protection of your Excellency, and find an opportunity to see his fine talent more generally recognised." Clearly Meyerbeer could have done no more: these extracts from authentic documents surely place it beyond question that he had behaved throughout in a perfectly honourable way to Wagner, with the sincerest desire to help him. It can be readily understood, then, how, in the light of Wagner's attacks on him later, he joined in the general chorus of condemnation of Wagner for ingratitude towards his benefactors. Henri Blaze de Bury, who knew Meyerbeer intimately, has told us that towards the end of his life " there was only one name that could set him on edge — that of Richard Wagner. He could not hear it pronounced without experiencing a disagreeable sensation, which he never tried to conceal — he who as a rule was so discreet, so ingenious in picking out the least quality of each individual. . . . I repeat, the name of the composer of *Tannhäuser* and *Lohengrin* produced on Meyerbeer the effect of a dissonance." [1]

Blinded by his later hatred of Meyerbeer, Wagner nowhere mentions in *Mein Leben* that he had been largely indebted to his powerful elder rival for the acceptance of *Rienzi* at Dresden and of the *Flying Dutchman* at Berlin. The libretto of the latter opera had been already sent by Wagner to Ringelhardt, the director of the Leipzig theatre, and to Küstner, the manager at Munich. The former had declined the work on the ground that the subject was too gloomy; the latter, because in his opinion it was not suited to the

---

[1] See BMC, pp. 215, 217.

German taste — a remark that gives us a hint of the subservience of the German theatres to French and Italian opera modes at that time. Two months after the score had been sent to Meyerbeer, the composer received from Count Redern, the Berlin Intendant, the gratifying news that the work was accepted. But on his return to Germany in the following spring Wagner learned, according to his account of the matter in *Mein Leben*, that Redern, at the time of the correspondence, had " long since retired from the management of the Berlin Opera," that the fulfilment of his promise therefore depended not on him but on his successor, and that this successor, who was already appointed, was none other than that very Küstner who had declined the work for Munich. In the mood of general resentment and suspicion in which *Mein Leben* was written, he regarded himself as having been merely the dupe of the treacherous Meyerbeer. But that is a conclusion that can by no means be accepted without more evidence than we possess at present.

17

With the disarming optimism that pervades all opera houses, the Dresden authorities, when accepting *Rienzi* in June, 1841, had fixed " the beginning of next year at the latest " as the date of its production. Wagner at once got into touch with the practical men of the theatre, and gave them a taste of his quality. Fortunately for him, the two who mattered most, so far as *Rienzi* was concerned, were men of character and high artistic ideals, who were not repelled by an insistence that later, in other theatres, was to raise enmities wholesale for him. These two men were the stage manager and chorus master, Wilhelm Fischer, and the costume designer, Ferdinand Heine. Fischer, who was some twenty-three years older than Wagner, had begun as a bass singer; his connection with Dresden had dated from 1831. He had officiated as chorus master at Leipzig during Wagner's residence in that town as a youth, but Wagner did not make his personal acquaintance until after his own return to Dresden in 1842. Heine, who was an actor as well as a designer, had been a friend of Geyer. On Fischer and Heine the young composer opened his batteries almost as soon as he had received word from Lüttichau of the acceptance of his opera. The correspondence gives us our first glimpse of Wagner as a practical man of the theatre, solidly sure of himself, with a keen eye for every musical and scenic detail, and determined to leave nothing undone that was essential for the full realisation of his aims. Politely, but none the less firmly, he makes it clear that young as he may be, obscure as his name at present may be, he is no mere novice in the theatre. He makes no attempt to gloss over the unusual difficulties in the matter of staging that *Rienzi* will present; but he is flatteringly confident that these difficulties will vanish before the intelligence and good will of Fischer. He goes into the minutest details as to the disposition of the members of the chorus both on and behind the stage — for the latter he will need the choir of the Kreuzschule — as to the great tragic pantomime in the finale of the second act, the ensuring of pure intonation in the chorus of the Messengers of Peace, the adequate planning of the ballet, the distribution of the solo parts, and a hundred other points. Objections had been raised in high quarters to the introduction of the Pope, a Legate, and Cardinals into the work. He argues strenuously against the notion that his opera is really concerned with the catholic religion; it is a matter more of the " catholic costume," he insists, than of the " catholic idea." Still, he is willing enough to be accommodating, and to make such superficial alterations in the manner of presentation of these matters as may be thought necessary.[1]

Schröder-Devrient, whom of course he had in his mind as Adriano, while Tichatschek was the only possible Rienzi in all Germany, had employed her good offices on his behalf even before the work was accepted: now, at the least slackness on her part in the matter of correspondence, he dreads a weakening of her interest, and begs Heine to find out for him how the affair stands in that quarter. He was resigned to waiting till the new opera of the local Kapellmeister, Reissiger, had been rehearsed: that had been understood from the beginning. But after *Adèle de Foix*, the opera in question, had been duly produced on the 26th November, 1841, followed by Halévy's *Guitarrero*, and this again by an opera by

---

[1] He had written eagerly to Heine on this point while the opera was still under consideration by the management; he did not want to risk a refusal of the work for religious reasons.

Mercadante, which had been put on for the benefit of a guest singer, he learned, to his dismay, that Schröder-Devrient, with the caprice of her sex and her profession, had suddenly conceived a desire to distinguish herself in Gluck's *Armida*. He was promised that *Rienzi* should be taken in hand after that; but at the best this meant that the work could not be given before the Easter of 1842. At once, of course, he assumed that Schröder-Devrient had ceased to feel an interest in him. He implores Heine to see her and tell her of the " misery " she is preparing for him, and induce her, if he can, to give up this " whim " for his sake; failing that, he urges Heine and everyone else to get on with this inconvenient *Armida* at once, and then prepare *Rienzi* with all possible speed. But Easter came and went, and still *Rienzi* was not in proper rehearsal, though Fischer had commenced to teach the chorus their music, and Heine had begun to be busy with the new costumes, of which no fewer than 537 would be required, while two completely new stage settings had been put into commission. There was no production of *Armida*, but a general exodus from the Dresden theatre; Schröder-Devrient had gone to Berlin, while Winkler, the manager of the theatre, talked of taking a holiday in Italy. It was now nine months since *Rienzi* had been accepted, and Wagner, to whom Paris was daily becoming more repugnant, was beginning to despair.

One of the difficulties of the management was the abnormal length of *Rienzi;* it had been calculated that it would play for four hours without taking intervals into consideration — and the work was in five acts! Wagner discusses the question at great length in his letters to Fischer, who had become more perplexed the more he tried to work out a practical system of cuts. As usual with him, Wagner was reluctant to admit that his work was excessively long; but in any case, he insists — and this was to be the burden of his argument in kindred cases in the later years — the length was a necessary condition of the clear exposition of the *drama*. It was this, indeed, that made cuts so difficult; he had nowhere, he says, expanded the numbers for purely musical reasons — in which case an abbreviation here and there would have been an easy matter; so that the work was not long in virtue of its separate parts but purely by its nature as a dramatic whole. He hoped that even four hours was not too long a time to ask an audience to take an intelligent interest in a lively and closely-knit action. He ends, however, by making numerous suggestions of his own as to possible cuts, and for the rest he leaves the matter entirely in the hands of Fischer and Reissiger. His one desire was to have the opera produced, and as quickly as possible.

Lüttichau, Winkler, Schröder-Devrient, Reissiger, Fischer and Heine could never before have been plagued with so much correspondence from an unknown composer over his first opera. They must all have felt that this young man was of harder stuff than the average. But they took it all in good part, for they seem to have been convinced from the first that the work would be a success, while the cultivated and conscientious Fischer and Heine never for a moment lost patience with the voluble and troublesome and decidedly exacting young man.

18

The longer the negotiations dragged on, the more ardent became Wagner's desire to see Germany again. He had long ago become completely disillusioned with regard not only to his prospects in Paris but to French taste in general; almost the only good thing Paris had done for him was to make a German of him once more. The production of *Der Freischütz* at the Opéra in June, 1841, grotesque as it must have been in some respects, brought him a breath of the German forest and German legend in the depths of the Paris desert. The rehearsals he had heard of the Ninth Symphony at the Conservatoire had not only made that work clear to him: the stupendous experience had purged his soul of all the musical frivolities and basenesses to which he had surrendered himself for so many wild and wasteful years. It was under the influence of Beethoven that he had written, in January, 1840, his *Faust* overture, which was originally intended to be the first part of a *Faust Symphony*.[1] In the spring of that year he had asked the Conservatoire

---

[1] That, at any rate, is his statement in *Mein Leben*, where he says he got as far as to work out the Gretchen motive for the second movement. But in a letter of the 17th December, 1843, to Kittl he speaks of it as "an Overture to the First Part of Goethe's *Faust*"; and in his letter of the 30th January, 1848, to Liszt he calls it "my Overture to Goethe's *Faust*." See RWKK, II, 97, 264. He revised the work towards the end of 1854. See his letters of the 1st January and 16th February, 1855, to Liszt (RWLZ, II, 46, 51). There is no mention in any of these letters of a *Faust Symphony*.

Orchestra to rehearse the work, but this request was not granted. When, some time later, Schlesinger offered to give a work of his at one of his subscription concerts, Wagner chose the *Columbus* overture: he knew the orchestra was to be a second-rate one, and moreover he doubted whether the quiet ending of the *Faust* would sufficiently impress the Parisians. His failure to get *Das Liebesverbot* produced in Paris had probably been no great grief to him for any but financial reasons, so rapidly was his inner self turning away in disgust from the superficialities of Paris musical life. Unfortunately he never dared tell Minna of the spiritual change that was going on within him. She would not have understood: they had made this mad excursion for the express purpose of Richard's establishing himself as a composer at the Opéra, and the poor woman would have been as incapable of understanding his seemingly unpractical idealism then as she was later in the Zürich years.

Partly from necessity — shortness of money, shabbiness of clothes, his retirement to Meudon, and so on — but in large part also through choice, he came to care less and less for visiting the Paris theatres, though he saw *Les Huguenots* and was impressed by the scale of the handling of it and the lavishness of the stage production. According to *Mein Leben,* during the whole of his two-and-a-half years in Paris he went to the Opéra only some four times. The Opéra-Comique repelled him because of the mediocre quality of most of the works given there. The greatest impression of all — after the Ninth Symphony — was made on him by the music of Berlioz, whose *Symphonie fantastique, Harold in Italy* and *Romeo and Juliet* he heard in the winter of 1839–40, and the *Symphonie funèbre et triomphale* in the summer of 1840. He confesses that after hearing these works he felt like a schoolboy: he was not insensible to their faults of construction and their occasional lack of artistic control, but the ardent imagination revealed in them, and above all their hitherto unheard-of richness of orchestral texture, shook him through and through. He was perhaps more attracted to Berlioz than to any other musician in Paris; but the Fates then, as later, decided that the two greatest musicians of their epoch should never become really intimate. Wagner respected Berlioz for his artistic idealism: " alone among his Parisian colleagues," he said in the *Autobiographical Sketch* of 1843, "he does not make music for gold." But Berlioz, fighting with his back to the wall, wholly absorbed in his own problems of life and art, was not easily approachable; while even then the German composer, as he says in the *Sketch*, felt that the Frenchman " lacked the sense of beauty " and of " pure art." [1] Of the influence of Berlioz upon him, however, there can be no question: while Beethoven had deepened his feeling that he was at heart a German, Berlioz undoubtedly gave him a new standard of contemporary values: the brilliant, audacious Frenchman must have made the bulk of the modern music of Germany seem very provincial to him.

He resolved to leave Paris as soon as possible after Easter 1842. To provide himself with the necessary funds he turned out an article on Halévy's *Reine de Chypre* for the *Abendzeitung*, and another on the same subject, running to four issues of the paper, for the *Gazette musicale*. Unexpected assistance came to him from another quarter. The acceptance of *Rienzi* at Dresden, and the favourable view taken of its value and its prospects by the leading people at the theatre, had changed the attitude of his relations towards him. It began to dawn on them at last that Richard was not quite so mad as he had appeared to be in insisting on being a composer; and since his prospects were so good, obviously the rational thing to do was to help him to come to Dresden. At Christmas 1841 he received, inserted in the back of a goose, a five-hundred-franc note that had been placed there by Avenarius; it was a loan that Luise had obtained from Schletter. There must certainly have been debts to clear off before he could leave Paris, and perhaps the five hundred francs went, in part, to the payment of these, for Wagner had to borrow funds for the actual journey from Friedrich Brockhaus, who now, like the rest of the family, proved as approachable as he had formerly been coy. On the 7th April, a bright spring morning when Paris looked its best, Wagner said good-bye to Anders, Lehrs and Kietz; the two former, in view of their tottering health, he hardly dared hope to see again. The faithful Kietz

---

[1] Which did not mean much more, at bottom, than that the minds of the two geniuses were fundamentally antipathetic to each other. In the *Sketch* of 1843 Wagner added to the words quoted above, "with a few exceptions his art is grimace." This does not appear in the modern reprint of the *Sketch:* Wagner deleted it when preparing his prose works for collected publication.

pressed into his hand, as the coach was leaving, a final five-franc piece towards the expenses of the journey, and a packet of snuff for solace on it; and with their eyes blinded by tears, Wagner and Minna passed the barrier of the town in which they had endured miseries and privations unspeakable for thirty months of their young lives.

In after years he could hardly speak of his Paris days without bitterness. He had not only suffered material miseries: his pride as an artist had been grievously wounded, his idealism had been outraged, and the luxury-loving soul and body of him were resentful of the wealth enjoyed by others but denied to him. In 1870, when Malwida von Meysenbug happened to turn the conversation on to Minna and Paris, the tears came into his eyes. Paris, he said, had been for him the bottomless abyss of vulgarity: " the main moment of his early life, and everything connected with it, had ended in utter derision." " He told me I must be patient and forbearing with him," Cosima notes in her diary after the conversation, " for I could have no conception of the atmosphere in which he had lived." [1]

---

[1] MECW, I, 509.

CHAPTER XV

THE RETURN TO DRESDEN

1

AFTER FIVE days and nights of uncomfortable travelling, the stream of pilgrims to the Leipzig Easter Fair being especially a nuisance from Frankfort onwards, Richard and Minna saw Dresden once more after so many years. They had left Paris looking its best on a bright spring day; and the sensitive Richard was a little depressed by the decided fall in the temperature after they had crossed the frontier. On the one bright day and hour of the journey they passed the Wartburg: the sight of the venerable place, so rich in associations for the German mind, sent his thoughts back to the Tannhäuser subject that had occupied them during the last few months in France, and he at once visualised the setting for his future third act so vividly that when *Tannhäuser* was being prepared for production in Dresden more than three years later he could still give the French scenic artist, Desplechin, the most detailed description of what he wanted. Cheered by what struck him as a good omen, he bore with more equanimity " the wind and the weather, the Jews and the Easter Fair "; and at last, on the 12th April, he arrived in Dresden.

For the moment the town affected him disagreeably. Except for brief occasional visits, most of them in connection with matters of an unpleasant nature, he had not been there since the family had removed to Leipzig in 1827; none of his boyish friendships had survived, and he now felt himself miserably alone in the city that was to be the scene of his next gamble with fortune. They put up for the night at the " Stadt Gotha " inn. Minna's parents being too poor to lodge the pair, Wagner had to look round for rooms appropriate to his exiguous purse. He found them, at the rate of twenty-one marks a month, at No. 7 in the Töpfergasse. Having installed the exhausted Minna there, he set out at once for Leipzig, impelled thither less by the sentimental desire to meet his relations again than by the necessity of seeing what he could do in the way of raising funds to tide him over till his ship came home with *Rienzi*. He found his mother enjoying, thanks to the generosity of Friedrich Brockhaus, a comfortable and happy old age in a pleasant apartment. Living with her was her son Julius, for whom neither she nor Richard seems to have had any particular affection at any time. He talked with his mother about the dead Rosalie, whose steadfast belief in him at last appeared likely to be justified. He saw Friedrich and Luise, Hermann Brockhaus and Ottilie, all of whom made a great fuss of the returned prodigal. Klara was in Chemnitz; Albert, who at that time was connected with the Halle theatre, was on tour.

He stayed only three days in Leipzig, and then, on the 19th, set out for Berlin, in quest of Meyerbeer. Berlin was of far more importance than Dresden to a young composer of his soaring ambition. A success in Dresden might or might not impress the rest of Germany; but a success in Berlin meant certain fame and probable fortune. For one thing, Berlin paid rather more handsomely than other German towns; for another, it was from the Prussian capital that Germany as a whole took its tone in opera. Even Weber, though Kapellmeister at Dresden, elected to have *Der Freischütz* produced first in Berlin, for, as Edward Holmes said in 1828, "this last place is one in which a young artist may be sure of having a liberal judgment passed upon his abilities, with the advantage that if he really achieve a good thing his fame spreads more rapidly from this part of Germany than any other." [1] Energetic and persistent as usual, Wagner meant to give the Berlin authorities no rest until the question of the acceptance of the *Flying Dutchman* was settled. From there he wrote to Avenarius and Cäcilie. The tone of this and of all his subsequent letters to Paris during this period is one of the warmest affection. Whatever the bruised and embittered man who dictated *Mein Leben* might say some twenty-four years later, it is clear that his and Minna's relations with Cäcilie and her husband had been of the most affectionate kind during their stay in Paris. "God!" he writes to Cäcilie on the 22nd October, 1843, "when I think, my good Cäcilie, of the time when you knew no

---

[1] HRMG, p. 171.

greater joy than to give me help and support! How completely and purely the genuine and fine in your nature revealed itself then! Believe me, we never forget it. . . ." Minna positively regretted Paris so much that she wept and longed to return to it; failing that, her only possible consolation, Richard kept assuring the Paris friends, would be a visit of Cäcilie and Eduard to Dresden as soon as it could be arranged.

He tracked Meyerbeer down on the evening of the 20th, but found him to be on the point of " going away," " a state," he cynically adds in *Mein Leben*, " in which I always found him later whenever I sought him out in Berlin." An appointment was made for the following day, and presumably Meyerbeer took him then to Count Redern. Küstner had not yet arrived in the town; but Redern, who received Wagner " with great distinction," assured him that the *Flying Dutchman* would be put into rehearsal after the production of the *Huguenots*, which was set down for the end of May. The snag, of course, was that Küstner had already refused the *Flying Dutchman* in his capacity as Intendant at Munich; but Wagner was buoyed up with the belief that Küstner would be hardly likely to repudiate an arrangement that had already been made at Berlin, and he was given to understand that Redern would still be in fact, if not in name, Director of the Opera for the first six months after Küstner's entry into office.[1] Wagner could obviously get no further at the moment; but he resolved to return to Berlin as soon as might be necessary, to deal at first hand with Küstner on his arrival there.

During his stay in Berlin he called on Mendelssohn, whose personal acquaintance he had already made long ago in Leipzig. In his letter of the 3rd May to Avenarius he says that he has " struck up quite friendly relations " with Mendelssohn — a statement which is not really inconsistent, as some have supposed, with his statement in *Mein Leben* that he found Mendelssohn " cold," and that he (Wagner) " was not so much repelled by him as that he recoiled from him." Mendelssohn was probably polite and friendly enough on the surface: but he could have felt no particular call to be vastly interested in this visitor and his business with the Court Theatre, he never seems to have been greatly attracted to Wagner

---

[1] See RWFB, p. 48.

the man, and his own affairs were too worrying at that time for him to be able to feel a passionate concern for those of others. He had been induced by the King of Prussia (Friedrich Wilhelm IV), the year before, to leave Leipzig to take the official lead in an ambitious attempt on the monarch's part to make his capital the centre of German musical culture: but the work was not congenial to him,[1] he had a great deal to contend with in Court circles and from vested interests, and, as he told Wagner at this time, he had no faith in the outcome of his work in Berlin and longed to be back again in the more congenial Leipzig. He made no reference to the symphony the score of which Wagner had sent to him in years gone by; he appeared, indeed, to have no recollection whatever of it, and Wagner forbore to recall it to his memory.

Armed with a letter of introduction from Friedrich Brockhaus, Wagner called also on Ludwig Rellstab, the then greatly feared critic of the *Vossische Zeitung*, but the fourteen-years-older man received him with so marked an absence of cordiality that any further cultivation of the acquaintance was impossible. All in all, he found Berlin depressing and its inhabitants uncongenial: he was painfully conscious of his dire poverty and the handicap it imposed on him, and already dimly suspicious that the path to fame and fortune in his native land was not to be so easy a one as he had thought at first. He found himself, indeed, actually prepossessed for a time in favour of Paris — " that desert," as he calls it in one of his letters of this period, " for the German soul."

On his way back to Dresden he stayed for a few days in Leipzig in the house of the kindly Hermann Brockhaus, where the atmosphere of domestic comfort and the serenity of an existence devoted to an absorbing intellectual pursuit (Brockhaus was now Professor of Oriental Languages at the University) so affected him, in contrast with his own ceaseless buffeting by the world, that his self-control broke down, and he burst into tears in the course of an intimate talk with Ottilie, who showed the greatest sympathy with him in his trials. The family was at last beginning to believe in him; all felt that the acceptance of *Rienzi* at Dresden was a public testimony to his musical gifts, and that the time had come to help him. There was no occasion now for him to go to them, as of old,

---

[1] See DRFM, p. 212 ff.

hat in hand: at the instigation of Hermann, they voluntarily offered him 200 thalers to maintain him during the half-year or so before *Rienzi* could become a paying proposition. It seems incredible that he and Minna, or anyone else, could live on some 35 thalers a month (about £5); but as Wagner himself had fixed upon this sum as adequate, it is evident that the thing was approximately possible in the Germany of that epoch, though existence could hardly have been maintained on it above the privation limit. On the whole, Wagner's relations with the well-to-do section of his family were better at this period than they ever were before or later. They knew how grievously he had suffered in Paris; they felt that by those sufferings he had atoned for his youthful follies; they took the acceptance of *Rienzi* at Dresden as a proof that he had been justified in following at all hazards the bent of his genius; and it was obviously impossible for them to live so close to him in luxury and to remain utterly insensitive to the spectacle of his poverty.

2

He needed all the sympathy and encouragement that friends and relations could give him, for he soon realised that events were going to move at a much slower pace than he had imagined at first. The *Flying Dutchman* had ostensibly been accepted at Berlin, but there were the usual theatrical delays to look forward to there. He would be able to overcome the normal inertia of the opera house and the normal chicaneries of vested interests only by asserting himself vigorously in person; and as Berlin was nearly a hundred miles from Dresden, and he could not afford to make the journey often, the chances were that the business would drift along indefinitely. At Dresden, where he arrived from Leipzig on the 26th April, he had the chilling sense of not being altogether welcome in the theatre. It is true that in his letter of the 3rd May to Avenarius and Cäcilie he speaks of Reissiger, the Kapellmeister, falling on his neck and smothering him with kisses. But he is obviously painting the situation in the most glowing colours to hearten his Paris friends; and even from this letter it is evident that what he had heard about Reissiger in musical circles in the town was not re-assuring. Everybody, he says, is certain that Reissiger means honestly by him —

[329]

which of itself implies a doubt having been expressed in some quarters; but, he continues, " the man has become such a lazy Philistine that I should be in a nice mess if I were to leave the artistic execution of my opera to his tender care alone." Fischer and Heine received him with open arms. Schröder-Devrient, he found, was at the moment making guest-appearances in other towns. Tichatschek was also on the point of leaving Dresden when Wagner arrived, but he gave the young composer a friendly greeting. In *Mein Leben* he tells us that " the results of my talks with the Intendant [Lüttichau] and the Kapellmeister [Reissiger] left me cold and incredulous. They were sincerely astonished at my arrival in Dresden. I received the same impression from my frequent correspondent and patron, Hofrath Winkler, who also would have preferred my remaining in Paris." He, for his part, was already secretly disillusioned about Dresden. Since he had seen it last he had seen also London and Paris; and in comparison with these, Dresden must have seemed cramped and provincial. As we shall see shortly, his first thought after the resounding success of *Rienzi* was that if only this had happened in Paris how much better off he would have been! For in Paris he would have drawn good royalties from each performance, sold the piano score at a handsome figure, and seen the German theatres clamouring for permission to produce the work. In Dresden, under the best circumstances, he could hope only for a single meagre fee, and for a relatively slow spread of the work to other German towns and to foreign territories.

The explanation of the coolness of the theatre authorities towards him is probably that they had already had a taste, in his correspondence from Paris, of his persistence where his interest was concerned; and as they knew well, though as yet he did not, that there was no immediate likelihood of the work being mounted, they were not cheered at the prospect of having this terrier barking at their heels day in and day out until the bone he wanted could be flung to him. In distant Paris he could be put off with epistolary promises and smooth assurances of good will: in Dresden he was more than likely to prove a nuisance. We can estimate his persistence there from the energy with which, hampered as he was by his poverty, he kept on pushing his claims in Berlin. Hearing that Küstner, on his way to take up his new duties, had arrived at Leipzig and was spending a few days in the town, he went thither on the 5th May and had a talk with him. Küstner was manifestly embarrassed at the discovery that the opera he had refused at Munich had been accepted in Berlin. He diplomatically told Wagner he would see what he could do in connection with it. But if he thought that this down-at-heels young starveling, who must have been indistinguishable in his eyes from a hundred other respectful applicants of the same genre in the Germany of the period, was to be fobbed off with vague words he was soon to find out his mistake. A threat to call on Küstner in Berlin, on the 2nd June, brought from the latter an appeal to wait a little longer for his final verdict. And as there was nothing more to be done, for the time being, in either Berlin or Dresden — it manifestly being impossible now for the promise to produce *Rienzi* in July to be fulfilled — Richard made up his mind to take a summer holiday, for the sake of Minna's sorely damaged health as much as for his own pleasure. From Leipzig he slipped over to Halle to see Albert. He found his elder brother meanly provided for at the small theatre there, and numbly resigned to a fate from which now, at the age of forty-three, there seemed no hope of escape for him. His daughter Johanna, who was ultimately to retrieve the family fortunes, was as yet only fifteen. She sang for Richard, who was impressed by the unusual quality of her voice and her precocious instinct for dramatic expression; but it was not for some time yet that he could launch her, in Dresden, on a career that was to prove so brilliant and profitable a one.

His holiday he spent in Teplitz, where, on the 9th June, he arrived with Minna and her sister Jette. They had lodgings in a farm, " Zur Eiche," only a few paces away from the Turna Garden. Teplitz had long been a favourite resort of his mother. The old lady arrived there for her summer holiday at the same time as they did; she was housed much more luxuriously than they, in the " Blue Angel." She and her daughter-in-law now met for the first time, and apparently got on quite well together; the quaint little old lady, if a trifle eccentric, was cheerful and talkative, and, in spite of a stiff knee, able to take a fair amount of exercise. Feeling the urge of the *Tannhäuser* subject in him, and therefore longing to be alone, Richard soon left the women and started off on a ramble of several days in the Bohemian mountains. At Aussig, on the Schreckenstein, he took humble quarters for a few days, sleeping at night on an improvised shakedown in the one room available for a guest. He spent most of his time on the Wostrai, the highest peak of the neighbourhood: and there he worked out the scenario for *Tannhäuser* in full detail, in a small note-book that is now in the Burrell Collection. Ten pages are in pencil, fourteen in ink, the latter evidently having been added after his return to Teplitz, for the commencement of the sketch is dated " June 22, 1842, Schreckenstein bei Aussig," and the conclusion " Teplitz, July, 1842." The title he had intended for the opera was *The Venusberg;* the change to *Tannhäuser and the Contest of Song on the Wartburg* was forced on him later by his having heard that certain ribald wits were giving too Rabelaisian a sense to the earlier title. One day, during his ascent of the Wostrai, he heard a goatherd piping a merry tune in an adjacent valley. The scene of the pilgrims and the shepherd boy in the first act of the opera at once came to life within him; but when, later, he searched his memory for the tune he found he had forgotten it completely, and he " had to help himself out," as he says, " in the usual way." The world can have been no great loser by the exchange.[1]

3

His stay in Teplitz was cut short by the news that Schröder-Devrient and Tichatschek had returned to Dresden. He had been assured that *Rienzi* would be produced at the end of August; and although he did not doubt everyone's good will towards him, he meant to leave nothing to chance. He was wise, for in spite of all his urgency one delay followed on another. He was back in Dresden on the 18th July. On the 21st he sends word to Minna, who is still in Teplitz, that the production has now been postponed to the end of September. He feels he ought to have hastened back earlier; " the

---

[1] Glasenapp, however, says that some leaves from a sketch-book of this period have survived, on which are noted themes for "The Venusberg," "The Pilgrims," "End of Act 1," "Commencement of Act 3," etc.; and that the melody of the Shepherd Boy appears "in a form completely different from the one finally selected." (See GRW, I, 445, 446.) Did Wagner, after all, jot down the melody he heard on the Wostrai, but reject it later for one of his own?

Devrient, Tichatschek, and Reissiger have already been here three weeks, and nothing whatever has been done. It's abominable! " Evidently he found it difficult to conceive that the Dresden Opera could have any other reason for its existence just then than the production of *his* work. He found that at the beginning of September Tichatschek was to go to Salzburg for twelve days, which, of course, meant more delay. But he cajoled or bullied the theatre authorities into starting the piano rehearsals at the commencement of August. On the return of Tichatschek there was to be another week of these, then a week of stage rehearsals, and all would be ready for a production on 26th September. Tichatschek was keen enough about his job, and Schröder-Devrient could be managed fairly easily. The great trouble was the laziness of Reissiger. " However," he assures Minna, " I'll soon remedy that! " Reissiger's easy-going ways were a perpetual annoyance to Wagner, who had finally to stand over him while he affixed his signature to the parts, without which formality the rehearsals could not begin. After that, Wagner called on the Intendant to get the final authorisation to commence. He must have been a thorn in the flesh of everyone in the theatre administration.

He took furnished apartments at No. 5 in the Waisenhausgasse, for which he had to pay twelve thalers a month, and settled down in grim earnest to the business of floating *Rienzi*. Fortunately for him, Fischer and Heine were not only delighted with the work but soon conceived a great personal liking for its composer. Heine, as has been said, had been a theatrical colleague and friend of Geyer in days gone by; Fischer, a much older man, Wagner had not met in the flesh before his return from Paris, though, as we have seen, he had carried on an extensive correspondence with him from there. Wagner never forgot the thousand kindnesses shown him by this good soul, and after Fischer's death, in November 1859, he published a moving eulogy of him in the *Neue Zeitschrift für Musik*.[1] In his scanty spare time Fischer used to copy out ancient musical works, especially of the polyphonic kind, that were almost unknown to the generality of musicians in those days; and no doubt he introduced Wagner to many a work of the remote past that played its part in deepening his musical nature and revealing to

[1] Reprinted in RWGS, Vol. 5.

him new aspects of choral technique. Most of his evenings at this time were spent with Fischer at Heine's house, a highly intellectual conversation being sustained on a frugal supper of potatoes and herrings.

The two persons on whom the success or failure of *Rienzi* virtually depended were of course the soprano and the tenor; and it was one of Wagner's none too frequent strokes of luck to find, at the outset of his operatic career, two stars of such magnitude so favourably disposed towards him. Each of them was the idol not only of the Dresden public but of all Germany. Schröder-Devrient was now thirty-eight, vocally somewhat past her best, and becoming decidedly matronly in figure, but still the most magnetic artist on the German operatic stage. Though she was not at first in love with her part (that of Adriano), her old liking for Wagner and her admiration of his genius ensured her doing her best for him.[1] Everyone, including Wagner, counted on a rousing effect with the groundlings at the end of the opera, when Adriano was to *ride* on to the stage to rescue Irene from the burning Capitol, Schröder-Devrient recklessly bestriding her charger like a man! Tichatschek was at this time thirty-five, and at the very summit of his powers. He had been first tenor at the Dresden Opera since 1838; he retained the post for thirty-four years — till his retirement on a pension in 1872.[2] Not for many years — till, in fact, the more modern race of Wagner singers came into being — could an adequate substitute be found for him anywhere in Germany in the earlier Wagnerian parts. As late as 1867, when *Lohengrin* was being prepared at Munich, Wagner could still think of no other German tenor on whom he could even approximately rely. King Ludwig's idealistic conception of the ethereal nature of the Knight of the Graal was outraged by the old tenor's now unromantic figure and the stiffness of his gestures, especially when the King remembered the ideal performances, a few years before, of Schnorr von Carolsfeld. But Schnorr was dead, Niemann was unsuited to the part, Vogl was not yet ripe for it; so Tichatschek it had to be.[3]

---

[1] It is doubtful, however, whether she was ever really enamoured of his music. What drew her to him was his temperamental energy and his artistic idealism. See WSD, p. 307.

[2] He survived Wagner, dying in 1886, at the age of seventy-eight and a half.

[3] See MECW, I, 350–359.

His voice was powerful, ringing, and brilliant — apparently one of those voices that by some sensuous magic of their own can move the listener emotionally in defiance of all doubts of the intellect as to the extent of the singer's mental equipment.[1] In many respects Tichatschek was just a great lovable boy. He was quite childishly in love with his part in *Rienzi*, with the opportunities it gave him for deploying all the finest resonances of his voice, and not less with the prospect of wearing several new costumes, and, above all, of flaunting it in a suit of silver armour. He showed his friendliness to Wagner and his passion for the coming rôle by asking Lüttichau to relieve him of his part in Lortzing's *Casanova* — which was set down for performance shortly — in order that he might devote the whole of his time to the study of his part in *Rienzi*; and he was even ready to give up his engagement in Salzburg if that would help Wagner. At all times he was ready, in his boundless good-nature, to behave in the most unprofessional way for the benefit of the young composer he so admired; when, for example, he detected, from his dressing-room, signs of flattening in the Pilgrims' Chorus in the third act of *Tannhäuser*, he would rush out and sing with them to restore the pitch. As for Reissiger, who of course would conduct the work, Wagner was certain that, as he tells Minna,[2] he " had him quite in his pocket," mainly as the result of that gift of the *Hohe Braut* subject the story of which has already been told. With the orchestra and the stage arrangements he was secretly dissatisfied: they seemed mediocre and provincial after what he had heard and seen in Paris. This inner dissatisfaction was to have tragic results a few years later; but for the present it was over-ridden by his delight in the nearer and nearer approach to his immediate goal. The overwhelming need of his life at the moment was the money which he hoped *Rienzi* would bring him.

---

[1] According to the contemporary Sincerus, he was at home not only in Heldentenor parts but in those calling for a romantic softness and sweetness of tone. The range of his voice in both directions made practically all the tenor parts of the German and French repertory possible to him. His production was so natural that it was seldom he was out of voice. His intonation and his diction were alike above suspicion; but his coloratura left something to be desired. Even his occasional little faults as a singer were of a type that endeared him to his listeners. As an actor he was at times a little awkward. See SDH, pp. 198–210.

[2] RWMW, I, 5.

One passage in his letter of the 28th July to Minna leaves us somewhat puzzled as to its full meaning. The moment he had got settled in his new apartment, which was on the 27th, he wanted Minna to return from Teplitz; as usual, he was longing for the domestic comfort that only she could provide. But he was disturbed by finding her hinting, in her reply, at " the necessity for a *longer* parting." There can be no doubt that this meant a parting for more than the term of even a prolonged holiday; the terms of his answer make this clear enough. Had she made the suggestion at any one of half a dozen earlier times he could have understood it, he says — when, for instance, he had disclosed to her his soaring plans in Riga, and persuaded her to share in them; when he had induced her to embark at Pillau upon the voyage to an utterly uncertain goal; when, in Paris, Frau von Zech and Fräulein Leplay had offered to save her from starvation by taking her back to Germany with them; yet her love and devotion had kept her by his side in these and other times of trial. " Why did you not speak *then* of the necessity for us to part? *Then* I could have found nothing to reply to you. But now, when I feel that I have my future more and more in my own hands, why, I ask you, do you speak of this necessity? Tell me, what makes you so faint-hearted? " No hint is discernible of there having been any difference between them; and the only speculation we can permit ourselves — it is one that seems to be suggested by the remaining portion of the letter — is that Minna had become appalled at their pennilessness, at the expense she saw before them if they were to keep up the necessary appearances in Dresden, and at the consequent likelihood of their always being dependent upon the charity of others, and had perhaps suggested leaving him to carve out his career in Dresden alone while she maintained herself elsewhere.

An echo of the Paris days had come to him in Teplitz in the shape of a request from the publisher Schlesinger for the delivery of an arrangement, presumably of Halévy's *Reine de Chypre*, which he had contracted to do before he left there, and for which, it is not improbable, he had been paid in advance.[1] He polished off the job

---

[1] In view of the impression he conveys, in *Mein Leben*, that Schlesinger had over-driven and under-paid him in Paris, it is worth noting that his tone in his contemporary letters to the publisher is always one of genuine gratitude to him. In his letter of the 25th June, 1842, announcing the despatch of the Halévy arrange-

by working at it until midnight. He scoured the town to raise money for Kietz, who seems to have been in a desperate way just then; ultimately he managed to borrow 200 thalers from Schröder-Devrient. " You see," he writes cheerfully to Minna, " she is an artist, and Kietz and I are artists, and artists ought to have to do with none but each other: no trader ought to be mixed up in the matter, for that leads to disagreeable conflicts " — a side blow, no doubt, at the rich Leipzig merchant Schletter, who had more than once come to Richard's own rescue, and from whom he had recently borrowed a little both on his own account and on behalf of Kietz. Before very long he was to extract a much larger sum from the sympathetic Schröder-Devrient, this time not for Kietz but for himself.

4

One extraordinary feature of *Mein Leben* is Wagner's omission to record the fact that Natalie had at some time or other been sent to him and Minna in Paris: there is no mention whatever of her in the autobiography from the moment when she and Minna set out on that flight from Richard in Königsberg at the end of May, 1837, till the year 1849, when the two women followed the fugitive revolutionary to Zürich. When or how Natalie had arrived in Paris we do not know, or what had been done with her there. But from Wagner's letters to Paris after his return to Dresden we gather that she had been left in the care of Avenarius and Cäcilie. On the 3rd May we find him inviting them to gratify him with a visit in Teplitz: " Natalie," he says, " could be disposed of somewhere or other by then — perhaps through the good Kühnes." (Herr Kühne was a German friend of Avenarius who kept a private school in Paris; Wagner used to spend a pleasant evening now and then at his house during the last few months of his stay in France.) On the 13th June he sends Natalie greetings through Cäcilie, exhorting her to " grow tall and slim " — a playful reference to that stumpiness of body of which he speaks later in *Mein Leben*. There was talk of Cäcilie bringing Natalie with her to Germany in the spring

---

ment referred to above, he calls Schlesinger his "protector," and asks him for a continuance of his sympathy, "which has so often brought me help in my need." RWKK, I, 269–271.

of 1843; but as this scheme did not materialise, the rather dull-witted girl had finally to be started off on the journey alone. Apparently she had some wild idea in her head that, as Wagner puts it in a letter of the 8th April, 1843, to Cäcilie, she could be of use to herself and the world by learning French, of which, we gather, she still knew next to nothing in spite of her long sojourn in Paris. This plan, says Wagner grimly, is a delusion on her part, as she would soon discover if she would submit her *German* letters to an examination in cold blood. At no period of his life had he a high opinion of Natalie's mental powers. " Success can bloom for Natalie," he tells Cäcilie, " only in a sphere of life that, be it as satisfactory and as honourable as it may, has nothing whatever to do with the French language." Avenarius was to pack up her things for her, put her in charge of the conductor of the coach, and she would be bound somehow or other, some time or other, to reach her destination (Leipzig) in safety, where her brother-in-law, Tröger, the husband of her sister Charlotte,[1] would meet her and take her off to his home in Zwickau. Evidently neither Wagner nor Minna wanted to be burdened with this backward and unresponsive girl in their new sphere of life in Dresden. She was duly transplanted to Zwickau some little time later, according to Wagner's plan; and it was not until January, 1845, that she paid her first visit to her mother in Dresden.

5

Minna and Wagner's mother returned from Teplitz on the 1st August: in a letter to Cäcilie and Eduard he speaks optimistically of the good that the holiday, the baths, and the dieting have done Minna, but it is fairly clear, reading between the lines, that her health and spirits had been seriously affected by the buffetings and the privations of the last three years. With hardly a groschen to call his own he still could not refrain from hiring a grand piano for his new lodgings, though this and the first instalment of the rent of the " rather genteel apartments " made away with more than the half of his monthly allowance. He was already in dire financial straits,

---

[1] Cäcilie and Avenarius, of course, believed, like everyone else, that Natalie was Minna's sister.

but he felt it necessary to keep up appearances while he threw all his energy into the business of whipping up what he called his " Dresden drones." With Fischer and Heine and Tichatschek he had no trouble. Tichatschek had become convinced that as Rienzi he had the rôle of his life. It is true that he was often a trial to Wagner. As he was a good reader, he never troubled to learn a part at home by the ordinary processes of study: all he had to do was to sing from his copy at the rehearsals and the words and music became firmly imprinted on his excellent memory. But as he brought no reflection and no particular intelligence to bear upon the inner musical or dramatic meaning of his part, the result of his always singing from the copy was that any mistakes in that became fixed in his mind with the rest; and he would fret Wagner by singing a piece of accidental balderdash with as complete and as cheerful belief in it as if it were what the author had intended. Against the tenor's sunny temper and his unshakable belief in himself Wagner soon grew tired of struggling: there was evidently nothing for it but to let the amiable and affectionate fellow go about his job in his own way, and to trust to things somehow or other coming right in the end.

With Schröder-Devrient Wagner began to have a little more trouble. She did not learn new parts easily; she did not take kindly at first to the rôle of Adriano, as it was not that of the heroine; she was " temperamental " in the theatrical sense of the term, was capable of acrid professional jealousies, and the language that occasionally came from the lips that were to give expression to the lofty sentiments of Adriano jarred on Wagner's ears. Now and then they all had to suffer from her tantrums: one day, in a sort of hysteria brought on by some modulations that she had difficulty in mastering, she flung her copy at Wagner's feet and stormed out of the room, and of course had to be coaxed into coming back. But Wagner's profound admiration for her great talent, and his canny sense of how much depended on the success of this his first real venture into the theatre, made it possible for him to handle her with a patience and tact that were rare with him; and her enthusiasm for the work, like that of everyone else in the company, increased as the rehearsals went on. Tichatschek's geniality communicated itself to them all. He notoriously preferred, as a rule,

[339]

a shooting party to a piano rehearsal; but for *Rienzi* he would give up anything, even his sport. In the finale to the third act there was a passage in B minor that later disappeared from performances of the opera owing to the excessive length of the work. Tichatschek was so enraptured with the effect of this that he vowed the composer ought to be specially paid for it; so at each rehearsal each of the soloists contributed a silver groschen to the fund that Tichatschek had started. These pence were duly handed over to Wagner every day, and no one suspected that what was an amiable joke for them was the means of buying him an extra morsel of sorely-needed food.[1] That, at any rate, was Wagner's view of the matter; but we may hazard the guess that the company knew quite well the straits he was in, and took this tactfully humorous way of helping him with their pennies. He himself tells us that during an intermission at the final rehearsal, while the others went out to refresh themselves with lunch, he remained seated on some boards on the stage, so that no one would perceive his inability to follow their example; whereupon " an invalid Italian singer " who sang a small part in the opera kindly brought him a piece of bread and a glass of wine. This good Samaritan was Gioachino Vestri, the singer of the small bass part of the Papal Legate, Raimondo. " It grieved me," says Wagner in his account of the incident, " that in the course of the year I had to deprive him of this small part, as a result of which action on my part he was so worked upon by his wife that from that time onward he was driven by conjugal tyranny into the ranks of my enemies. When, after my flight from Dresden in 1849, I learned that I had been denounced to the police by this same singer for my supposed complicity in the Dresden revolt, I thought of this lunch during the final rehearsal of *Rienzi*, and I believed I was being punished for my ingratitude, for I felt that I was guilty of having created matrimonial trouble for him." [2]

Sympathy with Wagner's pinched face and hollow chest must have played a large part in creating an atmosphere of good will

---

[1] The passage in question is that commencing with the words "Jungfrauen, weinet, ihr Weiber, klaget." It was omitted from the published editions of the opera that used to be current, but will be found on p. 418 of the complete vocal score published a few years ago by Breitkopf & Härtel.

[2] Apparently this singer was not attached to the Dresden Opera when Sincerus wrote his book in 1852, or else he was considered to be too insignificant for mention.

towards him in the theatre before the production of *Rienzi* and for some little time after. But the work itself roused an extraordinary enthusiasm among those who were to take part in it, and as their good reports of it soon spread through the town, a success was certain from the first. The production, after various delays, had been fixed for 12th October. A postponement to the 19th was found necessary, then another to the 20th. Writing on the 8th to Avenarius, Wagner looks forward eagerly to what is already an assured triumph. The actual result, however, surpassed the expectations of the most optimistic. The performance on the 20th was of course conducted by Reissiger; the leading singers, in addition to those already mentioned, were Fräulein Wüst (Irene), Dettmer (Colonna), and Wächter (Orsini). Wagner sat in a pit-box with Minna, the Heine family, and his sister Klara, who, with all her stage illusions shattered and all her hopes from that quarter vanished, was now dragging out a bourgeois existence in Dresden. Minna, knowing from her own experience the nervous horrors of a theatrical first night, had at first wanted to remain at home, but Frau Heine took her under her wing and brought her to the box. According to Heine, she looked " green and miserable." Wagner sat for most of the time in one of those semi-cataleptic states that were frequent with him in moments of crisis. At the large audience he did not dare to look; its torrential applause affected him, he says, like some stupendous natural phenomenon, such as a storm of rain. From his own work he stood completely aloof; it neither gave him pleasure nor created any anxiety in him; he was in a somnambulistic state in which he appeared to be watching an event with which he had no personal connection; and at the end of each act he had to be roused by Heine and driven on to the stage to acknowledge the applause. In only one respect did the affair come home to him as being personal to himself. The performance had been announced to begin at six o'clock and to end at ten. How a miscalculation of that kind could have come about is inexplicable; one would have thought that the many rehearsals would have made it clear to everyone that *Rienzi* could not possibly finish at so early an hour. But a woeful miscalculation there obviously had been. When he observed that the first two acts had taken as long as the whole of *Der Freischütz*, Wagner began to be nervous. When, at ten o'clock, the curtain came

[341]

down on the third act, he began to curse himself for not having taken the business of cuts more seriously in hand at the rehearsals. For there were still two acts to come! He took the applause at the end of the third act to be merely a final polite expression of the audience's regard for him before it left for home; while behind the curtain the high spirits of the singers, and particularly of Ticha-tschek, were obviously put on, he was convinced, to cheer him up in this hour of coming catastrophe. But when he saw the audience still in its seats for the fourth act, and again for the fifth, his original feeling of the utter unreality of the whole proceedings came over him again. In *Mein Leben* he tells us that it was " towards midnight " when the fifth act began, and " past midnight " when it ended. His memory, however, seems to have been at fault here; for in a letter to his brother Albert of a few weeks later he speaks of the opera having finished at a quarter past eleven.

About the stupendous success of the work there could not be the slightest doubt. This was the first time the Dresden musical public had been called upon to pass judgment on a brand new work of any importance — for the town was not then regarded as being in the very front rank of European music — and it made no mistake about its verdict. We might be inclined to discount the story of everyone's enthusiasm as told even in Wagner's own letters of the period, were it not that we have the fullest confirmation of it in a letter from Ferdinand Heine to Kietz in Paris, written almost immediately after the first performance. Heine tells how at the first rehearsals the singers and orchestral players vied with each other in cursing the work for its " unreasonable difficulties "; how the music gradually took complete possession of them all, down to " the last of the chorus "; how difficulty after difficulty that at first seemed insuperable had been vanquished by the zeal and patience of " Father Fischer "; how Tichatschek and the orchestral leader, Lipinski, were never able to find words strong enough to express their admiration for the opera; how Schröder-Devrient had sent Wagner's heart into his boots by being the last of all to master her part, and then, at the performance, had astonished and transported everyone with the sheer genius of her impersonation of Adriano. The opera, according to Heine, had lasted till half past eleven, yet no one left the theatre before it was over; " the Dresdeners," he says ironically,

" were no longer Dresdeners." The applause had been terrific: in the intervals Heine had made a point of mixing with the crowd in each and every part of the house, and " often could not believe his ears " at what he heard. " In one place all the note-gormandisers and counterpoint-cocks laid their heads together and declared openly that with this opera Wagner had placed himself in line with the worthiest masters; in another, some loathsome Italianised fools, such as the fat Count Solms and his friends, who peck like sparrows at Beethoven, Mozart, Weber and Marschner, were of the opinion that the work ' surpassed even the divine Donizetti.' " Wagner, when the evening was over, had said that if by some magic he could transport the whole production to Paris he would be " a saved man "; to which Heine's hopeful reply was that this would prove to be the case without Paris. " You and the other Paris friends of Wagner should have seen him on the night of the performance," says Heine. " He looked like a spectre; he laughed and wept at the same time and embraced everybody who came near him, while all the while the cold perspiration ran down his forehead. When he was first called for he did not want to go on the stage, and I had to give him a huge push; he flew out of the wings, but not an inch further than the shock of the kick carried him; then he recoiled again before the roar of the audience. Fortunately he has so famous a nose that at any rate the left half of the spectators could refresh themselves with the sight of the point of it." [1]

It is to Heine also that we owe the delicious story of Minna and the laurels. Like a good wife, she rejoiced in the triumph of her husband; and like a good German wife, she thought the triumph of an artist ought to be celebrated in the poetic way traditionally associated with heroes and the muses. So on the night of the production she placed some laurel leaves in his bed, so that he might not merely figuratively but literally rest on his laurels. But Richard slept so soundly that it was not until the next morning that he became conscious of Minna's touching tribute to his genius. Perhaps he had been celebrating with a few of the faithful before he came home that night.

Heine and a few others saw, or fancied they saw, at any rate one snake lurking in the figurative laurels of the happy young man.

---

[1] KW, pp. 6–13.

Rienzi had had the imprudence to create more stir in the town than even the *Huguenots* had done when it was produced there in March, 1838; and it was feared that, as Heine put it, "Meyerbeer, who is so infinitely influential for Wagner both in Berlin and in Paris, may become envious; he is ambitious." That Meyerbeer might come to take a rather different view of Wagner now that he had been transformed from a partial dependent into a potential rival was not improbable. For the moment, however, there was no need to be too apprehensive. Indeed, Meyerbeer unconsciously did Richard a good turn. For the known fact of the great man's interest in him soon became transformed into a legend in the town that he was a " pupil " of Meyerbeer, he having been sent to Paris, at the expense of Brockhaus, to " study " for three years under the master; the general feeling was that so young and hitherto so unknown a man could not possibly have achieved a work like *Rienzi* by his own unaided efforts. If Meyerbeer ever heard this story, which is not unlikely, he no doubt consoled himself with the reflection that if after all this young unknown were to develop into a sought-after composer, he would be eternally grateful to *him* for having helped him so unmistakably at the first. He little dreamed what the years had in store for him from his *protégé*.

With a fear in his heart that owing to the insane length of his opera the first performance of it would be the last, Wagner hastened to the theatre office at eight the next morning, and in his agitation " cut " the score mercilessly. He came back at midday to see how the copyists were getting on with their work. He found that they were not getting on at all, Fischer having ordered them to wait awhile, while Tichatschek had flatly forbidden the carrying out of the composer's orders, on the ground that the portions deleted from his own part were " too heavenly " to be sacrificed. The dazed Wagner was gradually made to realise that what he had thought to be a fiasco from which there was no recovery was in fact an unprecedented success. However, some cuts were clearly necessary if the thing were to continue to be practicable. He managed to force these on the reluctant company, and *Rienzi*, lasting now till about half past ten, was given again on the 26th. This time the King was present. He had been unable to attend the first performance owing to a fall from his horse on the morning of the day. When Lüttichau warned him that the new opera finished very late, the King replied that in that case he would sleep in town. (He was staying at his country seat at the time.) Among the warmest admirers of the work were the Princesses Amalie and Augusta — especially the former, who herself dabbled in musical and dramatic composition. Six performances were given, all at increased prices, and still the public's appetite for the work showed no signs of abating. Its unusual length, however, was felt to be a source of danger, so at the suggestion of Lüttichau it was now given in full but spread over two evenings at a time, the first part being labelled *Rienzi's Greatness* and the second *Rienzi's Fall.* But after three performances in this form the attendances began to fall off, the frugal Dresdeners objecting to paying twice, as they put it, for the one work; so the previous arrangement, with cuts, was reverted to, and in this form the opera continued to be such a success as Dresden had rarely known. People came from as far afield as Leipzig to hear it. " Society " descended upon the successful composer, as it always does in cases of this kind. For a time he was a " lion." Invitations rained upon him: the embarrassed but gratified Minna told Cäcilie that in many a week they hardly dined at home twice.

One result of this triumph was that the Dresden authorities were now anxious for the honour of the first performance of the *Flying Dutchman;* and as Küstner had informed the composer that there was no possibility of the work being given in Berlin before February, as Lachner's *Catarina Cornaro* took precedence of it, Wagner demanded his score back, promising to return it in time for the February production. Küstner was reluctant to give up the score, in the first place because the success of *Rienzi* had suddenly made Wagner a figure of some importance, in the second place because he did not want to get on the wrong side of a composer who had been shown such signal favour by Redern and Meyerbeer. Wagner's high-handed reply was that Küstner must either produce the *Flying Dutchman* at once or return him the score, otherwise he would hold Küstner responsible for any financial loss he might reckon himself to have suffered. So the score came back, and the new work was at once put into rehearsal at Dresden. The gods thus seemed to be showering their favours on Wagner: the production of two new operas by the same composer — and that an unknown one — within

[345]

a few weeks of each other at the same theatre was an unprecedented thing.

6

The decision to give the *Flying Dutchman* in Dresden seemed also to solve a problem that had been worrying Wagner more and more during the last few weeks. It was true that in the new opera he would have to do without Tichatschek, for there is no Heldentenor part in the *Flying Dutchman*. Tichatschek, however, was too good-natured to feel any resentment on that account; and Wagner knew that there was a part very much to the tenor's liking coming along for him in due time in *Tannhäuser*. But Schröder-Devrient was a more difficult proposition. She had not been able to reconcile herself to seeing Fräulein Wüst taking the leading soprano part in a highly successful opera on the stage on which she had so long been supreme. But as Senta in the *Flying Dutchman* she would virtually have to carry the new work on her own shoulders, for the only possible Vanderdecken — the baritone Wächter — could not be looked upon as entirely equal to the part.[1] In spite of all her wounded *amour propre*, the big-hearted woman remained faithful to Wagner, whose genius had hypnotised her from the first. Her great personal liking for him was shown, among other ways, in her making him her confidant and adviser in what he calls " her truly dreadful love affairs ";[2] and though, as he says, this had its risky side for

---

[1] Sincerus, in 1852, describes Henriette Wüst's voice as being, in its best days, "a beautiful, extensive, powerful, pure soprano," and herself as a talented actress who had worked hard to perfect herself. In spite of the competition of Schröder-Devrient, she had managed to make her way to the front. By 1852 something of the old quality of the voice had apparently departed.

Wächter had been at Dresden since 1827. His voice is described as "sonorous, with a metallic ring"; its range placed the ordinary bass and baritone parts within his power. He was so decidedly on the decline in 1850, and his corpulence made so incredible a stage figure of him, that Sincerus declared bluntly that he had "outlived himself." See SDH, pp. 225, 226, 237–239.

[2] She was notoriously amorous. The anonymous and scandalous work, *Aus den Memoiren einer Sängerin*, of which there is a modern French version edited by Guillaume Apollinaire (Paris, 1913), is probably apocryphal; but the fact that the book should have been attributed to her at all is significant. Her two deadliest enemies, says her biographer Alfred von Wolzogen, were "passionateness and sensuality"; and as her youthful ideality as an actress faded, she was inclined to import these qualities half-mechanically into the parts she played. Married at nineteen, divorced at twenty-four, and deprived by the judgment of the court of her four children, she found anything like balance in her life impossible. She alternated incessantly between a Bacchantic lust for life and a profound melancholy: even in

him, he was probably, as a bit of a connoisseur himself in these matters, not uninterested in her singularly frank confidences.

Tichatschek and she carried him off with them to Leipzig, where, at a concert on the 26th November for the benefit of her mother Sophie Schröder, the former queen of the German stage, she sang Adriano's big aria, Tichatschek contributing Rienzi's Prayer, and Wagner himself conducting. The grey-haired and now almost toothless old Sophie could still electrify an audience with her recitation of things like Bürger's *Lenore;* and she, not the two Dresden operatic stars, was the real success of the evening. The Leipzig Press was cool towards the selections from the new opera: it was the correct thing in busy, prosperous, self-satisfied Leipzig at that time to be critical, and a little contemptuous, of Dresden. The city of books and fairs prided itself on being everywhere in touch with the great world: in comparison with it, Dresden, though the capital of the country, was regarded as provincial.[1] At the same concert Mendelssohn conducted his *Ruy Blas* Overture, which was then a novelty. He and Wagner met at the house of Friedrich Brockhaus, where Mendelssohn accompanied Schröder-Devrient at the piano in some Schubert songs. Wagner, in his talks with Mendelssohn during this two-days' visit, was painfully aware not only of the rather fevered condition to which his colleague had been reduced by his experiences at Berlin,[2] but of a slight but unmistakable subconscious resentment on his part of the sudden success of the younger man. With all Mendelssohn's excellent qualities, he was not innocent of self-esteem and of a tendency to take offence on very slight grounds.[3] After making all possible deductions for error on Wagner's part, we are driven to the conclusion that his early and

the theatrical world she was notorious for her recklessness of speech and behaviour, though it is also said of her that she could adapt her manners perfectly to the society she happened to be in at the moment. See WSD, pp. 78 ff, 90 ff.

[1] On the relations between the two towns, see FE, I, 33 ff. Somebody in that epoch summed the matter up in the remark that Leipzig was a big small town, and Dresden a small big town.

[2] In a letter of the 28th November to his mother, Mendelssohn complains of the load of routine business on his shoulders in Leipzig. It is rather significant, by the way, that while he tells his mother of the success of Sophie Schröder and of the wild caprices of her daughter, and mentions "Tichatschek, Wagner, Döhler, and Mühlenfels" as being in Leipzig, he says nothing whatever of the *Rienzi* selections. See MRB, II, 351.

[3] See the not always flattering analysis of him by his close friend Eduard Devrient in DRFM.

swift successes were not particularly pleasing to either Mendelssohn or Schumann, neither of whom had any great opinion of the musical ability of their younger rival, and each of whom was secretly fretted by his own inability to realise himself in opera. Wagner seems to have had good reason to complain later of the way in which his first triumphs were ignored in Schumann's journal, the *Neue Zeitschrift für Musik.*

In Leipzig, Wagner once more came across Laube, who had just resumed the editorship of his old paper, the *Zeitung für die elegante Welt.* Wagner being the man of the moment, Laube desired a biography of him for an early number. On his return to Dresden, accordingly, Richard drafted the desired account of his career. Apparently he had intended only to supply Laube with notes to be worked up into a formal article by someone on the paper; but Laube's journalistic instinct for a good thing told him that Wagner's cakes would be best served hot from the oven. He accordingly printed the *Autobiographical Sketch,* as it is now called, in Wagner's own words in the issues of the 1st and 8th February, 1843, accompanying it with the drawing that Kietz had made of the young composer in Paris — the first, and, for some time still, the only portrait of Wagner obtainable.

He was back again in Dresden on the 29th. In December, 1842, he went to Berlin with Schröder-Devrient, who had to sing at a Court concert at which Liszt had also been commanded to appear. After their two abortive meetings long ago in Paris, Liszt had passed completely out of Wagner's life. Wagner had told the story of these meetings to Schröder-Devrient, who now, in Berlin, took it into her head to tease the pianist for his failure to recognise, in Paris, the worth of the unknown young German who had lately become so famous. Wagner was in her hotel room, remonstrating with her for her lack of tact, when from the next room they heard the bass passages in Donna Anna's " Revenge " aria, from *Don Giovanni,* being thundered out in octaves on the piano. They both recognised the unmistakable sign manual of Liszt, who soon afterwards entered to take Schröder-Devrient to the rehearsal. The mad creature bantered the pianist again in the wildest fashion, to the great discomfort of Wagner, and to the distress of Liszt, whose generous soul was pained at the thought that he had in any way failed to come to the aid of a colleague in need. He promised to take the first opportunity that might present itself of hearing *Rienzi*, while Wagner, for his part, at once fell under the spell of Liszt's fundamental nobility of character. As yet, however, the acquaintance did not develop into anything approaching a friendship.

Schröder-Devrient was more incomprehensible and unmanageable than usual at this time, owing to the collapse of one hectic love affair of some years' standing and her entry upon another. But the constant state of agitation in which she was living was an excellent thing for Wagner, for the singer carried over into her study of the part of Senta the excess of fever that was wasting her in her private life. The first performance of the new opera, on the 2nd January, 1843, was a cold douche for Wagner. The Dresden audience was a little repelled by this cold and gloomy subject after the brilliance and *panache* of *Rienzi;* Laube, who was present at the first performance, probably expressed the general feeling when, many years later, he described the opera as being " ghastly pallid." The phlegmatic Wächter carried no conviction as the Dutchman.[1] The setting was unimaginative, and the handling of the sea and ships incompetent. Wagner became painfully conscious that his daemon was to drive him along a road on which the general public would have some difficulty in following him at first. It was not in his music that the trouble lay, but in the fact that to appreciate even his music to the full it would be necessary for the German public to acquire a new sense of drama in opera; and this, as he soon learned to his cost, was going to be made extremely difficult for them by reason of the intellectual shortcomings of the interpreters on whom, unfortunately, the theatrical creator has to rely for the transmission of his thought to his hearers. Schröder-Devrient had practically to carry the new opera on her own shoulders. When Wagner asked himself whether the comparative failure of the *Flying Dutchman* was not due to the inability of Wächter to get to the inner significance of the character of the Dutchman, he had to admit that Tichatschek's Rienzi was psychologically no nearer what he had

---

[1] The Daland was Risse; Reinhold was the Erik. The work was given in three acts, and was timed to commence at six o'clock and end at nine. Glasenapp says that it was during the rehearsals that the action, which was originally set on the Scottish coast, was transferred to Norway. In the first sketch of the *Flying Dutchman,* by the way, the heroine's name is not Senta but Minna.

intended. Tichatschek, however, could always fascinate the audience with the brilliance of his voice and the charm of his personality; while the plentiful pomp and circumstance of *Rienzi*, its piquant ballet, its brisk movement, its sheer weight and momentum, all played their part in the stupendous popularity of the work. Wagner began to feel, as he says, " a presage of a divergence between my inner aspirations and my outward success." And in a sense it was a misfortune for him that just at the moment when he was becoming dimly conscious of having thus outgrown the ordinary material, human and musical, of the theatre, necessity should have forced him into a closer union with these woefully imperfect instruments.

After three more performances of the *Flying Dutchman*, Schröder-Devrient, on the 1st April, 1843, left the Dresden company for a whole year. That of itself would have been sufficient to account for the work disappearing from the bill; [1] but the management no doubt welcomed the event as solving what might have been a difficult problem for them in the easiest way. *Rienzi* was put on once more; the public went back to its first love; the management rejoiced once more in full houses; only Wagner felt, not the old elation, but a sinking at the heart.

The comparative failure of the *Flying Dutchman* may have been due to the fact that just about that time the German public was beginning to be a little weary of operatic subjects of the romantic, and especially the gloomy romantic, type. Meyerbeer had given people a liking for historical subjects; the " actuality " of these was more to the taste of the new generation than the world of myth and saga. A. B. Marx was probably the spokesman of his epoch when he impressed it on Mendelssohn that " supernatural subjects, such as the *Freischütz*, were henceforth exhausted, and the hopes of opera rested upon the working up of subjects from grand historical events." [2] As late as 1855 Marx refused to believe that saga and

---

[1] It was not given again in Dresden until 1865. This must not be taken to mean that nobody wished to hear the opera again. When there was some talk of reviving it with Wagner's niece Johanna as Senta, that young lady showed no enthusiasm for the scheme, as the character gave her no opportunity of making an effect with fine costumes!

[2] DRFM, p. 41. Devrient, with whom Mendelssohn discussed the point, held, on the contrary, that music was "the art best fitted to deal with the marvellous

legend could furnish subjects worthy of the music drama of the new epoch: " *This* drama [*Lohengrin*] the drama of the future? " he said: " the Middle Ages a picture of our future, the out-lived, the quite finished, the child of our hopes? Impossible! These sagas and fables of the wicked enchantress Venus and the Holy Grail, with all their clash of weapons, their worthy heroes, their ordeals by combat, come to us now only as the echo of the long-dead times that are quite foreign to our spirit." [1] Marx undoubtedly expressed the feeling of many thousands of Germans of his epoch. It was only by the magic of his music that Wagner succeeded in imposing the old sagas on the dramatic world of his own and a later time.

7

Eight days after the first production of *Rienzi*,[2] Francesco Morlacchi, who had been Kapellmeister at the Italian Opera in Dresden since 1810, and had continued to be connected with the theatre after the later merging of the Italian Opera in the German, died at Innsbruck. In little more than another fortnight (on the 15th November), the institution suffered a further loss in the death of Joseph Rastrelli, the subordinate conductor, who bore the title of Music Director. It was natural that the young composer of the successful *Rienzi*, who was himself a practised conductor, should at once be talked of in the theatre and the town as the most suitable man for one of the vacant posts.[3] He was very reluctant to accept it. It is true that when writing *Mein Leben* he may have unconsciously read into this early period of his life a little of the disgust with the theatre that became so pronounced in him in later years. But a certain mistrust, if not disgust, there undoubtedly was within him already. He could hardly have understood himself then as he did later, and as we have learned to do. But he must have had an

and supernatural," while historical subjects were "in their very nature unmusical." Ibid., p. 42.

[1] MMNJ, p. 176.

[2] I.e., on the 28th October, 1842, not 1841, as given in Riemann's *Musik-Lexikon* and in Grove's *Dictionary*.

[3] There were many applicants for the posts, which were regarded as highly desirable ones. Among those who applied for them were, according to Glasenapp, Schindelmeisser, Gläser, Louis Schuberth, Reuling (of Vienna), the brothers Ricci (Venice), Skraup (Prague), Stein (Freiburg), Röckel (Weimar), and Eberwein (Weimar).

obscure instinct even then that he had outgrown the German theatre of his time, that there was something struggling towards being in him that the theatre as it then was could not realise, and that he would be torn in twain by the inevitable conflict between his creative genius and the unintelligence and routine of a Court Opera. He sets forth his perturbations of soul in a letter of the 3rd December to his brother Albert.[1] He would have preferred, he says, to keep his freedom for a few years, for he has two new operatic subjects in hand which he could work out in two years if he had the necessary leisure.[2] He can surely count on good financial returns from *Rienzi* and the *Flying Dutchman;* at the same time he recognises how slowly matters operatic move in Germany, and meanwhile there is the problem not only of living but of his debts — for one of the results of the resounding success of *Rienzi* had been that his old Magdeburg and other creditors had promptly swooped on him, believing his fortune to be now made. He is not uninfluenced, also, he tells Albert, by the prospect of having an instrument like the Dresden Opera under his hands for the possible realisation of his artistic ideal, which was to take up Weber's work at the point where it had been interrupted seventeen years before.

Minna, of course, would be all for his accepting the Court offer, as it meant an assured income for life, while further pressure was put upon him by Weber's widow, who, like many other people in the town, lamented the low level to which many of the Dresden performances had latterly fallen under the slothful Reissiger. It was pointed out to him, too, that at the theatre he would have quite as much leisure for composition as if he had to earn his living by other work; in Paris and afterwards, for example, he had not been able to write any music for a full year after finishing the *Flying Dutchman*. He could not resist the pressure of all these forces. He did indeed tell Lüttichau that on no account would he accept the subordinate post of Music Director. He told the Intendant frankly that there was a good deal in the discipline and the playing of the orchestra that he would have to set himself to improve, his experiences of the Paris orchestras having made him critical of the local

---

[1] RWFB, p. 87.

[2] One of them, of course, was *Tannhäuser*. The other may have been either *Die Sarazenin* or *Die Bergwerke zu Falun*.

forces; and, he said, he could not possibly carry out the reforms he had in mind if his office were merely a subordinate one.[1] So anxious was the management to secure him that he was thereupon offered the post vacated by Morlacchi, even the regulation, to which Weber himself had had to submit, that he should first serve a year in the minor position being relaxed in his favour. As a matter of form he conducted a " trial " performance on the 10th January: for this he chose *Euryanthe*. And so, on the 2nd February, 1843, he was appointed Royal Kapellmeister for life at a salary of 1,500 thalers.[2]

To everyone but himself he must have appeared the luckiest young man in Germany: within ten weeks he had had two operas produced, one of which had set all Germany talking, and had received a life-appointment at one of the principal theatres of the country. Minna was in the seventh heaven of delight; there would be no more pinching, no more blacking of lodgers' boots, no more dodging of creditors: she would even be a person of some importance in the town. Richard's relatives thought they saw him at last on the way not only to increasing honour but to financial independence. It was only he who felt a chill at his heart, deep down within himself he knew that for the redemption of his half-starved body he had sold his soul into slavery. Had he had a presentiment, months before this, of his some day becoming connected with the Dresden theatre? On the 12th June, 1842, when in Teplitz, he had written to Lehrs, saying that " a shudder came over him " when he thought that some day " a banal, tiresome ' good fortune ' " may await him, where he must find his satisfaction " not in fowls and goats [he is referring to the delights of the farm at Teplitz] but in Court Councillors and asses." Poor as he was, he evidently dreaded being dragged into the practical world of the theatre again: he would have preferred leisure and tranquillity in which to develop the ideas that were now germinating in him. He loathed almost everyone connected with opera houses: " my future," he wrote to Lehrs, " lies in the hand of the theatre riff-raff: may God enlighten their lordships and open their hearts to virtue! Amen! " He loves no town, he says, enough to want to live in it: " my heart

---

[1] See his letter of the 5th January, 1843, to Lüttichau, in RWKK, I, 323.

[2] Reissiger's salary was 2,000 thalers.

cannot refresh itself among stones and humanity; I must have Nature and friends." Nearly a quarter of a century was to elapse before he could have his heart's desire at Triebschen. " My future and final welfare," he wrote from that haven to the still faithful Heine in 1868, " depends upon whether I can bring my manner of life, and consequently my disposition, to a state of greater tranquillity and freedom from excitement. Talking, letter-writing, business complications — are my life's-enemies: quiet, undisturbed creation and work, on the other hand, are my life's-preservers. . . . I have nothing whatever to do with the theatre, and this is the very foundation of the peace I have won for myself. So long as my nerves hold out, I attend important rehearsals of my works in Munich; but I never go to a performance — by the time one occurs I am back among my mountains." [1]

Soon after his installation as Kapellmeister at the Dresden Royal Opera, he and Berlioz met again. Berlioz was in Dresden for two or three weeks in that month, giving two concerts of his own music in the theatre. He was an old friend of Lipinski, the leader of the orchestra, whom he had known in Paris. Being completely ignorant of German, Berlioz had to rely a good deal on the services of Lipinski; and as Wagner was already, in all probability, becoming a little suspicious of the Pole, for reasons that will appear later, the intimacy of these two would hardly commend Berlioz to him. The French composer heard the fourth performance of the *Flying Dutchman*, and another of the last three acts of *Rienzi*. In his contemporary account of his German tour Berlioz speaks of Wagner being " naturally exhilarated " over his appointment as Kapellmeister, which meant an end of the kind of privations he had suffered in Paris. Berlioz tells of Wagner's dazzling success in Dresden. He never, at any time, had any more insight into the musical nature of his German rival than Wagner had into his; but he praises Rienzi's Prayer and the triumphal March in the opera, and the handling of the orchestra for sombre effects in the *Flying Dutchman*, though he censures Wagner for " an abuse of the tremolo," the continued use of which in both operas he regards as an indication of " a certain indolence of mind against which the composer is not sufficiently on his guard ": " the sustained tremolo

---

[1] RWUF, pp. 406, 407.

is," he says, " of all orchestral effects the one of which we weary most quickly: it calls for no invention on the part of the composer when it is not accompanied above and below by any striking idea." He had a rather poor opinion of Schröder-Devrient, whose " affected poses " and " spoken inflections " he disliked; but he praised warmly the baritone Wächter, with whom, as we have seen, Wagner himself was very dissatisfied. The explanation, of course, is that Wagner found Wächter inadequate psychologically; while Berlioz, knowing no German, and therefore standing outside the drama of the *Flying Dutchman*, listened to Wächter purely as a singer, and found his voice musical and moving in its expression. He was enchanted with Tichatschek. In his contemporary letter to the *Journal des Débats* dealing with his Dresden experiences, and again in the reprint of all these German letters in his *Voyage musical* (1844), he praises Wagner for the " energy and precision " of his conducting. This passage he deleted when preparing his *Mémoires*.

Wagner, for his part, was not greatly drawn to Berlioz, though he seems to have helped him loyally in the preparations for his Dresden concerts. In a letter of the 7th April to Lehrs he says that the success of his operas was " an abomination " to Berlioz. " He is an unhappy man, against whom I certainly would not have written anything if I had previously been to the concerts he gave here: I was sorry for him." Wagner's conscience was perhaps not easy in the matter. In the *Autobiographical Sketch* he had spoken rather freely and not too complimentarily of the Frenchman, whom he accused of " lacking all sense of beauty " and of being spoiled and misled by his admirers, " who, shallow as they are, and destitute of the slightest judgment, hail him as the creator of a brand new musical system and completely turn his head, while the rest of the world avoids him as a madman." Lehrs had apparently protested against these lines, and Wagner was perhaps not altogether comfortable in his mind with regard to them, for in his letter of the 7th April he tells Lehrs that he had " given himself naked " to Laube in the belief that he was only supplying notes for a biography by another hand, and he had been " surprised " at the literal reprint of his words. He and Berlioz were by their very natures incapable of any real understanding of each other's music, and while the older and more experienced Frenchman was perhaps a little patronising to one who must have seemed to him, at that time, just a talented amateur, Wagner probably felt a little secret jealousy of the undoubted superiority of Berlioz in some respects, particularly as regarded the handling of the orchestra. But a good deal of their lifelong failure to draw nearer to each other must be put down to Wagner's public expressions of contempt for his rival. When the pair were in London at the same time in 1855, Wagner conducting the concerts of the " Old " Philharmonic Society, Berlioz those of the " New," the friends of the latter made mischief between them by translating for his benefit the slighting remarks that Wagner had made about him in his *Opera and Drama*. We may be sure that friends in Dresden did him the same kind service with regard to the remarks in the *Autobiographical Sketch* which had appeared in the *Zeitung für die elegante Welt* at the very time Berlioz was in the town. Wagner's conscience probably pricked him over the matter, and he may in consequence have read Berlioz's comparative coolness towards him personally as the outcome of jealousy over his success.

CHAPTER XVI

THE EARLY YEARS IN DRESDEN

1

IN SPITE of the fact that it was the capital of Saxony, the seat of government, and the *Residenzstadt* of the King, Dresden was at this time still a small town; it had only some 70,000 inhabitants as against the 400,000 or so of Berlin and the half million of Vienna. Baron Max von Weber, the son of Carl Maria von Weber, has given us, in his biography of his father, a description of the town as it was in the twenties and thirties of the nineteenth century. It had boasted an Italian Opera since the middle of the 17th century. The superficial foreign genre was of course looked down upon by the more serious German musicians; one of Johann Sebastian Bach's jokes was to suggest to his son Friedemann that they should trot over from Leipzig to Dresden, go to the Italian Opera, and "hear their pretty little songs." The normal musical tie between Dresden and Italy was strengthened by the fact that from the time of Augustus the Strong (1697–1733) the royal house of Saxony had been catholic in religion. By the early nineteenth century there was a fairly large Italian colony in Dresden, whose polished manners, it was admitted more or less reluctantly, gave a certain tone to the place, though it did not make itself any too popular by failing to conceal its contempt for the natives as "German barbarians." [1] There was little business transacted in the town; culture centred almost entirely in the Court and its hangers-on; the mass of the people, debarred from participation in politics and accustomed to having their lives and affairs regulated for them from above, were distinguished by the absence of anything salient in either their character, their mentality or their taste: "mediocrity

---

[1] Holmes, in 1828, noted that in Dresden "may be found a more polished society, a greater attention to the established formalities and etiquette of genteel intercourse, than in other cities of Germany." HRMG, p. 192.

had become the key-note of public life, *point de zèle* the guiding maxim." [1] Exclusion from politics, however, had had the effect of driving the intelligentsia of the town into literature and art: the " poetry tea," at which the newest flights of the muses were launched and discussed, was an institution in high favour among the dilettanti of Dresden.

The town had not greatly changed between 1826, the year of Weber's death, and 1842, when Wagner settled there. As we have seen, a German Opera had been founded in 1817, to run side by side with the Italian, which latter remained for some time the darling of the Court and high society. In 1832 the Italian Opera had ceased to exist as a separate institution, though a few of the singers were kept on, and occasional performances were given in the Italian tongue for some years after. A change in taste was brought about by King Friedrich August II (1836–1854), who had a passion for Gluck's operas and other relics of the old sober, solid times. A handsome new theatre, the creation of the famous architect Gottfried Semper, who was to be intimately concerned, much later, in some of Wagner's ambitious plans, had been opened in April, 1841.[2] This was the building in which *Rienzi*, the *Flying Dutchman* and *Tannhäuser* were produced. Its acoustic was generally excellent; the actors had no need to strain to be heard, while the singing voices and the orchestra sounded brilliant in it.[3]

While the Dresden Opera did not stand in the very front rank of the European opera houses of the period, it occupied a high place in the second. It had the services of two of the leading German singers of the day — Schröder-Devrient, who, with a few short breaks, remained connected with it from 1823 till her retirement from the stage in 1847, and Tichatschek, who remained faithful to it from his first appearance there in January, 1838, to the end of his career in 1872. There was a very competent second soprano, Henriette Wüst, who was the first Irene in *Rienzi*, and later re-

---

[1] See WCMW, Vol. II, Chap. XVI.

[2] It was burnt down, in a couple of hours, in 1869. For a full description of it, by the designer himself, with plans, see SKHD.

[3] See FLT, pp. 210 ff. Friesen, who in the course of his life occupied various political and administrative posts under the Saxon Government, was a resident in Dresden for several years. He was a cultured dilettante, and his reminiscences of the personalities and the artistic life of the town in the Wagner period and earlier are valuable first-hand documents.

placed Schröder-Devrient as Venus in *Tannhäuser*.[1] In addition there was a capable baritone, Mitterwurzer, who was attached to the theatre from 1839 till his retirement in 1870, and another baritone, Wächter, of rather less distinguished quality. Wächter, as has been said, was the first Vanderdecken in the *Flying Dutchman*. Mitterwurzer was the first Wolfram in *Tannhäuser*: he distinguished himself later as Telramund in *Lohengrin*, and lived to sing Kurvenal in *Tristan* and Hans Sachs in the *Meistersinger*. During Wagner's term of office at Dresden the Opera acquired his niece Johanna Wagner, who was the first Elisabeth in *Tannhäuser*, and became later one of the most distinguished German singers of her epoch.

The orchestra was quite a good one for the country and the period: it contained some players of excellent quality, but also, like all but one or two of the German orchestras of that time, a number of mere " passengers." It was at Dresden, it will be remembered,[2] that Berlioz found a contrabassist " too old to play several notes in his part, and indeed, hardly able to support the weight of his instrument," a circumstance that moved Berlioz to comment on the practice in the German orchestras of allowing players to retain their jobs long after they were physically and technically unequal to their work. The leader of the violoncellos was the renowned Dotzauer: among the violins was Theodor Uhlig, who, after being anything but well disposed towards Wagner at first, soon became one of his most devoted friends and most passionate and intelligent admirers. We have constantly to bear in mind that while the Dresden orchestra compared favourably with the average German opera orchestra of that epoch, it was almost hopelessly inadequate, by modern standards, for works like Wag-

---

[1] She married the Dresden actor Hans Kriete, who was one of the people from whom Wagner borrowed money for the printing of the scores of *Rienzi*, the *Flying Dutchman*, and *Tannhäuser*. As a result of the extremely tardy liquidation of this debt she became, in time, decidedly unfriendly to Wagner. See RWAP, *passim*.

[2] See p. 141. Wagner tells an amusing story of his violas. When Spontini was rehearsing his *La Vestale* at Dresden in 1844, the viola tone not being to his liking he asked, "in sepulchral tones, 'Are the violas dying?'", whereupon the two pale and incurably melancholy old greybeards at the first desk, who, to my sorrow, stuck tenaciously to their jobs, in spite of their having qualified for a pension, stared affrightedly at Spontini, believing he had threatened them; and I had to explain his wishes to them in less dramatic and drastic terms in order to win them gradually back to life."

ner's. The official list for the 1st January, 1842, shows it to have consisted of Lipinski, another concertmeister (leader), a vice-concertmeister, 14 violins, 4 violas, 4 'cellos, 4 basses, 4 flutes, 4 oboes, 4 clarinets, 3 bassoons, 5 horns, 4 trumpets, 3 trombones, 1 kettle-drummer, and 1 harpist.[1] (The wind, of course, was not used at this paper strength at any performance; the men took duty in turns.) We can dimly imagine what such a piece as the *Tannhäuser* Overture, which was immensely difficult for that period, must have sounded like on an orchestra of this kind, especially when we remember that all but the chief players in each section were technically inefficient.[2]

The leader of the orchestra was the Pole Karl Lipinski, one of the most brilliant violinists of the day. At the time Wagner took office, Lipinski was a man of fifty-two. He was an admirer of the young composer of *Rienzi* so long as the latter was not officially attached to the theatre; but when Wagner became Kapellmeister he had to take exception to certain bad habits of Lipinski, who had been attached to the Dresden theatre too long, and was too vain of his vogue in the town, to take the newcomer's criticisms in good part. Discipline in German theatre orchestras at that time was not what it is now. A player who fancied himself was inclined to indulge in various little Italian-opera tricks in order to draw attention to himself; we have seen how Berlioz had to complain of the Dresden oboe player ornamenting his part with trills and mordents.[3] Wagner's grievance against Lipinski was that the violinist's inordinate vanity made him, in one way, a hindrance rather than a help to a conductor who had a mind and a will of his own. Not only was his peculiarly telling tone audible above that of the rest of the violins, who, as a whole, were probably not of first-rate quality, but he had a habit of coming in a little in advance of them; as Wagner ironically puts it, he was a leader in a dual sense, in that he was always ahead of the rest.[4] That Wagner's description

---

[1] PGHD, pp. 489, 490.

[2] For further information on this point see Chapter XIX below. The orchestra for the Italian opera in the old days had numbered 68; but expenses were cut down when the theatre went on the Civil List in 1831 and the Italian opera was given up. See BKMK, p. 11.

[3] This was Hiebendahl, who also will come into our story later as a long-term creditor of Wagner.

[4] See Wagner's account of his warfare with Lipinski in RWML, p. 344 ff.

of him is correct is proved by a passage in the reminiscences of Friesen, who says he could " always hear this virtuoso even when the orchestra was at its strongest."[1] The result of this difference of opinion between the violinist and the new Kapellmeister will be told later.

2

The senior Kapellmeister, Francesco Morlacchi, had died, as has been said, a few days after the production of *Rienzi*, at the age of fifty-eight. After a career as composer and conductor in Italy, he had come to Dresden in 1810, and in the following year was appointed head of the Italian Opera there for life. He had always been in high favour at the Court; among his German colleagues his polished manners were looked upon as merely a cloak for Southern deception and intrigue, though this may have been merely the verdict of the rougher Teuton mind upon a courtliness of manner and a smoothness of speech that were so alien to its own national habits that they aroused suspicion. The memory of Morlacchi has been covered with opprobrium by the biographers of Weber for his alleged intrigues against the German master, whose position at the head of the newly-founded German Opera he is said to have done all he could to render difficult. Friesen, however, who knew Morlacchi, was inclined to think that Baron Max von Weber, the composer's son, who is the main source of all these allegations, is not an ideally impartial witness. No one who knows anything of musicians in general, and of opera houses in particular, will require much demonstration that there was a good deal of jealousy and intrigue in the Dresden musical life of the second and third decades of the nineteenth century; but that they were the exclusive property of one party is hardly credible *a priori*. That Weber

---

[1] FLT, p. 223. See PGHD, p. 489, on Lipinski's "extraordinary intensity of tone" and "animation of expression." The Concertmeister was a more important person relatively to the conductor than he is now: "he acts as first violin when not conducting," says Berlioz in his description of the German orchestras, "in which case he conveys the Kapellmeister's remarks and directions to the further end of the orchestra, superintends the material details of the rehearsals, sees that nothing is wanting in the way of music or instruments, and sometimes indicates the bowing or phrasing of a passage — a task forbidden to the Kapellmeister, who always conducts with a baton." See BM, II, 3.

believed himself to be scurvily treated is undeniable, and he must often have had good reason for his belief. But the always ailing Weber was inclined to be ill-tempered and suspicious, and, like every man driven onward by an ideal, was sometimes undiplomatic and hard to get on with; and it may be mere common prudence not to believe everything that is said against Morlacchi by the Weber camp, for what one musician has to say about another cannot, as a rule, be regarded as evidence. Morlacchi, of course, being a practising musician, was not, for all his exquisite manners, a model of disinterestedness; it is said that the reason why Rossini's *Barbiere* was so long excluded from Dresden was the fact that Morlacchi had perpetrated a *Barbiere* of his own. But according to Friesen, who may be taken as representative of ordinary Dresden opinion at that time, Morlacchi was a competent enough musician, and his performances, in his best days, were generally admired for their distinction, and especially for their fine shading.[1] Dresden opinion, it is true, may not have counted for much, for in those days, with their system of life-appointments and the tendency of each musical centre to be virtually self-contained and self-sufficing, there were not the chances for comparison there are now. There were star singers who " guested " in this town or that, and so afforded their provincial hearers the opportunity of comparing the local opera singers with those of the larger cities; but once a Court Opera had settled upon its conductor he remained with it, as a rule, to the end of his active days.

Morlacchi's colleague, Karl Gottlieb Reissiger, had had a busy career as singer, pianist and teacher, in Germany, Italy, and at The Hague, before he came to Dresden in 1828, at the age of thirty, to take Marschner's place as Musical Director at the German Opera; later he rose to the rank of Kapellmeister. Wagner paints a not very flattering portrait of him, but in his earlier days at any rate he was held in considerable esteem in the town. Friesen speaks of him as being " solidly schooled and diligent," [2] and says the Dresden Opera owed much of its standing to him. Sincerus, another of Dresden's inhabitants, writing in 1852, describes him as " lively and energetic," " a sound musician ": no doubt he had in view

---

[1] FLT, pp. 225 ff.
[2] FLT, p. 241.

the Reissiger of the earlier Dresden years.[1] Wagner, on the other hand, specifies indolence as Reissiger's distinguishing feature. The explanation seems to be that as the years went on he lost whatever idealism he may have had in his younger days. He was not made of the same uncompromising stuff as Wagner: having discovered, from experience, that it was difficult, if not impossible, to carry any reform through in the theatre or to change the mentalities and the habits of the curious fauna indigenous to such places, he had settled down into a placid routine, getting through his job with the minimum of trouble to himself, and counting the years to the pension that would come to him some day. When Wagner tried to inspire him with something of his own ideals he merely told the younger man that he too would some day see the uselessness of that kind of thing and resign himself to his fate; then he would smite approvingly a stomach that had grown fat with a life of ease, and express the cordial wish that it would not be long before the starveling Wagner would be able to boast of one as comfortably round. When the Royal Saxon Orchestra celebrated its tercentenary in 1848, the rank of Knight of the Civil Order of Merit of Saxony was conferred not on Wagner but on Reissiger. Wagner came to suspect him of jealousy and none too great friendliness as the years went on, and above all of allying himself secretly with his younger colleague's enemies on the Dresden Press; but this latter charge is necessarily impossible of proof today. Practising musicians have never been notable for an excessive belief in either the abilities or the honesty of their colleagues or rivals.[2]

The Intendant of the theatre was Wolf Adolf August Freiherr (Baron) von Lüttichau, who had succeeded Könneritz in that office in 1824.[3] He was an authority on forestry, and until that year had

---

[1] See SDH, p. 24. Of Reissiger's numerous compositions in many genres nothing is heard today but a few chamber music works, which still enjoy a certain popularity among amateur string players and unsophisticated listeners.

[2] When Berlioz visited Germany in December, 1842, he found he could not give a concert of his works in Frankfort, as the theatre was not free: but he had no doubt whatever of the good will towards him of the local Kapellmeister, Guhr, whom he always regarded as a genuine friend. The cynical Hiller, however, who was living in Frankfort at the time, tells us that Guhr "took good care" that the theatre should not be available for Berlioz. See BM, II, 10, 11, and HKL, p. 90.

[3] He was born in 1786, and died in 1863: he consequently did not live to see the final triumph of his former Royal Kapellmeister. The Dresden authorities declined to produce *Lohengrin* in December 1848: and no later work of Wagner's was given anywhere in Germany till the production of *Tristan* in Munich in June 1865.

been Saxon Master of Forests. In the Germany of that epoch there was nothing strange in a career of that kind being regarded as a guarantee of fitness to be in control of an art-institution; but as a matter of fact Lüttichau owed his connection with the theatre, at any rate in part, to quite another circumstance. During the imprisonment of the royal family in the years 1813–1815 he had functioned as hunting-page, in which capacity he had particularly endeared himself to the future King. An exhausting illness having made it difficult for him to carry on his duties as Master of Forests, and King Friedrich August II still wishing to have him near him at Court, to make him Intendant of the theatre seemed the easiest solution of the problem. Lüttichau had no great familiarity with the arts; but in some quarters it was held that this was, if anything, an advantage, as it preserved him from the influence of the coteries and enabled his purely human qualities to find freer play. He may have been, as Wagner said, dry and hard: what the scientists call occupational psychology would be sufficient to account for that. A Royal Theatre Intendant would have to keep his subordinates at a certain distance, and would undergo too many deceptions and disillusions to have any great faith in human nature as modified by life in the theatre. But at any rate Lüttichau was a gentleman and a polished man of the world. The actors, singers, musicians and authors of a State theatre are, at the best, a difficult team to drive: Lüttichau held them together and got on with them, in the main, as agreeably as any man could have done, by virtue of his breeding, his tact, his obvious zeal for the institution that had been committed to his charge, his equanimity in periods of storm, his desire to be fair in all things and towards all people, and the courtesy combined with authority with which he treated his subordinates.[1] Wagner, though he came into frequent collision with him

---

[1] See the description of him in FLT, pp. 80 ff. Baron Max von Weber paints a less kindly portrait of him: he says Lüttichau combined "an imposing personality" with "considerable lack of consideration": and so he was able to "overcome many difficulties in face of which a more finely feeling, more deeply cultivated man, would perhaps have been helpless." Baron Max, however, as has been said before, is not a wholly impartial witness; he saw Lüttichau and everyone else in Dresden through his father's eyes. He could probably never forgive Lüttichau for his now celebrated remark to Weber during the *Euryanthe* rehearsals in Berlin. Lüttichau was astonished at the respect paid to his little German Kapellmeister in the Berlin theatre: even the people in the street raised their hats to him. "What, Weber," said Lüttichau, "are you then really a famous man?" (See WCMW, pp. 582–3, 631.) He could not

later, manifestly had a considerable respect for the man's character; the two would probably have been good friends had one of them not been the Royal Intendant and the other a young idealist with more ideas, and better ideas, than his official superior, and a bulldog tenacity in the assertion and pursuit of them. Though there was much in Wagner that he could not possibly understand, Lüttichau undoubtedly admired and valued him, and on more than one occasion showed him considerable kindness; he was reproached by the local critics, indeed, with too much indulgence towards Wagner. It was the fault of neither of them that they belonged to two entirely different worlds, and that one of them was the incarnation of a new force in music and in social life that was destined to destroy most of what the other had stood for so long.

Wagner speaks, as does everyone else, in the warmest terms of Lüttichau's wife, a woman of great culture and even greater refinement, who occupied a prominent place in the intellectual life of the Dresden of that epoch. She had a keen and kindly eye for all that was best in that life; and her breadth of mind and beauty of disposition were a help and a consolation to many an artist besides Wagner. She had been a good friend, twenty years before this, to Weber. She showed Wagner marked favour, and must have done a good deal in secret to relieve the strain that his warfare in the theatre imposed on him. But anything like real friendliness between a lady of her rank, who was in addition the wife of the General Director of the theatre, and the employee who had to wear a livery on ceremonial occasions, was manifestly impossible. The day when Wagner, in virtue of his genius alone, could meet the great ones of Germany without bending his back was not yet.

The King, Friedrich August II, was a man of culture and good feeling, who was universally respected by his subjects. He seems

---

understand how the public could greet Weber with applause even when he was not conducting: "that is natural," Weber writes to his wife; "he does not yet know the power of an artist who is honoured everywhere." (WRB, p. 138.) But all this, we must bear in mind, was within a year or two of the former Master of Forests having been pitchforked into a musical world that had till then been foreign country to him. Naturally he would at first share the Dresden Court's opinion of the inevitable inferiority of all German musicians to the Italians; and there is evidence that at that time his manner towards Weber was the normal one of the Saxon nobleman and Court official towards a servant. In his first years in a sphere of activity with which he was unfamiliar he would naturally be on his guard. The Lüttichau with whom Wagner was brought into contact twenty years later was a very different man.

to have been sufficiently musical to play Wagner's works on the piano for himself.[1] He too had a high opinion of the abilities of his young Kapellmeister, and it was not only a political shock but a personal grief to him when Wagner joined the ranks of the revolutionaries in 1849. Wagner, for his part, had a sincere esteem for the mind and the human qualities of his royal master. The two met only four times in the seven years that Wagner spent in Dresden — a few days after Wagner's appointment as Kapellmeister, when he was formally presented to the King; again in September 1844, when the composer presented the newly published piano score of *Rienzi* to the monarch, to whom the work had been dedicated; in February 1847, when the King stopped him in the street to congratulate him on his production of Gluck's *Iphigenia in Aulis;* and finally in the winter of 1847, when Wagner petitioned in person for an increase of salary.

3

Trouble with Reissiger and the members of the orchestra was inevitable sooner or later, and more likely to come sooner than later. It was one thing when they had simply to admire the creative talent of the composer who had given the opera house a work that filled it lucratively night after night, and to sympathise with the wasted young man the story of whose long privations was everywhere known in the town. It was quite another thing when this young intruder began to shake them all out of their sloth, break down their cherished routine, and generally to let them see that they did not come up to the exalted standard he had set himself to attain. It was not merely that during the last four years he had been silently maturing as composer and dramatist, and was no longer able to tolerate the facile theatrical formulae and stereotyped methods of the past. He was also a conductor with a new ideal of orchestral playing — the founder, indeed, of the modern art of

---

[1] The royal house of Saxony rather prided itself on its culture. The late King, Anton, was a prolific, if not inspired, composer: fifty volumes of his manuscript works exist in the Dresden archives. These works were produced in the family circle, the King himself deigning to appear as performer in them. Prince Max was also musical, while the Princess Amalie played the piano, sang, and composed. An opera of hers, *Die Siegesfahne,* was actually given in the Dresden theatre in 1834.

conducting — and not merely a visionary in these matters but a thoroughly practical technician.

Weber, in his day, had had experience of the difficulty of altering the routine of a Court Opera orchestra, for he too, like Wagner a generation later, had tried to impose more modern ideas upon the drowsy institution under him, and had been unmercifully snubbed by his masters for his pains. Weber found the Dresden orchestra arranged in a parallelogram, the longer sides of which ran level with the stage on the one side and the parquet on the other. Under the King's proscenium box on one of the narrow sides were placed the trumpets and the kettledrums: a good deal of their tone was necessarily lost, while the players could not see the conductor, who sat at a piano in the middle of the orchestra. Wrong entries of these assertive instruments were consequently frequent and disturbing. Further, the position of the conductor made it almost impossible for him to communicate his wishes to the singers, or to keep the orchestra in touch with the stage action. This arrangement worked well enough in the Italian opera, with its standardised forms, its thin scoring, its reliance, for the main effect, on the solo singers, and the relative unimportance of the chorus in the action: the Kapellmeister had little concern with anything else beyond accompanying the arias, the stage manager attending to the dramatic conduct of the work. By the time Weber took charge of the German opera at Dresden a new style of orchestration had come into vogue, and the dramatic action, as well as the singing, had begun to acquire a significance of its own in opera. Weber, like Wagner, held that the production should be an organic unity, under the control, from moment to moment, of the conductor. But with the Dresden orchestra as he found it his ideal was frustrated at every point. Behind him sat a violoncellist and a contrabassist, who were supposed to read from the conductor's score, but were constantly having their view of it obstructed by the movement of his arms. In front of him sat another couple of the same kind. The thick tone of these four players, so close to his ear, made it difficult for him to perceive what was going on in more delicate instruments further away from him. The third contrabassist sat by the royal box, so that he was quite out of touch with his colleagues; when a fourth double-bass was required, room was made for the extra player in the parquet. First and second violins were mixed up together, reading from the same desk. The strings were arranged on the right and the left of the conductor: and the two groups were separated from each other by the three trombones. On the further left of the conductor were the wood wind, two horns, and two trumpets; if two extra horns happened to be required, the trumpets were packed off to the hollow below the royal box.

The arrangement seems, to modern ears and eyes, the fantastic invention of a grimly humorous lunatic. After putting up with it for eight months, Weber made a more rational disposition of the orchestral forces for a production of Spontini's *La Vestale*. But the trombones now happened to be placed near the royal box; and as Spontini makes liberal use of them in this work, the King had rather a bad time. The arrangement might still have been allowed to stand, however, had not Weber committed the imprudence of sending to the Press a rather tart reply to a local critic, in which he virtually said that what had been good enough for the Italian opera in the unenlightened days of old would not do for the German opera and the new spirit in music. This roused the Italian partisans in the town and the Court, and Weber received a peremptory order from the Minister in whose department the Opera lay to revert at once and for ever to the old arrangement. In his anguish he laid before the Minister a full and reasoned statement of his objects in making the change, but in vain: a mere German Kapellmeister could not be allowed to initiate any changes in a Court institution.[1]

Wagner, when his turn came, would have liked to improve the Opera orchestra by drafting in fresh players of proved competence whenever a vacancy occurred, instead of filling it up with the next player on the list in order of seniority. When, however, he tried to bring in a contrabassist from Darmstadt in place of one who had died, the whole orchestra rose against him; and Lipinski, by whom this very bassist had been recommended to him, actually turned round and sided with the malcontents. The disturbance must have been serious, for Lüttichau hesitated to leave Dresden while it was in progress; but Wagner assured him bitterly that he now saw the folly of his attempting any reform of this kind, and would not concern himself with such matters in the future. Already, he says, the

---

[1] See the whole story in WCMW, II, 138–147.

conviction had rooted itself in him that wherever and however he might die, it would not be as Kapellmeister at Dresden. When, at a later period, he tried to alter the absurd arrangement of the orchestra at concerts, where it sat in a long thin semicircle round the singers, he was told that this plan had come down unquestioned from the days of Morlacchi, who, as an Italian, would have only the faintest notion of the modern orchestra and its capabilities. Wagner's novel readings of the German classics, again, often got him into trouble at first with the orchestra, and still more with the critics. He was censured for his " Paris tempi "; he was accused of not understanding Mozart.

4

He had accepted the post of Kapellmeister none too willingly; but it was characteristic of him that once he had undertaken it he threw all his energy into the efficient performance of his duties. There has been a vast amount of quite mistaken talk about Wagner's mind being " theatrical." The people who thus use the term as one of contempt have failed to perceive that, in reality, it is they who are " theatrical " in the bad sense of the term, while Wagner, in reality, was nothing of the kind. People use " theatrical " as a term of disparagement only because to them the theatre is something inferior to life. They look upon the theatre as a place of entertainment where their sympathies are played upon for a time by stage devices in which they do not really believe, and which strike them as calculated, if not actually insincere. But for Wagner the theatre — the *ideal* theatre in which alone he lived and moved and had his being — was not a collection of devices and effects to draw the gaping multitude in their hours of relaxation, and extract money from them for an entertainment in which the author and the actors believe no more sincerely than they do, but a temple in which all that was best in humanity was, or ought to be, put to uses as noble, as uplifting, as those of any temple devoted to the exercise of religion. That may be an idealistic point of view to which it is hopeless to expect ordinary humanity to rise; but at any rate credit should be given to the passionate, self-sacrificing sincerity of the artist whose point of view it was. Neither the theatre nor the concert room was ever, for Wagner, a mere place of business routine

[369]

or of self-advertisement. For him, art was not simply an emanation from life; rather was life only a sorry counterfeit of the ideal world of art in which alone he had his spiritual home. No man was ever less fitted by nature than Wagner to earn his living as a theatre conductor, for the simple reason that it was impossible for him to reconcile himself to the shifts, the compromises, the surrenders to which the most conscientious practising artist has to agree if he is to realise even half of his ideal. With Wagner it was all or nothing; either the ideal world that had been created by a great artist in this masterwork or that should be shown forth in its full ideality, or it would be better not to present the work at all. It was this uncompromising strain in him that made him later refuse his permission to more than one production of his own operas, sorely as he needed the fee it would have brought him, because he could not bear the thought of a performance that would fail to exhibit the work as he had conceived it.

That this was not mere pride and egoism in him, the mere prickly esteem of the artist for his own work, is shown by the fact that he insisted on precisely the same scrupulousness in the performance of the works of other composers. For him a work of art was not just a piece in a programme, something to fill up the bill of an evening's entertainment. It was a living thing: to destroy it utterly, as the average performance of a Beethoven symphony in those days destroyed the work, was nothing short of murder; to maltreat it in a lesser degree hurt him as it hurts one to see a defenceless child being ill-used. In time his zeal, the purity of his aims, and his indisputable competence won over to him not only the more intelligent part of the Dresden public but the orchestra itself: players and spectators lived to see with regret the dull routine into which the masterpieces of opera and instrumental music once more fell after he had fled the town. But he was very young when he found himself, as Kapellmeister at Dresden, in the sudden possession of an instrument that, it seemed to him, could be put to great uses; and in his artistic enthusiasm and his ignorance of human nature he made the mistake of forcing the pace. It seems probable that he had lent too willing an ear to people in the town and about the theatre who were weary of Reissiger's easy-going ways, and who looked to the ardent young newcomer to revitalise the Dresden

Opera. On the 7th April, 1843, he wrote to Lehrs, in Paris, congratulating himself on his life-appointment to so important a post, and saying, " I have been openly told that a really artistic reorganisation of the musical life here is expected of me, and consequently any suggestions I may make will be unconditionally accepted [1] — which adds not a little to the respect that is shown me, for people have been accustomed for some time to see Reissiger reduced to complete impotence. In order that my time shall not be too fully taken up with business, a new Musical Director has been appointed [to assist me]. More I could not ask for." Clearly he was held in considerable esteem by his superiors, and much was expected of him.

He had not been in the saddle three months before he had raised a storm about his head. The opposition was in part the honest protest of musicians who saw their previous conception of this work or that being held up to obloquy, in part the revolt of established interests that suddenly saw themselves threatened. Reissiger, it is clear, was by this time not much more than a cipher in the theatre. The most ambitious and energetic spirit there was Lipinski, who could not resign himself to becoming a subordinate where hitherto he had been virtually master.

A month or so after his installation, on the 5th March, 1843, Wagner had produced Gluck's *Armide;* it was the first time the work had been given in Dresden. He had put all his knowledge and enthusiasm into the performances: Friesen, who was not a musician but a cultivated and experienced amateur, still remembered, when writing his reminiscences in 1871, the delicate nuancing of the orchestra under Wagner, and especially the soft but perfectly clear piano he obtained from it at times.[2] On the 26th April Wagner conducted *Don Giovanni,* apparently with only one rehearsal. The praise bestowed on him in the town for his *Armide* had been taken by Lipinski as a slight upon himself: he had become too accustomed to regard all triumphs in the theatre as due to his inspired leading. After the *Don Giovanni* performance, which, owing to Wagner's conception of the work cutting across that of the performers, was not a success, he stirred up the orches-

---

[1] This seems to indicate that these assurances had been given him by Lüttichau himself, or at any rate by some other highly placed official.

[2] FLT, I, 247–249.

tra to protest against Wagner's novel reading: it was on this occasion that a local critic took the young Kapellmeister to task for what he called his " Paris tempi " — that is to say, too slow in andante movements, and too fast in allegri. The quarrel in the theatre developed to such a pitch that on the 1st May a meeting of the governing authorities was held to hear what both sides had to say. (Presumably this is the trouble to which reference has already been made on p. 368, though Wagner does not specify any date in his account of the affair in *Mein Leben.*) He was unfortunately unable to control that quick temper of his at the meeting; and conscious, no doubt, that he had not done himself justice there, he addressed, on the following day, a formal letter to Lüttichau, in which, while apologising for the impetuosity of his behaviour and the violence of his language, he put his own case on record. He does not mince his words about Lipinski, whom he accuses of impossible vanity, of double-dealing, and of being the fountain-head of the agitation in the theatre. He declares openly that the Dresden performances of some of the older operas have in process of time become grievous parodies of the works; he cites, in particular, *Euryanthe*, and quotes in support of his contention Weber's widow and Schröder-Devrient, both of whom agreed that he had rescued this work from the malefactors who had so long mishandled it. Not only the actual letter but Wagner's draft of it has survived. Either the latter lay before him when he dictated his memoirs or his memory for detail was remarkably good after some twenty-three years, for his summing-up of the matter in *Mein Leben* [1] agrees almost verbally with his final words to Lüttichau. After an expression of regret for his inability to keep his temper in hand at the meeting, he goes on to say that the experience has taught him one lesson — not to take people for his friends who pretend to be such. " I now see, of a sudden, the path I must take in order to arrive gradually at the goal which, in the ardour of my zeal for the desired things, I thought to be quite close; and I promise Your Excellency that in my future relations with Herr Lipinski I will forget entirely the disturbing experiences I have had of his character as a man, and will see in him only the artist to whom I will not deny my most admiring esteem." [2]

---

[1] RWML, p. 346.   [2] RWKK, II, 37.

The truth is that intellectually and musically he had already out-grown the theatrical environment into which his lot had once more been cast; and the new broom was not welcome because no one in that world as yet realised the necessity for it. Early in January, 1843, he had spent a few days in Berlin on business connected with the long-delayed production of the *Flying Dutchman*, and had formed no favourable opinion of the music-making even there. " A little while ago I was in Berlin," he writes to Schumann on the 27th January; " everything there is in a sorry state, and I came away with the conviction that nothing of any value to art can come about there. The demoralisation comes from above: everything is half, half! I was disgusted." [1] But it was some time yet before he became fully conscious of his complete inner divorce from the surrounding world of public art.

5

We must now turn to a rapid summary of the main outer events of Wagner's life during the first couple of years of his activity in Dresden.

In the spring of 1843 he moved to a new apartment in the Marien-strasse, No. 9, where he remained until the following October. In January he had allowed himself to be elected to the committee and the conductorship of the Dresden Liedertafel (Choral Society), which was a social rather than an artistic body. It was run chiefly by a Professor Löwe, whose great ambition in life it was to bring back to Dresden the remains of Weber from London. He was planning at this time a big choral festival in which all the male voice choirs of Saxony were to take part. Wagner was persuaded to write for the occasion *The Love-Feast of the Apostles*, for male voices and orchestra, which was given in the Frauenkirche on the 6th July, 1843. Though he dwells, in a letter of the 13th to Cäcilie,[2] on the success of the work and the imposing effect of a choir of 1,200 and an orchestra of 100, he saw clearly that experiments on this huge scale finally lead to nothing of any value. In later life he himself had a poor opinion of this composition of his, which

---

[1] RWKK, I, 329.
[2] This letter is not included in RWFB. It will be found in RWKK, II, 70.

had been dashed off at high pressure between the 14th May and the 16th June, in the midst of peculiarly exhausting labours at the theatre.

In this first year of his in Dresden everything conspired to make him feel that the ball was at his feet. The resounding success of *Rienzi*, the swift succession of the *Flying Dutchman* production and the appointment as Kapellmeister, carried his name through all the German-speaking countries. In May, 1843, he was asked by the Direction of the Vienna Court Opera for a new work for the coming season. He replied that he had a new opera on the stocks (*Tannhäuser*), but this was already promised to Dresden; he has, however, in his mind another work (*Lohengrin*), which will be admirably suited to the personnel of the Vienna theatre; and this he could have ready for a production in the season of 1844–45. Meanwhile he suggests that Vienna should take up *Rienzi:* he is willing to modify the text so as to placate the Austrian censorship, and he will provide a score suitable for performance in one evening or in two, as may be desired. The negotiations, however, came to nothing, probably because the subject of *Rienzi* did not commend itself to the religious Censor. Vienna was rather peculiar in these matters. Edward Holmes noted with amusement, in 1828, that while the Devil was not allowed to appear on the Austrian stage, his own " English proprieties were somewhat scandalised at finding [at the Leopoldstadt and Josephstadt Theatres] a number of young ladies introduced on the stage . . . in short tight jackets without tail, [in] silk breeches, and stockings equally tight, a dress calculated to delineate the form with excessive accuracy "; and Holmes could only " leave it to casuists to settle whether the gentleman in black, whom, out of respect and ceremony, they will not engage for the *Freischütz*, would conduce half the mischief to public morals and delicacy by appearing on the stage that these abandoned and profligate exhibitions do." [1] The Vienna Censor could hardly be expected to countenance *Rienzi*, with its Papal Legate and its occasional religious atmosphere.

One curious result of Wagner's swiftly-won fame was that Schotts took advantage of the fact that he had no copyright protection in Germany for his Paris song *The Two Grenadiers* to issue

---

[1] HRMG, pp. 136, 137.

a pirated edition of the work. Wagner published a protest in the *Neue Zeitschrift für Musik* for the 15th May, 1843, whereupon Schott threatened him with an action for libel, declaring that his edition was not a *Nachdruck* (pirated reprint), but an *Abdruck* (reimpression); and poor Wagner, though he was unable to grasp the subtle distinction, and knew only that he had been defrauded, had to apologise in a later edition of the *Neue Zeitschrift* (the 19th June). Wagner never forgot or forgave an injury. Twenty-six years later, when Judith Gautier was his guest at Triebschen, a telegram arrived. " ' It is nothing! Only rather a bore! ' said Cosima after reading it. ' Two elderly people named Schott, husband and wife, announce that they will visit us this evening for supper. They are very worthy people, but he, at one time, did Wagner a serious wrong, and Wagner, without exactly holding resentment (!), yet has not been able to forget.' " [1] The rankling memory of this little piracy of 1843, together, no doubt, with certain minor irritations of the later years, sufficed to blot out from his mind all sense of the vast consideration Schott had shown him in financial matters since he had become Wagner's publisher.[2]

Wagner's position as a Court servant made it either necessary or desirable for him to produce music, from time to time, for this or that official celebration. For the 7th June, 1843, he had written a festal chorus for male voices, to be sung at the unveiling of the statue of the late King Friedrich August I in the Zwinger. Its broad outlines made it more effective in the open air than the work contributed by Mendelssohn for the occasion. Mendelssohn had had the unlucky idea of combining contrapuntally with the choral song the melody of " God save the King " (which was sung in Saxony to the words " Heil Dir im Rautenkranz ") on the brass. The only result had been to puzzle the good Dresdeners, who could not understand why the instruments did not play the same tune as the vocalists were singing. Wagner received for his work a gold snuffbox from the gala committee. On inspecting this, no doubt with a view to determining its possible cash value in some future moment of financial stringency (he tells Cäcilie that it is worth about 100 thalers), he was disgusted to find that the hunting scene

---

[1] GWH, p. 238.

[2] For a detailed account of the business relations of the pair, see NFF, pp. 105–139.

embossed on the top had been so badly executed that in several places the metal was cut through.

In *Mein Leben* he tells us that he had finished the *Venusberg* poem by May, 1843: but from the letter to Lehrs that has already been cited it would appear that the book had been completed by the early part of April. Although he had now served only some six months at the theatre, the Director gave him a month's holiday in July, partly to enable him to proceed with the composition of his new opera — of itself a testimony of unusual good will towards him and admiration for him — partly because of late he had had an extra amount of work thrown on him by the absence of Reissiger on holiday. Minna, whose health had still not recovered from the Paris trials, had already gone to Teplitz with Richard's mother; he followed them there about the 13th of July. This time he allowed himself the luxury of better rooms than on his last visit to the place. He was troubled with rushes of blood to the head: his hard work in Dresden had told on him, the " cure " did not suit a man of his temperament, and he was in a restless, excited condition, as always when the music to a new work was beginning to shape itself within him. He devoured Grimm's *German Mythology*, his organising brain at once reducing the incoherent mass to plastic dramatic forms. All in all, he wrote very little of the *Tannhäuser* music at Teplitz. He made an excursion to Prague, saw once more his old friend Kittl (who was now Director of the Conservatoire) and was rejoiced to find that Jenny and Auguste Pachta had made advantageous marriages. By the middle of August he was back in Dresden again, where he at once set to work in such earnest at the music of *Tannhäuser* that he was able to complete the first act by January of the following year.

The unaccustomed sensation of being in receipt of a salary that was both respectable in itself — for that epoch — and certain of regular payment, and the optimistic conviction that before long he would be receiving solid fees from all the German theatres for his operas, led him to feel that he could now permit himself a little luxury. In October, 1843, he took a pleasant second-floor apartment in the Ostra-Allee, No. 6, with an outlook on the Zwinger; the rent was 220 thalers a year. He furnished it in a way that was certainly beyond his means; " everything was done solidly and well," he says, "as was only right when a man of thirty settles down at last for the remainder of his days." On this occasion, however, Minna did a little borrowing on her own account, obtaining a loan, on Richard's behalf, from the actor Hans Kriete; while the 200 marks he received (in advance) from Hamburg for a production of *Rienzi* proved very useful. He had already obtained a concert grand piano from Breitkopf and Härtel, who in those days were in the instrument-making as well as the publishing business. The price was 440 thalers. He had paid 240 thalers down — two months' salary of a man who was already deeply in debt! For the remaining 200 thalers and accumulated interest the firm had to wait until 1851, when they acquired the publishing rights of *Lohengrin* in liquidation of the debt. He permitted himself the further extravagance of forming an extensive library of books on all kinds of subjects in various tongues, including some that he could not read. On his flight from Dresden in 1849 this library passed into the hands of Heinrich Brockhaus, to whom he owed 500 thalers; and, to his enduring annoyance, Wagner never saw his beloved books again. Undisturbed by the new load of debts that he was thus piling on his shoulders, he settled down to the composition of *Tannhäuser* in his comfortable new home, that was brightened by the presence of his new dog, little Peps, and, later, by an intelligent parrot, Papo (a present from Cornet, the theatre director at Hamburg), which, under the tuition of Minna, soon acquired quite a repertory of parlour tricks, including the whistling of selections from *Rienzi*.

On November 19th *Rienzi*, which had been temporarily suspended owing to the absence of Schröder-Devrient from Dresden, appeared on the boards once more, Henriette Wüst having been persuaded to exchange her old part of Irene for that of Adriano. In January, 1844, he was surprised to learn from Berlin that the *Flying Dutchman* had at last been put into rehearsal there — not at the Court Opera House, however, which had been burnt down in August, 1843, but in a smaller building, the Playhouse that was used for the dramatic performances. The news gave him anything but pleasure. He had counted on the big stage and the exceptional financial and technical resources of the Berlin Opera to remedy the bad impression made by the inadequate staging of the work at

Dresden; he had the suspicion that he was being played with, for it was hardly likely that when the new theatre that was now in process of building was opened the management would go to the expense of a second set of scenery for his work. The hopes he had built on Berlin were thus dashed to the ground. Any production, however, being better than none at that time, and Schröder-Devrient having been promised him for the part of Senta, he went to Berlin in January. He conducted a full rehearsal and two performances — on the 7th and the 9th — in neither of which, however, did Schröder-Devrient appear. On the whole he was satisfied with the singers and the staging, but less so with the orchestra, the size of the theatre necessitating a cutting down of the strings to something like half. The first act was coldly received, the second went better, and after the third he appeared to have scored a success.[1] But the Press next day was decidedly hostile, and the fate of the *Flying Dutchman* in Berlin was sealed before the theatre opened for the second performance. The public as a whole seems to have liked the work, but the management was no doubt influenced by the Press. A third performance was given on the 23rd February, and a fourth on the 25th, Schröder-Devrient appearing in both; and though both performances were sold out, the opera now disappeared from the Berlin repertory for some twenty-five years. The leading local critic, Rellstab, who had been severe on it at first, soon had to admit that it became " more accessible " to the understanding at each hearing, and protested against the neglect of " an art-work which, with its uncommon individuality, and its rugged forms, must beat out for itself a pathway to more general understanding "; but for all that it received no production in the newly-built Royal Opera House.

Wagner met Mendelssohn several times during his visit to Berlin, but the latter was too weary in himself and too cool about Wagner for their relations to become any more intimate than they had been before.

After the second performance Wagner went with his Dresden

---

[1] In his letter to Minna the day after the first performance he speaks of having "scored a remarkable triumph" with this "fantastic opera, that is so completely different from everything people have been used to." He says also that Mendelssohn had embraced him and congratulated him quite warmly. It is probable that, on this as on other occasions, he concealed his inner doubts from the anxious Minna.

friend Heine to a dismal wine bar, where for the first time he read the criticisms of the first performance. Cut to the heart by the brutal unfriendliness of them, he drank more than was good for him. On his return to his hotel he found waiting for him a man with a pale, refined face, who had been waiting since the conclusion of the performance to see him and express the profound emotion that the *Flying Dutchman* had aroused in him. He talked earnestly about it for some time in Wagner's cold room, undisturbed by the young man's frank protestations that having taken too much wine he was not in an ideally rational condition. The man, who was dressed entirely in black, and seemed to Wagner like some figure out of a tale by Hoffmann, had finally to write down his name, Wagner being afraid he would be unable to remember it next day. He was a Professor Werder. The episode was typical of many another in Wagner's career, the thoughtful amateurs being irresistibly drawn to him while the professional musicians and the journalists were mostly against him. Werder brightened up many an hour for him in Berlin in later days; and when Wagner was escaping from Germany in 1849 he blandly assumed the name of " Professor Werder, of Berlin," in order to avail himself of a few days' shelter at Magdala, near Weimar.

Though he does not say so in *Mein Leben*, he once more paid court to Meyerbeer during this few days' visit to Berlin, and the opportunity may be taken now to survey the general relations of the two men. It is impossible to acquit Wagner of a certain amount of double-dealing with regard to Meyerbeer. For the view of the older Wagner partisans that Meyerbeer " double-crossed " him from first to last, and that even the delays in the production of *Rienzi* at Dresden and of the *Flying Dutchman* at Berlin were due to the " machinations " of his apparent friend but secret enemy, it is impossible to discover any foundation in fact. Ellis, in his addition to the text of Glasenapp (ELW, I, 339), declares that ". . . we have good reason for concluding that the same machinations which eventually deferred the production of the *Holländer* at Berlin had something to do with the endless delays in the production of *Rienzi* at Dresden." Ellis gives no " reason " whatever, good or bad, for this " conclusion." Delays were common enough in the German theatres of that epoch, while the documents we now possess prove beyond question that both at Dresden and at Berlin it was a letter of warm recommendation from Meyerbeer that finally determined the acceptance of the two operas.[1] The older Wagner partisans of the type of Glasenapp and Ellis really seem to have been incapable of thinking rationally where Meyerbeer and Mendelssohn were concerned. The *Flying Dutchman* was given six times at Riga between June, 1843, and February, 1844. Then it dropped out of the repertory until the 7th November, 1864, "half a year after Meyerbeer's death," says Glasenapp darkly, adding, in heavy type, "a strange piece of art-history lies in these dates."[2] The leaded type he uses for these words is plainly intended to suggest to the reader that it was Meyerbeer's "machinations" that were answerable for this neglect. As usual, of course, not a particle of evidence is given in support of the malicious suggestion. We do not know which to wonder at most — the immense amount of energy which, according to these people, Meyerbeer must have devoted every day of his life to keeping his rivals out of the theatre, not only all over Western Europe but so far away as Russia, or the mental unbalance of some of these stout old Wagnerian henchmen. Glasenapp, by the way, finds it convenient to refrain from answering the question why, if Meyerbeer was so jealous and so powerful as all this, *Tannhäuser* should have been produced in Berlin in 1856, and *Lohengrin* in 1859.

Ellis[3] adds an absurdity of his own to this footnote of Glasenapp's: "remembering that the fifth Dresden performance [of the *Flying Dutchman*], did not take place until 1865, we here have surely something more than mere coincidence," — the suggestion,

---

[1] The archives of the Berlin Opera, of which Meyerbeer had been appointed General Music Director in 1842, show him to have been in favour of the production of the *Flying Dutchman* there. On the 5th December, 1843, he writes to Küstner, from Paris (discussing the coming repertory), "for the second opera we had agreed on Wagner's *Flying Dutchman*, and as the cast for that was chosen some time since by the composer himself, I have nothing to add on that subject." See William Altmann's article, *Meyerbeer-Forschungen*, in SIM, IV, 519 ff. It was commonly said, even by friends of Meyerbeer, such as Moscheles, that his ostensible letters of recommendation were insincere and were generally cancelled-out by other and more secret letters: but there seems to be no documentary proof of this. See KM, p. 54.

There can be no doubt that he and his wife were lavish with expensive presents when a Meyerbeer opera was in the making. See Verdi's indignation over a case of this kind in 1865, in TGV, pp. 134, 135.

[2] GRW, II, I, 53n.
[3] ELW, II, 50n.

of course, being once more that the opera could not be given until the evil hand of Meyerbeer had been removed, by death, from the Dresden theatre. These good people seem to have been as ignorant of ordinary theatrical phenomena as they were of ordinary human nature. There are dozens of reasons, some of them general, some purely local, why this opera or that, in this town or that, is dropped for a long time and then revived. Public taste may turn against it for a while, other works by the same composer being preferred; the people in power at the moment may not particularly care for the work; the theatre may lack the special voices required for it. The Dresden Theatre had bought Marschner's *Hans Heiling* shortly after its first performance at Berlin in May, 1833; but it was not until January, 1844, that the work was produced in Dresden. It has been said that the delay was due to the jealousy of Reissiger; but a comparison of dates seems to suggest another reason both for the long forgetfulness of the score and its sudden unearthing (by Wagner) in 1844. The opera had had a fair success at first, being given at Leipzig and Hanover in 1833, in Cassel and Bremen in 1834, in Copenhagen in 1836, and in Frankfort in 1837. The next production was at Prague in 1840. Then the demand for the work dried up. But in 1844 it began a new tour of the German theatres, Dresden and Weimar producing it in that year, Vienna, Hamburg, Dessau and Schwerin in 1846, Munich and Mannheim in 1847. Then came another long spell of quiescence, followed by another belated wave of demand, Stuttgart producing the opera in 1853, Coburg in 1856, Gotha in 1857, Carlsruhe in 1859.

The inference clearly is that there are cycles in these matters. Evidently there was a new wave of interest in *Hans Heiling* towards the end of 1843, and it was the pressure of this wave that induced Wagner to dig up the score out of the Dresden archives and produce it in January, 1844. There is no particular need to assume " machinations " anywhere, either in the case of Wagner or in that of any other composer. There are times when certain works simply cannot be given, owing to the unsuitability of the local forces to the task. Wagner, in a letter of 1844 to Fräulein Wüst, begging her to help him out of a difficulty by singing Agathe (in *Der Freischütz*), says that the repertory is in a mess — *Norma* cannot be given for this reason or that, *The Daughter of the Regiment* cannot be given because of the illness of a certain singer, *Czar and Zimmermann* and *Der Wildschütz* cannot be given because of gaps in the cast, Tichatschek will not sing in *La dame blanche* without a rehearsal, and so on. This is the normal condition of things, in detail and in gross, in opera houses; and delays and neglects of this opera or that are amply accounted for in these and a dozen other natural ways, without resorting to the childish theory of the " machinations " of some rival composer or other.

Mendelssohn's reputation, as well as Meyerbeer's, calls for defence against the blinder Wagner partisans. Ellis complains that Mendelssohn " said nothing " when Leipzig, in 1844, was refraining from taking up *Rienzi* or the *Flying Dutchman*. Why Mendelssohn *should* say anything is not explained. Apparently Ellis thought that it was the duty of every musician to divine, in the composer of these early works, the future creator of *Tristan*, the *Meistersinger*, the *Ring* and *Parsifal*, and put aside his own business to devote himself to worrying the local theatre to perform Richard Wagner's works. There was not the slightest reason why Mendelssohn could be expected to concern himself with the interests of a composer whose personality he disliked, and of whose music he had no great opinion.

The score of Spohr's elsewhere successful opera *Die Kreuzfahrer*, which had been specially asked for by the Dresden management, remained in possession of the latter more than twelve months, and was then returned to the composer in a dilapidated condition, the performance of it being declined.[1] But Spohr, furious as he was, and had a right to be, at this " insult " to a man of his standing, had too much sense to put it down to the " perfidy " and the " machinations " of Kapellmeister Wagner. He knew that other explanations, connected with the management and the subject of the work, amply met the case. But where Wagner is concerned, Glasenapp and Ellis refuse to admit the possibility of any explanation of neglect but the intrigues of Meyerbeer and Mendelssohn!

Meyerbeer's side of the story of his connection with Wagner will perhaps never be known in full; but it certainly cannot be said that Wagner's record presents a clean sheet. Even in Paris, while still accepting eagerly anything that Meyerbeer could do for him, either

---

[1] See SA, pp. 274 ff.

there, in Dresden, or in Berlin, he had not scrupled to strike at his benefactor behind his back. There are some things in Wagner's career that it is not a pleasure to dwell upon; and one of them is his resort to anonymity or pseudonymity when he wanted to deal a blow, either at an enemy or a friend, without publicly facing the responsibility for it. In May, 1836, he sent to Schumann an article intended for the *Neue Zeitschrift für Musik,* in which he made a violent attack on the influential Berlin critic, Rellstab — but signed, not Richard Wagner, but " Wilhelm Drach " (an anagram of " Richard "). The violence of the polemic made it impossible for Schumann to print the contribution. In the article on *Paris Amusements* contributed to Lewald's journal *Europa* in 1841, Wagner vented his spleen on various Parisian notabilities, such as Scribe, Auber, Dumas, and the opera singers Rubini, Duprez, and Mme. Dorus-Gras; and as it would have done him no good in Paris to have it known there what he had said about all these influential people, he discreetly signed the article " W. Freudenfeuer " ("Feu de joie "). He expressly tells Lewald that " a false name " is necessary " as German articles are read here " — in Paris — so that the opinions he expresses might do him harm if they were traced to him. On the 28th December, 1841, there appeared in the *Neue Zeitschrift für Musik* an article from Wagner's pen in which Rossini and his *Stabat Mater* were handled maliciously and with heavy Teutonic humour. Obviously emanating from a correspondent in Paris, it was signed " H. Valentino." Now Henri Valentino was a well-known Paris conductor of that epoch; it was he, indeed, who had conducted the abortive performance of Wagner's *Columbus* Overture on the 4th February, 1841. It was inevitable that many readers of the article should regard it as coming from him, and it is impossible to avoid the conclusion that Wagner maliciously intended to create that impression; he did not use that pseudonym for any of his articles that appeared in Paris — where, of course, exposure would have been prompt — and in choosing a pseudonym for an article in Leipzig it is extremely unlikely that he hit by pure accident upon a name, out of all the thousands of names that were open to him, that happened to be that of a well-known Paris musician who had incurred his displeasure a little while before.[1]

---

[1] Examples from the later years of this resort to the anonymous or pseudonymous

From Paris, again, on the 5th February, 1842, he sent a " Letter from Paris " that appeared in the *Neue Zeitschrift für Musik* on the 22nd. It was signed " H.V." — initials which the readers of the journal would be tolerably certain to translate once more as " H. Valentino." In this article, after speaking of Halévy's lack of private means, he adds, " He is frank and honest — no sly, deliberate *filou* [pickpocket] like M." No contemporary reader of ordinary intelligence could fail to read the " M." as Meyerbeer; Glasenapp and every other Wagner biographer reads it in that way, and Glasenapp must have received his information from Wahnfried; so that the identification of the " M." with Meyerbeer may be taken as authentic. It thus appears that while still pestering Meyerbeer for recommendations, and being quite willing to accept any favour that Meyerbeer might be able to confer on him, Wagner was not in the least unwilling to disparage him publicly under the safe shelter of a pseudonym. Ellis says that " it is beyond conceivability that he should have written these words unless some crying proof of Meyerbeer's duplicity had recently come to his knowledge." [1] On the contrary, we who know the frequent meanness of the Wagner of the later portions of *Mein Leben* can quite easily conceive him to have been capable of penning these words in a moment of suspicion or of pique. If he really believed at that time that Meyerbeer was playing fair before his face and trying to injure him behind his back, the decent and dignified thing to have done was to drop him. But to believe in his heart of hearts that Meyerbeer was a sly *filou* and yet do all he could to use him for his own purposes is in its turn a piece of slyness that can be justified, if at all, only by the necessity he felt himself to be under of making his way by hook or by crook.

As we have seen, the historians are in error who allege that on the completion of the *Flying Dutchman* Wagner sent the

---

when Wagner wanted to hit without the blow being traceable to him include: (1) The articles of 1850 on *Judaism in Music* (signed "K. Freigedank"); (2) the merciless ridicule of his old friend Eduard Devrient in the article *Herr E. Devrient and his Style* (1869; signed "Wilhelm Drach"); (3) the farce, *A Capitulation*, in which he jeered, in 1870, at the beleaguered French. He wanted Richter to write the music to this, but concealed from his young friend the fact that *he* was the author of the text. He offered it anonymously to a Berlin theatre, but it was refused.

[1] Not much more than a year before this, on the 29th December, 1840, he had written to Schumann asking him not to let Meyerbeer be abused so much in the *Zeitschrift:* "I owe the man everything, especially my fame, which is coming soon."

score to Meyerbeer in Berlin. His letter of the 20th November, 1841, to Count Redern shows that he had sent the score to that gentleman direct. But about the same time [1] he wrote also to Meyerbeer, assuring his " highly honoured protector " that without him he could begin nothing and only through him could he attain to anything. " The first has been an instinct with me for the last two years: the second has recently been demonstrated most strikingly. Your kind intervention with the Direction of the Dresden Court Theatre, as I have learned, has borne the best fruit; I expect my *Rienzi* to be produced there before January. Thanks, thanks, heartfelt thanks! I now bespeak this glorious intervention for Berlin." As he has no friends in that town, he begs Meyerbeer to use his influence in his favour with Count Redern, in doing which he will only be adding to " the thousand proofs you have already given me of your kind sympathy." A few days later, having been once more assured by Meyerbeer of this sympathy, he writes another letter of effusive thanks. He quotes the exact words of Meyerbeer's letter — " I will try to get Count Redern to accept the work "; and he concludes, " That God may give joy to each day of your beautiful life and preserve your eyes for ever from grief is the sincere prayer of your sincerest pupil and servant, Richard Wagner." That Meyerbeer kept his promise is proved by his letter of the 9th December to Redern, which has already been cited on p. 317. Wagner had never received any reply from Redern to his first letter of the 27th June, covering a copy of the libretto of the *Flying Dutchman*. He was a person of so little importance that the Berlin Direction did not even trouble to acknowledge receipt! But a recommendation from Meyerbeer was a different matter altogether; and on the 14th December the Direction wrote to Wagner saying that the libretto and the score had been received " and had been particularly warmly recommended by Meyerbeer." Wagner immediately dashed off a letter of thanks to his " protector " for "the priceless friendly service " he had done him. " If I thought you could be happier than you are, I would wish you the attainment of the highest happiness; but I must be just an egoist, and beg you to share with me a small portion of your felicity and fame." [2] Yet within a few days of send-

---

[1] The letter is apparently undated, but it must belong to the end of November.
[2] RWKK, I, 207–212.

ing off this epistle, Wagner, under what he took to be the safe shield of a pseudonym, was holding Meyerbeer up to the opprobrium of the German musical world as a pickpocket! There is not a particle of evidence that in the interim he had had any good reason to change his opinion of Meyerbeer. The irresistible conclusion seems to be that he thought Meyerbeer a " pickpocket " all along, but was willing to flatter him and grovel to him whenever he wanted anything of him.

We have seen how, immediately on his arrival in Germany, Wagner rushed off to Berlin, tracked down Meyerbeer, and persuaded him to take him to Redern for a personal interview: evidently the pickpocket could still be very useful. Wagner must have been already spiritually alienated from Meyerbeer the musician even at the time when he was still signing himself his " pupil." He carefully kept the knowledge of that fact from his " master "; but he made no secret of it to others whom he could count on to share his own poor opinion of the composer of *Robert the Devil* and the *Huguenots*. A letter of his to Schumann, of the 25th February, 1843, shows him decidedly irritated at the suggestion that his own works had a touch of Meyerbeerism about them. " I don't know what ' Meyerbeerish ' signifies," he says, " except a cunning angling for shallow popularity. Anything really achieved [*etwas wirklich Gegebenes*] cannot be ' Meyerbeerish,' for in this sense Meyerbeer is not ' Meyerbeerish,' but Rossini-ish, Bellini-ish, Auberish, Spontini-ish, and so on. But if there really were anything actual, anything consistent that could be called ' Meyerbeerish,' as we can speak of something Beethovenish or, to my thinking, Rossini-ish, then I must confess it would be a marvellous joke on Nature's part if I had drawn anything out of *that* stream, the mere odour of which from a distance is repugnant to me. This would be a sentence of death on my own productive powers; and that you [Schumann] could think such a thing shows me clearly that you simply have no unbiassed opinion at all — which perhaps comes from the knowledge of the outer circumstances of my life, for these have indeed brought me into relations with the *man* Meyerbeer, for which I have had reason to be grateful to him." There is no reason whatever why he should admit this gratitude to Schumann unless he really felt it: and if, as his own words and Meyerbeer's letters show,

WILHELMINE SCHRÖDER-DEVRIENT
(*Courtesy, J. B. Lippincott Co.*)

Semper's Theatre in Dresden, in which "Rienzi," "The Flying Dutchman," and "Tannhäuser" were first performed

he had decided cause for gratitude, his conduct in maligning his benefactor pseudonymously in public while still begging favours of him privately, becomes all the more objectionable.

As has been pointed out, while speaking in *Mein Leben* of his intercourse with Mendelssohn in Berlin on the occasion of the production of the *Flying Dutchman,* he refrains from mentioning that he once more sought out Meyerbeer also. Yet his letter of the 4th January, 1844, to Minna makes it clear that he did so, and that for the sole reason of exploiting Meyerbeer's influence once more. " Meyerbeer returned here yesterday.[1] I haven't managed to catch him yet; I will try again at eight to-morrow morning. After all, he can be of great service to me, especially with the King." [2] That, in his determination to get on, he pursued and flattered and cajoled Meyerbeer while running him down in private cannot be doubted in face of all the evidence we have from his own letters; and though the story is at present not anything like complete, we know enough to understand why, in later years, at the mention of Wagner's name a grimace should pass over Meyerbeer's usually impassive face, as if he had been jarred by a " dissonance." [3]

6

A couple of months after these performances of the *Flying Dutchman* in Berlin, *Rienzi* was produced in Hamburg, where Wagner, who had been invited to conduct the first performance, arrived on the 14th or 15th March, 1844. The town had recently suffered from a disastrous fire: the theatre finances were in a bad way, and the Director, Cornet, hoped that the sensational *Rienzi* would revive his sinking fortunes. A comparison of Wagner's letters from Hamburg with the corresponding pages of *Mein Leben* will show the difficulty of relying implicitly on either the one record or the other. No doubt the accounts in *Mein Leben* of the

---

[1] Is it too wild an assumption that Meyerbeer had returned to Berlin expressly to hear the work he himself had recommended to the management?

[2] RWMW, I, 26.

[3] We may know more about it all some day. Only fragments from Meyerbeer's diary have as yet been published. He did not wish the diary and his letters to be made public until fifty years after his death, which occurred in 1864. His heirs, however, are said to be withholding them from publication until 1934. See the *Nachwort* to KM.

first productions of his earlier operas are unconsciously coloured by his later experiences: he had by that time conceived an intense hatred of the German theatres and all they stood for, and his exact‑ ing taste made him perhaps more critical of the early productions of his operas than he was at the time. On the other hand, it seems likely that in his contemporary letters he slightly exaggerated his successes and his delight in them in order to keep up Minna's spirits. Neither the personnel nor the stage apparatus at Hamburg could have inspired him with much confidence; but in his letters to Minna he glosses over the defects of everyone, and, while declar‑ ing the performance, which took place on the 21st, to have been a success, he insists that it was in spite of the theatre material rather than in consequence of it.[1] It astonished and gratified him, indeed, that the work should go down so well without Tichatschek. In *Mein Leben*, however, he speaks in the most uncomplimentary terms of the Rienzi — one Wurda, whom he describes as " an elderly, flabby, voiceless tenor " — and of the wretched costumes. The only person he was pleased with was the Adriano — a Madame Fehrin‑ ger, who, a few years later, when she was past her best, however, sang Ortrud in Liszt's production of *Lohengrin* at Weimar. It was to placate the composer, who made no secret of his ill-humour, that Cornet gave him the grey parrot to which reference has already been made. The opera proved an undeniable popular success in Hamburg. In *Mein Leben* Wagner grumbles that Cornet not only fobbed him off with a smaller fee than was right, but suggested the payment of it by instalments. What he forgets to mention is that for the eighth performance Tichatschek was engaged, and Cornet gen‑ erously gave Wagner a third of the gross receipts — which were certainly large — by way of a benefit.[2]

At the end of March, 1844, Schröder-Devrient resumed her con‑ nection with the Dresden theatre, and in June a youthful rival to her came along in the person of Wagner's niece Johanna. The girl, who was still only in her eighteenth year, made such an impression in the two trial rôles she undertook in May that she was promptly given a three years' engagement from the 1st July. One of her

---

[1] A local journalist, while critical of the Rienzi, pronounced the success of the work to be "very considerable." The second performance followed on the 24th.

[2] See Wagner's humorous letter of thanks to Cornet of the 29th August, in RWKK, II, 134.

earliest appearances as a regular member of the company was as Donna Anna in *Don Giovanni;* a few weeks later she took the part of Irene in *Rienzi,* eclipsing, on Wagner's testimony, all her Dresden predecessors in the part. She was so decided a success in all she did that the management, early in 1845, changed her three years' contract for one of much longer duration. Her father, who for a long time had been making no headway of his own, gave up his professional career and settled in Dresden, to attend not only to the artistic development of his daughter but to her business affairs. At first relations between him and Richard were friendly; but trouble soon arose between them, owing to the latter objecting to his niece taking the business-like course of singing whatever part, by whatever composer, she could make a success with, instead of evolving exclusively along Wagnerian lines, which he thought it her duty to do. Schröder-Devrient, who was by now obviously on the decline, did not welcome the coming of this dangerous young rival; and, as will appear later, her resentment had certain disagreeable consequences for Wagner.

7

Outwardly his life at this time seemed successful enough; he was esteemed by the Court, and his excellent work at the theatre was beginning to make its effect in the town. Part of his official duty was to direct the Catholic services occasionally; and he was of course called upon to supply music when required for state ceremonies. In his zeal he once even anticipated the wishes of his superiors in this latter regard. On the return of the King from a visit to England, where the London public had shown its dislike for the Czar of Russia, who had also been in England at the time, by lavishing extra enthusiasm on Friedrich August, Wagner wrote the words and music for a male voice chorus and orchestra,[1] and hastily improvised the arrangements for its performance before the monarch at his country seat in Pillnitz. He was called over the coals by Lüttichau for taking into his own hands what was strictly a matter in which the Intendant should have been consulted; but

---

[1] *Gruss seiner Treuen an Friedrich August den Geliebten.* The work will be found in the Complete Edition, Vols. XV and XVI.

Wagner pacified him by diplomatically turning over the conducting of the work to Reissiger — Wagner himself singing with the
tenors — and the performance, on the 12th August, 1844, was a
conspicuous success. The King said the comprehensively tactful
thing when he complimented Wagner on " composing so well " and
Reissiger on " conducting so well "; and the success of the day's
proceedings, combined with Wagner's evident willingness to co-
operate amicably with his older colleague, smoothed out the
wrinkles in the brow of the worried Lüttichau. From that time the
relations of Wagner with his Director became for a while more
friendly and confidential than they had been of late; but unfortunately this happy state of affairs did not last.

In September Wagner went for his holiday to Fischer's Vine-
yard, near Loschwitz — a few miles away from Dresden, on the
other side of the Elbe — where he spent six happy weeks on the
composition of *Tannhäuser,* finishing the second act on 15th October. He interrupted his holiday for a few days to run up to Dresden
for the twentieth performance of *Rienzi* on the 20th September.
The performance was witnessed by a distinguished company that
included Meyerbeer, Spontini, and General Lwoff, the composer
of the Russian National Anthem. Wagner would have us believe, in
Mein Leben, that he made no attempt to discover what impression
his work had made on these great ones, and that the one thing that
gave him pleasure was to find that his little dog Peps had run all
the way from Loschwitz after him. But from his letter of the 5th
June, 1845, to his friend Carl Gaillard in Berlin it appears that
Meyerbeer had been greatly impressed by the enthusiasm of the
audience, " and he promised me to work with might and main to
get the opera produced as soon as possible in Berlin. I have no
doubt of the honesty of his intentions with regard to me," he continues; " but I am likely to be driven to despair by the as yet
irremovable reason for the impossibility of giving my work — the
lack of a Heldentenor." [1] That, indeed, was always the main obstacle in the way of progress of *Rienzi* to other German theatres.

Back in Dresden again for good from his holiday, Wagner settled
down in earnest to the composition of *Tannhäuser,* and had the
satisfaction of finishing the music of the third act by the 29th De-

---

[1] RWFZ, p. 52.

cember, 1844. This winter was brightened up for him by a visit of Spontini to Dresden. The long reign of the old Italian master in Berlin had come to an end in 1841. For twenty-two years, thanks to the infatuation of the former King of Prussia, Friedrich Wilhelm III, he had been the dictator of the Berlin Opera, at a salary that made the mouth of every impecunious German musician water. Now, at the age of seventy, his rule in Berlin was at an end, though he still drew a generous pension from the Court. Though he himself was unaware of the fact, his day as an operatic composer was already almost over; public taste was decidedly veering away from the post-Gluckian genre of which he had been the greatest representative. But his belief in himself was as illimitable and as unshakeable as it had always been. He amused Wagner by telling him, kindly but firmly, that while *Rienzi* was a work of genius, the composer of it " had done more than he could do." By this cryptic utterance he meant that Wagner had tried to carry opera a stage further than himself, Spontini, which, in the nature of things, was a pure impossibility for any mere human being. It was he, he said, who had effected, in *La Vestale*, the only revolution in music achieved since Gluck. In that score he had introduced the suspension of the sixth into harmony and the big drum into the orchestra. With *Cortez* he had made a further step in advance; with *Olympie*, another three steps, and with *Agnes von Hohenstaufen* no less than another hundred steps; here he had utilised the orchestra in such a way that it abolished the organ. How then, he asked Wagner, could anyone hope to invent anything new in opera, " seeing that I myself, Spontini, can in no way surpass my existing works, and that since *La Vestale* not a note has been written elsewhere that was not stolen from my scores? "

Wagner's respectful arguments in favour of the possibility of a new type of opera, based on a new conception of drama-in-music, were summarily brushed aside by the old Olympian. What new kind of dramatic subject *could* be discovered? he asked. He himself had dealt with, and of course exhausted the possibilities of, every conceivable type of subject — a Roman one in *La Vestale*, a Spanish-Mexican one in *Cortez*, a Greco-Macedonian one in *Olympie*, and finally, a German one in *Agnes von Hohenstaufen*. There was nothing left; for he hoped Wagner was not thinking of a

" romantic " subject, such as that of the contemptible *Freischütz*? He demonstrated, indeed, by all the laws of logic, that with himself music as a serious art had come to an end. For what nation could produce any composer who could go beyond him? Not the Italians (he was himself an Italian), for they were merely *cochons;* not the French, who only imitated the Italians; and of course not the Germans, who were and always would be children in music, while such trifling natural aptitude as they might possess for the art would come to nothing now that they had given themselves up to the leadership of the Jews. " There was some hope for Germany," he said, " when I was the Emperor of music at Berlin; but since the King of Prussia [the new King, Friedrich Wilhelm IV] has abandoned his music to the disorder brought into it by the two Wandering Jews [Meyerbeer and Mendelssohn] the last hope has been lost."

Spontini had come to Dresden at the suggestion of Wagner, who saw an excellent part for Schröder-Devrient in *La Vestale*. The old despot gave everyone in the theatre a vast amount of trouble by the rigour of his demands, and amused them by asking to have specially made for him a heavy ebony baton, with an ivory knob at each end, which he grasped in the centre like a field-marshal's staff. He evidently expected productions not only of *La Vestale* but of his other operas, and the prospect of being burdened with him in perpetuity struck terror into them all, from Lüttichau downwards. Schröder-Devrient got them out of their difficulty by a diplomatic " indisposition " after a solitary performance of *La Vestale*. Wagner, accompanied by the Music Director Röckel, whose excellent French was useful in interviews with Spontini, hardly dared approach the great man to break it to him that further performances of his opera would have to be postponed indefinitely; but fortunately for them all, they found Spontini in high spirits at having received a summons to Rome, where the Pope intended to create him Count of San Andrea, while simultaneously a minor order of nobility had been conferred on him by the King of Denmark. So the troublesome guest left Dresden, and the harassed company could breathe again. While Wagner had been amused at the vanity of the old man, he profited by his observation of Spontini's handling of the production of his opera; and he was all the less likely

[392]

to take offence at the Italian master's disparagement of all his contemporaries as he himself secretly entertained the same unflattering opinion of them.

8

In the latter part of 1844 Wagner threw all his energies into the fight that was necessary before an object dear to the hearts of all Dresden music lovers could be attained — the transference of Weber's remains from London. The movement had been set on foot as early as 1841, Wagner's friend Ferdinand Heine taking a prominent part in it. After a subscription had been opened for the purpose, and a fair sum of money been raised, the usual difficulties arose, and the scheme languished for a couple of years. In 1844 a new committee was formed in Dresden, that included Wagner, Heine, and Professor Löwe, the ruling spirit of the Liedertafel: and it was resolved not only to bring the remains to Dresden but to erect a monument to Weber. The King was against the plan, owing to religious scruples as to disturbing a dead man's remains; while Lüttichau was lukewarm, fearing that a precedent might be established for the exhumation of the bodies of all Kapellmeisters who might choose to die elsewhere than in Dresden! But Wagner was determined to carry the scheme through; by this time it had been taken up enthusiastically by other Saxon towns, ample funds being raised by benefit performances at this theatre and that. At last the dead composer's son, Max, who was at that time a student in London, was able to have the remains exhumed from their resting-place in Moorfields Chapel and carried to Dresden. There, on the 14th December, a torchlight procession greeted them, to the strains of music arranged by Wagner for eighty [1] wind instruments and twenty muffled drums, based on two motives from *Euryanthe*.[2]

At the ceremony of the burial of the body in the Friedrichstadt cemetery the next day, Wagner delivered an oration that is perhaps the best of all his efforts in this line; the full text will be found in RWGS, Vol. II. He had a natural gift for rhetoric, and on this occasion he was moved to his depths by his subject, for Weber was

---

[1] Not eight, as given in the English version of *Mein Leben*.
[2] The music will be found in Vol. XX of Wagner's Complete Works. There the specification is for seventy-five wind instruments and six muffled drums.

not only his beloved master in music but the immortal symbol of that struggle against routine on the one hand and foreign corruption on the other in which he himself was now engaged. For the only time in his life, he learned his speech by heart; and he delivered it in a style that drew warm praise afterwards from the actor Emil Devrient. In the course of it he fell into one of those cataleptic states that were not infrequent with him in moments of extreme emotional tension: he both heard and saw himself as another being than the speaker; and at one point, to the momentary embarrassment of his hearers, he paused for quite a time, expecting the other to continue. After his oration, a choir of men's voices sang a setting of a poem of his own, *An Webers Grabe*, the text of which is also given in Vol. II of his literary works. The music will be found in Vol. XVI of his complete musical works.

During this winter of 1844–5 he completed the scoring of *Tann-häuser*, the last page of the manuscript being dated the 15th April, 1845. Largely as the result of his having a hundred copies of the full score lithographed — the full story of his venture into publication on his own account, and the financial complications in which it involved him, will be told later — he was in more than his normal financial difficulties at this time; and he made desperate efforts to float his two available operas outside Dresden. He sent the abbreviated score of *Rienzi* to several theatres, but with the exception of that at Königsberg, which gave the opera in the spring of 1845, every one of them returned it to him: Munich even sent the parcel back unopened. The impression seems to have prevailed everywhere that *Rienzi* was an exceptionally difficult and expensive work to produce, and that its success depended on Tichatschek, the equivalent of whom was not to be found in any other German theatre; while the unfriendly tone of the Dresden journalists who communicated local news to the musical journals of other towns must have influenced more than one theatre director. In Dresden everything augured well for the coming *Tannhäuser*. So confident was the management of the success of the new work that it had ordered special scenery from the eminent Paris scenic artist, Desplechin, while Heine had been given *carte blanche* with regard to the costumes. On only one point was Lüttichau unresponsive; in a spasm of economy he insisted on using, for the Hall of Song, a setting that had already done duty for the Hall of Charlemagne in *Oberon*.

With the assurance that *Tannhäuser* would be produced in the autumn of 1845, Wagner went with Minna, in July, to Marienbad for a holiday and " cure," taking with him the anonymous old epic of Lohengrin, and Simrock's edition of the poems of Wolfram von Eschenbach. The Lohengrin subject, which had been slumbering within him since his Paris days, now took definite dramatic shape in his mind; and in a state of excitement that made him oblivious to the demands of his health and the warnings of his doctor he had worked out, by the 3rd August, the sketch of a new opera. His momentary effort to escape from this exhausting obsession, indeed, led only to the conception of yet another work. A recent reading of Gervinus's *History of German Literature* had revived his memories both of Hans Sachs and of the street brawl in Nuremberg the story of which has been told in Chapter XI; and in a highly feverish state he sketched out, on the 16th July, the scenario for another opera on the subject of Sachs and the Mastersingers. His " cure " lasted nominally five weeks; but long before it was over, the baths doctor had given him up as a hopeless subject: anything in the nature of rest, physical or mental, was impossible for him just then. When he returned to Dresden, in mid-August, he had thus within him two fresh dramatic subjects to be left to undergo that slow process of half-unconscious gestation that was customary with him. In the highest spirits he now settled down to preparing *Tannhäuser* for production.

9

Schröder-Devrient, whom jealousy of Johanna had made more than usually clear-sighted, did, it is true, suggest certain looming difficulties that had perhaps not occurred to the composer. She was all too aware that her generous figure would make her anything but an ideal Venus. She pointed out that the part of Elisabeth called for an actress of a more matured psychological insight than could reasonably be expected of the nineteen-year-old Johanna; would the youthful innocence of the girl's voice be of itself sufficient to realise all Wagner's intentions? As for Tichatschek, her acute and experienced eye saw at once that the part of Tannhäuser was dramatically, because mentally, beyond him; as Wagner himself had to admit, the tenor's strength lay mainly in the joyous brilliance of his tones; to give them the colour of searing grief and self-doubt and despair would be at all times impossible to him. Wagner fought down his misgivings; but at the first performance, on the 19th October, 1845, he had to recognise that Schröder-Devrient had been mainly right in her forebodings, while it was borne in on him that at a dozen points he had presented singers, stage managers and public alike with dramatic problems they were not yet in a position to solve. Do what he would, he could not force the right point of view upon any of them in the Contest of Song in the second act; old habits of thought could not be broken down in a moment. It was inevitable that all should see in this scene merely a succession of " numbers," in the old operatic manner, designed to give each of the principals an opportunity to make his individual mark; for the first time in the history of opera, as Wagner says, they had been asked to follow the gradual working-out of a poetic idea over a large area, and they failed. Moreover, not only then but even at a much later date he could not get the singers to phrase the lyrical portions that were not cast in the obvious " aria " mode in any way but that of the old-style recitative. For them, vocal music must be one thing or the other; a type of arioso that lay midway between the two, that was certainly not in the set aria-form but at the same time needed to be sung as melody, not declaimed as recitative — the germ, in fact, of the Wagnerian melos, spread over a whole opera — was outside their comprehension. Their method of delivery in passages of this kind not only deprived the music of all naturalness but confused and chilled the audience: these ariosi failed on the one hand to afford the customary gratification expected from an aria, and on the other hand seemed to drag intolerably when looked upon as recitative. It was many years before Wagner could force his new conception of " endless melody " on the German singers, or even induce them to sing this midway order of vocal music in strict time, instead of with the almost rhythmless articulation of the ordinary operatic recitative.

Johanna's fresh, youthful tones, slender figure, and *ingénue* manner made Elisabeth a credible figure enough; but Schröder-Devrient could not have been at her expected best as Venus, while

Wagner soon became painfully conscious that the opening scene had not been worked out by him in close enough detail and with sufficiently drastic dramatic power, a defect that he was not to remedy until many years later. Mitterwurzer, the Wolfram, after betraying the blankest incapacity, at the first rehearsals, to conceive this new type of music as being anything else but the old-fashioned recitative, had finally, by dint of the most conscientious pondering of the composer's instructions, so mastered the novel conception that Wagner still had some hope left in him that it would not be utterly impossible to train a new race of singers of the kind his music would need in future. Tichatschek, as Schröder-Devrient had foreseen, failed completely to do anything but *sing* the music of Tannhäuser. Where he could give his ringing voice full play, in moments of lyrical expansion that called for no psychological subtlety, as at the end of the first act, he carried the audience enthusiastically with him; but he failed abjectly in the crucial scene of the work — Tannhäuser's remorse and despair at the conclusion of the scene in the Hall of Song. He reduced Wagner to despair by one characteristic tenor touch. At the vital moment when Tannhäuser, revolted by the pale ardours of ideal love as hymned by other knights, bursts into his frenzied praise of sensual love, Wagner was horrified to see Tichatschek cross the stage and pour his unholy sentiments into the chaste ear of the virginal Elisabeth! Tichatschek, of course, reasoned according to his lights. He was the principal tenor, Elisabeth was the prima donna; and to whom should the leading tenor address himself in a supreme moment if not to the prima donna? In his story of Tannhäuser's excommunication by the Pope, where his splendid voice easily dominated the brass of the orchestra, he did something to re-establish his accustomed hold on the Dresden audience; but the upshot of it all was that Wagner had to resign himself to the feeling that his latest opera was doomed to failure for lack of the right kind of interpreters.

The scenery had been a disappointment to him. Lüttichau had indeed, in the end, changed his mind about that for the Hall of Song; but the order for the fresh setting had gone to Paris too late, so that after all the familiar *Oberon* setting had to be utilised. Its effect on the audience was chilling. The French artists had sent a set for the grotto in the Venusberg which, as Wagner says, was suggestive of Versailles rather than the Hörselberg. For the third act the same set was used as for the second scene of the first act; and no amount of art could make a leafy spring landscape look like a leafless autumn one. Finally, the dénouement was undoubtedly ineffective. In this first version of the opera Venus did not appear to Tannhäuser in the flesh, but only as a figment of his fevered brain, suggested by a roseate light over the distant Hörselberg, while the death of Elisabeth, instead of being announced by Wolfram, was merely indicated by bells tolling and torches flickering far away on the Wartburg. All in all, it was little wonder that the audience on the first night failed to grasp Wagner's novel dramatic ideas in all their subtlety of poetic detail. He came away exceedingly depressed, feeling that he had achieved only a failure, which meant not only a grievous wound to his artistic idealism but the shattering of his hopes that the success of this new work would start *Rienzi* and the *Flying Dutchman* on a triumphal career throughout Germany. To Tichatschek he dared not express his real feelings, for that would probably have led to the tenor refusing to appear in the work again. He prudently affected to take the whole blame on himself, and, with the ostensible object of remedying certain weaknesses in it, he cut out several passages in which Tichatschek had been least effective, though in doing so he necessarily weakened the dramatic appeal of the work still further.[1]

Unfortunately for him, Tichatschek had become hoarse at the first performance, so that there could be no question of another for at least a week. The delay gave full opportunity for gossip and malice to do their deadly work in the little town. As was to be the case more than once in later years, Wagner was accused of writing in a way that spelt vocal ruin for his singers. Lüttichau was so scared at the lukewarm reception of the opera that he was in half a mind to cancel the order that had been given for a new setting for the Hall of Song. The absurd story was started that Wagner had written *Tannhäuser* as propaganda for certain Catholic ideas that

---

[1] The pianist Justus Dietz, who was present at the first performance, told Kohut that all round him he could see people asleep during the Minstrels' Contest. Even the finale to the second act was received tepidly. "Wagner himself was so depressed over this lukewarm reception of the work that at the conclusion of the performance he flung away his baton and hurried out of the orchestra." See KRW, p. 112.

were in the air at the time, so that the crude passions of religious partisanship now raged around the work: he was even sought out by the editor of a Prussian paper, who was acting as the agent in north Germany of the Catholic party in Austria, and who gratefully hailed the composer as a gallant soldier for " the cause." And while rumour after rumour thus spread through the town, the local critics had a full week in which to disparage the new work before the public could get a chance to correct, possibly, its first impressions of it. By this time there was already that definite cleavage between a Press almost uniformly unfriendly to Wagner and a small but growing body of staunch adherents with which the later Wagner story has made us so familiar. He was surprised to find the inventions and the malice of his enemies countered by anonymous paragraphs in the local papers; these paragraphs, he discovered to his amusement later, were the secret work of Röckel and Heine. Röckel's unshakable conviction that the tide of public approval would inevitably turn in favour of *Tannhäuser* was one of the few things that gave Wagner strength to bear the trials of that miserable week.

For the second performance, on the 27th, the new setting for the Hall of Song had arrived, and Wagner was greatly pleased with it. The theatre, however, was nearly empty. But the word soon went round the town that the audience, small as it was, had been decidedly more enthusiastic than on the first night, and for the third performance, a few days later, the house was full; even Lüttichau was convinced now that the work was saved. A fourth performance, before a packed house, followed on the 2nd November. Thereafter *Tannhäuser* proved a steady draw, and though Wagner could not persuade himself that it had been such a success as the inferior *Rienzi*, he saw, with great gratification, that it appealed particularly to the more cultured and thoughtful section of the public, and that this section grew steadily in numbers. In his heart of hearts he felt that he and the general public were already at the parting of the ways, not because his music was not to its taste, but because it was slow to perceive his dramatic intentions.[1] Those who believed in

---

[1] Here, however, as elsewhere, we must be wary of accepting *in toto* the story given in *Mein Leben*. It represents, in part, Wagner's later reflections rather than his contemporary experiences. His letters, such as that to Carl Gaillard of the 3rd November, 1845 (RWKK, II, 174), show him exulting over a success. The truth

him, not in his own immediate circle alone but in the town generally, tried to hearten him by demonstrations of increased affection and respect. The opera was given with its changed ending — i.e. with Venus appearing in person, and the body of Elisabeth carried in on a bier — on the 1st August, 1847, and by the 1st December, 1848, the nineteenth performance had been reached.

10

It soon became clear enough, however, that the work was not being sought after by other theatres. Naturally Wagner's thoughts turned eagerly first of all towards Berlin. In May, 1845, the King of Prussia had heard the twenty-fifth performance of *Rienzi* in Dresden; he had been so taken with it that he attended another performance when on a visit to the town again in the following summer. No good had been done Wagner's cause by a wretched performance of the *Tannhäuser* overture at a Leipzig Gewandhaus concert on the 12th February, 1846, under Mendelssohn; the music was voted incomprehensible, and the unfavourable opinion of the Leipzig critics, none too well disposed, at the best of times, to look with a kindly eye on anything that came from Dresden, must have had its repercussions throughout musical Germany. Bülow, in an article written in 1851, enlarged sarcastically on the "exclusive and intolerant local patriotism" that made Leipzig the natural enemy of Wagner. With its local pride in its own concerts and in Mendelssohn, it could not stomach the importance that Dresden was rapidly acquiring in the musical world under the leadership of Wagner. Leipzig being, on its own admission, the pre-ordained temple of "classical" art, the admired new product of the rival town could necessarily be only an inferior imitation, Wagner himself a mere pretentious amateur, and the new spirit in music mere charlatanism. There was accordingly a decided antipathy in Leipzig towards Wagner's music even before it was known there. Mendelssohn's "ostentatiously ill-humoured" demeanour when conducting the *Tannhäuser* overture was a clear hint to his parti-

---

seems to be that the work *was* a popular success from at any rate the third performance onward, but that Wagner gradually persuaded himself that this success was not of the kind he desired: the public took to *Tannhäuser* as an opera, but missed the drama of it.

sans that he thought little of it, and the performance of the then extremely difficult work was, according to Bülow, an " execution " in not only the figurative but the literal sense of the term.[1]

Still, if only Berlin could be won over to the new work, the rest of Germany would soon follow its lead. Early in December, 1845, two months or so after the production of *Tannhäuser* in Dresden, Wagner obtained leave of absence to go to Berlin. He called at Leipzig on his way. He found the Leipzig Opera " pitiable," the leading tenor being particularly poor. He was deluded into believing that the *Flying Dutchman* would be produced in February, and he thought Kindermann would make an excellent Dutchman; but nothing, of course, came of all this. In Berlin he saw a performance of *Don Giovanni* that did not please him greatly; Donna Anna, he told Minna, was not Jenny Lind's best part; he admired some of her singing, but thought nothing of her as a dramatic artist. He was very pleased with the new opera house, the acoustic of which seemed to him better than that of Dresden. Meyerbeer was away and would not be returning until Christmas; but Frau Meyerbeer showed him much cordiality. He sent the scores of his operas to Jenny Lind, who returned them to him, unopened, on the eve of his departure from Berlin.

He left a copy of the text of *Tannhäuser* with Count Redern, and was mortified to learn, a little later, that while the Intendant was favourably impressed by it, the Director, Küstner, thought the work " too epic " for Berlin. Wagner asked for permission to dedicate his score to the King, but was told that in the first place His Majesty accepted the dedication only of works already known to him — which was reasonable enough — and in the second place that in order to bring *Tannhäuser* before the King's notice it would be advisable for him to make an arrangement of airs from it for a military band, so that the selection could be played at a change of guard. Perhaps nothing in his bitter experiences up to this time wounded Wagner so grievously as this: he could no longer doubt that between him and the rest of the musical world there was a gulf that it would take years of effort to bridge.

His account of the matter in *Mein Leben,* however, is somewhat misleading. He did not greatly mind which of his operas was given

---

[1] BAS, I, 18 ff.

in Berlin; all he wanted was to get a footing there, for financial as much as for artistic reasons. The slow spread of his works outside Dresden had been due primarily to two things — the report that had got about that they were exceptionally difficult, *Rienzi* because of the heavy demands made on the tenor, the *Flying Dutchman* because of certain problems of staging; and the fact that, for all the excellence of certain of its singers, the Dresden theatre still ranked only as a provincial stage. A success in Berlin, on the other hand, would have repercussions not only over all Germany but, in all probability, in Paris and London as well. Moreover, a Berlin success meant royalties for him. By this time he had got himself into the gravest financial difficulties through his over-sanguine publication of his operas at his own expense, a venture of which the details will be given later. From the Dresden theatre he could hope for no more money: *Rienzi* continued to draw full houses, and *Tannhäuser*, after its first set-back, became very popular, but his first modest fee for each of these operas and for the *Flying Dutchman* was the last. If he could plant one of his works permanently in the Berlin repertory he would be assured of a certain small regular income from that quarter. It is evident from his letters of this epoch that with regard to the *Lohengrin* that was now on the stocks he intended to follow Weber's example in the matter of *Der Freischütz* — to pass over Dresden and, if he could, have the work produced in the first place in Berlin. During his visit to that town in December, 1845, he had scanned the singers critically and at first hopefully, but on his return to Dresden he had to admit to himself that they would be unequal to the unaccustomed vocal and dramatic problems set them by the coming work.

His Berlin campaign was fruitless. Küstner promised to give *Rienzi*, though not until September, 1846; but Wagner doubted whether the King of Prussia could be present then, and it was on the King that he was mostly building his hopes. Nothing whatever could be done in the way of a production of a Wagner opera before the coming Easter. Redern was cordial enough. He dined Wagner sumptuously at his house, and was willing to try to arrange for a reading of the text of *Lohengrin* to the King; but as the latter had gone hunting, it meant Wagner's staying at least another week in Berlin, and that was impossible. With a heavy heart he made his way back to Dresden, unable to delude himself that his visit had resulted in anything but failure. " And so," he writes to Alwine Frommann on the 27th December, " good-bye to honour and fame! I now write *Lohengrin* for Dresden." Lüttichau, in fact, had expressly asked for the new work; no doubt he had remembered the parallel case of Weber and *Der Freischütz*, and had been a little perturbed at the interest that was obviously being taken in his Kapellmeister in Berlin. But though for the moment Wagner had to resign himself to the immediate inevitable, he had by no means given up his designs on Berlin. He hoped for a great deal from Friedrich Wilhelm IV, who had more than once shown a keen interest in *Rienzi* and its composer. With all his faults as man and as statesman, the King had a strong vein of idealism running through him; he was sincerely anxious to further the cause of German culture according to his lights, and to give his capital a foremost position in the world of art. Wagner, already conscious of the gulf that was beginning to yawn between himself and the ordinary world of the theatre, believed he saw in this royal idealist an instrument pre-appointed by Providence for the realisation of his ideals. " Richard tells me," Cosima notes in her diary in April, 1871, at the time when Wagner had become alienated from King Ludwig, " that once more he has had the dream he had so often dreamed long before his meeting with the King of Bavaria: the Prussian King Friedrich Wilhelm IV overwhelmed him with thoughtful kindness and showed him boundless love, so that when he first saw King Ludwig he believed he was going to see the realisation of his dream." [1]

It is even doubtful whether, in 1845, he revolted as strongly against the idea of arranging selections from *Tannhäuser* for the King's military band as he imagined he had done when, some twenty years later, he was dictating *Mein Leben*. To such arrangements in themselves he could have had no *a priori* objection at that time; he was used to the Dresden open-air bands performing the overture to *Rienzi* and other especially popular excerpts from his early operas. And as a matter of historical fact we find him quite willing that an arrangement from *Tannhäuser* shall be made for the King of Prussia. " Whether there are *many* pieces in my opera,"

---

[1] MECW, I, 554.

he writes to Redern on the 26th June, 1846, re-opening the question of the desired permission to dedicate the score of *Tannhäuser* to the King, " that are suitable for production as military music I am rather doubtful; consequently I permit myself to draw your attention particularly only to *one* number, which has gone exceedingly well on parades here in Dresden; I refer to the first section of the fourth scene of the second act (the entry of the guests into the Wartburg); it is a kind of March with chorus, in B major, that lends itself well to treatment as an effective piece for military band. If now a pendant to this is required, perhaps the Pilgrims' Chorus in the first scene of the third act could be chosen, in which case I want the person who will make the arrangement for military music [1] to take note of the first tempo in the overture, where this chorus appears in the instruments alone; while for a close to it, as a separate piece, I would like him to look at the accompanying separate edition of this chorus, where he will find a close which I have myself written." [2] He goes on to say that while he regrets that His Majesty should not have the opportunity of learning more of the work than this, he hopes that these extracts will suffice to win his approval of it. He presses Redern for a quick reply, as the long delay is damaging both him and his publisher, the public issue of the full score and the piano score of *Tannhäuser* having been held back all this time because of the uncertainty whether the leaf containing the dedication to the King is to be inserted or not. But Redern replied, some two months later, that he had still had no opportunity of bringing the pieces before the notice of the King; and finally, in November, 1846, Wagner's last hope of the King's acceptance of the dedication vanished, and the scores had to be put on sale without the coveted honour.

---

[1] This was to have been Wieprecht, the director of the King's military music. He was a man of ability. He invented (with Moritz) the bass tuba, and, with Skorra, the bathyphone (a species of bass clarinet), and effected several improvements in other instruments and in the way of playing them. He had made a sensation in Berlin with his brilliant handling of military band masses; so there was nothing at all derogatory to the dignity of an ordinary composer in the King's desire to hear something from *Tannhäuser* as arranged by Wieprecht for the band of the Guards.

[2] RWKK, II, 213, 214.

CHAPTER XVII

THE MIDDLE YEARS IN DRESDEN

1

WITH THE final shattering of his hopes in connection with Berlin he realised that nothing short of a miracle could ward off a storm that might not, indeed, break for some time yet, but the sinister mutterings of which were daily drawing nearer. The *Flying Dutchman* had disappeared from the Dresden repertory. *Rienzi* still pursued its triumphal course there, and *Tannhäuser* was becoming more unmistakably popular with each performance. A new public, the nucleus of the later Wagner phalanx, was forming in Dresden; *Tannhäuser* in particular was increasingly attended by thoughtful lovers of the theatre who previously had fought shy of opera because of its general intellectual feebleness; and this public, each time Wagner conducted the work, applauded him with an ardour that was manifestly intended as an *amende honorable* for the town's first cool reception of the work. For any other German composer of that epoch, the situation as it was now developing would have been a flattering and promising one. But Wagner was passing through a difficult phase of spiritual development that of itself gave him an odd sense of the unreality of the outer world; while the growing disorder in his finances made his life for the next three years one of constant privation and anxiety. He could not separate in his mind the two cardinal factors in his perplexity and misery. He found himself, at every point, rapidly outgrowing the theatrical world in which his lot had been cast; both as original creator and as interpreter of the music of other composers he had visions of an ideal for which neither the public in general nor his singers and players in particular — to say nothing of his employers — were yet ready. He saw himself not only suffering physically from his poverty but hampered by it in his creative work, for it was rarely that the mountain of debt that was now

[405]

weighing on him left him with any heart or any peace of mind for composition; while his pride was galled by the knowledge that, in spite of the genius of which he was rightfully conscious, he was the servant of a Court Intendant who, for all his undoubted good will towards him, was incapable of reaching out into the future with him. He became, he said in later years, a revolutionary for love of the theatre. But his love for the theatre was alternately fed and poisoned by his hatred of the state of society that made it possible for men like himself to suffer in their pride as he did, and to have a purse as empty and a stomach as pinched as his. Generalising, as he always did, from his own case, he came to identify his personal difficulties and sufferings with the very constitution of modern society; and it was not long before he had persuaded himself that as that constitution was intolerable to *him*, it was therefore an offence in the sight of the gods.

The determining factors of his life at this epoch were perhaps even more financial than artistic.

For a man of his age, position, and prospects, he was already uncomfortably in debt before he left Riga. Paris added to the load. That he suffered greatly there is beyond question; but one cannot quite do away with the suspicion that he might have just supported himself on his earnings there, meagre as they were, had it not been for his incurable tendency to indulge himself occasionally in luxuries beyond his means. It seems a little unkind to harbour this suspicion, and there is no direct documentary evidence for it; but we know that on more than one occasion Avenarius and Cäcilie were astonished, when they called on him, to find him treating himself and his friends on a scale that seemed to them, under the circumstances, extravagant; and we know also that Friedrich Brockhaus angered him by refusing him money but advising him to mend his way of life. Having regard to the cost of living in that epoch, and the prices generally paid for literary and musical work — Berlioz, for instance, received only 100 francs for each of his articles in the *Journal des Débats*, and did not look upon himself as underpaid, though he revolted against the necessity of having to earn his living in this way when he would have preferred to be composing — we feel that Wagner, on his earnings from Schlesinger, ought at any rate to have been able to support existence on the

modest scale accepted as inevitable by thousands of other intellectual workers of the time. The trouble was that every franc that
came into his possession was mortgaged in advance. Whatever he
may have said against Schlesinger in later years, it is evident from
his contemporary letters that he regarded him as a benefactor
without whom he would have starved, and that he was correspondingly grateful to Meyerbeer for having procured this literary and
musical hack-work for him. His letter to Schlesinger of the 27th
April, 1841, shows that the publisher had paid him *in advance* as
much as 2,440 francs for arrangements and articles. Wagner makes
out a list of the work he has done, showing a final balance in Schlesinger's favour of 10 francs 12½ sous; whereupon he proceeds to
ask for a fresh advance of 100 francs to save him from ruin.[1] As
we have seen, he borrowed from time to time from Avenarius, from
Pecht, and from the always impecunious Kietz in Paris, and, when
he could, from friends, acquaintances, and even strangers in Germany; and as he did not trouble himself in the least about repaying
the creditors he had left behind him when he fled his own country,
one suspects that there must have been some peculiar imprudence
or recklessness on his part to account for the straits to which he
was now and then reduced in Paris.

2

Be that as it may, he came back to Dresden with a fresh load of
debts. His salary as Court Kapellmeister, as has been said, was
1,500 thalers. It seems little enough by our present-day standards;
but for the time, the place, and the contemporary cost of living it
was regarded as a comfortable sum enough for a man with no ideas
above his station. Weber and Morlacchi received precisely the
same salary as Kapellmeisters in the earlier years of the century.
No figures are available as to the salaries of the orchestra in 1843,
but it is improbable that they differed very much from those paid
in Weber's time, and of these we have a record in a report drawn
up by Weber himself on his entry upon his duties in Dresden in
1817. From this it appears that the leader of the orchestra received
1,500 thalers per annum, the leader of the violas 450 thalers, the

[1] RWKK, I, 173–175.

leader of the 'cellos the same amount, and the leader of the basses 500 thalers. The pay of the rest of the orchestra varied from 800 thalers in a few exceptional cases to 150 thalers. The theatre copyists received from 250 to 325 thalers a year.[1] All these people must presumably have had other minor sources of income, from teaching and so on; the Kapellmeister, for his part, could count on occasional fees for his operas and from a concert or two. As posts went in the Germany of that epoch, where musicians were accustomed not to expect too much as the reward of their work, that of Wagner, with its life-tenure and its ultimate pension, was regarded in the profession as a good one; and it was eagerly desired by many composers and Kapellmeisters, the experienced Nicolai among them, when Wagner fled from Dresden in 1849.

Unfortunately he never came into real enjoyment of his salary. Some debts, such as those to Avenarius and Kietz, he regarded as debts of honour, which at once, on settling in Dresden, he professed his willingness to liquidate according to his powers. But the news that spread so quickly through Germany of the unexampled success of *Rienzi* brought upon him demands from all his creditors of years ago, who now regarded his fortune as made. He was reminded of debts which he had long ago comfortably forgotten, some of them dating even from his school days. If only for the sake of appearances it was as well not to let these often threatening demands become too public; and of course it was possible to meet them only by further borrowing. Schröder-Devrient generously lent him, on her own initiative, 1,000 thalers without security, besides making handsome presents to Minna. Nearly half of this sum promptly went to Paris; with the other half he proposed to settle with his Magdeburg creditors, who were talking of legal proceedings. But as their demands, with accumulated interest, amounted to some 657 thalers, in the end not a groschen of the 1,000 thalers remained for himself; and there were still outstanding the debts he had incurred in Riga and other towns, to say nothing of his indebtedness to friends such as Apel. A few days after receiving Schröder-Devrient's contribution he sent Avenarius, in January, 1843, 1,500 francs to be distributed in Paris as follows:

---

[1] WCMW, II, 37–40.

To Kietz	600	francs
" M. Loizeau (his tailor)	400	"
" redeeming his pawned watch, silver, etc.	350	"
" Fechner	100	"
" his shoemaker	40	"
Interest, at Avenarius's discretion, " to the highest bidders "	10	"
	1,500	"

He calmly tells Avenarius that he will discharge his debt to *him* later — and then asks him to buy Natalie what she needs and defray the cost of her journey to Dresden.

The ordinary fee for an opera at Dresden was about 100 thalers, but for *Rienzi* he received the quite exceptional payment of 300 thalers; and fast on the heels of this came the fee for the *Flying Dutchman*, the amount of which is not known. These fees were first and final so far as Dresden was concerned. But he thought he could count on the quick diffusion of the two works throughout Germany, and his optimism in this respect is shown by his removal first of all from the Töpfergasse to the Waisenhausgasse, where his rent was twelve thalers a month, then to a better apartment in the Marienstrasse, and then to a still better one in the Ostra Allee. His position in the town making it necessary for him to keep up appearances, he had to borrow once more to furnish this last place " well and substantially," as he says, to pay the first instalment on the Breitkopf & Härtel piano, and to provide himself with the luxury of a library. His rent was 220 thalers a year. This was in the autumn of 1843; he remained in the Ostra Allee, where his rooms looked out on the Zwinger, until April, 1847, when he was driven to cheaper rooms — his rent was 120 thalers less than before — in the old Marcolini palace, which, having become the property of the town council, was now let out in sections. There he had a pleasant outlook on the garden; the only drawback was that the Friedrichstadt suburb in which the building stood was a considerable distance from the theatre. As the cab fare was a serious item, he had to resign himself to a good deal of walking, which told on his meagrely nourished frame after a fatiguing day in the opera house.

The removal to this suburb was in itself a confession of the gradual failure of his hopes for financial betterment. He had launched out at first in the comfortable belief that his first two operas would be taken up by all the German theatres. Five months after the production of the *Flying Dutchman* in Dresden, Riga and Cassel gave the work; from the former town he received 15 Louisdor, from the latter 20. " You see," he writes jubilantly to Lehrs in Paris, " how modestly I have to begin. But it will soon be very different." As he had to provide himself about this time with a Court uniform, costing 100 thalers, not much of this sum would in any case have remained to him. But just at this very time he received unexpected demands from two old creditors for a total sum of 900 thalers plus interest! [1] Other towns nibbled at the new works, but performances eventuated nowhere but in Berlin, where the *Flying Dutchman* was given in January, 1844, and Hamburg, where *Rienzi* was given in the following March. Then nothing happened until 1845, when Königsberg gave it, Berlin following suit in 1847. He was resolved, he told Lehrs in his optimistic letter of the 7th April, 1843, not to offer the scores of his first two operas to the publishers until they had been taken up by other theatres, when he would make these gentlemen pay a proper price. But in the following July he asks Breitkopf & Härtel to publish the *Flying Dutchman*, of which his colleague Röckel was willing to make a piano score for him. The firm was quite willing to issue the work, but without an honorarium. (He had suggested 1,000 thalers.) He told them, politely enough, what he thought of this attempt on the part of a German publisher to rook a poor German composer, at the same time that they were ready to bring out French operas that had made no particular sensation in the musical world; and he assured them proudly that he would not offer his scores to a publisher again, but quietly wait until their successes in other towns had given these gentry a better idea of their worth.

There the matter rested for the present; but he seems to have

---

[1] Letter to his brother Albert, 17th May, 1843: "One unpleasantness after another has come upon me. For instance, one of my old acquaintances has demanded from me 600 thalers he lent me — or, as was tacitly assumed — gave me, with interest for eight years at five per cent. [Apel?] A Königsberg Jew, who had come to the [Leipzig] Fair, called on me in Dresden and made it clear to me that I owed him 300 thalers." JKJ, p. 34.

approached the firm again in January, 1844. The stumbling-block was once more the question of an honorarium for a work of which the publishers were not willing to take the success for granted. They suggested a royalty, which, however, was not to commence until after the sale of the first hundred copies. This offer he refused. Relations with the firm continued, however, to be friendly. Breitkopfs accepted *The Love-Feast of the Apostles* in October, 1843, issuing, in the following year, both the full score and an arrangement for piano.[1] Wagner dedicated this work to the widow of his old teacher Weinlig.

3

One of the oddest of the many odd contradictions in his character was a strong conviction, on the one hand, that his ideals were too far in advance of the ordinary theatrical humanity of the time for there to be much hope of his realising them, and the conviction, equally strong, that some day they would be realised in full; perhaps the explanation of the seeming paradox is that he hoped nothing from Intendants, committees, singers, actors, conductors, and all the other degenerate and unregenerate fauna of the theatre, but felt that if only he could cut his way through this stupid and obstructive mass and get into direct touch with the ordinary man, his message would quickly strike home. Be that as it may, the feeling never left him, even in the most discouraging circumstances, that victory would be his sooner or later. In the depth of his misery in London in 1855, an exile from his own country, with the Press almost entirely against him, and with apparently little chance of ever seeing his newest works performed, he astonished and amused Berlioz by saying that in another fifty years he would be the master of the musical world — a prophecy that was to become fact. And in 1844 he was so certain that his works had only to be known to become popular that he plunged into the mad business of making his scores available to theatre directors and the public by publishing them himself.

He selected as his unconscious victim the Court music-dealer C. F. Meser, a person in a humble way of business, who, according to Wagner, had so far never published anything more ambitious

---

[1] For further details see the whole correspondence in RWBV, I, 2–12.

than a waltz. This is not strictly true; but it is beyond question that Meser had neither the capital to carry through a slow-moving proposition of this kind with any hope of success, nor any " pull " with the music trade or the theatres. Wagner began in 1844 with *Rienzi* — the score of which, as he says, was as large as that of three ordinary operas — and the *Flying Dutchman*. To these, in due course, *Tannhäuser* was added. Schröder-Devrient had shown her belief in his future by offering to sell out some of her investments in order to furnish him with a loan at a rate of interest equivalent to what these had been earning; but when he applied to her for the first advance, to meet Meser's account for the first batch of expenses, he learned that she had recently acquired a new lover, a young Lieutenant von Döring, of the Guards, to whom, with the infatuation of an amorous woman verging on middle age, she had given control of all her money, and who had no intention of wasting any of it on anyone but himself.[1] The embarrassed Wagner had consequently to turn to other sources. He seems to have had little difficulty in inspiring some of his Dresden friends with his own confidence in the coming vogue of his operas. He borrowed from several of them, presumably. Among them were two or three whose names figure prominently in his later story — Hiebendahl, the oboist of the orchestra, the actor Hans Kriete (the husband of Fräulein Wüst), and Anton Pusinelli.

The last-named, who was some two years younger than Wagner, was at that time beginning to establish a high reputation as a doctor in Dresden. One of the earliest enthusiasts for *Rienzi*, he had introduced himself to the composer after a serenade given Wagner by the Dresden Liedertafel on his thirtieth birthday. Pusinelli soon became Minna's physician and Richard's creditor; it was to prove a life appointment in each case. Apart from a short period of coolness after 1849, the pair remained the closest friends until the death of Pusinelli in 1878: in certain private matters of his life, as will be seen later, Wagner confided in and sought the advice of

---

[1] She married him in August, 1847; before the ceremony she signed, without reading it, a contract he himself had drawn up, under which she surrendered to him not only all her savings but her future earnings, even to the half of her pension. After the wedding he "threw off the mask," as Wolzogen says. Broken in health, and almost completely beggared, she parted from him in February, 1848; but it was not until the end of that year that she obtained her release from him: his terms for being bought off were magnificent in their cynicism. See WSD, pp. 316–320.

Pusinelli to the exclusion of all his other friends. The first documentary evidence of financial transactions between them is a letter of Wagner's of the 16th December, 1844, in which he promises to repay the 150 thalers that Pusinelli has lent him " by Easter of next year at the latest." The debt was still unredeemed in 1873, when Pusinelli cancelled it.[1]

The agreement with Meser, who was to receive ten per cent. commission on the sales of the operas, was made in June, 1844, and the scores of *Rienzi* and the *Flying Dutchman* were published by the end of that year. In addition to the engraved piano arrangements,[2] Wagner had twenty-five copies of the full score of each work struck off by a lithographic process. When the turn of *Tannhäuser* came, he wrote down the orchestral version direct on the special paper intended for the stone, and had a hundred copies struck off. His only hope of covering his heavy expenses was by the sale of the full scores to the theatres in return for the right of performance; but the scores were returned to him by all the theatres to which he sent them, Munich even returning its copy unopened. Coburg approached him with regard to *Rienzi* in June, 1844. He asked for a fee of 25 Louisdor. His terms were agreed to on his desperate assurance that the opera was not nearly so difficult as rumour alleged, and that it could be adapted quite easily to a small stage and to modest personal resources — for the ballet, for instance, a few of the ducal soldiers could pose! — and on his promise that when the time for production arrived he would himself make whatever small changes might be necessary in the score. Nothing came of it all, however, no doubt mainly because the tiny Coburg establishment had no singers equal to the parts of Rienzi and Adriano. Negotiations with Darmstadt later in the same year had no better result. *Rienzi* was given in Königsberg in 1845, in 1847 in Berlin. The *Flying Dutchman* was given in Riga and in Cassel in June, 1845. These were the only productions of his early operas outside Dresden during the period of his Kapellmeistership. It was not until 1850, when Liszt gave *Lohengrin* in Weimar, that his real vogue in Germany as a whole began.

---

[1] RWAP, pp. 18, 19.
[2] That of *Rienzi* was made by one Klink. Röckel did the *Flying Dutchman*, and Wagner himself *Tannhäuser*.

4

By 1845 it became clear even to him, in spite of his incurable optimism, that only a miracle could avert the catastrophe that was looming. He could pay — or partly pay — his growing account with Meser, and satisfy a particularly pressing creditor or two now and then, only by further borrowing. His sheet anchor at this time was the faithful Pusinelli. On the 31st March, 1846, we find him carrying through one of his characteristic financial transactions: he tells Pusinelli that the 30 thalers which the doctor had recently lent him are now at his disposal — and then asks for a new loan of 500 thalers; this, of course, is positively the last time he will trouble his dear friend. In February, 1845, he had tried, but apparently without success, to borrow 2,000 thalers from Ferdinand Hiller.[1] He was driven to borrow from Röckel, who was himself as poor as a church mouse. In April, 1846, he was dunned by Breitkopf & Härtel for the 225 thalers still outstanding in respect of the piano, and could only promise to liquidate the debt by Michaelmas [2] — a promise, which, of course, it was impossible for him to fulfil when the time came. As a matter of fact, the debt was still undischarged in 1851. In October, 1846, we find him turning to the Leipzig merchant Schletter, who had helped him in Paris, with a desperate request for 1,000 or 1,200 thalers to enable him to put his affairs in order and win some peace of mind for his work. The fees for the first dozen performances of *Rienzi* in Berlin, he says, would cover this small amount.[3] In December, Breitkopf & Härtel, while venturing once more to remind him of his little debt to them in connection with the piano, mentioned that a bill of his for 65 thalers had been put in their hands, for collection, by the Paris Schlesinger.

By this time, thanks in part to the threat, if not the actual commencement, of legal proceedings by some of his creditors, his affairs had become the subject of very free comment in Dresden. His enemies in the theatre and the Press were delighted with the weapon his bad reputation gave them against him. In March,

---

[1] RWKK, II, 145.
[2] RWBV, I, 13, 14.
[3] As we have seen, *Rienzi* ran to only eight performances in Berlin in 1847 and 1848. We do not know what reply Schletter made to Wagner's request.

1846, he was driven to write a letter to Pusinelli — authorising him, if he thought fit, to have it published in the *Anzeiger* — professing his unbounded contempt for the " disgusting town talk," and protesting against the exaggerated public interest taken in his " humble person." Pusinelli published the letter, as desired; but the obvious bluff could hardly have taken anyone in. It was a few days after this episode that Wagner appealed to Pusinelli for the loan of 500 thalers to which reference has already been made.

His friends might be willing to give him latitude, but the usurers to whom he had had to resort would not. And just when these gentlemen became most active in their demands, counting on the hunted man being willing to do anything rather than risk disgrace at the theatre, Schröder-Devrient precipitated the long-threatened catastrophe. Unhinged by her wretched love-affair, jealous of Johanna Wagner's rapidly growing popularity in the town, and convinced that Wagner had brought his young niece to Dresden only to secure her own dismissal, she suddenly changed from devoted friend to venomous enemy, and placed in her lawyer's hands Wagner's IOU for the 3,000 marks she had lent him some four years before. The lawyer at once commenced an action, and there was nothing for it now but for Wagner to go to Lüttichau and make a clean breast of everything — or almost everything.

It speaks volumes for the esteem in which the Court held him as an artist, and the sympathy he inspired as a man, that a loan for the large amount of 5,000 thalers was granted him from the Theatre Pension Fund at five per cent. interest. Such favour had certainly never been shown to any Court Kapellmeister before. He had to take out a policy on his life to cover the amount, at a premium of three per cent. on the capital. He had doubts whether, in his wretched state of health, the risk would be accepted by the company; but a certificate from the obliging Pusinelli got him over that difficulty. As it was, Wagner had concealed some of his debts from Lüttichau, confessing only those, as he puts it, " of an un-friendly nature," and believing that he could in process of time liquidate the others out of the profits of his publishing venture. The position, then, in August, 1846, when the arrangement with Lüttichau was made, was that in addition to considerable private debts Wagner owed 5,000 thalers — merely three and a half years' salary! — to the Pension Fund. Obviously it would be many years, under the most favourable circumstances, before he could hope to be free, even by practising the most rigid economy; and economy, beyond a certain point, was never welcome to Richard Wagner.

5

Reserving the further history of his financial troubles to a later page, we must now take up again the thread of the story of his life in general at the point where he returned from Berlin, at the end of 1845, his effort to induce the King of Prussia to accept the dedication of *Tannhäuser* having failed.

Racked with anxieties of every kind, and, within himself, wholly absorbed in the subject of *Lohengrin*, which was now beginning to germinate and define itself according to the secret laws that govern the processes of the creative artist's mind, he felt himself growing more and more out of touch with the world of men around him. He had become, by this time, a person of importance in the intellectual world of Dresden. IIis social circle was widening; as *Tannhäuser* gradually consolidated its victory, the conviction spread among the more thoughtful elements of the town that here were no Kapell-meister and no opera of the ordinary type, but two driving forces of a kind new to German music. But apart from a receptive amateur or two he nowhere found a really kindred spirit. The professional musicians were becoming more and more doubtful about him, for his new ideal of the relations of drama and music in opera was necessarily not as clear to them as it was to him and as it is now to us. In November, 1845, he had read the poem of *Lohengrin* to some of his friends, and though they praised it and voted it " effective," none of them could conceive how such a thing could be set to music. Schumann was especially puzzled in this respect; and Wagner found ironical amusement in reading it to him a second time as if it were a " libretto," throwing this part or that into high relief as " aria," " cavana," and so on, whereupon Schumann smilingly declared himself satisfied. At a slightly later stage Wagner was urged by his friend Hermann Franck to give the work a happier ending, and for a time he actually thought of a dénoue-ment in which Elsa went away with Lohengrin; but the sound artistic sense of Frau Lüttichau, to whom the point was submitted, decided emphatically against Franck, and there was no more talk of a remodelling of the subject.[1] It is inconceivable that under any circumstances Wagner would have allowed the feeling of another to override his own artistic judgment; but the episode is interesting for the light it throws on the operatic mentality of the time, and on the deadweight of conservatism, even amongst his most intelligent friends and well-wishers, which he had slowly, and by dint not of argument but of practical demonstration in the theatre, to overcome.

Nervous, excited, and unhappy, longing to settle down to the composition of his new work but unable to win the necessary peace of mind for it, he turned away from the lively social and artistic life around him and plunged into the intensive study of literature, history, and mythology, and especially into the world of the old German and Scandinavian legends. The Lohengrin subject became, paradoxically, all the dearer to him because of the secret conviction that the work, when finished, would isolate him still further from the ordinary world of men. He had had difficulty in forcing on them so new a conception of the musical drama as was embodied in *Tannhäuser*; indeed, he had to confess to himself that, in spite of the outward signs of a growing popular success, the work, though it pleased as an opera, was still not understood as a drama. He felt that the still longer stride he was taking in *Lohengrin* would inevitably carry him yet further beyond ordinary comprehension, and that this process of estrangement would be intensified with each successive new creation of his. *Tannhäuser* was wanted nowhere outside Dresden: he foresaw a similar fate ahead of him with regard to *Lohengrin*; the more his genius expanded, the more he would be restricted to the tiny local terrain that he had already outgrown intellectually; and without a spread of his vogue to the rest of Germany there was no hope of escape from the ever-rising tide of his debts. He could drug his distracted and unhappy soul only with practical work connected with his public duties.

---

[1] See Wagner's extremely interesting letter of the 30th May, 1846, to Franck (in RWFZ, pp. 70–75), in which he gives his reasons for declining to re-model the dénouement, drafts some new lines to make the psychological relation of Lohengrin and Elsa clearer, and insists that the music will throw the needed light on the words and the action.

6

I have already referred to that curious " compensating mecha. nism " in him that in later life was to be his salvation in more than one moment of emergency — the mechanism that enabled him to abstract himself psychologically from his surroundings just when they were becoming intolerable, his mind, for instance, at the very height of a quarrel with Minna, when the whole cosmos must have seemed to both of them as foul a thing as their speech to each other, suddenly quitting the immediate scene and soaring serenely into an ideal world round which the outer storm raged in vain. Like every other great dramatist, he never described anyone or anything but himself in his art, his own experiences, actual or potential. Shakespeare may never have committed a murder, but he must have had it in him to commit a thousand murders, and to know how each murderer would feel after his particular crime. Every character, every mood, in Wagner is potential Wagner, just as every character and every mood in Shakespeare was potential Shakespeare. That mystical abstraction from the real world to which we find Tristan and Isolde trying to give expression was merely the sublimation of a frame of mind that was quite common with Wagner. The quaintest commentary of all on the naïve theory that his mind was " theatrical," in the vulgar acceptation of the term, is the patent fact that the world in which he really lived and moved and had his being was one so mystical that again and again he broke his life in pieces in the effort to realise it in the form of dramatic " show " — the only form, of course, in which it could be made actual to others — and, as every performance that has ever been given of a Wagner opera proves, failed sadly in the end to realise his symbols through the crude flesh and blood, the sorry paint and canvas, that are all with which the theatre can provide the mystic. We shall never understand him as a man, to say nothing of understanding him as an artist, unless and until we see that many an action of his that in another man would be explicable simply in terms of one of the cruder moral failings was in his case the outcome of a native inability to see the real world as other people saw it. For example, with all his calculation — and he could be calculating enough at times — there was a vein of intel-

TICHATSCHEK

lectual honesty in him so completely pure that he could never see the necessity for tact. He was too much given, as one of his friends said, to thinking aloud. He made countless enemies in the world of art through pure inability to soften, by any euphemism whatever, the expression of his opinion as to the badness of another man's work. He aroused many antagonisms in Dresden by this outspokenness; personal friends and fellow-workers thought they were entitled to rather more tactful handling; he, for his part, saw nothing but the artistic problem, utterly detached from questions of personalities and friendships.[1] The trouble was that the ideal world in which he did his thinking impinged at a hundred points on the real world in which he, like the rest of us, had to do his bodily living; and wherever the two met, the ideal had to submit to tarnishment by the real. The prime cause of his estrangement from Meyerbeer was undoubtedly the revolt of his own serious soul as an artist against the cunning calculation of effect that constituted the main stock in trade of the other: but once the conviction of the complete immiscibility of their two minds had taken possession of him, he fell an easy victim to his suspicions, and the suspicions of certain of his friends, that Meyerbeer had played him false from the first.

He was, as I have said, a born borrower. At the same time we have to recognise that many of his financial transactions looked quite different to him from what they did to his creditors, or those he would fain have made his creditors. He was so convinced from the first that some day he would have an enormous vogue that the money he asked for, and generally received, appeared to him not as a loan granted as a favour, but a mere business advance on values that would be realised to the full later. He was talking the soundest of business sense when, as we shall shortly see, he implored one person after another to pay off his debts for him and take over his copyrights in exchange; any one of his friends or acquaintances or business connections who had had the inspiration to do this would have found it, in time, by far the most profitable investment all Europe could have afforded for his funds. In 1848,

---

[1] This was one of the few points in which he resembled Brahms. No amount of adoration on Herzogenberg's part could induce Brahms to praise his friend's music: while Wagner, in Paris in 1861, in spite of Gounod's championship of his cause, refused to go to hear *Faust*, though he gave Gounod a copy of the *Tristan* score.

anyone could have become the out-and-out proprietor of *Rienzi,* the *Flying Dutchman,* and *Tannhäuser* for about £750 in all — an investment that would have one day brought him in some hundreds per cent. The commonsense of the thing seemed so self-evident to Wagner that he frankly could not understand why it was not equally and immediately self-evident to others.

At a later period of his life he was completely unable to understand why, with success certain some day, the world in general, or, failing that, his friends in particular, should not maintain him till then. We are constantly faced with the necessity of dissociating the artist in him from the man. It was the man who pocketed all the money that was lent to him or given him; but the curious mentality of the man regarded it as going not to him but to the artist. This remains true even after we have taken into consideration all that can be said on the other side of the account. He was luxurious, and constitutionally incapable of accommodating his desires to the state of his purse. He had not the slightest sensitiveness with regard either to asking for money or to forgetting a debt until he was forcibly reminded of it. But running through all this seemingly calculating and selfish realism was a vein of idealism that none but the rarest spirits among those with whom life threw him into contact ever understood. A few of them, although they were as conscious as the rest of the world how his borrowings looked to the realistic eye, were yet aware that at bottom the problem was not a material but an ideal one, that Wagner's chief difficulties came primarily from his poverty, and that it was their duty to sacrifice themselves to any extent to relieve his poverty in order that he might endow humanity with the treasures of his unique mind. Wagner himself would have agreed with Balzac that it was the duty of society to maintain him for this purpose. " Let one of my millionaire friends," said Balzac, " or some banker who does not know what to do with his money, come to me and say: ' I recognise your immense talent; I know your cares; you need so much money to be free; accept it without scruple; you will discharge your debt; your pen is as good as my millions ' . . . It is something to be able to say, ' I saved a Balzac.' " It is an ironic commentary on the human intelligence that it was reserved for a King who was looked upon as half-mad to win for himself the eternal glory of being able to say " I saved a Wagner."

In 1862, when he was leaving Leipzig for Vienna, Bülow helped to defray the expenses of the journey by selling a ring that had been presented to him by the Grand Duke of Baden. Wagner, says Du Moulin, " accepted it without the smallest scruple, in a spirit that soared above all ordinary outer considerations. He even wrote to Hans with a desperation that reminds us of the epoch of the Renaissance: ' Whoever else still possesses valuables he does not care about must cheerfully and confidently [*getrost*] sacrifice them to me — in all seriousness.' " [1] Nothing is easier than to misunderstand a remark of this kind; and we certainly misunderstand it when we look at it as we would look at a similar remark in any other man's correspondence. What we have to do is to consider who wrote it, and to whom it was written. Wagner, as a passage following in his letter to Bülow shows, was once more confident that the tide was about to turn, and that, with the production of *Tristan* in Vienna, no further sacrifices would be necessary from his friends: " As I am now," he says, " I have suddenly regained full confidence that I shall redeem and return all the stuff, splendidly and gloriously." A few of his friends, of whom Bülow and Cosima were at that period the chief, had themselves sufficient idealism to see that this was fundamentally not a case of a wastrel borrowing for a wastrel's ordinary purposes, but an artist accepting the willing sacrifices of kindred spirits till the time should come when sacrifices would no longer be required. The more carefully we study Wagner, in the light of all the material now available, the stronger becomes our conviction that a sharp line of distinction must be drawn between two elements in his mentality that to a crude psychology seem one — between the man demanding sacrifices from his friends for the man's sake, and the artist expecting similar sacrifices for art's sake and the world's sake. In the innocence of his first belief that the world of men was what his fancy as an artist conceived it to be, he became so entangled in the net of the real world that escape from it very soon began to look a sheer impossibility, then or at any future time. And so, as he was to explain to Pusinelli much later, in one of the most self-

[1] MECW, I, 212.

illuminative letters that we possess of his, it was not long before this puzzling outer world, in which he could find his bearing neither as artist nor as man, came to seem to him utterly unreal, a shadow world through which his legs carried him from day to day, but the principles of whose structure, the rationale of whose purpose, the artist simply could not understand. In his first instinctive revolt against it he became a revolutionary; and then, as he says, even his debts ceased to have any real significance for him, for the burden of them, and the processes by which, and the reasons for which, he had come under this burden belonged to a world essentially more fantastic to him than the Hörselberg or Monsalvat.

7

And so, in the winter of 1845–6, he had tried to forget the outer world by pressing ever more inward towards the ideal heart of music. Though the poem of *Lohengrin* had been completed by the 27th November, at no time during that winter could he find the necessary peace of mind for its composition. To brace himself and still his longing for the ideal he plunged into the preparation of the Ninth Symphony for the Palm Sunday concert of 1846. The choice of this was in itself significant; subconsciously he made for a mystical region in which he knew he would be alone. The work was virtually unknown in Dresden: it is true that it had been given twice in 1838 by Reissiger, but these performances must have been little better, if at all, than a parody of the work, which was consequently regarded in Dresden, as in so many other towns, as one of the last incoherent outbursts of a composer who had become crazier as he grew older. Lüttichau was appalled at the choice; even the players did all they could to have it set aside — going so far as to threaten an appeal to the King — for they dreaded an empty house and consequently poor receipts for their Pension Fund. But the symphony meant more to Wagner just then than merely a piece to be performed at a concert. He absorbed himself in the study of it, finding in its vast idealisation of humanity a haven of refuge from his miseries. The orchestral parts had to be borrowed from Berlin,[1] the Pension Fund Committee

---

[1] Not Leipzig, as stated by Wagner in *Mein Leben.*

being unwilling to go to the expense of buying them. Wagner took infinite pains over both the technical and the imaginative study of the work by the orchestra; merely for the phrasing of the recitative of the 'cellos and basses at the commencement of the finale he had no less than twelve special rehearsals for those instruments alone. He used his practical knowledge of the orchestra to bring out the spirit of the music by an occasional ignoring of the letter of the printed page. He coached the solo singers, lashed the choir to an enthusiasm that was new to it, and even wrung from the reluctant Lüttichau the money for a reconstruction of the old platform that enabled him to concentrate the tone of the orchestra to better effect, and at the same time to group the choir round the players in such a way that the former would all be facing the conductor.[1] Finally he stirred up public interest in the work in advance by the adroit insertion, at his own expense, of anonymous paragraphs in the local *Anzeiger*, and for the programme book of the concert he wrote an " explanation " of the symphony that mostly avoided technical details, for which the Dresden public of that period was perhaps not ripe, but correlated the spirit of the work with certain passages from Goethe's *Faust*.[2]

The result of it all, at the performance on the 5th April, 1846, was a popular success so great that not only were the receipts higher than they had been at any previous Pension Fund concert, but the symphony became the surest card for the committee to play on similar occasions in the future. His professional colleagues, among them Reissiger and Hiller, were mostly either mildly critical of his novel reading of the symphony, or blankly unreceptive of the work itself; Gade, on the other hand, who came over from Leipzig expressly to hear the final rehearsal, was greatly impressed,

---

[1] The concert was given, of course, in the "old" opera house. See Wagner's energetic letter of the 4th March, 1846, to Lüttichau, in which he explains the suggested alterations in detail, points out that they will be of lasting benefit for the orchestral concerts, and, as the Pension Fund cannot meet the necessary expenditure, asks for a special grant — which he obtained — of 200 thalers from the King. RWKK, II, 194.

[2] His programme note will be found in RWGS, Vol. II, the *Anzeiger* paragraphs in Vol. XII. It is significant that in one of these paragraphs he speaks of Beethoven's spiritual "loneliness," and of the Ninth Symphony being the expression of his longing to escape from that loneliness by bringing a message of beauty and joy to mankind. This, as Wagner's later writings show, was the root-idea of his own Lohengrin, over whose psychology he was brooding at this time.

especially by the recitative for the 'cellos and basses. Wagner, at the end of it all, was left, as the result of so many difficulties overcome, with "an agreeable feeling of the capacity and power to carry to a successful conclusion whatever I desired with sufficient earnestness." But he could not help asking himself why he had been able to achieve his end with the difficult Ninth Symphony of Beethoven, which was still very much of a problem to the crowd, and yet, in spite of the regular performances of *Tannhäuser*, he could not regard the opera as an assured success.[1] He could give little time to the conscious examination of this problem, for his outer affairs were weighing heavily on him then and for some time afterwards; but it was always at work in his subconsciousness, gradually forcing on him the conviction that for an artist like himself there was no possibility of genuine understanding in a society constituted like that around him. And so his feeling of loneliness increased; it needed only the addition, a year or two later, of the feeling that in this society there was no hope for him as an economic being, to drive him into the arms of Revolution.

8

His relations with other composers had never been very cordial, and were destined to become decidedly less so as the years went on. Against Meyerbeer as an artist he had definitely turned, though he still thought Meyerbeer might be of practical use to him. He had a genuine respect for Spontini, but there could be no question of intimacy between the old Olympian whose twilight had already set in and the new-comer of whose ultimate significance he had not the faintest perception. Marschner, who was nearly twenty years older than Wagner, never attracted him as an individual, though he learned from him as he did from many others in his first period:

---

[1] One gathers, from a letter of his to Henriette Wüst of the 8th August, 1846, asking her to study the part of Venus, that he had become dissatisfied with Schröder-Devrient in that rôle. About this time, too, his troubles in connection with his niece were beginning. Her grasping father had communicated to her his own lack of idealism: she was turning more and more to the French and Italian operas in which an easy success could be won and easy money made. In September, 1846, Wagner had to explain that he could not put on a performance of *Tannhäuser* for Kittl when the latter was in Dresden, as Johanna was too absorbed in the study of *Les Huguenots* to be willing to play Elisabeth. "I could die of annoyance," he writes to Kittl, "but I cannot change anything."

it is probable, for instance, that Senta's ballad, which Wagner himself described as the musical core of the *Flying Dutchman*, was modelled on the ballad-scene in Marschner's *Vampyr*, while the gloomy romanticism of that work undoubtedly influenced Wagner, not so much at the time when he was actually writing the *Flying Dutchman* as in the years of his nonage between Würzburg and Riga. It is possible that memories of *Der Templer und die Jüdin* (first produced at Leipzig in 1829) remained with Wagner in later life, and played their part ultimately in influencing certain scenes in *Lohengrin*.[1] Schumann and Mendelssohn, in spite of all his efforts at a rapprochement, and in spite of his undoubted regard for their music, never drew really close to him. The one composer who brought some warmth into his life was Spohr, who had produced the *Flying Dutchman* at Cassel in June, 1843, and had apparently written the young composer a letter of unusually warm appreciation. Wagner was deeply touched by this evidence not only of esteem but of personal kindliness on the part of the veteran Spohr, who had the reputation everywhere of being cold and self-centred; and his contemporary letters to Spohr, and to his friends concerning Spohr, are proof sufficient of his essential modesty in those days, of his gratitude for a kindness, of his youthful respect for men of eminence, and of a general likeableness of character the diminution of which in later years was the world's fault at least as much as his own.

Through one accident of time and place after another, he did not meet Spohr in the flesh until June, 1846, when he made a special journey to Leipzig to see him. Spohr was at that time a man of sixty-two. Why he had taken so strong a liking to the *Flying Dutchman* is something of a mystery, for his tastes were extremely conservative. He had written to his friend Lüder, in 1843, that though the work was " somewhat new-romantic à la Berlioz," and " immensely difficult," it had interested him in the highest degree, " for it is written apparently with true inspiration, and, unlike so much of the modern opera music, does not display in every bar the striving after effect, or effort to please." " I think I am so far correct

---

[1] See WM, pp. 47, 48. Wagner, though he criticised Marschner searchingly in later life, paid tribute to his power in certain great moments in the *Templer*. See his article *Über das Opern-Dichten und Komponiren im Besonderen*, in RWGS, Vol. X.

in my judgment when I consider Wagner as the most gifted of all our dramatic composers of the present time. In this work at least his aspirations are noble, and that pleases me at a time when all depends upon creating a sensation, or in effecting the merest ear-tickling." To *Tannhäuser* he reacts less favourably: he paid tribute to its earnestness of purpose, and admitted that, after repeated hearings, certain things in it were not so disagreeable to him as they had been at first: but he could not reconcile himself to what he called its " want of rhythm," to some of its bold modulations, and to its continuity of musical texture, unbroken by the customary restful " closes." For all that, he was anxious to give *Lohengrin* in Cassel, and pending the time when that would be possible he asked for permission to perform some scenes from it in concert form.[1] In Leipzig he and Wagner got on very well together. They met at dinner at the table of Hermann Brockhaus, and listened to music at the houses of Mendelssohn and Moritz Hauptmann. Spohr was impressed not only by Wagner's vivacity of temperament but by the breadth and depth of his culture, and was astonished at the boldness of his views on politics and the ardour with which they were expressed. Spohr took away with him a copy of the *Lohengrin* libretto, which he found " original and interesting."

Wagner had made the journey to Leipzig to see Spohr from Gross-Graupe, a village between Pillnitz and Pirna (at that time three-hours' distance from Dresden), whither he had gone about the middle of May, 1846, for a three months' holiday — a proof of the damage done to his health by his too conscientious labours in the cause of music in Dresden, and by his anxieties with regard to his finances. For company on his country walks he had his little dog Peps, and, as a second string, Minna. With Peps, at any rate, his fretted soul could retire into itself. He brooded over *Lohengrin,* and made a rough sketch of the music of the whole work. On his return to Dresden in August he began the composition in detail, writing the third act first; in his troubled state of mind, however, and with the many interruptions to which he was subjected, the act was not completed until the 5th March, 1847. This was the sole occasion on which he worked backwards at the music of an opera: his reason for doing so in this case seems to have been that he had

---

[1] See SA, II, 276 ff., 307, 308.

been a little disturbed by the comments of his friends on the dénouement of the work, and wanted to settle the matter once for all by realising in music the dramatic conception which his instinct told him was the only possible one. The composition of the first act was finished on the 8th June, and that of the second on the 2nd August, the Prelude being added on the 28th. The scoring was not completed until the end of March, 1848.

Early in 1847 he gave the Dresden public another proof both of his artistic disinterestedness and of the restlessness of his eager and sensitive mind in its quest for perfection. He recast Gluck's *Iphigenia in Aulis* in the light of more modern feeling, ridding it of the conventionalities of structure and of presentation that had been imposed upon Gluck by the French eighteenth century stage. He acted not only as arranger and conductor but as producer: he gave the singers a special coaching, though he could do little with any of the older hands except Mitterwurzer, the one singer in the company who seemed capable of learning from him, and whose Agamemnon seems to have been a powerful and impressive piece of work.[1] By ignoring the generally accepted Berlin score, with the emendations of Spontini, and going direct to the original Paris score, Wagner was able to correct many misapprehensions that in the course of the years had clustered round the ordinary German performance of *Iphigenia*. Above all, he corrected a long-standing error with regard to the tempi intended by Gluck in the overture; for which, and for other restorations of the spirit of the original, he was of course looked at askance by the critics and by professional musicians of the type of Hiller. To-day no one would dream of questioning Wagner's reading of the overture.[2]

---

[1] Sincerus (SDH, p. 222) pays tribute to Mitterwurzer's desire to perfect himself in his dramatic as well as his vocal art by constant study.

[2] For a performance of the overture at Zürich in 1854 he wrote an ending for concert purposes. (In the opera, the overture runs on without a break into the opening scene.) This ending is always used now at concert performances of the piece. Wagner set out his views on the tempi of the work in detail in an article on *Glucks Ouvertüre zu Iphigenia in Aulis*, which originally appeared in the *Neue Zeitschrift für Musik* of the 1st July, 1854; it will be found in Vol. V of RWGS.

The actual orchestral score used by Wagner for the Dresden production is now in the Burrell Collection. From a note in the Catalogue it appears that the vocal score (by Bülow) published in 1859 is only a "very abbreviated version" of the one prepared by Wagner. "At least 200 pages," of the Paris score, "have undergone alterations and comments in his hand, and on practically every page he has written musical indications and instrumental directions: in nine places he has inserted small

His niece Johanna, who had recently returned from Paris, she having been granted six months' leave of absence in order to study under Garcia, played the part of Iphigenia in the production, which took place on the 22nd February, 1847: Schröder-Devrient was the Clytemnestra. In its new form the opera was a great success; and as the Ninth Symphony was re-demanded for the Palm Sunday concert of that year, even the local critics and rival composers must have begun to feel, by this time, that in Wagner the Dresden Opera possessed not only the most promising German composer of the day but a conductor with a new and unique insight into the great works of the past. But unknown to them all — King, Intendant, musicians, critics, and public — he had already turned his back on Dresden in spirit; and his departure from them in the flesh was now only a matter of time and circumstance.

---

pieces of paper with more considerable alterations." "His own additions in his own hand . . . occupy no less than 40 folio pages, including 8 complete pages that constitute a new close to the opera." It is to be hoped that some day Wagner's version will be published in its entirety.

CHAPTER XVIII

FRIENDS AND ENEMIES

1

IN WAGNER's life everything tended to the extreme. His music deals with problems of organisation and of architecture to which there is no parallel elsewhere. His dramas cover an area of action and psychology that makes that of the ordinary opera seem small. Other composers have suffered in their lives, but there is nothing in the record of any other composer comparable to his record in this respect in its totality, from the prolonged misery of the Paris days to the heartbreak of the last two or three years in Dresden, from this to the despair of the Vienna epoch, from this to the shattering of all his hopes in Munich, and from this again to the exhausting struggle to force the conception of Bayreuth upon a mainly indifferent or apathetic world. In no other composer's life does the pendulum, again and again, swing so far first to one side, then to the other. From the depths of poverty and neglect he was suddenly lifted, in the winter of 1842–1843, to what must have seemed to his friends and other contemporaries the very height of good fortune. He left Dresden in 1849 apparently ruined for ever. In the next few years, in spite of all the handicaps his exile imposed on him, he became the leading figure in not only German but European music. In 1861, in an alien country, this proscribed German had placed at his disposal, for the production of *Tannhäuser*, such forces, artistic and financial, as had never before fallen to the lot of any composer. From seemingly utter and irreparable ruin, artistic, financial, and moral, he was dramatically rescued by King Ludwig in 1864. In Bavaria he rose to a position of such power, not only in matter of art but affairs of state, as no other artist in the world's history has ever attained. Once more he fell to the bottom of the pit: Munich drove him out, pursued by stupendous hatreds and bespattered with incredible contumely, and engendered in him a detestation of mankind in the mass that never left him to the end of his days. In such long silence and seclusion from the world as no other dramatic artist has ever achieved, he won for himself, in Triebschen, the strength to embark upon his last and greatest practical enterprise, the founding of Bayreuth. He died not only the greatest figure in contemporary art but the dictator of the monarchs and the Intendants to whom at one time he had had to go hat in hand.

In his personal relations with individuals there is the same violent oscillation between wide extremes as in his relations, as artist, with the world in general. No other artist's friendships have the saga-like quality, the intensity and tragedy and pathos, of some of his: no other artist has ever passed through such a furnace of hatreds. No other artist suggests as he does two completely different men, according to the source of the testimony to which we listen. And it is during the Dresden years that we see the beginnings of this cleavage of opinion with regard to him, not only as artist but as man. As in his art, so in himself, he developed according to the inexorable laws of his inner being; and when, about 1847, the Fates cast, for good and all, the hard statue that had been implicit in the more or less plastic clay of which the youthful Wagner had been composed, men soon found that there could be no middle course with regard to it: they were either attracted to it and succumbed, often in spite of themselves, to the power and fascination of it, or they hated it with a furious and irreconcilable hatred. As I have said, two completely different portraits of the man can be painted, according to which set of testimonies we accept to the exclusion of the other. One side of the record shows enough meanness, malice and selfishness in him to justify all that has been said against him by those who detested and despised him. But on the other side is the record of the attachment of some of the finest spirits of that or any other time, who either saw no evil in him at all, or, if they could not be quite blind to what they saw, counted it as less than nothing as against the purer and nobler aspects of him.

No man inspires such love — not merely admiration for his qualities as an artist, but glowing love for his qualities as a man — unless either there is a great deal that is lovable in him, or, what in the last resort is no less remarkable, something in him that weaves a veil of illusion about the minds of those who worship him.

It was not the fools or the amiable weaklings who loved Wagner most; it was precisely the best, the strongest, the most high-minded of those with whom he came into contact. If ever any man had cause to dislike and scorn him, on the basis of the mere outer factual relations between them, it was Pusinelli, who suffered under Wagner's borrowings for many years, and in the end forgave him a very considerable debt. Yet Pusinelli's last act, almost, was to place on record his profound love for, and his unshakeable belief in, this man who, as the cruder judgment of the world would phrase it, had done little but prey upon him financially and in a variety of ways use him for his own purposes. On his deathbed he murmured, with tears in his eyes, " My Richard, oh my Richard, how you have had to fight, how you have been misjudged — only the next centuries will know how to value you! And you were my friend! "[1] And Cosima, who knew Wagner to the very marrow of his bones, from whom none of his weaknesses were hidden, and who herself suffered grievously from him at times, noted in her diary on one occasion that he was as noble as Goethe, and, on another, wrote to King Ludwig that " to anyone who has become intimate with him, anyone whose spirit has become interwoven with his, everything else becomes a matter of indifference; the cleverest people seem to me as flat as a field since I became intimate with his pure nature, which is as lofty as the glaciers." [2] Evidently we are faced, when we try to estimate Wagner as a man, with a psychological problem of peculiar complexity.

2

The final years in Dresden make a dividing line between the earlier and the later Wagner; it was then that the artist came to something like full consciousness of himself and of the differences that marked him out from the musicians and poets around him, with the result that in certain quarters he began to stir up first of all doubts and then resentments that were soon to develop into bitter enmities. The only real friend of his boyhood was Apel, from whom he had soon become estranged, partly by reason of his borrowings, partly through the long separation of the Paris days, during which Apel's developing blindness cut him off more and more from every-

---

[1] RWAP, p. 281.   [2] MECW, I, 656, 344.

thing but the world in his immediate vicinity. There seems to have been no friendly communication between the two men from 1840, when Wagner was seeking Apel's help to save him from a debtors' prison, until 1853, when Wagner replies to a letter he has received from his old associate. Apel died in 1867. Of the Paris friends, Lehrs died in 1843, soon after Wagner's return to Dresden. Anders virtually passed out of his life. With Ernst Kietz he maintained a friendship to the end; but Kietz remained in Paris until 1870, so that he took no part in the development of the intellectual life of the later Wagner. (He survived Wagner some nine years, dying in 1892, impecunious to the last.)

At the time of his settling in Dresden, then, Wagner had about him no friends to whom he was particularly attached, either in the town itself or elsewhere. The acquaintances brought him by his earliest activities had been mostly older than himself, and their relations to him had been that of helpers and protectors rather than friends. From the nine-years-older Dorn, who had assisted him to get a hearing for some of his earliest work, he was now estranged by his conviction of Dorn's perfidy in the matter of the Riga musical directorship. Laube, who was six years older than Wagner, was a man of importance in the German literary and theatrical world when Richard was a mere beginner. The basic differences between their natures became evident to both of them during the Dresden years; and Laube, who survived Wagner (he died in 1884) became in time one of his most implacable enemies. When Wagner returned to Dresden in 1842 he knew practically no one in the town except Schröder-Devrient, Winkler and Ferdinand Heine. (Soon after his arrival he made the acquaintance of Kietz's brother Gustav Adolph Kietz, the sculptor, who was living in Dresden at this time, and who became a regular visitor at Wagner's house. He has left us (in KW) some interesting and valuable reminiscences of Wagner.) Heine had been one of Geyer's actor friends; Wagner had not seen him since his childhood. Winkler (Theodor Hell) was a Court Councillor, the secretary of the Dresden theatre, and the proprietor of the local *Abendzeitung*. He was a much older man than Wagner — he dated from Weber's time — and Richard's relations with him were never other than those of an employé. Dresden brought Wagner a new and always faithful friend in the person of old Fischer, while

Heine also became strongly devoted to him. The third of the solid Dresden friendships, that with Theodor Uhlig, was of rather later growth. Uhlig was a violinist in the Dresden orchestra, of which he had become a member in 1841, at the age of nineteen. He was an excellent musician apart from his fiddling, and a man of considerable culture. He seems to have felt at first no particular attraction towards Wagner personally, and to have been rather opposed to his ideals as an artist until 1846, when a sense of the uncommon quality of his chief came upon him partly through a study of the score of *Tannhäuser*, partly through a reading of the explanatory programme issued by Wagner for his performance of the Ninth Symphony in April, 1846. Once a bond had been established between them, Wagner, in his walks with Uhlig, found an intelligent and appreciative listener to his plans for theatre reform; and after the catastrophe of 1849 Uhlig did Wagner more than one valuable service with his pen.

For his superior in the Royal Kapelle, Reissiger, he had no feeling but one of more or less good-humoured contempt; the man was a mere survival from that older musical world of routine and commonplace which it was one of Wagner's missions in life to sweep away. Reissiger was perhaps too slow-witted and too indolent to be capable of doing much that would confer on him the dignity of the title of active enemy; but Wagner believed, probably with reason, that he intrigued against him in private, especially in quarters connected with the Press. We have seen that Wagner quickly made an enemy for himself in the person of Lipinski, though after the first fierce brush between them their official relations, at any rate, became conventionally correct again. Wagner's *fidus Achates* in the opera house was his assistant August Röckel, who joined the institution not long after himself. Each of the Dresden Kapellmeisters had assigned to him a subordinate with the official title of Music Director, one of the conditions of whose appointment was that he should be a Catholic, for the Catholic Court and clergy necessarily felt themselves somewhat inadequately served by Reissiger and Wagner, both of whom were Protestants. Röckel, who was a nephew of Hummel, the brother-in-law of Lortzing, and the son of that J. A. Röckel who had once been a tenor at the Theater an der Wien, where he had sung the part of Florestan in the revised version of

[433]

Fidelio in 1805, was an excellent all-round musician and a good linguist. For a time he had ambitions as a composer; but he practically relinquished these for ever when he came under the powerful spell of Wagner. The two soon became close friends: Wagner, as usual, needed some one to whom he could pour out his sorrows and his aspirations, and for both he found a sympathetic and understanding listener in Röckel; while the latter felt himself amply repaid by the fertilising contact with the lucid and far-reaching mind of Wagner.

With Tichatschek his relations were always those of one crony with another. The tenor had the greatest admiration for the young composer who had provided him with such brilliant parts in *Rienzi* and *Tannhäuser;* and though he was incapable of ever understanding the real Wagner, his dog-like devotion was strong enough to withstand many a temporary strain, while Wagner, for his part, had a genuine liking for Tichatschek as a cheery soul who was always good company outside the theatre. Wagner's other operatic friend and admirer, Schröder-Devrient, turned in time, as we have seen, into something like an enemy, owing in the main to her unjustified suspicion that Wagner had brought his niece to Dresden with the express object of supplanting her in the affections of the public.

So much for his friends and acquaintances in the opera house. As regards the theatre, he seems to have had no very close relations with anyone but Eduard Devrient, the later historian of the German stage. Tieck, who had been the *Dramaturg* of the Dresden theatre for some years, had been badly shaken by the death of his daughter in 1841, and in the autumn of the following year he left the town, carrying with him his broken illusions about mankind and the theatre to a similar post in Berlin. Wagner does not appear to have made his acquaintance in the few months that elapsed between his own arrival in Dresden and the departure of Tieck, for when he called on the old poet in Berlin in October, 1847, at the time of the production of *Rienzi* there, he was provided with a letter of introduction from Frau von Lüttichau. For a time, Tieck's former functions in Dresden had been carried on by his enemy Winkler, who had been largely instrumental in driving him from his post; but in August, 1844, a new " Oberregisseur für Schauspiel und Oper " was appointed, in the person of Eduard Devrient. He in his turn left

Dresden in February, 1846, having wearied of the hopeless struggle against the prima donna superficialities of his brother Emil, whose hold as an actor was so strong on the Dresden public that the management was indisposed to quarrel with him for the mere sake of an ideal. Eduard Devrient, who had himself been an actor and a singer, was a man of solid if rather sober intellect, who is remembered today chiefly by his painstaking four-volume history of the German theatre, which appeared between 1848 and 1861. The functions of the *Dramaturg* were not very clearly defined: nominally the opera as well as the drama came within the sphere of them, so that there were plentiful opportunities for friction between him and the Kapellmeisters. This division of responsibilities was to have serious consequences when Devrient's successor, the playwright Gutzkow, came upon the scene. Devrient, however, worked harmoniously enough with Wagner, each of them having at that time a genuine respect for the other that was fated not to endure. Devrient's verdict upon his more imaginative musical colleague was that he was too much given to fantastic abstractions to possess any real historical sense, while Wagner gradually turned against his old friend as he did against so many others; in 1869 he published, as a pamphlet under his old pseudonym of " William Drach " a savage review of Devrient's book *My Reminiscences of Felix Mendelssohn-Bartholdy*, in which he tore the poor man's slovenly German to pieces.[1]

3

It was perhaps inevitable that Wagner should have hardly one real friend among the professional musicians. In later years he took comparatively little interest in other living composers, especially those whose temperaments or whose ideals of art were different from his: he had the good sense to see that he had been sent upon earth to do his own work in his own way, and that the ways and the works of other people had no vital bearing upon the matter. In his younger days his interest in other men's work was insatiable; and he was generous with his admiration when he came across anything that seemed to him worthy of admiration. His youthful judgments upon the French and Italian operas of the early nineteenth century

---

[1] Reprinted in RWGS, Vol. VIII.

were often piercingly critical; but he had a keen sense of what was really good in these alien genres. He had been deeply impressed by Berlioz's *Symphonie funèbre et triomphale,* which he heard in Paris in 1840. His record at Dresden as a conductor shows him to have always been at the service of any composer who had anything to say. He was more sensible than the majority of his contemporaries of the weaknesses of Marschner; yet he urged the Dresden authorities to secure the first performance of the latter's *Adolph von Nassau,* and it was not Wagner's fault that the opera proved a failure. His relations with Meyerbeer are a little puzzling; but the rational thing to do seems to be to ignore most of what the later Wagner had to say about his one-time idol, and rely on the testimony of his contemporary letters. From these it is tolerably clear that even in the Dresden epoch, long after he had turned in secret against Meyerbeer as a musician, he still had considerable respect for him as a man, and remembered with a certain gratitude all that Meyerbeer had done for him.

In 1845, as his letter of the 5th June to Carl Gaillard shows,[1] he was still convinced that Meyerbeer was sincere in his promise, after having heard the twentieth performance of *Rienzi* in Dresden, to do what he could to have the work produced in Berlin. " I have no doubt of the honesty of his feeling towards me," he says; he admits that the real obstacle to the production of *Rienzi* in Berlin, as elsewhere, is the lack of a Heldentenor. Writing on the 1st January, 1847, to Hanslick, who had published an appreciative, if not particularly intelligent, article on *Tannhäuser* in the *Wiener Musikzeitung,* he says, " What separates me by a whole world from you is your high estimate of Meyerbeer. I can say this with the fullest impartiality; for I am personally friendly with him, and have every reason to prize him as a sympathetic, amiable man." [2] A few months before that, in a letter to his Berlin friend Alwine Frommann, he had suggested that Meyerbeer might help him by becoming Director of the Berlin Opera and lending him 1,000 thalers at four or five per cent.[3] The touch is half-whimsical, but certainly not more than half: Wagner would have welcomed either form of assistance on Meyerbeer's part. When he was in Berlin in September, 1847, for

---

[1] RWFZ, p. 50.
[2] RWKK, II, 230.
[3] Letter of the 9th October, 1846, in RWKK, II, 220.

the production of *Rienzi*, he was so pleased at first with the atmosphere round him that he indulged in the hope of settling there some
day, as the town was " undeniably a better field for his art than
Dresden." He would most assuredly not have thought that had he
felt the slightest doubt of Meyerbeer's good intentions towards him.[1]
He sought out Meyerbeer as usual, and dined at his house on the
3rd October. Whatever he may have thought in later years, his contemporary letters reveal him to have been perpetually receiving
favours from Meyerbeer and feeling a proper gratitude for them.
The difference between the social circles of the two men would have
been, however, in itself a bar to any real friendship between them;
while Wagner's inner alienation from Meyerbeer as an artist would
of itself make him reluctant to be brought into any closer relation
with the older man than was necessary for strictly practical
purposes.

4

With regard to Mendelssohn and Schumann, Wagner's conscience was quite clean in those days; it was decidedly not his fault
that he and they never drew closer together. He had a sincere admiration for Mendelssohn's talent; his letters to him are couched in
a tone not only of courtesy but of genuine respect.[2] From *Mein
Leben* we gather that Mendelssohn was almost invariably cool
towards Wagner's music, but that is not always borne out by the
letters. In *Mein Leben* he tells us that after the production of the
Flying Dutchman in Berlin Mendelssohn merely murmured, " with
accentless bonhomie," " Well, you ought to be satisfied now," and,
though the pair met more than once during the next few days, never
breathed another word about the matter. Wagner's letter to Minna
of the 8th January, 1844, however, says that " Mendelssohn, with
whom I dined once, gave me great pleasure; after the performance
he came on the stage, embraced me, and congratulated me most
heartily." But all in all there can be no doubt that Wagner's warm
admiration for his colleague's music was not reciprocated. His own
mental world was outside Mendelssohn's limited range; all that

---

[1] RWMW, I, 38.

[2] See, for instance, his letters of the 17th April and 15th May, 1845, asking for
Mendelssohn's interest in the plan for a monument to Weber. RWKK, II, 150, 153.

Mendelssohn could find to praise in *Tannhäuser* was an admirable piece of canonic imitation in the second finale of the opera! Wagner was convinced that the inadequate or unfriendly treatment he received in the Leipzig *Allgemeine Musikzeitung* was traceable to the influence Mendelssohn was held to have with that journal, and he put this down, perhaps not without reason, to Mendelssohn's jealousy of his success.[1]

Wagner's liking for Schumann's music in those days, and his respect for him as a fellow-fighter in the cause of German art, can hardly be questioned; but the response was much less cordial on Schumann's part. He was probably unable at first to see in Wagner anything more than just another of the young German composers who were trying to win an easy success in opera, a genre after which Schumann himself had a hankering, but for which he had not much aptitude. As editor of the *Neue Zeitschrift für Musik*, which he founded in 1834, he had published various articles by Wagner during the Magdeburg and Paris periods. In May, 1836, Wagner had sent him an article (now lost) on music in Berlin, which Schumann, for prudential reasons, declined to print, as it contained a violent attack on the powerful Berlin critic Rellstab. A commendatory notice of the first production of *Rienzi*, by the Dresden correspondent of the *Neue Zeitschrift für Musik*, appeared in the issue of the journal of the 1st November, 1842; in this, Wagner was hailed as " one of the most important talents of the present day." [2] After the

---

[1] See Wagner's letters to Schumann (25th February, 1843) and Lehrs (7th April, 1843), RWKK, II, 21, 25. Mendelssohn was curiously cold towards Schumann also in spite of the latter's warm admiration for him. Niecks is reluctant to attribute jealousy to Mendelssohn, preferring to put his coldness towards Schumann down to the fact that "he was one of the many great creative artists who, by the nature of their genius, were incapable of appreciating their differently-gifted contemporaries." (NRS, p. 304.) But the old legend of Mendelssohn's super-angelic nature is nowadays discredited to an extent that would have surprised our fathers. "In his personal relations," a contemporary tells us, "Mendelssohn was most amiable, but in large social gatherings his extraordinary vanity demanded that people should concern themselves with him, and him alone, and he would get quite out of humour when now this other person, now that, would attract attention to himself." See Johannes Nordmann's reminiscences of 1847 in RWJK, p. 73 ff.

[2] See KRW, pp. 97, 98. Since the above passage was set up in type there has come to light a hitherto unpublished letter from Wagner to Schumann — evidently the first that passed between the pair. It is dated "Magdeburg, 14 September" [1835]. It was offered for sale on the 9th December 1932 by the Berlin firm of Leo Liepmannssohn, in whose catalogue it is summarised thus: "He regrets not to have had the opportunity of approaching Schumann when he [Wagner] lived

production of the *Flying Dutchman* in Riga, Wagner sent Schumann a eulogistic notice from that town, asking him to insert it in his paper: " Don't be angry with me," he wrote, " and don't take me for one of those people who fish for journalistic praise; but I am making my first step in fame, and as nowadays this is a vital matter for our production, I have to give some thought to this kind of support." Schumann, however, printed not this notice but one sent him by his own correspondent in Riga. This was laudatory enough; but, as is shown by the manuscript, which has survived, Schumann toned the Riga writer's description of Wagner as a genius down to " talent," and suppressed a passage hailing Wagner as " the hope of the coming years."

In the years immediately following, Wagner believed himself to be unduly and unjustly ignored in the *Neue Zeitschrift für Musik,* and after Schumann's retirement from the editorship (in 1844), the Dresden correspondent of the journal was not precisely friendly to Wagner. The latter's explanation of it all was probably the correct one: so long as he was a poor and unknown young composer who happened to have had a bit of luck with *Rienzi,* everyone was willing enough to be patronisingly kind; but as soon as this first success led to a life-appointment as Kapellmeister at the Dresden Opera, and the young man began to look like being somebody, " the milk of sympathy began to run sour." In December, 1844, Schumann left Leipzig and settled in Dresden. There he and Wagner saw each other fairly frequently, without, however, becoming really intimate. The often-quoted story told of them may or may not be true — that Schumann, when Wagner's name was mentioned to him, spoke sadly of his colleague's devastating fluency of speech, that allowed of no one else getting a word in, while Wagner, when asked his opinion of Schumann, complained that you could get no further with a man who never opened his mouth — but it certainly

---

in Leipzig. 'I love you and your friends, and this is by no means insipid flattery.'. . . . In words of the greatest significance Wagner expresses the opinion that they are living in an epoch of political, scientific, and artistic reform, and it is the mission of youth to grasp this trend of the time energetically. He says that youth must take the field ruthlessly 'against the old lies' . . . 'and we need no authorities for this fight, for we do not want to be recognised by the Philistines — . . . In your journal you have opened out to us a splendid battleground, and I long to try my own powers in it. . . . I offer myself to you heart and soul; make whatever use of me you think I am worth.'"

sums the matter up to perfection. Wagner must have poured out on Schumann, as he did on everyone else, the flood of his new ideas about music, opera, drama, politics, and every other subject under the sun; and the taciturn Schumann must generally have remained unresponsive even when he understood.

Schumann himself, like Mendelssohn, wished to be an opera composer. It was at Dresden, in 1847 and 1848, that he wrote his *Genoveva,* a work in which some fine music has been lost to the world through a bad piece of libretto-construction. Wagner saw from the beginning what was wrong with the drama, and gave Schumann a friendly warning; but Schumann merely sulked, believing that his rival wanted " to spoil his best effects," went his own way, and achieved a failure. Like so many professional musicians of that time, he chose to regard Wagner as only a gifted musical amateur with a knack for the stage, and the younger man's success, if not an actual offence to him, was at any rate a puzzle. Wagner had sent him the full score of the *Flying Dutchman* in February, 1843; Schumann found fault with the " gloomy colouring " of the work, and made the mistake of seeing echoes of Meyerbeer in it — a mistake that of itself would be sufficient to rule him out once for all as a judge of Wagner. In due course Wagner presented him with the score of *Tannhäuser.* Again he failed either to understand Wagner's purpose or to estimate his achievement at its real value; writing to Mendelssohn on the 22nd October, 1845, he rhapsodises over the latter's organ sonatas, and then continues: " What . . . does the world in general (many so-called musicians included) understand of pure harmony? There is Wagner, who has just finished another opera. He is certainly a clever fellow, full of crazy ideas and audacious to a degree. Society still raves over *Rienzi.* Yet he cannot write or think out four consecutive bars of beautiful, hardly of good music. All these young musicians are weak in harmony, in the art of four-part writing. How can enduring work be produced in that way? And now we can see the whole score in print, fifths, octaves and all. It is too late now to alter and scratch out, however much he may wish it. The music is no fraction better than *Rienzi,* but duller and more unnatural, if anything. If one says anything of the sort it is always put down to envy, and that is why

I only say it to you, knowing you have long been of the same opinion." [1]

It is true that some three weeks later he wrote to Mendelssohn, " I must take back one or two things after reading the score. It makes quite a different effect on the stage. Much of it impressed me deeply "; and in a letter of the 8th May, 1853, to Carl Debrois von Bruyck he warns his correspondent that he must not judge Wagner by his piano scores, as " many parts of his operas could not fail to stir you deeply if you heard them on the stage." But he still held to it that Wagner was " not a good musician," that he had " no sense of form or euphony," and that " the music, considered apart from the setting, is inferior — often quite amateurish, meaningless and repugnant; and it is a sign of decadence in art when such music is ranked with the masterpieces of German drama." [2] When Schumann wrote this letter he had had the score of *Lohengrin* in his possession for five years; so that the only conclusion we can come to is that he was a true critic — that is to say, a hopelessly bad judge of music that lay beyond his own intellectual and aesthetic range. To Dorn he had written, on the 7th January, 1846, " I wish you could see Wagner's *Tannhäuser*. It has depth, originality; altogether a hundred times better than his earlier operas — along, indeed, with much that is musically trivial. In summa, he may become of the greatest importance to the stage, and by what I know of him he has the spirit for it. The technique, the orchestration I find first-rate, beyond comparison more masterly than before." It looks as if Schumann could not help being moved by a Wagner work in the theatre, but broke down when it came to the test of understanding Wagner purely and simply as a musician from the score. *Lohengrin*, of course, he never saw on the stage.

5

The truth is that about 1846 it became evident to a large number of people that as regards Richard Wagner there could be no middle course; one had either to go joyfully with him or react violently against him. He not only envisaged a future that was beyond the

---

[1] LRS, pp. 250, 251.   [2] Ibid., p. 278.

ken of most of his professional colleagues; he also understood the past better than they. It would hardly be too much to say that in the Europe of that epoch he alone really understood the greater Beethoven. He did not arrive at this understanding, as Habeneck and his like did, by pounding away at the symphonies, at rehearsal after rehearsal, till something of the meaning of the works dawned on them, but by penetrating to the heart of them in the solitude of his study. We have seen how he forced a comprehension of the Ninth Symphony upon his orchestra and the Dresden public. He found it less easy to endow some of his fellow-composers with a real understanding of Beethoven. He tells us, in *Mein Leben,* how he managed to argue Reissiger into a proper conception of the tempo of the third movement of the Eighth Symphony, which was to be given at the Palm Sunday concert of 1843. Reissiger promised to refrain from taking the movement " in the meaningless waltz time " that was customary in that epoch; but at the concert he had not sufficient command of the orchestra to impose the new reading on it, with the result that he fell helplessly into the old foolish tempo. Wagner had previously put his own view of the matter before Mendelssohn, who agreed with him. When the orchestra broke out into the third movement, Mendelssohn, imagining that Reissiger was carrying out his colleague's instructions, nodded gratified approval to Wagner, who was sitting with him in a box. The incident is one of the many proofs we have of Mendelssohn's congenital inability to get to the essence of Beethoven. Berlioz complained of the way he raced through the symphonies; even Schumann, after hearing Wagner's performance of the Ninth, confessed how he had suffered in Leipzig, year after year, under the rapid pace at which Mendelssohn was accustomed to take the first movement.

Ferdinand Hiller, as has been said, was dubious about the rightness of Wagner's tempi in the symphony; and Hiller was one of those who, before long, drifted by inevitable necessity into the anti-Wagnerian camp. He had settled in Dresden in 1844; he was a well-to-do, cultured, travelled young man of thirty-three, with a Polish wife. They entertained a good deal, particularly among the Polish colony. Their house became a centre of music and letters in Dresden; it was there that Wagner met the youthful Joachim.

When Wagner resigned the conductorship of the Liedertafel in 1845 he induced the committee to take Hiller as his successor; and Hiller occupied the post until he left for Düsseldorf in 1847. He gave orchestral concerts in Dresden, at which he astonished Wagner by the unintelligence of his readings of some of the masters, especially of Bach and Beethoven: Wagner tried to get him to see the error of his ways, but though Hiller confessed himself convinced, particularly with regard to the *tempo di menuetto* of the Eighth Symphony, he could not realise in performance a conception he had probably never inwardly grasped. From time to time he produced works of his own in Dresden, without being able to convince anyone but his immediate circle that he was a composer by the grace of God. Like so many of the composers of the time, he asked for Wagner's advice and help in the choice of a subject for an opera, and Wagner's letter of the 10th April, 1845, shows him sending Hiller " an opera book which can form the theme of our next conversation." But, again like most of the others, Hiller chose to go his own way rather than Wagner's, and the result was *Konradin von Hohenstaufen*, which was a ghastly failure.

He seems to have been one of the numberless academics who could never see that Wagner was anything more than a mediocre musician with a gift for " bringing it off " on the stage. Meissner, who was no fanatical admirer of Wagner, tells a delicious story of a chance meeting with Hiller during the Dresden days. Hiller was carrying the recently completed poem of *Lohengrin*. " Richard Wagner has written a new opera text and given it to me to read," he said. " It is called *Lohengrin*, and deals with the saga of the Knight of the Swan. It is a quite excellent libretto — most effective! What a pity that Wagner means to set it to music himself! His musical gifts are not equal to that. In someone else's hands it would make quite another effect " — in Ferdinand Hiller's, no doubt.[1] Even in 1876 Hiller was frankly puzzled at the stupendous success that Wagner had achieved by that time, especially with the production of the *Ring* at Bayreuth. In his agreeable literary way — for, like Hanslick, he was one of those people who write much better than they think — he compared Wagner with Napoleon III, at the same time regretfully admitting that there was little chance

[1] MGML, I, 174.

of Wagner meeting his Sedan, for there was no " musical-dramatic Bismarck or Moltke " in view at the moment. Hiller could only console himself with the reflection that Wagner's *art* would certainly find its Sedan, " for it is built, like that of the once so powerful Emperor, on a falsehood." [1] It must have been a great consolation and encouragement to Wagner, quite early in his career, to realise that he and men like Hiller stood at the opposite poles of music. The fact that Wagner had tried to borrow 2,000 thalers from him would, of course, hardly be likely to correct Hiller's impression that his colleague was no musician.

6

Wagner was no more fortunate with some of the gentlemen of the Press; as he says himself, he had not been long in Dresden before he became the victim of an animosity on the part of the German critics to which there had hitherto been no parallel in music. The Glasenapp-Ellis school maintained that " the Reissiger clique " had " nobbled " the Dresden critics. It may have been so, but there is really no need for any assumption of that kind: anyone who has had much experience of musical critics knows that they are honestly capable of making their blunders of judgment without the smallest stimulus from others. Every artist who suffers under criticism believes the critic either to be personally prejudiced against him or the hireling of a rival artist. The critics, however, are generally quite honest according to their lights: the trouble, as a rule, is merely with the quality and the degree of the illumination.

The leading Dresden critic — so far as musical critics can ever be said to lead anybody or lead to anything — was Carl Banck, with whom Wagner had been very friendly in the Magdeburg days: Wagner had played him some scenes from *Das Liebesverbot*, and the then budding critic had been graciously pleased to express approval. In Dresden he developed into an open enemy: Wagner attributed this to the fact that he had been unable to provide Banck with tickets for the first performance of *Rienzi*. It may have been so; but, human nature being what it is, the simplest course is to as-

[1] HMP, p. 281.

sume that Banck's hostility was the result of Wagner's music and theories rubbing him the wrong way. As he survived Wagner by six years, dying in 1889 at the age of eighty, he no doubt had ample opportunity to reflect on the fallibility of aesthetic judgment, so far as musical critics are ever given to reflection on that somewhat uncomfortable subject. Banck seems to have been possessed by the complacent notion that whatever appealed to Carl Banck was right in the sight of God, and whatever failed to appeal to him was wrong. A young English musical critic of the present day has told a trembling world that he " has no use for the romantic epoch." He had a spiritual ancestor in Carl Banck, who, if not quite as wholesale as this in his contempt for the ways of Providence, at any rate had no use for romanticism as it revealed itself in the leading composers of his day. He hated Wagner and Liszt, and loftily patronised Berlioz. " I have had a visit," Berlioz writes to Liszt from Dresden on the 26th April, 1854, " from M. Banck, the *influential critic,* who overwhelmed me with his self-sufficiency and his patronising phlegm. It seems he has written some Lieder of his own, and he admires Mozart to the exclusion of everyone else. He granted me, I am told, a few pieces such as the Ride to the Abyss, the Chorus of Sylphs, the March [from *Faust*], and a certain gift for orchestral combinations; but I am totally lacking in ideas." [1]

Banck's stupidities on the subject of Mozart goaded Wagner into an energetic public reply in 1846. Banck had found fault with the Kapellmeister's performance of *Figaro*. Wagner did not deny that things were far from perfect in the Dresden Opera, but he protested against the malicious assumption that the imperfections were peculiar to Dresden: they were rooted in the very being of German public music as it then was. He would be willing to take such praise or blame as might be due to him for a production of a Mozart opera that was wholly his own. But in Dresden he has to try to impose his own conception of Mozart, and that with insufficient rehearsal, upon an orchestra and singers that have been ruined by a thoughtless and slovenly tradition. As for his tempi, they were Mozart's own, as communicated to him by Dionys Weber, who had often seen Mozart rehearse; and as for the flexi-

[1] BAMC, p. 197.

bility of phrasing for which he was censured, the sensitive music of Mozart is the last that ought to be taken with metronomic rigidity: the spirit is more important than the letter. He bluntly asks Herr Banck what proofs *he* has ever afforded that he knows what he is talking about in affairs of the theatre in general and of the Dresden theatre in particular, and pointedly hints at personal prejudice on Banck's part, the result of his too friendly association with other people in the Dresden Opera.[1]

The other leading critical light of the town was Julius Schladebach, who was later to bring out a *Neue Universallexikon der Tonkunst* (1854) that is now a rich mine for the researcher into the musical criticism of the past. He was by no means the hopeless fool the older Wagnerians would have us believe; his book on the Dresden Theatre, published in 1852 under the pseudonym of Al. Sincerus (the SDH of the " Sources " enumerated at the commencement of the present volume), shows him to have had an intelligence quite up to the average in matters of this kind. Here again there is no need to assume, with Wagner and the older Wagnerians, any particular prejudice or specific corruption: the man honestly disliked all that Wagner stood for, as he was fully entitled to do. But, like Banck, he was utterly incapable of sensing the new life that was being brought into music by Wagner, Berlioz, and Liszt. In 1846, in a journal (*Teutonia*) that devoted itself especially to music for male choirs, he solemnly warned German singers against *The Love-Feast of the Apostles*, a work of the " opera Messiah " Wagner, who had no " specifically musical talent " but was only an imitator of Berlioz, though without the latter's originality: " his inventive power is weak, he lacks depth of feeling and truth of sentiment," and so on.[2]

Wagner himself, like all musicians, never objected to criticism, except when it was unfavourable to him. It is true that he never had a very high opinion of his own journalistic partisans, who, for all their good will, often came no nearer understanding the real essence of him than his enemies did. But at the beginning of

---

[1] The article — *Artist and Critic, with reference to a particular case* — appeared in the Dresden *Anzeiger* of the 14th August, 1846. See GS, Vol. XXII.

[2] Quoted in TWSK, p. 96. The term "opera Messiah" is undesignedly significant: it suggests that, in spite of his critics, Wagner's works and theories were already concentrating public attention on him.

his career he was naturally glad of Press publicity, and we find him more than once complaining that the Schumann and other journals are not taking enough notice of him. It was only when he found the majority of the critics were against him that he came to the pardonable conclusion that critics are congenitally imbecile and criticism a curse. And if musical criticism could have had the slightest permanent influence on public opinion he would have been damned beyond redemption before he was forty. The German system at that time was a thoroughly bad one: this or that critic in this or that town would act as correspondent to journals in various other towns, so that the original stupidity of someone or other in Dresden would be further dished up for the misguidance of music lovers in Leipzig, Berlin, Vienna, and other places; and there the local journalistic wits would get to work on the Wagner subject before they or their fellow-townsmen had heard a single note of his. In this way they could indeed delay the production of a Wagner opera for years, by inspiring a certain fear in the heart of the local theatre director; though once the work had been produced, the public did its own thinking about it.

One suspects, however, that in Dresden, in the late 1840's, Wagner's character and manners had something to do with the attitude of the critics towards him. Their dislike for his music and his theories may have been based primarily on a natural personal reaction against them; but the public duty of expressing an unfavourable opinion on the artist was turned into a private pleasure, in many cases, by dislike of the man. Wagner at this time laboured under a double disadvantage: he was right, and he knew he was right. He really knew more about music than his theatre associates or his critics. He had thought harder than they about the problems of the combination of music, poetry, and drama in opera. He could see a future that was hidden from them. He was right in his views as to the meaning of Beethoven and the way to perform Beethoven, and he was founding a new school of conducting. He was full of bold schemes for the improvement of orchestral playing, of operatic production, of the finance and the routine of the institution with which he was connected, of the musical culture of the town. He was no visionary, but a thoroughly, indeed exceptionally, practical man; as Mr. Bernard Shaw has

[447]

put it, he talked such sound sense that naturally he was regarded as a lunatic. But if to be right in a world of half-rights or quite-wrongs is of itself generally dangerous, to be superlatively right without tact is almost invariably fatal. No one is more in need of tact than the one man who is in possession of the truth in a society of dullards; the surest way of setting them against the truth is for him to make it too evident to them that he regards them as dullards. But tact was a virtue with which the gods had not endowed Wagner. His incorruptible idealism made it impossible for him to compromise on the facts, while his eagerness and his intellectual loneliness prevented him from seeing how the matter looked to other people, and from realising the necessity of winning them over slowly by diplomacy. We have to take into account also the fact that he was almost always in bad health, physical no less than mental, and prone to become irritable and abusive under opposition. Never, at any period of his life, could he bear contradiction in argument or even opposition to the most trifling of his plans. When Judith Gautier was staying at Triebschen in 1869 she did not take kindly, at first, to a project he had sketched for an excursion into the William Tell country. Cosima whispered to her, " Do not refuse: he would be angry. And let him manage it all; let him take the lead, if you do not wish to grieve him." " He grows listless and loses his good humour," said Cosima to her on another occasion, " when he is not allowed to dominate." [1] Meissner tells us of a conversation he had with Wagner about 1847, in which Wagner set forth his views on the necessity and certainty of revolution. They were joined by Gutzkow, who argued as ably on the other side. " Wagner lost his self-control and broke off the debate with strong and ill-tempered words." The adoring Glasenapp puts a mark of interrogation against this, but we have too many testimonies of a similar kind to be in any doubt about it. Wagner was all of a piece: without a passion for domination and for self-realisation so overwhelming that it flowed over into the most trifling affairs of his life, he would never have accomplished, in face of such opposition, the work he was sent on earth to do.

We get a taste of his quality in the matter of undiplomatic and inconvenient frankness in a recorded episode that must have been

[1] GWH, pp. 58, 239.

typical of many that have remained unrecorded. We have accounts by two eye-witnesses, Alfred Meissner [1] and Pecht,[2] of what happened after the production of a play by Laube, *Die Karlsschüler*, in November, 1846. (Pecht tells the story in connection with another play of Laube's, *Struensee*, which had been produced the year before; but the error is of no importance.) After the performance, a large company met at Wagner's house to pay honour to the hero of the evening. The facile, half-sincere compliments usual on these occasions had been passing for some time, when Wagner, who was not in the best of humours, splashed tear gas into the incense with the awkward question, " Whether the playwright who puts Schiller on the boards ought not to have something of Schiller's own genius? " The query was a legitimate one from the abstract point of view of the higher aesthetic; whether it was tactful to launch it just then is another matter. Wagner then proceeded to an unfavourable criticism of the play in detail — he was " too conscious of his own superiority," says Pecht — and succeeded in depressing the temperature of the atmosphere to such a degree that even the champagne, at a later stage, failed to raise it again. Wagner seems to have been slightly conscious that his criticism had not contributed much to the gaiety of the evening, for Meissner describes him looking round him uneasily at the supper, and getting more and more peevish. While he smiled with the side of his face that was turned to the company, the other was expressive of his real feelings. At last he hissed at Minna, out of the corner of his mouth, still trying to keep his temper under, " Where's that damned champagne? " [3] (Wagner was never so hard up that he felt he had to go without his champagne; he might have to deny himself the bare necessities of life, but no artist can get along without the luxuries.) But poor Laube's evening was spoiled even beyond the redemptive power of champagne; after leaving Wagner's house he wandered disconsolately with Meissner through the dark streets by the river. It is a safe surmise that Wagner's uncompromising expressions of opinion on the works and the ideas of others, combined with the heat of his language when he was opposed, played their part in making enemies for him in Dresden.

---

[1] MGML, I, 176 ff. [2] PAMZ, p. 266. [3] MGML, I, 177.

We have to bear in mind his ill health at this time, his financial worries, his frustrated idealism, his growing sense of loneliness, none of which would be likely to improve his temper in the company of people who were not particularly congenial to him. Meissner, who made his acquaintance during this period, describes him as " rather under the middle height — almost small, in fact — with piercing eyes, tightly compressed lips, sharply curved nose, a remarkably broad forehead, a projecting chin, and something of the look of a professor. Early struggles had given him, though so young, an unusual irritability; there was always something excitable, exasperated, virulent [*giftkochendes*, poison-brewing] about him." [1]

7

But, though he himself would hardly be conscious of it at the time, there was already forming in Saxony the nucleus of the later body of true Wagnerians, for the most part thoughtful people who were either very slightly or not at all connected with music professionally. In Dresden he made several friends in literary and artistic circles, some of whom, it is true, were to fall away in later years. In the artistic group were the architect Semper, the sculptors Hähnel and Rietschel, the painters Schnorr, Bendemann and Hübner; in the literary group were Berthold Auerbach, the novelist, and the poet-painter Reinick. The meeting-place of these celebrities was Engel's restaurant in the Postplatz, where the air, especially when Wagner and Semper were present and in form, often became thick with argument. Wagner's contact with them all, however, with the exception of Semper, was purely intellectual; none of the others became part of his later life. At the theatre, and on his walks, he had Röckel and Uhlig to talk to; each was an ideal listener from the Wagnerian point of view. Laube, on his occasional visits to the town, he found less responsive, that is to say, less willing to see the cosmos exclusively from the Wagnerian angle. The pair would argue for hours as they walked, till late into the night, up and down the Zwinger Terrace. " He was a very adroit, fluent disputant," says Laube: Wagner would expound his " system," and Laube would object, with some justice, that he

---

[1] MGML, I, 169.

merely wanted to make his personal way of looking at things a rule for the universe.

For a time it looked as if a friendship might form between Wagner and Hanslick. Fortunately for Hanslick, it did not develop very far; it is better to be notorious than to be forgotten, and by becoming Wagner's enemy Hanslick did at all events achieve a kind of negative immortality. In 1845, when the pair first met, he was a young man of twenty, studying philosophy and law at the University of Vienna. Happening to be spending his holiday at Marienbad when Wagner was there, he introduced himself at the dinner table of the Kurhaus as an admirer of the composer of *Rienzi* and the *Flying Dutchman,* with which works he had become acquainted in the piano scores. He called on Wagner in Dresden in September, 1846, on which occasion he heard a performance of *Tannhäuser.* On his return, he indulged himself in an analysis of the work that occupied no fewer than eleven numbers of the *Wiener Musikzeitung.* He sent the articles to Wagner, who favoured him, on the 1st January, 1847, with a long and interesting letter in which he set forth his views on the respective claims of music and drama in opera. He expressed his alienation from Meyerbeer as a musician, at the same time that he admitted his obligations to him as a man; and he set himself patiently and courteously to correct some of the errors into which his young admirer had fallen.

"Do not under-rate the power of reflection. The unconsciously-produced art-work belongs to epochs remote from ours: the art-work of the epoch of the highest culture can be produced only in consciousness. The Christian poetry of the Middle Ages, for instance, was spontaneous, unconscious; but the completely valid [*vollgültig*] art-work was not achieved then — that was reserved for Goethe, in our epoch of objectivity. The rarity of the appearance of works of the highest order is due to the fact that only the richest human nature can achieve the marvellous union of this strength of the reflective intellect with the fullness of immediate creative power. . . ."

His own works, both those already written and those on the way, he says after some remarks on Gluck and Spontini, are only studies to see if opera is possible. He ends by asking his young friend to write to him again. Presumably this invitation was not accepted, for we have no further letters from Wagner to Hanslick, who no doubt preferred to go his own way and that of Meyerbeer.[1]

Here and there, however, Wagner's work and tendencies were already beginning to be discussed by writers who sensed the novelty and the future importance of them. An article on *Tannhäuser* in the Augsburg *Allgemeine Zeitung*, in November, 1845, earned from Wagner the high praise, when he was writing *Mein Leben*, that, although it was the first essay of its kind on *Tannhäuser*, he still regarded it as the most far-reaching and exhaustive that had ever appeared on the subject. But though he assures us that it was written without any persuasion on his part, there can be no doubt that its sympathetic tone and trustworthy quality were the result of his conversations with the author. This was Dr. Hermann Franck, formerly of Breslau, who had settled in Dresden a little while before. Wagner valued him highly, not less for his thoughtfulness and breadth of culture than for the unfailing courtesy of his manner in argument. The story of Wagner's discussion of the ending of *Lohengrin* with Franck has already been told. The article on *Tannhäuser* has been reprinted in full in BBW, 1885, pp. 320, et seq.; it is still worth reading. It only remains to be added that Franck was taken angrily to task in the Dresden *Abendzeitung*, presumably by Schladebach, for ranking Wagner and his *Tannhäuser* so highly, while " absolute silence is maintained with regard to works like Ferdinand Hiller's *Traum in der Christnacht*, which unquestionably has more music in it than *Tannhäuser*." There is clear enough contemporary evidence that what angered critics like Banck and Schladebach was the knowledge that, in spite of all their efforts, Wagner was becoming highly popular in Dresden, and already being regarded as the man of the future. The critic of the *Abendzeitung* was very wroth with the writer of an

---

[1] Hanslick's account of his personal acquaintance with Wagner will be found in HMS, pp. 268–276. Like so many others, he could not forgive the later Wagner for treating his confessed enemies with the contempt he felt they deserved. There can be little doubt that many of them would have liked to draw nearer to him after he had so unmistakeably triumphed; but instead of being welcomed with the outstretched hand they were repelled by the extended boot-toe. "Yes," says Hanslick pettishly, in reply to an enquiry whether Wagner had answered his youthful letter. "Yes; at that time Wagner was not yet at the height of his fame. For all his self-confidence, he was then a man, not a god, as he has been since the Bayreuth ascent into heaven. He thanked those who greeted him, and sometimes answered those who wrote to him."

article in the Leipzig *Deutsche Allgemeine Zeitung* for praising *Tannhäuser* so highly. " A man is all too easily persuaded that he is a genius, for pride and vanity are very human sins, and there is already a solid phalanx that tries to persuade the world that Richard Wagner is one. This is not the first passage of arms for a disputed genius. If only this phalanx, the ranks of which are already becoming significantly thinned, would reflect that the well-intentioned exaggeration in conduct of this kind soon becomes apparent, and that it easily calls forth an opposition, so that the really good and worthy no longer receives its due! " [1]

After the production of the *Flying Dutchman* in Berlin in January, 1844, Wagner received an earnest letter from one Carl Gaillard, a young art-lover of perhaps more enthusiasm for music than technical knowledge of it, but with at any rate an intuition of the new operatic values that Wagner was creating. He set himself at once to help the Wagnerian cause in a journal he had recently founded — the *Berliner Musikalische Zeitung*. Wagner, on his return to Dresden, wrote his new admirer a letter that is one of the most valuable documents we possess in connection with Wagnerian aesthetic: he sets forth clearly his views on the relations of poetry and music, and the essential differences between opera and drama, and explains that before he writes a single line of one of his texts, before even he lays out a scene in detail, the characteristic musical motives already live their own life in his mind, so that once the poem is put on paper the opera is virtually complete, for the detailed musical working-out then follows easily of itself. The pair met for the first time in Dresden in the following September, when Gaillard showed Wagner some of his poems. Wagner saw at once that the young man, for all his culture, would never attain eminence in any field; but he took to him personally, recognising the purity of his motives and the loftiness of his ideals. He had a sympathetic listener in Gaillard, to whom, in later letters, he poured out all the sadness of his lot, all the bitterness of his frustrated hopes. He sent Gaillard the full score of *Tannhäuser* as soon as it was lithographed, and Gaillard went to Dres-

---

[1] From the Dresden *Abendzeitung* of the 19th October, 1845, cited in KRW, p. 109. A paragraph in the Dresden *Anzeiger* for the same year expresses the resentment of "the man in the street" against the malice of Wagner's critics, and stresses the growing admiration in the town for his genius. See KRW, p. 112.

den for the first performance of the opera in October, 1845. Wagner found later that Gaillard dabbled in the writing of dramas; but even his sense of the worthlessness of these did not diminish the genuine liking and respect he had for the simple, honest fellow. Gaillard began to fall on evil days about 1847. He had to suspend publication of his little journal, for lack of capital on his side and lack of support on that of the public: his modest business — he kept a shop for the sale of music — declined, and the incurable disease from which he was suffering was already making terrible inroads on him. He died in 1851, sincerely mourned by Wagner, who, in his stormy voyage through life, had met all too few fellow-passengers of this congenial type.

Another Berlin friend who was to bring him encouragement in difficult times and remain faithful to him in the after years was Alwine Frommann, one of those devoted women with whom he had the occasional good luck to meet, whose interest in him endured to the end because it was purely intellectual. She was another of those who had felt, after hearing the *Flying Dutchman* in Berlin, that a new era had dawned for German opera. She wrote him an enthusiastic letter after the two performances in which Schröder-Devrient had taken part, but it was not until the occasion of the first performance of *Tannhäuser* that they met, though she had previously made the journey to Dresden to hear *Rienzi* in October, 1844. She was the sister of the Jena bookseller Frommann, who had been an intimate of Goethe. She was reader to the Princess Augusta of Prussia, very poor but nobly independent: she was highly respected by the Princess, and through her was able to exercise a certain amount of influence in Court circles in favour of Wagner. No longer in her first youth when Wagner met her, her attractiveness lay mostly in her expressive eyes, that bespoke a character of unusual strength and nobility. Wagner, in his eternal hunger for a companionship that would be both intellectual and humanly sympathetic, asked her, in November, 1847, to take up her abode with him and Minna; but this project came to nothing. She died in 1875, having to the last done all she could to further Wagner's interests in Berlin.

During these middle Dresden years the relations between Wagner and Liszt were gradually becoming closer, though as yet in an indefinite kind of way. It took Wagner a long time to rid his mind of its first prejudice against Liszt as the money-making and tuft-hunting virtuoso who played down to the Philistine public, who, wherever he went, allowed himself to be made ridiculous by foolish women, and who flaunted it in Berlin, in the days of his triumphs as a pianist, in a carriage drawn by six horses. But Liszt's gradual abandonment of his virtuoso career and his growing concentration on the work of making Weimar a centre of musical culture must have given Wagner a higher opinion of him; and we find the two drawing tentatively nearer to each other about 1845. Liszt, with his passion for progress, could not fail to be aware, by that time, of the coming importance of Wagner to German music. He attended a performance of *Rienzi* in Dresden on the 9th February, 1844; Wagner met him in Tichatschek's dressing-room during the intervals, and was touched and heartened by his enthusiasm for the work; while he was gratified later to hear that Liszt sang its praises in every town he visited. Liszt was the first man, Wagner told Cosima in Triebschen, to give him the impression of nobility.[1] It was not until Liszt was firmly in the saddle at Weimar — from about 1848 onwards — that he could be of service to Wagner at first hand; but he did his best to help him in Vienna in the spring of 1846. Pokorny, the Director of the Theater an der Wien, had apparently been angling for *Rienzi* a year or so before, but the negotiations had lapsed. As Tichatschek was about to undertake some guest-engagements in Vienna, Wagner thought there might now be a chance for *Rienzi* there. He accordingly asked Liszt, who was in Vienna at the time, to use his influence with Pokorny on his behalf; and he sent Liszt the full scores of *Rienzi* and *Tannhäuser*, which latter opera, of course, Liszt had not yet heard. Nothing was done by Pokorny with regard to *Rienzi*, however. At a later stage than the present one of our story, in January, 1848, Liszt asked Wagner to let him have the score of the *Faust Overture:* when sending it to him, Wagner says he is not greatly pleased with it now, and with grim humour condoles with Liszt on being now well on the way to realising what it means to be a Kapellmeister! The day had not yet come when Wagner was to regard Liszt as his sheet anchor, but it was not far distant.

---

[1] MECW, I, 509.

Two or three other acquaintances made by Wagner in these middle years were to play a considerable part in his later life. Through Lipinski he met Marie Kalergis, a niece of the Russian Chancellor Count Nesselrode; Liszt had spoken to her so enthusiastically about Wagner that she had made a special journey to Dresden to be present at the first performance of *Tannhäuser*. She was half Russian, half Polish: she had been a pupil of Chopin, and was an excellent pianist. Her exceptional beauty had not only impressed the susceptible Liszt but had stirred Heine and Theophile Gautier to song. She seems to have been a little disillusioned by the inadequate presentation of the work, so that the acquaintance developed no further at that time. It was not until some years later that, as the Countess Mouchanoff, she came to play an important part in the life of Wagner and Cosima.[1]

It was in 1848 that he met, in Dresden, Jessie Laussot, who was to figure prominently in his emotional life a couple of years later. She was a young Englishwoman, a former Miss Taylor, who was now married to a Bordeaux wine merchant, Eugène Laussot. In Dresden she used to stay at the house of Frau Julie Ritter, a well-to-do widow who was before long to have thrust on her the burden of maintaining the exiled Wagner in Switzerland. Madame Laussot presented herself to him shyly one day in the company of Frau Ritter's eighteen-year-old son Karl — one of the ardent youths who about this time were beginning to be drawn into the orbit of Wagner's powerful personality. Wagner's account of the meeting with Jessie Laussot is studiously ambiguous — it must be remembered that he was dictating his reminiscences to Cosima, and moreover his one-time passion for Jessie had long ago burnt itself out completely; but even through the calculated obscurity of his language it is evident that the pair, at this first meeting, made an impression on each other that neither could at the moment understand.

With a former school-friend of Karl Ritter — Hans von Bülow — Wagner's later life was destined to be very closely connected.

---

[1] She had married the Greek diplomatist Johann Kalergis in 1839, at the age of sixteen, but the marriage was unhappy from the first, and they separated in the following year.

The Bülow family had taken up its residence in Dresden in 1842, when Hans was a boy of twelve. He had heard the first performance of *Rienzi* in that year — his ticket had been given him by Lipinski — and, as he told his daughter more than forty years later, had been so thrilled that he longed to throw himself at the feet of the pale little man in the brown coat who came on the stage at the finish to acknowledge the applause of the audience.[1] A nervous, over-excitable boy, already suffering from the bad health that was to pursue him relentlessly his whole life long, sensitive to the strain in the atmosphere at home, where the imaginative and choleric father and the bigoted mother had long ago realised their lack of anything in common, it was a necessity of his being to attach himself to some one stronger than himself. In his childhood he divided his dog-like devotion between Wagner and Liszt; as a young man he relied upon Cosima Liszt, whom he married in 1857, to an extent that sometimes gave that sympathetic but strong-minded young woman no very high opinion of his strength of character. He had been allowed to study music in Leipzig under Moritz Hauptmann and Plaidy, but his pious aristocratic mother would not hear of a professional career for him, on religious as much as on social grounds. For a time he took piano lessons in Dresden from a Fräulein Schmiedel; he had for fellow-student the little Jessie Taylor; the friendship of the two survived all the storms of the later years, and was terminated only by the death of Hans in 1894.

It was a great grief to the boy that his family and all their connections were anti-Wagner. He would have converted them if he could, but failing that, he clung passionately to what he felt to be the true faith. " It grieves me," he wrote to his mother from Leipzig in July, 1844, " not to have been at the Dresden concert, particularly because of the Wagner Overture [i.e. the *Faust Overture*, which had been given by Wagner at a concert in the Grosser

---

[1] "It was the birth-hour of Bülow's apostolate," says his widow. "Thirty-six years later, after having conducted a performance of *Rienzi* at which Liszt was present, he wrote in his music-calendar 'historic date'!" BBLW, p. 14. At the time when he first heard *Rienzi*, the boy knew nothing of opera but the lightly-scored works of Mozart and the Italian school. His sensitive ear was so affected by Wagner's powerful orchestration that during the third act he went completely deaf, seeing the characters move about on the stage without hearing a sound: at the commencement of the fourth act his hearing had returned. See RWHB, p. iv.

Garten on the 22nd]. It cannot possibly be what you say it was."
" On Thursday they gave *Tannhäuser* in Dresden! " he writes to
her from Leipzig in August, 1848. " I was filled with ecstasy and
misery. What would I have given to be there! I would have gone
on foot had that been possible; as Tannhäuser made his pilgrimage
to Rome, I would have made mine to the theatre, to win for myself a long refreshment and exaltation. I often say: I thank thee,
God, that I am not like others (that is, not the publicans, but the
Pharisees); that I am able to grasp the full holiness and divinity
of the music revealed to our inner contemplation by this work,
and to comprehend the mission of the apostle Wagner. And so I do
not contemn his enemies, unless they have a personal prejudice
against him [obviously a reference to the ill esteem in which
Wagner was beginning to be held in some quarters, in part because
of his notorious borrowing habit, in part because of his growing
political activities]; but I pity them because they are incapable of
raising themselves out of the dust! " [1] And again, a few months
later, " I hope you have been to hear *Tannhäuser* again. This
alone would console me a little for the fact that I was not there
myself. But if you have missed the opportunity yet again, don't
take it ill of me, but I shall be furious." [2]

In July, 1846, the Bülow family left Dresden for Stuttgart. The
boy felt he could not go so far away without meeting in the flesh
the man he adored. He went with Lipinski to Gross-Graupe, where
Wagner was on holiday, and was there introduced to him. He
begged for an inscription in his album: Wagner wrote, " If there
gleams in your breast the sincere, pure glow of art, assuredly the
lovely flame will some day burst forth: but it is knowledge that
nourishes this glow and turns it to strong, pure flame." From
Stuttgart he corresponded with Wagner, to whom he sent some of
his own compositions: Wagner wrote back very kindly and sensibly, saying that they had given him much pleasure but that he
would not criticise them in detail, " for you will receive criticism
enough without me, and I am the less disposed to dwell upon

---

[1] BB, I, 123. On the Palm Sunday of 1846 Bülow had heard Wagner's performance of the Ninth Symphony: not only was he overwhelmed by the revelation of
the music, but he realised that in Wagner there was a marvellous conductor as
well as a great composer.
[2] BB, I, 138.

weaknesses and points that have not pleased me because I can see that you will soon be fully able yourself to criticise your first attempts. Continue to write, and let me see something else of yours soon." [1] Bülow was even more delighted to learn that Wagner had shown Karl Ritter the manuscripts, and had commented, "An unmistakable talent."

In May, 1848, Bülow saw Tieck, who was an old friend of the family, in Leipzig, and was angered because the old poet did not approve of the poem of *Lohengrin.* " I only shrugged my shoulders," Hans wrote to his mother, " and thought to myself, ' Cobbler, stick to your last '; then I thought sorrowfully of the obstinacy and the inertia of mankind against everything new, everything it cannot immediately understand, and therefore undervalues. Doubly sad is it to me when I reflect that some day I myself will be no better, perhaps in some other connection. But neither in thought nor in speech will I fret myself over the ' judgment ' of this kind of aesthetic ' expert '; the thing isn't worth it, and Wagner's divinity remains unsullied." [2] Nor were his experiences with his own family any happier. His cousin Woldemar Frege used to leave the room when Hans played *Tannhäuser,* while Woldemar's young wife Livia revoked a promise to go through the score with him, as she thought the music " bad or crazy." But as compensation he found an occasional enthusiast of his own type. " A few days ago," he writes to his mother from Leipzig on the 24th July, 1848, " I made what is to me the very agreeable acquaintance of a student here who is studying philosophy and more particularly music. He has already composed a good deal — a symphony, overtures, etc. — and is an extraordinary admirer and idolator of Wagner's music, which he knows down to the minutest detail. His name is Dietrich; he knows Wagner personally, and me by name, because Wagner once said something to him in my praise. He possesses many full scores; in short, he is a most acceptable acquaintance, that came to me through his whistling in front of me, perhaps not without intention, a Wagner melody." [3]

All this testimony is valuable as showing the new orientation that German music was on the point of taking. There must have

---

[1] Letter of the 7th September, 1847, in BB, I, 78.   [3] BB, I, 118.
[2] Ibid., I, 95.

been hundreds of ardent young spirits of this kind beginning to rally round Wagner as their leader in the campaign against the old-world routine, feeling that with the *Flying Dutchman* and *Tannhäuser* a new world of music drama was coming into being. It is a mere chance that Bülow's letters of the period have survived: we may take it as certain that they are representative of a general ferment among the youth of the day and the more intelligent of their elders. The Wagner-battle had been joined: the vested official and academic interests were now confronted with an army that was not only willing but eager for a fight: Wagner was no longer alone, though it was not until after his flight from Dresden that he was to realise how strong his following had grown in the few years that had elapsed since the production of *Rienzi* there. The reactionaries and his personal enemies could still make his entry into this or that theatre difficult for him, but now they were under constant observation, and decidedly unfriendly observation at that. " I have managed to get several short paragraphs in Wagner's favour inserted in the local papers," writes Bülow from Leipzig on the 8th August, 1848. " For one of them I made use, quite innocently, of some private communications from Rietz.[1] Woldemar was very angry with me because I would not believe in the infallibility of Rietz's judgment. What had happened was this: the Leipzig theatre director, some time ago, wanted to give the *Flying Dutchman*, and had all the parts copied out. But Rietz said ' I can't do anything good, but at any rate I will prevent bad being done, namely, the rehearsing of this opera, which would not go down here.' " [2]

The day, in fact, was over when officials and reactionaries could treat Wagner *du haut en bas;* and it was probably the consciousness, on his part, of the rising tide of enthusiasm for him that made him now face his employers not as a servant but as at least an equal, and a similar consciousness on their part that made them

---

[1] Julius Rietz, at that time Kapellmeister at the Leipzig Opera and conductor of the Gewandhaus concerts. He was a protégé of Mendelssohn, and was in every respect typical of the Leipzig musical clique that would have no truck with Wagner. Rietz remained in power in Leipzig for several years, and was always an obstacle in the path of the "New German Music" there. In 1860 he left Leipzig to succeed Reissiger at Dresden, so that Wagner found an irreconcilable enemy entrenched in the very citadel he himself had built.

[2] BB, I, 121.

take from him a defiance hitherto unheard-of on the part of a German Kapellmeister, and show him a consideration without parallel in the annals of German music until that time. They too must have become rather uncomfortably aware, by about 1848, that the old order was passing and a new one well on its way. A dividing line had been drawn across German musical life, a new set of values brought into being. In a very little while the Reissigers, the Rietzes, the Spohrs, the Marschners, the Laubes, the Winklers, the Lüttichaus and the rest of them were to appear as little more than fossils belonging to an epoch that was no more, the very names of some of them being of significance to posterity only in so far as they come into the story of the pushful, quarrelsome little man they despised or detested. A new generation, filled with belief in the future, eager for a fight *à outrance* with the forces of reaction, was rallying round Wagner. He was making men in his own image, men who, like Bülow and Liszt, were willing to go through fire and water for one in whom they believed all that was best in the new Germany to be concentrated.

CHAPTER XIX

THE STORM BREWING

1

IN ORDER to preserve the unity of our survey of the position of Wagner relatively to public opinion about this time, we have had to leap a little ahead, at one or two points, of the story of his life as we left it at the end of Chapter XVII. We have now to take up again the purely biographical threads from February, 1847, after the production of *Iphigenia in Aulis* in Dresden.

On the Palm Sunday of this year (the 28th March) he gave, by general request, the Ninth Symphony once more, and in April he moved to his new quarters in the Marcolini Palace.

The importance of the year 1847 consists less in its outer events than in the inner change that was taking place in Wagner: 1847, indeed, may with reason be taken as the actual turning-point in his career. It was in that year that he became completely convinced that no good would ever come out of the Dresden Theatre as it was then constituted; [1] and, as he saw the matter, the central object of his existence — the regeneration of German life and culture through a new national attitude towards the theatre — could be realised only through a political revolution. And it is virtually certain that his whole life and the whole story of music in Dresden would have been different had the Dresden Theatre Direction not made the greatest mistake in its whole history — the rejection of Wagner's plans for reform. Had those been accepted, he might never have left Dresden. Their rejection not only made him withdraw more and more from co-operation in the administrative business of the theatre but convinced him, once for all, that he would either have to stifle his idealism or cut himself loose from the Ger-

---

[1] Before him, Marschner, who had been Musical Director at Dresden since 1824, had insisted, after two years' service, on his resignation being accepted, it being impossible to effect the reforms he had desired. See WM, p. 36.

man theatre as it was, and wait until he could create a theatre after his own heart.

It is in connection with 1847, therefore, rather than with 1846, when his Report *Die Königliche Kapelle betreffend* (*Concerning the Royal Orchestra*) was actually written, that that historic document calls for consideration. Paradoxically enough, while it is one of the three or four most vital documents in the Wagner story, it is as yet hardly known even to Wagner students. This long Report, running apparently to some hundred pages of manuscript, was not included by Wagner himself in the Collected Edition of his Prose and Poetical Works, perhaps because he did not possess a copy of it. It is dated the 1st March, 1846, and was sent to Lüttichau, with a covering letter, on the following day. It was unearthed in the Saxon Archives by Julius Kapp, and published by him for the first time in *Der Junge Wagner* (1910).[1] Later it was included in Volume XII of the Collected Edition of Wagner's literary Works, the editor of these, Richard Sternfeld, having gone direct to the original manuscript and corrected sundry errors in, and omissions from, Kapp's reprint. There is consequently no analysis of it in Glasenapp, whose final volume was issued in 1911, nor, of course, in Ellis, whose sixth volume appeared in 1908. Ellis, in the eighth volume of his English version of the Prose Works, translated as many of the posthumous writings as were then available, but as his final volume was published in 1899, necessarily the Report is not accessible to English readers. It is not even mentioned in the article on Wagner in the new *Grove* (1928), which, indeed, nowhere refers to the existence of the two supplementary volumes, XI and XII, of the German edition of the Collected Works.

The Report represents three months of hard work on Wagner's part. It deserves analysis in some detail, not only because of its cardinal importance in the story of Wagner's outer activities and inner disillusion in his Dresden days, but because of the light it throws on the musical conditions of the epoch.

Wagner evidently had in mind a plan for the complete reorganisation of the Dresden Opera; in his letter to Lüttichau he says, indeed, that if the present Report is favourably received by

---

[1] JKJW, pp. 341–415. Brescius had summarised it in 1899 in BKMK.

the authorities he will follow it up with one on the Opera as a whole.[1] For the moment, however, he will address himself only to the simpler problem of the orchestra — simpler because, for one thing, it is not complicated by the question of a vocal personnel. With his usual clear-sightedness, he foresaw the danger to German music of the growing rapacity of the public's favourite singers, who were cramming into their pockets a quite undue share of the funds that ought to be devoted to the Opera as a whole; and in his covering letter to Lüttichau he warned the Intendant that if this tendency was not checked, and more money spent on the orchestra, it meant, in time, the sure ruin of opera as an artistic whole. The fact, he says in his Report, that there are considerably more good orchestral players than good singers has the paradoxical result that the all-important orchestra is underpaid relatively to the singers, who, as the whole world knows, cannot compare with the average good instrumentalist in musical understanding or equipment.[2] But precisely because the egoism and the vanity of the singers are such serious factors in the operatic situation he will not deal with the Opera as a whole now, but will confine himself to the more concentrated and more immediately practical question of the orchestra. To every institution, he says, there comes a time when either the faults that have developed in it in the course of the years must be eradicated or it must go to ruin; and this time has now arrived so far as the Royal Kapelle is concerned.

The duties of the Dresden orchestra, in the theatre and in the church, have been increasing steadily since it was founded, till now it is overworked. The men have neither the time nor the inclination to think of either their technique or the inner meaning of their music except when they are actually in the theatre, while the system of life-appointments makes for slackness, moral as well as physical. Nor is the best conceivable use being made of the orchestra relatively to the construction of the theatre and the de-

---

[1] He did, in fact, draw up, in May, 1848, an elaborate *Plan for the Organisation of a German National Theatre in the Kingdom of Saxony*, which we shall consider later.

[2] Semper's theatre had a seating capacity of 1712, as against the 814 of the old theatre. But the new house had been specially planned to provide a large number of cheap seats; and as there were only 134 seats at one thaler, the remainder costing from 4 groschen to 16 groschen (about sixpence to two shillings), it is evident that an excessively large proportion of the receipts went into the pockets of the more highly-paid singers. See PGHD, p. 493.

mands of the repertory. He begins with the strings, to the resonance of which, he contends, the new theatre is not very favourable; in any case there are too few of them. The present establishment provides for 22 violins, 8 violas, 7 'cellos, and 6 basses: there should be 24 violins, 8 violas, 7 'cellos, and 6 basses.[1] The second violins are at present unsatisfactory, especially in the matter of precision. Owing to the heavy work thrown on the strings, there is a great deal of sickness among them — *Armida* had recently to be given with only 15 violins — and the absence of the invalids throws extra work on the others, who are already tried to the limit of their strength. The violins were especially prone to these breakdowns; quite recently an excellent young violinist, Kühne, had died of consumption; another exceptionally gifted player, Winterstein, had been compelled by reason of his ruined health to petition for his release; another, Franz, has been unable to take his place in the orchestra for nine months, and, by all appearances, will never regain his health; Morgenroth, one of the leaders, has been absent through illness for nearly a year; Lind can carry on only by the most conscientious efforts; and so on. Under these circumstances only a few of the younger men and an older one here and there can be expected to bring zeal and fire to the performance of their duties. Moreover, the orchestra is weakened in the summer by leaves of absence and by the drafting of some of the members to the Linke'sches Bad — though it is precisely in the summer that the opera performances should be at their best, because it is then that Dresden is full of visitors.

Wagner's plan is to economise the strength of the players by a more rational distribution of them between the heavier operas, the lighter operas, the plays in which incidental music is required, the farces, vaudevilles and so on; divided and combined as he suggests, there would be no waste of men or of effort, and the pick of the forces would be in full strength for the more exacting works. Players who are manifestly no longer equal to their task should be

---

[1] The players were divided into two classes — the full members of the Kapelle (the Kammermusiker), and the Accessists. Wagner's proposals call for more of the former and less of the latter. This of course means not only an improvement in quality but an increase in the total of the salary list.

The paper strength of the orchestra had been raised, in January, 1847, from 53 to 61; but the Accessists sometimes numbered as many as 22. See BKMK, p. 13.

pensioned forthwith: the veteran part-leader of the second violins, for instance (Schmiedel), is now so feeble that precision among the seconds is difficult to obtain when he is there: he is old, his eyes are bad, and he is musically dull-witted.

The rule at Dresden used to be that there were four players for each wood-wind instrument — not all employed at once, of course, but in relays. Now there are four players for the flute and clarinet only; Wagner recommends that a fourth should be added for the oboe and another for the bassoon. The leader in each of these departments, he says, is really as important as any of the singers: he must be a virtuoso upon his instrument and a sensitive artist as well, for many expressive solo passages fall to his lot. His strength should therefore be economised: he should be called upon to play only in the more important works if the quality of the performances is not to suffer. This applies also to the solo horn, whose lips are essential to his tone, and who therefore should be reserved for the more exacting operas. The second horn should be taken more care of, so that in time he may be able to take the place of his leader. There are actually eight hornists on the register at present, but by a better distribution of the work seven would be sufficient. The present first horn, Haase, is too old to be of any real service to the institution: his embouchure is uncertain, his breath inadequate, his lips weak; he is a hindrance rather than a help to the Kapelle. It is impossible to relegate him to second horn, for his faults would be equally disturbing in that capacity: moreover, a player who has been used to the high notes of the first horn-part for so many years would not be equally at home among the lower notes of the second horns. Haase should either be pensioned or relegated to plays and vaudevilles — though, to be sure, in these there is already a hornist, Kretschmar, who is not fit for anything better than these. Perhaps the best thing to do, under the circumstances, would be to pension Kretschmar and put Haase in his place.

The trumpets and trombones are of so much importance in modern operatic scores, and even in farces and ballets, that the players of these instruments should be as well paid as the others. The salaries of the four trumpets should be raised to at least 500, 450, 400, and 300 thalers respectively. At present the bass trombone gets only 300 thalers a year, the other two 200 thalers each. These amounts are insufficient; the bass trombone, at any rate, in consideration of the importance of his work, should receive a gratuity in addition. A tenor trombone should be provided, especially for the modern French operas, in which the tenor alone is used: at present these parts have to be played by the alto, who has either to omit many notes or to transpose them an octave higher.

One kettle-drummer is not enough for an orchestra like that of the Dresden Opera. A supernumerary should be engaged: Wagner recommends Pfund, of Leipzig, as being of exceptional promise. New kettle-drums are an imperative need, as those now in the orchestra are old and quite inadequate. They should be obtained from London, the English make being the best. The orchestra cannot do with less than three of these: they may be more expensive at first, but they are more lasting.

Germany in general, and Dresden in particular, have not yet realised the importance of the harp in modern scores. Dresden should set an example to other theatres by paying a harpist sufficient — Wagner suggests 300 thalers — to permit of his giving his whole time to the instrument. The present harpist is paid only 200 thalers; as he cannot live on that, he is forced to give lessons on other instruments, especially the piano, which is bad for his harp technique. The Dresden orchestra possesses only two single pedal harps, which are not equal to all that modern composers demand of them. They should be replaced by double pedal instruments, even though these be dearer.

The Dresden orchestra possesses no big drum, cymbals, or triangle; when anything of this kind is required a town musician is engaged. But his instrument is generally of inferior quality and he himself is so crude an executant that his efforts are frequently in disharmony with the tone of the orchestra as a whole.

The time-honoured position of the conductor — close to the stage — is a fundamentally bad one. He is placed there because the singers are supposed to be his principal charge, these people requiring most watching and guidance. But in this position he has his back to the orchestra; necessarily he cannot communicate his intentions to the players as he would like, while, facing the stage

[467]

as they are bound to do, a great deal of their tone is lost to the audience. The conductor should be at the other side of the orchestra, where the players can face him. But this might make the singers nervous unless they were perfectly sure of their parts; more rehearsals are therefore imperative, and this is difficult with the constantly changing German repertory, which is consequently too often under-rehearsed. Further, the construction of the orchestral space is basically faulty. It is insufficiently deep relatively to its length: perfect precision is impossible, owing to so many of the players being too far away from the conductor; the back desks are apt to lose confidence and are incapable of fine shading, while an unnecessary burden of anxiety is imposed on the conductor. It often happens that the players at one extreme of the long line hear those at the other end entering *after* the beat. The orchestra should be more concentrated.

> " An orchestra that is to form a good ensemble should not stretch laterally more than twice its depth or breadth; the players at the extremity of each wing should be no further from the conductor than he himself is from the centre of the depth. Therefore in the big operas the depth of the orchestra should be one of four desks, there being consequently only four rows on each side of the conductor. On this principle, he can easily overlook all the players and guide them more surely: they, being closer to each other, will hear each other better; the general body of strings can follow the leader's bowing better; the wood-wind will form a concentrated harmonic body, and will be in a magnetic *rapport* with the phrasing of the solo players that is impossible when they cannot hear and see each other."

This, of course, will mean a certain amount of rearrangement of the seating in the auditorium; but what is lost in one quarter will be made up in another. Because the original construction of the theatre is faulty in this respect, there having been no one who could advise the architect on such points, is the error to be perpetuated? The architect should now bring the theatre in this matter into line with other theatres, that of the Paris Opéra, for instance; it should be taken as a maxim that an orchestra should not be more than twice as long as it is deep or broad, whereas the Dresden orchestra is four times as long as it is broad.

The old-fashioned wooden music stands are too massive: they afford the players insufficient room and interfere with the sound.

They should be replaced by stands of thin iron, resting on small iron feet. Each wind player should have his own desk, so that he may in all circumstances face the conductor. The orchestral seats should be without backs, so that they may occupy the minimum of space and be easier to handle.

Concerts should be given regularly by the orchestra in the winter months — six of them at least — so that the public may become acquainted with those masterpieces of instrumental music that are the glory of the German school: Dresden is shamefully behind other towns in this regard. Acquaintance with these masterpieces would be good also for the style of the players. Two objections may be raised to this proposal — that the orchestra lacks time and energy for concert rehearsals in addition to its duties in the opera, and that a regular series of concerts might damage the yearly Pension Fund concert on Palm Sunday. As to the latter, the Pension Fund concert could only benefit by the increased appetite for instrumental music that would be the certain result of regular winter concerts: while the Palm Sunday concert could always be given special significance, partly by the employment of exceptionally large forces, partly by the production of works of more than ordinary calibre. As to the first objection, that could be met by giving the orchestral players the receipts from the winter concerts. Their salaries are much too low: they were fixed at a time when living was less expensive than it is now, and when the men had more leisure for supplementing their theatre pay by other work.[1] It will be difficult for the King to increase salaries all

---

[1] The archives of the Berlin theatre show that Meyerbeer, in 1843, had tried to secure better pay for everybody connected with the Opera. They were nearly all, he says in his letters to the Intendant Küstner on the subject, better off twenty-five years ago, when living was cheaper. The lower ranks of the orchestra were in a lamentable economic condition: salaries of 400 thalers and under should be increased by 100 thalers, those over 400 thalers by 60 thalers. In 1819, the Berlin Kapelle of 88 members had cost 43,785 thalers per annum: in 1843, 104 members received only 47,237 thalers. Orchestral players in the Germany of that epoch were evidently grossly underpaid. See the documents in Altmann's article *Meyerbeer-Forschungen*, in SIM, IV, 528 ff.

It is little wonder that most German artists of ability forsook the opera orchestra at the earliest opportunity. In 1850, when Joachim was leader of the Weimar Kapelle, his salary was only 500 thalers; while his colleague Cossmann, who was later to become one of the most eminent 'cellists of the day, received only 350 thalers. The salaries of the rank and file of the Weimar orchestra ranged from 325 to 100 thalers per annum. In 1851 Liszt made an attempt to improve the pay of the Kapelle. One of the players, with a large family and a salary of 200 thalers, had told him he was

round from the Civil List; but here is a simple means by which the economic condition of the players can be improved. Part of the receipts from the concerts could be set aside as a Sustentation Fund for needy members of the Kapelle — Wagner suggests that one quarter of the total shall be allotted to this Fund, the other three-quarters to the players. At present, requests to the management for advances upon salaries are frequent; and the players would feel less embarrassment, when in temporary difficulties, in applying for relief to the custodians of a Fund they had created solely by their own exertions than in approaching the Direction of the Kapelle.

The King should issue an order for the commencement of these concerts in the coming winter: the artistic management of them should be in the hands of the conductors and leaders of the orchestra, the supreme administrative control being vested in the Intendant. But where are the concerts to be given? The opera house is unsuitable, because each concert there means the sacrifice of an operatic or dramatic performance. The " old " opera house, in which concerts are given at present, would do if the necessary structural alterations were made. The town, however, should look ahead. Dresden should have a permanent concert building; and it is certain that the recent plans for the beautifying of the town will be carried further, which will mean, sooner or later, the destruction of the " old " opera house. The sensible thing would be to make away with certain buildings — among them the Royal laundry — that are at present a blot on the best part of the city, and construct a new and handsome street, containing a restaurant, a larger and a smaller concert hall, with ample cellars in which the theatre pro-

---

starving. The man was granted an extra 10 thalers, on the strict condition that he did not "importune the Grand Ducal Court Marshall's Bureau again." Liszt asked for better pay for his players, the pensioning of seven of them, and the addition to the orchestra of a second and a third trombone, a bass clarinet, cymbals, triangle, big drum, two klappenhorns, a harp, and an organ — which, of course, meant the engagement of so many more players. He was informed that it was impossible to comply with his wishes. In 1857 he tried again, but again in vain, to secure better pay for the players, whose salaries were what they had been forty years before, though the cost of living had increased. (See RLL, p. 105 ff.)

It is clear that Wagner's revolt against the economic conditions to which German musicians were subject was part of a general protest against a state of affairs that had become intolerable. In 1829 the Dresden orchestra served in the theatre 257 days, and had 108 days free. For 1844 the respective figures were 344 and 22. See BKMK, p. 12.

perties (now in the " old " opera house) could be stored. These concert halls could be let for balls, redoubts, etc.; and the buildings would prove a sound commercial proposition.

Appended to the Report are two detailed statements of the numbers of the orchestra, the present salaries paid, and the changes and additions suggested by Wagner, with the estimated extra cost of these. The present yearly cost of the orchestra is 28,000 thalers. The proposed changes, with all that they mean in the way of easier conditions for the players and greatly improved performances, would cost only a further 3,050 thalers; and against this could be set the financial advantages accruing from the suggested winter concerts.

2

There is not a sentence in the whole of this long Report that does not carry its own justification and conviction even now, nearly a century after it was written. It is the work of an idealist indeed, but not of a visionary: from the first page to the last it is the quintessence of practical commonsense. Moreover it is the work of a man who puts the claims of art and the interests of the institution with which he is officially connected above all thoughts of self. There was no reason, in the outer nature of things, why Wagner should have troubled himself in the least about the present conditions or the future prospects of the Royal Kapelle; he could quite easily have turned away, with a cynical shrug of the shoulders, from the waste and the folly and the artistic incompetence of the Opera, as Reissiger and the others did, and contented himself, like them, with earning his salary with the minimum of work and worry on his part. For a man in constant bad health,[1] and racked

---

[1] "Wagner has been in ill health for some time," writes Ferdinand Heine to Ernst Kietz in Paris in October, 1846. "On the one hand he overstrains his spirit; on the other, his enemies and enviers strew so many thorns among his scanty but well-deserved laurels that he is beginning to feel wounded in body and mind. I am afraid it will go with him as with many another really great genius: he will not live to see his triumph, and himself estimated at his true value. Everything cuts too deeply with him and swiftly eats away his vital spirits. Of what use is it to him that nine-tenths of the Dresdeners are enraptured with his *Rienzi* and his divine *Tannhäuser?* The papers tear him to pieces; other theatres take their cue from these papers, so that his works are not given elsewhere — and will not be until he is dead, when people will fight to have them! I am convinced he will not live to be old." (Quoted by G. A. Kietz in KW, p. 59.)

with anxieties of all kinds, to spend three months of his none too plentiful leisure working out a scheme of this sort is to give an example of selflessness so complete as to be almost without a parallel in the history of musical institutions. The people who so glibly accuse Wagner of " egoism " and of having " a vulgar personality " simply do not know him. Egoism he may have shown, like the rest of us, in plenty in later life in the satisfaction of his personal desires; and there were elements in him, as a man, that jar upon the taste of the purist in human character. But as an artist he was from first to last beyond fear and above reproach. There is not a solitary instance in his whole career in which he yielded an inch of his artistic idealism for personal ease or profit. He loathed and despised the theatre as it actually was; but being in it he could not bring himself to do anything less than his best for it, at serious cost to his time, his health, his creative work, his peace of soul.

It would have been well for the Dresden theatre and for Dresden had the authorities listened to him and taken his advice; they would almost certainly have kept him for many more years and raised their city to the foremost place in German music. But no one in a placidly self-satisfied institution welcomes a reformer; and for the reformer to be so devastatingly right in every one of his criticisms and so unerringly practical in every one of his suggestions is merely an extra reason for suspecting and opposing him. Wagner's proposals would not be welcomed in the theatre: Reissiger would resent his junior colleague's taking so much upon himself and, by implication, telling him that *he*, for all his years of service, had neither the eyes to see what was wrong with the institution over which he presided nor the brains nor the wish nor the will to set it right. The players who were threatened with transplantation or superannuation would all be against Wagner, and the herd instinct would carry most of the others with them. (It is true that Wagner tells Lüttichau that he has discussed his Report with no one in the theatre; but at a hundred rehearsals and performances and in a hundred conversations he could not have failed to reveal the trend of his thought.) The Intendant and the Committee would be against him because it was an unheard-of thing for a second Kapellmeister to be showing them so plainly how little he thought of them: every fault pointed out in the institution, every suggestion

[472]

for reform, carried with it the implication that in his opinion they did not know their business and were incompetent to have the direction of the town's Opera in their hands. And so was laid the basis for that charge of " vanity " that it now became the fashion to bring against him in Dresden. Nothing could have been more unjust: there was no vanity and no self-seeking in Wagner's proposals — nothing but the revolt of the exasperated idealist against the slovenliness and the cynicism of the routine work of the theatre, and the revolt of the highly practical man against the unskilled handling of the theatre forces by people who had neither the intelligence to see the need of something better nor a perception of how to realise it when it was pointed out to them. It was intolerable that a poverty-stricken young man of thirty-three, after a mere three years' duty in the Dresden theatre, should have so low an opinion of its artistic products, and presume to know so much more about the running of an opera house than men who had been in their posts a whole generation before *he* arrived on the scene.

Wagner heard nothing about his Report for a whole year after he had handed it in: then, in 1847, he was informed that his proposals were rejected. He could no longer have any illusions now with regard to either Dresden in particular or Germany in general, for everywhere in Germany the same irrational conditions prevailed; only through the theatre, he was convinced, could the desired regeneration of German culture come about, and the theatre was in the hands of people utterly unworthy of such a trust. And as these people were as a rule Court Intendants, he became the irreconcilable enemy both of Intendants and of Courts. The sense of his spiritual loneliness increased; more than ever he identified himself with his own Lohengrin. He had already separated himself as well as he could from the professional musicians of the town, and turned for intellectual companionship and moral support to the artists and the men of letters. Now he began to shun the society even of these. He buried himself in the past, in German and Scandinavian antiquities and in the literature of ancient Greece; out of these he created for himself an ideal world into which he could retire at will and forget the murk and moil, the meanness and ugliness and superficiality of the life around him.

And, as was so often to be the case with him, he achieved at times a serenity of soul that astonished not only himself but his associates. He took long walks with little Peps; he buried himself in the bushes or sat in the branches of the tall trees of the Marcolini garden; he lost himself in the soul of Lohengrin — like himself, a temporary visitor to a world that could not understand him.

His relations with Lüttichau worsened steadily during all this time. As long ago as May, 1846 — two months, it will be noted, after his sending in his Report, about which, it is probable, not a word had as yet been said to him from high quarters — he had expressed himself freely with regard to Lüttichau in a letter to Spohr. Wagner is writing from Gross-Graupe. " I am indebted to my General Director," he says ironically, " for having permitted me to have nothing to do with him for a whole three months. . . . His behaviour [in the matter of the long retention and final rejection of Spohr's *Kreuzfahrer*, the story of which has already been told],[1] the exact details of which I learned from your letter, shows a crudity in the man that struck me as almost comical: whom shall we pity — these Junkers, these foxes put in charge of the geese, who make themselves ridiculous in everything they do, or the artists who have to suffer from their impertinences? . . . Anyhow you have given Herr von Lüttichau a drastic lesson, of the kind you were particularly fitted to give him, and for my part I hope to God I shall be able some day to make you a proper atonement for this piece of Dresden incivility." [2]

From this time onward, and more especially after the rejection of his Report in 1847, Wagner showed his resentment and his contempt for his employers by either absenting himself wholly from the meetings of the theatre committee at which the weekly affairs of the Opera were arranged, or, if he deigned to put in an appearance, by treating Lüttichau, Reissiger and the others with studied indifference. They could not follow him into the ideal world from the heights of which *he* contemplated the theatre; he, for his part, could no longer take any interest in the petty matters of routine that were all in all to them. He had found that the best-laid plan for raising the standard of performance or improving the repertory was liable to be upset at any moment by the

---

[1] See p. 382. [2] RWKK, II, 203.

caprice of some singer or other, or the superior wisdom of some minor official at the theatre; and after many a heated discussion he had come to the conclusion that it was a waste of time and energy for him to try to extract more intelligence out of these people than Providence had seen fit to endow them with at their birth. And matters became worse after Gutzkow was firmly settled in the saddle as *Dramaturg.*

3

Wagner may not have done complete justice, in *Mein Leben,* to Gutzkow as a man of letters and as the representative of certain phases of contemporary German thought; but that is not the specific concern of the Wagner biographer, who has to deal solely with the relations of the pair in Dresden during these critical years. Gutzkow, though completely unmusical, still thought himself entitled to have an opinion upon music and musicians, apparently on the strength of the fact that his wife played the piano. He probably had the sense not to stress the abstract powers of the *Dramaturg* too far where the opera was concerned; but at the same time there was more interference on his side in matters upon which he was profoundly ignorant than Wagner could tolerate. A few conversations between the two had sufficed to enable Wagner to take his new colleague's intellectual measure. As it happens, we have accounts by Wagner and by Gutzkow, each written independently of the other,[1] of what is evidently the same episode. Gutzkow was not averse to the occasional employment of music in drama, though his views on the subject were the conventional ones of the unmusical man of letters. In his play *Uriel Acosta,* which was produced in Dresden in 1846, he wished the scene of the hero's recantation of his supposed heresy to be accompanied by a soft tremolo in the orchestra. The effect was musically so ludicrous, and so harmful to the effect of the play, that Wagner felt impelled to try to come to an understanding with Gutzkow as to the real nature of music and drama, and the lines upon which the

---

[1] Gutzkow's reminiscences were published in 1875, some ten years, therefore, after Wagner had written the (as yet, of course, unpublished) pages relating to him in *Mein Leben.*

two arts could be made to co-operate to the maximum advantage
of both. He soon came to the conclusion, however, that Gutzkow
was constitutionally incapable of ever arriving at a solution of the
problem, or even understanding that there *was* a problem — all
he wanted was a little orchestral sound, of no significance in itself,
to relieve, as he thought, this situation or heighten that — and
Wagner saw the uselessness of pursuing the question with him any
further. Gutzkow's account of the matter is that Wagner invited
him to "tread the same path with him," the second and fourth
acts of *Uriel Acosta* having demonstrated his capacity to do so,
but that he (Gutzkow) could not be convinced of the possibility of
the perfect union of opera and drama; opera, he contended, would
always have to remain opera, and drama remain drama. There was
evidently no possible point of contact between the two minds. Of
this Wagner could no longer remain in doubt after Gutzkow had
seriously asked him why he had not introduced Klingsohr into
the singers' contest in *Tannhäuser,* as this would have given him
" the opportunity to introduce a powerful bass part à la Bertram
in *Robert the Devil.*" [1] Were it not Gutzkow himself who tells the
story, in all its exquisite fatuity, we might have been inclined to
regard it as a humorous invention on Wagner's part or on that of
one of his friends. " There were no more meetings after this frankness on my part," says Gutzkow, still blissfully unaware of the
immortal stroke of humour he had achieved. We find no difficulty
in accepting his statement.

The pair must soon have found it more and more impossible to
work together. Wagner's great popularity in the town after *Tannhäuser* had thoroughly established itself in public favour was an
annoyance to Gutzkow. He speaks of Wagner in his memoirs as
being " much-glorified "; he protests against the " disgraceful "
applause after each performance of a Wagner opera, which he
regards as " the beginning of that organised claque that is now
[i.e. in 1875] spread over all Germany ": he could not understand
this " fanaticism." [2] He disliked Johanna, and, when he could,
struck through her at her uncle. He allied himself with that spoiled
darling the actor Emil Devrient — the " prima donna in breeches "

[1] GRML, p. 319.
[2] Ibid., p. 319.

— against what he called " the Tichatschek-Wagner despotism." [1]
Wagner, for his part, came to regard Gutzkow as the evil genius
of the Dresden theatre. " At the commencement of this year," he
writes to Carl Gaillard on the 31st August, 1847, " I found myself
on such friendly terms with Gutzkow that I could speak warmly to
him with regard to your play . . . but soon after that my relations with him became very unfriendly, a condition which I must
deliberately preserve if I am to safeguard my honour. This affair
brought me into what was an inevitable conflict with my Intendant,
leading, a little while ago, to a breach between us which, I earnestly
hope, will end in my leaving." [2]

When Eduard Devrient left Dresden, Wagner would have liked
Laube, who was not only a personal friend but a man of considerable attainments, to be appointed *Dramaturg* in his place.
Wagner must have known something of Gutzkow's writings, though
apparently he had not met him as yet. Gutzkow, like Wagner, was
in Paris in 1842, studying the French stage: but there is no record
of Wagner having met him there. He joined the Dresden theatre
early in 1847. In July of that year we find Wagner, who was no
doubt sufficiently irritated already at the rejection of his scheme
for the reform of the Kapelle, protesting to Lüttichau against the
Dramaturg's interference with matters that did not concern him.
Wagner speaks bitterly of his own disappointment and discourage-
ment at finding himself unable to realise the ideals he had set before him since his appointment as Kapellmeister. But his difficulties, he says, have increased since Gutzkow came — a journalist,
he calls him, who had indeed had a certain connection with the
stage, though mostly under the aspect of a *chronique scandaleuse,*
but who had given no proof of any real understanding of its problems. This man is suddenly appointed to the highest technical, and in
some degree administrative, control of an institution that had won
a distinguished place for itself. Wagner, however, had no real

---

[1] See his letter of the 5th July, 1847, to Devrient, in HED, p. 314. Pecht, who
was living in Dresden at this time, was unfavourably impressed by Gutzkow, whom
he met at Hiller's house. "I felt an antipathy towards the lurking quality, the sense
of ambush, in this man, whose nature was consumed by a burning ambition. . . .
He had the profile of a shrew-mouse . . . and his narrowed eyes harmonised only
too well with his snuffling nature, that was utterly incapable of giving itself." See
PAMZ, I, 291.

[2] RWKK, II, 242.

right, he says, to feel aggrieved so long as Gutzkow confined his activities to the spoken play — though even there his incompetence and bad taste and pretentiousness have earned him the contempt of the dramatic personnel. But Gutzkow has presumed to meddle with the opera also: he had taken it on himself to act as producer of Halévy's *Les Mousquetaires de la Reine*. He not only operates through a clique at the theatre, but acts as correspondent of the *Deutsche Allgemeine Zeitung*, in which journal he pulls wires in order to influence the engagement of singers in Dresden. He is in alliance with Wagner's enemy Carl Banck, who accuses Wagner of intriguing against other singers for the benefit of his niece Johanna.

Wagner resents these attacks on his honour, and feels so deeply the impossibility of doing his best for the Opera with these journalistic cliques scheming against him, that if only his material circumstances were better he would ask the King to dismiss him.

" Nevertheless I cannot continue to be the slave of these circumstances; and unless Your Excellency can see his way at least to bar Herr Dr. Gutzkow officially from all connection with the affairs of the Opera, and especially from our Opera conferences, and unless Your Excellency can decide to confide to me the conduct of the Opera more unreservedly than has hitherto been the case . . . then I am firmly resolved to leave it to the wisdom of His Majesty to decide in what manner, and to what extent, my proved capacity as dramatic composer and conductor can be utilised for the service of His Majesty in such a way that an honorarium could be granted me that would safeguard the obligations I have entered into with regard to the Pensions Fund,[1] but would cease to lay upon me official duties and relations in connection with the affairs of the Opera which, consistently with my oath, I cannot fulfil. . . . Rather would I deliver myself naked and defenceless to the care of God alone than seek any longer a protection in a situation in which my conscience and my honour alike are to be further outraged." [2]

The tone is aggressive, the language often undiplomatic: but the too conscientious artist had evidently been goaded beyond endurance. Lüttichau, however, who had been hypnotised by the assurance and vanity of Gutzkow, chose to side with the latter. Once more the chance of binding the most brilliant musician and con-

[1] I.e., in connection with the loan granted him on his life assurance. See p. 415.
[2] RWKK, II, 232–237.

ductor in Germany to the Dresden Opera with links of steel was lost: once more Wagner sank into utter despair of ever realising his ideals in the German theatre as it then was. His employers and his enemies were unconsciously pushing him yet a step nearer revolution.[1]

To the fact that Ferdinand Heine was away from Dresden at the time, taking a cure, we owe a letter in which Wagner, on the 6th August, 1847, pours out the whole story of his clash with Lüttichau and his disgust with theatre conditions.

"Perhaps you have already heard something of my having definitely broken with Lüttichau about three weeks ago, so that, from my side at least, there is no hope at all of a reconciliation: Gutzkow was the cause of it. The circumstances in themselves are really a matter of complete indifference; it is the eternal strife of knowledge and conviction against incomprehension. Agreement is quite out of the question; but when the conflict has come to such a pitch as this, then even a settling down together is unthinkable, and so I keep to my firm resolve to put an end to the matter. However, I took counsel of prudence, recognising that if only I could put a big Berlin success into my end of the scale this would be bound to help me. If therefore I can keep Lüttichau at arm's length until I have won that advantage, and *then* approach the King, I should much prefer this; but if, before this, he will not leave me in peace, well, this step must be taken sooner. Naturally I have no inclination to make a great sacrifice of my salary; but if there is no other course open, I must put up with that." [2]

Wagner's behaviour towards his Intendant at this period was certainly not what the Directors of German Court Operas were accustomed to from their employees; and we can account for Lüttichau's tolerance of it only on the supposition that he and everyone else, from the King downward, knew well that Wagner's ability not only as composer but as conductor gave a decided prestige to the Dresden theatre. Wagner, for his part, traded on his extraordinary popularity among the opera-going public of the

---

[1] Lüttichau's reply being unconciliatory, Wagner, in a letter of the 10th August, asks to be excused from further attendance at committee meetings. He asks for a week's leave (to go to Berlin; Küstner had invited him to go and hear two possible tenors for the forthcoming production of *Rienzi*). Whether this request could be granted at the time is not certain: but Wagner spent nearly two months in Berlin later in the year. He might complain, with reason, of Lüttichau's lack of understanding of his ideals; but in other respects the Intendant certainly showed him great consideration.

[2] RWUF, p. 378.

town. The lust of combat was in him; he never doubted that some day he would be in a position to dictate terms to all his adversaries. Gutzkow gives us a pathetically humorous picture of Lüttichau's difficulties with his Kapellmeister. All musicians were a trouble to Lüttichau, but the " contumacious Richard Wagner " was the greatest trouble of them all. At this period, says Gutzkow, Wagner " lived in a suburb, like an exile. He had had differences with his chief, perhaps with the Court. His reappearance at the Kapell-meister's desk and at the meetings of the committee seemed to be bound up with conditions on both sides of which I was ignorant." At committee meetings it was Lüttichau's practice never to decide a point till he had heard what each of the Kapellmeisters had to say. Reissiger, on these occasions, always acted the dear friend and tender father; he was, says Gutzkow, a quiet fellow of the old school, whose misfortune it was to be one of the first to undergo the shock of " the storm-trooper of the ' future.' " Reissiger al-ways tried, or affected to try, at these conferences, to say a good word for Wagner; " I admire the man, I esteem his talent," but at the same time " one can't run one's head against a wall." Gutzkow calls him " the first of the Wagner martyrs." " One day the sulk-ing Achilles left his ship to attend a committee meeting "; he was " in the full flood of his Saxon gift of the gab." The subject under discussion was the casting for a coming operatic production. Wag-ner, no doubt to show his contempt for the whole proceedings, kept switching the conversation over to other themes — Gluck and Piccinni, Gluck and the pure forms of the antique, the relations of music and the drama, the difference between melody and rhythm — on all of which he discoursed fluently; until at last poor Lütti-chau, unable to bear it any longer, cried out, " But, Herr Jesus, all we want to know is whether Frau Kriete can sing the part or not! " Thereupon Achilles once more retired to his ship, and henceforth left the theatre committee to settle grave matters of that kind among themselves.[1]

---

[1] GRML, pp. 315–318. The utter unreliability of Glasenapp and Ellis where Wagner's enemies are concerned, and the necessity of checking their use of every document, are charmingly illustrated in their respective accounts of this episode. Glasenapp (GRW, II, 212) conceals from the reader the real nature of what he calls Wagner's "discourse," and regards Gutzkow's account as merely "malicious." But the whole point of the story is that Lüttichau's outburst was wrung from him by the sheer irrelevance of Wagner's talk to the business in hand. Ellis (ELW, II, 215),

In so small a town as the Dresden of that epoch the differences between the leading personages of the theatre could hardly be a secret from anyone; so it is not surprising to find an ironic announcement in the Leipzig *Signale für die musikalische Welt* for 1847 (communicated by its Dresden correspondent), that "the Dresden Opera has been threatened with a calamity: the matter, however, has been happily settled, and Germany is saved. Herr Kapellmeister Richard Wagner has resigned, owing to differences with the *Dramaturg*. Also Tichatschek is sulking with Herr Wagner. These are weighty matters for Dresden."

4

We have seen that on the 1st August, 1847, *Tannhäuser* was put on the stage again, with a changed ending.[1] It was an immense success with the public; but what Wagner must have felt about it can be deduced from his brochure — intended as a guide to singers, regisseurs, conductors, and scenic artists — *On the Performing of Tannhäuser*, written towards the end of 1852. We can understand his inner despair in spite of his outer success; what with the cuts, the almost all-round incompetence of the singers to realise his dramatic idea, the wretched scenery, and the unskilled lighting, the best of the Dresden performances in these miserable years must have seemed to him little better than a parody. But at the moment he welcomed all these dubious successes because there was a probability of their helping him towards his real objective — a triumph in Berlin. The King of Prussia still showed a flattering interest in him: he had been in Dresden at the end of July, 1847, and had asked that *Rienzi* should be put on for

---

while professing to be translating Glasenapp, garbles the latter's text for his own ends. "As a fact," he makes Glasenapp say, "when Wagner had brought forward some important scheme, he was simply cut short by von Lüttichau with 'Herr Jesus! All we want to know is whether the Kriete can sing the part or not.'" There is nothing whatever in Gutzkow about Wagner having "brought forward some important scheme" at the conference: what Wagner had done had been to talk all round the subject. Ellis had evidently not consulted Gutzkow at first hand.

[1] Wilhelm Tappert, after having consulted various old text-books of *Tannhäuser*, and talked with the old Dresden copyist, Karl Mehner, came to the conclusion that in 1846 Wagner had tried yet another ending, in which Venus appeared in person and the young Pilgrims entered bearing the staff in flower. See his article *Die drei verschiedenen Schlüsse des Tannhäuser*, in DM, I.

his benefit. And to Wagner's gratification, for his creditors were pressing him and Berlin royalties would be very useful, *Rienzi* was now put into rehearsal there, the Queen of Saxony having apparently approached, at Wagner's request, her brother Friedrich Wilhelm IV. To Berlin, accordingly, he went in September.

At first he was highly pleased with everything and everybody there. The word having gone round that he was in favour with the King, the Kapellmeister (Taubert), the singers and the chorus could not do enough to impress him with their enthusiasm for the work. Optimistic as usual, he tells Minna that he is sure Berlin is a field in which he can become influential: " God keep you in good health and good spirits," he writes. " You have now more reason than ever to be cheerful, when you reflect that the long-awaited turn for the better is at last near at hand. Everything will be first-rate with us in the end, in a nice country house. That wouldn't be bad, would it? " The Rienzi (Pfister) is not a Tichatschek, but he is full of good will. The Adriano (Frau Köster) has a very agreeable voice: she will make a very good Elsa — a hint as to the direction his thoughts were taking with regard to the first production of his new work. He is rehearsing incessantly. The only flaw in his contentment is the separation from Minna; but he looks forward to the time when they will be settled for good in Berlin. " When I walk about here and turn this Berlin over in my mind, and reflect what may possibly be awaiting me here, that we might finally transfer ourselves hither, I get a strange enough feeling: as yet I cannot figure out what it would be like. Well, I won't brood upon it too much, for perhaps in the long run I am fretting myself unnecessarily. Lord, how contented one could be with Dresden if the nest had only a little higher standing! That *this* place is more the right field for my works is undeniable! But no more of these fantasies! "

The more he rehearsed the company the better pleased he was with them. He had " the best Irene imaginable " (Fräulein Tuczek), while Frau Köster, he tells Minna, is almost too good for Adriano — in comparison with his niece Johanna she is " very virginal." Everyone, including the landlord of the hotel at which he is staying, is making a great fuss of him; but he is so lamentably short of money that he has to draw upon the good Röckel for

Minna as well as for himself. There were the usual postponements, due to the indisposition or the caprice of this singer or that; and the first performance did not take place until the 26th October, before a house sold out at double prices. The King, whose active patronage meant so much to Wagner, was for some reason or other not present. The performance, according to his later account in *Mein Leben*, was ruined by the utter inadequacy of the Rienzi. The reception of the work by the audience was flattering enough, taking into consideration the notorious frigidity of the Berlin public; but the Press, as usual, was hostile. Wagner conducted two more performances. These were followed by a further five in the course of 1848: then *Rienzi* disappeared from the Berlin repertory until 1865. An innocent remark by Wagner at the final rehearsal had been put to malicious use by the critics. He had apologised to the singers for the heavy demands made on them by this " sin of his youth " — meaning the over-loading of the texture of *Rienzi* owing to his inexperience at that time: this was construed as meaning that the composer himself had no great opinion of his work, with the inference that the public, in that case, need be no more indulgent towards it than he was.

In truth he had far outgrown *Rienzi* by this time, and would have preferred either of his other operas, or the forthcoming *Lohengrin*, to represent him in Berlin. But he had had to suppress his real feelings; *Rienzi* had been such a constant success in Dresden that there was a possibility of its making a public for itself in Berlin also, in which case the financial ruin that was impending might have been staved off. The desperate man had had to do further violence to his nature by acting the diplomatist during his stay in Berlin, humouring this person, concealing or toning down his real opinion of another, professing an acquiescence here, a satisfaction there, which he could not honestly feel. And all for nothing! He came away from Berlin not only depressed at his failure but furious with himself for having shown the Philistines a complaisance that was secretly abhorrent to him. He was dimly conscious that the great crisis of his life was arriving. A month or so after his return to Dresden he writes to a Berlin friend, Ernst Kossak, admitting his Berlin defeat, but, characteristically enough, assuring him that his ambition will yet be realised in some other way. The

King of Prussia has just heard a performance of *Tannhäuser* in Dresden that seemed to give him great pleasure: he himself was pleased with the performance — another proof, among so many, that his later comments upon the Dresden days are not an accurate representation of his feelings at the time, but in some degree the product of maturer reflection, with all the dissatisfaction and disillusionment that later experiences had brought in their train. Then comes a significant passage:

> "Best of friends, what is the use of all our preaching at the public? How sorry I am that you give yourself so much trouble over them on my account. There is a barrier to be broken through, and the only way to do that is — Revolution! The positive basis must be won; what we regard as good and right must become the firmly and unalterably existent, and then the bad that dominates at present will dissolve of itself into a stupid, easily vanquished opposition. A single rational decision on the part of the King of Prussia for his Opera, and at a stroke everything would be in order." [1]

5

One of Wagner's objects in visiting Berlin had been to read the libretto of *Lohengrin* to the King, and to interest him in his future art-plans as a whole. He found it, however, impossible to obtain an audience. The rabid Wagner partisans of the old school have attributed this, of course, to the machinations of the bogy-man Meyerbeer. All this is pure assumption; Wagner himself, in *Mein Leben*, gives us a much more rational explanation — the notoriously weak and vacillating character of the King, who started a hundred hares for one he caught. When in Berlin, Wagner had called on the celebrated theorist and critic A. B. Marx. That once ardent enthusiast had lost all his old-time fire. He had found himself unable to realise any of his schemes for the improvement of music in Berlin. He had managed to interest the King in a plan for a new school of music: he was passed on from one official to another, each of whom, so long as the King appeared to be interested, professed himself warmly in favour of the plan: but in the end nothing had been done. Wagner found Tieck equally disillusioned and even more bitter; out of the wealth of his own sad

---

[1] RWKK, II, 258, 259.

experience the poet assured Wagner that while the King would listen to his (Wagner's) theories with the greatest interest, and profess himself anxious for the realisation of them, there was not the smallest hope of any practical result, for the King had no strength and no central point in himself, but was all for this scheme of reform and this work of art today, and all for another tomorrow. A conversation with the Countess Rossi, the former celebrated singer Henriette Sontag, who was then living in Berlin, yielded the same discouraging result: the more influential portion of the Berlin public, he was told, was apathetic towards everything good and new, while the King, for all his apparent keenness for progress, failed everyone when the time came for talk to be translated into action. And as the Sontag herself, after graciously reading the poem of *Lohengrin,* returned it to the author with the assurance that she had been so fascinated when reading it that she had actually " seen the little elves and fairies dancing in front of her," Wagner could hardly feel that even the circles in Berlin that prided themselves most on their musical culture were as yet ripe for his message. He needed all the consolation that his faithful friends Werder and Alwine Frommann could give him in those depressing days.

The hostility of the Berlin Press to *Rienzi* was of course made as much of as possible by his enemies in Dresden; and he had to undergo the further chagrin of a tussle with Küstner over the vital matter of his Berlin expenses. Wagner had spent two months in the town. Küstner refused to pay him more than the bare royalties for the three performances he had conducted, alleging that while they had been delighted to have his co-operation at the rehearsals and in the coaching of the singers, no formal invitation to visit Berlin for those purposes had been sent him. Wagner would have appealed to Redern, but he found the Count prostrated by the news of Mendelssohn's death, which had taken place on the 4th November. As Küstner's letters bore out his legal contention, Wagner had to be satisfied with what was given him — a pleasing situation for a man whose debts were by now well on the way towards engulfing him!

He was under the disagreeable necessity of confessing the failure of his financial hopes to Lüttichau, and, in view of the mounting liabilities of his publishing venture, of petitioning for an increase in his salary that would place him on a par with Reissiger, whose salary was 2,000 thalers. The opportunity for putting him in his place was too good to be missed. The request, of course, had to be submitted to the King, and one day Lüttichau handed him the monarch's reply. Wagner was too stupefied to read to the end; but he realised that he was being severely censured for allowing his successes and the praise of his friends to turn his head. It might be necessary, the document went on, to dismiss him. However, in consideration of the zeal he had shown in certain matters, such as the production of *Iphigenia in Aulis,* he would be given another chance. Lüttichau had then to explain to the dazed man that his request for a rise in salary had been granted, and that he could draw an extra 300 thalers at once. Wagner's first impulse was to refuse the favour, but he soon changed his mind; he gives us, as the somewhat paradoxical reason for this, the encouragement he derived from the presence of the King of Prussia at that performance of *Tannhäuser* to which reference has already been made, and the obvious interest Friedrich Wilhelm took in the work.

This, it should be said, is the story as told in *Mein Leben.* It is not strictly consistent, however, with the facts; as on one or two other occasions, Wagner has the sequence of events wrong. The three concerts must have been decided upon in December, for they are foreshadowed in the Leipzig *Neue Zeitschrift* in its last number for 1847, and in the *Signale* a week later. The first was given on the 22nd January, 1848, the programme consisting of a Mozart symphony in D, Bach's motet *Singet dem Herrn ein neues Lied,* a scene from Cherubini's *Medea,* and the Eroica. The second concert, with a Haydn symphony in D, Beethoven's Seventh, a *De Profundis* by Gluck, and the 42nd Psalm of Mendelssohn, followed on the 12th February, and the third on the 8th March, the programme on this occasion containing Mendelssohn's A minor symphony, the C minor of Beethoven, and Palestrina's *Stabat Mater* in a new version by Wagner.[1] It was probably to arrange about these concerts that Wagner consented to attend the committee

---

[1] Wagner is in error when he says, in *Mein Leben,* that the *Stabat Mater* was given at the first concert. His arrangement of the work was published by Kahnt in 1871. See W. Kleefeld's article, *Richard Wagner als Bearbeiter,* in DM, IV, p. 231 ff.

meetings again after his long absence from them; and it is possible that the decision to give the concerts may have come out of his conversations with Lüttichau on the subject of the desired increase of salary. This, indeed, may be the meaning of Gutzkow's remark as to the reappearance of the sulking Achilles being connected with " conditions on both sides of which I was ignorant."

It is certain, however, that the matter of the increase in salary was not put officially before the King until early in February, 1848 — a fact which it is difficult to reconcile with Wagner's statement that he was encouraged to pocket his pride and accept the increase by the news that the King of Prussia had been greatly pleased with the performance of *Tannhäuser* in the previous November. Lütti-chau's letter to the King of Saxony is dated the 8th February. Glasenapp and Ellis almost foam at the mouth at what they regard as the impertinence of this " disgraceful " document: " A very ugly stroke of work! " says Ellis. " Had it not been that the original document figures as one of the inalienable archives of the Dresden Royal Court Theatre, we should have considered it a gross and wicked forgery, perpetrated by some scoundrel of not the smallest education." [1] This virtuous indignation is quite misplaced, how-ever. Lüttichau's letter is a perfectly rational and temperate state-ment of the case as he and others saw it; we have to remember, in justice to him, that he was dealing not with the great artist and world-conqueror we now know, but with the person and the facts as they appeared in 1848. He points out, quite fairly, that through his former residence in Paris Wagner had

" unfortunately acquired so light a view of the relations of life that he can probably be cured of it only by experiences as serious as those he is going through in his present harassed condition — if, indeed, he can rescue himself at all. He has not known how to value the good fortune which fell to him here in his appointment as Kapellmeister at a salary of 1,500 thalers; and the praises, in part exaggerated, bestowed by many people on his talent and his compositions have merely encouraged him the more in his too exalted ideas; so that he deludes himself with the notion of successes and profits from his operas as great as those that have indeed fallen to Meyerbeer and other composers in Paris and London, but are incompatible with things as they are in Germany. Through a more expensive establish-

[1] ELW, II, 220.

ment than he really needed, he fell into debt here from the first; [1] and his whim of not leaving to the bookseller the profit from the publication of his works, but hoping to secure it all for himself, misled him into undertaking their publication at his own risk and expense; whereby, the sales being small and the costs having to be met in cash, he has been plunged into the greatest embarrassment. He hoped for big gains from the production of his *Rienzi* in Berlin last autumn; but as that also miscarried, he finds himself now in very straitened circumstances, which fact has given him the courage to appeal directly to Your Majesty for an increase of 500 thalers in his salary.

Now whether his retention here is of such moment as to justify so exceptional an advance being made to him, I must admit that this does not appear to be in proportion to what, in general, he has achieved here up to now. Nevertheless it cannot be denied that in particular cases, such as the production of *Iphigenia in Aulis* last year and the present subscription concerts, he has put forth all his powers and shown a zeal for which he deserves all praise, and which would make his loss a matter for regret. It must therefore be left to Your Majesty's sovereign grace to decide whether, and to what extent, his humble request can be granted; in which case I venture, without presumption, to suggest that,

In fulfilment of the sum besought by Kapellmeister Wagner there be most graciously granted to him 300 thalers, not as an addition to his salary — which would make it equal to that of Kapellmeister Reissiger, who has served much longer — but simply as a gratification to enable him to regulate his debts, to come out of the fund for extraordinary Kapelle expenses; and 200 thalers as a grant from the receipts of the yearly subscription concerts, a portion of which receipts, as I humbly suggested in my report on these concerts, should in any case be graciously devoted to the relief of needy members of the Kapelle, among whom Wagner may certainly be reckoned . . . but that he be threatened with instant dismissal should he plunge into further pecuniary embarrassments or be unable to regularise his present ones, in which worst of events there would undoubtedly be nothing to be done but to deprive him of his post." [2]

There is no justification whatever for the obloquy poured by the Wagnerians on Lüttichau's head for this letter. It is the work of an

---

[1] It is both disingenuous and useless for Glasenapp and Ellis to say, in reply to what Ellis calls "this idle slander," that "even Meissner speaks with malicious disparagement of Wagner's 'modest dwelling' in the Ostra-Allee." Meissner took his standard from the more expensive establishments to which he was accustomed. Wagner himself, in *Mein Leben*, admits that he indulged himself, on the strength of his hopes, in an expenditure not warranted by his income. The facts must have been known to everyone connected with the Dresden theatre.

[2] GRW, II, 217, 218.

honourable official doing his best according to his lights. It is absurd to demand of him that he should always have acted, in his relations with Wagner, as if he were consciously dealing with the future composer of *Tristan,* the *Meistersinger,* the *Ring* and *Parsifal.* The person he had to do with was merely the second Kapellmeister of the Dresden Opera in the year 1848. Lüttichau simply states the facts as practically everyone in Dresden, from the King downwards, would see them — that Wagner had been raised from poverty and obscurity to a respected and, according to the notions of the time, a reasonably well-paid post at the Royal Theatre; that while he had done a great amount of good work, for which he was given general credit, he was inclined to be insubordinate; that he forgot the difference between Germany and France or England, and expected a shorter cut to wealth than the circumstances of his native country could supply; that he had consistently lived beyond his means; that his enormous debts were a matter of common talk and had brought him into ill odour in the town; that he had been badly advised to plunge into the business of publishing his scores on his own account without the necessary capital; that, all in all, the situation was becoming dangerous for Wagner and intolerable to his employers; that in his own interests he should be made to realise that he lived in a world of hard reality, not of poetic fancy; that he should be helped, but only in such a way as to relieve him of his more pressing burdens, not in such a way as to encourage him to believe that there was any possible ultimate escape from his difficulties except through a prudence and self-restraint of which he had shown too little so far; and that in the event of his proving that he was unteachable by experience, there would be nothing for it but to replace him by a Kapellmeister who would give less trouble and bring less personal discredit upon the town.

It was as unfortunate for them as for him that they could not see that he was the living symbol of a new epoch in German music, to which the old standards, of talent in composition and performance, of economic reward, of social standing, of conditions of service, would no longer apply. It would have been better not only for Wagner but for Dresden and its Opera had he been given the powers and the salary he thought his due. But to have perceived his due at that time would have implied, on Lüttichau's part, a future-piercing genius equal to Wagner's own: and Lüttichau is not to be blamed for not possessing that. His main concern was to do his best, according to his lights, for the institution of which the King had made him the head. He showed Wagner great consideration in many ways through the whole seven years of his service in Dresden; and we may be sure that it was no pleasure to him to have to paint the situation in 1848 to the King as we have seen him do. Even Wagner had to admit, in the following year, the consideration shown him by the Intendant in very trying circumstances; while in a letter of 1859 to Lüttichau, in which he pleads for an amnesty, he refers gratefully to the " sympathy with his aims " that was the cause of his Dresden appointment, and that was constantly extended to him " in spite of the great anxiety I gave you." He hopes that whatever recollections Lüttichau may have preserved of him have now lost their bitterness. For the loan of 5,000 thalers from the Pensions Fund, which he sees no means of repaying in the ordinary way, he professes the deepest and most loyal gratitude to the King, to whom he acknowledges he owed this exceptional favour.[1]

---

[1] See LWV, pp. 110, 115.

CHAPTER XX

NEARING THE END IN DRESDEN

1

IN THE middle of the short concert season of this winter he was summoned to Leipzig to lay his mother in earth. The old lady had passed away serenely on the 9th January. With her death, Richard felt that the last link between himself and the family was broken; each of the children had definitely gone his or her own way, and only by accident would his path cross theirs again in the future. In Leipzig he met Laube again; the pair talked despondently of the clouds that seemed to be descending upon Europe, in politics as in art.

A few weeks later, near the end of February, Paris was in revolution. The flames spread with lightning rapidity to Germany: in the middle of March there was a rising in Vienna, followed, on the 17th, by troubles in Berlin. It was only to be expected that the artists of the epoch would be infected with the general excitement, and share the general illusions as to the coming of Utopia. It was at this time that Spohr wrote his sextet, op. 140; when entering the work in the list of his compositions the seventy-year-old man added, " Written in March and April, at the time of the glorious revolution of the peoples for the liberty, unity, and grandeur of Germany." [1] The normally gentle Peter Cornelius, then a youth of twenty-four, helped to man the barricades in Berlin; he had been an ardent republican since the age of thirteen. [2] The long-desired emancipation of the peoples seemed at last to be at hand. The finer spirits in art and letters had long been hoping for the coming of a society in which their dreams of an ideal world would be realised. Liszt, in his mystical youth, had plunged into Saint-Simonism; even the opera singer Nourrit had cherished the idea of a national theatre in which the humble and oppressed would be able to enter freely into

---

[1] SA, II, 292.   [2] See CPC, I, 50, 94 ff., etc.

the heritage of music that was supposed to be their natural right.[1] The time seemed ripe for not only political emancipation but a spiritual catharsis. In the naïve political philosophy of that and every similar time, it was " the princes " who were primarily at fault, the rich who were answerable for all the economic woes of humanity: the virtuous " Folk " had only to be " freed," and the millennium would arrive by the next post. Wagner was not by any means alone in his idealisation of that rather dubious entity " the Folk." The poet Georg Herwegh, who had fled to Zürich to escape military service, had set the more progressive world of Germany on fire, in 1841, with his *Gedichte eines Lebendigen* (*Poems of a Live Man*); so extensive were the repercussions of these that even the King of Prussia, Friedrich Wilhelm IV, was moved to discuss politics with their author in the following year and to attempt to convert him. " The Folk," Herwegh wrote to the Countess d'Agoult in 1843, " alone can bring back vigour into our polished, blasé, civilised society; by it will art be fecundated and renewed " — an eminently Wagnerian sentiment.[2] And again, " When I use the term *man* I mean always the human species, man eternal, humanity itself, to which belong the greater number of the attributes we have until now bestowed on an alien being, a certain Lord God " [3] — an anticipation of the " truly human " that plays so large a part in Wagner's writings of his post-Dresden period.

The storm-clouds had been gathering for years. " The philosophy of the schools," said Herwegh in 1844, " is finished in Germany, and the philosophy of *life* has begun; " and again, " From Morocco to Berlin an electric battery runs; at the least contact the sparks will flash out." [4] In that same year the sufferings of the Silesian weavers, to which, in our day, Gerhart Hauptmann has given such fine dramatic expression in his play *Die Weber,* had stirred the conscience of all Germany.[5] Wagner was only one of tens

---

[1] See LSAS, II, 131.   [3] Ibid., p. 23.
[2] HAPD, p. 19.   [4] Ibid., p. 100.
[5] See also Heine's passionate poem, *Die schlesischen Weber:*
    Im düstern Auge keine Träne,
    Sie sitzen am Webstuhl und fletschen die Zähne;
    "Deutschland, wir weben dein Leichentuch,
    Wir weben hinein den dreifachen Fluch —
      Wir weben, wir weben!"
        etc.

of thousands of earnest Germans who felt that the history of civilisation had arrived at a major crisis; the only difference between himself and the others was that he had had mournful practical experience of the impossibility of the pure artist shaping the world according to his heart's desire in face of the power of the Courts and the notorious lethargy of the German spirit. In the early years of the century, Hölderlin, in his *Hyperion*, had lashed the Philistinism of his fellow-countrymen in a style that anticipated Nietzsche — "Barbarians from of old, now still worse barbarians by dint of their labours and their science, even of their religion, utterly incapable of any godlike sentiment." At a slightly later date Platen, in a poem (*Farewell to Germany*) that was suppressed in every edition of his works, had said that " in all this base world there can be nothing baser than a German "; while still later Herwegh was to tell his countrymen that they were only lackeys and would never be anything else but lackeys. It took Wagner some time, and many a bitter disillusionment, to turn even against his idealised " Folk " — against the slowness of the plodding German mind of the period, the dullness of German sensibility, the bovine females who took their knitting to the theatre.[1] In his Dresden days he still cherished agreeable illusions about the Folk: all his rage and contempt were reserved for the bureaucracy which, generalising from his own experience, he held to be the real obstacle to the Folk's demonstrating its direct descent from the angels. It was against the Courts, rather than against the Kings, that he ultimately flung himself into the combat.

2

At the commencement of 1848 he had found himself, probably out of sheer exhaustion, a trifle more reconciled, if only passively, to conditions at the Dresden theatre. He had many a cause for irritation, it is true, not the least among them being his niece Johanna, who was by this time taking advantage of her popularity in the town to play the prima donna, and, as far as she could, to turn the repertory into channels of which he did not approve.[2] But he had schooled

---

[1] See his outburst to Judith Gautier, in GWH, p. 21.

[2] In a letter to her of the 3rd June, 1857, when he was hoping his niece would be the first Brynhilde in the *Ring*, the fretted idealist spoke frankly but sensibly and

himself by this time into a comprehensive indifference towards the Dresden theatre and the people with whom his duties there brought him into contact: and during the early months of the year he could forget them all in the company of his *Lohengrin,* the scoring of which he finished by the end of March, 1848. The conclusion of this task coincided with the full coming of the crisis in German public affairs; and he could now turn his always superabundant energy into the business of politics, for which, as for everything else, he felt he had particular qualifications and a special mission from the Deity.

Only one event of this period had any significance for him as an artist — the real beginning of his friendship with Liszt. On his way from Vienna to Weimar, where he was now settling down for good as Court Kapellmeister, Liszt took in Dresden *en route,* and astonished Wagner by suddenly appearing in his room. Finding himself once more in Dresden in November, 1857, in the same room in the same Hôtel de Saxe, he wrote to Wagner recalling their talks there nine years earlier — " How could I fail to think of you always with love and fervent devotion, especially in this town, in this room, where we first drew nearer to each other, and your genius flashed its light on me? " [1] They spent an evening at Schumann's house, where they all made music together; an argument broke out with regard to Mendelssohn and Meyerbeer, that led to their host — unable, no doubt, to bear up against the combined assault of Liszt and Wagner — retiring to his room in a temper. After this meeting, Wagner was so sure of Liszt's affection that it was not long before

---

kindly of the old differences between them in Dresden. "I thought you would follow the same path as myself, the path along which I was fleeing, with ever-increasing repugnance, from the false, to refresh myself only with the true. Briefly, you were to be my singer, my representative; and one night, when I had been particularly pleased with you as Donna Anna in *Don Giovanni,* I felt a really passionate inclination towards this — hope. Your heart was good and willing, but as yet you could not comprehend me: while I was sketching my Brynhilde I had to conduct *La Favorita* for you, and see you and Tichatschek fling yourselves into *Zampa.* Believe me, what estranged me irresistibly from you was not poisonous innuendo but simply the tragic feeling, *she is going to be just like the others!* "

He explains that at that time he had also turned against her father for a similar reason. Albert had in earlier days shown talent as a singer, but had given up all his ideals, for himself and for Johanna, merely in order to go with the crowd and make money. "As a father he may have acted for the best; but from him also I had hoped too much not to watch him now, with bitter grief, from a distance." JKJ, p. 74 ff.

[1] RWLZ, II, 179.

he began to look hopefully in his direction for assistance in his financial troubles.

He spent part of April and May in the drawing up of a comprehensive *Plan for the Organisation of a German National Theatre for the Kingdom of Saxony*.[1] The turn-over of public opinion, as shown by certain electoral results in Saxony, pointed to the probability of the election of an extreme Radical Chamber, composed mostly of men who were resolved on cutting down the Civil List. Rumour had it that one of the institutions the funds of which were to be curtailed or withdrawn was the theatre, which was looked upon by these noble purists as a mere place of entertainment for the frivolous. Wagner took the sensible view that since the theatre was certain to continue to exist in some form or other, to deprive it of State countenance and State direction would be to deliver it over, bound hand and foot, to the very influences that were held to have made for its degradation. He thought it his duty, therefore, to point out that the nation ought to continue to contribute the same amount as that hitherto furnished by the King through the Civil List, but that the institution should cease to be a Court Theatre and become a National Theatre. He drafted, with his usual thoroughness, a complete scheme for the working of a theatre on these lines.

In Germany, he pointed out, the theatre was mostly an appanage of, and financially dependent on, the Court, with an Intendant possessing no real qualifications for his task, and responsible to the King or Grand Duke alone. Hence at once the degradation of the theatre as an artistic institution and its failure to play its due part in influencing the moral life of the community. It should everywhere cease to be Royal and become National. There should be a national union of dramatists and composers, whose informed opinion should decide which works should be given; and the " immoral trade of theatre reporter " should be done away with. Workers for the theatre should receive an adequate return for their labour. Detailed plans are drawn up for the constitution and the routine of the proposed governing body.

As the State can have only one National Theatre, the locale of this must obviously be the capital, Dresden. One other city in the

---

[1] Reprinted in RWGS, Vol. II. When he was preparing it for publication in the Collected Edition of his writings he wrongly dated it 1849.

Saxon kingdom — Leipzig — maintains a theatre out of its own purse. But it suffers from all the evils natural to a theatre that is dependent for its very existence on its box office takings, a system which subjects the impresario to a constant temptation to sacrifice the ideal to the real. As Leipzig, however, cannot reasonably be asked both to support its own theatre and to contribute to the upkeep of the National Theatre, the Leipzig theatre shall also become a secondary National Theatre, with a subvention from the State, and regulated by the same organisation as that in Dresden. The smaller Saxon towns have never been able to support theatres of their own; they have been dependent upon touring companies, working under concessions from the government. No more of these concessions should be granted, and those in existence should be allowed to run out or be withdrawn as soon as is practicable. These theatres have brought about a deplorable degeneration in public taste: a better theatrical fare can be provided by the central institution.

A school is to be founded in the capital in which everyone who intends to take up a musical or theatrical career can receive adequate instruction in every branch of the art he will have to practise, and at the same time a sound general culture. Promising students can begin their actual stage career in the smaller towns, and from there be drafted gradually into the two central theatres. The small local theatres will be permitted, on the one hand, to produce only works of real artistic value, and on the other hand only such works as are within the range of their modest resources: in this way a fight can be made against "that utter ruin of taste and manners resulting from the production of operas and pieces, calculated originally for the colossal dimensions of the largest Paris theatres, with the most horrible mutilations and the most deficient personnel, and on the most unsuitable stages."

In towns with so few inhabitants as Dresden and Leipzig it is inevitable that the public that patronises the theatre shall sooner or later have seen this or that play or opera as often as it wants to for the time being; and the result is that to attract an audience each night of the week there has to be an incessant change of bill. This means a large repertory, inadequate rehearsals, and mediocre productions. The theatre should be open not more than five nights a week, instead of seven as at present. Bad performances not only dis-

[496]

gust the public but ruin the taste and the morale of the performers. The conventional reply to this, says Wagner, will probably be that in a town like Dresden there are many people, particularly visitors, who would not know what to do with themselves on evenings when the theatre was closed. But that reply is the severest condemnation imaginable of the current view of the theatre. If it is true that people only go to the theatre to escape from boredom and from themselves, that is an admission that the theatre has been allowed to lose sight of its lofty mission. The fault can only be corrected by making the theatre less common. As for the feared loss of income, the returns from five good houses a week would be larger than from seven middling houses.

The official church music in Dresden is equally in need of reformation. The music of the Catholic church has everywhere been allowed, in the course of generations, to drift away from its old severity of ideal. Under the influence of the Italians it has become operatic, being written and performed, in great part, for the vain display of vocal virtuosi. Since the Royal Kapelle is used for the church service, this results in the absurdity that an orchestra of fifty accompanies a choir of twenty-four or twenty-six. The orchestra should be abolished in the church: the music should either be a cappella or accompanied only by the organ. In a country that is predominantly Protestant while the Court is Catholic, there must necessarily be a difficulty in providing a full and adequate Catholic personnel for the choir; Protestant singers should therefore be admitted, as well as a certain number of female voices. There should be a school for the proper training of the chorus singer: " the State neither can nor ought to tolerate his being turned into a slave for the purpose of its higher pleasure, which is what he has been and is, his time being so fully occupied with these duties that no other means of livelihood is open to him, yet his wages barely sufficing for the commonest necessities of life; while only in exceptional circumstances can the care of him when he is infirm be recommended to the King's grace." [1]

---

[1] I have already said that opera was a sweated industry in the Germany of those days. One sometimes wonders how the rank and file of the theatre managed to keep body and soul together, even with living as cheap, relatively, as it was then. At Leipzig, in the 1820's, the Concertmeister received 400 thalers per annum, the leaders of each section of the orchestra 200 thalers, the remainder only 150 thalers.

By a more rational redistribution of material and duties the orchestra of the opera would not only be more efficient but would cost less, for at present there is a good deal of wasted effort. The orchestra should not be expected to perform in the entr'actes of the spoken play. The men despise the trivial stuff they have to perform on these occasions, and resent the manifest indifference of the audience, with the result that they become mechanical and cynical. The public acquires such a contempt for this kind of music that when really worthy incidental music is put before it, as in the case of Goethe's *Egmont* with the music of Beethoven, it hardly troubles to listen. Out of the five nights a week to be devoted to performances in the theatre, only two, or three at the most, should be allotted to opera if the best results are to be obtained from the men.

Instead of an orchestra composed of a limited number of full "Kammermusiker" plus a number of inferior "Accessists," the latter receiving only half the salary of the weakest regular member of the band,[1] and consequently being recruited from a very inferior class of musicians, the National Theatre should have an orchestra of good material throughout, the payment offered, and the conditions of service, being such as will attract first-rate men. The orchestra should be allowed to give regular concerts of its own each winter, up to the number of twelve, the proceeds to be devoted to ameliorating its deplorable economic lot; this would relieve the Civil List of the onus of the care for members in distress.

The Leipzig Conservatoire should be transplanted to Dresden, and made into a National School for the kingdom of Saxony.

There should be a Union of the composers of the country, who, along with representatives from the players, should elect the Kapellmeister for the Opera, determine the repertory, select new works for performance, and so on, functioning through a properly con-

---

They were paid 8 groschen (a shilling) for small rehearsals, and 16 groschen for costume rehearsals. They were engaged for 110 operas and 110 plays a year, plus 50 rehearsals, so that they could not have found much time for other occupations. In the 1830's the Leipzig orchestra cost in all only 6,000 thalers a year, including extra rehearsals. The chorus was paid from 4 thalers 4 groschen to 10 thalers 10 groschen per month. See SHJ, pp. 22, 90, etc. For figures relating to the Gewandhaus Orchestra at that period see DGG, pp. 66–77.

[1] Sometimes, after as many as fifteen years' service, an Accessist would be receiving a salary of only 150 thalers!

stituted managing council. The King will remain the national head of the national institution, but the person in control will be a responsible Minister of State, not a mere Court placeman with no qualifications whatever for his task; while the purely artistic conduct of the theatre shall be entrusted to an artist — i.e. the Kapellmeister.

The Plan, as was always the case when Wagner was dealing with the practical side of music or the theatre, was the quintessence of common sense. After his experience in connection with his previous Plan for the reorganisation of the Kapelle, and in view of his strained relations with the Intendant at this time, he no doubt thought it useless to approach Lüttichau in the matter, especially as the political events of the moment seemed to herald a change in the relations of the Court to the business of the Kingdom. He wrote to Oberländer, the Minister of the Interior, on the 16th May, 1848, asking for the favour of an hour in which to read his Plan, and hoping that the Minister of Education, von der Pfordten, might also be present, as he was not sure to which department a matter of this kind really belonged. Pfordten, who, by the way, was to come into sharp conflict with Wagner in the hectic Munich days of the 'sixties, did not prove particularly responsive. Oberländer was more receptive and sympathetic, but could hold out no hope of success, the Ministers of the moment not being *personae gratae* with the King. He advised Wagner to try to work through the Chamber of Deputies. The attempt to do so brought him into close contact with a number of democratic politicians, for whose wits and culture he soon conceived a fitting contempt. They were wholly preoccupied with the facile formulae and the oratorical platitudes that do duty for political and economic thinking in times of national stress; and, as is the quaint way of their kind, they were either frankly indifferent to questions of high art, or held the complacent theory that the last person to be entrusted with the control of a national artistic institution is a practical artist. Wagner's scheme consequently came to nothing; and as Lüttichau got wind of it, heard that Wagner had deliberately ignored him in a matter that vitally concerned his office, and no doubt learned from the Report itself that Wagner was audaciously proposing to take the control of the theatre out of the hands of aristocratic " Court placemen " like himself, the relations of the pair during these weeks of political tension became more strained than ever. Wagner, for his part, could no longer cherish any illusions as to the possibility of a reform of the theatre through Court officials. The only hope now was in revolution.

3

Thus for the second time the Dresden authorities threw away their chance at once of retaining the good will of the most gifted composer and most practical musical organiser of the day, and of gradually raising the Dresden Opera to the front rank among contemporary institutions. And Wagner being what he was, he now turned his back on music and plunged into political agitation not merely for music's sake but for political agitation's sake. His remark that he " became a revolutionary for love of the theatre " is in part true, but only in part. For this extraordinary man, music was never quite enough, just as poetry was never quite enough for Goethe or painting for Leonardo. It is no paradox to say that it was really Wagner's peculiar constitution as a musician that made him, at more than one period of his life, abandon music for other activities. From the world's point of view, it has always seemed a pity that he should have spent so much time, his whole life long, in writing so many prose works and letters, and meddling so much with politics, and confidently dogmatising in a dozen intellectual spheres in which he was only an amateur, instead of turning his back resolutely on all this and concentrating on his real work. Had he done that, it has often been said, he might have dowered us with another half-dozen operatic masterpieces. But that view of the matter, which would be reasonable enough in the case of any other composer, leaves out of consideration the one vital factor in the problem — Richard Wagner himself.

He could never write music, as so many composers do, for mere music-writing's sake — the equivalent of talking for mere talking's sake. In one of the rare direct glimpses he affords us into his psychology as an artist, he says that he finds it impossible to embark automatically upon a new work as soon as the one in hand has been finished. Each new work, he held, should represent a new phase in its creator's inner life, a new extension of experience, a new conquest of material and of technique, a new crystallisation not only of aesthetic but of spiritual wisdom and power. Planning his works on the scale he did, to cover so vast an area of thought and emotion, this point of view was inevitable: for art-works of this ultimate stature and complexity of organisation the long preliminary period of unconscious gestation is far more important than any amount of conscious reflection. The subjects of virtually all his works, down to *Parsifal,* were settled upon, more or less definitely, at quite an early stage of his career: but for the working-out of them he had to wait almost passively for the right psychological moment in each case. Thus there is really no mystery, in the last resort, in this extraordinarily musical mind refraining altogether from the writing of music for a period of something like six years — from August, 1847, when *Lohengrin* was completed, to about October, 1853, when he began work upon the music to the *Rheingold.* Busoni has aptly spoken of the almost "animal instinct" that led Mozart and Schubert to do the right thing again and again in their music without reflection. This "animal instinct" Wagner had in the highest degree, though in him it took another form — that of unconsciously holding aloof from the specifically musical part of each new work until a new experience of life and the slow self-gestation of the poetic subject within him had brought about the needful new enrichment of his musical powers. It was not that he needed a "libretto" to set his musical faculty working, and that when he had settled upon the text he proceeded doggedly to "set it to music." His musical imagination kept playing incessantly upon the subject through every stage of its progress, from the first thrill at meeting with it, through the various prose sketches for it, down to the final casting of it in poetic form. But for the complete release of the musical imagination at its highest pressure, and for the organization of these innumerable moods into living forms, a sound instinct always bade him wait until the operations of his subconsciousness rose of themselves to the conscious surface of his mind and clamoured imperiously for outward realisation in line and colour.

Already, in his last Dresden years, the *Ring* was shaping itself in the depths of his subconsciousness; but he knew instinctively that the time for dealing with it as a whole was not yet. Yet his

[501]

stupendous physical and mental energy, to which there is hardly
a parallel in the artistic, scientific, or political world of the nineteenth century, made quietism impossible for him; he had to be
fructifying even in his fallow seasons. If he was not writing music
he had to find some other outlet for his high-voltage dynamism,
that was allied with so illimitable and unshakeable a belief in
himself. In his earliest years he managed to work off this excess
of energy in the practical routine of the theatre; we have seen him
more than once incurring resentment there not only by his passion
for perfection but by his lust for pedagogy and leadership; and to
have had to give all this up in Paris, to have been compelled to
realise that he was nobody in that rich swirl of cosmopolitan life,
to have been from first to last the provincial under-dog, impotent
to impose his will upon others, must have been the bitterest of all
the pills he had to swallow there. His kingdom there was a very
tiny one, with only an Anders, a Kietz, a Pecht for his subjects.
It was no doubt this constant sense of subjection and frustration
that accounted for the surliness that unsympathetic observers noted
in him at the time. On his appointment as Kapellmeister in Dresden the young zealot at once made the pace so hot for everyone
in the theatre that, as we have seen, he raised a camp of enemies
for himself. German Kapellmeisters and composers had hitherto
been content to serve. Wagner was bent on governing; but the time
had not yet come when a mere musician could dictate his own
terms to Intendants and impresarios. He was part of a Court establishment, and not only a servant but a liveried servant: in the after
years he would sometimes amuse his guests by coming down ar-
rayed in his old Dresden uniform, bending his back and rubbing
his hands in the style that Reissiger, no doubt, used to adopt in the
presence of his official superiors.

There are no universal geniuses in art: the thing is a contradiction in terms. But there are geniuses whose energy is too colossal
to permit of their confining themselves to any one form of intellectual activity. Goethe was not satisfied to be a poet: he had to be
a politician as well, an administrator, a theatre producer, a critic
and aesthetician, a speculator in purely scientific territories such
as those of botany, geology, and the theory of colour. The result
was, as Brandes has pointed out, that, for all his greatness, he

achieved hardly a single perfect work of art on the large scale.[1] Wagner's was really the more remarkable artistic mind of the two; no matter in how many directions he might waste the surplusage of his vast energies, he gave to each of the completed works of his maturity the finish, the organic unity, that one expects of an artist who has never thought of anything else but his art. But when, as was so often the case, the creative impulse was lying dormant in him, wisely biding its appointed time, some other outlet had to be found for his inexhaustible intellectual and physical energy, some other means of gratifying his considerable self-esteem, some other channel through which he could exercise his lust for shaping men and things to his own end. In the whole course of his life he never seems to have doubted himself. He was as certain that he could solve the knottiest problems of art, of science, of economics, of politics, or run a kingdom, or guide a strayed civilisation to the new Jerusalem, as that he could write better music than any of his contemporaries. We shall see, at a later stage, the trouble he made for himself in Munich by his obstinate belief in his God-given mission for politics.

Could the Dresden authorities have been as wise at the time as it is easy for us to be now, they would have seen to it that his energy was canalised for the benefit of the music of the town, instead of

---

[1] "The masterpieces are relatively few . . . because, with the exception of a short period, Goethe never applied himself unreservedly to his true vocation — to the writing of poetry. He allowed business to sap him of his strength. For ten long years, and these the very best for a poet, from his twenty-seventh to his thirty-seventh, he gives up poetic activity entirely and dedicates himself to the wearisome affairs of statecraft in Weimar. During all this time he writes practically nothing but poetry for set occasions. Hence the lack of unity in his more pretentious works. He let them lie too long; they are as a rule heterogeneously or poorly constructed. He constantly took them up anew and revised them, or he worked new pieces into them, or he continued them after he had half-forgotten the original plan.

"*Götz von Berlichingen* exists in three different forms, not counting detached scenes. *Iphigenie* was revised five times. *Wilhelm Meisters Lehrjahre* lay so long that it was finally completed after a plan that differed entirely from the original one; two versions exist. *Wilhelm Meisters Wanderjahre* was elaborated according to no plan whatsoever: it is a mere compilation. And finally we come to his main work, *Faust*, which was outlined and laid aside and then taken up again and then laid aside again and taken up again, so that its composition extends over a period of sixty years. It is consequently difficult to say how many Fausts there are in *Faust;* one there certainly is not. The entire work contains a series of geological strata, and these strata lie at times as they do when a great mass of material tumbles over — in one confused and conglomerate pile." Georg Brandes, *Wolfgang Goethe,* I, xix, xx.

being dammed in the quarter in which it could have been the most useful and driven into channels where it was bound to be a danger to himself and others. For the overruling impulse of his being, apart from his artistic creation, was to plan, to organise, to pontify, to govern. It was this impulse that led him finally, to the lasting benefit of the world, to call Bayreuth out of the void — the fighting spirit that made him, once he had become disillusioned about King Ludwig, refuse to exist in a theatrical world in which he could not be absolute master. Even the task of founding and running Bay-reuth — a colossal task for any man, but most of all for an elderly man whose health was already undermined — was not sufficient to absorb all his energy, as is shown by the lengthy list of his prose works during the last ten years or so of his life; but at any rate we can congratulate ourselves on the fact that the greatest and most continuous outward effort of his whole career was directed to a purely artistic, not a political end. Dresden would have had reason to congratulate itself later if in 1847 and 1848 it had only had the wisdom to turn the overplus of Wagner's energy, which at the moment he did not need for the creation of a new work of art, into the business of the reorganisation and regeneration of the local theatre.

4

The last chance there might normally have been of his keeping his head in this atmosphere of political excitement was destroyed for him by the parlous state of his finances. Unless a miracle hap-pened, and soon, he was ruined; and the only hope for a miracle lay in the birth of a new theatre in a new world of German culture.

We have seen him, in October, 1846, endeavouring to get a loan of 1,000 or 1,200 thalers from Schletter to help him to discharge his growing debt to Meser. In June, 1848, he had to swallow his pride and approach Breitkopf & Härtel once more. To liquidate his debt to them he offers them the score of *Lohengrin*, which opera, he says, is to be produced in Dresden in the coming winter. He then reminds them of his unlucky publishing venture on his own ac-count. This would have been fully justified, he says, had the capital been his own; for the sales have more than covered the interest, and that at a time when his works have been given hardly anywhere but in Dresden, so that with the spread of them to the rest of Germany he can reasonably count on an improvement in this respect. But situated as he is he can no longer carry the huge load of the capital indebtedness. Owing to his already having become a political suspect, various creditors had called in their loans; he wants to settle down again to creative work, but cannot win the necessary peace of mind. Breitkopf & Härtel have already informed him, he reminds them with a touch of irony, that they would have no objection to publishing his works if he did not expect payment for them. Very well; will they now become the proprietors of *Rienzi,* the *Flying Dutchman,* and *Tannhäuser* by paying Meser the capital sum still outstanding, he himself receiving nothing? " If I thus renounce, once for all, the profit from my works, this sacrifice seems a small one to me in comparison with the so ardently desired regulation of my external affairs."

The Leipzig firm threw away this chance of acquiring an ultimately most valuable property for very little. He has himself admitted, they say in their reply, that his works have as yet not been taken up by the German theatres in general. They are polite enough not to question the rightness of his belief that some day the operas will be very successful. At the same time, as business men, they feel bound to point out to him that experience shows that an opera rarely conquers a big public for itself a long time *after* its first production. The thing is not impossible, of course; this belated fame, they assure him soothingly, has been the lot of some of the greatest musical works. But there is a technical difficulty in the way of their taking over the three operas from Meser. That gentleman has already sent out specimen copies to the trade; this process cannot be repeated, so that Breitkopf & Härtel would simply have to rely, for sales, upon such orders as might come along from intending purchasers, and, in the terms of the case, not many of these can be hoped for. Wagner's operas present great difficulties for the smaller German stages; and there is no demand anywhere for vocal scores until after a work has been heard in the theatre. Moreover, owing to the fact that Meser has no music-engraving plant of his own, he has necessarily had to pay more for the production of the works than Breitkopf & Härtel, with their own workmen and machines, would have had to pay in the first place.

Finally, the times are bad for art: " many of the theatres are closed, everyone is taken up with politics, no one has the necessary peace of mind to think about art." They will not even ask him to go into details as regards his new opera *Lohengrin,* " for we take the most mournful view of the future, especially with regard to works that call for elaborate staging, and which will consequently present even greater difficulties to the German theatres in the coming time than has hitherto been the case." [1]

Wagner's situation was now indeed desperate. Within a couple of days of receiving Breitkopf & Härtel's letter the distracted man turns to Liszt, in Weimar, for help: his creditors are pressing him, he says, and the times are so difficult that no one will take over his liability to Meser. Will Liszt do so — the sum required is 5,000 thalers — and so become his publisher? " Do you know what this would mean for me? I should become a human being again, one to whom existence is possible — an artist who will never again in all his life ask for a groschen, but will simply turn joyously to work. Dear Liszt, with this money you would buy me out of slavery! " But Liszt, who had abandoned his virtuoso career, and had already parted with perhaps most of the fortune he had made as a pianist, could for the moment do nothing.

At the end of July, the situation having become intolerable, Wagner asked Pusinelli to come to his rescue by buying Meser out. As he saw it, it was a rational business deal that would some day pay handsomely whoever might undertake it. But Pusinelli shrank from the further large sacrifice it would involve. In a letter to Wagner's attorney, Fleck, which has lately been published for the first time, he points out that he would have to pay Meser at least 3,000 thalers, and as Wagner already owes him capital and accumulated interest amounting to between 5,600 and 5,800 thalers, he would be involved to the extent of some 9,000 thalers, and moreover, " compared to the other creditors, be at a most conspicuous and unfair advantage." He could not raise so large a sum except at a high rate of interest, or alternatively by the sale of securities at a loss, or by using his wife's means. " My friendship for W——, my great regard for his talent, my enthusiasm for his art, must not mislead me into any further unwarranted

---

[1] RWBV, I, 14, 16.

steps. I have proved that I am ready to make sacrifices, great sacrifices, but my conscience forbids my going any further, and I have decided quite firmly not to enter into the purchase proposal under any circumstances. *In fact, I claim the same rights as Wagner's other creditors.* Although I may lose much, very much, by doing so, I shall have to content myself with the conviction that I have been enthusiastic over an ideal and that I am paying dearly for an enthusiasm, a lofty enthusiasm; I shall regret only this one thing, and on this account I shall not think any less of Wagner than hitherto, but it would be senseless to make any further sacrifices, it would be unfair to my family, to the property entrusted to me. Actually, Wagner's published works already belong to me.[1] He promised them to me as surety for the loans I made him. He neglected making over this guarantee to me — I was too considerate to demand it. Now I shall renounce these claims in Wagner's favour, so that he may dispose of his property — his works — as he likes, to his advantage." [2]

Pusinelli could hardly have done any more: it was generous of him to have done so much. Fearing, no doubt, that his resolution might weaken if Wagner were allowed to exercise his familiar blandishments on him in person, he wrote to him to ask him not to approach him directly on the matter. This brought a characteristic reply from Wagner, in another letter recently published, by Mr. Elbert Lenrow, for the first time from the Pusinelli papers. Though he recognises the friendship Pusinelli has shown him, and admits the obligation he is under with regard to him, he cannot refrain from expressing a certain irritation. " Many and bitter were the thoughts which this [i.e. the request not to write to Pusinelli personally] roused in my mind. Perhaps you might — speaking frankly! — not comprehend what I perceive in this wish to have me keep away. In this I don't see any change in your feelings towards *me* in particular, but rather a fresh confirmation of my views regarding the ruinous effects of money and its attendant vile worries upon the human mind: we are not guided by any purely humane sentiment, but the more we perceive anything godlike in

---

[1] Wagner had overlooked this trifling fact when he asked Breitkopf & Härtel and Liszt to set him free by buying out Meser.

[2] RWAP, pp. 27, 28.

us, the greater our inclination becomes to yield this up to another baser — but unfortunately, prevailing — principle: we prefer to give way to it consciously, perceiving its superior force. It is to be hoped that last evening you did *not* expect a visit from me, in consequence of your request." [1] The expression is not ideally lucid, but one gathers that Wagner was annoyed at Pusinelli's refusal, even though he recognised that Pusinelli acted as he had done because of " the ruinous effects of money and its attendant vile worries upon the human mind "; the " purely humane," the " god-like " thing to have done, apparently, was for Pusinelli to bleed himself and his family to the bone for Richard's benefit. One detects in this letter the first hints of the later exacting spirit and rancorous mood of Wagner towards those who had helped him, or, in his opinion, ought to have helped him on demand. As the years went on, his needs became more and more pressing, while at the same time his sensibilities both as borrower and as hypothetical repayer became progressively blunted. The key to the mentality and the events that were now and then to come so near to wrecking his life in the future is to be found, not, as the more romantic biographers have supposed,[2] in his escapades with women, which were for the most part of the ordinary male kind, but in the cumulative story of his debts. As he himself said, in a passage to which reference has already been made in the foregoing pages, he ceased, in time, to believe in the reality of them and of finance in general, so monstrously disproportionate were his desires and his liabilities to his income, past, present, or, as it seemed, future. According to Pecht, when Wagner fled from Dresden in 1849 he owed 20,000 thalers. From all that we know, the figure is not incredible. It is easy to understand how a man with a debt of anything approaching that amount, and a salary of only 1,500 thalers, would come to regard it all as so fantastic that it had the minimum of relation to reality; and when even that small income ceased, as it did when he fled from Dresden, it became an imperative necessity, if he were to go on living and working, that he should complacently declare not only a financial but a moral moratorium.

[1] RWAP, p. 28.
[2] See, for instance, JKWF, Introduction and final chapter.

This is virtually what we find him doing in the years following 1849, which present us with the spectacle of a Wagner differing in several respects from the Wagner of the first half of his life. And in 1848 and 1849 he drifted into revolution not merely " from love of the theatre " but from lack of thalers. Even while he was endeavouring to bring some sort of order into his finances with the aid of Breitkopf & Härtel, of Liszt, and of Pusinelli, and in each case failing, he was already up to the waist in the revolutionary activities of the epoch. The story of his complete plunge into them, which brought him near drowning, must be reserved for another volume.

INDEX

A NOTE ON THE TYPE IN WHICH
THIS BOOK IS SET

This book is composed on the linotype in Bodoni, so called after Giambattista Bodoni (1740–1813), son of a printer of Piedmont. After gaining experience and fame as superintendent of the Press of the Propaganda in Rome, Bodoni became in 1766 the head of the ducal printing house at Parma, which he soon made the foremost of its kind in Europe. His Manuale Tipografico, *completed by his widow in 1818, contains 279 pages of specimens of types, including alphabets of about thirty foreign languages. His editions of Greek, Latin, Italian, and French classics, especially his Homer, are celebrated for their typography. In type-designing he was an innovator, making his new faces rounder, wider, and lighter, with greater openness and delicacy. His types were rather too rigidly perfect in detail, the thick lines contrasting sharply with the thin wiry lines. It was this feature, doubtless, that caused William Morris's condemnation of the Bodoni types as "swelteringly hideous." Bodoni Book, as reproduced by the Linotype Company, is a modern version based, not upon any one of Bodoni's fonts, but upon a composite conception of the Bodoni manner, designed to avoid the details stigmatized as bad by typographical experts and to secure the pleasing and effective results of which the Bodoni types are capable.*

THE BOOK WAS COMPOSED, PRINTED, AND BOUND BY THE PLIMPTON PRESS, NORWOOD, MASS. THE BINDING WAS ADAPTED FROM DESIGNS BY W. A. DWIGGINS.